THE PROCESS OF
Research in Criminal Justice and Criminology

Riane M. Bolin
Radford University

Margaret C. Pate
Radford University

Jeffrey C. Dixon
College of the Holy Cross

Royce A. Singleton, Jr.
College of the Holy Cross

Bruce C. Straits
University of California, Santa Barbara

Oxford University Press is a department of the University of Oxford.
It furthers the University's objective of excellence in research, scholarship,
and education by publishing worldwide. Oxford is a registered trade mark of
Oxford University Press in the UK and in certain other countries.

Published in the United States of America by Oxford University Press
198 Madison Avenue, New York, NY 10016, United States of America.

© 2023, 2019, 2016 by Oxford University Press
© 2025 by Oxford University Press

The Process of Social Research, 3e was originally published in English in 2016 by Oxford
University Press, 198 Madison Avenue, New York, NY 10016, United States of America.
This adapted edition has been customized for US criminal justice and criminology departments
and is published by arrangement with Oxford Publishing Limited. It may not be sold elsewhere.
Oxford University Press US is solely responsible for this adaptation from the original work.
Copyright © 2016 by Oxford University Press

> For titles covered by Section 112 of the US Higher Education Opportunity
> Act, please visit www.oup.com/us/he for the latest information about
> pricing and alternate formats.

All rights reserved. No part of this publication may be reproduced,
stored in a retrieval system, or transmitted, in any form or by any means,
without the prior permission in writing of Oxford University Press,
or as expressly permitted by law, by license or under terms agreed with
the appropriate reprographics rights organization. Inquiries concerning
reproduction outside the scope of the above should be sent to the Rights
Department, Oxford University Press, at the address above.

You must not circulate this work in any other form
and you must impose this same condition on any acquirer

Library of Congress Cataloging-in-Publication Data

Names: Bolin, Riane Miller, author. | Pate, Margaret, author.
Title: The process of research in criminal justice and criminology / Riane
  M. Bolin, Radford University, Margaret C. Pate, Radford University,
  Jeffrey C. Dixon, College of the Holy Cross, Royce A. Singleton, Jr.,
  College of the Holy Cross, Bruce C. Straits, University of California,
  Santa Barbara.
Description: First edition. | New York : Oxford University Press, [2025] |
  Includes bibliographical references and index. | Summary: "The Process
  of Research in Criminal Justice and Criminology introduces students to
  the fundamentals of research, from topic selection and research design
  to data collection, analysis, and interpretation. A unique feature of
  the book is its emphasis on process. Every chapter contains flowcharts
  of research processes—for example, the process of measurement, the
  process of sampling, and the process of planning and conducting a
  survey—that provide step-by-step guides to conducting research in
  criminology and criminal justice and evaluating the research of
  others"—Provided by publisher.
Identifiers: LCCN 2024010780 | ISBN 9780197605912 (paperback) | ISBN
  9780197605943 (epub)
Subjects: LCSH: Criminology—Research. | Criminal justice, Administration
  of—Research.
Classification: LCC HV6024.5 .B66 2025 | DDC 364.072/1—dc23/eng/20240516
LC record available at https://lccn.loc.gov/2024010780

Printed by Integrated Books International, United States of America

Brief Contents

Preface xviii

CHAPTER 1 **Introduction:**
Why Care About Research Methods? 1

CHAPTER 2 **Science and Social Research:**
From Theory to Data and Back 19

CHAPTER 3 **Reading and Writing in Criminal Justice Research:**
It Is All About Communication 44

CHAPTER 4 **The Ethics and Politics of Research:**
Doing What's "Right" 69

CHAPTER 5 **Research Designs:**
It Depends on the Question 100

CHAPTER 6 **Measurement:**
Linking Theory to Research 130

CHAPTER 7 **Sampling:**
Case Selection as a Basis for Inference 173

CHAPTER 8 **Experiments:**
What Causes What? 203

CHAPTER 9 **Surveys:**
Questioning and Sampling 238

CHAPTER 10 **Field Research and In-Depth Interviews:**
Systematic People-Watching and Listening 271

CHAPTER 11 **Existing Data Analysis:**
Using Data from Secondhand Sources 314

CHAPTER 12 **Evaluation Research:**
Assessing Program Need and Impact 346

CHAPTER 13 **Multiple Methods:**
Two or More Approaches Are Better Than One 377

CHAPTER 14 **Quantitative Data Analysis:**
Using Statistics for Description and Inference 400

CHAPTER 15 **Qualitative Data Analysis:**
Searching for Meaning 444

Glossary 471
References 480
Credits 502
Index 505

Contents

Preface xviii

CHAPTER 1 **Introduction:** Why Care About Research Methods? 1

Introduction 2
1.1 The Process of Social Research 7
1.2 Four Criminal Justice Studies 10
    An Experiment 10
    A Survey 11
    A Field Research Study 13
    An Analysis of Existing Data 15
    Summary 16

<u>BOXES</u>
    1.1 READING CRIMINAL JUSTICE RESEARCH: Empirical vs. Anecdotal: Who Do We Trust? 5
    1.2 PRACTICE WHAT YOU LEARNED: Formulate a Research Question 9
    1.3 CHECKING YOUR UNDERSTANDING: Limitations of Methodological Approaches 17

CHAPTER 2 **Science and Social Research:** From Theory to Data and Back 19

2.1 The Characteristics and Process of Science 21
    Theory 21
    Verifiable Data 22
    Systematic Observation and Analysis 23
    Logical Reasoning 25
    Summary 30
2.2 Logics of Inquiry: Deductive and Inductive Logic 30
    How Do Career Criminals Disengage from Criminal Behavior? An Answer from Inductive Inquiry 31
    Do Social Bonds Matter? An Answer from Deductive Inquiry 32
    Combining the Logics of Inquiry 33
    Moving Between Deductive and Inductive Inquiries: Domestic Violence Responses 34
    Summary 36

2.3 Evaluating Scientific Knowledge: Possibilities, Cautions, and Limits 36
Tentative Knowledge 36
The Ideal and Reality of the Scientific Process 37
The Sociohistorical Aspect of Science 38
The Human Element of Science 39
Summary 40

BOXES

2.1 READING CRIMINAL JUSTICE RESEARCH: Verify This! 23
2.2 CHECKING YOUR UNDERSTANDING: Identifying and Evaluating Deductive and Inductive Reasoning 26
2.3 CHECKING YOUR UNDERSTANDING: Testing Our Reasoning: Is It Deductive or Inductive? 29
2.4 CHECKING YOUR UNDERSTANDING: Which Logic of Inquiry? 40

CHAPTER 3 Reading and Writing in Criminal Justice Research: It Is All About Communication 44

3.1 Read, Take Notes, and Write a Research Proposal 45
Locate Relevant Research Literature 46
Read and Evaluate Prior Research 50
Formulate Research Question 52
Design Research and Prepare Proposal 54
Summary 54

3.2 Write a Research Report 55
Outline and Prepare to Write 56
Write a First Draft 56
Revisions and Other Writing Considerations 63
Summary 65

BOXES

3.1 DOING CRIMINAL JUSTICE RESEARCH: How to Search the Literature 46
3.2 READING CRIMINAL JUSTICE RESEARCH: Questions to Ask in Evaluating a Research Report 53
3.3 CHECKING YOUR UNDERSTANDING: Research Proposals 55
3.4 DOING CRIMINAL JUSTICE RESEARCH: APA Guidelines for In-Text Citations and References 62
3.5 CHECKING YOUR UNDERSTANDING: Parts of a Research Report 66

CHAPTER 4 The Ethics and Politics of Research: Doing What's "Right" 69

4.1 Overview: Ethics 71
4.2 Ethical Issues in the Treatment of Research Participants 71
Potential Harm 72

Informed Consent 73
Deception 74
Invasion of Privacy 75
Summary 77

4.3 Federal and Professional Ethical Guidelines **78**
Evaluating Potential Harm 79
Informed Consent Procedures 81
Deception Ground Rules 82
Privacy Protection: Anonymity and Confidentiality 84
Summary 86

4.4 The Process of Ethical Decision-Making **87**
Review Federal Regulations and Professional Ethics Codes 88
Assess Costs and Benefits of Proposed Research 88
Identify and Address Areas of Ethical Concern 89
Prepare and Submit Application for IRB Approval 89
Collect Data and Secure Participants' Rights 90
Summary 91

4.5 Politics and Social Research **92**
Topic Selection, Political Ideology, and Research Funding 93
Data Analysis and Interpretation and Political Ideology 95
Dissemination of Research Findings: Science, Politics, and Public Policy 96
Summary 96

BOXES

4.1 READING CRIMINAL JUSTICE RESEARCH: Privacy Invasion in the Public Identification of Participants 76
4.2 CHECKING YOUR UNDERSTANDING: Ethics Practice Questions I 78
4.3 CHECKING YOUR UNDERSTANDING: Ethics Practice Questions II 85
4.4 CHECKING YOUR UNDERSTANDING: Human Subjects Training 86
4.5 DOING CRIMINAL JUSTICE RESEARCH: Online Resources on Research Ethics 88
4.6 CHECKING YOUR UNDERSTANDING: Federal and Professional Ethical Guidelines Review 92

CHAPTER 5 **Research Designs:** It Depends on the Question **100**

5.1 Initial Steps in the Research Process **102**
Select a Research Topic 103
Review the Literature/Consider Theory 103
Formulate a Research Question 104
Prepare a Research Design 106
Summary 107

5.2 Designing Research to Answer Quantitative Questions 108
Select a Research Strategy 108
Identify and Select Units of Analysis 109
Measure Variables 110
Gather Data and Analyze the Relationships Among Variables 114
Summary 120

5.3 Designing Research to Answer Qualitative Questions 121
Select a Research Strategy 122
Select Field Setting, Social Group, and/or Archival Records 123
Gain Access and Establish Relationships 124
Decide Whom to Observe or Interview or What to Read 124
Gather and Analyze Data 124
Summary 126

BOXES
5.1 PRACTICE WHAT YOU LEARNED: Crafting a "Good" Research Question 106
5.2 CHECKING YOUR UNDERSTANDING: Qualitative or Quantitative? 107
5.3 READING CRIMINAL JUSTICE RESEARCH: The Ecological Fallacy 110
5.4 CHECKING YOUR UNDERSTANDING: Quantitative Research Questions, Units of Analysis, and Variables 113
5.5 READING CRIMINAL JUSTICE RESEARCH: How to Interpret Correlations and Tests of Statistical Significance 117
5.6 PRACTICE WHAT YOU LEARNED: Expand on Your Research Question 119
5.7 CHECKING YOUR UNDERSTANDING: Identifying Variables 120
5.8 CHECKING YOUR UNDERSTANDING: Designing a Research Review 126

CHAPTER 6 Measurement: Linking Theory to Research 130

6.1 Overview: The Measurement Process 131

6.2 Conceptualization and Operationalization 132
Conceptualization 132
Operationalization 134
Summary 137

6.3 Variations in Operational Definitions: Data Sources 138
Manipulated vs. Measured Operations 138
Sources of Measured Operational Definitions 139
Summary 143

6.4 Variations in Operational Definitions: Levels of Measurement 144
Nominal Measurement 145
Ordinal Measurement 146
Interval Measurement 147

Ratio Measurement   148
Summary   149

6.5 Select and Apply Operational Definitions to Produce Data   151
Summary   153

6.6 Assess the Quality of Operational Definitions   154
Forms of Reliability Assessment   158
Forms of Validity Assessment   161
Summary   165

6.7 The Feedback Loop: From Data Back to Concepts and Measurement   167
Summary   169

BOXES

6.1 PRACTICE WHAT YOU LEARNED: Create a Conceptual Definition   134
6.2 CHECKING YOUR UNDERSTANDING: Measurement Process Review   137
6.3 CHECKING YOUR UNDERSTANDING: Operational Definition Review I   143
6.4 CHECKING YOUR UNDERSTANDING: Inferring Level of Measurement from Operational Definitions   149
6.5 PRACTICE WHAT YOU LEARNED: Identify Variables and Empirical Indicators   153
6.6 CHECKING YOUR UNDERSTANDING: Operational Definition Review II   154
6.7 READING CRIMINAL JUSTICE RESEARCH: Indexes, Scales, and Scaling Techniques   157
6.8 READING CRIMINAL JUSTICE RESEARCH: Measurement Error and the Social Desirability Effect   163
6.9 CHECKING YOUR UNDERSTANDING: Matching Definitions   166
6.10 CHECKING YOUR UNDERSTANDING: Models of Inquiry   169

CHAPTER 7 Sampling: Case Selection as a Basis for Inference   173

7.1 Overview: The Sampling Process   174

7.2 Principles of Probability Sampling   176
Probability and Random Selection   176
Probability Distribution and Sampling Error   179
Statistical Inference   180
Summary   182

7.3 Steps in Probability Sampling   183
Define Target Population   183
Construct Sampling Frame   184
Devise Sampling Design   185
Draw Sample   189
Summary   191

7.4 Nonprobability Sampling 192
Overview of Nonprobability Sampling 192
Steps in Nonprobability Sampling 193
Making Inferences from Nonprobability Samples 197
Summary 198

BOXES
7.1 DOING CRIMINAL JUSTICE RESEARCH: How to Select Things Randomly 177
7.2 CHECKING YOUR UNDERSTANDING: Probability Sampling I 182
7.3 READING CRIMINAL JUSTICE RESEARCH: Assessing Nonresponse Bias and Overall Sample Quality 190
7.4 CHECKING YOUR UNDERSTANDING: Probability Sampling II 191
7.5 READING CRIMINAL JUSTICE RESEARCH: Methodological Issues Related to Sampling via Crowdsourcing and Online Panels 196
7.6 CHECKING YOUR UNDERSTANDING: Matching Exercise: Sampling 199

CHAPTER 8 Experiments: What Causes What? 203

8.1 Introductory Example: Misconduct in Criminal Prosecution 204

8.2 The Logic of Experimentation 206
Summary 210

8.3 Variations on the Experimental Method 211
Variations in Experimental Design 211
Variations in Experimental Context 213
Summary 216

8.4 The Process of Conducting Experiments 217
Pretesting 218
Participant Recruitment and Informed Consent 219
Introduction to the Experiment 219
Experimental Manipulation and Random Assignment 221
Manipulation Checks 221
Measurement of the Dependent Variable 223
Debriefing 224
Summary 225

8.5 Strengths and Weaknesses of Experiments 226
Internal Validity 226
External Validity 229
Reactive Measurement Effects 231
Content Restrictions 233
Summary 233

BOXES

8.1 DOING CRIMINAL JUSTICE RESEARCH: The Difference Between Random Sampling and Random Assignment 208
8.2 CHECKING YOUR UNDERSTANDING: Experimental Design Review I 210
8.3 CHECKING YOUR UNDERSTANDING: Experimental Design Review II 217
8.4 DOING CRIMINAL JUSTICE RESEARCH: Informed Consent Form for an Experiment 219
8.5 CHECKING YOUR UNDERSTANDING: Experimental Process 225
8.6 READING CRIMINAL JUSTICE RESEARCH: Thinking Critically About Research Designs and Threats to Internal Validity 227
8.7 CHECKING YOUR UNDERSTANDING: Internal and External Validity 234

CHAPTER 9 Surveys: Questioning and Sampling 238

9.1 General Features of Survey Research 239
Large-Scale Probability Sampling 240
Structured Interviews or Questionnaires 240
Quantitative Data Analysis 242
Summary 242

9.2 Variations in Survey Designs and Modes 243
Survey Research Designs 243
Data-Collection Modes 245
Summary 253

9.3 The Process of Planning and Conducting a Survey 254
Choose Mode of Data Collection 255
Construct and Pretest Questionnaire 255
Choose Sampling Frame/Design and Select Sample 261
Recruit Sample and Collect Data 261
Code and Edit Data 262
Summary 263

9.4 Strengths and Weaknesses of Surveys 264
Generalization to Populations 265
Versatility 265
Efficiency 265
Establishing Causal Relationships 265
Measurement Issues 266
Summary 266

BOXES

9.1 CHECKING YOUR UNDERSTANDING: Survey Research and Questions 242
9.2 CHECKING YOUR UNDERSTANDING: Types of Data Collection 253
9.3 DOING CRIMINAL JUSTICE RESEARCH: Writing Survey Questions 256

9.4 PRACTICE WHAT YOU LEARNED: Wording Questions   260
9.5 CHECKING YOUR UNDERSTANDING: Question and Survey Framing   264
9.6 CHECKING YOUR UNDERSTANDING: Survey Review   267

CHAPTER 10 **Field Research and In-Depth Interviews:** Systematic People-Watching and Listening   271

Introduction: Prisonization and the Problems of Reentry   273

10.1 General Features of Qualitative Research   274
- Observation   274
- Interviews   275
- Supplementary Archival and Other Data   277
- Nonprobability Sampling   277
- Qualitative Data Analysis   278
- Reflexivity   278
- Summary   280

10.2 Variations in Qualitative Research Methods   280
- Degrees of Participation and Observation   280
- Overt vs. Covert Observation   282
- Between Overt and Covert Observation   284
- Interview Structure   285
- Individual vs. Group Interviews   286
- Impact of Technological Developments on Observations and Interviews   287
- Summary   289

10.3 The Process of Conducting Field Research   290
- Select Setting/Group   291
- Gain Access   291
- Establish Roles and Relationships   294
- Decide What to Observe/Whom to Interview   295
- Gather and Analyze Data   296
- Leave the Field   297
- Write the Report   298
- Summary   298

10.4 The Process of Conducting In-Depth Interviews   300
- Select and Recruit Interviewees   300
- Develop an Interview Guide   301
- Gather Data   303
- Analyze Data   304
- Summary   305

10.5 Strengths and Limitations of Qualitative Research   306
- Naturalistic Approach   306
- Subjective and Contextual Understanding   307

Flexible Research Design 307
Generalizability 308
Reliability and Validity 308
Efficiency 309
Summary 309

BOXES

10.1 CHECKING YOUR UNDERSTANDING: Reflexivity in Criminological Research 279

10.2 READING CRIMINAL JUSTICE RESEARCH: Parts Unknown: Undercover Ethnography of the Organs-Trafficking Underworld 283

10.3 CHECKING YOUR UNDERSTANDING: Qualitative Research Review I 289

10.4 CHECKING YOUR UNDERSTANDING: Field Research 299

10.5 DOING CRIMINAL JUSTICE RESEARCH: Preparing for an In-Depth Interview 302

10.6 CHECKING YOUR UNDERSTANDING: In-Depth Interviews 305

10.7 CHECKING YOUR UNDERSTANDING: Qualitative Research Review II 310

CHAPTER 11 Existing Data Analysis: Using Data from Secondhand Sources 314

11.1 Sources and Examples of Existing Data 315
Public Documents and Official Records 316
Private Documents 318
Mass Media 318
Physical, Nonverbal Evidence 320
Criminal Justice Data Archives 321
Summary 321

11.2 Content Analysis 322
Content Analysis Example: Portrayal of Mental Illness in US Crime Dramas 323
The Process of Content Analysis 324
Summary 331

11.3 Comparative Historical Analysis 332
An Example of Comparative Historical Analysis: The Emergence of Mass Imprisonment 332
The Process of Comparative Historical Analysis 335
Summary 339

11.4 Strengths and Limitations of Existing Data Analysis 340
Studying Social Structure, History, and Social Change 340
Nonreactive Measurement 341
Cost Efficiency 341
Data Limitations 341
Summary 342

Contents   XIII

BOXES

    11.1 READING CRIMINAL JUSTICE RESEARCH: The Big Data Revolution   319

    11.2 CHECKING YOUR UNDERSTANDING: Data Sources   322

    11.3 CHECKING YOUR UNDERSTANDING: Identifying Units of Analysis   326

    11.4 DOING CRIMINAL JUSTICE RESEARCH: Analyzing the Content of Cell Phone Use   331

    11.5 CHECKING YOUR UNDERSTANDING: Comparative Historical Analysis   339

    11.6 CHECKING YOUR UNDERSTANDING: Data Analysis Review   342

CHAPTER 12   Evaluation Research: Assessing Program Need and Impact   346

12.1 Overview of Evaluation Research   348
Evaluation Research Defined   348
Components of Evaluation Research   349
Summary   351

12.2 Types of Evaluation Research   352
Needs Assessment   352
Evaluability Assessment   355
Process Evaluations   358
Outcome Evaluations   360
Efficiency Evaluations   363
Summary   364

12.3 Conducting Evaluation Research   365
Program Theory   365
Orientation of Research   366
Feasibility   368
Quantitative, Qualitative, or Mixed Methods   369
Summary   370

12.4 Experimental, Quasi-, and Nonexperimental Designs   371
Experimental Designs   371
Quasi-Experimental Designs   371
Nonexperimental Designs   373
Summary   373

BOXES

    12.1 CHECKING YOUR UNDERSTANDING: Research and People Involved in Research   351

    12.2 DOING CRIMINAL JUSTICE RESEARCH: Comparing and Contrasting Evaluability Assessments and Process Evaluation   359

    12.3 DOING CRIMINAL JUSTICE RESEARCH: Randomized Controlled Trials   362

12.4 CHECKING YOUR UNDERSTANDING: Types of Evaluation Research 364
12.5 DOING CRIMINAL JUSTICE RESEARCH: Action-Research Partnerships 367
12.6 CHECKING YOUR UNDERSTANDING: Research Terminology 370
12.7 CHECKING YOUR UNDERSTANDING: Research Design 374

CHAPTER 13 Multiple Methods: Two or More Approaches Are Better Than One 377

13.1 A Comparison of Four Basic Approaches to Criminal Justice Research 379
Summary 382

13.2 Examples of Mixed Methods Research 383
Bullying and Victimization During Childhood and Adolescence 383
What Employers Say vs. What They Do 385
Explaining Discrimination in a Low-Wage Labor Market 388

13.3 Purposes of Mixed Methods Research 390
Triangulation 390
Complementarity 391
Development 391
Expansion 392
Summary 392

13.4 Mixed Methods Research Designs 393
Sequential Designs 395
Concurrent Designs 395
Component Designs 395
Integrated Designs 396
Summary 396

BOXES
13.1 CHECKING YOUR UNDERSTANDING: Approaches to Criminal Justice Research 382
13.2 CHECKING YOUR UNDERSTANDING: Mixed Methods Research 392
13.3 DOING CRIMINAL JUSTICE RESEARCH: Limitations and Guidelines for Doing Mixed Methods Research 393
13.4 CHECKING YOUR UNDERSTANDING: Mixed Methods Research Design 397

CHAPTER 14 Quantitative Data Analysis: Using Statistics for Description and Inference 400

14.1 Introductory Overview: The Process of Quantitative Analysis 403

Contents XV

14.2 Prepare Data for Computerized Analysis: Data Processing 404
Coding 404
Editing 404
Entering the Data 405
Cleaning 408
Summary 408

14.3 Inspect and Modify Data 409
Nominal- and Ordinal-Scale Variables 410
Interval- and Ratio-Scale Variables 412
Summary 416

14.4 Carry Out Preliminary Hypothesis Testing 417
Nominal- and Ordinal-Scale Variables 418
Interval- and Ratio-Scale Variables 423
Summary 428

14.5 Conduct Multivariate Testing 429
Elaboration of Contingency Tables 430
Multiple Regression 433
Summary 438

BOXES

14.1 DOING CRIMINAL JUSTICE RESEARCH: Codebook Documentation 406
14.2 CHECKING YOUR UNDERSTANDING: Quantitative Data Analysis 409
14.3 CHECKING YOUR UNDERSTANDING: Quantitative Data Concepts 416
14.4 CHECKING YOUR UNDERSTANDING: The Meaning of Statistical Significance and Strength of Association 427
14.5 READING CRIMINAL JUSTICE RESEARCH: The Impact of Statistical Assumptions in Quantitative Data Analysis 437
14.6 CHECKING YOUR UNDERSTANDING: Multivariate Testing 438

CHAPTER 15 **Qualitative Data Analysis:** Searching for Meaning 444

15.1 Overview: A Process of Analyzing Qualitative Data 446
15.2 Prepare Data 447
Transform the Data to Readable Text 447
Check for and Resolve Errors 448
Manage the Data 449
Summary 451

15.3 Identify Concepts, Patterns, and Relationships 452
Coding 452
Memo Writing 455

Data Displays 455
Summary 459

15.4 Draw and Evaluate Conclusions **460**
Summary 461

15.5 Variations in Qualitative Data Analysis **462**
Grounded Theory Methods 462
Narrative Analysis 464
Conversation Analysis 465
Summary 467

BOXES

15.1 CHECKING YOUR UNDERSTANDING: Working with Data 451
15.2 DOING CRIMINAL JUSTICE RESEARCH: Coding Textual Data 454
15.3 CHECKING YOUR UNDERSTANDING: Coding Terms 459
15.4 CHECKING YOUR UNDERSTANDING: Evaluating Data 461
15.5 CHECKING YOUR UNDERSTANDING: Qualitative Data Analysis 467

Glossary 471

References 480

Credits 502

Index 505

About the Authors

RIANE M. BOLIN, associate professor and chair of the Department of Criminal Justice at Radford University, received her PhD from the University of South Carolina.

MARGARET C. PATE, former associate professor of criminal justice at Radford University, received her PhD from the University of Florida.

JEFFREY C. DIXON, professor of sociology at the College of the Holy Cross, received his PhD from Indiana University, Bloomington, with a minor in research/quantitative methods and also holds a BS in secondary education from Wright State University.

ROYCE A. SINGLETON, JR., professor emeritus of sociology at the College of the Holy Cross, received his PhD from Indiana University, Bloomington, with a minor in mathematics.

BRUCE C. STRAITS, professor emeritus of sociology at the University of California, Santa Barbara, received his PhD from the University of Chicago.

Preface

The Process of Research in Criminal Justice and Criminology introduces students to the fundamentals of research, from topic selection and research design to data collection, analysis, and interpretation. A unique feature of the book is its emphasis on process. Every chapter contains flowcharts of research processes—for example, the process of measurement, the process of sampling, and the process of planning and conducting a survey—that provide step-by-step guides to conducting research in criminology and criminal justice and evaluating the research of others.

We have tried to make the book student-friendly in many ways: by writing in a conversational style, by illustrating concepts with familiar everyday examples, and by carefully selecting criminal justice research examples that are timely and relevant.

Many chapters include studies that are current and methodologically rigorous.

They also cover a wide range of cutting-edge topics, including drug treatment courts, gang use of social media, desistance from crime, prosecutorial misconduct, mass incarceration, and substance use and academic performance. To fully describe study methods, additional information on methodology was provided from the researchers that was not contained in their original published work. In this way, our readers see how research is sometimes a bumpy road and how researchers negotiate the bumps along the way.

In writing this book, we drew material from Dixon, Singleton, and Straits' *The Process of Social Research*. Those familiar with the book will find, however, while much of the core content is the same, the examples throughout the book are specific to criminology and criminal justice. In addition to its criminology and criminal justice examples, the book also features a new chapter on evaluation research.

ORGANIZATION

The book is organized into 15 chapters, grouped as follows:

Contexts of Criminal Justice and Criminology Research

Chapter 1 includes an overview of the research process. Chapter 2 shows how the essence of research as a scientific enterprise is a constant interplay between theory and data. Chapter 3 offers guidance for reviewing the criminal justice and criminology literature, writing a proposal, and writing a research report. Chapter 4 considers how research is shaped by ethical and political choices.

Designing Criminal Justice Research

Chapter 5 introduces basic terminology as we discuss topic selection and research designs in quantitative and qualitative research. The next two chapters then examine two key considerations in planning or designing a study: measurement (Chapter 6) and sampling (Chapter 7).

General Approaches to Criminal Justice Research

Chapters 8–11 cover basic approaches to criminal justice research: experiments, surveys, qualitative field research and in-depth interviews, and the use of existing data. Chapter 12 discusses how to assess program needs and impacts through evaluation research. Chapter 13 presents strategies for combining methods and approaches.

Analyzing and Interpreting Criminal Justice Research

Chapters 14 and 15 discuss data analysis and interpretation, respectively, for quantitative and qualitative data.

FEATURES

The book has several special features that will be useful in teaching and learning about the process of social research.

- **Learning objectives** are listed at the opening of each chapter, previewing key topics being discussed.
- **Section summaries** highlight the main ideas after each major section of a chapter.
- **Boxes** *assess comprehension of key concepts* (Checking Your Understanding), provide practical advice to *conduct social research* (Doing Criminal Justice Research), *clarify and evaluate research* (Reading Criminal Justice Research), and *encourage students to demonstrate their knowledge* (Practice What You Learned).
- **Key Terms** are highlighted and defined in each chapter and included in the book's comprehensive glossary.
- **Key Points, Review Questions,** and **Exercises** at the end of each chapter reinforce learning objectives.

TEACHING AND LEARNING SUPPORT

Oxford University Press offers students and instructors a comprehensive teaching package of support materials for adopters of *The Process of Research in Criminal Justice and Criminology*.

OXFORD LEARNING LINK

Oxford Learning Link at https://learninglink.oup.com/ is a convenient destination for all teaching and learning resources that accompany this book. Accessed online through individual user accounts, Oxford Learning Link provides instructors with access to up-to-date ancillaries while guaranteeing the security of grade-significant resources. In addition, it allows OUP to keep users informed when new content becomes available. Oxford Learning Link for *The Process of Research in Criminal Justice and Criminology* includes a variety of materials to aid in teaching:

- Digital copy of the **Instructor's Manual**, which includes:
  - Lecture and demonstration ideas
  - Exercises
  - Online resources
  - Answers to review questions
- A **Test Bank**, including:
  - Multiple-choice questions
  - True/false questions
  - Essay prompts
- **PowerPoint lecture slides**
  - Sample syllabus

ACKNOWLEDGMENTS

As all researchers know, completing any major project requires reliance on and support from others. This was certainly the case in the development of this book. As we reflect on the journey of completing this book, we are filled with gratitude for the many individuals who contributed their time, advice, and support along the way. There are several persons whose contributions deserve special acknowledgments.

First and foremost, we would like to thank the authors of the original text from which our book was adapted, Jeffrey C. Dixon, College of the Holy Cross, Royce A. Singleton, Jr., professor emeritus at the College of the Holy Cross, and Bruce C. Straits, professor emeritus at the University of California, Santa Barbara. Without their hard work and dedication to producing a solid and student-friendly research methods textbook, our book would not have been possible.

We would like to extend our deepest appreciation to the editors with whom we have worked at Oxford University Press, Steve Helba and Sherith Pankratz. Their unwavering belief in this project and constant encouragement and patience kept us motivated during the challenging moments. Your support and guidance have been invaluable, and we are endlessly grateful for your belief in us.

In the Oxford production department, we would like to thank content development manager, Lauren Wing, art director Sherill Chapman, production editor Mairi

Patterson, and copy editor Elise Davies. Your expertise and attention to detail were instrumental in transforming the manuscript into a polished work. And last, but certainly not least, we would like to acknowledge and thank the Oxford marketing team, including marketing manager Laura Ewen, marketing assistant Kaylee Williams, and the other hardworking people who are getting our book into the hands of the students for whom we wrote it.

We owe a huge debt of gratitude to our spouses for their unwavering support and understanding throughout this process. Your patience, love, and encouragement sustained us through the long hours of writing and revision. We would also like to acknowledge our friends and colleagues who provided moral support and encouragement.

We would like to extend special thanks to those instructors, both named and anonymous, who took the time to offer thoughtful reviews of our book:

Cindy Michelle Britton, Chowan University
Julie Campbell, University of Nebraska at Kearney
Jason Cantone, George Mason University
Nicole Doctor, Ivy Tech Community College
Sheila J. Foley, Bay Path University
Tina Freiburger, University of Wisconsin-Milwaukee
Huan Gao, California State University, Stanislaus
Jonathan Grubb, Georgia Southern University
Emily M. Homer, UNC Wilmington
Patrick Jackson, Sonoma State University
Vesna Markovic, Lewis University
Shelly A. McGrath, University of Alabama at Birmingham
Robert McNamara, The Citadel
Rebecca Petersen, Kennesaw State University
Rae Taylor, Loyola University of New Orleans
Sarah Tosh, Rutgers University-Camden
Diane Zorri, Embry-Riddle Aeronautical University

Introduction

Why Care About Research Methods?

CHAPTER OUTLINE

Introduction 2
1.1 The Process of Social Research 7
1.2 Four Criminal Justice Studies 10
  An Experiment 10
  A Survey 11
  A Field Research Study 13
  An Analysis of Existing Data 15
  Summary 16

LEARNING OBJECTIVES

By the end of this chapter, you should be able to

1.1 Identify the four major steps in the research process.

1.2 Describe the four major approaches to social research.

▲ PHOTO 1.1 "Is social media ruining students?" That is one of many headlines that question the impact of Facebook and other such forms of online communication.

INTRODUCTION

Launched in 1999 "for students, by students," Rate My Professors claims to be the largest online source of professor ratings. Students visiting the website may rate a professors' overall quality and level of difficulty, indicate whether they would take a course with the professor again, and add comments. Students may even select classes based on the "data" reported on this website. But how credible is the website? Can you trust such ratings?

According to the Pew Research Center, the majority of individuals aged 18–29 use social media, suggesting that most college students use social media (Auxier & Anderson, 2021). The expansive use of social media by college students has led researchers to explore the effects of such use on various aspects of students' lives, including academic performance. (See Photo 1.1.) In April 2009, Aryn Karpinski, then a graduate student at The Ohio State University, presented a coauthored paper at a professional meeting indicating that students who use Facebook have lower grades than those who do not (Karpinski & Duberstein, 2009). These findings generated a media frenzy, triggering such headlines as "What Facebook users share: Lower grades" and "Study: Facebook hurts grades" (cited in Pasek et al., 2009). Given the ever-expanding number of social media sites such as Snapchat, TikTok, and YouTube, the impact of social media on academic performance has remained in the news, with recent headlines including:

- "Why social media diminishes student performance and wellbeing" (Whelan & Golden, 2023),
- "Social media addiction takes toll on academic performance" (Kigotho, 2023),
- "Teachers Say B.C. school teens showed improved grades and social skills after a ban on phones" (Shen, 2023), and
- "Social media usage negatively impacts the schoolwork of students from adolescence to college research suggests" (Newswise, 2023).

Like many students today, you probably spend some time on social media. Should you believe these findings? A working knowledge of research methods can help you answer this question along with many more. The utility of studying research methods begins with our daily exposure to vast amounts of information. As you encounter information on websites, in the news media, through advertisements, and from other sources, it is important to know what information to believe, for much of it can be inaccurate, misleading, or conflicting.

Suppose, for example, it is time to select classes again, and you are thinking about a particular course. You are interested in the course topic, and the days and times when it meets are compatible with your schedule, but you do not know anything about the professor. So you decide to find out what students think about the professor by visiting Rate My Professors. According to the posted ratings, your potential professor is good, but difficult. You also read some of the student comments: some say the professor is very challenging; others complain about the heavy amount of assigned reading and unfair tests. How trustworthy is this information? Should you use it to decide whether to take this professor's course?

The answer: it would be hard to trust the ratings on Rate My Professors and make a good decision based on them. The problem is that these ratings are not based on a representative group of students who have taken the professor's course but rather on self-selected students who took the time to go to the website. Very few students choose to rate their professors on Rate My Professors. It is also possible that those few students who do visit the website have strong feelings about the professor, either favorable or unfavorable. As a result, you might find that responses fall at the extremes: they rate the professor as either very good or very bad. In addition, there is ongoing debate about whether such ratings reflect gender, racial, and other biases against professors, to which some recent large-scale studies of Rate My Professors speak (Murray et al., 2020; Rosen, 2018). Furthermore, there is no guarantee that the same students are not "voting" more than once. Thus, it is hard to accurately predict what this professor will be like from these ratings.

Sometimes, faulty, or misreported evidence and research can have other consequences, such as causing false alarm. Reports of the research on social media use and grades are an example. Though attention-grabbing, the headlines we cited are misleading. To conclude from this type of study that using social media *causes* bad grades violates a cardinal principle of social research: a relationship between two phenomena does not mean that one thing caused the other. To put it more succinctly, association does not equal causation. There could be other plausible explanations of the findings. For example, an equally likely interpretation is that receiving bad grades causes students to become social media users. Still another possibility is that there is no causal link between social media and grades. Social media use and poor grades may both be the result of procrastination. Or the association could be due to another common factor, such as a student's major, with some majors having more stringent grading standards than others (Pasek et al., 2009).

It is also problematic to rely upon anecdotal evidence from someone in a position of authority. Consider Project S.T.O.R.M., a prison-awareness program for youth, which was run by the Chester County Sheriff's Office in Chester County, South Carolina from 2013 to 2019 as a delinquency prevention initiative (Kimball & Alexander, 2019). This prison-awareness program was designed to deter wayward youth from a life of crime by showing them the realities of prison life. Children aged 8–16 were "arrested" and taken to jail to spend the night in an attempt to "scare them straight" (WBTV, 2016b). The program received much media attention both locally and nationally, being featured on both *The Steve Harvey Show* and A&E's *Beyond Scared Straight*. The sheriff at the time, Alex Underwood, estimated the program had a success rate above 90 percent, though no official studies of the program's effectiveness were conducted (WBTV, 2016a). Interestingly, prior studies exploring the effectiveness of similar programs have found them to be unsuccessful in reducing delinquent behavior, with some studies even finding that program participation increases delinquent behavior (Petrosino et al., 2013; van der Put et al., 2021). Given the mixed findings, which should you believe?

The sheriff had a vested interest in the success of the program since he was the founder. Thus, this potentially limited his ability to be objective about the program outcomes; the cases where youths' lives were turned around stuck out to him because they aligned with his beliefs about the program. Further, given that there had been no systematic evaluation of Project S.T.O.R.M., one could not make definitive conclusions about the overall success of the program. Lastly, the sheriff's purported success of Project S.T.O.R.M. could not be generalized to state that all "Scared Straight" programs were effective, as his experience with prison-awareness programs was limited to Project S.T.O.R.M. and there was likely variability in how these programs were implemented. Studying research methods will enable you to critically evaluate and identify other limitations of reported research.

It is also not unusual to encounter conflicting information in everyday life and in social science research. One website presents different ways to lose weight, complete with percentages of people who successfully applied each weight-loss method. Another website is filled with stories of those who used the same strategies and *gained weight*. One news report cites studies showing the harmful effects of drinking coffee; another report claims that scientific studies refute most of these effects. Specific to research within the field of criminal justice, mixed findings have been reported on the effectiveness of sex offender registration and notification (SORN) on reoffending. In their meta-analysis of the effectiveness of SORN on reoffending, Zgoba and Mitchell (2023) found seven of the 18 studies included in their analysis reported reductions in recidivism. However, five other studies included found increases in recidivism and the six remaining studies reported nonsignificant findings. When you come across conflicting information or evidence such as this, knowledge of research methods can help you sort out what is most credible. For an example, see Box 1.1.

BOX 1.1
READING CRIMINAL JUSTICE RESEARCH

Empirical vs. Anecdotal: Who Do We Trust?

What, if anything, should you believe about the effectiveness of "Scared Straight" programs? As a student of research methods, you will learn to evaluate research by asking tough questions. For example, where is the evidence coming from, who is making the claim, was a systematic study conducted, and who were the participants in the study?

Thinking back to the former sheriff's conclusions about the success of Project S.T.O.R.M., a prison-awareness program for preventing juvenile delinquency, we must evaluate these claims with a critical eye, by asking the questions listed below. Let us consider his claims as compared to empirical research on the topic (see Table 1.1). If you had to make a conclusion on the effectiveness of "Scared Straight" programs, would you trust the opinion of the former county sheriff, or would you prefer more robust evidence?

Table 1.1 Project S.T.O.R.M. vs. Empirical Research

	Project S.T.O.R.M.	Meta-analysis of "Scared Straight" (Petrosino et al., 2013)
Who was the evaluator?	Former Chester County Sheriff Alex Underwood, founder of the program.	Petrosino, Turpin-Petrosino, Hollis-Peel, & Lavenberg; Petrosino is the director of the WestEd Justice & Prevention Research Center; coauthors Turpin-Petrosino, Hollis-Peel, & Lavenberg are academics at universities.
Who were the participants?	"About" 700 participants went through this program from 2013–2019. Participants were mainly from South Carolina, with some from Texas and California.	Exactly 946 participants were part of this review. Participants came from studies conducted in 8 different states during the years 1967–1992.
What was the process of evaluation?	No formal evaluation was conducted, and there were no formal documents describing how the program should be implemented.	This study was a meta-analysis of 9 studies. All 9 studies evaluated the "Scared Straight" program using a randomized control trial, meaning there was a comparison of individuals who were randomly assigned to a program and individuals in a no-treatment control.

continues

continued

	Project S.T.O.R.M.	Meta-analysis of "Scared Straight" (Petrosino et al., 2013)
What evidence was found?	After youth left the program, deputies were supposed to follow up with their parents. According to these reports, "only a small percentage have reported that their children got into trouble afterward" (Kimball & Alexander, 2019, para. 51). This "evidence" is only available for those who have gone through the program.	Studies were only included in the review if they had at least one measure of post-program criminal behavior. Results of the meta-analysis produced evidence that the programs do not work and can actually have a negative effect; individuals in the programs were slightly more likely to engage in criminal activity after the program than individuals who had never gone through a program, even though random assignment to treatment would have made the two groups of individuals relatively equal at the start.

As you read this book, you will develop the ability to understand and evaluate the accuracy and limits of social scientific research so that you can draw *your own* conclusions about it. You should find this useful in numerous ways. As a student, you may be required to read published research articles for class or to prepare a term paper or other course project. After graduation, you may need to know the policy implications of research findings or read research reports to keep up in your field. And as an ordinary citizen, you may want to use information from published research to make informed decisions or simply evaluate information reported online and in the media every day.

You will learn from this book not only how to evaluate research but also how to conduct it yourself. In this way, you will become both a critical *consumer* of research and an active *producer* of knowledge. Students often enjoy doing their own research. It can be empowering to learn how to find out something *you want to know*. It can also be fun to "get one's hands dirty" in the research process itself.

Learning how to conduct research also has many benefits. First and foremost, it may be an essential skill for the course you are currently taking. Later in your undergraduate academic career, you may conduct research for another course, a capstone project, or a thesis. If you plan to further your education, knowing how to do research may be a prerequisite for gaining admission to graduate or professional school and successfully completing a postbaccalaureate degree. These and related skills are also quite valuable in the world of work (Hart Research Associates, 2018). As instructors, we have had former students ask for our advice on research projects they were working on for their employers. For example, one project consisted of a client survey; in another, the student wanted to assess the effectiveness of a new reentry program that was being implemented at the prison where she was employed.

Now that you can see how useful it is to study research methods, we want to give you a better idea about the nature and process of social science research. When we say *social science research*, we mean that the topic must have some social aspect such as studying people, interactions, groups of people, social networks, or whole nations. It also means that this research is *scientific*, or based on systematic and verifiable observations. Like all sciences, social research aims to arrive at explanations of the natural world through systematic observations and logical reasoning. In the remainder of this chapter, we provide an overview of the process of social research found in criminology and criminal justice.

1.1 THE PROCESS OF SOCIAL RESEARCH

We believe that the best way to learn how to do something is to understand the underlying *process*. As an example, consider the process of course registration. The first step in this process is to see which courses are offered. As a next step, you might consult with others, such as an academic advisor, friends, or family, about the courses. (We hope, though, that you now understand the drawbacks of consulting Rate My Professors!) At the same time, you need to consider your schedule and time preferences to ensure there are no conflicts. Once you have decided on your course schedule, the final step is to actually register.

Likewise, if you want to learn how to do social research so that you can evaluate reported studies as well as conduct your own study, you need to understand the research process. Figure 1.1 shows the major steps in this process. As the figure illustrates, research begins with a research question. Once you have posed a research question, you need to determine how best to answer it. That is, you need to devise a plan, called a research design (step 2 in the figure). Step 3 is to carry out your research design by gathering data to answer your research question. Finally, step 4 consists of the analysis and interpretation of your data. This book is organized to follow these steps. After a discussion of the scientific, ethical, and political contexts of research in Chapters 2 and 4, Chapters 5–7 cover steps 1 and 2. Chapters 8–13 cover step 3, and Chapters 14 and 15 cover step 4.

Each major step in a process is often a series of other steps. For instance, there is more to the process of course registration than we described, as you probably know. Consider the step of consulting with others. This may also involve getting course approval from advisors and professors, filling out additional forms, and ensuring that all of your fees are paid before you can register. Even these steps are processes themselves. To get approval

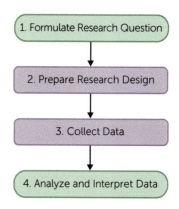

FIGURE 1.1 The Research Process

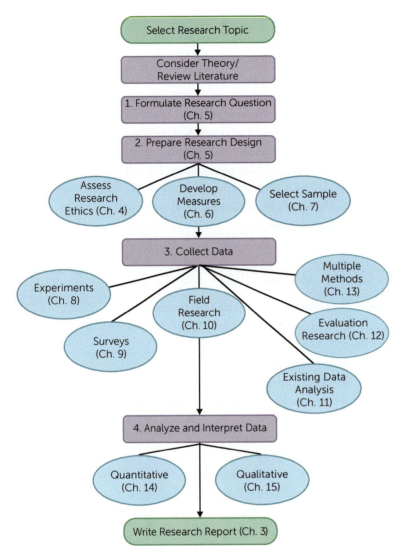

FIGURE 1.2 The Research Process Elaborated

for the course, for example, you may need to set up an appointment, meet with your advisor or professor, and then get this approval put into the system.

Although we hope it is not as frustrating as the process of course registration (!), the process of social research also involves other steps, which are processes in and of themselves (see Figure 1.2). The chapters of this book describe these steps and their underlying processes. Consider, for example, the first major step of formulating a research question: for beginning researchers, this initially depends on the selection of a *general* topic. There also may be questions about criminal behavior or the justice system that led to your interest in criminal justice as a major. For example, while scrolling through TikTok, you come across a story of an offender who has recently been released from prison who has gone on to commit a heinous crime. This causes you to wonder, does punishment really deter crime? Is rehabilitation an effective tool for reducing recidivism? Media headlines, personal interest, course content, and curiosity are all worthwhile motivators for the study of a general topic. However, a general topic must be narrowed to a more specific research question. This narrowing process requires a consideration of theory and prior research, which involves reviewing the literature: locating scholarly books or articles and reading, synthesizing, and evaluating them. Once you have reviewed the literature on, say, deterrence and rehabilitation, you can formulate a research question. You might learn about specialized courts in your criminal justice course and then wonder whether drug treatment courts, a specialized court for the treatment of drug offenders, are more effective than traditional courts at rehabilitating offenders and reducing recidivism for drug-related offenses (Mitchell et al., 2012). You might instead want to know about the effectiveness of the death penalty in deterring others from engaging in violent crime (general deterrence) (Hong & Kleck, 2018). Outside of the effectiveness of punishment, as a criminal justice major, you might have other questions, such as how citizens' perceptions of the redeemability of people who commit crimes impact their level of punitiveness (Burton et al., 2020) and how gangs use social media to challenge their rivals (Stuart, 2020). To practice formulating a research question, please refer to Box 1.2.

Finally, whether we are considering course registration, social research, or some other process, one size rarely fits all. While an understanding of the general process will help you to complete the steps, each step in the process will shape those that follow. For example, in designing research to answer your question (step 2), the steps will depend largely on the *type* of research question you ask (see Chapter 5). The question also will shape, in particular, which method you choose to collect data (step 3). Among the numerous methods available, the most essential differences occur among the broad approaches into which these methods can be grouped: **experiments**, **surveys**, **qualitative research**, and **existing data analysis**. We discuss the process of doing research with each of these approaches in Chapters 8–11. In Chapter 12, we will discuss how to use these methods for a specific purpose of research, evaluating the process and outcomes of criminal justice programs. Then we discuss strategies for using a combination of approaches in Chapter 13. Reading these chapters will enable you to decide which approach or combination best answers your research question as well as how to use the approach in your own research. Finally, the process of analyzing data (step 4) varies according to whether your data are in numerical form. We explain how to analyze quantitative (numerical) data in Chapter 14 and how to analyze qualitative (nonnumerical) data in Chapter 15.

---

experiment basic approach to social research that entails manipulating an aspect of the environment to observe behavior under different, controlled conditions

survey basic approach to social research that involves asking a relatively large sample of people direct questions through interviews or questionnaires

qualitative research basic approach to social research that involves directly observing and often interviewing others to produce nonnumerical data

existing data analysis analysis of data from existing sources of information that were not produced directly by the researcher who uses them

---

BOX 1.2

PRACTICE WHAT YOU LEARNED

Formulate a Research Question

Consider your current interests in the field of criminal justice. Identify the interests you have that can be formulated into a research question. For example, if you have an interest in the death penalty as a punishment, maybe you can generate a research question like this one: Does the death penalty deter crime? Write out a research question or two based upon your general interest(s).

1.2 FOUR CRIMINAL JUSTICE STUDIES

Now that you have a general idea of the overall research process, we want to give you a "sneak preview" of this process by briefly describing studies that address each of the earlier questions we posed about criminal behavior and the justice system. We chose these questions, in part, because each is best answered with a different methodological approach. In this way you can see how the specifics of the research process vary depending on the approach. Our discussion of these studies is necessarily limited and selective; we encourage you to consult the original sources for further exploration.

An Experiment

Have you ever wondered what a drug treatment court is? What about the effectiveness of a drug treatment court at reducing reoffending for drug-related offenses? To answer this question, Gottfredson et al. (2003) conducted an experiment. An experiment is a distinctive methodological approach with two key features: manipulation and control. Researchers introduce changes into the environment (manipulation) so that behavior is observed under different conditions, and the conditions are the same except for the manipulation (control).

Wanting to know whether being assigned to a drug treatment court had a causal effect on likelihood to commit another drug offense post-release, Gottfredson and colleagues (2003) designed an experiment by manipulating whether participants were assigned to a drug treatment court or "treatment as usual." What varied was the type of treatment assigned: The treatment group was assigned to the Baltimore City Drug Treatment Court (BCDTC) and the control group was assigned to a traditional court. The BCDTC includes "intensive supervision, drug testing, drug treatment, and judicial monitoring over the course of approximately two years" (Gottfredson et al., 2003). Ultimately, drug treatment courts offer more intensive drug treatment and monitoring of offenders. In contrast, those assigned to traditional courts may be given some variation of incarceration, probation, and/or drug treatment (Gottfredson et al., 2003). The participants included 235 drug offenders; 139 of these offenders were randomly assigned to BCDTC, and 96 were randomly assigned to traditional courts. After a two-year follow-up period, researchers utilized official arrest and conviction data to determine differences in recidivism between the two groups (Gottfredson et al., 2003).

What did the analysis of data reveal? Participants assigned to the drug treatment court were significantly less likely to be rearrested compared to those assigned to traditional courts (Gottfredson et al., 2003). Additionally, drug treatment court participants had fewer new charges brought against them at follow-up than control group participants. Gottfredson and colleagues (2003) conclude that drug treatment courts can have a positive impact on recidivism for individuals arrested for drug offenses, particularly for those who consistently participate and complete certified drug treatment during the program.

Well-conducted experiments can help us understand the *cause and effect* relationship between two or more variables. In Chapter 8 you will learn how they do this effectively. As you will see, more than any other approach, experiments emphasize the design phase of criminal justice and criminological research. Once you have figured out how to manipulate the causal factor and how to control other factors, data collection and analysis are fairly straightforward. Yet experiments have limitations: you cannot manipulate everything of interest to criminologists, and experiments are usually performed on a select group of people at a certain place and time, such as the drug offenders in Baltimore where Gottfredson and colleagues (2003) conducted their research. Experiments also often involve deception, which raises questions about research ethics (see Chapter 4).

A Survey

While watching the evening news, you run across a story about an individual who recently committed a heinous crime. It leads you to question the redeemability of the individual: Can this person turn their life around or are they unlikely to change for the better? Further, you wonder whether perceptions of redeemability impact support for punitive and rehabilitative policies. Burton et al. (2020) sought to explore such questions in their national online survey of 1,000 individuals in the United States. A survey involves asking questions, usually of a randomly selected group of people. They partnered with YouGov, an international research data and analytics group, to administer a survey to a national sample of 1,000 US respondents. Below are some questions adapted from the survey, which you can also answer.

- To what extent do you agree that most offenders go on to lead productive lives with help and hard work?
  - o Strongly agree
  - o Agree
  - o Somewhat agree
  - o Somewhat disagree
  - o Disagree
  - o Strongly disagree
- To what extent do you agree that most criminal offenders are unlikely to change for the better?
  - o Strongly agree
  - o Agree
  - o Somewhat agree
  - o Somewhat disagree
  - o Disagree
  - o Strongly disagree

- Are you in favor of the death penalty for a person convicted of murder?
    - Favor
    - Oppose
    - No opinion
- In general, do you think the courts in this area deal too harshly or not harshly enough with criminals?
    - Too harsh
    - About right
    - Not harsh enough
    - Don't know
- To what extent do you agree that it is important to try to rehabilitate adults who have committed crimes and are now in the correctional system?
    - Strongly agree
    - Agree
    - Somewhat agree
    - Somewhat disagree
    - Disagree
    - Strongly disagree
- To what extent do you agree that it is a good idea to provide treatment for offenders who are supervised by the courts and live in the community?
    - Strongly agree
    - Agree
    - Somewhat agree
    - Somewhat disagree
    - Disagree
    - Strongly disagree

What were your answers? Burton and colleagues (2020) found that the public held a nuanced view of the redeemability of those who commit crime. Over three-quarters of the sample agreed that most offenders can go on to lead productive lives. However, at the same time, almost 60% indicated agreement that most criminals are unlikely to change for the better. Similar nuances were found for support for punitive and rehabilitative policies. Just over half (54.43 percent of the sample) favored the death penalty, while only 40 percent supported harsher courts. Further, respondents tended to support the idea of rehabilitation for those who commit crime. Examining the relationship between perceptions of redeemability and support for punitive policies and rehabilitation, redeemability was found to be associated with decreases in support for the death penalty and making courts harsher, but increases in support for rehabilitation. Additional analyses were conducted using data collected in 2019 from MTurk (see Burton et al. (2020) for more information).

Surveys help researchers to understand patterns and relationships that may be generalizable to a larger group of people. As you will see in Chapter 9, survey researchers take great care in writing questions, designing the questionnaire, and selecting respondents. Like experimental data, survey data typically are numerical and thus amenable to quantitative analysis (see Chapter 14). There are drawbacks to the survey method, however. Although the numbers generated by survey responses provide a snapshot of what a generally large group of people has to say, what people *say* may not always be truthful or even predictive of what they *do*. Furthermore, it can be difficult to establish "what causes what" with survey data, especially if the survey is conducted at only one point in time. Another limitation is that surveys may not adequately represent the group under study. Recall that only 1,000 US individuals were surveyed. Can we assume that these 1,000 individuals' opinions are representative of the US population as a whole? Discussion of generalizability of research findings will be discussed in later chapters.

A Field Research Study

Given the ubiquity of social media today, some scholars and law enforcement figures assume that gang-related violence may not begin in the streets but rather in tweets and other online activity (Stuart, 2020). To understand how young Black people associated with gangs use social media to challenge rivals, Forrest Stuart (2020) conducted field research in Chicago's South Side. **Field research** involves observing people in their natural settings and often interviewing them. Both field research and **in-depth interviews**, which may be used as a stand-alone method, produce *qualitative* (nonnumerical) data. Although field research is akin to engaging in "people-watching" and deep discussions in everyday life, it is systematic, requiring careful observation, listening, and analytic skills.

Stuart (2020) gained access to Black youth associated with gangs through his role as a "director of an after-school youth violence prevention program" (p. 196). For two years, he spent anywhere from 20 to 50 hours a week observing participants in a variety of settings, such as at home, work, in local neighborhoods, and in criminal justice settings. In addition, he conducted formal and informal interviews, asking "participants to review each day's social media activity" with him (p. 196).

Synthesizing data from his observations and interviews, Stuart (2020) found that his participants engage in different ways of presenting themselves and responding to rival gangs on social media. For instance, one participant, Tevin (a pseudonym), posted several photographs on Instagram of himself in various settings and in different outfits while holding a gun. Tevin explained that rival and fellow gang members would be checking his Instagram profile to see if he is as violent as he claims. He said, "That's why I got them pictures . . ." (p. 197). Tevin admitted to Stuart, however, that he took the pictures in five minutes with his cousin's gun; he never owned a

field research basic approach to social research that involves directly observing and often interviewing others to produce nonnumerical data

in-depth interview a type of formal interview intended to yield deep responses through open-ended questions and a flexible format

gun himself during Stuart's fieldwork. Such posts were common, according to Stuart (2020), as he "regularly observed members of all five gang factions upload pictures to social media that contained inoperable firearms, fake narcotics, and counterfeit money" (p. 197). Thus, it would be a mistake to take online activity at face value, as some police have.

Some communication strategies Stuart (2020) observed were less likely to lead to offline violence than others. Using a strategy he calls "cross referencing," he found that youth associated with one gang would post pictures of a rival gang member intended to undercut their personas. For instance, a gang member dug up an old Facebook photo of Will (a pseudonym), a person associated with a rival gang, in a tuxedo getting ready to go to a high school dance to cross-reference Will's recently posted selfie "standing menacingly on a street corner" (p. 198). Compared to other strategies Stuart discusses, this one was the least likely to lead to offline violence because it could be settled through a further online refutation, as Will did when he posted another picture of himself, gun in hand, seemingly taken around the same time.

Another strategy called "catching lacking" refers to confronting a person associated with a gang who is going about their non-gang-related daily business. This "involves physical assault . . . by definition" (p. 201) and can lead to even further violence, as one gang may retaliate against another. Sometimes these confrontations are recorded and uploaded to social media. But Stuart emphasizes that this strategy does not always lead to more violence. In one case, a young man named Nicky (a pseudonym) was caught lacking by another gang, which was recorded and appeared on Facebook feeds. Instead of retaliating against the rival gang, however, the gang with which Nicky was associated ostracized him.

Field research is distinct from experiments and surveys in several ways. Although both experiments and field research rely on observations, field researchers do not intentionally attempt to change people's behaviors. Rather, field researchers describe what they observe in people's natural settings and try to understand the broader social context of people's behaviors. The interviews used in field research—and in-depth interviews more generally—are distinct from survey interviews because researchers are less interested in the number or percentage of people who provide a certain response than the social meanings and processes behind those responses. Such qualitative research requires a more open-ended type of inquiry that, in contrast to other approaches, places less emphasis on design and more on the collection and analysis of data. Thus, early findings from observations and/or interviews tend to shape the direction of the research. The data are reported in ordinary language, such as in Tevin's quote. As you'll see in Chapter 15, the analysis of qualitative data requires a different set of tools than the analysis of quantitative data.

Although field research can deepen our understanding of the context and meanings behind behaviors and emotions, conclusions may not apply beyond the sometimes-narrow group being studied. Indeed, a criticism of Stuart's research is that his conclusions were based on observations and interviews in a selected area of Chicago, which makes it difficult to know how generalizable the findings are—that is, to whom they apply. Moreover, interviews in this form of research are subject to the same criticism as surveys: they capture what people say, but are not necessarily reflective of what people do. To counter this limitation of interviews, however, Stuart attempted to cross-check these data with observations.

An Analysis of Existing Data

A hotly debated topic in the field of criminal justice and in society generally is the use of the death penalty. One specific argument for the use of the death penalty is that it has a deterrent effect on violent crime. This argument generates a relevant research question: Does the death penalty actually have a deterrent effect on homicides? Hong and Kleck (2018) explored this question using existing data, which represents the fourth general approach in social research. Existing data analysis is the analysis of data from sources of information that were not produced directly by the researcher who uses them. Vast sources of existing data are available for analysis; these include books, historical documents, official statistics, and data compiled by other researchers.

Hong and Kleck (2018) answered their research question by examining a number of data sources, including state-level data on daily homicide rates, size of the state prison population, whether an execution had occurred, and national news coverage of executions. They predicted that the deterrent effect of executions on homicide rates should be largest around the time when news coverage is at its strongest. They found that both television and newspaper stories tended to peak the few days before and after an execution. Then, through a sophisticated quantitative analysis, they concluded that there was no significant pattern for homicide rates around the time of execution, like the pattern that was seen with news coverage. Ultimately, Hong and Kleck conclude that there were no drops in the homicide rate during the two weeks post-execution, therefore, their analysis does not support a short-term deterrent effect of the death penalty.

The enormous variety of existing data is limited only by the researcher's imagination. The challenges are to find data that are appropriate to answer the research question and to figure out how to analyze them. In Chapter 11, we examine diverse data sources and some of the major forms of existing data analysis. As you will see, the analysis of existing data often is well suited to studying the past and understanding social structure and social change. Compared with other approaches, a major strength is that existing data analyses tend to eliminate the tendency of research participants to change their behavior in the presence of a researcher. Yet this strength can also be a weakness: the distance between the researcher and the people they are studying can be problematic.

SUMMARY

Once you become aware of research findings and other evidence, you will realize that they surround us all on a daily basis. In the news, in everyday life, and even in our college classrooms, we hear: "Research indicates *this*"; "Research shows *that*." We see numerical ratings of professors (e.g., Rate My Professors), and even our colleges or universities, online (e.g., *U.S. News and World Report*'s rankings, available online). Knowledge of research methods can empower you to become a critical *consumer* of research findings and other evidence by asking tough questions. It can also enable you to pose research questions and answer them yourself, thereby becoming a *producer* of knowledge. The goals of this book are to provide you with the tools to do both.

In order to carry out a systematic investigation, social scientists follow a research process. The four major steps in the process are to

1. formulate a research question,
2. prepare a research design,
3. collect data, and
4. analyze/interpret data.

Each of these major steps in the process requires taking other steps to complete. The formulation of a research question, for example, involves selecting a general research topic, reviewing previous research and theory, and narrowing the topic to a more specific research question. These steps, in turn, are processes in and of themselves. Reviewing previous research and theory, for instance, requires reading, synthesis, and evaluation. Although this may seem complicated, it is similar to what you do in everyday life. As in registering for courses, the process goes much more smoothly if you know what it is and take it one step at a time.

Like other processes in everyday life, the process of social research provides you with options about how to carry out your study and collect data. We discussed several general methodological approaches: experiments, surveys, field research and in-depth interviews, and existing data analysis. We gave you a "sneak preview" of each of these approaches using specific examples. Each approach has its own set of strengths and weaknesses. The approach you use will depend on your research topic, question, and the available resources at your disposal. To check your understanding of the concepts learned within this section, please refer to Box 1.3.

1.2 Four Criminal Justice Studies

BOX 1.3

CHECKING YOUR UNDERSTANDING

Limitations of Methodological Approaches

Identify two limitations from the word box below for each of the methodological approaches listed. Write the corresponding letter for the limitation in the blank space after the methodological approach. Note: One limitation may be used for more than one methodological approach.

A. Responses may not be truthful	B. Finding data that is appropriate to your research question
C. Reduced generalizability, only uses a select group of people at a certain place and time	D. Involves deception, ethics concerns
E. The distance between the researchers and the people they are studying	F. Capture what people say, but not necessarily what they do
G. Inability to manipulate all variables of interest	

1. Survey _____

2. Experiment _____

3. Qualitative Research _____

4. Existing Data Analysis _____

KEY TERMS

existing data analysis, p. 9
experiment, p. 9
field research, p. 13
in-depth interview, p. 13
qualitative research, p. 9
survey, p. 9

KEY POINTS

- The study of research methods can enable you to become a more critical consumer of research evidence.
- The study of research methods can enable you to conduct your own research.
- The research process begins with the formulation of a research question and moves to the preparation of a research design, data collection, and data analysis.
- The four basic approaches to social research are experiments, surveys, qualitative research, and the analysis of existing data.

REVIEW QUESTIONS

1. What do the authors mean when they say that you can benefit from the study of research methods as both a *consumer* and a *producer* of research evidence?
2. What are the four major steps in the research process?
3. Briefly describe each of the four major approaches to social research. What are some strengths and weaknesses of each approach?

EXERCISES

1. Find a story or article in the media (e.g., newspaper, magazine, television) that reports the findings of a criminal justice study or of a contention purportedly based on social scientific evidence (i.e., the death penalty deters crime). What information, if any, is given about the methods of the study or the limitations of the findings? Does the author report where the data came from, how they were collected, or how many observations the findings were based on?
2. Select a recent issue of a major criminal justice journal, such as the *Criminology, Crime & Delinquency, Journal of Criminal Justice,* or *Justice Quarterly*. Based on your reading of the abstracts (the concise summaries on the first page) of each article, identify the basic approach (experiment, survey, qualitative research, or analysis of existing data) that is used in each study reported in the issue.

2

Science and Social Research

From Theory to Data and Back

LEARNING OBJECTIVES

By the end of this chapter, you should be able to

2.1 Define science and describe its characteristics.

2.2 Distinguish between deductive and inductive logic and describe how deductive and inductive logic are used in research to move between theory and data.

2.3 Identify the possibilities and limits of scientific knowledge.

CHAPTER OUTLINE

2.1 The Characteristics and Process of Science 21
Theory 21
Verifiable Data 22
Systematic Observation and Analysis 23
Logical Reasoning 25
Summary 30

2.2 Logics of Inquiry: Deductive and Inductive Logic 30
How Do Career Criminals Disengage from Criminal Behavior? An Answer from Inductive Inquiry 31
Do Social Bonds Matter? An Answer from Deductive Inquiry 32
Combining the Logics of Inquiry 33
Moving Between Deductive and Inductive Inquiries: Domestic Violence Responses 34
Summary 36

2.3 Evaluating Scientific Knowledge: Possibilities, Cautions, and Limits 36
Tentative Knowledge 36
The Ideal and Reality of the Scientific Process 37
The Sociohistorical Aspect of Science 38
The Human Element of Science 39
Summary 40

When you think of a scientist, what do you think of? For many years, Royce Singleton asked his sociology methods students this question. If you are like most of Singleton's students, you associate science first and foremost with the natural sciences—chemistry, physics, and biology. Moreover, you probably picture a scientist wearing a white lab coat in a laboratory, surrounded by test tubes and microscopes. Like many other students, you also might think of a scientist as a researcher or experimenter (Singleton, 1998).

These responses suggest two important patterns. First, students rarely think of criminologists or other social scientists as "scientists." The American public distinguishes between natural and social sciences in a similar way: whereas 71.3 percent of a national sample of American adults think that biology is "very scientific," only 10 percent say the same of sociology (Smith et al., 2019). Even though social scientists do not always agree on exactly what science is, their disciplines strive to be scientific (Academy of Criminal Justice Sciences, 2024; American Psychological Association, 2024; American Society of Criminology, 2023). To understand how they practice their craft, we therefore need to understand how science guides their activities. In this chapter we identify a characteristic process of inquiry that defines and unifies all the sciences—natural and social.

Second, students picture scientists almost exclusively as researchers. Singleton's students also referred to invention, discovery, exploration, and data analysis as other research activities. But they rarely thought of *theorists* when they thought about scientists (Singleton, 1998). Neither does the American public: when a national sample of adults was asked in 2018 to express in their own words "what it means to study something scientifically," only 13.85 percent mentioned the "formulation of theory" or "testing hypotheses" (Smith et al., 2019). This is a glaring omission because the best overall characterization of the scientific process is that it involves a continuous interplay between theory and data. This interplay is at the heart of every scientific discipline. It is why, for example, virtually every undergraduate and graduate student in criminology and/or criminal justice is required to take at least two courses: one in theory and one in research methods.

This chapter introduces you to the characteristics and process of science. It also outlines how scientists use logical reasoning to move back and forth between theory and data. This movement is illustrated in Figure 2.1, which shows that theory shapes data just as data shape theory. Lastly, we examine the possibilities and limits of scientific knowledge, which you should keep in mind when reading reports of research and conducting research yourself.

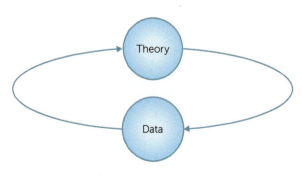

FIGURE 2.1 The Theory–Data Relationship

2.1 THE CHARACTERISTICS AND PROCESS OF SCIENCE

Scientific studies are guided by a cumulative body of knowledge, or theory; they also add to this body of theoretical knowledge. As noted in Chapter 1, science is based on verifiable data that have been systematically collected and analyzed. Scientists use the principles of logical reasoning to move back and forth between theory and data. Let us further examine each of these characteristics of science, beginning with theory.

Theory

We all have abstract ideas about how the social world works; a **theory** is no more than a formal statement, or system of statements, of these ideas. Sociologist Robert Merton (1996) defines theory as "logically interconnected sets of propositions from which empirical uniformities can be derived" (p. 41). The goal of science is to produce knowledge in the form of theory. If you have taken natural science courses, you are probably familiar with Darwin's theory of evolution, which holds that humans evolved from nonhuman animals through a process of natural selection over many, many years. In your criminal justice courses, you may have encountered numerous theories, including those of Robert Agnew, Ron Akers, Edwin Sutherland, or Michael Gottfredson.

theory an interconnected set of propositions that shows how or why something occurs

As an example, consider a theory that addresses a question you might have asked yourself about criminal behavior: What causes people to *not* engage in crime? In *Causes of Delinquency* (1969), criminologist Travis Hirschi put forward a theory of the social bonds that individuals have that could keep them from engaging in crime. The theory contains the following four elements:

1. attachment to others,
2. commitment to conventional norms,
3. involvement in prosocial activities, and
4. belief in the conventional norms and values of society.

When people are bonded to society via attachment to others, particularly parental figures, commitment to obeying and living by conventional rules of society (i.e., having educational and occupational aspirations), involvement in prosocial activities (i.e., church, school, extracurricular activities), and a belief in the validity of the law and rule structure, they are less likely to engage in criminal or deviant behavior (see Photo 2.1). If any of these individual elements (bonds) are weakened, the likelihood of criminal and/or deviant behavior is increased. The bonds are also interconnected, so if one bond is weak, it is likely that the other bonds are also weak. For example, imagine that a group of friends are hanging out, and one of them suggests breaking into an abandoned building for the purposes of vandalism. Steve says no because he realizes he has a lot to lose if they were to get caught. Steve has a strong bond with his parents and would not want to

▲ PHOTO 2.1 Hirschi suggests that people who are bonded to society through involvement in prosocial activities, such as being part of a sports team, are less likely to commit a crime.

disappoint them (attachment). Steve also has a scholarship to attend a prestigious state university in the fall and would not want to jeopardize his future (commitment). While he is concerned about his future, he also has to think about the present; Steve also has to show up for his job in a few hours and does not have time to engage in vandalism (involvement). Lastly, Steve believes that breaking and entering, even into an abandoned building, is a crime that he should not take part in (beliefs).

Characteristic of both the natural and social sciences is an emphasis on theory testing and development. That is, theories such as Darwin's or Hirschi's inform data and are informed by data, as illustrated in Figure 2.1. Contrary to popular belief, scientists rarely come up with brilliant ideas themselves and then test them; rather, their research is often guided by theories of their predecessors (Merton, 1996). Neither does research end after the collection and analysis of data. The patterns observed by researchers may support an existing theory, modify it, or lead to the generation of a new theory altogether.

In short, theory is integral to science. It both inspires and is inspired by research. Even more, beyond the scientific goal of producing theoretical knowledge, theory underlies the entire research process, from formulation of a research question to choices about how to conduct a study to the interpretation of data. While theory is a fundamental characteristic of science, science also depends on verifiable data.

Verifiable Data

data information recorded from observation; may be in numerical or nonnumerical form

Sometimes referred to as facts or empirical evidence, **data** are another characteristic of science. Their most important quality is to be verifiable. To verify is to check. And for this to be possible, the data must be observable to both the researcher and others in the scientific community. The terms *observable* and *empirical* are interchangeable; they mean that data must be tangible or "sensed" in some way—through sight, hearing, taste, smell, or touch. Evidence that cannot be sensed, such as appeals to authority, tradition, revelation, or intuition, cannot be verified; thus, they are not scientific data.

In Chapter 1, we provided several examples of criminal justice data: data from interviews and surveys, existing data sets, and experimental designs. Each of these

> **BOX 2.1**
>
> ## READING CRIMINAL JUSTICE RESEARCH
>
> ## Verify This!
>
> Imagine that you have just read a research report on crime in the United States. The report stated that in 2022 there were over one million reported violent crimes and cited the Uniform Crime Report (UCR) as its source. This number seems alarmingly high to you, as you do not witness or hear about violent crimes occurring regularly within your community. You decide to verify the data presented using the steps below:
>
> 1. Search online for the Federal Bureau of Investigation's Crime Data Explorer.
> 2. On the left-hand side of the screen, click the button for the "Data Discovery Tool."
> 3. Once the next screen comes up, under the "Dataset" option, select "Crime Data" and under the "Query Level" select "National or State" from the list.
> 4. Next, under the section titled "National or State Query" for the dates "to" and "from," select "2022" for each, for "Crime Select," choose "All Violent Crimes," and for "Location Select," choose "United States." Then click the "Submit" button.
> 5. Once finished, you will see a line chart that displays a single point of national data for violent crime in 2022. If you hover your mouse over the data point, this number should read 1,268,880,022. This confirms the information reported in the article you read!
>
> This example gives an idea of how to verify something. It also introduces you to the UCR, which is useful for learning about reported crime in the United States.

kinds of data is observable by the researcher and can also be checked by others. For example, it is theoretically possible to verify research reports containing extensive verbatim statements of people who participated in in-depth interviews by going back to the transcription or recording of the interview. Likewise, for a research report presenting survey data in numerical form, it is possible to verify these data by reviewing the questionnaires that respondents completed. And in the case of available survey data, it is possible to check with the organization that collected these data, as in Box 2.1.

Scientific knowledge is only as good as the data upon which it is based (Lieberson, 1985). Even if data are verifiable, they may not be systematically collected and analyzed. This brings us to another characteristic of science: it is systematic.

Systematic Observation and Analysis

Science is systematic in that it follows a typical process or a series of steps, which we outlined in Chapter 1. This process, which includes the collection and analysis of verifiable data, gives the broader scientific community greater confidence in the knowledge that is produced. Understanding that knowledge is based on a series of steps—and knowing what those steps are—lends credibility, or believability, to the conclusion (Gieryn, 1999).

If you have any doubt about the need to be systematic in order to arrive at credible conclusions, think about the grades you receive on the papers you write for your courses. Would your reaction to a grade differ depending on whether it was graded systematically or unsystematically? Suppose you had worked extremely hard on the paper: you logged long hours at the library, reading whatever you could on the topic; spent many sleepless nights writing and rewriting; and proofread the paper more times than you can remember. A week after you turned in the paper, your instructor returned it with a grade of a "C." You are not happy with a "C," but under which of the following scenarios are you most likely to accept the instructor's conclusion?

In the first scenario, the instructor explains to the class how he graded the papers. First, he developed a grading rubric that weighted certain components of the paper: for example, 10 percent of your grade was based on the clarity of your writing, 25 percent was based on the thesis development, and so on. Then, he read all the papers, marking them up with point deductions and comments explaining the point deductions. After adding up points, your instructor explains, he then reread the papers to check for consistency in how he applied the rubric. Finally, he made sure that he did not make any calculation errors and determined final grades from the grading scale.

In the second scenario, the instructor does not offer an explanation for how he graded the papers. When one student asks about this, the instructor replies that students' grades are based on their demonstrated knowledge of the material. Another student then asks: "How do you know that we know the material?" The instructor says, "I just know based on my reading of the papers."

Our guess is that, even if you are unhappy with the grade in either case, you are more likely to accept the grade as credible under the first scenario, and you are less likely to think that the grade reflects the instructor's personal values or biases. This is because the grading is systematic: the instructor has a process, or series of steps, by which he reads the papers, analyzes them, and ultimately assigns grades. In the second, by contrast, there is no system or method.

Just like the instructor under the first scenario, scientists attempt to be systematic. Being systematic minimizes the influence of scientists' personal values and lends credibility to their conclusions. But in practice, what does it mean to conduct research systematically? In the natural sciences, researchers may follow protocols; these are explicit statements, for example, of which chemicals should be combined in a test tube, how they should be measured, and what should be done next. This can be contrasted with an unsystematic approach, such as that of the second instructor's grading. Like natural scientists, social scientists follow a series of steps in their research, which we further discuss in Chapter 5 and describe in detail throughout the book. However, these steps depend on the specific research approach they use (discussed in Chapters 8–11) and on the logic of their inquiry, which we will now consider.

Logical Reasoning

When you answered the question in the chapter introduction about your mental image of a scientist, you may have said that you think of a scientist as logical. Science is often said to follow the principles of logical reasoning, which are also standards by which science is evaluated.

Whenever we reason, we proceed from certain information to conclusions based on that information. One of the true masters of reasoning would have to be Sir Arthur Conan Doyle's famous detective, Sherlock Holmes. In "Silver Blaze," the police investigating a murder identify someone unknown to the victim as the prime suspect. Holmes is certain, however, that this suspect is innocent. To make his point, he draws attention to "the curious incident of the dog in the night-time." When the police inspector protests, "the dog did nothing in the night-time," Holmes utters, "that was the curious incident." The fact that the dog did nothing (i.e., did not bark) shows that the perpetrator was someone the dog knew well. Therefore, the suspect could not have committed the crime (Doyle, 1894, p. 22).

We use logic to evaluate the correctness of our reasoning—to determine how justified a conclusion is, based on the evidence. There are two different types of reasoning: deductive and inductive. The primary difference between the two is how certain we are that the conclusion is true based on the evidence. When we use **deductive logic**, we are claiming that the conclusion must be true if the evidence is true. With **inductive logic**, by contrast, the conclusion is uncertain even if the evidence is true because the content of the conclusion goes beyond the evidence.

You are likely familiar with these logics even if you have never formally studied them. Popular books, movies, and television shows—especially involving criminal investigations—often feature them prominently. As described above, for example, Sherlock Holmes reasoned deductively as follows: Dogs bark at strangers. If the intruder were a stranger, the dog would have barked. The dog did not bark. Therefore, the intruder was not a stranger (i.e., they were someone known to the dog). This reasoning is said to be deductively valid—that is, correct—because the conclusion must be true if the evidence (or premises) is true.

In everyday life, however, we often use inductive, rather than deductive, logic to make choices about everything, from which foods to eat to which course to take. Suppose, for example, you observed a pattern of getting a stomachache whenever you consume a soda; therefore, you choose not to drink a soda when you are thirsty. Or you think that you will enjoy a history course and decide to take it because you have always liked history courses. In neither case does the conclusion necessarily follow if the evidence is true: it is possible that you will not have a stomachache the next time you drink a soda, and you may also not like the history course.

deductive logic
reasoning in which the conclusion is implied by, but goes beyond, the evidence at hand and, hence, may or may not be true

inductive logic
reasoning in which the conclusion necessarily follows if the evidence is true

Unlike deductive reasoning, which may be either valid or invalid, inductive reasoning may be weak or strong depending on how strongly the evidence supports the conclusion. Thus, the inductive conclusion that you will get a stomachache from drinking a soda in the future would be stronger if this had happened to you 20 times than if it had happened only once. To check your ability to reason deductively and inductively, complete the two questions presented in Box 2.2.

> **BOX 2.2**
>
> **CHECKING YOUR UNDERSTANDING**
>
> ## Identifying and Evaluating Deductive and Inductive Reasoning
>
> If you are thinking of going to law school or graduate school, or even applying for a job, you may have to take a logical reasoning test. These tests gauge people's ability to analyze reasoning. Your success on the tests would be enhanced greatly if you have taken a course in logic, which would provide the tools for identifying and evaluating different types of reasoning. Short of taking a logic course, however, you can learn a few skills that will aid your critical thinking.
>
> The official website of the Law School Admissions Test (LSAT) lists several skills that are central to legal and logical reasoning. The first skill consists of "recognizing the parts of an argument and their relationships" (Law School Admissions Council [LSAC], 2020). The second consists of "recognizing similarities and differences between patterns of reasoning." By examining each of these skills, in turn, we can help you understand a little more about the logic of scientific reasoning and maybe even improve your performance on the LSAT.
>
> 1. *Recognize the parts of an argument and their relationships.* The first skill provides a starting point for logical analysis. In our Sherlock Holmes example, Holmes stated a conclusion along with supporting evidence. He proceeded from certain information that he held to be true (the dog did not bark; dogs do not bark at people they know) to a claim (the suspect is innocent) that he inferred from them. Logical analysis concerns the relation between the evidence and conclusion. It begins when people like Holmes make an *argument*, which is to claim that one proposition (the *conclusion*) follows from one or more other propositions (the evidence, usually referred to as *premises*).
>
> 2. *Recognize similarities and differences between patterns of reasoning.* There are many patterns of reasoning, but two of the most important, which also are central to scientific inquiry, are deduction and induction. Understanding this difference is critical for analyzing reasoning because the evidence (or premises) bears a different relation to the conclusion in each argument type. In a valid deductive

argument, if the premises are true, the conclusion is true. In an inductive argument, if the premises are true, the conclusion may or may not be true.

Manhattan Review (found online), a test preparation company offering LSAT preparation courses and tutoring, gives a sample question from the LSAT that tests your ability to apply deductive reasoning:

> If Amy were a tall and fair actress from the mainstream film industry, she would have won the best actress award. She is not a tall and fair actress since she has not won the best actress award.

The conclusion about Amy is flawed because the author does not consider that Amy could

a) have won an award for scriptwriting,
b) be a singer from the mainstream film industry,
c) be a tall and fair actress from a non-mainstream film industry,
d) be an actress belonging to a mainstream theater group,
e) have won an award for some other mainstream work.

To determine the correct answer, let us first identify the premises and conclusion of the argument. By doing so and putting the root of the question in standard argument form, you can determine if it involves deductive or inductive reasoning. The word *since* in the second sentence (or proposition) suggests that the first part of the statement is a conclusion. Now, if we rearrange the premises and conclusion, we can reconstruct the argument as follows:

> If Amy were a tall and fair actress from the mainstream film industry, she would have won the best actress award. (Premise)
>
> She (Amy) has not won the best actress award. (Premise)
>
> Therefore, she (Amy) is not a tall and fair actress. (Conclusion)

Arguments of this form, in which the second premise affirms or denies the truth of the antecedent (the phrase following "if") or consequent (phrase following "then") are deductive. If the first two premises are true, it follows deductively that "Amy is not a tall and fair actress *from the mainstream film industry*." Notice, however, that the conclusion of the argument is flawed because it does not contain the italicized phrase. Therefore, the argument is not deductively valid. Now, which answer addresses the flaw "Amy could still be a tall and fair actress from a non-mainstream film industry"?

Theoretical explanations should be deductively valid, and whenever scientists formulate hypotheses, they use deductive reasoning. It is therefore important to evaluate the reasoning that underlies theoretical arguments. As you can see, this

continues

continued

involves identifying the parts of the argument (i.e., the premises and conclusion) and determining if the relation between premises and conclusion is deductively valid.

Other tests of logical reasoning gauge people's ability to reason inductively. Recall that inductive reasoning means that the conclusion is uncertain even if the evidence is true because the content of the conclusion goes beyond the evidence. Often, these tests present people with some sequence of shapes, symbols, or even numbers; test takers are then asked to complete the next part of the sequence. Consider the following example:

12, 15, 19, 24, 30

Which of the following numbers best completes the sequence?

a. 33
b. 34
c. 35
d. 36
e. 37

For this question, "e" is the best answer. The evidence is the numbers. The answer, or conclusion, is reasonable because there is a (linear) pattern to the order of the numbers: they increase by 3, then 4 (= 3 + 1), then 5 (= 4 + 1), then 6 (= 5 + 1), and finally 7 (= 6 + 1), making 37 (= 30 + 7) the best answer. However, the conclusion goes beyond the evidence and is by no means certain. For example, who is to say that the rest of the pattern would not be a (circular) repetition of the first, such that the next number might be 12 (a choice not given in the answer)?

Inductive reasoning in science involves the same uncertainty. Scientists use inductive reasoning whenever they attempt to arrive at theoretical generalizations based on observations or data. To evaluate this type of reasoning, you must first identify the parts of the theoretical argument, as in deductive reasoning. However, because inductive conclusions exceed the information contained in the premises, the concept of validity does not apply, and you can only evaluate inductive arguments in terms of their strength or weakness. This amounts to determining the probability or likelihood that the conclusion is true, based on the evidence. One way of strengthening inductive conclusions is to consider additional evidence; imagine, for example, obtaining additional numbers in the sequence 12, 15, 19, 24, 30. As you will see in later chapters, scientists have developed various methods for strengthening conclusions, such as increasing sample size (Chapter 9) and replicating studies (Chapter 8).

Deductive and inductive reasoning represent two different ways of moving between theory and data, based on two different starting points for conducting social research. On the one hand, deductive inquiry—that is, research based on deductive reasoning—represents a top-down approach, moving from abstract theory to concrete data (refer to the right-hand side of Figure 2.1). Along the way, a scientist deduces conclusions, albeit tentative, based on premises or theoretical propositions, which are then tested with data. Inductive inquiry, on the other hand, is a bottom-up approach, moving from data to theory (see the left-hand side of Figure 2.1). Here, a scientist infers a generalization or conclusion based on a pattern of observations or data. In the next section, we will explain exactly how scientists employ these logics of inquiry. To check your understanding of the concepts learned within this section, please refer to Box 2.3.

BOX 2.3

CHECKING YOUR UNDERSTANDING

Testing Our Reasoning: Is It Deductive or Inductive?

Indicate whether each of the following inferences represents deductive or inductive reasoning.

(a) A pollster interviews 2,500 randomly chosen US adults and finds that 69 percent of them say they are in favor of capital punishment. He concludes that 69 percent of the US adult population favors capital punishment.

(b) The presence of others strengthens people's dominant (prevalent or most likely) responses. If the dominant response is correct, people will perform better in the presence of an audience than when they perform alone. (This is called the "social facilitation effect.") Assuming these statements are true, it follows that good pool players will make a higher percentage of their shots when an audience is watching them play than when they are shooting pool by themselves.

(c) Research with University of Hawaii students found that women, Asians, and students living at home were less likely to smoke cannabis than men, non-Asians, and students not living at home, respectively. Noting that each of the former groups has more to lose (e.g., is likely to experience more disapproval) from smoking cannabis, the researcher concluded that the more social constraints a student has, the less likely they are to smoke cannabis.

SUMMARY

The goal of science is to produce knowledge. Science is characterized by theory, verifiable data, systematic data collection and analysis, and logical reasoning. In the process of moving between theory and data, scientists primarily use two forms of logical reasoning: deductive and inductive. These logics also represent two ways of conducting research.

hypothesis an expected but unconfirmed relationship among two or more phenomena

2.2 LOGICS OF INQUIRY: DEDUCTIVE AND INDUCTIVE LOGIC

Having now examined the characteristics and process of science, including the two different types of logical reasoning, how exactly do we put these logics into practice when conducting research? One way of thinking about deductive and inductive inquiry is to imagine two funnels (see Figures 2.2 and 2.3). At the ends of both funnels, you see familiar terms: theory and data. Reflecting the top-down approach of deductive inquiry, the arrow in Figure 2.2 is pointing down, indicating that this process moves from (broad) theory to concrete data. The arrow in Figure 2.3 is inverted, or flipped, reflecting the fact that inductive inquiry begins with data and moves to theory. In Figures 2.2 and 2.3 you also see other terms, which means that there is more to the process than just theory and data.

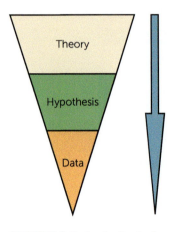

FIGURE 2.2 Deductive Logic of Inquiry

Let us first consider the deductive (top-down) logic of inquiry in Figure 2.2. To understand how the world works, a researcher begins with a broad and abstract theory, or multiple theories, comprised of interconnected propositions. Recall, for example, Hirschi's (1969) social bond theory, which suggests the following are important in reducing the likelihood of involvement in criminal and deviant behavior:

- attachment to others,
- commitment to conventional norms,
- involvement in prosocial activities, and
- beliefs in the validity of the law.

From the theory and its propositions, a researcher deduces a **hypothesis**, which is a tentative, but unconfirmed, expectation about the relationship between two or more phenomena. In formulating a hypothesis from a theory, a researcher is using the deductive reasoning described earlier by effectively saying, "If theoretical propositions A, B, and C are true, then we should expect the following relationship in the data." To return to Hirschi's theory

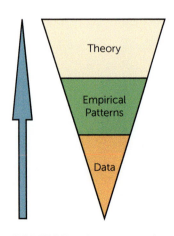

FIGURE 2.3 Inductive Logic of Inquiry

and our example of engaging in vandalism, we might expect individuals to be less likely to engage in criminal activity if they are strongly bonded to society. As suggested by this example and illustrated by the funnel in Figure 2.2, a hypothesis is a more specific—and less abstract—statement than theory. A hypothesis is then tested with concrete data, which is represented by the narrowest part of the funnel.

Whereas the "line of sight" is from theory to data in deductive inquiry, it is from data to theory in the bottom-up approach of inductive inquiry (see Figure 2.3). In analyzing the data, a researcher infers empirical patterns, which are regularities or uniformities in the data. An **empirical pattern** represents general tendencies based on data, much like the pattern of effects from drinking soda, mentioned earlier, or the sequence of numbers in Box 2.2. These patterns are at a higher level of generality or abstraction than individual pieces of data, such as a single experience drinking soda, or in the case of research, a single observation of students' classroom behavior, individual words spoken by interviewees, or a specific answer provided by survey respondents. At the highest level of abstraction is theory, which may be generated from—or "grounded" in (Glaser & Strauss, 1967)—data and the empirical patterns that emerge from analysis.

As you will see throughout this book, deductive inquiry is most characteristic of quantitative research, such as experiments and surveys, and inductive inquiry is most characteristic of qualitative research. This is true of the next two examples, which illustrate how criminologists use inductive reasoning and deductive reasoning in their research.

> **empirical pattern**
> a relationship among phenomena usually inferred from data

How Do Career Criminals Disengage from Criminal Behavior? An Answer from Inductive Inquiry

When researchers study criminal behavior, they tend to focus on one of three stages: the emergence, the patterns, and the abandonment of criminal behavior. Meisenhelder (1977) explored this third stage, the abandonment of criminal behavior, posing the following research questions: "(1) What are the subjectively significant contingencies that induce an actor to attempt a disengagement from a criminal career? (2) What subjectively significantly contingencies influence the successful accomplishment of an exit from crime?" (p. 320).

In order to answer these questions, Meisenhelder (1977) conducted unstructured interviews with 20 "nonprofessional" property offenders. These offenders were inmates at a southeastern US correctional institution and had been convicted of felony property offenses. Themes were identified from the transcripts of the interviews in order to establish similarities across participants' responses and experiences.

Meisenhelder (1977) found that participants' motivations for exiting their career as a criminal were twofold: one was to avoid reincarceration and the second was a desire to gain or regain a sense of a more "normal" life. For example, one inmate said,

> *I just didn't wanna get no more time or anything. I seen what was gonna happen if I get caught again, and I said, "This ain't worth it." I just didn't wanna come back to do more time.* (p. 323)

Another inmate stated,

> I just decided I wanted to be like any other person, settle down, have me an old lady, a place to stay at, a good job. I was just tired of it. I really wanted a chance to live a normal, straight life. (p. 324)

To summarize, Meisenhelder (1977) found the offenders were "pushed by the deterring threat of 'doing more time' in prison, and pulled by a growing desire to 'settle down.'" (p. 322). In regard to his second research question, Meisenhelder found that offenders were able to successfully exit, although temporarily, their career criminality through the development of meaningful attachments and investments in conformity. These conditions, the men believed, would provide them support for exiting and significant reasons not to deviate back.

On the basis of his data, analysis, and inferred empirical patterns, Meisenhelder used the inductive, or bottom-up, approach to research in order to identify patterns that help explain the exit from a criminal career. His findings tended to support control theories of crime, such as Hirschi's social bond theory, noting that success in exiting a life of crime revolves around the development of social bonds.

Do Social Bonds Matter? An Answer from Deductive Inquiry

With the invention of the internet, there has been an increased focus among criminologists on understanding why individuals engage in cybercrime. Based upon prior research, juveniles engage in cyber delinquency at a disproportionate rate (Yar, 2005); most hackers begin to engage in this specific type of cyber delinquency around the ages of 11 to 18 (Sterling, 1994). Therefore, in order to understand why juveniles begin engaging in hacking, Back et al. (2018) conducted a study testing the self-control and social bonding theories. They wanted to know if these traditional criminological theories could help explain juvenile hacking. Given that they were utilizing theory as a framework for their study, this illustrates the process of deductive inquiry. Moving from theory to hypothesis, the authors deduced hypotheses from Hirschi's (1969) social bonding theory and Gottfredson and Hirschi's (1990) self-control theory. In regard to social bonding theory, they hypothesized that higher levels of parent attachment, attachment to parental supervision, involvement, and school attachment would all lead to decreased computer hacking.

The next step in the research process is to examine data to test hypotheses. Back et al. (2018) utilized self-report survey data that was part of the second International Self-Report Delinquency Study (ISRD-2). Data were collected from middle and high school students in eight countries: the United States, Venezuela, Spain, France, Germany, Poland, Hungary, and Russia. The data used for this study consisted of students' responses to survey questions about whether they had engaged in hacking and whether they liked to engage in risky behavior. In addition, researchers utilized a nine-item social bonding scale which consisted of four subscales:

1. students' attachment to parents ("How do you usually get along with your father/mother?"),
2. attachment to parental supervision (i.e., "Do your parents usually know who you are with when you go out?"),
3. involvement (i.e., "How often do you and your parents do something together, such as movies, hike, sporting event?"), and
4. school attachment (i.e., "I like my school").

Based on their data analysis, do social bonds matter in regard to juvenile involvement in hacking? Back et al. (2018) found partial support for social bonding theory. For six of the eight countries, strong attachment to parental supervision reduced the likelihood of computer hacking. Interestingly, none of the social bonding variables were significant in predicting computer hacking among juveniles in the United States.

Back et al.'s (2018) study illustrates deductive inquiry, or the "top-down" approach to research: they began with theory and its propositions, derived hypotheses, and used data to test their hypotheses. Their study added knowledge about the strengths and limits of social bonding theory as applied to juvenile hacking in different cultural contexts.

Combining the Logics of Inquiry

There are strengths and limitations to both deductive and inductive inquiry. One advantage of deductive, top-down inquiry is that theory focuses the research. At the same time, researchers must be cautious not to get "funnel vision" or otherwise let the sides of the funnel depicted in Figure 2.2 blind them to other theoretical insights. As for the inductive, bottom-up approach, development of new theory is one of its greatest advantages (Glaser & Strauss, 1967). One of inductive reasoning's drawbacks, however, is that the empirical patterns it generates are likely to be subject to multiple (theoretical) interpretations.

In reality, researchers often combine both deductive and inductive logics of inquiry to some extent. The two logics of inquiry may be combined in a way that essentially puts together the funnels in Figures 2.2 and 2.3. On the one hand, researchers may begin with theory, deduce a hypothesis, test the hypothesis with data, infer empirical patterns, and

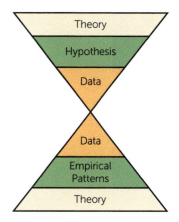

FIGURE 2.4 Combining Logics, Starting with Theory

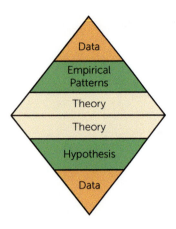

FIGURE 2.5 Combining Logics, Starting with Data

put forth a new or revised theory (see Figure 2.4). On the other hand, they may begin with data, infer empirical patterns, put forth a theory, deduce a hypothesis, and then analyze (still other) data (see Figure 2.5). We next describe a study that illustrates how researchers may combine the logics of inquiry, as depicted in Figure 2.4.

Moving Between Deductive and Inductive Inquiries: Domestic Violence Responses

Police response to domestic violence often varies between four options:

1. talking through the incident,
2. threatening to take legal action for subsequent calls,
3. asking one of the parties to leave, or
4. making an arrest.

Researchers have explored the effects these varying police responses have on reoffending. A classic example of the process of moving from deductive to inductive research comes from researching police response to domestic violence.

Through a set of three studies, researchers were able to understand the effects of mandatory arrests on domestic violence reoffending (Pate & Hamilton, 1992; Sherman & Berk, 1984; Sherman et al., 1992). Not only did this set of studies help to establish the effects of police response on reoffending for domestic violence cases, but they also illustrate both the deductive and inductive approaches to research. In this case, this research on mandatory arrests for domestic violence started with one theory and ended with another, as in Figure 2.4.

Sherman and Berk (1984) conducted a test of two competing theories, the specific deterrence doctrine and the labeling theory, to determine the effect of mandatory arrest as a police response to domestic violence. At the time of their study, these theories conflicted on how the predicted punishment would impact recidivism, and there had been few empirical studies assessing the claims of these theories. For instance, the specific deterrence doctrine predicted that punishment of an offender should deter that individual from reoffending, while labeling theory posited that punishment would lead to a criminal label that would perpetuate offending.

To examine the competing hypotheses from specific deterrence and labeling theories, Sherman and Berk (1984) conducted what is now known as the Minneapolis Domestic Violence Experiment with cooperation from the Police Foundation and the Minneapolis Police Department. In order to execute the experimental design, police officers were randomly assigned to one of three responses for simple domestic assault cases, where both the victim and suspect were present, and police were allowed to make an arrest at their discretion but an arrest was not mandatory. The three responses included:

1. arresting the suspect,
2. separating the suspect and the victim for a minimum of eight hours, or
3. providing advice, including mediation, to the suspect and victim.

Sherman and Berk's (1984) analysis revealed several empirical patterns, which supported the hypothesis deduced from specific deterrence. They found that the "swift imposition of a sanction of temporary incarceration may deter male offenders in domestic assault cases" (Sherman & Berk, 1984, p. 270). In addition, they did not find support for labeling theory. In concluding, they do emphasize that arrest should not be required in all cases, but that there should be a presumption of arrest; arrests should be made unless police have specific reasons as to why an arrest may prove detrimental to the individuals involved. They also caution that replications of their study may not produce consistent findings depending upon the populations and contexts involved. In fact, between 1984 and 1992 their experiment was replicated in five cities across the United States: Omaha (NE), Milwaukee (WI), Charlotte (NC), Colorado Springs (CO), and Dade County (FL). Through these additional deductive inquiries testing the deterrent effect of arrest in domestic assault, inconsistent results were found. In some cities, Sherman and Berk's (1984) original findings were supported and long-term deterrent effects were found. However, in other studies contradictory findings were reported; researchers found long-term increases in reoffending for suspects who had been arrested.

In order to make sense of the inconsistent findings, Sherman and colleagues (1992) and Pate and Hamilton (1992) reanalyzed recidivism data from Milwaukee and Omaha (Sherman et al., 1992), as well as Dade County (Pate & Hamilton, 1992). Following the inductive process of research, these follow-up studies examined the data from the original experiments and found new empirical patterns, which supported a control theory perspective. Sherman et al. (1992) found that the "effectiveness of legal sanctions rests on a foundation of informal control" (p. 688). Individuals with a high "stake in conformity" (i.e., married and employed) were more likely to be deterred by arrest than those with a low "stake in conformity" (i.e., unmarried and unemployed). Pate and Hamilton (1992) found similar patterns: individuals with high levels of commitment (i.e., married and employed) were more likely to be deterred by arrest than those with low levels of commitment (i.e., unmarried and unemployed). Although these studies are not without criticism, which we discuss next, it is a good illustration of the continuous process of deductive and inductive reasoning and going "from theory to data and back."

SUMMARY

Scientists may use a deductive logic of inquiry, which provides researchers with theoretical focus; however, deductive logic may blind researchers to other theoretical insights. In contrast, an inductive logic of inquiry has the advantage of generating new theory but may be especially subject to multiple theoretical interpretations. Researchers may combine the logics of inquiry in one of two ways: they may move from "Theory to data and back," as Sherman and others did, or they may start with data, move to theory, and then go back to new data. The constant interplay of theory and data over time and across many studies best characterizes science as a whole. Each study is part of a continuous, unending cycle of inquiry.

2.3 EVALUATING SCIENTIFIC KNOWLEDGE: POSSIBILITIES, CAUTIONS, AND LIMITS

Scientific knowledge is advanced through the process of moving between theory and data. As such, science has an amazing potential to offer new knowledge that might not be gained through other means. It can help to dispel "common-sense" notions that may not be true; conversely, it can help to confirm information that we long believed was true but were not sure of (Berger, 1963). Science can help us to make informed decisions in our everyday lives, ranging from which beverages are safe to drink to recognizing the potential dangers of simply following an authority's orders (Milgram, 1974). Equipped with the latest scientific knowledge, scientists and others can improve the human condition with technological innovations and new treatments or social programs. For example, studies of suicide inform treatment of its causes (Wray et al., 2011). In the 1950s, research on the positive effects of interpersonal contact between racial groups helped inform the US Supreme Court's decision to desegregate schools (*Brown v. Board of Education of Topeka*, 1954).

Yet, just as we need to critically evaluate other forms of knowledge, we need to critically evaluate scientific knowledge. Despite the possibilities that science presents, it also has limits that we need to be aware of when we read scientific studies or conduct research ourselves; we also need to be cautious about putting too much weight on what we know now.

Tentative Knowledge

The goal of science, as we noted, is to produce new knowledge. This also means that our current scientific knowledge is tentative. Regardless of how good scientists' theories are, how systematically scientists collect and analyze data, or how logical scientists' reasoning is, we must always remember that scientific knowledge changes. Today's knowledge may be tomorrow's "old news"; yesterday's knowledge may be today's "old news." New discoveries may be made that change scientific knowledge (Popper, 1959/1992) or the way we think about science (Kuhn, 1970).

The reason scientific knowledge is tentative is that patterns inferred from data may not recur and inevitably are open to alternative theoretical interpretations. This was clearly demonstrated in continuing research on arrests in domestic assault cases. Since Sherman and Berk (1984) conducted their study, the Minneapolis Domestic Violence Experiment, replications of the research were conducted in the early 1990s. As we saw earlier, some of the studies supported the pattern Sherman and Berk found, that is the deterrent effect of arrest (Berk et al., 1992). However, in other cities contradictory results were actually found, showing that arrests may be harmful to victims, leading to an escalation in reoffending (Dunford et al., 1990; Sherman et al., 1991). You might also recall that Sherman and Berk's (1984) data, along with data from additional cities, were explored even further to find that a commitment or stake in conformity (i.e., marriage and employment) mattered in order for arrests to have a deterrent effect for offenders. The replication studies reveal that the relationship between arrest and re-offending is quite complex. Due to the complexity of the association between police response to domestic violence and future offending, as well as the need to protect victims, this is an ongoing process of scientific inquiry. Recent research has called into question the creation of domestic violence policies based solely upon Sherman and Berk's (1984) original findings, as a meta-analysis of 11 different studies found that arrest for domestic violence did not significantly reduce repeat offending and may actually lead to a slight increase in re-offending (Hoppe et al., 2020).

Science, then, is a double-edged sword. On the one hand, the tentative nature of scientific knowledge is suggestive of endless possibilities for theory and research. On the other hand, the tentative knowledge that science produces cautions us against putting too much faith in a single study, including our own. We also have to be realistic about the scientific process.

The Ideal and Reality of the Scientific Process

The process of moving back and forth between theory and data is an idealized version of how science operates. It is not unusual for scientists to deviate from this ideal (Freese & Peterson, 2017; Molina & Garip, 2019). Scientists may, for example, begin with a theory, deduce hypotheses from it, and find that the data do not support the hypotheses. Then, they may start with another theory, repeat the process, and find support for a different hypothesis. It is also possible that scientists will discover something through intuition, by making an educated guess (Popper 1959/1992), or by chance, which Merton (1996) calls the **serendipity pattern**.

serendipity pattern unanticipated findings that cannot be interpreted meaningfully in terms of prevailing theories and, therefore, give rise to new theories

▲ PHOTO 2.2 Assembly line workers at the Western Electric Hawthorne plant, the site of a study that suggested people's behaviors change when they are being observed.

An example of the reality of the scientific process—and, more specifically, the serendipity pattern—comes from the famous Hawthorne studies, so named after the Western Electric Hawthorne plant in Cicero, Illinois. F. J. Roethlisberger and William J. Dickson (1939) wanted to know how changes in working conditions would affect workers' productivity in a controlled experiment. In one of these studies, six women with the task of assembling a telephone part were placed in a special test room for observation (see Photo 2.2). Then, changes in the working conditions were introduced over a period of time.

To the astonishment of Roethlisberger and Dickson (1939, p. 86), the workers' productivity increased uniformly, no matter what the change. After questioning the women, Roethlisberger and Dickson concluded that the workers' increased productivity was a response to the special attention they received as participants in what was considered an important experiment. The fun of the test room and the interest of management simply made it easier for the women to produce at a higher rate. This chance, or "serendipitous," finding came to be known as the **Hawthorne effect**, which generally refers to the tendency of research participants to change their behavior as a result of their awareness of being studied. This study is but one example of research that does not strictly follow the deductive logic of inquiry, and, interestingly enough, it is also an example of tentative knowledge in science. Although many other studies showed how researchers' mere presence could change the behavior of study participants, later analyses showed that Roethlisberger and Dickson's conclusions were unsupported by the evidence (Carey, 1967).

In short, the scientific process of reasoning between theory and data that we outlined in this chapter is an ideal. While many scientists likely strive toward this ideal—and so can we—it may be difficult to achieve in practice.

Hawthorne effect a change in behavior, such as an improvement in performance, that occurs when research participants know they are being studied

The Sociohistorical Aspect of Science

Science does not occur in a vacuum. Rather, it is a product of the society and culture in which scientists live. Discoveries, the emergence of scientific disciplines, and revolutions in scientific thinking are products of the times (Kuhn, 1970). When we evaluate research and conduct it ourselves, we need to be aware of its broader sociohistorical context. Social scientists who study the "problems of their times" may have an understanding of those problems that an outsider lacks (Merton, 1996). However, it is also possible that their research interpretations and findings may be biased by the broader sociohistorical context.

In fact, Sherman and Berk's (1984) findings on the deterrent effect of arrest for domestic assault cases were likely interpreted as proof of the effectiveness of mandatory arrest legislation by politicians who were strongly influenced by social and historical factors. At the time of Sherman and Berk's study in the 1980s, "tough on crime" policies were beginning to emerge with "truth in sentencing" laws developed in some states in 1984 (Ditton & Wilson, 1999). In addition, by 1994, the Violent Crime Control and Law Enforcement Act was in place, supported by both Democrats and Republicans. This legislation provided more federal aid to law enforcement, supported truth in sentencing laws, and established more mandatory minimum penalties. Despite Sherman and Berk's caution and recommendation for future research before the adoption of mandatory arrest laws, by 1991 the results of their study had already contributed to 15 states' passage of mandatory arrest laws (Zorza, 1992). Now it is known, through replications and further inductive inquiry, that mandatory arrest laws may actually do more harm than good; yet these laws still exist today.

Science is also a project of its times in more insidious ways. One of the foremost examples is research on racial and ethnic minorities. Undoubtedly influenced by waves of immigration and the prejudiced environment of the time, as well as spurred by Darwin's theory of evolution, some scientists in the late 19th and early 20th centuries looked for "proof" that African Americans and other racial and ethnic minorities were "inferior." Their research ran the gamut of examining facial features of prisoners (and concluding that "Black" features were associated with criminality) to applying culturally biased IQ tests (and concluding that the low scores of minorities "proved" their intellectual inferiority). Ignoring the widespread discrimination against minorities, as well as the cultural bias in IQ tests, this research had the unfortunate consequence of perpetuating prejudice and racism. While less prominent today, this kind of "science" is still around (Zuberi, 2003; Zuberi & Bonilla-Silva, 2008).

Scientific knowledge is thus a product of social and historical factors, sometimes quite harmful ones. This should give us pause as we evaluate and conduct research.

The Human Element of Science

Behind every scientific study is an imperfect human. If you think that scientists do not make mistakes, let us quickly disabuse you of that notion. Moreover, scientists have their own motivations, values, and interests that may shape their research.

Scientists are not perfect, and this must be borne in mind when we evaluate and conduct research. However, before you dismiss science, consider a question that we sometimes ask our students, "Would you dump a romantic partner because they are not perfect?" Probably not, we would guess. Similarly, we need to give some leeway to scientists and the process as a whole because science has its own set of checks that ensure greater accuracy over time. One of these checks is **replication**, broadly the repetition of a study, which may be carried out by the original researcher or another researcher using similar or different procedures and data.

replication the repetition of a study

SUMMARY

Through the never-ending process of scientific inquiry, science produces new knowledge that can benefit humankind by informing decisions and fostering innovations in technology, social programs, and treatments. Scientific knowledge is tentative and subject to revision; it does not always strictly follow the scientific process; it is shaped by sociohistorical factors; and it is, after all, produced by imperfect humans. Thus, it should be critically evaluated and treated with caution. These are by no means fatal flaws, however, as science can better itself through its own checks. Indeed, the ability of science to critique itself is one of its major strengths. To check your understanding of the concepts learned within this section, please refer to Box 2.4.

BOX 2.4

CHECKING YOUR UNDERSTANDING

Which Logic of Inquiry?

1. Susie is interested in examining whether low self-control impacts one's involvement in crime. She hypothesizes that individuals with lower self-control will be more likely to engage in crime. To conduct her study, she surveys 125 high school students about their level of self-control and engagement in crime. Susie's study represents which logic of inquiry?
    a. Deductive
    b. Inductive
    c. Theoretical
    d. Data-driven

2. John observed college student drinking behavior at an off-campus party he attended. He noticed that males at the party were more likely to drive themselves and their friends to the event, whereas female partygoers were more likely walking to the party. Through the patterns in his observations, he concludes that males are more likely to engage in reckless behavior, like drinking and driving, than females. John's study represents which logic of inquiry?
    a. Deductive
    b. Inductive

> c. Theoretical
> d. Thought-driven
>
> 3. When John evaluates his observations and notices consistencies in behaviors among males and females, he is identifying a/an:
>   a. hypothesis
>   b. theory
>   c. empirical pattern
>   d. serendipity pattern
>
> **Answers: 1. a, 2. b, 3. c**

KEY TERMS

data, p. 22
deductive logic, p. 25
empirical pattern, p. 31
Hawthorne effect, p. 38
hypothesis, p. 30
inductive logic, p. 25
replication, p. 39
serendipity pattern, p. 37
theory, p. 21

KEY POINTS

- The constant interplay between theory and data best characterizes science as a whole.
- Science involves theory, verifiable data, systematic data collection and analysis, and logical reasoning (deductive and inductive).
- Deductive and inductive reasoning are used in research to link theory and data.
- A deductive logic of inquiry represents a "top-down" approach to research, whereby researchers deduce hypotheses from theory and then test these hypotheses with data.
- An inductive logic of inquiry represents a "bottom-up" approach to research, whereby researchers infer empirical patterns from observations, and empirical patterns form the basis of theory.
- Researchers often use both logics of inquiry, sometimes starting from theory and sometimes starting from data.
- Science produces new knowledge that may be used to improve the human condition.
- Scientific knowledge is tentative, shaped by sociohistorical factors, and subject to human error.

REVIEW QUESTIONS

1. Identify the relationship between theory and data in scientific inquiry.
2. Describe how data in science should be (a) verifiable and (b) systematically collected and analyzed.
3. Describe deductive and inductive logic or reasoning and provide an example of each.
4. Explain why deductive and inductive inquiry are described, respectively, as "top-down" and "bottom-up" approaches to scientific research.
5. From this chapter, identify two examples each of theories and empirical patterns.
6. How is scientific knowledge (a) tentative, (b) shaped by sociohistorical factors, and (c) subject to human error?

EXERCISES

1. Indicate whether each of the following inferences represents deductive or inductive reasoning.

    a. A pollster interviews 2,500 randomly chosen US adults and finds that 69 percent of them say they are in favor of capital punishment. The pollster concludes that 69 percent of the US adult population favors capital punishment.

    b. The presence of others strengthens people's dominant (prevalent or most likely) responses. If the dominant response is correct, people will perform better in the presence of an audience than when they perform alone. (This is called the "social facilitation effect.") Assuming these statements are true, it follows that good pool players will make a higher percentage of their shots when an audience is watching them play than when they are shooting pool by themselves.

    c. Research with university students found that women, Asians, and students living at home were less likely to smoke cannabis than men, non-Asians, and students not living at home, respectively. Noting that each of the former groups has more to lose (e.g., is likely to experience more disapproval) from smoking cannabis, the researcher concluded that the more social constraints a student has, the less likely it is that he or she will smoke cannabis.

2. Select a recent issue of a major criminal justice journal, such as *Criminology*, *Criminal Justice and Behavior*, or *Justice Quarterly*. Find an article that reports the results of empirical research. Read the first part of the article to see how the researcher(s) presents the theory underlying the research. What theory or theories does the researcher present? What hypotheses, if any, does the researcher derive from theory?

3. The UCR database provides violent crime statistics at the national and state level. Select a state of interest to you and make a hypothesis about whether you believe violent crimes have increased, decreased, or stayed the same from 2012 to 2022. To determine whether your hypothesis is supported, complete the following steps:
   a. Search online for the Federal Bureau of Investigation's Crime Data Explorer.
   b. On the left-hand side of the screen, click the button for the "Data Discovery Tool."
   c. Once the next screen comes up, under the "Dataset" option select "Crime Data"; and under the "Query Level" select "National or State" from the list.
   d. Next, under the section titled "National or State Query," select "2012" for "from" and select "2022" for "to"; for "Crime Select" select "All Violent Crimes"; and for "Location Select" choose a state of interest to you. Then click the "Submit" button.
   e. Once finished, you will see a line chart that displays the state data for all violent crime from 2012 to 2022. Discuss whether your hypothesis is supported.

3

Reading and Writing in Criminal Justice Research

It Is All About Communication

CHAPTER OUTLINE

3.1 Read, Take Notes, and Write a Research Proposal 45
  Locate Relevant Research Literature 46
  Read and Evaluate Prior Research 50
  Formulate Research Question 52
  Design Research and Prepare Proposal 54
  Summary 54

3.2 Write a Research Report 55
  Outline and Prepare to Write 56
  Write a First Draft 56
  Revisions and Other Writing Considerations 63
  Summary 65

LEARNING OBJECTIVES

By the end of this chapter, you should be able to

3.1 Explain how to locate, read, and evaluate criminal justice research.

3.2 Apply your knowledge by writing a research proposal or report.

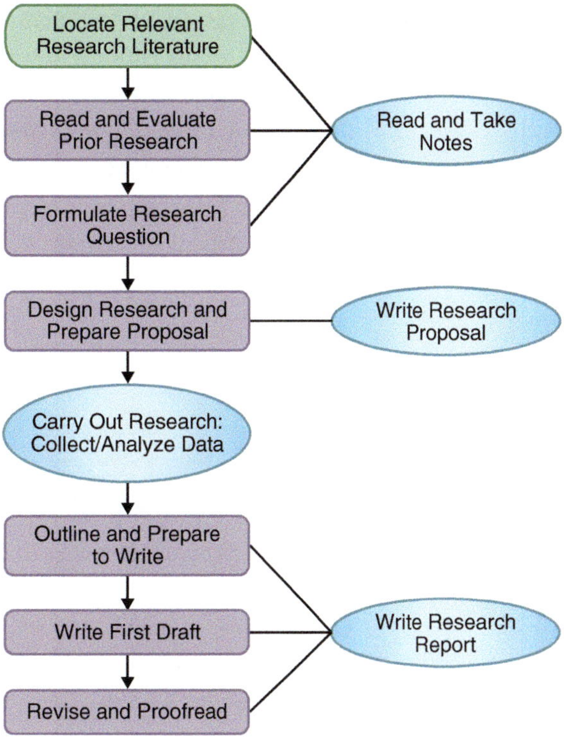

Science could not exist without communication. Only through communication can scientists learn about and contribute to the shared body of knowledge that defines each scientific discipline. Much scientific communication takes place orally, but the advancement of science is not based on the oral tradition; it ultimately depends on writing. Through written research reports, books, and articles, researchers communicate with others who review, apply, and extend their work.

A major purpose of this chapter is to enhance research writing skills. Yet, we consider not only how to write about research but also how to read the research of others. This reading/writing interface is the essence of communication in everyday life. For communication is (or at least it is supposed to be) a two-way street: one person speaks (or signs); the other listens (or sees) and responds. And so it is in criminal justice research: we read prior research to understand what others have done; we write reports to accurately communicate our findings.

Like conducting research, there is an underlying process of communication—or reading and writing—in criminal justice research. Figure 3.1 presents an idealized model of this process. In quantitative research, the reading phase typically comes first, leading to the formulation of a research question and a proposal, and the writing phase generally follows data analysis. In qualitative research, as we discuss in Chapters 10 and 15, reading and writing occur throughout the research process, including data collection and analysis.

In this chapter, we elaborate on the steps in Figure 3.1 to show you how to read and write criminal justice research.

FIGURE 3.1 The Process of Reading and Writing Criminal Justice Research

3.1 READ, TAKE NOTES, AND WRITE A RESEARCH PROPOSAL

Reading criminal justice research entails understanding and evaluating studies reported in the criminal justice literature. In this section, we provide tips on how to locate relevant studies, evaluate them, and use them as a basis for formulating a research question and developing a research proposal.

Locate Relevant Research Literature

Research begins with the selection of a topic. However, topics must be transformed into answerable research questions, which researchers are expected to relate to existing theory and research. The first step in "reading," therefore, is to locate the criminal justice literature that is relevant to your topic. Box 3.1, How to Search the Literature, provides guidelines for using the library's electronic databases to *search* the scientific literature. Here we elaborate on how to *read* the literature to formulate a research question.

> **BOX 3.1**
>
> **DOING CRIMINAL JUSTICE RESEARCH**
>
> # How to Search the Literature
>
> The object of a literature review is to grasp the current state of knowledge on a particular topic. More than likely there will be a lot of information on the topic you choose; therefore, you must (a) identify the relevant criminal justice literature and (b) decide which parts of this literature to read. Below is a set of guidelines to help you search the literature.
>
> 1. *Start your search by using the library's online resources.* The library's online resources usually include an online catalog and databases. This is where you will find references to books and scholarly articles in which criminal justice research is most likely to be reported. Beware, however, that the online catalog may only list the library's holdings. In addition, the most current information may be found in journal articles rather than in books.
> 2. *Conduct a subject or keyword search of the library's electronic databases*, which will enable you to find relevant journal articles as well as books, book chapters, technical reports, and other written materials. Be sure to check with your instructor on preferred source type for your class and assignments. Of particular value for criminologists are discipline-specific databases such as Criminal Justice Abstracts, Criminal Justice Database, and National Crime Justice Reference Service (NCJRS) Abstracts Database.
> 3. *View initial results with the aim of narrowing your topic.* It is not unusual for initial searches to yield results numbering in the thousands. If this occurs, the topic is probably too broad, and you will need to refine your search. By looking at a few of the initial screens, you can quickly see what kind of research is being done and then choose a term to add to the search in order to narrow the results. You can narrow your search by inserting the operators AND or NOT between search terms or by enclosing exact phrases in quotation marks. For example, "drug use

AND grades" is much more targeted than just "drug use." Also, be aware that the words you choose can make a difference—decreasing or increasing the number of relevant citations—so, try different words, like "drug use" or "substance use," and "grades" or "academic performance."

4. *Locate relevant references by reading titles and abstracts.* It is usually impossible—and, fortunately, unnecessary—to read the full text of every article, book chapter, or other citation you find in your search. Rather, it will be sufficient to locate relevant literature by reading titles and—if available—abstracts, which are concise summaries of the content of an article. Once you have begun to narrow your topic and have identified relevant articles, you should read the full text. Fortunately, databases usually indicate whether the "full text" of an article is available online; if the article is not available online, you will need to see if the library has a print copy of the journal or can order a copy of the article through interlibrary loan.

5. *Read the most recent literature first and then work backward.* Given that all researchers place their work in the context of prior research and theory, the latest articles will provide the most up-to-date references. Citations in many databases are listed in reverse chronological order or can be listed by date, which makes it easy to find the latest published research. In addition, some databases, such as Google Scholar, indicate which studies have cited a reference, so that you can trace a line of inquiry backward or forward in time. The search images shown below illustrate this for the topic of "police use of force," showing that Terrill and Reisig's (2003) article, "Neighborhood Context and Police Use of Force," is the most widely cited reference in Figure 3.2; selected literature that cites this article is shown in Figure 3.3. (Be aware, though, that not everything in Google Scholar has been published nor are all publications of the same quality.) Finally, if the full text of an article is available online, citations in the text may be hyperlinked. By examining these additional articles and books for further references, you can "reference-hop" your way through the literature, which should enable you to quickly gain a command of research and theory on the topic.

6. *Search for review articles that summarize the literature on the particular topic,* as these are the best sources of information on existing research and theory. Database results will include several types of references. Most articles will consist of reports of empirical research; a few will present a new theory or theoretical synthesis; a few others will consist of commentaries. In addition, there are serial publications, such as the *Annual Review of Criminology,* that specialize in review articles. You may want to do a keyword search that combines your topic with the term "review" or "annual review."

continues

continued

FIGURE 3.2 Search Results in Google Scholar for Police Use of Force

7. *Use database information to evaluate the quality and importance of a citation.* Some databases indicate whether a journal publication is *peer-reviewed* (that is, subject to the evaluation of fellow academics and researchers), an important distinction between scholarly and popular publications. Some databases also indicate the number of times an article has been cited by other references in the database. This could be very useful information, as it might indicate the significance of the reported study.

8. *Use the internet sparingly and selectively.* Although in today's world students are understandably inclined to start any quest for information by searching online, it is important to recognize that the internet has limited utility for reviewing the criminal justice literature. Internet searches tend to yield extremely large lists of citations or "hits," many of which will be irrelevant to your interests. It is also necessary to evaluate internet search results carefully because authorship can range

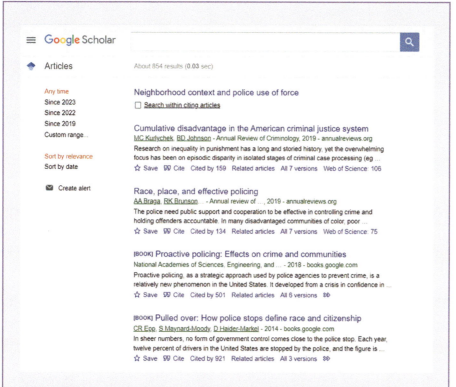

FIGURE 3.3 Selected Literature That Cites Terrill and Reisig's (2003) Article

from grade-school students to government agencies to political interest groups to profit-making businesses that seek to promote a given viewpoint or body of knowledge. On the other hand, once you have narrowed your topic, the internet has many valuable resources to help you conduct your research. One of the largest depositories of social science data is the Inter-university Consortium for Political and Social Research (ICPSR). The website of the General Social Survey (GSS) offers data files, codebooks, and other documentation available to download or order. You also can obtain data online from numerous US government agencies, which are outlined in Chapter 11.

9. *Organize your references, perhaps with reference management software.* Although the authors of this textbook are "old school," in that we simply download references to folders on our computers, there are a variety of programs, such as EndNote, Zotero, Mendeley, and RefWorks, that not only allow you to store bibliographic files but also create reference pages from these files.

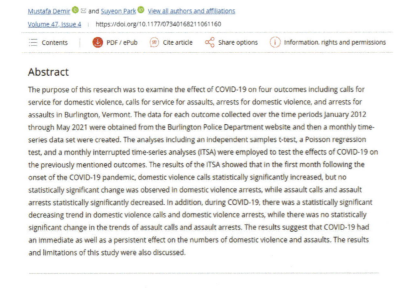

FIGURE 3.4 Title and Abstract of a Journal Article

As a first step, you should identify relevant articles and books by examining titles and abstracts. Titles provide clues about the research topic, but abstracts are much more helpful in judging the relevance of the research to your topic. An **abstract**, usually only included in research articles, is a capsule version of the full report that briefly describes the research question, hypotheses (if applicable), data and methods, and the major findings or results. Figure 3.4 presents the abstract of Demir and Park's (2022) article on the effect of COVID-19 on domestic violence and assaults.

abstract A capsule version of a research report that briefly describes the research question or hypothesis, data and methods, and the major findings or results.

Note how Demir and Park's (2022) abstract briefly summarizes questions that the study addresses, the methods (collection of agency data), the setting/source of data (Burlington, Vermont/Burlington Police Department), and the main findings. Reading an abstract, such as Demir and Park's, helps to determine whether the study may be relevant for your research. If so, you may skim the "introduction" and the "methods" sections of the article for keys to the author's perspective, then dwell on the "findings" or "results" and their implications.

Books, which are often the publication venue of qualitative research, do not have abstracts. A good way to get an overview of the study is to skim the introductory and concluding chapters of the book. The introduction is likely to frame the research and the conclusion is likely to summarize major findings or results. Regardless of whether the study is quantitative or qualitative, the methods section may be reported in an appendix rather than in the main text of the book.

Read and Evaluate Prior Research

At step two, you decide what to read in detail; keep a separate record of references; evaluate the credibility of each reference; and take notes and ask questions about the research. As you read, you should ask two kinds of questions:

1. How does the study contribute substantively to research on the topic?
2. Is the study credible and methodologically sound?

If you are interested in how COVID-19 impacted domestic violence and assaults, for example, you may decide to read Demir and Park's (2022) article in detail. Assuming it is relevant for your research, you should keep a record of this reference. To do so, you need to locate the pertinent publication details, which for journal articles—such as Demir and Park's—usually can be found on the first page.

In addition, reference management programs (e.g., *EndNote*, *Zotero*, *Mendeley*, *RefWorks*) can automatically find and import these details. Look closely at Figure 3.4 and you will see the publication details that are necessary for many reference formats:

- Author(s): Mustafa Demir and Suyeon Park
- Article Title: "The Effect of COVID-19 on Domestic Violence and Assaults"
- Year of Publication: 2022 (located at the top right of the page)
- Journal Title: *Criminal Justice Review* (also located at the top right of the page)
- Volume and Issue: 47 and 4 (sometimes journals only list one number, which is the volume; if the issue number is listed, it is usually enclosed in parentheses)
- Page Numbers: 445–463

For books, you can usually find the pertinent publication details on the first few pages. These include the name of the author, the title of the book, the year in which it was published, and the publisher. For a study of race and mass incarceration, you may decide to read Michelle Alexander's book *The New Jim Crow: Mass Incarceration in the Age of Colorblindness*. It was first published in 2010 by The New Press; the 10th anniversary edition was released in 2020.

Knowing the publication details can help you evaluate the credibility of the reference. One such detail, a relatively hard and fast standard that is provided in many databases, is whether a research publication is peer-reviewed. **Peer review** is a system in which researchers' reports are evaluated by other scholars in the field. These scholars, or peers, read the reports, provide comments and critiques, and offer an overall evaluation of the research concerning whether it should be accepted or rejected for publication. An important part of the peer-review system is that it is usually double-blind, which means that the authors do not know who the reviewers are and the reviewers do not know who the authors are. Although we believe it is sufficient for your purposes to determine whether a reference is peer-reviewed, credibility can be gauged in other ways. For example, there are measures to evaluate the impact of a journal on the field, which are often taken as signs of journals' prestige. We are unaware of such measures for books, but a general rule of thumb is that university presses, such as the University of California Press or Oxford University Press, are more highly regarded than nonuniversity presses.

Having evaluated the credibility of the reference, you can proceed to understand how a study contributes substantively to a research topic. You will find a researcher's claims about a study's contribution in the literature review and discussion sections of

peer review system in which researchers' reports are evaluated by fellow academics and researchers

Table 3.1 Matrix of Studies and Their Key Features

	Study #1	Study #2	Study #3
Research question(s)			
Argument/Hypothesis			
Data			
Method(s)			
Results/Findings			
Conclusions			

journal articles. And by reading the latest references, you can begin to trace the line of inquiry on a topic and identify the key studies. Then, as you read and take notes, you should begin to see similarities and differences and thus determine what each study distinctively contributes. One way to facilitate comparison is to make a matrix with the names of the studies (i.e., the citations) on one axis and key features of studies on another axis, as we have done in Table 3.1.

In addition to identifying key features and substantive findings, you should also evaluate each study's claims. Throughout this book, we describe methods of assessing the quality of research, and we identify the relative strengths and weaknesses of various approaches. Box 3.2, Reading Criminal Justice Research, provides a guide for reading and critiquing research. We present this box, however, with a word of caution: understanding and applying all of these questions requires that you read all of this book.

Formulate Research Question

Reading the literature prepares you for the next step: transforming your general topic into an answerable research question. Research questions often attempt to fill a "gap" in the literature. For example, Sinchul Back, Sadhika Soor, and Jennifer LaPrade (Chapter 2) found that few studies had empirically tested whether Gottfredson and Hirschi's (1990) self-control theory of crime and Hirschi's (1969) social control theory could be used to explain participation in computer hacking. So, they conducted an empirical test of whether these theories could be used to explain involvement in juvenile hacking.

Although finding "holes" in the literature is a worthy goal, sociologist Mark Edwards (2012) points out that it can be difficult to find them or to have the resources to fill them, especially for beginning researchers. On the other hand, it is worthwhile for small-scale projects to replicate previous studies. In so doing, the project may contribute to the literature simply by confirming prior research. Additionally, it may expand the literature

BOX 3.2

READING CRIMINAL JUSTICE RESEARCH

Questions to Ask in Evaluating a Research Report

The questions below are presented in the order in which they are most likely to be answered in a research report, such as a journal article. Keep in mind, however, that the information needed to answer a question may be found in one or more parts of the report.

1. Has the researcher posed a question or problem that can be addressed through criminal justice research?
2. How is the research question/hypothesis related to prior research and theory? Is the theoretical foundation of the research clear? Does the hypothesis clearly follow from the theory that is presented?
3. Which general methodological approach (e.g., experiment, survey, field research, etc.) is taken? Is the approach or combination of approaches well suited to addressing the research question or testing the hypothesis?
4. Does the author adequately address ethical concerns? Are procedures implemented that adequately protect participants' rights and welfare?
5. For quantitative studies, what are the independent and dependent variables? What other key variables are identified?
6. How are central concepts defined and operationalized? Does the author present prior evidence regarding the reliability and validity of measures? Does the present study assess reliability and validity?
7. What is the unit of analysis? Is probability or non-probability sampling used to select units? How many are selected and from where? What inferences does the author make from their observations? If population characteristics are estimated, what is the margin of error? Do the author's generalizations about research results seem reasonable?
8. What other evidence is reported regarding the quality of the data? In an experiment, does the design contain appropriate means of control? In a survey, what is the response rate, and does the author address the issue of nonresponse bias? In field research and in-depth interviews, does the author discuss relationships with participants and reflexivity? For existing data analysis, what is the quality and source of the data and how well does it fit the research question?
9. For quantitative studies, does the author describe the statistical analyses that are applied to the data? Are the findings clearly presented, with appropriate inferences about the strength and direction of association and statistical significance of hypothesized relationships? Does the author make causal inferences? What evidence is presented regarding direction of influence and nonspuriousness?
10. For qualitative studies, what form of qualitative analysis (e.g., grounded theory, narrative analysis) does the author apply? Are the analytic techniques (e.g., coding) adequately described? Does the analysis lead to an in-depth understanding of the topic? Does the author discuss member checking and/or negative cases?
11. What substantive conclusions are drawn from the study? Does the author discuss alternative explanations of research findings or results? Does the author discuss limitations of the study and the implications of study results for future research?

by improving on the methodology or by showing how findings apply to different settings, time periods, or populations. (For some useful steps in conducting a replication study for a quantitative class research project, see Stojmenovska et al., 2019.)

Design Research and Prepare Proposal

Once researchers come up with a research design to address their research question, they may prepare a research proposal. You may be asked to write a proposal to gain the approval of an instructor or thesis chair to carry out research, or you may submit a proposal to request funding to support your research. A research proposal is a written description of how the researcher intends to address the research question. The outline of a proposal is essentially the same as the first three parts of a research report (which we discuss in detail in the next section): an introduction, literature review, and description of methods and data to be used to address the research question. The difference is that a proposal describes what the researcher plans to do rather than what they did. In addition, it is usually shorter than the parallel parts of the final report (in fact, funding agencies usually have word and/or page limits).

In preparing to do research, you also may be required to submit a proposal to the Institutional Review Board (IRB). As we will discuss in Chapter 4, this usually means completing a form that asks you to describe the aims and methods of your proposed research and to specify how participants' rights are to be protected. Although requirements vary somewhat across institutions, Chapter 4 outlines a set of issues that you will likely need to address. These include the potential risks and benefits of the research, as well as the steps you will take to gain informed consent, protect confidentiality, and otherwise secure the data and, if deception is involved, to debrief participants.

SUMMARY

The initial aim of reading criminal justice research is to locate relevant literature, so that you can transform a general topic into a researchable question and place your research in the context of prior research and theory. Reading the abstracts of journal articles and the opening and concluding chapters of books should indicate whether a study warrants further attention. Once relevant works are identified, you should record bibliographic information, determine how the study contributes to the topic, and evaluate its methodology. Determining the contributions of previous studies can be aided by forming a matrix that compares key features across each reference. From this comparison, you can decide how your research may contribute to a line of inquiry and then formulate a research question and develop a research proposal. To check your understanding of the concepts learned within this section, please refer to Box 3.3.

> **BOX 3.3**
>
> **CHECKING YOUR UNDERSTANDING**
>
> ## Research Proposals
>
> 1. Before reading the full text of an article, it is recommended that you read the _____, which is a summary of the research question, methods, and findings.
>   a. Introduction
>   b. Hypothesis
>   c. Abstract
>   d. Title
>
> 2. When considering the credibility of a source, it is often preferred to have a source that has been evaluated by fellow academics and researchers. This means the source is:
>   a. Reliable
>   b. Peer-reviewed
>   c. Original
>   d. Quantitative
>
> 3. Which of the following would be the best option for finding additional criminal justice sources?
>   a. Searching the internet with a keyword
>   b. Using the reference list of a recent article
>   c. Using a sociology database
>   d. Going to the library and walking through the aisles
>
> **Answers: 1. c, 2. b, 3. b**

3.2 WRITE A RESEARCH REPORT

Either during or after the collection and analysis of your data, you turn your attention to writing—to communicating what you did and what you found. The objective is to communicate precisely and accurately what questions framed the research, what literature informed it, what you did, what you found, and what conclusions might be drawn. When this is done well, the report clearly conveys what was learned, and others are able to make an informed evaluation of the study.

Outline and Prepare to Write

Before you begin to write, you should have a conception of the overall organization of the research report. Although there are differences in the organization of reports based on quantitative and qualitative research, as discussed below, we recommend writing an outline that organizes the paper in terms of the following sections:

- An introduction that includes a statement of the problem under investigation
- A literature review that summarizes and places the problem in the context of related theory and research
- A description of the design and execution of the study
- A presentation of the data analysis that identifies the method of analysis and the specific results/findings of the study
- A discussion that offers a broad interpretation of the results/findings

Within each of these major headings you should list subtopics and important points. As you may discover, outlining frequently brings out the recognition of new ideas and the necessity for transition topics that lead from one point to the next. You should ask the following continually as the outline becomes detailed:

- How can I move logically from this point to that point?
- Does the organization make sense?
- Have I left out anything essential?

A report-length paper of 15–20 pages requires an outline of at least one and possibly two or more single-spaced pages.

Write a First Draft

With your outline in hand, the next step is to write a draft of your research report. As you begin to write, we have a few recommendations:

free writing An exercise to overcome the difficulty in beginning to write by quickly recording thoughts, without regard to grammar and punctuation or reference to notes, data, books, and other information.

1. Avoid so-called "writer's block" by **free writing**—recording your thoughts quickly, without regard to grammar and punctuation and without referring to your notes, data, or other information. As experienced writers, we know how difficult it is to write. More often than we care to count, our minds have been blank as we faced a blank document on our computer screen. Sociologist Howard Becker (2007) is one of many advocates of free writing: when his students were having trouble getting started, he advised them to simply sit down and write whatever came into their heads without pausing to look at notes, books, data, or other aids. In free writing, the idea is to write continuously as quickly as you can for a time without worrying about grammar, spelling, and so forth. Although the topics in free writing may be completely open, Becker seems to suggest—and we agree—that it is important to at least stay on the research topic.

2. Related to the first point, consider your first draft a "draft" and not the final report. Too often, because of time and other constraints, students treat writing as a kind of test in which a paper is a problem that they get only one shot at answering (Becker, 2007). All professionals who write fully expect to go through multiple drafts: they know that their first draft is not the finished product. Rather, they see writing as a form of thinking, in which early drafts may show some confusion and lack coherence. As Becker (2007) says, "the rough draft shows you what needs to be made clearer"; rewriting and editing "let you do it" (p. 17). (We have more to say about revisions below.)
3. Make sure you have a clear grasp of the audience's level of knowledge and sources of interest. For the criminal justice reader familiar with the area of study, the report may include technical language, an abbreviated presentation of previous research, and a detailed presentation of methods and findings. For lay readers, in contrast, it should omit technical terms and provide a more detailed presentation of the background of the research and a more general presentation of methods and findings. Because students commonly err in providing too little information about research methods and using too many technical terms, we recommend that you gear your writing to a lay audience.
4. Use the active voice. The use of active rather than passive verbs is standard advice in writing texts. Becker believes this practice is particularly important for those writing in the social sciences, such as criminology and criminal justice. The reason, he explains, is that:

   > Active verbs almost always force you to name the person who did whatever was done . . . We seldom think that things just happen all by themselves, as passive verbs suggest, because in our daily lives people do things and make them happen. Sentences that name active agents make our representations of social life more understandable and believable. "The criminal was sentenced" hides the judge who, we know, did the sentencing and, not incidentally, thus makes the criminal's fate seem the operation of impersonal forces rather than the result of people acting together to imprison him or her. (Becker, 2007, pp. 79–80)

   In addition to using the active voice, unless you are instructed otherwise, we recommend that you write in the first person. Like Johnny Saldaña (2011), who recommends the first person when writing about qualitative research, we think this makes the writing more personal and engaging.
5. Communicating accurately and clearly requires proper grammar, punctuation, and style. The principles of being concise and direct, of avoiding unnecessary jargon, of providing examples to clarify points, and so forth apply just as strongly to technical as to any other form of writing.

6. Finally, no matter how much advice we may impart about writing, the best way to learn how to write in an academic manner is to read academic publications (i.e., journal articles, monographs, research reports, etc.). Reading publications by criminologists and other academics will help you to gain a better understanding of what "good writing" looks like in criminal justice.

With these points in mind, let us consider in some detail the topical outline suggested above. It is important to note that this is only one of many possible outlines, and it applies best to quantitative research. Moreover, considerations of length, subject matter, purpose, and audience may influence the organization and elaboration of this outline in the actual report. A report may emphasize measurement, sampling, or something else, depending on the study. No perfect outline exists ready to be adopted for every research report. The important point is that the outline should be functional and should facilitate your writing.

INTRODUCTION TO THE REPORT

This section sets up the rest of the paper. It is the place, Edwards (2012) points out, "where you try to hook the reader with an answer to the question, 'Why should I care?'" (p. 43). To answer this question requires a clear statement of the problem and why it is of general interest and importance. General interest and importance may be demonstrated by relating the problem briefly to the theoretical context of the study or by pointing to its social and practical significance. For example, Sherman and Berk (1984) begin their article in the journal *American Sociological Review* (see Chapter 2) with a discussion of the competing predictions of specific deterrence and labeling theories. The theories make opposite predictions regarding the effects of punishment on behavior. They note that neither prediction has established consistent empirical support. They then point out that their study will add knowledge to the current debate by examining the "impact of punishment in a particular setting, for a particular offense, and for particular kinds of individuals" (p. 262).

In some ways, the introduction can be the most difficult part of the report to write. In fact, we have struggled at times to introduce chapters in this book. In these cases, we have followed some sage advice that Becker received while in graduate school: write the introduction last, after you have a complete draft of the report. You can never be certain when you begin a report of exactly what you will write. So, it is often easier and more effective to write the introduction after you know how the paper turns out.

LITERATURE REVIEW

The literature review is where you are expected to present the theoretical context of the problem under investigation and how it has been studied by others. The idea is to cite relevant literature in the process of presenting the underlying theoretical and methodological rationale for the research. This means providing a "selective but fair treatment of the state of current knowledge about a topic" (Edwards, 2012, p. 21) rather than trying to report every study ever done on the topic.

In studies designed to test specific hypotheses, the aim of this section should be to show, if possible, how the hypotheses derive from theory or previous research. When this is not possible—for example, because the research question or hypothesis is based on everyday observations and experiences—one should still show the relevance of the study to previous research and theory, if only to show how it contradicts existing evidence or fills a gap in scientific knowledge.

Finally, it is a good idea—especially for lengthy literature reviews—to end this section with:

1. a concise restatement of the research question or hypothesis,
2. a presentation of the theoretical model in a figure, such as an arrow diagram (see Chapter 14), and/or
3. a brief overview of the study.

METHODS

In the Methods section you should state clearly and accurately how the study was done. The following subtopics may help you to accomplish this objective.

DESIGN First you must state what type of study you have done: experiment, survey, field research, or some other approach. The particular approach determines the primary design and procedural issues that must be addressed. Key issues for the different approaches are as follows:

- In the case of an experiment, the type of experimental design and the procedures of its implementation
- In a survey, the mode of data collection and the sampling design
- In field research, the nature of the setting(s) and the researcher's relationship to informants
- In in-depth interviews, the type of interviews conducted (in terms of structure, number of participants, and content) and the extent of rapport established
- In research using existing data, the sources of data and their completeness

SAMPLE This section should make clear who participated in the study, how many cases were sampled, how they were selected, and whom or what they represent. It is necessary to discuss sampling procedures, the limitations of the sample data (including nonresponse bias for surveys), and types of inferences that it is possible to make from the data.

MEASUREMENT Here, operational definitions are described. In quantitative research, you should define concepts and describe how variables were measured. In an experiment, this means specifying the procedures for manipulating the independent variable and measuring the dependent variable. In a survey, this should include the specific questions that were asked as measures of each variable in the theoretical model. In field research, you should describe fully the kinds of observations that were made and, if relevant, other sources of information such as documents and in-depth interviewing. Longer reports may contain appendixes with some of these materials, such as copies of the complete questionnaire or interview guides.

In addition, this section should include any evidence on reliability and validity that is not presented in other sections, such as the outcome of manipulation checks and tests for measurement reliability and validity.

PROCEDURES This section, which may be a part of the description of sampling and measurement, presents a summary of the various steps in the conduct of the research. This is especially important for an experiment and in qualitative research. Experiments should include a step-by-step account of the study from the participant's point of view. Qualitative researchers often give a chronological account of the research, telling how they selected and gained entry into the setting, how they met and developed relationships with informants or interviewees, and how long they were in the setting. In fact, the research report of a field researcher usually follows a narrative, from either the researcher's or informant's point of view, which begins with a discussion of these methodological issues.

FINDINGS/RESULTS

The heart of the research paper is the findings/results section, toward which the entire report should be aimed. This is where questions or hypotheses that framed the research are answered. In quantitative analyses, the researcher should describe what sort of statistical analyses were performed on the data. This description should be very specific with regard to the kind of analysis (e.g., three-way analysis of variance, paired *t*-tests, and ordinary least squares regression), and it may include (which we recommend for the student researcher) descriptions of the statistical techniques or references to the computer software package (e.g., SPSS) used to carry out the analysis. Furthermore, the researcher often constructs tables, charts, and graphs to facilitate the presentation of findings. Here, we have some specific recommendations.

- Use tables and figures sparingly, to summarize large amounts of information. During the course of research, investigators usually generate many more tables than they can possibly present in the research report. These interim tables guide the researcher in determining the course of the analysis, but more often than not they contain single facts that can be communicated in the text of the report.

- Organize this section around the major hypotheses or theoretical questions and/or major findings. If there is a single main hypothesis, then a single table may suffice to summarize the findings.
- Discuss the data in terms of what they show about the research problem or hypothesis. Do not let the data speak for themselves, and do not discuss the data merely in terms of the variables or the numbers in a table. In other words, subordinate the data to your argument and use the data and tables to help tell a story.

This last point also applies to qualitative research. The data in such studies are usually not numbers but quotations, concrete observations, and historical events. As we will see in Chapter 15, various visual displays (e.g., typologies, taxonomies) may be used to communicate findings. Still, the data should be used in the same way as in quantitative analysis: organized around the thesis of the report and presented to support arguments. More generally, the presentation of data should convey an understanding of how research participants think and act within their social contexts.

DISCUSSION

Research reports end with a summary of the major findings and a general interpretation of the study results. The summary serves as a sort of "caboose abstract," reviewing the highlights of the report. This is particularly useful in cases in which the paper is long or necessarily complex. It is important to avoid excessive repetition in the summary: do not lift passages from earlier parts of the paper but, rather, restate the basic problem and basic findings.

Beyond summarizing, the discussion section may accomplish several goals. First, it provides a place to point out the shortcomings of the research. For example, the data may be drawn from populations or under conditions that limit the generalizability of the findings. Honesty regarding such limitations is important in preventing readers from making more from the research than is warranted. Second, it provides a chance to point out inconsistencies, account for anomalies, and suggest improvements in the research design. Third, the discussion section allows the writer an opportunity to place the whole project into broader perspective, to mention the theoretical and practical implications of the study, and to discuss possible future work.

Finally, researchers often conclude reports with a succinct statement of the major point of the study. For example, Back, Soor, and LaPrade (2018) conclude that self-control appears to be associated with a juvenile's likelihood of engaging in computer hacking.

REFERENCES

Lastly, the report needs to include some sort of bibliography or reference list. It is best practice to list only works cited in the body of the report. The format of the references varies slightly from one discipline to another. Box 3.4 should help you understand and apply a style guide often used in criminology and criminal justice courses.

BOX 3.4

DOING CRIMINAL JUSTICE RESEARCH

APA Guidelines for In-Text Citations and References

The American Psychological Association (APA) has established formal guidelines that apply to all articles published in journals and books sponsored by the association. Many instructors ask their students to use the *Publication Manual of the American Psychological Association* (2020). Below are a few of its rules. If you plan to major in or pursue graduate studies in criminal justice or criminology, we recommend that you read the complete manual.

Whenever a publication or presentation is the source of claims or ideas, you must give credit to the source. Giving credit begins with citations inserted in the text that include the author(s) and year of publication. If you are quoting directly from a work, you must also include page numbers. Below are examples that show how these rules apply under different conditions:

- Author's name in the text.

    Sherman and Berk (1984) explore the impact of mandatory arrest . . .

- Author's name not in the text.

    Research indicates . . . (Sherman & Berk, 1984).

- A work by three or more authors.

    Low self-control . . . impacts likelihood of juvenile hacking (Back et al., 2018).

- Citations with more than one reference: use semicolon to separate and list alphabetically.

    . . . (Bachmann, 2010; Back et al., 2018; Bossler & Burruss, 2012).

- Direct quotation or reference to specific passage: author, year of publication, and page number for the reference are needed.

    Sherman and Berk (1984) find that "swift imposition of a sanction . . ." (p. 270).

    "Computer hacking has received considerable academic attention . . ." (Back et al., 2018, p. 41).

All names cited in the text should be placed in a reference list following the text. This section is headed "References," and all references are listed alphabetically by the first author's last name. The APA includes last name and first and middle initials for all authors, as in the following examples.

- References for books.

    Alexander, M. (2010). *The New Jim Crow: Mass Incarceration in the Age of Colorblindness*. The New Press.

- References for journal articles with one author.

    Terrill, W. (2005). Police use of force: A transactional approach. *Justice Quarterly, 22*(1), 107–138. https://doi.org/10.1080/07418820420003333663

- References for journal articles with more than one author.

    Sherman, L. W., & Berk, R. A. (1984). The specific deterrent effects of arrest for domestic assault. *American Sociological Review, 49*(2), 261–272.

- References for chapters in edited volumes.

    Meade, B., & Bolin, R. M. (2018). Religion and prison violence. In K. R. Kerley (Ed.), *Finding freedom in confinement: The role of religion in prison life* (pp. 93–119). Praeger.

- References to websites.

    American Society of Criminology. (2016). *American Society of Criminology Code of Ethics*. ASC. https://asc41.org/wp-content/uploads/ASC_Code_of_Ethics.pdf

Revisions and Other Writing Considerations

Your draft should go through multiple revisions, and when the final draft is completed, you should carefully proofread it. As noted earlier, many students make the mistake of treating the first draft as the only draft. Most professional writers, on the other hand, assume that the first draft will be one in a series of drafts designed to sharpen and improve the final product. The purpose of a first draft is to transfer ideas, thoughts, and facts from the mind of the writer into some material form that can be reflected on. We cannot put a number on how many subsequent drafts should be written; however, it is hard to imagine a polished report that is not the product of numerous drafts. Good writing requires attention to detail; it means writing as if every word and sentence should be taken seriously. And that requires extensive rewriting.

For many people the best time to revise a paper is after taking some time away from the work. Writers who wait until the last few hours or days to write a paper will not produce a good paper—among other reasons, because they simply will not have time to "sleep on it" and reread their work in a refreshed frame of mind. Authors' judgments about the quality of their work may vary directly with the recency of the effort. The passage of time tends to bring perspective and a renewed energy to tackle a job that perhaps did not seem necessary earlier. Much revision, of course, can be of the "cut and paste" variety. This job usually involves the revision of what is unclear, the deletion of what is extraneous, and the addition of what had been omitted.

Finally, at some point in the successive drafting of a report, you will have a "working" draft ready to be shown to others who can provide critical feedback. We realize that much of the writing students do, with its rigid time constraints, does not allow for this. But there is no better way of judging the clarity of your writing than asking others if they understand what you are saying. Professionals know this and often develop a circle of friends who will read their work. We encourage students to do the same.

LENGTH

Probably the most frequently asked question regarding student papers is: How long should it be? The most appropriate but usually unsatisfying answer is: As long as it needs to be. Many students make the mistake of underestimating the length that thoroughness demands; they may omit vital information and thus seriously weaken the impact of the report. On the other hand, some students make the mistake of thinking that the longer a report is, the better it is. The techniques of "padding" a paper through overuse of citations, excessive use of full quotations instead of summarizing the findings of cited sources, and reliance on vocabulary and jargon intended to "impress" the audience are mistakes that experienced readers usually see through. Jeffrey Katzer, Kenneth Cook, and Wayne Crouch (1998) refer to these smoke screens as "paraphernalia of pedantry" and conclude that they are more likely to be distracting than to facilitate communication. And it is communication that is the essence of the research process.

AVOIDING PLAGIARISM

One form of scientific misconduct is plagiarism. Plagiarism, according to the US Department of Health and Human Services, is "the appropriation of another person's ideas, processes, results, or words without giving appropriate credit" (Steneck, 2007, p. 21). Plagiarism in any form, whether intentional or accidental, is a serious and often punishable offense. As you write your report, therefore, you must be careful to properly cite all work that is the source of the ideas presented.

Leonard Rosen and Laurence Behrens (1992, p. 582) believe that much plagiarism is unintentional, occurring because of writers' carelessness or ignorance about the conventions of quotation and citation. They offer two general rules for avoiding unintentional plagiarism. First, "whenever you quote the exact words of others, place these words in quotation marks and properly cite the source." To quote a source is to extract a word, phrase, sentence, or passage from the original and insert it into the text. Quoted material should be enclosed within double quotation marks or, if lengthy (more than 40 words, according to the *APA Manual*), indented as a block quote. Second, "whenever you paraphrase or summarize the ideas of others, do not use whole phrases, many of the same words, or sentence structures similar to the original," and be sure "to identify the source of the paraphrased or summarized material." To summarize is to condense the original into a sentence or two in your own words; to paraphrase is to follow the original statement more closely but still restate it in your own words. In general, your report will be easier to read and better convey your understanding of what you read if you summarize or paraphrase others' ideas rather than present a stream of quotations. Use direct quotations only when the original words are particularly well chosen—clear, incisive, and powerful.

SUMMARY

Writing the research report is facilitated greatly by preparing an outline, keeping in mind the intended audience and how they will read the report, and writing several drafts as well as soliciting others' critical comments on early drafts. Most research reports contain the following components:

1. an introduction to the problem pointing out its theoretical, practical, and/or social significance;
2. a literature review relating the research problem to previous theory and research;
3. a methods section outlining precisely how the research was done, including the overall approach and design and methods of sampling and measurement;
4. a findings/results section;
5. a discussion of the limitations and anomalies as well as the broader theoretical and practical implications of the research; and
6. a list of references cited in the report.

To check your understanding of the concepts learned within this section, please refer to Box 3.5.

> **BOX 3.5**
>
> **CHECKING YOUR UNDERSTANDING**
>
> ## Parts of a Research Report
>
> 1. Which of the following is the correct order of the various parts of a research report?
>   a. Introduction, Literature review, Methods, Findings/Results, Discussion, References
>   b. Introduction, Methods, Literature review, Discussion, Findings/Results, References
>   c. Introduction, Findings/Results, Methods, Literature Review, Discussion, References
>   d. Introduction, Discussion, Methods, Findings/Results, Literature Review, References
>
> 2. What is the purpose of an APA formatted reference list?
>   a. Avoid plagiarism
>   b. Give credit to sources
>   c. Allow other researchers to locate relevant studies
>   d. All of the above
>
> 3. Cite the following reference according to proper APA format.
>   Article title: The Role of Entertainment Media in Perceptions of Police Use of Force.
>   Page numbers: 1261–1281
>   Authors: Kathleen M. Donovan and Charles F. Klahm, IV
>   Year of publication: 2015
>   Journal name: Criminal Justice and Behavior
>   Volume number: 42
>   Issue number: 12
>
> **Answers: 1. a, 2. d**

KEY TERMS

abstract, p. 50   free writing, p. 56   peer review, p. 51

KEY POINTS

- The process of reading and writing social research usually begins by identifying relevant literature, reading and evaluating it, and formulating one or more research questions.
- Writing often begins with the development of a research proposal, which synthesizes relevant literature, poses one or more research questions or hypotheses, and describes the methods and data to be used to address the question.
- Research reports typically include an introduction, literature review, a description of data and methods, presentation of results or findings, a discussion/conclusion, and references.
- In writing a research report, researchers may develop an outline, write a draft, and revise it multiple times based on proofreading and comments from others.
- Ultimately, writing requires attention to detail, including the careful citation of sources.

REVIEW QUESTIONS

1. What does the textbook recommend as the primary means of evaluating the credibility of published articles?
2. Besides identifying gaps in research on a topic, what does the textbook recommend as a worthwhile research question?
3. For whom or for what purpose may a research proposal be written?
4. What are the major components of a research report?
5. What is an effective way of overcoming the difficulty in beginning to write?
6. In a sentence, describe the objective of each of the following sections of a research report: (a) introduction; (b) literature review; (c) results/findings; (d) discussion.
7. Identify two rules for avoiding unintentional plagiarism.

EXERCISES

1. To practice locating literature relevant to a research topic, suppose that you are interested in the perceptions of police. More specifically, you want to know what factors influence citizens' perceptions of police. First, following the guidelines presented in Box 3.1, use the comprehensive criminal justice database National Criminal Justice Reference Service (NCJRS) abstracts (which should be available in your library's online research databases) to conduct a search on this topic. What keywords seem to produce the most relevant list of references? Do you need to add additional key terms in order to further narrow your search? Second, begin reading the titles and abstracts that you find. List the first five references that you believe are relevant to your topic.

2. Choose a topic and repeat the steps in Exercise 1. For the first five journal articles that you deem relevant to your topic, determine whether the article is peer-reviewed. Now summarize the contents of each reference using Table 3.1 as a framework.
3. Addressing the questions outlined in Box 3.2, write a critique of the following article: Brady, P. Q., Nobles, M. R., & Bouffard, L. A. (2017). Are college students *really* at a higher risk of stalking?: Exploring the generalizability of student samples in victimization research. *Journal of Criminal Justice, 52*, 12–21.

The Ethics and Politics of Research

Doing What's "Right"

4

CHAPTER OUTLINE

4.1 Overview: Ethics 71

4.2 Ethical Issues in the Treatment of Research Participants 71
Potential Harm 72
Informed Consent 73
Deception 74
Invasion of Privacy 75
Summary 77

4.3 Federal and Professional Ethical Guidelines 78
Evaluating Potential Harm 79
Informed Consent Procedures 81
Deception Ground Rules 82
Privacy Protection: Anonymity and Confidentiality 84
Summary 86

4.4 The Process of Ethical Decision-Making 87
Review Federal Regulations and Professional Ethics Codes 88
Assess Costs and Benefits of Proposed Research 88
Identify and Address Areas of Ethical Concern 89
Prepare and Submit Application for IRB Approval 89
Collect Data and Secure Participants' Rights 90
Summary 91

4.5 Politics and Social Research 92
Topic Selection, Political Ideology, and Research Funding 93
Data Analysis and Interpretation and Political Ideology 95
Dissemination of Research Findings: Science, Politics, and Public Policy 96
Summary 96

LEARNING OBJECTIVES

By the end of this chapter, you should be able to

4.1 Define ethics.

4.2 Identify and describe the four major ethical issues in the treatment of research participants: potential harm, informed consent, deception, and privacy invasion.

4.3 Recall the federal regulations and professional guidelines concerning the ethical treatment of research participants.

4.4 Apply the process of ethical decision-making to your own research.

4.5 Discuss the relationship between politics and criminal justice research.

"Let's talk about sex," sang the music group Salt-N-Pepa (1991) in their classic hit of the same title. Well, that is easier said than done. It can be difficult for people to "talk about sex" because they may view it as a private matter. The topic of sex is also politically charged, evoking ideological and religious values in debates over public issues ranging from abortion to same-sex marriage, parenting, and adoption. In social science research, generally, sex is among the most ethically and politically sensitive topics, according to sociologist Janice Irvine (2012).

Within criminal justice research, many of the topics covered involve private matters, or what we call "sensitive subjects." These topics can include, but are not limited to, risky sexual behaviors, substance use, criminal activity, and victimization. Not only do these topics include sensitive information that a participant may not wish to divulge to a researcher, but studying sensitive issues can also become very political. Let us consider, for an example, research that the authors of this text conducted on college student substance use. Bolin, Pate, and McClintock (2017) collected self-report data from undergraduate students; survey items included questions about alcohol use, marijuana use, and academic achievement. In addition, but not published in the 2017 manuscript, students were asked about risky behaviors such as sexual activity, drinking and driving, and other criminal activity. Students who completed the survey revealed a lot of sensitive information about their backgrounds and behaviors. While this research is important because of the real-world implications it can have for college campuses, it can be very political from start to finish. For instance, a university might deny the use of such a survey instrument on campus for fear of the impact the results may have on the university's reputation (luckily this was not the case for Bolin et al.). In addition, a university might become concerned with the results and ask for information about specific students who admitted to violating school policies, or even the law, on the self-report survey. Finally, instead of considering how research like this can be used to tackle a real problem on college campuses, the media, politicians, or society may use the information to bring negative attention to universities.

As criminal justice researchers, we have to consider the ethical ramifications of research for participants, organizations, society, and ourselves. We also have to consider the politically polarizing nature of much of the research that we do on crime and delinquency. These controversial topics found in criminal justice research illustrate the twin topics of this chapter: ethics and politics. Both topics further establish the broader context of criminal justice research. Just as research is guided by the elements of scientific inquiry, as discussed in Chapter 2, it also is shaped by moral and political considerations. The first part of this chapter will sensitize you to ethical issues in research. Later in the chapter we consider how politics enters into research.

4.1 OVERVIEW: ETHICS

As a subject matter, **ethics** consists of standards of conduct that distinguish between right and wrong. When you were a child, you were probably told that honesty is right and lying is wrong. Similar ethical standards exist in the world of research. Researchers are expected, for example, to make sure that their data are trustworthy by honestly and accurately conducting and reporting their research. They are also expected to give proper credit when they use others' ideas, to accept authorship of a paper only when they have made a significant contribution to it, and to guard against the improper application of their research findings.

ethics Standards of moral conduct that distinguish right from wrong

Most of the ethical standards that guide criminal justice research are derived from the larger society; some standards are codified in professional codes of conduct and in federal regulations. Generally, these standards are not hard-and-fast rules by which researchers are expected to abide but rather depend on the situation and are subject to multiple interpretations. Is it necessarily wrong, for example, to deceive a research participant? By an absolutist standard, the answer is yes; because deception is a form of lying, it should not be tolerated. Yet, according to professional organizations, such as the Academy of Criminal Justice Sciences (ACJS, 2000) and the American Society of Criminology (ASC, 2016), the answer to this question is "it depends." What it depends on are the risks posed to the rights and welfare of research participants, the benefits of the research, the steps taken to protect participants' rights, and the plan for debriefing participants—providing the full purpose for the study after participation.

In discussing ethics, we focus on issues regarding the treatment of research participants, as in our example of deception. Every social scientist, including criminal justice researchers, has a personal and professional obligation to protect the rights and welfare of research participants. It is important to become aware of these ethical issues and how to address them, whether you are evaluating the research of others or conducting your own research. First, we consider how scientific research may violate participants' rights and welfare. Next, we review federal and professional ethical guidelines for protecting participants. Then, we briefly outline an ethical decision-making process intended to guide you in carrying out research.

4.2 ETHICAL ISSUES IN THE TREATMENT OF RESEARCH PARTICIPANTS

Four issues have been identified most often regarding the ethical treatment of human participants: potential harm, lack of informed consent, deception, and privacy invasion (Diener & Crandall, 1978). It is considered a violation of basic human rights to harm others, to force people to perform actions against their will, to lie or mislead them, and to invade their privacy. To illustrate these ethical issues, we cite several studies, including landmark cases of unethical or ethically questionable research, some of which were instrumental in the development of current ethical standards.

Potential Harm

The first right of any research participant is the right to personal safety. Atrocities committed in World War II (1939–1945), which came to light in the Nuremberg Trials (1945–1946), brought attention to this issue. During the war, Nazi scientists used prisoners in experiments that resulted in pain, suffering, and even death. In one experiment, subjects were kept naked outdoors in below-freezing temperatures until parts of their bodies froze; in others, they were infected with malaria, typhus, poisons, and bacteria in deliberately inflicted wounds (Katz, 1972). This research clearly violated the most fundamental right of research participants: that they should not be harmed by their participation.

Research that would endanger the life or physical health of a human subject is simply not acceptable in the scientific community. But harm is not only physical. Participants in social research may experience anxiety, the loss of self-esteem, feelings of embarrassment or humiliation, or even the loss of trust. These forms of harm often are difficult to anticipate and may occur despite researchers' best intentions. An example is the prison simulation study conducted at Stanford University by Philip Zimbardo et al. (1973; Haney et al., 1973). To examine how the roles of "prison guard" and "prisoner" influence behavior, these investigators created a mock prison in the basement of a campus building in which male student volunteers played the roles of a "prison guard" or "prisoner." (See Photo 4.1) The study was scheduled to run for two weeks; however, it had to be terminated after only six days because guards physically and psychologically abused prisoners and prisoners broke down, rebelled, or became submissive and apathetic. The participants got so caught up in the situation, became so absorbed in their roles, that they began to confuse role-playing and self-identity.

In another example, there is potential harm that can come when sensitive information, such as engagement in delinquent activity, is revealed and confidentiality cannot be maintained. One well-known instance is the set of subpoenas issued by the US Attorney General, on behalf of the United Kingdom, to Boston College for interview transcripts from Boston College's Belfast Project (BP) (Palys & Lowman, 2012). In this study, researchers interviewed participants who had been involved in paramilitary activity, including bombings, abductions, murder, etc., during the Northern Ireland conflict (also known as The Trouble). Recognizing that release of participants' identities could bring them harm, researchers told participants that their interviews would not be released until after their deaths (Inckle, 2015). Legal authorities in the United Kingdom eventually

▲ **PHOTO 4.1** Student participants in the Stanford Prison simulation study, shown here, quickly absorbed the roles of guard and prisoner. Reactions were unexpectedly intense and pathological, with the potential for harm so great that the study was prematurely stopped after only six days.

became aware of the BP archive and subpoenaed the college for the interviews. A US court ruled the data be handed over to the UK authorities, and despite protestations by the researchers, Boston College abided, handing over dozens of interview transcripts. The release of the interviews caused many participants to fear for their safety. Confidentiality will be discussed in more detail later in this chapter, however, examples such as this one illustrate how information given by participants to researchers can lead to potential personal consequences should it be released, including damaged reputations, legal issues, or embarrassment.

Informed Consent

The second ethical issue arises from the value placed on freedom of choice. The significance and meaning of this ethical principle are illustrated by the Tuskegee study of syphilis (a sexually transmitted and life-threatening disease) conducted over the course of four decades by the US Public Health Service. The research participants consisted of about 600 African American men, many of whom were uneducated sharecroppers. Of these men, about two-thirds had the disease when the study began in 1932; the other third did not. The men were told that they had "bad blood" (see Figure 4.1), which could include a range of illnesses not limited to syphilis; they agreed to participate on the promise of medical care for "minor ailments," burial insurance, and other benefits (Jones, 1981; U.S. Centers for Disease Control and Prevention, 2022). For those who had syphilis, though, "there was nothing to indicate that ... [they] knew they were participating in a deadly serious experiment," according to historian James H. Jones (1981, p. 7). The purpose of the study was to follow the course of untreated syphilis. When penicillin was accepted as a treatment in the late 1940s and early 1950s, the men were not given it. It was not until 1972 that the study was exposed and terminated (Jones, 1981; U.S. Centers for Disease Control and Prevention, 2022).

Both the atrocities committed by Nazi scientists and the Tuskegee study raised the issue of **informed consent**. "Informed" means that research participants must be given enough information about the research to make a rational decision about whether to participate. In the case of Tuskegee, participants were given incomplete

informed consent
The ethical principle that individuals should be given enough information about a study, especially its potential risks, to make an informed decision about whether to participate.

FIGURE 4.1 This Letter to Participants in the Tuskegee Study, from the National Archives, Shows How the Participants were Enticed to Participate and were Not Informed About the True Purpose if the Study.

and misleading information (i.e., "bad blood"), and they did not know that treatment for their true underlying condition would be withheld. "Consent" refers to *voluntary* participation, a principle established at the military tribunal at Nuremberg (Katz, 1972). Nazi prisoners were, by definition, not free to consent. To volunteer is to have the freedom to choose to participate and to discontinue participation; however, firsthand accounts indicate that the men at Tuskegee were discouraged from seeking treatment, and they would lose benefits if they withdrew from the study (Jones, 1981, pp. 5–7).

Two controversial social science studies also violated the principle of informed consent. The first is Stanley Milgram's (1974) shock experiment, which was designed to study obedience to authority. Participants in this study volunteered to take part but were not given enough information to make an *informed* decision to participate. They were told beforehand that they would be administering harmless electrical shocks to another human being as part of a learning experiment. However, they were *not* told that being in this position could be highly stressful and that they might experience great stress and anxiety.

Another example is Laud Humphreys's (1970/2009) study on male–male sexual encounters. Humphreys observed men in *public* places, which generally does not require participants' consent. Many critics point out, however, that his observations *could have* posed a risk—of blackmail, for example—to participants if they were exposed (Glazer, 1972/2009; Von Hoffman, 1970/2009; Warwick, 1973/2009). Furthermore, when Humphreys went back to interview many of these men in their homes, he *misinformed* them about the nature of the study. Not knowing that they previously had been observed, they believed that they had been selected to participate in a survey on social and health behavior (Warwick, 1973/2009). Thus, research participants did not consent in the early stage of the study; then, in a later stage, they consented on the basis of false information (Glazer, 1972/2009).

Deception

Both Humphreys's and Milgram's studies involved deception: Humphreys lied and disguised himself; Milgram misled participants in several ways. Volunteers in Milgram's experiment agreed to participate in what they thought was a learning experiment but was actually a study on obedience. When the research participants arrived at the setting, they chose a card designating whether they would be the "teacher" or "learner." In reality, the drawing was rigged, with "teacher" written on both cards. Thus, research participants ended up playing the "teacher" role, whereas an actor, who was a confederate of the experimenter, played the role of "learner." Participants were then told they would be reading word pairs to the learner, and when the learner responded incorrectly, they were to shock him by pressing a lever on a "shock generator." (See Photo 4.2) The shocks, the experimenter told the research participants, could be extremely painful but would not cause permanent damage; however, the learner never actually received any shocks.

While these examples of deception raise serious concerns, it is important to realize that researchers rarely give complete information about the purpose of their research and that this is not in itself considered deceptive. Deception in social research, including criminal justice research, involves intentionally misleading or misinforming participants about aspects of a study (Sell, 2008). As we noted earlier, deception is allowed in certain circumstances, but its use is controversial. On the one hand, some scholars argue that deception is sometimes necessary to place research participants in a mental state where they will behave naturally. Had Milgram informed research participants that he was studying obedience, they almost certainly would have disobeyed. Only by deceiving them about the true purpose of his research could he observe their naturally obedient behavior. Karen Cook and Toshio Yamagishi (2008) further write that "a ban on deception would make it impossible or extremely difficult to investigate non-rational aspects of behavior" (p. 216), as many social scientists do.

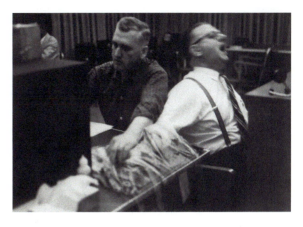

▲ **PHOTO 4.2** Teacher (left) and learner (right) in Milgram's obedience study. The study involved several experimental conditions. In this condition, the teacher forces the learner's hand down on a shock plate.

On the other hand, many social scientists oppose deception on moral and pragmatic grounds. For some, the most telling argument is that lying is immoral. Similarly, some critics contend that deception invariably violates participants' rights to informed consent because consent obtained by deceit, by definition, cannot be informed (Baumrind, 1985). Although social scientists debate this position, most agree that Milgram's and Humphreys's use of deception went too far, as both investigators misled participants about the *potential risk of harm*, thereby clearly violating the principle of informed consent. Critics who argue against deception on pragmatic or scientific grounds contend that it may make participants suspicious and not produce the spontaneous behavior it intends (Baumrind, 1985; Hertwig & Ortmann, 2008). Evidence about the impact of suspicion generally fails to support this position, however, with recent research showing that exposure to deception does not affect the validity of experimental results (Barrera & Simpson, 2012; Krasnow et al., 2020; Rahwan et al., 2022).

Invasion of Privacy

Criminal justice research also presents many possibilities for invading the privacy of research participants. One dramatic case is the 1954 Wichita Jury Study (Vaughan, 1967). In an effort to understand and perhaps even improve the operations of juries, researchers secured the permission of judges to record six actual jury deliberations in Wichita, Kansas, without the knowledge of the jurors. When news of the study became known, it was roundly criticized by columnists and commentators across the country and investigated by a Senate subcommittee, which ultimately led to the passage of a law prohibiting the recording of jury deliberations. The argument against this study was that jury deliberations must be sacrosanct to protect the inalienable right to trial by impartial jury. Surveillance such as that used in the study "threatens impartiality to the extent that it introduces any question of possible embarrassment, coercion, or other such considerations into the minds of actual jurors" (p. 72).

The right to privacy is the individual's right to decide when, where, to whom, and to what extent his or her attitudes, beliefs, and behavior will be revealed. New forms of technology and advanced systems of information technology make privacy invasion in research a major concern today. For instance, states collect criminal histories on offenders and compile the information into electronic databases (Myrent, 2019). This criminal history record information (CHRI) is used by agencies for public safety reasons and criminal background checks. Additionally, this computer-based information can be useful for criminal justice researchers. According to Myrent (2019), "CHRI is a particularly valuable source of data for evaluation studies seeking to determine the effectiveness of programs designed to prevent new or persistent criminal behavior, as well as for criminal career and desistance research" (p. 2). Researchers seeking to use CHRIs for their studies are required to follow federal guidelines regarding confidentiality and to receive Institutional Review Board approval. However, offenders are not required to provide consent for the use of this information in research. While researchers are required to keep information secure, maintain confidentiality, and limit the dissemination of research findings using CHRIs, individuals may still have concerns over the privacy of offenders whose information is being used without their consent. Even with de-identified data (data that is missing participant names or other identifying information), there are concerns about the ability for researchers to trace sensitive or private information back to an individual. To illustrate how it may be possible to identify specific participants in data sets, Box 4.1 describes a hypothetical example related to the concerns raised about even de-identified data.

BOX 4.1

READING CRIMINAL JUSTICE RESEARCH

Privacy Invasion in the Public Identification of Participants

Consider the data in Table A from a hypothetical online survey on voting among US college professors. In the columns from left to right, you see identification numbers for these professors as well as data on whether they work at Hudson University (= 1) or not (= 0), whether they are criminologists

4.2 Ethical Issues in the Treatment of Research Participants

Table A Hypothetical Data on Professors' Voting

ID	Hudson University	Law & Order	Male	Hometown	Voted '20
1	0	1	0	Chicago	1
2	0	1	1	L.A.	1
3	1	1	1	New York	1
4	0	0	1	Dallas	1
5	0	0	0	Dayton	0

(= 1) or not (= 0); whether they are male (= 1) or not (= 0), their hometowns, and whether they voted in the 2020 election (= 1) or not (= 0).

You can see from these data how it might be possible to identify professor #3. The table indicates that this professor works at Hudson University, is in the Department of Law & Order, is a male, and hails from New York City, New York. After going to the department's home page through Hudson University and looking at the faculty profiles, you see that one (male) professor was "born and bred in good ole' New York City, New York": Jack McCoy. Knowing this, you also now know that McCoy voted in the 2020 election. This is not very sensitive information, but if McCoy did not want his voting behavior to be publicly revealed, you can see how this would raise privacy concerns.

SUMMARY

Ethics consists of standards of conduct that distinguish between right and wrong. Researchers are expected to act ethically in conducting their studies and in their treatment of research participants. We identify four recurring issues concerning the welfare and rights of research participants: potential harm, especially to one's physical health and mental well-being; lack of informed consent in terms of the ability to make a rational, voluntary decision to participate; deception by being intentionally misled or misinformed about a study; and privacy invasion stemming from a study's revelation of personal information. Some unethical and ethically questionable studies concerning these issues have led to the development of federal and professional standards to protect participants' rights and welfare. See Box 4.2 to assess your understanding of this section.

> **BOX 4.2**
>
> **CHECKING YOUR UNDERSTANDING**
>
> ## Ethics Practice Questions I
>
> 1. Which of the following is not one of the four main ethical principles discussed above in section 4.2?
>   a. Potential harm
>   b. Lack of deception
>   c. Privacy invasion
>   d. Lack of informed consent
>
> 2. _____ is an individual's right to decide when, where, to whom, and to what extent their attitudes, beliefs, and behavior will be revealed.
>   a. Right to consent
>   b. Right to privacy
>   c. Right to confidentiality
>   d. Right to anonymity
>
> 3. The Tuskegee Syphilis Study is used as an example of which of the following ethical issues?
>   a. Potential harm
>   b. Lack of deception
>   c. Privacy invasion
>   d. Lack of informed consent
>
> Answers: 1. b, 2. b, 3. d

4.3 FEDERAL AND PROFESSIONAL ETHICAL GUIDELINES

Now that you are aware of the four main areas of ethical concern in scientific research with human subjects, let us examine the federal and professional standards that have been developed to protect participants' rights and welfare. In general, ethical practices are set forth in codes of ethics that were established in response to the worst abuses, such as the Nazi experiments and Tuskegee Syphilis Study. In the United States, congressional hearings on the Tuskegee Study led to the National Research Act (1974), which created a commission charged with the task of making recommendations for the protection of human subjects.

In 1979, the commission issued the *Belmont Report* (National Commission, 1979), which presented three broad, unifying ethical principles that formed the basis for specific regulations: respect for persons, beneficence, and justice. **Respect for persons** means that researchers must treat individuals as "autonomous agents" who have the freedom and capacity to decide what happens to them. It also requires that researchers protect those with diminished autonomy, such as children, prisoners, and the mentally disabled. **Beneficence** requires researchers to consider the welfare of participants so that they "maximize possible benefits and minimize possible harms." Included in this consideration are longer-term benefits that may result from the advancement of knowledge and betterment of humankind. **Justice** means that the benefits and burdens of research should be fairly distributed (National Commission, 1979). In particular, the burdens of research should not fall upon one group, while the benefits accrue to another. The exploitation of unwilling prisoners by Nazi scientists is an extreme example of injustice.

Based largely on the *Belmont Report*, federal regulations for protecting research participants were put into place and have been revised several times (Code of Federal Regulations, Title 45, Part 46—Protection of Human Subjects [CFR], 2024). Subpart A of these regulations, known as the **Common Rule**, provides information about the application of regulations and presents criteria for approval of research. The Common Rule applies to all research conducted or funded by a federal department or agency; it is also applied to "all human subjects research," regardless of funding, conducted at nearly every college and university in the United States (Meyer, 2020, p. 62, fn. 20).

Professional organizations' ethical codes articulate general principles and rules that apply to research situations often encountered in a particular discipline. They are designed at once to protect the welfare of the individuals with whom scientists work and to guide researchers in making ethically responsible choices. Some examples include the American Society of Criminology's Code of Ethics (2016) and the Academy of Criminal Justice Science's Code of Ethics (2000). Below we highlight portions of professional ethical codes and federal regulations as they relate to the four issues concerning the ethical treatment of participants.

respect for persons the Belmont principle that individuals must be treated as autonomous agents who have the freedom and capacity to decide what happens to them, and researchers must protect those with diminished autonomy

beneficence the Belmont principle that researchers have an obligation to secure the well-being of participants by maximizing possible benefits and minimizing possible harms

justice the Belmont principle that the benefits and burdens of research should be fairly distributed so that the group selected for research also may benefit from its application

Common Rule label given to the federal policy for the protection of human subjects

Evaluating Potential Harm

Federal regulations specify two main criteria for evaluating potential harm:

1. the level of risk to research participants and
2. the risks of the research in relation to the benefits ((CFR), 2024 46.111).

With respect to the first criterion, the level of risk should be "minimized" by using sound research procedures that "do not unnecessarily expose subjects to risk" (CFR, 2024, 46.111 [a] [1]). To distinguish studies in which special precautions should be taken, the Common Rule creates a criterion of "minimal risk": "The probability and magnitude of harm or discomfort anticipated in the research are not greater in and of themselves than those ordinarily encountered in daily life" (CFR, 2024, 46.102[j]). Surveys, for instance, often involve no more than minimal risk because the researcher is asking questions of respondents that they may encounter in everyday life (e.g., "What is your age?"). But when a study poses more than minimal risk (e.g., on a sensitive topic, particularly if participants may be identified) or involves special populations (e.g., children or prisoners), researchers need to take greater precautions to minimize risks.

The second criterion, derived from the principle of beneficence, is that "risks to subjects are reasonable in relation to anticipated benefits" (CFR, 2024, 46.111[a][2]). If there is little to no scientific value from a study that knowingly exposes participants to harm, the study should not be done, no matter how small the harm. But if a study has considerable scientific merit, some degree of potential risk may be justified.

Assessing the costs and benefits of social research is difficult. Unlike biomedical research, where participants may benefit directly from a new drug or treatment, such as a COVID-19 vaccine, the main benefit to participants in criminal justice research is simply what they may learn—about the research or themselves—from their experience. The primary benefits accrue to others: investigators gain knowledge that may contribute to professional success and recognition; the profession advances scientific understanding, which may lead to the betterment of humanity or development of policy and programs. In addition, costs and benefits may be hard to predict. Philip Zimbardo and colleagues (1973) did not foresee the emotional costs to participants in their prison simulation study; neither were they likely to have anticipated the study's contribution to ethical and scientific knowledge. The same can be said of Moloney, McIntyre, and McArthur, researchers from The Belfast Project, who did not anticipate the disclosure of their interview transcripts at the start of their project.

Although difficult, conducting a cost–benefit analysis is an important first step in evaluating the ethics of a proposed study. In addition to assessing risk of harm as well as costs and benefits, the following guidelines also help to minimize harm:

1. Researchers should *inform* participants of any reasonable or foreseeable risks or discomforts before the study begins and should give participants sufficient opportunity to consider. This is an important part of informed consent, which is mandated by federal regulations and discussed in the next section.
2. Where appropriate, researchers should screen out research participants who might be harmed by the research procedures. In the prison simulation study, the investigators gave several personality tests to the student volunteers in order to select participants with "normal" personality profiles and thereby minimize the possibility of harm (Zimbardo, 1973). By contrast, another criticism of Milgram's research is that he did *not* screen participants to see if they could withstand the stress that they would experience. In effect, participants were placed in a highly stressful conflict situation: Should they obey the experimenter in administering the shocks, or

should they refuse to continue in the experiment? The participants showed many obvious signs of stress; indeed, one person had a convulsive seizure that made it necessary to terminate their participation.
3. If stress or potential harm is likely, measures also should be planned to assess harm after the study and, if necessary, provide resources to ameliorate it. To this end, researchers conducting laboratory experiments or doing interviews on sensitive topics should probe participants' feelings and reactions immediately after the study (see discussion of debriefing later in this section). After discussing such feelings, the researcher may ask participants if they want to talk more and then provide contact information for people or groups who are trained to help, such as counselors and medical professionals.

Informed Consent Procedures

The Belmont Principle of respect for persons underlies the ethical requirement of informed consent. According to federal regulations, to make an *informed* decision about whether to take part in a study, research participants must be given adequate information about the study, including foreseeable risks of participating. Furthermore, obtaining their *consent* must "minimize the possibility of coercion or undue influence" (CFR, 2024, 46.116[a][2]), which means participation must be voluntary. Even greater protections should be taken when working with special populations, such as children and prisoners. Children, for example, cannot directly give their informed consent; rather, their parent or guardian needs to do so (CFR, 2024, 46.408[b]). On the other hand, school-aged participants may be required to give their *assent*—that is, agreement to participate in the research—if they are deemed capable of doing so, as determined by their "ages, maturity, and psychological state" (CFR, 2024, 46.408[a]).

Federal regulations generally dictate the use of a *written* consent form, *signed* by the participant or the participant's legal guardian. This not only protects participants, it also protects the researcher. Participants are protected from harm by being able to make up their own minds about the risks of participation; researchers are protected legally by obtaining a record of participants' explicit voluntary agreement. An exception to this rule is that a signed informed consent agreement is usually not necessary and may be waived in research involving minimal risk (CFR, 2024, 46.116[f]). In most surveys, for example, it is sufficient to read or have participants read a consent statement and then ask them if they wish to continue with the survey (Citro, 2010).

What should an informed consent statement include? Federal regulations spell out in detail the basic elements of informed consent statements. As applied to social research, these elements include the following (CFR, 2024, 46.116[b]):

1. a statement that the study involves research,
2. an explanation of the purposes of the research,

3. the expected duration of the participant's participation,
4. a description of the procedures to be followed,
5. a description of any reasonably foreseeable risks or discomforts to the participant,
6. a description of any benefits to the participant or to others which may reasonably be expected from the research,
7. a statement describing how, if applicable, the confidentiality of records identifying the participant will be maintained,
8. an explanation of whom to contact for answers to pertinent questions about the research and research participants' rights and whom to contact in the event of a research-related injury to the participant,
9. a statement that participation is voluntary, refusal to participate will involve no penalty or loss of benefits to which the participant is otherwise entitled, and the participant may discontinue participation at any time without penalty or loss of benefits.

All of this information, according to federal regulations (CFR, 2024, 46.116[a][3]), needs to be conveyed in clear and understandable language; anything less undermines participants' ability to make an *informed* decision. In Chapter 8, we provide a sample informed consent agreement from a laboratory experiment (see Box 8.2).

Deception Ground Rules

Federal regulations make one brief reference to deception in research but say nothing about the management of its use. Some professional ethical codes do permit deception, but these codes also refer to deception as a method of "last resort" (Hertwig & Ortmann, 2008, p. 223). For instance, the American Psychological Association (2017) Ethical Principles of Psychologists and Code of Conduct states:

> *Psychologists do not conduct a study involving deception unless they have determined that the use of deceptive techniques is justified by the study's significant prospective scientific, educational, or applied value and that effective nondeceptive alternative procedures are not feasible.* (8.07[a])

At the same time, these codes highlight the anticipated *benefits* of a study as a standard by which the use of deception is evaluated, and they establish "ground rules" for studies that use deception.

The first ground rule is that deception is banned when there is substantial *risk* of harm or stress. According to the APA (2017), "Psychologists do not deceive prospective participants about research that is reasonably expected to cause physical pain or severe emotional distress" (8.07[b]). In this case, researchers should undertake a different research design that does not involve deception.

A second ground rule is that researchers must "come clean" about the true nature of their study. According to the ACJS (2000) code of ethics, "Human subjects have the right to full disclosure of the purposes of the research as early as it is appropriate to the research process, and they have the right to an opportunity to have their questions answered about the purpose and usage of the research" (IIIB[13]). Debriefing is the practical implementation of this requirement.

Debriefing consists of a short interview that takes place between an investigator and research participants after they have finished their participation. Ideally, debriefing should occur in all studies with human participants, not just in studies involving deception, as it serves methodological and educational as well as ethical purposes. By interviewing participants after their participation, researchers may gain valuable information about participants' interpretation of research procedures; and, by understanding the nature of the study, participants can gain a greater appreciation for their research experience. If participants are deceived, however, the debriefing session becomes critically important to reveal the nature and purpose of the deception.

debriefing session at the end of a study in which an investigator meets with a participant to impart information about the study, including its real purpose and the nature and purpose of deception (if used), and to respond to questions and concerns

The nature of the debriefing depends on the topic, type of study, and, if deception is used, the extent of the deception. For surveys on nonsensitive topics, it is generally sufficient to answer any questions that respondents may have. Researchers also may provide a brief written statement of the purpose of the research and offer to send a summary of findings. For mild forms of deception, such as not disclosing the full purpose of the study in the consent, it may be enough to answer participants' questions and briefly inform them of the deception, pointing out its purpose and necessity.

If deception is more extensive or likely to cause discomfort, however, the debriefing should be more thorough and probing. In such cases, it is essential to make sure that participants (1) fully understand how they were misinformed and (2) do not leave the experiment feeling worse about themselves than before they began (Kelman, 1968). Milgram was obligated, for example, to convey the truth about his procedures—that he was really studying obedience, the drawing was rigged, the shock apparatus was phony, and so forth; he also needed to explain why it was not unusual or abnormal for participants to follow the commands of an experimenter to administer shocks to the learner. Milgram (1974) claimed that he carried out his debriefing slowly and sensitively, eliciting participants' reactions, acknowledging that he had placed them in a difficult position, and having the "learner" enter the laboratory so that the participant could see that he was not harmed. However, based on new evidence, including interviews with former research participants and unpublished materials from the Stanley Milgram archives at Yale University, psychologist Gina Perry (2013) compellingly shows that the debriefing was not as sensitive as Milgram suggests, and many participants did not know the true nature of the experiment when they left the lab.

Privacy Protection: Anonymity and Confidentiality

Federal regulations (CFR, 2024, 46.102[e][4]) specify two kinds of information that are private: (1) information that is revealed when "an individual can reasonably expect that no observation or recording is taking place," and (2) information provided for specific purposes (e.g., a medical exam) "that the individual can reasonably expect will not be made public." Such information is personally "identifiable" when a research participant's identity can be ascertained from the information.

Federal regulations further state that researchers need to ensure that "there are adequate provisions to protect the privacy of subjects and to maintain the confidentiality of data" (CFR, 2024, 46.111[a][7]). Moreover, the informed consent statement should explain to participants *how* their privacy would be protected. There are two forms of protection: anonymity and confidentiality.

Anonymity means that participants cannot be identified. Of the two means of protecting participants' privacy, anonymity is the highest standard, but it is also the most difficult to achieve. Often at least the investigator can identify participants. Examples of research that provides anonymity include self-administered surveys without names or identifying information attached as well as some existing data.

Confidentiality means participants "can reasonably expect that the information they provide will not be made public in a personally identifiable manner." This becomes critical when public disclosure "of the information could be harmful to the person to whom it refers" (ASA, 2018:10[a]). Investigators can ensure confidentiality in a variety of ways: by conducting research (especially surveys and in-depth interviews) in a private place, by removing names and other identifying information from the data as soon as possible, by keeping the data in a secure place, by not disclosing individuals' identities in any reports of the study, and by not divulging the information to persons or organizations requesting it without research participants' permission.

Field research usually requires ingenuity to safeguard confidentiality. The traditional approach is to use fictitious names for individuals, groups, and locations. For example, a researcher might assign pseudonyms to participants in a field research study on gangs, such as "Bo" and "Ace." Further, a researcher can report broad geographical areas, such as the Midwest and Northeast of the United States, that do not allow for the possibility of identification.

Yet it may not be possible to guarantee complete confidentiality. Unlike physicians, lawyers, and the clergy, criminologists along with other social scientists are *not* generally shielded by laws that allow them to keep their data secret if they are subpoenaed (Palys & Lowman, 2012; Scarce, 2005). Participants have a right to know about the limits of confidentiality (ACJS, 2000), which should be included in the informed consent statement.

Having now read about federal guidelines on privacy and other issues of concern, can you apply this knowledge? Box 4.3 provides the opportunity to do so.

---

anonymity ethical safeguard against invasion of privacy in which data cannot be identified with particular research participants

confidentiality ethical safeguard against invasion of privacy by which data obtained from participants are not shared with others without their permission

BOX 4.3

CHECKING YOUR UNDERSTANDING

Ethics Practice Questions II

Below are three questions about a hypothetical study. Answer the questions as you read them, then read the answers at the bottom of the box.

1. You are conducting an online anonymous survey of students at your university for your undergraduate research thesis. The topic of your research is students' online activities. You provide respondents an informed consent statement, and part of your survey includes a set of yes/no questions about students' experiences with cyberbullying—namely, whether they have been perpetrators and/or victims of cyberbullying. Based only on this information and what you've read in the text, what are potential ethical issues in conducting this research?

2. Your informed consent statement for the research above reads as follows: "I am conducting a survey on social media use among students at our university for my undergraduate research thesis, the results of which I will present at a professional conference. The survey consists of 20 questions and should take about six minutes to complete. The survey is voluntary; you may refuse to take the survey or, if you take the survey, you may stop at any time without any consequences. The survey is anonymous: it does not ask for your name or any other information that could personally identify you." Based on the text's discussion of guidelines for an informed consent statement, what is missing from this statement?

3. After your informed consent statement and survey (in questions 1 and 2 above), you include the following statement: "Thank you so much for your participation in this survey. I truly appreciate your time." Is this a sufficient closing for your survey?

Answers:

1. When surveys include questions on sensitive topics such as cyberbullying, they pose more than minimal risk to respondents. Even if the survey is anonymous, the questions could be distressing; therefore, you must take extra precautions to minimize risk and protect students' welfare. Students should be forewarned that some questions may be unsettling, and they should be given contact information for people or groups trained to help if the survey upsets them.

continues

continued

2. The informed consent statement lacks the following: (1) a description of any foreseeable risks or discomforts to the participant, (2) a description of potential benefits of the research, (3) an explanation of whom to contact for answers to questions about the research and participants' rights (e.g., the professor supervising the research), and (4) information about whom to contact if the participant experiences anxiety about their participation and feels the need to talk to someone.

3. In addition to forewarning individuals of potential risks in the informed consent statement and noting information about whom to contact, it also can be a good idea to reiterate the contact information here. Moreover, as suggested by our colleague, Mark Hallahan, it may be helpful to provide information about resources for individuals (e.g., counseling center) which are available to everyone irrespective of their participation in this research.

SUMMARY

Federal regulations and professional ethical guidelines help clarify researchers' ethical responsibilities and provide measures that should be taken to protect participants' rights and welfare. Potential harm is evaluated by the risks it poses to participants and the risks relative to the benefits. Potential research participants should be informed of these risks and the nature of the research and should be assured that their participation is voluntary. Deception is considered a method of last resort, but when it is employed, research participants need to be debriefed about the nature of the study; debriefing should ideally occur in all research and especially in research that may pose risk. Finally, researchers need to protect participants' privacy through anonymity or confidentiality. See Box 4.4 to assess your understanding of human subjects research.

BOX 4.4

CHECKING YOUR UNDERSTANDING

Human Subjects Training

Before faculty members can engage in research with human subjects, university IRBs require that they complete a training program about issues involving human subjects research. One such training program is the CITI program. If the training modules are completed successfully, participants get a certificate; every few years, researchers are required to complete a refresher course. Below are three test questions, modeled after those in human subjects training, which you should be able to answer based on your reading of this chapter.

1. With respect to potential harm, the Common Rule states:
   a. There should be no risk of harm to research participants.
   b. The risk of harm should be no greater than the risks encountered in daily life.
   c. Risks should be reasonable in relation to benefits.
   d. Those who take the risks should also receive the benefits.

2. To obtain informed consent, a researcher must do all but which one of the following?
   a. Inform participants that their participation is voluntary.
   b. Forewarn participants about potentially harmful effects of participating.
   c. Fully disclose his or her research objectives or hypotheses.
   d. Forewarn participants about how their rights might be threatened.

3. In studies in which research participants' identities are known to the researcher, the principal way to protect their privacy is to
   a. Ensure anonymity.
   b. Ensure confidentiality.
   c. Ensure both anonymity and confidentiality.
   d. Back up the data.

Answers: 1. c, 2. c, 3. b

4.4 THE PROCESS OF ETHICAL DECISION-MAKING

What do you need to do to make sure, so far as possible, that you are protecting the rights and welfare of research participants? Figure 4.2 outlines a process of ethical decision-making as it applies to the treatment of research participants. The first step, reviewing federal regulations and professional codes, will sensitize you to potential problems and means of addressing them. Then, as you select a topic and design your research, you should consider the costs and benefits of proposed methods and identify and address areas of ethical concern. If you are conducting your own research, you likely will have to submit a proposal to a college- or university-wide committee called an **Institutional Review Board**, or **IRB**. The IRB reviews and approves research

Institutional Review Board (IRB) a committee formed at nearly all colleges and universities that is responsible for reviewing research proposals to assess provisions for the treatment of human (and animal) subjects

CHAPTER 4 THE ETHICS AND POLITICS OF RESEARCH

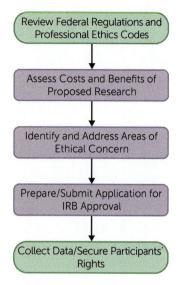

FIGURE 4.2 The Process of Ethical Decision-Making

involving human (and animal) subjects. Finally, researchers have an ethical responsibility to secure participants' rights in collecting and analyzing data. Let us examine each of these steps in greater detail.

Review Federal Regulations and Professional Ethics Codes

Having read the previous section of this chapter, you are well on your way to completing the first step in making ethically responsible decisions. We recommend that you also read the *Belmont Report*, Common Rule, and the professional code of ethics of the discipline within which you are working. Box 4.5 provides a list of federal regulations and several other resources that may be useful as you prepare to conduct your research.

Assess Costs and Benefits of Proposed Research

Ethical considerations should begin with the selection of your research topic, a good starting point for analyzing the potential costs and benefits of research. The potential for doing harm is greatest in social research that investigates negative aspects of behavior, such as aggression, violence, and

---

BOX 4.5

DOING CRIMINAL JUSTICE RESEARCH

Online Resources on Research Ethics

If you are preparing a research proposal or if you simply want to become more familiar with ethical codes and guidelines for conducting criminal justice research, there are many valuable online resources at your disposal.

- The Belmont Report

By scrolling down on The Belmont Report main page, you will find a short video clip ("Watch a video about *The Belmont Report*") or a longer video ("25th Anniversary Interviews").

- The Code of Federal Regulations
- American Society of Criminology Code of Ethics
- Academy of Criminal Justice Sciences (ACJS) Code of Ethics
- American Association of Public Opinion Research (AAPOR) Code of Professional Ethics and Practices
- Free online tutorials on the rights and welfare of research participants

norm or law violation. Research on sensitive topics, such as sex and drug use, also pose risks. There is potential harm, for example, in surveys that ask questions about illegal behavior such as drug abuse, which could prove embarrassing or put participants at risk for criminal prosecution if the information is disclosed.

In Chapter 5, we discuss the first few stages of research, from topic selection to reviewing the literature to creating a plan or design to carry out research. As you read the literature on your topic, you are likely to get a better understanding of the potential costs and benefits of doing research on this topic by examining the methods (e.g., deception, covert observation) and samples used in previous research (e.g., children, prisoners). Then, as you consider your research design, we recommend that you solicit opinions from others, including your faculty supervisor and potential participants. Ultimately, too, you should ask yourself, "How would *I* feel if I were a participant in my own research?"

Identify and Address Areas of Ethical Concern

The next step is to go through your research design carefully to determine areas of ethical concern and how you will address them. The best place to start is to review the requirements of an informed consent agreement. As we noted earlier, the agreement should describe foreseeable risks and benefits, indicate how you will maintain confidentiality, and assure participants that their participation is voluntary.

You also should devise a plan for debriefing participants. For research not involving deception, this may be no more than a written statement that describes more fully the nature of the research and reminds participants whom to contact if they have questions about the research or their rights. If the study involves deception, you will need a more elaborate protocol: the debriefing should probe participants' suspicions about the study, fully describe all deceptive elements and why deception is necessary, and explain the true purpose of the study. After the debriefing, APA ethical guidelines further dictate that you give participants the opportunity to withdraw their data (APA, 2017, 8.07[c]). The debriefing, in effect, fully informs participants about the study so that they are truly in a position to give their informed consent.

Prepare and Submit Application for IRB Approval

Once you have devised means of protecting participants, the next step is to prepare and submit a proposal to your school or organization's IRB, if required. This applies to all prospective studies meeting the federal definition of "human subjects research." "Human subject" refers to a "living individual about whom an investigator" gathers information; "research" refers to "systematic investigation . . . designed to develop or contribute to generalizable knowledge" (CFR, 2024, 46.102). You are likely to be doing "research" if you at least plan to present the results publicly (as in a conference presentation).

Students engaged in human subjects research should prepare their proposal in consultation with a faculty advisor who is responsible for reviewing and, ordinarily, signing off on all IRB applications. Generally, you must complete a form that describes the proposed research and specifies how participants' rights are to be protected. Although IRB forms vary across educational and other institutions, you should expect to at least address the following issues:

1. Is there the possibility of harm? Is the potential risk to participants beyond what they would experience in everyday life ("minimal risk")? What measures are you taking to mitigate risk and monitor the safety of participants?
2. What are the benefits of the research? Are risks reasonable in relation to the benefits?
3. How will participants be selected? Is the selection equitable; that is, are there sound ethical and scientific reasons for including some types of participants and excluding others?
4. What steps are you taking to gain the informed consent of participants?
5. Does the research involve deception?
6. What steps will be taken to debrief participants?
7. How is the privacy of participants going to be protected? What strategies are being used to secure the confidentiality of data?

When you submit your proposal, initially the IRB will decide whether the proposed study is *exempt*. Social research that is exempt from federal regulations includes the collection of existing data in which participants cannot be identified, research involving normal educational practices and educational testing, and the observation of public behavior when recorded information cannot be linked to individuals (CFR, 2024, 46.104[d]). Exempt research does not require IRB review; however, it is up to the IRB, not the investigator, to decide if the research qualifies as exempt (Shamoo & Resnick, 2009, p. 257). If the research is subject to review but presents no more than minimal risk to participants, it may be given an "expedited review" performed by either the chairperson or one or more designated members of the IRB (CFR, 2024, 46.110). Otherwise, the full committee will review it. In any case, the IRB may approve, disapprove, or require modifications to secure approval.

Collect Data and Secure Participants' Rights

Once the IRB has approved your proposal, all is not said and done. The final step is to secure participants' rights. For the most part, this consists of implementing the procedures presented in your IRB proposal. As you carry out your research, however, it is important to realize that your ethical responsibility to protect the rights and welfare of participants is ongoing, extending throughout, and sometimes beyond, the research process.

Consider, for example, potential harm. Although it may be sufficient to implement the means you have devised to protect participants from harm, it is possible that the research can unexpectedly threaten participants' welfare. This was the case in Zimbardo and colleagues' prison simulation study. The investigators had devised means to safeguard participants' welfare, such as screening for psychological problems; however, they did not anticipate the study's adverse effects. Because "guards" behaved inhumanely toward "prisoners," and "prisoners" showed signs of depression and extreme stress, Zimbardo and colleagues (1973, p. 45) took additional steps to secure participants' welfare. Not only did they terminate the experiment eight days earlier than planned, they also conducted encounter sessions immediately after the experiment to allow participants to vent their feelings and reflect on the moral issues they had faced. And to assess longer-term effects, they carried out follow-ups via questionnaires, personal interviews, and reunions.

Finally, circumstances may require additional means of securing participants' confidentiality if something unforeseen happens. Some researchers have gone to great lengths to protect participants' privacy when confronted with a potential breach. When Laud Humphreys (1970/2009, pp. 58, 229–230) realized that the confidentiality of his data could be compromised, he took his records out of his locked safe and burned them and vowed to plead the Fifth Amendment rather than divulge the identity of a single man whom he observed. Similarly, sociologist Rik Scarce spent 159 days in jail when he refused to testify about conversations he may have had with an animal-rights activist. He had met the activist in the course of research for his book, *Eco-Warriors: Understanding the Radical Environmental Movement*. Scarce (1999) believed that sociologists should "treat confidential information as confidential *no matter what*" (p. 981).

Finally, in addition to securing participants' rights, conducting ethical research also involves researchers' obligation to make sure their data are sound and trustworthy. Because scientific progress rests upon the trustworthiness of findings from the work of many investigators, dishonesty and inaccuracy in conducting and reporting research undermine science itself. Maintaining high standards of data collection also has ethical implications for research participants, as poorly conducted research is a waste of their time (Rosnow & Rosenthal, 2011).

SUMMARY

By reviewing federal and professional ethical guidelines and assessing the costs and benefits of our research, we become more familiar with exactly what we should do to protect research participants. On the basis of this knowledge, we can then take action, devising means to protect participants' rights, submitting a proposal to the IRB if required, and then securing participants' rights. See Box 4.6 to assess your understanding of this section.

> **BOX 4.6**
>
> **CHECKING YOUR UNDERSTANDING**
>
> ## Federal and Professional Ethical Guidelines Review
>
> 1. The _____ requires that all applicable institutions establish an IRB to review and approve research involving human (and animal) subjects.
>   a. Belmont Report
>   b. ACJS code of ethics
>   c. Common Rule
>   d. State governments
>
> 2. Which of the following is not a question likely to be asked on an Institutional Review Board (IRB) application?
>   a. What is your degree?
>   b. How will participants be collected?
>   c. What are potential harms?
>   d. Is there deception involved?
>
> 3. If research is under the exempt category, it does not require IRB review. Who decides if a research project is exempt?
>   a. The researcher
>   b. The university
>   c. The IRB
>   d. The researcher's direct supervisor or dean
>
> **Answers:** 1. c, 2. a, 3. c

4.5 POLITICS AND SOCIAL RESEARCH

At the outset of the chapter, we noted that politics also enters into social research. Underlying the influence of both ethics and politics is the concept of values. Values refer to guiding beliefs about what is good, important, useful, and desirable. As outlined earlier, values of respect, beneficence, and justice guided the creation of federal ethical codes that constrain criminal justice research. Similarly, values stimulate the influence of politics in criminal justice research, for politics essentially concerns the bargaining, negotiation, and compromise that occur in the pursuit of *valued* outcomes, such as the formation of policy (Pielke, 2007, p. 37). Whenever you debate social and political issues, you unavoidably base your position on your personal values, especially your *political ideology*, which refers to the set of values and beliefs associated with a political system or party.

Politics may influence the research process at an individual and a structural level. At the individual level, a researcher's personal values and ideology may shape their choice of what or whom to study. However, Max Weber (1949), one of the founders of sociology, believed that personal values should not influence the *collection and analysis of data* (see Photo 4.3). Otherwise, social scientists' findings will not be seen as credible and valid but rather as a projection of their personal beliefs. There is disagreement, nevertheless, about whether social science can and should be value-free, as you will see.

▲ **PHOTO 4.3** Max Weber

At the structural level, various groups in society, including the scientific community, professional associations, and local, national, and international political systems also may exert pressures that influence the course of the research (Sjoberg, 1967). Earlier in the chapter we described a very important source of political influence at the structural level: namely, the government regulation of scientific research as set forth in policies on research ethics and the protection of human subjects. In the remainder of this chapter, we touch on individual and structural influences, as we consider how politics enters into the research process, from topic selection to the application of findings.

Topic Selection, Political Ideology, and Research Funding

Research begins with the selection of a topic. In Chapter 5, we discuss factors that influence topic selection, including personal motivations of the researcher and the current state of scientific research and theory. Politics also enters into the equation, in terms of personal values and institutional support for social research.

Weber acknowledged that researchers' values shape their research topics and questions. This is unavoidable, for, as we pointed out in Chapter 2, science is always a product of the culture and the times. But the impact of values on topic selection especially applies in criminology and the other social sciences, which justify their work largely on its value relevance to human concerns. Criminologists have long been concerned about the causes, deterrence from, and prevention of criminal behavior, as well as the effective functioning of the US criminal justice system, which directly impacts society. The progressivism of the discipline of criminology and criminal justice has continued to the present day. Driven by the causes of civil rights and racial discrimination seen in the justice system, much contemporary criminological research is devoted to class and race inequality. For example, some criminal justice researchers have chosen to study the interaction of race and police use of force because of its relevance to issues of police use of force seen in the media. They also may do this research out of personal convictions regarding rights of all citizens.

Topic selection also may be hindered or promoted by the politics of research funding. Practically all criminal justice research requires financial support; so major funding sources exert considerable control over what gets studied (Leavitt, 2001). In the United States, sources of funding for scientific research include the federal government, corporations, private foundations, and professional organizations. The biggest single supporter of social science research is the federal government, which awards grants through agencies such as the National Science Foundation (NSF) and National Institute of Justice (NIJ). The NSF's Social, Behavioral, and Economics Sciences Directorate "provides 63% of the funding for all academic research in social and psychological sciences in the U.S." (NSF, 2024).

Funding sources influence topic selection in various ways. In allocating resources, funding agencies establish priorities for research on particular topics. The pattern of funding for criminal justice research has shifted over time (Petersilia, 1991). Funding agencies moved from grants for broad research agendas to unsolicited projects that the researcher had developed, to ultimately settle on strategic funding of research topics picked by agencies. This strategic funding is achieved through changes to the structure of award-granting agencies or carefully crafted calls for grant proposals. In an analysis of scholarly sources and the potential impact that funding institutions have had on criminal justice scholarship, Savelsberg, King, and Cleveland (2002) found that topic choice has been significantly impacted by funding. For instance, political funding increased the likelihood of research being conducted on drug use. The contemporary impact of politics on research funding is clearly illustrated in an amendment to the 2013 US spending bill. Senator Tom Coburn inserted language into the bill that restricts NSF funding in political science to research that the agency's director "certifies as promoting national security or the economic interests of the United States" (Mervis, 2013, p. 1510). Passed by Congress, the amendment elicited strong reactions from members of the academic community. The American Political Science Association (APSA) said in a formal statement:

> Adoption of this amendment is a gross intrusion into the widely respected scholarly agenda setting process at NSF that has supported our world-class national science enterprise for over sixty years. While political science research is most immediately affected, at risk is any and all research . . . funded by the NSF. The amendment makes all scientific research vulnerable to the whims of political pressure. (APSA, 2013)

Critics of the bill argued that the United States has benefited greatly from a government/science partnership that relies on sound scientific criteria in awarding grants (Farrell, 2013; Prewitt, 2013). The amendment sets a precedent that may lead politicians to "make sure that the research they like gets money, while the research they dislike does not" (Farrell, 2013).

Although the Coburn amendment presents new challenges, science has been a part of the political process by which the government allocates research funding for many years. When threatened with the loss of federal funding in the 1980s, the social sciences created the Consortium of Social Science Associations (COSSA), an organization that promotes funding for social research (Silver, 2006). And in 2013, the APSA hired a lobbying firm to endeavor to prevent the continuation of the Coburn language in future legislation (Stratford, 2014). In fact, the Coburn language was not included in a spending bill passed in early 2014, but as Michael Stratford (2014) writes, "advocates for social science researchers say the battle isn't over."

Data Analysis and Interpretation and Political Ideology

Aside from topic selection, the doctrine of value-free social science holds that the rest of the research process—that is, the collection, analysis, and interpretation of data—should not be influenced by one's personal beliefs and values. The following chapters of this book, in fact, present numerous methods by which criminologists attempt to control for investigator bias. In addition to these methods, all sciences have structural safeguards "to protest against the persistence of false, inaccurate, or misleading data and interpretations" (Leavitt, 2001, p. 27). Experts are called upon to evaluate grant proposals, so that only the most well-designed studies typically are funded. The best studies are published in refereed journals, in which reviewers judge whether the research is worthy of publication. And, over time, consistent results increase the credibility of data, and failed replications lead to the correction of misleading information (Leavitt, 2001). However, avoiding biases in the use and interpretation of evidence may be easier said than done, and some critics of the value-free ideology suggest that researchers "hide behind" the veil of "value-free" research when their research is anything but value-free. One way to address this criticism is to admit one's values and biases up front and allow others to evaluate the research with that information in hand.

Acknowledging personal and political sympathies is especially important in criminal justice studies of the marginalized, who are outside the societal mainstream, such as offenders, the poor, and racial/ethnic and sexual minorities. Charles Ragin and Lisa Amoroso (2011, p. 114) point out that field research often is undertaken and is best suited to give voice to these groups, whose views are rarely heard by mainstream audiences and whose lives are often misrepresented. In trying to understand reality from the perspective of the marginalized, field researchers may become sympathetic with their point of view. The way to deal with this, sociologist Howard Becker (1967) argues, is to adhere to the standards of good scientific work but also carefully consider and acknowledge "whose side we are on." Doing this clarifies the limits of a study and how its findings should be applied. Part of this "sociological disclaimer," Becker (1967) believes, should be a statement

> in which we say, for instance, that we have studied the prison through the eyes of the inmates and not through the eyes of the guards or other involved parties. We warn people, thus, that our study tells us only how things look from that vantage point—what kinds of objects guards are in the prisoner's world—and does not attempt to explain why guards do what they do or to absolve the guards of what may seem, from the prisoners' side, morally unacceptable behavior. (p. 247)

Dissemination of Research Findings: Science, Politics, and Public Policy

Another way in which science and politics relate to one another is in the use of scientific knowledge to inform public policy. The authority of science is undeniable in settling many questions about the physical world, such as the efficacy of medical treatments and effects of pollution. In such cases, scientists are likely to share the values of the decision makers and play the role of impartial experts, providing information to others without engaging directly in the politics of policymaking. However, when scientific knowledge is uncertain, and the policy options are based on different values, the role of scientists is more complicated. Scientists may be forced to take sides or become advocates for particular policies, and science itself may become a tool of political debate (Pielke, 2007).

When it comes to public policy, it is especially difficult for criminal justice researchers to play the role of the pure and impartial scientist. As noted earlier, the problems researchers choose to study often have immediate relevance to people's lives (and safety) and are inherently value-laden. Therefore, they must not only be aware of the possible influence of personal values and political views on their research but also must consider the practical implications of their research and how others may use their findings. In the article previously mentioned on the politicization of scholarship, Savelsberg et al. (2002) caution against the effects that institutions and funding agencies can have on the results of criminal justice research. Fortunately, through their quantitative analysis of almost 700 scholarly articles, they found that scholarly conclusions were given independent of institutional and funding agency variables.

SUMMARY

It is inevitable that criminal justice researchers make value judgments about what and whom to study, for these choices are a product of the culture and the times. Politics and its underlying values can also influence every stage of the research process. In conducting research, criminal justice researchers should identify and acknowledge their values, being alert to how they may affect the collection and analysis of data. And when they present their research, criminal justice researchers should consider the practical implications of their findings and how others may use them.

KEY TERMS

anonymity, p. 84
beneficence, p. 79
Common Rule, p. 79
confidentiality, p. 84
debriefing, p. 83
ethics, p. 71
informed consent, p. 73
Institutional Review Board (IRB), p. 87
justice, p. 79
respect for persons, p. 79

KEY POINTS

- Ethical standards of right and wrong guide the conduct of scientific research.
- Four common ethical issues in the treatment of research participants are potential harm, informed consent, deception, and privacy invasion.
- Risk of harm violates a person's right to safety; this risk arises in criminal justice research when procedures may result in physical pain, anxiety, loss of self-esteem, feelings of embarrassment, and so forth.
- Informed consent protects freedom of choice; consent is not informed if participation is involuntary or individuals have insufficient information to make a rational decision to participate.
- The use of deception in criminal justice research is controversial; some criminal justice researchers believe that without it, participants may not act spontaneously, while others question its ethical and methodological use.
- Privacy may be invaded in criminal justice research when participation results in the revelation of attitudes, beliefs, and behavior that the participant wishes to remain private.
- Federal regulations state that the risk of harm to research participants should be minimal and the benefits of participation should outweigh the risks.
- Regulations require informed consent, usually in written form.
- Most professional codes of ethics permit the use of deception, provided there is no substantial risk of harm, and participants are informed of the deception immediately after the study.
- Regulations require provisions to protect privacy, which may involve collecting data anonymously or taking steps to ensure confidentiality.

- The steps in ethical decision-making include assessing costs and benefits, identifying areas of concern and making provisions to meet those concerns, submitting a proposal to an IRB, and securing participants' rights.
- According to the doctrine of value-free science, values should not influence data collection, analysis, and interpretation.
- Values and politics may influence topic selection, data analysis and interpretation, and the dissemination of research findings.

REVIEW QUESTIONS

1. How does an analysis of costs and benefits apply to the ethical conduct of criminal justice research? What considerations are involved in conducting a cost–benefit analysis?
2. What are the basic ingredients of informed consent? How did Milgram violate this principle in his research on obedience to authority?
3. Briefly describe the arguments for and against the use of deception in criminal justice research. What are the conditions for its use?
4. How is research participants' right to privacy typically secured in (a) surveys and (b) field research?
5. What are Institutional Review Boards (IRBs)? What part do they play in the process of doing ethically responsible research?
6. Give examples of how values may enter into (a) topic selection, (b) the analysis and interpretation of data, and (c) the dissemination of research findings.
7. What obligations do criminal justice researchers have regarding the use of the knowledge they generate? How is this obligation an example of the intersection of ethics and politics in social research?

EXERCISES

1. Discuss the ethical problems raised in the following hypothetical research examples.
   a. A criminologist meets a professional fence through an ex-convict he knows. (A *fence* is someone who buys and sells stolen goods.) As part of a study, the researcher convinces the fence to talk about his work—why he sticks with this kind of work, what kind of people he deals with, how he meets them, and so forth. To gain the fence's cooperation, the researcher promises not to disclose any personal details that would get the fence in trouble. However, when subpoenaed, the criminologist agrees to reveal his informant rather than go to jail. Has the researcher violated an ethical principle in agreeing to talk to legal authorities?

b. A researcher gains access to a treatment center serving offenders (who have been court-ordered to substance use treatment) by responding to a hiring ad. While working at the center, the researcher makes a record of patients' names and later approaches them, identifies herself as a criminologist, fully explains the nature of her research, and asks them to participate in her in-depth survey on substance use in the United States. Most patients agree, although some react negatively to the request. What aspects of the researcher's strategy are ethically problematic?

2. Ethical issues arise when the pursuit of a research question or application of research procedures conflicts with general ethical principles. In a fascinating article in *Criminal Justice Studies*, Worley, Worley, and Wood (2016) interviewed several scholars on ethical dilemmas they faced and ethical questions that were raised in the midst of their criminal justice ethnographic research. The article shows how a study can raise ethical concerns in spite of a researcher's best intentions to conduct research ethically. Read Worley et al.'s article and address the following questions:

   a. What were some personal costs the researchers experienced when conducting criminal justice ethnographic research?
   b. How did the researchers struggle with the "insider–outsider dilemma" in their research?
   c. What are some ethical and IRB issues that were raised in this ethnographic research?

5

Research Designs

It Depends on the Question

CHAPTER OUTLINE

5.1 Initial Steps in the Research Process 102
- Select a Research Topic 103
- Review the Literature/Consider Theory 103
- Formulate a Research Question 104
- Prepare a Research Design 106
- Summary 107

5.2 Designing Research to Answer Quantitative Questions 108
- Select a Research Strategy 108
- Identify and Select Units of Analysis 109
- Measure Variables 110
- Gather Data and Analyze the Relationships Among Variables 114
- Summary 120

5.3 Designing Research to Answer Qualitative Questions 121
- Select a Research Strategy 122
- Select Field Setting, Social Group, and/or Archival Records 123
- Gain Access and Establish Relationships 124
- Decide Whom to Observe or Interview or What to Read 124
- Gather and Analyze Data 124
- Summary 126

LEARNING OBJECTIVES

By the end of this chapter, you should be able to

5.1 Describe the initial steps in the research process, from choosing a research topic to preparing a research design.

5.2 Discuss the purpose and steps in conducting quantitative research.

5.3 Discuss the purpose and steps in conducting qualitative research.

Having considered the scientific, ethical, and political contexts of research, we are ready to focus on the process of social research. The authors have embarked on this process many times. As a doctoral student, Maggie (Lisuzzo, 2014) Pate was casting about for an idea for her doctoral dissertation. With an interest in how juries interpret evidence in cases of wrongful conviction, she came across the work of G. Daniel Lassiter and colleagues (1986; 2001; 2002; 2010) who discovered that the camera angle in a videotaped interrogation could impact judgments about the coerciveness of an interrogation and voluntariness of a confession. In addition to the general work on camera angle, a study by Ratcliff and colleagues (2010) found that racial differences between the suspect and the interrogator could lead to biased judgments against the suspect. These works piqued the curiosity of Pate who wondered if other suspect characteristics may also influence viewers' perceptions of the interrogation and confession.

Based upon her prior knowledge of factors that impact false confessions, Pate narrowed her focus to juvenile suspects. She selected age as a suspect characteristic because research had shown that juveniles were more likely to falsely confess (Gross et al., 2005). Likewise, videotaped interrogations had been used previously in wrongful conviction cases involving juveniles, such as the Central Park Five and Michael Crowe. Thus, her final research question was "In videotaped interrogations, will perceptions of the coerciveness and voluntariness of a confession vary based upon perceived suspect age?"

To answer this question, Pate prepared a **research design**, or overall research plan. In this chapter, we introduce the basic terminology of criminal justice research as we consider the first few steps from topic selection through the preparation of a research design. Figure 5.1 presents these steps.

research design the overall plan of a study for collecting data

While the initial steps of conducting research are similar across different forms of research, research design depends on the research question asked and thus the type of understanding of the social world that the researcher hopes to achieve. Pate's question asked about the relationship between suspect age and perceptions of coerciveness and voluntariness of a confession. Based on her review of the literature, she derived a number of hypotheses, following the deductive logic of inquiry discussed in Chapter 2. Research and theory indicated that multiple factors influence one's perception of the voluntariness of a confession in videotaped interrogations. Research had found that camera angle, generally, and suspect characteristics, specifically, can cause laypeople to perceive a confession as voluntary which, in turn, could lead to more guilty verdicts. Ratcliff and her colleagues (2010) found support for an out-group salience bias with regard to race; when the suspect's race was different from the interrogator's, it drew observers' visual attention. These findings supported the concept of illusory causation; greater visual attention in an interrogation led to the belief that the suspect

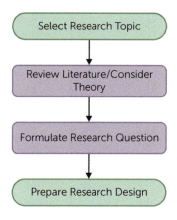

FIGURE 5.1 The Research Process: From Topic Selection to Research Design

was responsible for the outcome of the videotaped session (i.e., confession). Based on research showing that differences between the suspect and interrogator matter, Pate hypothesized that viewers of the interrogation would perceive that older suspects' confessions were less voluntary than younger suspects. In addition, she hypothesized that the probability of guilt ratings would be lower for older suspects. To test her hypothesis, she filmed mock interrogations with paid actors of various ages (e.g., 14 and 29). The interrogations were incorporated into an experimental design, and then the data were analyzed using quantitative analyses (Lisuzzo, 2014).

Other research, such as Thomas Meisenhelder's (1977) discussed in Chapter 2, is more concerned with the meanings and processes underlying phenomena than with testing explicit hypotheses. This form of research, which is more likely to follow an inductive logic of inquiry, calls for a different research design to uncover how people and social groups interpret the social world. Recall that Meisenhelder was interested in understanding the process of how career criminals desist from crime. As he carried out unstructured interviews with a small sample of nonprofessional property offenders, he asked: What factors influence an individual to attempt to desist from a criminal career, and what factors influence the successful accomplishment of desisting from crime? Based on the patterns that emerged in his data, he concluded that offenders are motivated to desist from crime both due to the offender's own desire to "settle down" as well as the deterrent effects of imprisonment. Further, he found successful desistance stems from the development of conventional social bonds. His findings lent support to social control theory, which argues those who are bonded to conventional society are less likely to engage in crime (Hirschi, 1969).

This chapter discusses the initial steps in the general research process leading to the formulation of a research question and development of a research design. As we point out, different questions call for different research designs with correspondingly different steps. We illustrate these steps with two featured studies: the first is Baumer et al.'s (2021) study on factors influencing decreases in juvenile delinquency rates, which shares the general design features of Pate's research; the second is Ida Johnson's (2015) research on female parolees' perceptions of parole experiences and parole officers, which shares the general design features of Meisenhelder's (1977) study.

5.1 INITIAL STEPS IN THE RESEARCH PROCESS

Pate's research on age and false confessions followed the research process outlined in Chapter 1: as initial steps, she selected a general research topic; next, she considered theory and narrowed her topic through a review of the literature; then, she posed a research question; and finally, she prepared a research design. Let us examine these initial steps in detail.

Select a Research Topic

The first step in the research process is the selection of a general topic. What topic areas in criminal justice are you most curious about? Are there subject areas in which you have some knowledge but want to know more? Have you ever studied a criminal justice problem and realized that its causes are not well understood? Or have you lived through something that makes you want to better understand your personal experience? All of these are motivations for choosing a general topic to research.

To begin, criminal justice researchers often select topics based upon the ongoing development of theory and research as well as current events. Criminologists, for example, frequently investigate causes of delinquency such as social class, race, ethnicity, gender, and sexuality, as well as examine aspects of the various parts of the criminal justice system, including police, courts, and corrections. For example, Pate developed her dissertation topic based upon recent research that had been published in the area as well as the topic's current relevance to criminal justice policy.

You may have been attracted to criminal justice because you want to understand what causes individuals to deviate from social norms as well as how the system responds to such deviations. Many of the founders of criminology concerned themselves with how crime was impacted by changing social conditions such as urbanization, the Industrial Revolution, and massive foreign immigration. Similarly, today's changing social conditions such as globalization, technological development, and the Information Revolution continue to stimulate topic selection.

Finally, your selection of a research topic may be affected by your personal background and experiences. Choosing a topic is not always easy, but we can offer you a bit of advice: first and foremost, you should choose a topic of interest to you, something that will *sustain* your interest for a period of time. You may be conducting research on the topic for weeks or months in the case of an undergraduate project, years in the case of a master's thesis or doctoral dissertation, and perhaps a lifetime in the case of an academic career. Second, the topic should be practical, which involves a whole series of considerations discussed further in this section.

Review the Literature/Consider Theory

Once you have selected a general topic, the second step in the research process is to conduct a literature review (see Figure 5.1). The "literature" includes theory and prior research on your general topic, which will inform your current research. To contribute to scientific knowledge, which is the ultimate goal of criminal justice research, we need to know the major theories, key research findings, and unresolved issues in an area of study. In addition, by reviewing prior research you will learn the methods that others have used to study a topic, which should be helpful in designing your research.

As you read the literature and learn about the current state of knowledge on your topic, you should have two related objectives in mind. First, how can I transform my topic into one or more questions that are amenable to research? Second, how can I contribute to ongoing research and theory on the topic? Pate's research on the effects of suspect age and videotaped interrogation illustrates both of these objectives. She began with a broad interest in the effects of camera angle on perceptions of the suspect, and transformed the interest into a more narrow, testable research question. The question contributed to ongoing research by exploring the effects of illusory causation with a new, not yet studied subgroup: juveniles.

Conducting a literature review is easier said than done, and we want to be frank with you: searching the literature can sometimes make you feel like you are in a maze trying to find your way out. You may find a path or a "gap" in the literature, just as Pate found an unanswered question in an ongoing line of inquiry. Be prepared to encounter a few dead ends, including irrelevant and questionable studies. You also may have to reroute your topic, as you may find that it is not amenable to research. For example, recall that Pate was interested in how age impacted one's perception of the voluntariness of a confession. It was not possible for her to measure perceptions of voluntariness with cases that had previously been decided, for example, the Central Park Five. Therefore, she had to instead create her own mock interrogations to assess the relationship. Further, you need to be flexible enough to realize that there is more than one path. For example, you may decide to recast your topic to fit a particular research strategy or some other need, such as the amount of time you have to undertake a study. Refer back to Box 3.1 for specific pointers to help you with the process of finding theory and research on your topic. Chapter 3 also provides information on how to take notes and write up the results of your review.

Formulate a Research Question

Once you choose a general topic, you must state it in researchable terms. This involves translating the topic into one or more research questions. A scientific research question is one that is answerable through the systematic collection and analysis of verifiable data. By way of contrast, some questions cannot be answered because they are beyond the realm of science (e.g., Does God exist? Is capital punishment morally wrong?).

Criminal justice researchers ask research questions for different purposes. One purpose is description. *Descriptive* research questions seek basic information, which may begin with questions of Who? What? When? Where? Descriptive research questions about the topic of capital punishment might include: What is capital punishment? When was it first implemented? Where is it practiced today? In this case, the answers define and describe the history and contemporary variation in capital punishment: capital punishment is the legal practice of killing people who commit serious crimes; it dates back to biblical times; and it is carried out in more than 50 countries today, including the United States, North Korea, and Iran (Smith, 2018).

All research must accurately describe the phenomenon under investigation, and some surveys and field research may have this as their primary purpose. More often, though, researchers want to go beyond description to explain how the social world works. *Explanatory* research questions ask why and how phenomena occur. For example, why is capital punishment practiced in the United States today but not in many European countries? Why does the majority of the US population support capital punishment? How and why has support for capital punishment in the United States changed over time?

Whether descriptive or explanatory, what makes for a good research question? First, research questions should be "interesting," according to Glenn Firebaugh (2008). What Firebaugh means is that beyond being interesting to you, research questions should contribute to ongoing conversations in a scientific field of study. Based on their literature review, Baumer and colleagues (2021) formulated an unanswered research question: What factors derived from criminological theory can explain reductions in youth offending since the early 1990s?

Baumer et al.'s research question was "interesting" because it extended prior research and applied criminological theory to explain an under-researched phenomena. Their question extended research in two ways: by applying multiple criminological theories to explain delinquency rather than just one; and by explaining reductions in crime, rather than explaining participation in crime.

Second, good research questions should be focused. To pursue the topic of female parolees' perceptions of parole experiences and parole officers, Ida Johnson (2015) formulated research questions that could be answered empirically. Focusing on female parolees' experiences, Johnson posed three questions:

1. How do reentry challenges impact women parolees' abilities to meet monthly parole obligations?
2. What are female parolees' expectations and perceptions of parole officers?
3. What strategies do female parolees utilize to avoid drug relapse and criminal behavior?

Finally, research questions must be manageable or feasible in terms of time, available resources, and other considerations. For example, if you were working on a term project, it clearly would be impractical to pose a research question that would require six months of fieldwork. Also, funding for criminal justice research is often limited; thus, researchers must develop research questions that can be explored using little to no money. An additional consideration is whether one has access to the study sample of interest. As both incarcerated individuals and juveniles are deemed special populations (see Chapter 4), researchers are often denied access to including them in studies. Thus, posing a research question that requires direct access to either population may not be feasible if one's IRB is reluctant to approve the study. If Johnson's IRB had been unwilling to approve her study to interview female parolees, she would have had to go back to the drawing board and either revise her study to address the concerns of the IRB or develop a new research question. See Box 5.1 to practice developing a research question.

> **BOX 5.1**
>
> **PRACTICE WHAT YOU LEARNED**
>
> ## Crafting a "Good" Research Question
>
> 1. Develop both a descriptive and explanatory research question based on a criminal justice topic of interest to you.
> 2. Explain how your questions are both interesting and focused, thus meeting Firebaugh's standards for a "good" research question.

Prepare a Research Design

Having formulated your research question, you are ready to plan your research. The overall plan, called the research design, should carefully spell out how you will answer your question: what kind of data you will gather and how you will gather and analyze the data. Of course, we cannot expect you to be able to fully prepare a research design at this point; to do so requires a more complete understanding of the research process, something you will gain from reading the whole book. Therefore, our objective in this chapter is to orient you to the design process by introducing the basic options for gathering and analyzing appropriate data. As we outline these options, we also will familiarize you with the language of criminal justice research.

In discussing issues of research design, we focus on explanatory research questions. Although the variety of explanatory research questions that could be asked is endless, many of them can be subsumed under two "ideal" types: quantitative and qualitative. Criminal justice researchers commonly use these labels to describe two broad methodological approaches to criminal justice research: a quantitative approach that tends to produce numerical (quantitative) data and a qualitative approach that results in nonnumerical (qualitative) data. However, the data and the methods used to generate them flow from the types of questions that are asked. Since each type has very different implications for research design, we discuss them separately in detail in the following sections. In brief, **quantitative research questions** ask: Is there a relationship between X and Y, controlling for other factors? To answer the question, X and Y must be carefully defined and measured *before* the researcher gathers data. **Qualitative research questions** ask about the meaning and cultural significance of social phenomena. They also ask if patterns or relationships exist in people's lives, but they focus on the social processes that produce these patterns and on what the patterns mean to the actors themselves and to the larger society. Unlike quantitative questions, qualitative questions do not necessarily specify relationships or define concepts before data collection and analysis.

quantitative research question a question that asks about the relationship between two or more variables

qualitative research question a question that asks about social processes or the meaning and cultural significance of people's actions

SUMMARY

The initial steps in the process of criminal justice research are choosing a topic, narrowing the topic through a literature review, formulating a research question, and preparing a research design. The selection of a research topic may be influenced by the ongoing development of theory and research, a concern with criminal justice problems, and/or one's personal background and experiences. A literature review not only helps to narrow the research topic, it also situates the proposed study in the context of ongoing research and theory. Knowing what has and has not been done on your research topic allows you to ask a specific research question, which should be "interesting," focused, and practically manageable. The research design is a detailed plan for how the research question will be answered: what kind of data will be gathered, how they will be gathered, and how they will be analyzed. The type of research question influences what kinds of research designs are appropriate. Quantitative and qualitative research questions are two main types. To check your understanding of the differences between quantitative and qualitative research questions, please refer to Box 5.2.

BOX 5.2

CHECKING YOUR UNDERSTANDING

Qualitative or Quantitative?

Instructions: Below you will find five research questions. Based upon what you read in the "Prepare Research Design" section, identify whether each question is a qualitative or quantitative research question.

1. What is the relationship between substance abuse and involvement in criminal activity?
2. What factors predict involvement in police use of force cases?
3. How do newly incarcerated individuals adapt to prison life?
4. Is there an association between victimization and offending?
5. How does neighborhood context shape individuals' gang membership experience?

Answers: 1. Quantitative; 2. Quantitative; 3. Qualitative; 4. Quantitative; 5. Qualitative

5.2 DESIGNING RESEARCH TO ANSWER QUANTITATIVE QUESTIONS

Social researchers addressing quantitative questions assume that the social world operates according to the same kind of universal laws found in the natural world. One example is Newton's second law of motion: Force = Mass × Acceleration. The force with which a bowling ball strikes pins is equal to the ball's mass times how fast the ball is rolled. Similarly, from a quantitative perspective, scientific understanding amounts to uncovering general relationships. Research on quantitative questions normally follows the deductive model of inquiry and has the immediate aim of testing hypotheses. You might remember that a hypothesis is an expected but unconfirmed relationship between two or more phenomena; it is essentially a tentative answer to a research question. Much of the time, the goal of quantitative research is to identify one or more **causal relationships**. For example, Baumer et al. (2021) asked what factors have influenced the decrease in youth crime since the early 1990s. They studied factors such as alcohol consumption, parental monitoring, community involvement, and school commitment, to name a few. Assuming that these factors cause decreases in the prevalence of delinquency, a follow-up question would ask how this could occur.

> **causal relationship** a relationship in which it is theorized that changes in one variable produce or bring about changes in another variable

To answer quantitative questions, what do you need to do? Because you want to establish general patterns, you need to examine data across many cases and then determine whether the phenomena of interest (e.g., parental monitoring and delinquency) are related to one another. To determine whether a relationship exists, you need to produce numerical data that can be analyzed statistically. Figure 5.2 shows the steps you will need to consider to gather and analyze this kind of data.

Select a Research Strategy

The first step is to select a data-collection strategy or approach. Your primary choices are to design an experiment, conduct a survey, or analyze existing data. Specifics of when and how to employ each of these data-collection methods will be discussed in later chapters. Baumer and colleagues (2021) analyzed data from the Monitoring the Future study (MTF), a longitudinal, nationally representative survey of 8th-, 10th-, and 12th-grade students' substance use patterns, attitudes, and beliefs. They chose this data set because it contained information from a representative sample of eighth and tenth graders that had been collected during the time period they were interested in (1990–2015). In addition, the MTF study collects data on the variables of interest

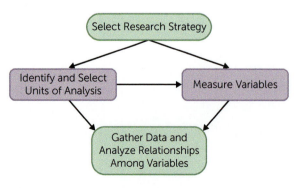

FIGURE 5.2 **Steps to Consider in Designing Research to Answer Quantitative Questions**

in their study: participants' delinquent activities, sociodemographic variables, and their involvement in school, the community, and risky behaviors.

Identify and Select Units of Analysis

After selecting a research strategy, you need to define your unit of analysis. **Units of analysis** are the cases or entities you study; they are the things you describe and compare. Criminologists study a variety of units, including individual people; a wide range of social groupings, such as families, police agencies, neighborhoods, and cities; and various social artifacts, such as books, periodicals, and television programs. Selecting a unit generally depends on the object of study. In Baumer et al.'s study, the unit of analysis was individuals or, more precisely, individual eighth- and tenth-grade students, for it is individual students who participate in delinquency and other activities.

units of analysis the entities such as people, nations, and artifacts that are studied, which are described and compared in terms of variables

In some areas of criminal justice research, however, criminologists may be less interested in individual differences than in the impact of the social context on people in general, the social relationships that individuals form, and large-scale social processes. To analyze "the social" often requires units other than individuals. For example, suppose a researcher wanted to determine whether wealthier neighborhoods report less crime than poorer neighborhoods. In this case, the researcher would treat the neighborhoods as the relevant unit and would gather data on the crime rates of different neighborhoods. When pursuing a question like this, however, researchers need to be careful about the conclusions they draw, as discussed in Box 5.3.

For studies of social and cultural change, or to determine how society is impacted by media, criminologists can make creative use of social artifacts as units of analysis. To examine the portrayal of the criminal justice system, including women and people of color, in popular crime shows, Color of Change (2020) conducted a study utilizing episodes from popular "crime-related scripted television series." Analyzing 353 randomly selected episodes from the 2017 to 2018 season, the researchers found that injustice and wrongful action on behalf of the criminal justice system was normalized across the episodes. In addition, the episodes depicted the criminal justice system as being race neutral and did not accurately portray the racial biases that are prevalent in the system. The researchers also analyzed the race and gender of those behind the camera, finding that a majority of those responsible for writing and producing crime shows are White males. By coding these scripted crime television shows, the researchers showed how the inaccuracies depicted in popular media could potentially be linked to misperceptions of how the criminal justice system actually works, leading to assumptions that injustices are forgivable and racism is not a problem.

Once you have identified the type of unit to study, you must decide how many of such units to choose and how to choose them—that is, what method of selection to use. Because Baumer et al. (2021) were using available survey data, they did not have to design a sampling procedure; nonetheless, it was an important aspect of the

> **BOX 5.3**
>
> **READING CRIMINAL JUSTICE RESEARCH**
>
> ## The Ecological Fallacy
>
> As a general rule, researchers should restrict their conclusions to the units of analysis to which their data pertain. Otherwise, they risk committing a logical fallacy. One such fallacy that seems to occur often in everyday life is called the "fallacy of division": assuming that what holds true of a group also is true of individuals within the group. Knowing that Sally lives in a neighborhood where the crime rate is relatively high, you would commit this fallacy if you assumed that Sally herself engaged in delinquency.
>
> The fallacy of division is quite similar to what social scientists call the **ecological fallacy**. This can occur in criminal justice research when relationships between properties of groups or geographic areas are used to make inferences about the individual behaviors of the people within those groups or areas (Robinson, 1950). In the past, criminologists analyzed the relationship between neighborhood crime rates and other characteristics of these neighborhoods in order to draw conclusions about characteristics of individual criminals. A typical erroneous conclusion might be that foreign-born persons commit more crimes than native-born persons because the crime rate is higher in areas with greater proportions of foreigners. But such a conclusion is clearly unwarranted because the data do not tell us who actually committed the crimes—foreign or native-born persons. In fact, studies in the United States consistently show that immigrants are less likely to commit crimes than the native-born (Hagan & Palloni, 1998; Martinez & Lee, 2000; see also Kubrin & Desmond, 2015, p. 346).
>
> It is not always wrong to draw conclusions about individual-level processes from aggregate or group-level data. Social scientists have identified conditions under which it is reasonable to make such inferences (Firebaugh, 1978), although it is often difficult to determine if these conditions are met. The implications of the ecological fallacy, however, are clear: When reading research, pay attention to the unit of analysis and ask whether it matches the conclusions. If you are interested in individuals but only group-level data are available, then be sure to recognize the possibility of an ecological fallacy.

ecological fallacy erroneous use of data describing an aggregate unit (e.g., organizations) to draw inferences about the units of analysis that make up the aggregate (e.g., individual members of organizations)

data they used. In many surveys that address quantitative research questions, units are chosen randomly from a specified population through some form of probability sampling. This was true of the MTF, which selected a nationally representative sample of students from just over 100 private and public schools nationwide. In Chapter 7, we describe sampling in depth.

Measure Variables

Once you have identified your unit of analysis, you are ready to consider the measurement of variables. We devote an entire chapter (Chapter 6) to this aspect of research design. For now, you need to understand what variables are and the different types of variables that appear in a quantitative research design.

WHAT IS A VARIABLE?

Measurement is the bridge between theory and research; it is the means by which criminologists translate abstract concepts into concrete variables. **Concepts** are the building blocks of theory; they are the terms researchers use to group together phenomena that have important things in common. Baumer and colleagues' research linked the concepts of school commitment and youth offending, among others. A **variable** is a *measured* concept that varies from one case to the next or over time within a given case. For example, individuals may differ with respect to age, sex, and class year (first, second, third, fourth); and a given individual may change in age, level of education (first grade, second grade, etc.), or income (dollars earned per year). One way Baumer et al. measured school commitment was by asking students' about their educational expectations and whether they expected to graduate from a four-year college or not. Note that individuals may place the same value on a variable, for example, two individuals could both indicate that they expect to graduate from a four-year college. However, individual responses may also vary, while one individual might expect to graduate from a four-year college, another individual might respond saying no, they do not expect to graduate from a four-year college.

Take care not to confuse variables with the attributes or categories they consist of. "Political party" (in the United States) is a variable consisting of categories such as Democrat, Republican, and so forth; "Democrat" and "Republican" by themselves are not variables but simply specific categories that distinguish persons who belong to different political parties. Likewise, "divorced" is not a variable but a category of the variable "marital status." To keep this distinction clear, note that any term you might use to describe yourself or someone else (e.g., sophomore, sociology major) is an attribute or category of a variable (academic class, major), not a variable in itself.

> **concept** a term scientists use to group together phenomena that have important things in common
>
> **variable** a measured concept that may vary across cases or across time

TYPES OF VARIABLES

In designing research to answer quantitative research questions, you need to know the differences among several types of variables. The most important distinction is between independent and dependent variables. A **dependent variable** is the outcome that one is interested in explaining or predicting. It is the variable that is thought to *depend on* or be influenced by other variables. The variables that do the influencing are **independent**. (Here is one way to remember this: **I**ndependent = **I**nfluences and **D**ependent = influence**D**). For example, when Baumer and colleagues explored whether school commitment would have an effect on youth offending, their independent variable consisted of whether students reported that they anticipated graduating from a four-year college, and the dependent variable was youth offending prevalence (i.e., whether they had engaged in any or all of six different delinquent behaviors).

Quantitative research questions are concerned with the relationship between independent and dependent variables. But as you design your research, you also need to consider the relevance of **extraneous variables**, which are other variables that are not

> **dependent variable** the variable that the researcher tries to explain or predict; the presumed effect in a causal relationship
>
> **independent variable** a presumed influence or cause of a dependent variable
>
> **extraneous variable** a variable that is not part of a hypothesized relationship

antecedent variable a variable that occurs before, and may be a cause of, both the independent and dependent variables in a causal relationship

intervening variable a variable that is intermediate between two other variables in a causal relationship; it is an effect of one and a cause of the other

control variable a variable that is not allowed to vary or otherwise held constant during the course of data collection or analysis

specified in your question or hypothesis. Especially important are extraneous variables that may affect the independent variable, the dependent variable, or both. For example, can you think of anything that might explain why students have low educational aspirations or engage in delinquent activity? In relation to specific independent and dependent variables, extraneous variables may be *antecedent* or *intervening*. An **antecedent variable** occurs prior in time to both the independent and dependent variable. Antecedent variables in Baumer et al.'s study were parents' education level and a student's race and sex; each of these variables can affect both educational expectations and delinquency. An **intervening variable**, on the other hand, is one that is both an effect of the independent variable and a cause of the dependent variable. Baumer et al. did not analyze any intervening variables, but we can look at their measures and assume that one in particular could be considered an intervening variable. Baumer and colleagues measured the amount of unstructured socializing that participants engaged in, including questions about how often during the week they rode around for fun, spent time with friends, and went out in the evening. A lack of commitment to school could affect unstructured free time spent with friends which, in turn, could affect a student's engagement in delinquent activity. Figure 5.3 depicts these examples of antecedent and intervening variables. Each arrow in the figure represents causal direction. Thus, "Parents' educational level → Participants' commitment to school" means that parents' education level may influence or cause students' commitment to school, and the absence of an arrow means that one variable does not cause another.

Extraneous variables also may be either controlled or uncontrolled. Controlled or, more commonly, **control variables** are held constant or prevented from varying during the course of observation or analysis. One aim of quantitative research design is for researchers to identify potentially relevant extraneous variables and then control as many as is feasible, often with the goal of ruling out these variables as possible explanations of the hypothesized relationship. Experiments control extraneous variables by creating experimental and control groups that are the same in all respects except for the independent variable, as discussed in Chapter 8. In nonexperimental studies, quantitative researchers attempt to measure and then *statistically* control for extraneous variables. This is what Baumer et al. did. Using quantitative data analysis techniques discussed in Chapter 14, they statistically controlled for numerous extraneous variables, including parents' education level and students' race, sex, and grade level. This enabled them to test the influence of these variables on the relationship between multiple independent

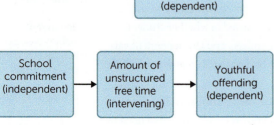

FIGURE 5.3 Antecedent and Intervening Variables

5.2 Designing Research to Answer Quantitative Questions

variables, including school commitment and prevalence of delinquency. As we discuss below, a researcher can only control what can be observed and measured, meaning that some variables in survey and other research may be uncontrolled due to their exclusion from the analysis.

You are now in a position to test your understanding of variables and units of analysis. Box 5.4 is designed to help you do this.

BOX 5.4

CHECKING YOUR UNDERSTANDING

Quantitative Research Questions, Units of Analysis, and Variables

Take a look at Table A. The first column presents six quantitative research questions or hypotheses; the second and third columns identify the relevant units of analysis and variables. For the sample research question in the first row ("Are older people more afraid …"), note that the unit of analysis is "Individuals" and the independent variable is "Age" and the dependent variable is "fear of crime." Fill in the numbered blanks for the remaining questions and then check your responses against the answers at the bottom of the table.

Table A Fill in the Blanks

Research Question/ Hypothesis	Identify the Unit of Analysis	Identify the Independent and Dependent Variables
Are older people more afraid of crime than younger people?	Individuals	Independent: Age Dependent: Fear of crime
The higher the proportion of female employees in a factory, the lower the wages.	1. _____	Independent: Proportion of employees who are female Dependent: Average wage
Does economic development lower the birth rate?	Nations	Independent: 2. _____ Dependent: Birth rate

continues

continued

Research Question/ Hypothesis	Identify the Unit of Analysis	Identify the Independent and Dependent Variables
The longer the engagement period, the longer the marriage.	3. _____	Independent: Length of engagement Dependent: 4. _____
Comic strips introduced in the 1930s were more likely to emphasize powerful heroes than strips introduced in the 1920s.	Comic strips	Independent: 5. _____ Dependent: Whether main characters in strip were powerful
Does the amount of alcohol that students consume have a negative impact on their grades?	6. _____	Independent: 7. _____ Dependent: Grade-point average

Answers: 1. Factories. 2. Level of economic development. 3. Couples. 4. Length of marriage. 5. When comic strips were introduced (1920s or 1930s). 6. Individuals (students). 7. Amount of alcohol consumed.

Gather Data and Analyze the Relationships Among Variables

Selecting units of analysis and measuring variables are the key design elements for gathering data to address quantitative questions. But to properly design research, you also must anticipate how you will analyze the data you collect. As we noted, one of the main goals of quantitative research is to identify causal relationships. So, what kind of evidence is necessary to infer that one variable causes another? In everyday terms, a cause is something that makes something else happen or change. It seems obvious that a rock thrown against a window will cause the glass to shatter. However, in contrast to this implicit understanding of causality that seems to exist in everyday life, the meaning of the concept of "cause" has been hotly debated by philosophers and scientists for centuries (Hume, 1748/1951). Although criminologists, and other social scientists, have continued to debate the notion of causality (Blalock, 1964; Bunge, 1979; Pearl, 2010),

5.2 Designing Research to Answer Quantitative Questions

researchers generally agree that at least three kinds of evidence are needed to establish causality: association, direction of influence, and nonspuriousness.

ASSOCIATION

The first criterion to establish causality is association. Two or more variables are associated, or form a relationship, to the extent that changes in one are accompanied by systematic changes in the other(s): if one variable changes, the other variable changes, and if one variable does not change, the other does not change. Suppose, for example, that you wanted to examine the relationship between a person's race and 2020 presidential vote choice. The kind of data you need could be gathered in a survey, where the units of analysis are individual respondents or voters. In fact, randomly selected voters from across the country were interviewed through a telephone survey and as they left voting stations before and on Election Day, November 3, 2020. In addition to whom they voted for, respondents were asked about their sex, age, race, and ethnicity among other questions. Table 5.1 provides answers for four hypothetical respondents. Notice that these data form a perfectly consistent pattern: if one variable changes (from White to Black), the other variable changes (from Donald Trump to Joe Biden); if one variable remains the same, as race does for the first and second respondents, both of whom are White, the other variable remains the same (i.e., both voted for Trump).

Of course, in real life we never see perfect relationships; so, researchers have devised statistics for determining whether there is an association between two variables. To understand how these statistics work, let us examine actual data from the 2020 presidential election exit polls, conducted by Edison Research. Table 5.2 presents the data for the 11,713 respondents who identified themselves as either Black or White and as voting for either Trump or Biden (excluded are other races, other candidate choices, and those who did not respond). As the table shows, 58.5 percent of White people as compared with 12.4 percent of Black people voted for Trump; therefore, White people were more likely to vote for Trump. The difference in vote choice for Trump between Blacks and White people is 46.1 percent (58.5–12.487), which represents a crude measure of association called the "percentage difference."

Table 5.1 Answers for Four Hypothetical Respondents

Respondent	Race	Vote for President
1	White	Donald Trump
2	White	Donald Trump
3	Black	Joe Biden
4	Black	Joe Biden

Table 5.2 Vote for Presidential Candidate by Race, 2020 Presidential Exit Polls

Candidate	Voter Race	
	White	Black
Joe Biden	41.5%	87.6%
Donald Trump	58.5%	12.4%
Total	100.0%	100.0%
Number of voters (approximate)	(9,803)	(1,910)

Source: National Election Poll 2020 Presidential Election Exit Poll; data provided by Edison Research.

The larger the percentage difference, the more likely that an association exists. In fact, another statistic, called a *test of statistical significance*, indicates that the difference is so large that, given the sample size, it is unlikely to have occurred at random or by chance. We have much more to say about statistics on quantitative data analysis in Chapter 14. See Box 5.5 to better understand the meaning of statistics commonly reported in criminal justice literature.

DIRECTION OF INFLUENCE

The second criterion needed to infer a causal relationship is direction of influence. The direction of influence should be from cause to effect. Thus, if A is a cause of B, then changes in A should bring about changes in B and not vice versa. For many relationships in social research the direction of influence between variables is easily determined by their *temporal order*—that is, which variable comes first in time. For example, characteristics fixed at birth, such as a person's age, come before characteristics developed later in life, such as a person's education or political party preference, and it is hard to imagine how changes in the latter could influence changes in the former.

Direction of influence is a common issue in criminological theories, such as social learning theory. Social learning theory posits that individuals who spend time with peers that engage in delinquency will adopt attitudes favorable to delinquency and begin engaging in it themselves. The problem is that it is difficult to tell whether an individual who is not delinquent is influenced to engage in delinquency by their delinquent peers, or if already delinquent individuals seek one another out as friends—a "birds of a feather flock together" sort of explanation. If a criminologist were to try to establish direction of influence for social learning, they would need to determine the time at which the individual began associating with delinquent peers and whether this preceded their own engagement in delinquent activity. As we discuss in later chapters, the timing of observations is an important dimension of research design. As you will

> **BOX 5.5**
>
> **READING CRIMINAL JUSTICE RESEARCH**
>
> ## How to Interpret Correlations and Tests of Statistical Significance
>
> As you read reports of quantitative studies and Chapters 6–14 in this book, you will encounter two kinds of statistics that indicate whether an association exists between variables: measures of degree of association and tests of statistical significance. Both kinds of statistics are explained in detail in Chapter 14. For now, we want to give you enough information to understand how to interpret study findings.
>
> Many statistics are available for determining the degree of association between variables. Which statistic is used depends largely on the types of variables being analyzed. The "percentage difference" in Table 5.2 may be applied to two variables with nonnumerical categories, such as "race" and "vote for presidential candidate." For variables with numerical categories, such as age and crime frequency, the most common statistic is the Pearson product-moment correlation coefficient, or *correlation coefficient*—often represented by the symbol r. Correlation coefficients vary from 0 to 1 (or –1), where 0 indicates that there is no association and 1 (or –1) indicates that there is a perfect association. (The correlation coefficient, including the meaning of the sign, + or –, is explained further in Chapter 14.) Imagine that while analyzing data from the MTF, Baumer at al. found a correlation of –0.74 between students' school commitment and prevalence of offending. This would be a strong, negative correlation, and it would indicate that students who were more committed to school tended to be less likely to engage in delinquency. Their analysis was much more complicated than this, but the imaginary example helps us understand a little bit more about correlations.
>
> If Baumer at al. did run a correlation analysis, they may have found that this coefficient was **statistically significant**, which means that the association is unlikely to have occurred at random or by chance. In research reports or articles, you may read that an association is "statistically significant at $p < .05$." The lowercase p stands for "probability"; "$p < .05$" means that the probability is less than .05, or 5 in 100, that the association could have occurred by chance, assuming that there is no relationship in the larger population from which the sample was drawn. With odds this low, we can be confident that the result would not have occurred by chance and that there is an association between the variables in the larger population.

see, experiments (Chapter 8) and longitudinal survey designs (Chapter 9) provide direct evidence of temporal ordering.

NONSPURIOUSNESS (NO COMMON CAUSE)

The final criterion for inferring causality is that two variables that are associated statistically should have no common cause. If two variables happen to be related to a common extraneous or third variable, then a statistical association can exist between the original two variables even if there is no inherent link between them. Therefore, to infer a causal

statistical significance the likelihood that the results of a study, such as an association between variables, could have occurred by chance

relationship from an observed correlation, there should be good reason to believe that there are no "hidden" factors that could have created an accidental or spurious relationship between the variables. When an association between variables *cannot* be explained by an extraneous variable, the relationship is said to be *nonspurious*. When an association has been produced by an extraneous third factor, and neither of the variables involved in the association has influenced the other, it is called a **spurious relationship**.

The idea of spuriousness was directly tested in a study conducted by Felson and colleagues (2008) as they analyzed whether the relationship between alcohol use and delinquency is causal or spurious. They found that for some types of delinquency, namely petty theft, such as shoplifting or stealing from your own home, alcohol use was related to sober delinquency (i.e., delinquency committed when one is not under the influence of drugs or alcohol) and total delinquency, showing that alcohol use is *correlated* with these types of delinquency, but does not *cause* the delinquency. Because alcohol use is associated with sober delinquency, it cannot be said that alcohol use causes delinquency, as the individuals are sober when they engaged in the delinquency, therefore the association between the two variables is likely caused by some third variable such as peer influence, low self-control, conflict at home, etc.

In actual research, spurious relationships are much less apparent, and the possibility often exists that an unknown variable may have produced an observed association. To infer that a relationship is nonspurious, researchers must identify and control for extraneous variables that might account for an association. Circumstances seldom allow for the control of all variables; therefore, researchers attempt to control the effects of as many as possible. The greater the number of variables controlled without altering a relationship, the greater the likelihood that the relationship is not spurious.

Recall that Baumer et al. statistically controlled for several variables, including students' race and sex. This is a very common practice in the analysis of survey data. The major drawback to this method is that one can control statistically only for those variables that have been observed or measured as part of the research. Hence, the effects of any unknown or unmeasured variables cannot be assessed. A stronger test of nonspuriousness is provided in experiments through a process called *randomization*. When participants in an experiment are randomly assigned to an experimental or "control" group, it is assumed that the groups are equivalent—that is, all extraneous variables have been controlled. We discuss randomized experiments in Chapter 8; we discuss causal analysis techniques involving statistical manipulation of nonexperimental data in Chapter 14.

CAUSATION, INTERVENING VARIABLES, AND THEORY

In addition to association, direction of influence, and nonspuriousness, the specification of an intervening mechanism or variable can strengthen causal inferences. Though

---

spurious relationship noncausal statistical association between two variables produced by a common cause, that is, an antecedent variable

not a necessary causal criterion, intervening variables are nonetheless an essential part of scientific inquiry. Often, in fact, this is what the development and testing of theory is all about. For example, a study by Riane Bolin, Margaret Pate, and Jenna McClintock (2017) looked at the relationship between substance use (alcohol and cannabis) and academic performance. Overall, we found that increased alcohol and cannabis use were associated with decreased GPA. The relationship between substance use and academic performance was partially explained by an intervening variable, the frequency with which the respondents skipped class. Therefore, substance use led to lower academic performance partially due to the fact that students who used substances, both alcohol and cannabis, were in class less often.

By specifying intervening variables, theories render a more complete understanding of the causal processes that connect events. Equally important, theories provide the general framework for investigating the nature of all relationships. Theories tell the researcher which relationships to observe, what extraneous variables are likely to affect the relationships, and the conditions under which a causal relationship is likely to exist. In short, it is in terms of some theory that the researcher can determine how to assess the meaningfulness of a "weak" association and how to test for direction of influence and nonspuriousness. Thus, we see again the importance of the interplay between theory and research in science. Theory guides research, and research provides the findings that validate and suggest modifications in theory. To practice selecting an appropriate research strategy, identifying units of analysis, and measuring variables, please see Box 5.6.

BOX 5.6

PRACTICE WHAT YOU LEARNED

Expand on Your Research Question

Using one of the explanatory research questions developed in the previous "Practice What You Learned" exercise, please complete the following:

1. Identify an appropriate data collection strategy. Explain why you chose this strategy.
2. Define your unit of analysis.
3. Identify the independent and the dependent variable from your research question.
4. List at least one extraneous variable (antecedent or intervening) that might influence your independent and/or dependent variable.

SUMMARY

Quantitative research questions focus on relationships between variables, often with the explicit aim of establishing *causal* relationships, in which the independent variable is the presumed cause, and the dependent variable is the presumed effect. Designing research to answer quantitative questions involves selecting a research strategy (e.g., experiments, surveys, or existing data analysis), selecting units of analysis, specifying and deciding how to measure variables, and considering how the data will be analyzed. Three criteria are assumed to be requisites of a causal relationship: association, direction of influence, and nonspuriousness. In addition, the specification of an intervening variable or mechanism can strengthen causal inferences. Theory plays an important role in quantitative research not only in specifying intervening variables but also in shaping the overall research design. To check your understanding of the concepts learned within this section, please refer to Box 5.7.

BOX 5.7

CHECKING YOUR UNDERSTANDING

Identifying Variables

1. Paul is interested in studying neighborhood crime; he surveys respondents about the level of crime in their neighborhood. Respondents could choose between no crime, occasional crime, and frequent crime. "No crime" is an example of which of the following?
    a. Independent variable
    b. Attribute
    c. Dependent variable
    d. Extraneous variable

2. Paul hypothesizes that individuals who live in rural environments will report lower levels of neighborhood crime than those who live in urban environments. "Type of environment" is an example of which of the following?
    a. Independent variable
    b. Attribute
    c. Dependent variable
    d. Extraneous variable

3. Stacey is conducting a study exploring the impact of substance use on academic achievement for a sample of high school students. Stacey includes the variable "parental supervision" in her research design. "Parental supervision" is an example of which of the following?
   a. Intervening variable
   b. Independent variable
   c. Dependent variable
   d. Antecedent variable

4. Three kinds of evidence are required to establish causality. First, a researcher must determine if the two variables of interest are related to one another. Which criteria for causality is being established?
   a. Association
   b. Direction of influence
   c. Nonspuriousness
   d. Mechanism

5. Research has found that as the number of storks in a geographic area increases, so too does the number of human births in that area. The association between the two has been deemed a consequence of a third variable, population size. Because storks like to nest in chimneys, storks are more prevalent in high population European cities, and in high population areas there are, by default, more births. The relationship between storks and births is thus a _____ relationship.
   a. Causal
   b. Non-existent
   c. Spurious
   d. Fake

Answers: 1. b, 2. a, 3. d, 4. a, 5. c

5.3 DESIGNING RESEARCH TO ANSWER QUALITATIVE QUESTIONS

One way in which the social sciences differ from the natural sciences is that, unlike nonliving things, plants, and lower animals, humans can interpret and interact with the world around them. To fully understand *human* action, therefore, we must take into account the actor's point of view (Simmel, 1972; Weber, 1905/1998). Qualitative questions take this perspective; they ask about the meaning and purpose of human

PHOTO 5.1 "Snow"?

actions, both for individuals and for social groups (Schwartz-Shea & Yanow, 2012). They also examine the social processes and interactions that produce patterns in society. The aim is to develop theory and deepen understanding by providing in-depth knowledge.

The importance of understanding meaning—and how one thing can mean quite another depending on people's interpretations of it—is evident when we consider a popular example from anthropology (Boas, 1911): When you look at Photo 5.1, what do you see? Whereas some people may see "snow," others may see something entirely different. In fact, Boas (1911) wrote that the Inuit group he studied had about 50 words for *snow*. The different words reflect different types of precipitation that the Inuit experience living in extremely frigid areas: wet snow, salt-like snow, hard-falling snow, and so forth. These interpretations also have consequences for action. Wet snow (*matsaaruti* in local dialect), for example, helps to ice the runners on one's sleigh (Krupnik & Müller-Willie, 2010; Robson, 2013).

Developing an in-depth understanding of human thought and action requires researchers to "get inside" the individual—to discover their interpretations, experiences, intentions, and motives (Schwarz & Jacobs, 1979). To represent this inside view, researchers tend not to count or assign numbers to observations but rather to produce data in the form of ordinary language consisting of quotations and detailed descriptions. Unlike research on quantitative questions, research on qualitative questions is more open-ended, as researchers generally aim to develop rather than test theory. Therefore, the research design is more flexible. Typically, researchers begin by carefully selecting a few research sites or cases, keep a record of observations, and then code, analyze data, and develop theoretical concepts throughout the process of data collection. Figure 5.4 depicts the steps you will need to consider in designing research to answer qualitative questions.

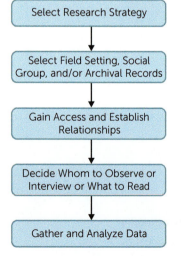

FIGURE 5.4 Steps to Consider in Designing Research to Answer Qualitative Questions

Select a Research Strategy

Just as in research designs for quantitative questions, the first step is to select a data-collection strategy. However, the strategies suitable for exploring qualitative questions are quite different. Researchers asking qualitative questions may conduct field research, carry out in-depth interviews, read and interpret archival records, or use some combination of these strategies. The research question will determine which strategy is most appropriate.

Johnson's (2015) interest in exploring the experiences of women on parole led her to conduct in-depth face to face interviews with 60 women on parole, asking about "the challenges encountered in monthly parole reporting, perceptions of parole officers, and the strategies used to sustain their freedom in the community" (p. 785). We explain when and how to do field research and in-depth interviews in Chapter 10.

Archival records are a form of existing data used in both quantitative and qualitative research, but the types of archival records used vary. Kai Erikson (1966), for instance, analyzed court records and personal journals to study three crime waves in Puritan New England, including the famous witchcraft hysteria in colonial Salem. More recently, Xiaochen Hu and colleagues (2018) examined Facebook pages of 14 police departments in the United States to explore police departments' practices of posting on social media. Our discussion of qualitative research design focuses here primarily on observations and interviews from field research, but we make mention of archival records below and discuss one method of analyzing archival records in Chapter 11.

Select Field Setting, Social Group, and/or Archival Records

In order to gain an in-depth understanding, qualitative researchers generally select a relatively small number of cases or often a single setting to extract the meaning of, or describe the processes shaping, people's actions in a given context. Qualitative research questions thus tend to be connected with a particular setting, time period, or group or with some combination of these (Schwartz-Shea & Yanow, 2012). To return to the snow example, you might see how a quantitative concern with the relationship between temperature and the amount of snowfall all over the world would obscure the local differences in the very meaning of snow and its consequences.

To see how the research setting is chosen to fit the question, let us consider Johnson's (2015) study. As Johnson was interested in studying women on parole, she had to first locate a state that still utilized parole. After that, she had to narrow her sampling frame, as it was not feasible for her to include in her study all female parolees in the state. She ultimately decided to draw her sample from three cities in one southern state; the two largest cities in the state as well as a third city that was in close proximity to the researcher and easy to access. For the two largest cities, a random selection process was used to select participants. All female parolees were asked to participate in the third city given the small number of parolees on its caseload.

Qualitative research making use of archival records must make similar decisions about what to analyze. To get a true "insider's view," diaries and personal journals, such as those used by Erikson, have traditionally been popular choices. More recently, researchers have begun using social media as data sources, including TikTok (Reid & Niebuhr, 2022) and Facebook profiles (e.g., Hu et al., 2018), among other forms of social media.

Gain Access and Establish Relationships

The second step is to gain access to the particular setting or group that the researcher has chosen to study, to decide how to interact and to present oneself, and to establish a working relationship with the observed or interviewees. Johnson, for instance, had to first get permission from the parole agencies in the three cities to interview the female parolees. Once she received permission from the agencies, she then had to obtain IRB approval before she was allowed to solicit participation. Gaining access and securing permission involves ethical issues, discussed in Chapter 4, as well as technical issues that are addressed in Chapter 10.

Decide Whom to Observe or Interview or What to Read

Quantitative and qualitative researchers typically select cases in different ways, reflecting the different understandings they hope to achieve. Unlike the quantitative emphasis on statistically generalizing findings to a larger population, qualitative research is concerned with gaining an in-depth understanding of particular individuals or social groups, which may lead to a more complete theoretical understanding of the meanings and processes being examined. This calls for a more flexible approach to selecting cases. Thus, beyond choosing an appropriate site or social group to observe and/or interview, qualitative researchers often decide what and whom to observe after they begin to gather data. Initial contacts in the field may suggest who will provide the best or most relevant information; then, as researchers observe and begin to analyze their data, they may choose to gather information that they believe will advance their theoretical understanding. Similarly, in archival research, as researchers develop theoretical insights, their exposure to initial texts or other materials may lead to still others.

In contrast to the probability sampling often used in quantitative research, qualitative research tends to rely on nonprobability sampling because of the different understanding it hopes to achieve. We discuss both forms of sampling in depth in Chapter 7.

Gather and Analyze Data

Qualitative researchers, seeking to understand the lived experience of those they study, tend not to fully specify concepts before they embark on their research. Instead, they assume that key concepts and their meaning will emerge in the study setting or will be captured in written words stored in archives (Schwartz-Shea & Yanow, 2012). Thus, rather than move from abstract concepts to observable variables, as in quantitative research, qualitative researchers are more likely to infer concepts from observations. In Chapters 10 and 13, we discuss the process of coding observations to extricate their larger meaning. This inductive process has several implications for research design.

When data are not generated to test a specific hypothesis, qualitative researchers understand that the direction of their research may be altered once they begin to gather and analyze data—indeed, this can be a major strength of qualitative research.

One of the greatest strengths of qualitative research is that its design lends itself to the generation of new theoretical insights, which stems from a very different interplay between theory and data than in quantitative research. Following the deductive logic of inquiry, quantitative researchers conduct literature reviews to assess the state of theoretical knowledge. Once they have devised their question or hypothesis, based on existing theory, they expect the data to provide a definitive answer or test—to support or reject the underlying theory—or to suggest ways to revise it. The research literature also informs qualitative research, identifying the issues that inform a research question and providing information about the setting where the research will be conducted (Schwartz-Shea & Yanow, 2012). But just as data are generated to understand actors' experiences, theorizing emerges in the process of data analysis to deepen one's understanding. In evaluating qualitative research, we can ask to what extent the theory, concepts, and data provide new and/or more complete understandings of the specific phenomena under investigation.

Johnson's study illustrates this process. Johnson (2015) gathered data through the use of in-depth, face to face interviews with the female parolees who participated in her study. The interview questions were developed after a review of the literature, along with discussions with parole district managers, parole supervisors, and an expert in parole research. The interview questions were broken into nine sections asking the women about their background and their experiences with parole, including perceptions of parole officers. The women were interviewed at the parole agency in a private location by the researcher. After receiving a signed informed consent, the researcher audiotaped and recorded through handwritten notes the contents of the interviews. She perceived the parolees to be open and honest when speaking about their parole experiences.

In describing her findings, Johnson points out that reconnecting and maintaining familial ties post-release is important for parolees' ultimate success. One parolee stated, "If I did not have my family to support me, I know I would fail on parole and end up back in prison" (Johnson, 2015, p. 794). Through the interviews it also became apparent that parolees' families often did not have a true awareness of the challenges of parole. Thus, Johnson suggested that parole informational sessions, facilitated by parole officers, be offered to family members as a way to further strengthen family support for the parolees.

SUMMARY

Qualitative research questions focus on achieving an in-depth understanding of meaning, action, and motive, particularly from an "insider's perspective." To do so, qualitative researchers begin by selecting a research strategy, such as field research or in-depth interviews, or the analysis of existing data, such as archival records. Then they select a field setting, social group, and/or archival records; gain and establish relationships, if applicable; decide whom to observe or interview or what to read; and proceed to gather and analyze data. One of the greatest strengths of qualitative research is its potential to develop theory. To check your understanding of the concepts within this section, please refer to Box 5.8.

BOX 5.8

CHECKING YOUR UNDERSTANDING

Designing a Research Review

1. As opposed to quantitative research, what is the main objective of qualitative research?
    a. To establish causal relationships
    b. To come up with general patterns that are true for a population
    c. To understand meaning and purpose of human actions
    d. Qualitative and quantitative research share the same main objective

2. Research strategies for _____ research often involve experiments, surveys, or existing data.
    a. Qualitative
    b. Quantitative
    c. Qualitative and quantitative

3. The first step in designing research to answer qualitative questions is to
    a. Gain access and establish relationships
    b. Select a research strategy
    c. Decide whom to observe or interview
    d. Gather and analyze data

Answers: 1. c, 2. b, 3. b

KEY TERMS

antecedent variable, p. 112
causal relationship, p. 108
concept, p. 111
control variable, p. 112
dependent variable, p. 111
ecological fallacy, p. 110
extraneous variable, p. 111
independent variable, p. 111
intervening variable, p. 112
qualitative research question, p. 106
quantitative research question, p. 106
research design, p. 101
spurious relationship, p. 118
statistical significance, p. 117
units of analysis, p. 109
variable, p. 111

KEY POINTS

- Research begins by choosing a topic, narrowing it through a literature review, and formulating a research question.
- Good research questions should be focused, contribute to ongoing research and theory, and be manageable in terms of time and other resources.
- Research designs differ according to the type of research question, which reflects the type of understanding researchers hope to achieve.
- Quantitative research questions aim to test hypotheses and establish general causal relationships.
- Qualitative research questions aim to establish context-specific meaning and contribute to the development of theory.
- Designing research to answer quantitative questions involves selecting a research strategy, selecting units of analysis, and specifying and determining how to measure variables.
- The primary objective of quantitative research—to generate data necessary to infer a causal relationship—requires evidence of association, direction of influence, and nonspuriousness (the absence of a common cause).
- Designing research to answer qualitative questions involves selecting a research strategy; selecting a field setting, social group, and/or archival records; gaining and establishing relationships, if applicable; and deciding whom to observe or interview or what to read.
- In gathering and analyzing data, the objective of qualitative research is to develop theories and concepts that make sense of one's observations.

REVIEW QUESTIONS

1. Explain and give an example of how a review of the scientific literature can help a researcher to narrow the focus of a research topic.

2. Explain the difference between quantitative and qualitative research questions. What is the scientific objective of each type of question? How is each related to deductive and inductive inquiry (discussed in Chapter 2)?
3. Give one example, other than those mentioned in the text, of (a) a positive and (b) a negative association between two quantitative variables.
4. What are the necessary criteria for establishing causal relationships in quantitative research?
5. Explain the function of intervening variables in establishing causal relationships.
6. Give an example of how research design in qualitative research is more "open-ended" than in quantitative research.

EXERCISES

1. Choose one of the following general research topics, conduct a literature review, and then formulate an appropriate research question related to the topic: (a) alcohol use, (b) sentencing disparities across race, or (c) crime.
2. In this chapter and throughout the book, we will ask you to examine data from the General Social Survey (GSS). GSS data may be accessed and analyzed by searching online for "SDA GSS 1972–2018" (this data is published by the University of California at Berkeley). Click on the data set and conduct the following analyses.
    a. First, opposite "Row:" enter DRUNK; opposite "Column:" enter SEX; opposite "Selection Filter(s):" enter YEAR (1994); and, opposite "Weight:" choose "No weight." Click on the "Output Options" tab and under "Cell Contents," you will see "Percentaging": check "Column" if it is not already checked; below you will see "Other options," and there you should check "Summary Statistics" and "Question text." Finally, click "Run the Table." The numbers in bold are the percentages in each column. Compare the percentages in the first row of the table. Who is more likely to say that they sometimes drink more than they think they should?
    b. First, opposite "Row:" enter CAPPUN; opposite "Column:" enter RACE; opposite "Selection Filter(s):" enter YEAR (2014); and, opposite "Weight:" choose "No weight." Click on the "Output Options" tab and under "Cell Contents," you will see "Percentaging": check "Column" if it is not already checked; below you will see "Other options," and there you should check "Summary Statistics" and "Question text." Finally, click "Run the Table." The numbers in bold are the percentages in each column. Compare the percentages in the first row of the table. Who is more likely to say that they favor capital punishment?

3. For each of the following statistical associations, identify a relevant extraneous (antecedent) variable and explain how it could create a spurious association.
   a. Research shows that as the number of police officers in a geographic area increases, the number of committed crimes for that area also increases.
   b. A study shows that as ice cream sales increase, so do incidences of burglary.

4. Referring back to the topics in Exercise #1, identify a field setting/social group that you could study to better understand the meanings and processes underlying each of these topics.

6

Measurement
Linking Theory to Research

CHAPTER OUTLINE

6.1 Overview: The Measurement Process   131

6.2 Conceptualization and Operationalization   132
Conceptualization 132
Operationalization 134
Summary 137

6.3 Variations in Operational Definitions: Data Sources   138
Manipulated vs. Measured Operations 138
Sources of Measured Operational Definitions 139
Summary 143

6.4 Variations in Operational Definitions: Levels of Measurement   144
Nominal Measurement 145
Ordinal Measurement 146
Interval Measurement 147
Ratio Measurement 148
Summary 149

6.5 Select and Apply Operational Definitions to Produce Data   151
Summary 153

6.6 Assess the Quality of Operational Definitions   154
Forms of Reliability Assessment 158
Forms of Validity Assessment 161
Summary 165

6.7 The Feedback Loop: From Data Back to Concepts and Measurement   167
Summary 169

LEARNING OBJECTIVES

By the end of this chapter, you should be able to

6.1 Describe the measurement process by identifying its major steps.

6.2 Apply your knowledge of measurement to operationalize a concept.

6.3 Distinguish between manipulated vs. measured operations and among types of measured operational definitions.

6.4 Identify and apply your knowledge of different levels of measurement.

6.5 Discuss the process of selecting and applying operational definitions to produce data.

6.6 Define reliability and validity, describe their relationship to each other, and identify the forms of reliability and validity assessment.

6.7 Explain the "feedback loops" in the measurement process, particularly how data can inform the development and refinement of concepts.

Have you ever "liked" something on TikTok? Rated a professor's level of difficulty as "easy" on Rate My Professors? Given a movie three out of four stars? Or simply stepped on a scale to find out how much you weigh? If you have done any of these things, you are already familiar with measurement.

	Number/label	To whom/what does it apply?	What does it represent?
	3 (stars) / ★★★	Movie (=unit of analysis)	Quality

FIGURE 6.1 Measurement of a Movie's Quality

Each of these examples contains the essentials of measurement: labels or numbers ("like," "easy," "three stars," a pointer reading on a scale) are assigned to people, objects, or events (TikToks, professors and others, a movie) to represent properties (likability, level of difficulty, the overall quality of a movie, weight) (see Figure 6.1).

There is a difference, of course, between these everyday examples of measurement and measurement in criminal justice research. In the examples the meaning of things, such as likability, are taken for granted, and the rules for assigning labels or numbers to units of analysis are more or less intuitive (e.g., you either like something or you do not). In criminal justice research, however, we often need to define the concepts we intend to measure (referred to as conceptualization) and we must spell out the rules in detail for how we will measure them (referred to as operationalization). Scientific norms require that we fully describe our methods and procedures so that others can repeat our observations and judge the quality of our measurements. In this chapter, we outline the measurement process, provide several examples of measurement in criminal justice research, discuss criteria for evaluating the nature and quality of measurements, and consider how data analysis and inductive inquiry may refine concepts and measurement. While there are some references to qualitative measures in this chapter, the main focus will be on quantitative measures. For a more detailed discussion of the qualitative research process, see Chapter 15.

6.1 OVERVIEW: THE MEASUREMENT PROCESS

Measurement is the process of assigning numbers or labels to units of analysis (people, objects, events, etc.) to represent their conceptual properties. In research addressing quantitative questions, the measurement process generally follows the deductive logic of inquiry, whereby theory leads to hypotheses and guides the collection and analysis of data. It begins as the researcher reviews the literature and formulates a research question. Next, the researcher develops a hypothesis based on the available research. The researcher must then determine how the key concepts of the hypothesis will be measured. This phase of the research process is known as the measurement process.

Figure 6.2 presents the steps in this process, in the order that research addressing quantitative questions tends to follow. The first two steps, called **conceptualization**, consist of defining and clarifying the meaning of a given concept. First, you must consider the concept's meaning by reviewing how it has been defined in the criminal

conceptualization
defining and clarifying the meaning of concepts

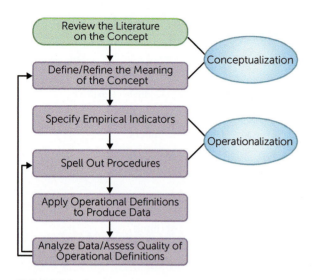

FIGURE 6.2 The Measurement Process

conceptual definition the meaning of a concept expressed in words that is derived from theory and/or observation (also called *theoretical definition*)

operationalization the process of identifying empirical indicators and the procedures for applying them to measure a concept

justice literature. As you invariably will encounter multiple definitions, you then must select or create an appropriate **conceptual**, or **theoretical, definition**, one that fits the theoretical framework of your research. The next two steps, called **operationalization**, involve identifying ways of observing the concept in real life and spelling out the procedures for applying these "indicators" when you carry out your research. The "final" steps in the process involve data collection and validation, which entail actually measuring the concept and assessing how well your measure represents the underlying concept.

We put the word *final* in quotes because, like all scientific inquiry, these steps are not really final, but rather part of an ongoing process of theory development. Reflective of inductive inquiry, feedback loops often occur, as represented by the arrows in the figure pointing upward. Thus, research addressing qualitative questions regularly undertakes these steps in a different order—beginning with data collection/analysis and ending with conceptualization—in hopes of developing a *new* theoretical concept (Glaser & Strauss, 1967). This process of defining concepts after data collection in qualitative research is discussed in more detail in Chapter 15. In addition, research addressing qualitative questions may refine existing concepts or operational definitions. In this chapter we also discuss research representing these feedback loops.

6.2 CONCEPTUALIZATION AND OPERATIONALIZATION

This section examines conceptualization and operationalization more closely.

Conceptualization

The first step in addressing quantitative questions is to define and clarify the meaning of the concepts embedded in your research question with words or examples. Recall from Chapter 5 that a concept is an abstraction that groups together phenomena with important things in common. The main goal of conceptualization is to make this abstraction more specific and ready to be measured. For simpler concepts such as age and class year, researchers may rely on common understandings. For instance, researchers exploring the impact of job tenure on community corrections officer burnout may choose not to define job tenure and rather use the implied definition of how long the officer has been employed as a community corrections officer (Rhineberger-Dunn et al., 2017). Another strategy researchers use for simpler concepts is to define them through examples. To illustrate, a researcher exploring the relationship between extracurricular activities and involvement and delinquency may offer examples, such as interscholastic sports, drama, music, and academic clubs.

For more complex concepts, on the other hand, it is important to review existing definitions in the criminal justice literature (step #1 in Figure 6.2). The concept of "use of force" in Ariel, Farrar, and Sutherland's (2015) study is an example. Ariel et al. were interested in exploring the impact of police body-worn cameras on use of force and citizen complaints against police officers. They hypothesized that the use of body-worn cameras by police would reduce the number of use of force incidents and citizen complaints against officers. This hypothesis included three concepts: "body-worn cameras," "use of force," and "citizen complaints." To begin the measurement process, Ariel et al. had to first conceptualize (or define) each of the concepts. To do this, they first reviewed how each of the concepts had been measured by previous researchers (pp. 513–515). After reviewing how researchers had previously defined use of force and identifying the "inherent subjectivity" (p. 513) and complexities of the concept, they derived their own definition of use of force: "the use of any physical force that is greater than basic control or 'compliance holds'—including the use of (a) OC spray, (b) baton, (c) Taser, (d) canine bite, or (e) firearm" (Ariel et al., 2015, p. 521). By providing a definition of use of force, the concept becomes less abstract and more "real." It also provides readers an understanding of the researchers' meaning of the concept, which allows them to assess the findings of the study accordingly.

There is more to conceptualization, however, than offering definitions. To further clarify the meaning of a concept (step #2 in Figure 6.2), researchers often distinguish the concept from similar concepts and ideas. As part of step #2, researchers may also break their main concept down into various *dimensions* and *types* to make it more manageable and concrete. Dimensions and types, as we use the words here, are progressively smaller and less abstract groupings of a concept.

Through conceptualization, researchers (1) refine and elaborate the theoretical foundation of their research and (2) provide a basis for linking theory to data. Having defined their concepts, Ariel et al. (2015) could generate a more precise statement of their hypothesis that could be linked more easily to data. Thus, beginning with the general theoretical relationship between body-worn cameras and use of force, Ariel et al. concentrated on the less abstract relationship body-worn cameras and official reports of use of force incidents as well as citizen complaints against officers. In this way, the measurement process moves from the abstract to the concrete, and the language shifts from "concepts" to "variables." To practice developing a conceptual definition, please refer to Box 6.1.

> **BOX 6.1**
>
> **PRACTICE WHAT YOU LEARNED**
>
> ## Create a Conceptual Definition
>
> Read the hypothesis below. Identify the concepts within the hypothesis. Provide a conceptual definition for each of the concepts.
>
> Hypothesis: Adolescents who are more involved in school will be less likely to engage in delinquent behavior.

Operationalization

In clarifying the meaning of a concept, the researcher begins the process of operationalization: identifying ways of observing variation (steps #3 and #4 in Figure 6.2). If you have already done good conceptual work, this process is a straightforward application of that work. To answer quantitative questions, you first need to find ways of indicating the concept in question. Second, you need to spell out the procedures by which you will apply these indicators. How you observe variation, though, depends on your research question and overall research strategy.

SPECIFY EMPIRICAL INDICATORS

Now that you know what your concept is, how would you recognize it if you saw, heard, or otherwise observed it? One way you would know is through one or more of its characteristics, as suggested by the popular saying, "If it walks like a duck and quacks like a duck, it is probably a duck." Walking style and quacking are **empirical indicators** of a duck. An empirical indicator is an observable characteristic of a concept.

> **empirical indicator**
> a single, concrete proxy for a concept such as a questionnaire item in a survey

Defining a concept and specifying its dimensions and types should point you in the direction of appropriate indicators. With respect to use of force, ask yourself: What sorts of police officer actions can be defined as forceful? At this point, it will be important to have a well-established conceptual definition. You must know whether you are simply measuring the presence of forceful actions by police, or whether you are measuring excessive force and the calculated proportionality of the suspects' actions and police officers' reactions. Once these actions have been identified, one possibility is to determine whether these actions have occurred or not, much like a yes or no response. Another indicator may be how *often* these actions occurred. These indicators may be measured from the official reports of the police themselves or via self-reports from citizens.

Recall that Ariel et al. (2015) were interested in the effect of body-worn cameras on police use of force incidents. Ariel et al. decided to indicate use of force incidents by determining whether or not a set of "forceful" actions had taken place, beyond compliance holds, as reported by the police to their department. Note how this "official report of force used..." empirical indicator follows from the concept of use of force.

A single empirical indicator of a concept may be inadequate, however, for two reasons:

1. It may contain errors of classification.
2. It is unlikely to capture the whole meaning of a concept.

We would probably make errors in determining whether an animal is a duck based on the sole indicator of quacking; after all, does "squawking" (as in the sound made by certain cranes, cockatoos, parrots, etc.) not sound a lot like quacking? And, just as the saying goes, there is more to a duck than quacking. Similarly, in Ariel et al.'s (2015) study, whether a forceful action took place in an officer–citizen interaction depends on whether the officer reports the action to the department. Likewise, this indicator does not measure how much force was used.

Because of the imperfect correspondence between indicators and concepts, researchers often choose to rely on more than one indicator when operationalizing a concept. Sometimes several indicators of a given concept are analyzed separately, yielding multiple tests or cross-checks of a hypothesis. At other times, distinct indicators are combined to form a new variable. Combining several indicators into a composite measure generally provides a better overall representation of the concept. The simplest and most common procedure is to create an **index** by adding or taking an average of the scores of the separate items.

Combining indicators is particularly useful in operationalizing complex or broad concepts. One common example in criminal justice research is the measurement of substance use. To operationalize substance use among a sample of individuals, a researcher may decide to create an index by summing or averaging responses to the questions that ask individuals to report whether they have ever used a variety of different substances. This allows the researcher to cover the full range of the concept of substance use. An example follows.

index a composite measure of a concept constructed by adding or averaging the scores of separate indicators; differs from a scale, which uses less arbitrary procedures for combining indicators

Have you ever used...

	No	Yes
1. Alcohol, any use	0	1
2. Cannabis	0	1
3. Inhalants	0	1
4. Cocaine	0	1
5. Amphetamines	0	1
6. Heroin	0	1

This should give you an idea of how researchers may use multiple empirical indicators, some of which they may decide to combine into an index. We have more to say about the use of multiple indicators later in this chapter (see Box 6.7), but for now, we turn to the next step.

SPELL OUT PROCEDURES

The next step in the measurement process involves spelling out procedures for applying empirical indicators when you carry out your research. With an indicator in mind, what specific observations will you make or what questions will you ask? Will you use more than one? If so, how will you combine them? In answering these questions, you are formulating an **operational definition**. The counterpart of a conceptual definition, an operational definition describes the exact procedures used to observe the categories or values of a variable.

Operational definitions must provide enough detail that others can replicate as well as assess what researchers have done. To see how this works, let us consider a simple illustration from everyday life. Suppose your friend bakes you a delicious carrot cake, so you ask your friend how they made it because you would like to make one. Your friend says, "Oh, you take some carrots, flour, sugar, eggs, and so forth, add some nuts, bake it, and *voilà*!—you have a carrot cake." Would you be able to make an identical cake with these directions? Not likely.

What you need is an operational definition of your friend's concept of "carrot cake." You would need to have details, such as all of the ingredients, the amount of each ingredient to use, the steps necessary to combine the ingredients, the oven temperature, and baking time. In short, your friend's operational definition should look like an ordinary recipe. Using the recipe (operational definition), you should be able to produce a very similar cake.

For Ariel et al. (2015), spelling out the procedures to formulate their operational definitions amounted to identifying the actions that would be considered "force" and determining whether these actions had or had not taken place, as indicated in the police department's system that was used to track officer reports of these incidents. To operationally define a broader concept, like substance use, a researcher may use a single item that asks about a specific substance, such as use of alcohol. As discussed previously in this section, the researcher may also operationally define substance use by adding the responses to multiple questions that ask about use of a variety of substances to create a "substance use" index.

In research, as in cooking, many operational definitions are possible. In the end, you have to decide for yourself which to apply to produce data (see Figure 6.2). To do so, you first need to be familiar with how operational definitions differ in the procedures they specify and in the variable categories or values they produce. Take the concept of

operational definition a detailed description of the research procedures necessary to assign units of analysis to variable categories

recidivism, for example. There are numerous ways in which this concept can be operationalized. A researcher may choose to:

1. ask an offender to self-report whether they have been rearrested since their last conviction,
2. collect rearrest information from official police reports, and/or
3. collect data from prisons on offender recommitments.

While all of these operational definitions provide a measure of recidivism, each goes about measuring it differently and captures different dimensions of the concept. In the next section, we illustrate how operational definitions vary with respect to the general research.

SUMMARY

To answer quantitative questions, the measurement process initially follows the deductive logic of inquiry in which theory informs hypotheses and guides the collection and analysis of data. The first major step is conceptualization, which includes reviewing the literature on a concept and defining/refining its meaning. The second major step is operationalization, which involves specifying empirical indicators of a concept and spelling out procedures by which these indicators will be applied. To check your understanding of the concepts within this section, please refer to Box 6.2.

BOX 6.2

CHECKING YOUR UNDERSTANDING

Measurement Process Review

1. A researcher is interested in studying the impact of substance use on delinquency. Establishing definitions from prior research of substance use and delinquency is one of the researcher's first tasks. The researcher is engaging in which step of the measurement process?
    a. Operationalization
    b. Conceptualization
    c. Data analysis
    d. Identifying dimensions

continues

continued

2. The researcher's decision to use official reports of arrest to measure delinquency is an example of which step of the measurement process?
    a. Operationalization
    b. Conceptualization
    c. Data analysis
    d. Identifying dimensions

3. A researcher decides to measure delinquency through the use of a self-report questionnaire. One of the questions asks respondents, "How many times have you been arrested in the past year?" This question represents a(n):
    a. Operational definition
    b. Concept
    c. Empirical indicator
    d. Dimension

4. If a researcher decides to use multiple indicators to measure delinquency by summing the responses, the researcher has created a(n):
    a. Index
    b. Concept
    c. Dimension
    d. Operational definition

Answers: 1. b, 2. c, 3. c, 4. a

6.3 VARIATIONS IN OPERATIONAL DEFINITIONS: DATA SOURCES

Our discussion of the process of operationalization, which focused on how Ariel et al. (2015) operationalized the concept of use of force, emphasized one data source—official reports whose data were obtained from official officer reports. We now distinguish between manipulated and measured operations and among sources of measured operations.

Manipulated vs. Measured Operations

There are two general types of operational definitions in criminal justice research: manipulated and measured. *Manipulation operations* are designed to change the value or category of a variable, whereas *measurement operations* estimate existing values or categories.

Both types of operational definitions are illustrated in Ariel et al.'s (2015) study. Recall that they asked the question: Do body-worn cameras reduce the prevalence of use of force and/or citizen complaints against police? Embedded in this question are several concepts, including body-worn cameras, use of force, and citizen complaints. To investigate their relationship, Ariel et al. randomly assigned officer shifts into experimental and control shifts. Officers on experimental shifts were provided body-worn cameras which they were instructed to utilize in every instance involving encounters with the public with the exception of sexual assault of minors and confidential police informants. Officers on control shifts were not assigned body-worn cameras. This is an example of a manipulated independent variable, as the researchers *created* the variable through random assignment. Manipulation of an independent variable is, by definition, experimental, and we have a good deal more to say about this in Chapter 8.

To operationalize the dependent variables, use of force and citizen complaints, Ariel et al. (2015) used measured definitions: whether the officer reported using force or not and the number of citizen complaints. For both dependent variables, official records were used. These are considered measured operations because they were naturally occurring, rather than manipulated by the researchers.

Sources of Measured Operational Definitions

There are three primary sources of measurement operations: verbal reports, observation, and archival records. Generally, these sources correspond, respectively, to surveys and in-depth interviews, field research, and the analysis of existing data. A given approach may use more than one data source.

VERBAL REPORTS

One way of measuring a concept—by far the most common form of social measurement—is to simply ask people questions. **Verbal reports**, or **self-reports**, consist of replies to direct questions, usually posed in surveys or in-depth interviews. Self-reports provide simple and generally accurate measures of background variables such as age, sex, marital status, and education. They also are used extensively to measure subjective experiences, such as knowledge, beliefs, attitudes, feelings, and opinions.

Criminal justice researchers rely on self-report measures particularly when exploring individuals' perceptions or behaviors. One example can be found in a research study by Schaefer and Williams (2018), who examined the impact of probation and parole officers' attitudes about offenders on professional practices. Most of the variables in their study were operationalized by means of self-reports. For example, in order to measure attitudes toward offenders, one of their key independent variables, they modified questions from the Attitudes toward Prisoners scale originally established by Melvin, Gramling, and Gardner (1985). Officers were asked to state their level of agreement with 33 different statements. Responses were summed into a scale to determine the

verbal reports an operational definition based on respondents' answers to questions in an interview or questionnaire (also called *self-report*)

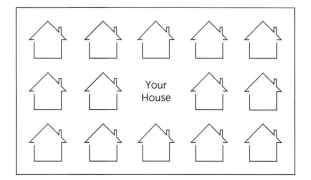

FIGURE 6.3 Neighborhood Card Used to Measure Residential Preferences

extent to which officers view offenders as "normal people capable of positive change" or as "deviants deserving of punishment" (Schaefer & Williams, 2018, p. 6). Schaefer and Williams also used a scale to measure their dependent variable: compliance with data entry processes for case management tools. Probation officers were asked to report the frequency with which they engaged in certain behaviors, such as how often they update the tool carelessly, exaggerate information, or put forth minimum effort. Responses to the individual items were averaged together, with higher scores indicating greater manipulation of case management tools.

Verbal reports also are elicited with pictures and diagrams, which can simplify complex issues. To measure attitudes toward residential integration, for example, Esther Havekes, Michael Bader, and Maria Krysan (2016) showed respondents diagrams depicting a neighborhood containing 15 homes, one of which was labeled "Your House" (see Figure 6.3). Respondents were told to "imagine an ideal neighborhood that had the ethnic and racial mix you personally would feel most comfortable in" (p. 124). The respondents were then asked to write the initials of the racial/ethnic groups that they would like to live by (e.g., "B" for "Blacks" etc.). Based on this information and respondents' racial and ethnic identification, the researchers calculated a measure of the extent to which people preferred to live with their "own racial/ethnic group" (p. 109).

OBSERVATION

Another means of measuring a concept is through observation. Observational measures are commonly used in field research. For example, in a field research study by Keuschnigg and Wolbring (2015), three field experiments were conducted to test the "broken windows" thesis. Originally proposed by Wilson and Kelling (1982), broken windows theory argues that physical and social disorder leads to an increase in further signs of disorder. The example for which the theory is named states that leaving a broken window unrepaired will lead to further disrepair and potential norm violation, as it indicates that there is a lack of investment in the property. One of the three field experiments will be discussed in detail below.

In Keuschnigg and Wolbring's (2015) third field experiment, which examined helping and stealing behavior at public mailboxes, a "lost" letter was placed in front of a mailbox in both a low and high local social capital district. Additionally, the area surrounding the mailboxes varied with a control condition consisting of a clean area surrounding the mailbox and an experimental condition of two heavily wrecked bicycles attached to the railing next to the mailboxes. The incentive to steal was also varied based on the amount of money that was displayed in the address window of the envelope (e.g., 5, 10, and 100 euros). Every individual who passed by the mailbox and noticed the letter was counted as a participant. To measure helping and stealing behavior, the researchers observed whether the individual took the letter, placed the letter in the mailbox, or ignored the letter. Observations took place over a two-month period resulting in 540 total observations. In the location where there was physical disorder, it was found that fewer individuals placed the letter in the mailbox, indicating less helping behavior. Likewise, the thieving rate was higher in locations with physical disorder. Refer to the article for further discussion of results.

Observation provides direct and generally unequivocal evidence of overt behavior. Besides direct, firsthand observation, technologies such as video recording, audio recording, counters, and mobile phones were used to observe and measure variables. Specific to criminal justice research, body-worn cameras have recently begun to be used to assess both officer and citizen behavior (e.g., Voigt et al., 2017). Additionally, mobile camera devices as well as surveillance cameras have been frequently used to measure offender decision-making (see Levine et al., 2011; Moeller, 2016). Others have utilized more sophisticated technology. For example, Jacques and colleagues utilized eye-tracking devices to monitor the behavior of would-be shoplifters (Jacques et al., 2015; Lasky, Jacques, & Fisher, 2015). Similarly, as an indirect means of observing everyday activities, social researchers have used time diaries, in which research participants are asked to report all their activities, usually for the previous day. For example, in their pilot study, Rokkan, Phillips, Lulei, Poledna, and Kensey (2000) utilized semi-structured diaries to get an understanding of the daily lives of probation officers across a number of European agencies. In a novel research study, Solymosi, Bowers, and Fujiyama (2015) used the Experience Sampling Method (ESM) to measure fear of crime. Respondents were required to download a mobile application and then periodically received a "ping" asking them to assess how worried they were about becoming a victim of crime at that moment. It was found that fear of crime is a dynamic variable that varies based on place and time as well as by individuals.

ARCHIVAL RECORDS

Archival records, which refer to existing recorded information, provide another invaluable source of measurement. The various types of archival data include statistical records, public and private documents, and mass communications. Archival records are used in approximately one-third of criminal justice research, making them a very common data source (Kleck et al., 2006). Examples of research in criminal justice using archival records include studies of crime rates, sentencing, and recidivism using police, court, and parole records. For example, Warren et al. (2019) utilized a variety of different types of archival data to assess the effects of racial and ethnic threat on sentencing departures for female defendants. Specifically, they utilized the 2003–2012

archival records
a source of operational definitions that consists of existing documents and institutional records

Florida Sentencing Guidelines and the Florida Department of Corrections' Offender Based Information System to obtain information on offender characteristics and criminal history. To capture county-level characteristics, the 2000 Census data were used to match respondents with the county in which they were sentenced. Lastly, the researchers utilized data from the Uniform Crime Report (UCR) to match crime rates with county context in order to assess its influence on sentencing departures. Combined, the data allowed for the researchers to examine the effect of both individual and contextual factors on sentencing departures. We have much more to say about the use of archival records in Chapter 11; here we focus on them in the context of operationalization.

An example of an operational definition based on statistics is the dissimilarity index, which measures residential segregation. The dissimilarity index[1] indicates the degree to which two groups (e.g., Black people and White people) are evenly spread throughout a given geographical area such as a city; more precisely, it gives the percentage of either group that would have to move to produce zero segregation. An index of 0 for a city would indicate that the percentage of Black people living in each neighborhood is the same as the percentage living in any other, so no one would have to move. An index of 100 indicates that Black people live in exclusively Black neighborhoods, and White people in exclusively White neighborhoods, so that 100 percent of either group (Black people or White people) would have to move to a different neighborhood for the groups to be spread evenly throughout the city. Values below 30 are considered low, and values above 60 are considered high (Logan & Stults, 2011, p. 25). Researchers exploring the relationship between racial, ethnic, and/or socioeconomic residential segregation and crime often utilize the dissimilarity index to measure residential segregation (e.g., Akins, 2009; Stacey, 2019).

Another example of operational definitions derived from archival records, specifically mass media, comes from a study by Dixon (2017), which assessed whether racial representations of police officers, perpetrators, and crime victims were being accurately displayed on local news channels. To operationalize race/ethnicity, for each news report, coders identified the victim, perpetrator, and officer as either African American, White, Latino, or Other. Coders relied primarily on physical characteristics shown during the newscast to determine race/ethnicity. To determine whether officers, perpetrators, and victims were being accurately represented in terms of race, the television portrayals were compared with perpetration and victim rates contained in data

---

[1] The formula for the Index of Dissimilarity measuring the segregation of White people from Black people in a city is:

½ Σ|(b$_i$/B) − (w$_i$/W)|, where
b$_i$ = the Black population in the ith neighborhood
B = the total Black population of the city
w$_i$ = the White population in the ith neighborhood
W = the total White population of the city

published by the California Department of Justice and the *Los Angeles Times*. Further, employment records published by the Los Angeles Police Department and Los Angeles Sheriff's Department were used to compare television portrayals of Los Angeles police officers. The data showed that African Americans were being accurately portrayed across all roles, while Latinos continued to be underrepresented as victims and officers. Consistent with previous research, White people received the most positive crime roles in the news, being overrepresented as homicide victims and officers on television news compared with official reports.

Finally, new forms of technology can also facilitate operationalization via archival records. For example, you may recall hearing a lot about "mobility data" during the COVID-19 pandemic. Collected through people's use of map and other applications on their cell phones, these data are aggregated to different geographical levels and can be made available to researchers. Using aggregate and anonymized mobility data for 25 counties in the US, Hamada Badr, and colleagues (2020) found that increased levels of mobility were associated with the growth of COVID-19 cases in these areas. In criminal justice, researchers are beginning to utilize mobility data as a tool for enhancing crime prediction (Kader & Pletikosa, 2018; Wu et al., 2022).

SUMMARY

There are two main sources of operational definitions: manipulated operations and measured operations, the latter of which include self/verbal reports, observation, and archival records. Each of these data sources typifies a general research approach. Experiments always involve manipulated operations; surveys and in-depth interviews involve self-reports, or replies to direct questions; field research involves direct observations of behavior; and the analysis of existing data may include a range of archival records. To check your understanding of the concepts within this section, please refer to Box 6.3.

BOX 6.3

CHECKING YOUR UNDERSTANDING

Operational Definition Review I

1. Manipulated observations estimate existing values or categories
    a. True
    b. False

continues

continued

2. Measured operations include which of the following?
    a. Self/verbal reports
    b. Observation
    c. Archival records
    d. All of the above

3. Warren et al. (2019) utilized the Florida Sentencing Guidelines and the Florida Department of Corrections' Offender Based Information System to obtain information on offender characteristics and criminal history. This is an example of
    a. Self/verbal reports
    b. Manipulated operations
    c. Archival records
    d. Observations

4. Ariel et al. (2015) randomly assigned officers into experimental and control shifts. Officers on the experimental shifts wore body cameras, while those on the control shift did not. This is an example of
    a. Self/verbal reports
    b. Manipulated operations
    c. Archival records
    d. Observations

Answers: 1. b, 2. d, 3. c, 4. b

6.4 VARIATIONS IN OPERATIONAL DEFINITIONS: LEVELS OF MEASUREMENT

Operational definitions specify procedures for sorting units into different categories (Davis 1971), such as the presence or absence of the use-of-force (as in Ariel et al., 2015) and amount of money displayed in the address window of an envelope set as either 5, 10, or 100 euros (as in Keuschnigg & Wolbring, 2015). Aside from the number of categories, another important way in which categories vary is in terms of their level of measurement. The four general levels usually identified are nominal, ordinal, interval, and ratio measurement. These levels indicate the kind of inferences you can make when you compare units (people, objects, or events) in different variable categories, which determines how the variables may be analyzed (Stevens, 1946). As we explain in this section, for example, it makes a difference whether you operationalize use of force by indicating (1) whether use of force was reported or not (nominal) or (2) the number of use of force incidents reported (ratio).

Nominal Measurement

The lowest level, **nominal measurement**, is a system in which cases are classified into two or more categories on some variable. As you may recall, Ariel et al. (2015) classified use of force into two categories as one indicator of use of force: whether force was used in a given shift or whether it was not. Other examples of variables that typically have a nominal level of measurement include race, religious preference, and political party preference.

In nominal measurement, the numbers are assigned to the categories simply as labels or codes for the researcher's convenience in collecting and analyzing data. For example, Ariel et al. (2015) likely would have assigned the number "1" to shifts where force was used and the number "0" to shifts where force was not used. Similarly, political party preference might be classified as:

1. Democrat
2. Republican
3. Independent
4. Other
5. No preference

Since we are merely using numbers as labels, no mathematical relationships are possible at the nominal level. We cannot say that 1 + 2 = 3 (Democrat plus Republican equals Independent) or that 1 < 2 (Democrats are "lower" on political preference than Republicans). We can say, however, that all 1s share the same political preference and that 1s differ from 2s in their political preference. With nominal measurement, the empirical rule for assigning cases to categories is that cases placed in the same category must be equivalent.

Nominal measurement has two characteristics that apply to all levels of measurement: variables must be both exhaustive and mutually exclusive. To be **exhaustive** means that the categories are sufficient, so that virtually all persons, events, or objects being classified will fit into one of the categories. The following set of categories for the variable "religious preference" does not meet the exhaustiveness criterion:

1. Protestant
2. Catholic

You can probably think of other categories that would need to be added to make this measure exhaustive: Jewish, Muslim, Hindu, Buddhist, other religions, or no religious preference at all. Even if one expected few non-Catholic or non-Protestant respondents, one would at least need to add the categories "None" and "Other" to cover all the possibilities.

nominal measurement a level of measurement in which numbers serve only to label categories of a variable

exhaustive the measurement requirement that a measure includes all possible values or categories of a variable so that every case can be classified

mutual exclusivity the measurement requirement that each case can be placed in one and only one category of a variable

The criterion of **mutual exclusivity** means that the persons or things being classified must not fit into more than one category. Suppose that a researcher hastily came up with the following categories for the variable "place of residence":

1. Urban
2. Suburban
3. Rural
4. Farm

You can see that some persons would fit into both categories 3 and 4. The following set of categories would be an improvement:

1. Urban
2. Suburban
3. Rural, farm
4. Rural, nonfarm

In the revised categories, the rural farmer would be able to easily identify the response category that best represents their place of residence (Option 3).

Ordinal Measurement

ordinal measurement a level of measurement in which different numbers indicate rank order of cases on a variable

In **ordinal measurement**, numbers indicate the *rank order* of cases on some variable. Psychologist S. S. Stevens (1946), who developed the idea of measurement level, used hardness of minerals as an example of ordinal measurement. We can determine the hardness of any two minerals by scratching one against the other: harder stones scratch softer ones. By this means we could number a set of stones, say five, from 1 to 5 according to their hardness. The numbers thus assigned, however, would represent nothing more than the *order* of categories. We could not say how much greater (or harder) one category is than another. Rather, we would only be able to say that one rock is softer or harder than another rock.

A common ordinal measure used within criminal justice research is a Likert scale. Likert scales, commonly used within survey research, provide 5–7 response options that an individual can choose from to indicate their opinion on a given topic. For example, a restaurant survey may ask visitors to indicate their satisfaction with their visit on a scale from "very unsatisfied" to "very satisfied." In the example below, the Attitudes toward Prisoners survey includes a number of indicators that utilize Likert scales.

The Attitudes toward Prisoners survey developed by Melvin, Gramling, and Gardner (1985) and modified by Schaefer and Williams (2018) consisted of 36 questions, all using an ordinal level of measurement. The survey measured probation and parole staff members' attitudes toward the offenders they supervised by providing statements such as, "Most offenders are victims of circumstance and deserve to be helped." Probation and parole staff members responded to each statement on a scale of 0 to 6, with the number "0" indicating that the participant *strongly disagreed* with the statement and the number "6" indicating that the participant *strongly agreed* with the statement. The numerical "ranking" here simply refers to the amount of agreement with each statement: smaller numbers indicate less agreement and greater numbers indicate more.

The study by Schaefer and Williams (2018) utilized another survey that included several ordinal level variables. They asked the probation and parole staff members to complete the Maslach Burnout Inventory developed by Maslach and Jackson (1981) to measure job burnout and stress. The burnout inventory consisted of several statements, such as "Working with offenders all day is a real strain for me," and participants were to indicate how frequently they experience these feelings as a result of their jobs. The responses again ranged from 0 to 6:

- 0 = never
- 1 = a few times a year
- 2 = once a month or less
- 3 = a few times a month
- 4 = once a week
- 5 = a few times a week
- 6 = everyday

Again, the numerical "ranking" of the responses refers to the frequency with which they experience certain feelings: smaller numbers indicate experiencing the feelings less often while larger numbers indicate experiencing the feeling more often.

One virtue of ordinal measurement, as Julian Simon and Paul Burstein (1985) note, is "that people can often make an accurate judgment about one thing *compared to another*, even when they cannot make an accurate *absolute* judgment" (p. 208). The ability of human observers to make comparative judgments permits a wide range of reasonably accurate social measurements at the ordinal level—for example, measures of socioeconomic status, intelligence, political liberalism, various preference ratings, and attitude and opinion scales. On the other hand, ordinal measurement is still rather crude. At this level, we cannot perform most mathematical (statistical) operations in analyzing the data. We cannot add, subtract, multiply, or divide; we can only rank things: 1 < 2, 2 < 3, 1 < 3, and so on.

Interval Measurement

Interval measurement has the qualities of the nominal and ordinal levels plus the requirement that equal distances or intervals between "numbers" represent equal distances in the variable being measured. An example is the Fahrenheit temperature scale: the difference between 20°F and 30°F is the same as the difference between 90°F and 100°F—a difference of 10°. We can infer not only that 100°F is hotter than 90°F but also how much hotter it is. What enables us to make this inference is the establishment

interval measurement a level of measurement that has the qualities of the ordinal level plus equal distances (intervals) between assigned numbers of a standard measurement unit, or metric. For Fahrenheit temperature, the metric is degrees; similarly, time is measured in seconds, length in feet or meters, and US income in US dollars. When numbers represent a metric, the measurement is "quantitative" in the ordinary sense of the word (Stevens, 1946, p. 679). Thus, we can perform basic mathematical operations such as addition and subtraction.

However, we cannot multiply or divide at the interval level. We cannot say, for example, that 100°F is twice as hot as 50°F or that 20°F is one-half as hot as 40°F. The reason is that interval measures do not have a true or absolute zero but an arbitrary one. That is, the zero point on the scale does not signify the absence of the property being measured. Zero degrees Fahrenheit does not mean that there is no temperature; it is simply an arbitrary point on the scale. Its arbitrariness is illustrated by the comparison with another interval scale designed to measure the property of temperature: 0°F equals about −18°C (Celsius or centigrade), and 0°C equals 32°F.

Although social researchers may aim to create interval measures, most of what passes for this level of measurement is only a very rough approximation. IQ score, for example, is sometimes treated as an interval-level measure, even though it makes no sense to add IQ scores or to infer that equal numerical intervals have the same meaning. (Is the difference between IQ scores of 180 and 190 equal to the difference between 90 and 100?) Pure interval-level measures are hard to find in the social sciences, which is why we used temperature as an example. Most variables in the social sciences with equal intervals between numbers have ratio measurement.

Ratio Measurement

The fourth level, called **ratio measurement**, includes the features of the other levels plus an absolute (nonarbitrary) zero point. The presence of an absolute zero makes it possible to multiply and divide scale numbers meaningfully and thereby form ratios. The variable income, measured in US dollars, has this property. Given incomes of $20,000 and $40,000, we can divide one into the other (i.e., form a ratio) to signify that one is twice (or one-half) as much as the other.

Many measures in social research have a well-defined metric and a zero point that meaningfully signifies none of the property being measured. Besides income, other examples are age in years, number of siblings, and years of employment. Ratio-level measures often are obtained by simply counting—for example, number of callbacks for interviews, number of siblings, number of people in a social network. In criminal justice research, examples include number of complaints filed against police officers (Ariel et al., 2015), number of flyers discarded on the ground (Keuschnigg & Wolbring, 2015), and crime seriousness as measured by "the number of points associated with the offense for which the defendant was convicted" (Warren et al., 2019, p. 14). Also, aggregate variables, which characterize collectivities of people, frequently are measured at this level by counting and then dividing by a population base. Some examples are crime

---

ratio measurement the highest level of measurement, which has the features of the other levels plus an absolute (nonarbitrary) zero point

6.4 Variations in Operational Definitions: Levels of Measurement

Table 6.1 Information Provided by the Four Levels of Measurement

Information provided	Nominal	Ordinal	Interval	Ratio
Classification	X	X	X	X
Rank order		X	X	X
Equal intervals			X	X
Absolute (nonarbitrary) zero				X

rate (number of crimes reported to the police per 100,000 people in the total population), divorce rate (number of divorces per 1,000 existing marriages), percentage of labor force unemployed, and percentage Democrat.

SUMMARY

An important variation in operational definitions is their level of measurement. Operational definitions may produce four different levels: nominal, ordinal, interval, and ratio. The four levels themselves form an ordinal scale with regard to the amount of information they provide. Each level has the features of the level(s) below it plus something else. Table 6.1 illustrates this. In most social science research, however, the distinction between interval and ratio levels of measurement is not very important compared with the differences between the interval and nominal or ordinal levels. Indeed, Chapter 12 distinguishes statistical analyses appropriate for nominal/ordinal vs. interval/ratio measures. See Box 6.4 to check your understanding of concepts within this section.

BOX 6.4

CHECKING YOUR UNDERSTANDING

Inferring Level of Measurement from Operational Definitions

How do you infer the level of measurement of a variable? You should keep in mind two important points. First, measurement level depends on the operational definition because a given variable may be measured at more than one level. A field researcher may form an ordinal measure of age, for example, by using people's appearance, manner, and other observed characteristics to classify them as "children," "young adults,"

continues

continued

"middle-aged," and "seniors." Or date-of-birth information might be used to measure age as a ratio scale.

Second, measurement level depends on the kinds of inferences that can be made when comparing units in different variable categories. Consider income. A common way of operationalizing this variable is to ask respondents, "How much money did you earn last year from all sources—that is, before taxes or other deductions?" and then present them with a set of categories, such as the following:

1. Less than $25,000
2. $25,000 to $49,999
3. $50,000 to $74,999
4. $75,000 to $99,999
5. $100,000 to $149,999
6. $150,000 to $199,999
7. $200,000 to $299,999
8. $300,000 or more

Now, what kind of inferences can you make if you compare people in different categories, say 3 and 5? (Think about this before reading further.) Clearly, you can infer that (1) they have different incomes and (2) one earns more than the other. But can you infer precisely how much more the person in Category 5 earns than the person in Category 3? No. Because of the range of possible incomes in each category, the difference could be as low as $25,001 ($100,000–$74,999) or as high as $99,999 ($149,999–$50,000). Therefore, this operational definition signifies ordinal measurement.

Below is a list of variables together with possible operational definitions based on self-reports. To check your understanding of level of measurement, identify the level of each. Be sure to think about what kind of inferences you could make when you compare persons or units in different categories.

1. *Educational attainment:* Ask respondents to check one of the following categories: eighth grade or less; ninth to eleventh grade; high school graduate; some college; college graduate.

2. *Religious preference:* What is your religious preference? Is it Protestant, Catholic, Jewish, another religion, or no religion?

3. *Attitude toward corporal punishment:* Do you strongly agree, agree, disagree, or strongly disagree that it is sometimes necessary to discipline a child with a good, hard spanking?

4. *Television viewing:* On the average day, about how many hours do you personally watch television?

5. *Educational attainment:* How many years of formal education have you completed?

Answers: 1. ordinal, 2. nominal, 3. ordinal, 4. ratio, 5. ratio

6.5 SELECT AND APPLY OPERATIONAL DEFINITIONS TO PRODUCE DATA

Now that you are familiar with sources of operational definitions and levels of measurement, how do you decide on an appropriate operational definition? Ultimately, the most basic requirement is to select an operational definition that fits the concept well, although this is often easier said than done. (See Steidl and Werum (2019) for an excellent discussion of some of the difficulties of operationalization.) Recall the carrot cake example: How could you be certain that your friend's recipe represents an authentic carrot cake? If your friend's recipe calls for walnuts, does that make them an essential ingredient? Suppose you used two large eggs instead of three as called for in your friend's recipe. Would you still have a carrot cake? What if you set the oven temperature to 400° instead of 350°? In the end, you would find that there is no correct recipe. Instead, you would have to decide for yourself whether your friend's operational definition (recipe) corresponded to your concept of what makes a carrot cake.

Similarly in social research, no operational definition can capture a concept's meaning perfectly or completely. However, this does not license the researcher to select just any measure. It is still desirable to get the best possible fit between concept and measure, and the best way to do this is by carefully considering the meaning of the concept as it relates to the theory in which it is embedded.

An example of a study in which theory guided the selection of an appropriate operational definition is Keuschnigg and Wolbring's test (2015) of Wilson and Kelling's (1982) broken windows theory, which states that physical and social disorder contributes to further norm violations leading to an increase in disorder. In turn, proponents of broken windows theory would argue that to curb disorder and crime, signs of disorder or disrepair must be removed or repaired promptly. Keuschnigg and Wolbring

(2015) conducted several experimental studies in which they manipulated conditions to determine the effects of physical and social disorder on norm violations (i.e., littering, stealing, jaywalking). As a reminder, this would be an example of a manipulated operation because the researchers are changing the categories of the variable. For their first experiment on the impact of social disorder on littering, the researchers attached flyers to dormitory residents' bicycles offering an incentive to litter. They conducted the experiment in a control setting which was clean as well as an experimental setting that was heavily littered. Thus, physical disorder was operationalized by the manipulated settings (i.e., clean vs. heavily littered). Norm violations were operationalized through the observation of the number of littered flyers (i.e., flyers left on the ground). The results showed that norm violations (i.e., littering) were higher in areas that were already heavily littered as compared to the clean areas, thus confirming the broken windows hypothesis.

Often, there is a disconnect between theoretical and operational definitions. For example, many criminological theories posit that peer delinquency is a predictor of individual delinquency. However, measuring peer delinquency is often problematic as research relies on respondents' perceptions of peer delinquency rather than direct measures of peer delinquency. Research has found that using respondents' perceptions of peer delinquency is flawed, as it is likely just a reflection of individual respondents' delinquency. Thus, studies that operationalize peer delinquency using respondents' perception of their peers' delinquency is actually measuring something different. One specific study by Meldrum and Boman (2013) found that self-reported delinquency from peers is inconsistent with respondents' perceptions of peer delinquency confirming the uniqueness of these two measures.

Though theory should guide your selection of an operational definition, selecting an operational definition also depends on your general research approach (experiments, surveys, field research, in-depth interviews, or existing data analysis). The approach you choose will determine the primary source of data and measurement, although some approaches may use more than one data source. We have more to say about measurement in chapters on each approach and in Chapter 13 on multiple methods.

Once you have selected a particular approach, another consideration is the number of variable categories and their level of measurement. Referring back to the study by Schaefer and Williams (2018), they utilized the Maslach Burnout Inventory which asked respondents to self-report the frequency with which they experienced feelings of strain, stress, and burnout. The response options ranged from zero ("never") to six ("everyday"). Therefore, they could analyze this type of burnout in terms of frequency of experiences or analyze it in terms of whether they ever experienced strain, stress, or burnout while on the job (= "a few times a year" to "everyday") or not (= "never"). Recall this is an example of a measured operation, as it comes from a self-report inventory.

If you are creating your own operational definitions, you need to determine how precise your measures need to be. As a general rule, we recommend creating a set of categories that will produce as much information as possible, which often means greater precision and a higher level of measurement. For example, it is usually better to ask respondents when they were born, which creates a ratio measure of age (current date–date of birth) than to provide a list of categories such as under 20, 20–29, 30–39, and so on, which creates an ordinal measure. However, survey researchers sometimes sacrifice precision to form questions that are clearer and more likely to be answered accurately. In operationalizing personal income, for example, research shows that respondents are less likely to answer questions requesting the exact amount that they earned than questions that provide a range of income categories (Yan et al., 2010).

Once you have decided on a theoretically appropriate operational definition in the context of your research approach, applying this definition to produce data creates *measures*. In the next section, we discuss methods of analyzing the measures to assess the quality of measurement. You can practice identifying variables and selecting empirical indicators in Box 6.5.

BOX 6.5

PRACTICE WHAT YOU LEARNED

Identify Variables and Empirical Indicators

Using the same hypothesis as the previous Practice What You Learned (Box 6.1, and listed again below), identify a variable to measure each concept. For each variable, provide an empirical indicator and spell out the procedures by which these indicators will be applied.

Hypothesis: Adolescents who are more involved in school will be less likely to engage in delinquent behavior.

SUMMARY

Researchers try to select operational definitions that best capture the meaning of the concept being measured. How you choose to operationalize a concept also depends on the data source or general methodological approach and the desired level of measurement. Use Box 6.6 to assess your understanding of the concepts within this section.

> **BOX 6.6**
>
> **CHECKING YOUR UNDERSTANDING**
>
> ## Operational Definition Review II
>
> 1. An operational definition always captures a concept's meaning perfectly and completely.
>   a. True
>   b. False
>
> 2. There is often a disconnect between theoretical definitions and operational definitions.
>   a. True
>   b. False
>
> 3. Respondents' perceptions of their peers' delinquency is an accurate measure of peer delinquency.
>   a. True
>   b. False
>
> 4. Both manipulated and measured operations can be theoretically appropriate.
>   a. True
>   b. False
>
> **Answers: 1. b, 2. a, 3. b, 4. a**

6.6 ASSESS THE QUALITY OF OPERATIONAL DEFINITIONS

In deductive inquiry, the final step in the measurement process is to assess the quality of one's operational definitions. Initially, assessment is subjective, based on the investigator's personal judgment of how well an operational definition fits the theoretical meaning of the relevant concept. And, sometimes, as in the case of variables like age, this may be satisfactory. But once you have applied an operational definition to generate data, there are more objective ways to evaluate its quality. Social scientists apply two criteria in evaluating measurement: reliability and validity.

Reliability is concerned with questions of stability and consistency: Is the operational definition measuring "something" consistently and dependably, whatever that "something" may be? Do you get the same results each time you apply the operational definition under similar conditions? If the operational definition is formed from a set of

reliability the stability or consistency of an operational definition responses or items, are the component responses or items consistent with each other? An example of a highly reliable measuring instrument is a steel tape measure. When you use it repeatedly to measure the length of a piece of wood 20 inches long, you will get, with negligible variation, 20 inches every time. Further, someone else measuring the same object should get the same results you do. A cloth tape measure would be somewhat less reliable because it may vary with humidity and temperature and you can expect some variation in measurements depending on how loosely or tightly the tape is stretched. Even less reliable would be an "eyeball measure"—that is, an estimate based on sight; chances are that two individuals could come up with widely different eyeball estimates of an object's length.

Measurement validity refers to the similarity or "goodness of fit" between an operational definition and the concept it is purported to measure. Does this operational definition truly reflect what the concept means? Are you measuring what you intend to measure with this operational definition? If so, you have a valid measure. An example of a valid measure is amniocentesis, a prenatal test performed in some pregnancies that reveals information about the health of the unborn child. Although generally used to detect genetic disorders, amniocentesis also reveals the baby's sex. It is a valid measure of biological sex because it indicates with near perfect accuracy whether the unborn child will be a male or a female. At one time, a number of invalid "measures" of the unborn child's sex existed in the form of folk wisdoms. One belief, for example, involves tying a string to the pregnant woman's wedding band and holding the band suspended over her abdomen. If the band swings in a circle, the baby will be a girl; if the band swings back and forth, it will be a boy.

Of the two criteria for assessing measurement quality, validity is more critical. Reliability is important; indeed, it is a necessary condition for validity. That is, a highly unreliable measure cannot be valid—how can you measure something accurately if the results fluctuate wildly? But a very reliable measure still may not be valid, because you could be measuring very reliably (consistently) something other than what you intended to measure. To take a facetious example, let us suppose we decide to measure the "intelligence" of students by standing them on a bathroom scale and reading the number off the dial (Davis, 1971, p. 14). Such an operational definition would be highly reliable, as repeated scale readings would yield consistent results. However, this obviously would not be a valid measure of an individual's intelligence.

The relationship between reliability and validity is illustrated in Figure 6.4, which displays a target. Measurement is an attempt to hit the bullseye, which represents the theoretical definition of the concept. A tight pattern, irrespective of its location

measurement validity the goodness of fit between an operational definition and the concept it is purported to measure

Low reliability   High reliability   High reliability
Low validity   Low validity   High validity

FIGURE 6.4 Analogy of Target to Reliability and Validity

on the target, reflects a reliable measure because it is consistent. Validity is a reflection, however, of how closely the shots cluster about the bullseye.

Researchers have devised several ways to assess the reliability and validity of operational definitions. To illustrate these forms of assessment, we will frequently reference Morris Rosenberg's (1965) Self-Esteem Scale, which Oser (2006) and many other researchers have used. Oser (2006) examined the relationship between self-esteem and crime, operationalizing self-esteem by using the 10-item Rosenberg Self-Esteem Scale. Each item is actually a statement, to which respondents are asked to indicate their level of agreement, as shown here.

	Strongly agree	Agree	Disagree	Strongly disagree
1. I take a positive attitude toward myself.	[ ]	[ ]	[ ]	[ ]
2. I feel I am a person of worth, at least on an equal plane with others.	[ ]	[ ]	[ ]	[ ]
3. I am able to do things as well as most other people.	[ ]	[ ]	[ ]	[ ]
4. On the whole, I am satisfied with myself.	[ ]	[ ]	[ ]	[ ]
5. I feel that I have a number of good qualities.	[ ]	[ ]	[ ]	[ ]
6. I certainly feel useless at times.*	[ ]	[ ]	[ ]	[ ]
7. At times I think I am no good at all.*	[ ]	[ ]	[ ]	[ ]
8. I feel I do not have much to be proud of.*	[ ]	[ ]	[ ]	[ ]
9. I wish I could have more respect for myself.*	[ ]	[ ]	[ ]	[ ]
10. All in all, I am inclined to feel that I am a failure.*	[ ]	[ ]	[ ]	[ ]

*Indicates an item that is a negative statement about the self.

Notice that the first five items are positive statements about the self, and the last five items, indicated by an asterisk, are negative. Agreement with positive statements suggests "high" self-esteem, whereas agreement with negative statements indicates "low" self-esteem. To take this into account, values between 1 and 4 are assigned to the response categories, with a 4 representing strong agreement with a positive statement about the self (or, conversely, strong disagreement with a negative statement). For example, for item 1, "strongly agree" = 4, "agree" = 3, "disagree" = 2, and "strongly disagree" = 1; for item 6, "strongly agree" = 1, "agree" = 2, and so forth. An individual's responses to these 10 items are then added together to produce a single scale score that could range from 10 (low self-esteem) to 40 (high self-esteem). (If you wish, you can take the full, 10-question Rosenberg self-esteem survey online. From some websites, you will receive a score. At least one website, however, also asks you for consent to use your score for research purposes.)

You may notice that what we are describing seems a lot like an index, defined earlier, but we refer to it as a **scale**. To understand why, see Box 6.7.

scale the combination of several indicators to measure a single dimension of a concept

unidimensionality a concept that measures just one dimension

BOX 6.7

READING CRIMINAL JUSTICE RESEARCH

Indexes, Scales, and Scaling Techniques

As we have noted, researchers frequently combine indicators to create an index or scale. Indexes and scales condense or reduce the data generated by multiple indicators into a single number or scale score. This not only simplifies the analysis but also increases the precision and provides a means of assessing the quality of the measurement.

There is a difference, however, between an index and a scale. An index usually refers to the arbitrary combination of indicators, such as when we simply add together the responses to separate items without regard to what each actually contributes to the measurement of the underlying concept. The chief problem with an index is that it may be measuring more than the intended concept. In other words, it lacks **unidimensionality**. Recall Keuschnigg and Wolbring's (2015) study of broken windows theory in which they used an index of local social capital to differentiate between dormitories that had high and low social capital. The index contained 13 items asking about relatedness to others, frequency of shared activities, depth of contact, and perceived cohesion among individuals living in their dorm. Although this may measure social capital, it is possible that it also measures the extent to which an individual is an extrovert or an introvert, whether the individual is too busy to engage with their dorm, and so forth.

A scale, on the other hand, combines indicators according to theoretical or empirical criteria that are ordinarily designed to reflect only a single dimension of a concept. Rosenberg's Self-Esteem Scale is an example: it is designed to only measure self-esteem. The construction of scales assumes that a concept can be understood in terms of an underlying continuum; in the case of an attitude, the continuum may range from favorable to unfavorable or positive to negative. It is further assumed that scores on individual items and composite measures represent specific points along the relevant continuum (or "scale"). Each score, in other words, should uniquely reflect the strength or degree of something, such as an individual's self-esteem. But whereas these assumptions are implicit in an index, scaling procedures make them explicit and are designed to test their validity.

Various scaling procedures have been developed. Some capitalize on each item's placement with regard to an underlying continuum, whereas others capitalize on the inherent pattern among a set of items. One scaling technique, *summated ratings*, assumes that each scale item reflects the entire range of the

continues

continued

> underlying continuum to the same degree. For many summated ratings scales, the response options for each item vary from "strongly agree" to "strongly disagree." Each item thus constitutes a separate rating, and an individual's score consists of the sum of his or her ratings (hence the label "summated ratings").
>
> To illustrate another scaling technique, *cumulative scaling*, we will describe the approach developed by Louis Guttman (1974). A cumulative scale is designed so that each item represents a particular point on the underlying dimension. Because the set of items is ordered and *cumulative*, an individual's total scale score not only denotes a place on the underlying dimension but also reveals his or her responses to each and every item. For example, suppose we measure people's reading ability by testing their reading comprehension of items ordered in terms of difficulty, such as portions of a third-grade reader, a ninth-grade textbook, and a college textbook. Participants would be tested on each item starting with the easiest, and the item at which someone changed from "passing" to "failing" the reading tests would indicate the subject's position on a scale of reading ability. Four response patterns are expected if the items form a perfect Guttman scale: (1) flunk each item, (2) pass only at the third-grade level, (3) pass all but the college text, and (4) pass all reading tests. Other response patterns, such as passing the ninth-grade test and flunking the other two, are called "nonscale" or "mixed types." By selecting a set of items that minimize the proportion of "nonscale" response patterns, the Guttman approach attempts to ensure a unidimensional scale.

Is the Rosenberg Self-Esteem Scale reliable? Is it a valid measure of "self-esteem"? As you will see, numerous studies provide answers to these questions.

Forms of Reliability Assessment

The three principal methods of reliability assessment are test-retest reliability, internal consistency, and inter-coder reliability.

TEST-RETEST RELIABILITY

test-retest reliability the association between repeated applications of an operational definition

The simplest way of assessing the reliability of operational definitions is **test-retest reliability**, which involves measuring (or "testing") the same persons or units on two separate occasions. For example, a researcher might administer the self-esteem scale to the same group of incarcerated individuals on consecutive days. The statistical correlation between the sets of "scores" obtained from the two measurements serves as an estimate of reliability. Such correlations range from 0 (indicating a completely unreliable measure) to 1.00 (indicating a perfectly reliable measure—that is, each incarcerated individual's score on the first day was the same as their score on the second day). Table 6.2 presents hypothetical data for five people on Rosenberg's Self-Esteem Scale, with scores recorded over two days.

For the test-retest procedure, correlation tends to be high, with anything less than .80 considered dangerously low for most measurement purposes. In the hypothetical data

Table 6.2 Self-Esteem Scores Among Five Incarcerated Individuals

Person	1	2	3	4	5
Self-Esteem Score (Monday)	25	20	13	10	18
Self-Esteem Score (Tuesday)	19	22	13	12	18

in Table 6.2, the correlation is .84. Test-retest reliability checks of the self-esteem scale have produced correlation coefficients of .82 to .88 for 1- and 2-week intervals (Gray-Little et al., 1997; Rosenberg, 1979). However, test-retest reliability coefficients for this scale are much lower for longer periods of 6 months (.63) and 1 year (.50) (Gray-Little et al., 1997).

Although it is simple in principle, the test-retest method is seldom used for several reasons. First, either the persons responding to questions or the persons recording observations may remember and simply repeat the responses they gave the first time, thereby inflating the reliability estimate. Second, real change in the concept being measured may occur in the interim between the two "tests." In attitude measurement, new experiences or new information may result in a shift in attitude. For example, positive or negative experiences between the administrations of the two surveys may raise or lower a respondent's self-esteem. Say for instance, an individual completed a GED program in between completions of the self-esteem scale. The data from the second administration would likely be much higher than data from the first, thus impacting the reliability of the measure. Because such true changes are inseparable from test-retest inconsistency, they falsely lower the reliability estimate. Third, the test-retest method often is impractical, as it requires time and resources to apply a measure more than once to the same group of respondents.

INTERNAL CONSISTENCY

The second method of reliability assessment, **internal consistency**, avoids the practical problem of repeating applications of the same operational definition; however, this method only applies to composite measures based on multiple items, such as the self-esteem scale. Rather than obtain a stability estimate based on consistency over time, as in test-retest reliability, this method estimates the agreement or equivalence among the constituent items of a multi-item measure. If we assume that each item represents the same underlying concept, a lack of agreement among the items would indicate low reliability. Table 6.3 illustrates the basic notion of internal consistency among 10 items in the self-esteem scale for five people.

Like the test-retest estimate, internal consistency estimates yield coefficients that run from 0 to 1.00. The most common measure of internal consistency is

internal consistency a form of reliability assessment; the consistency of "scores" across all the items of a composite measure (i.e., index or scale)

Table 6.3 Internal Consistency Among Responses to 10 Items

	Item #1	Item #2	Item #3	Item #4	Item #5	Item #6	Item #7	Item #8	Item #9	Item #10	Total Score
Person #1	4	3	4	4	3	4	3	4	3	4	36
Person #2	3	2	3	3	3	3	3	2	3	3	28
Person #3	2	3	2	2	2	1	1	2	3	1	19
Person #4	1	3	1	2	1	1	1	1	1	2	14
Person #5	4	1	2	4	2	2	3	4	1	2	25

Cronbach's alpha
a statistical index of internal consistency reliability that ranges from 0 (unreliable) to 1 (perfectly reliable)

Cronbach's alpha, which is based on the average of the correlations among the responses to all possible pairs of items. Numerous studies have reported Cronbach's alpha for the self-esteem scale, ranging from a low of .72 for a sample of men 60 years or older to a high of .88 for a group of college students (Gray-Little et al., 1997). For the hypothetical data in Table 6.3, Cronbach's alpha = .91.

INTER-RATER RELIABILITY

A third method of reliability assessment, **inter-rater reliability** (also called **inter-coder reliability**), examines the extent to which different observers or coders using the same instrument or measure get the same results. This method often is used to assess the reliability of observational and archival measures, where it is important to show that the data are not affected by the subjectivity of observers or raters. The assumption is that no matter who applies an operational definition, they should get the same scores or values. If two or more observers disagree, this suggests that the measure is unreliable. When Fouts, Callan, Piasentin, and Lawson (2006) measured the prevalence of demonizing in children's television and movies by coding references to 13 different words related to evil such as *monster, wicked, demon, devil,* or *evil,* they checked the inter-rater reliability of their coding scheme by having two researchers code a sample of the movies and television shows. They reported acceptable levels of agreement for all variables, with correlations of .88 and above.

▲ **PHOTO 6.1** Inter-rater Reliability in Action: Any given bird sighting might have everyone agreeing on what kind of bird they saw, or one or more members of the party disagreeing.

IMPROVING RELIABILITY

Partly because of the impracticality of applying the same measure twice to the same group of cases, the reliability of single-item self-reports is seldom checked. However, for composite measures, such as the self-esteem scale, researchers usually perform checks on internal consistency. It also is the norm in social research to check for inter-rater reliability whenever it is possible to have more than one observer or rater apply an operational definition. This can be easily carried out in studies where there is a large research team; however, it often is not possible in field studies in which a single individual is doing the research.

What, then, can you do to create the most reliable measures? First, if possible, you should conduct preliminary interviews with a small sample of persons similar to those you intend to study in order to find out whether your measures are clearly understood and interpreted similarly by respondents. The need for preliminary work with actual respondents before the final form of an instrument is completed cannot be overstated. Indeed, it is a topic we will consider again in relation to experiments and survey research. Second, it is not at all necessary to try to "reinvent the wheel" when it comes to measuring most variables. For many common background characteristics (age, level of education, income) and national statistics (economic growth, unemployment rate, poverty rate), survey organizations and the federal government have established standard indicators. And since your research inevitably will build on that of others, you should carefully consider the measures used in prior research. Each of these recommendations also applies to finding the most valid measures.

> **inter-rater reliability** the extent to which different observers or coders get equivalent results when applying the same measure (also called *inter-coder reliability*)

Forms of Validity Assessment

Validity assessment is much more difficult than reliability assessment. You can assess the stability and consistency of a measure without regard to what is actually being measured. By contrast, in assessing validity, the researcher is concerned precisely with what is being measured—with what a concept means theoretically and whether a given operational definition faithfully represents this meaning or something else. In addition, unlike the observation of consistency and stability, validity cannot be assessed directly—if we knew the value of a variable independent of a given measure, then there would be no need for the measure. Thus, validity assessment is indirect, and it generally boils down to one of two methods: convergent validation and construct validation (Adcock & Collier, 2001).

CONVERGENT VALIDATION

Suppose you had a perfectly valid, established measure of a concept. Assessing validity would simply be a matter of checking to see whether the scores obtained with your new operational definition correspond with the scores obtained with an existing one. If we invented a new measure of length, for example, we could easily check its validity by determining whether we get the same results with standard instruments—tape measure, yardstick, transit, and so on—for measuring length. Although there are few standardized measures in the social sciences, there may be alternative measures of the phenomenon under study. **Convergent validation** consists of examining the association between alternative measures of the same concept. An association between different measures is validating because it suggests that the two measures agree, or converge on, the same meaning—namely, the meaning conveyed by the underlying concept.

> **convergent validation** measurement validation based on an accumulation of research evidence indicating that a measure is related to other variables as theoretically expected

There is abundant evidence supporting the convergent validity of the Rosenberg Self-Esteem Scale. For example, based on a sample of 9th- and 10th-graders, David Demo (1985) showed that scores on Rosenberg's scale were positively associated with scores on another popular scale, the Coopersmith Self-Esteem Inventory, and with peer ratings of each individual's self-esteem. Other studies similarly have found positive associations between the Rosenberg Self-Esteem Scale and the Lerner Self-Esteem Scale (Savin-Williams & Jaquish, 1981) and with an indicator of general self-regard (Fleming & Courtney, 1984).

The strongest evidence of convergent validity occurs when one of the alternative measures is a well-established, *direct* measure of the concept. A popular example in criminal justice, and social science generally, is research assessing the validity of self-report measures of drug or alcohol use. Research on the correlates and causes of substance use might be limited by the inaccurate measurement of substance use when using self-report measures. Decades of research have assessed the validity of self-reported substance use by comparing the self-reports to more direct measures of substance use, including reports of parents and friends, polygraph tests, urine analysis, and hair analysis (Harrison, 1997). Urinalysis appears to be a valid, direct method of assessing individuals' substance use. However, studies have varied in agreement between self-reports of substance use and urinalysis results. Generally, individuals self-report less substance use than urinalysis tests detect. The first large-scale study to test the validity of self-reported substance use collected self-reports and urine specimen from individuals recently arrested for serious crimes (Harrison, 1989; National Institute of Justice, 1990 as cited in Harrison, 1997). This study consistently found that only half of those who tested positive for drug use also reported use in the past 2 or 3 days.

> **measurement error** a lack of correspondence between a concept and measure that is due to problems with an operational definition or with its application

> **social desirability** a tendency of respondents to answer self-report measures in a manner that they believe will be viewed as socially desirable by others

Convergent validation is enhanced in two related ways: by using multiple alternative measures and by using measures based on different operational methods (e.g., self-reports and observations). Because different methods are likely to be subject to different sources of bias, one of the most convincing signs of validity is a correspondence of results when a concept is measured in different ways. For

> **BOX 6.8**
>
> **READING CRIMINAL JUSTICE RESEARCH**
>
> ## Measurement Error and the Social Desirability Effect
>
> Validity refers to the accuracy of a measurement. An operational definition that does not match the true value of the concept it is intended to measure results in **measurement error**; this is equivalent to not hitting the bullseye in the target shown in Figure 6.4. A clock that is slow would produce error by overestimating time. Different methods of measurement tend to be subject to different sources of measurement error. Self-report questions may result in error if they are ambiguous or if they are worded in such a way as to encourage agreement rather than truthful answers. Observational measures may be in error if the observations are made at inappropriate places and times.
>
> One particularly vexing source of error in self-reports occurs when respondents are asked about socially approved or disapproved behavior. When asked, "How often do you attend church?" or "Do you exercise regularly?" respondents may inflate their estimates to feel better about themselves or to project a favorable image. And when asked how often they have received a traffic ticket or how often they drink alcoholic beverages, they may underestimate the frequency for the same reasons. This tendency, called the **social desirability effect**, has been demonstrated in numerous studies (Tourangeau et al., 2000).
>
> Another example from the substance abuse research has found further support for the social desirability hypothesis. Sloan, Bodapati, and Tucker (2004) questioned the validity of self-reported drug use hypothesizing that social desirability will impact self-reports. To assess validity, they compared self-reported drug use with urinalysis tests on arrestees. They were particularly interested in determining the characteristics that predict discordance between self-reports and urinalysis. They found that arrestees that use less socially acceptable drugs, such as cocaine, were more likely to misreport their drug use. Similarly, younger arrestees were found to be more likely to misreport their use. These findings support the social desirability hypothesis in the self-report of drug use.

example, self-reports of drug use may be biased by the social desirability effect and the tendency to overestimate socially desirable behavior or underestimate socially undesirable behavior such as drug use, but no such bias exists in a biological specimen. Therefore, a correlation between the two measures provides strong evidence of validity. To learn more about the social desirability bias and other sources of inaccurate measurement, see Box 6.8.

CONSTRUCT VALIDATION

According to the logic of **construct validation**, the meaning of any scientific concept is implied by its theoretical relations with other concepts. To validate an operational definition, therefore, you must first examine the theory underlying the concept being

construct validation measurement validation based on an accumulation of research evidence indicating that a measure is related to other variables as theoretically expected

measured. In light of this theory, you formulate hypotheses about variables that should be (and should not be) related to measures of the concept. Then you gather evidence to test these hypotheses. The more evidence that supports the hypothesized relationships, the greater one's confidence that a particular operational definition is a valid measure of the concept.

An example of construct validation is Rosenberg's validation (1965) of his self-esteem scale. Self-esteem refers to an individual's sense of self-respect or self-worth: those with high self-esteem have self-respect; those with low self-esteem lack it. Rosenberg (1965) reasoned that, if his "scale actually did measure self-esteem," then scores on it should "be associated with other data in a theoretically meaningful way" (p. 18) He then tested several theoretical hypotheses. Let us examine two of them:

1. Students with high self-esteem scores will be chosen more often as leaders by classmates than students with low self-esteem scores. This hypothesis follows from the sociological theory that an individual's self-identity is determined largely by what others think of him or her (Cooley, 1912; Mead, 1934). To test the hypothesis, Rosenberg asked 272 high school seniors, who had completed the self-esteem scale, to identify the person in their English class whom they would be most likely to vote for as the class leader. In support, 47 percent of those with high self-esteem scores received two or more choices as a leader, as compared with 32 percent of those with medium self-esteem scores and 15 percent of those with low self-esteem scores.

2. People with low self-esteem will display more depressive feelings. Supporting the theoretical link between self-esteem and depression, Rosenberg found a strong association when the self-esteem scale and a depression scale were administered to a random sample of 2,695 high school students in New York State. Only four percent of the students who were highest in self-esteem but 80 percent of those who were lowest in self-esteem were identified as "highly depressed."

These and other findings from Rosenberg's study helped to support the construct validity of his self-esteem scale.

Construct validity is not established, however, by confirming one or more hypotheses in a single study. Rather, "construct validation ideally requires a pattern of consistent findings involving different researchers using different" theories to test a range of hypotheses (Carmines & Zeller, 1979, p. 24). By 1990, 25 years after it was first reported in the literature, Rosenberg's Self-Esteem Scale had been used in more than 1,000 research studies (Blascovich & Tomaka, 1991). Many of these studies showed expected associations between self-esteem and other variables. Furthermore, they showed, as predicted, no significant correlations between self-esteem and gender, scores on the Scholastic Aptitude Test (Reynolds, 1988), age, and work experience

Table 6.4 Construct Validation of Rosenberg's Self-Esteem Scale

Self-esteem should be related to…	Self-esteem should NOT be related to…
Peer group ratings of leadership	Gender
(Relative lack of) depressive feelings	SAT scores
	Age
	Work experience

(Fleming & Courtney, 1984). This lack of association also supports the construct validity of the scale because there is no theoretical connection between self-esteem and any of these variables. Table 6.4 summarizes the logic of construct validation as applied to Rosenberg's Self-Esteem Scale.

You can understand the importance of accumulated evidence for establishing construct validity when you consider what would happen if data failed to support a theoretically derived prediction (Carmines & Zeller, 1979). One interpretation is that the operational definition is not a valid measure of the concept. But it also is possible that (1) the theoretical hypothesis is incorrect or (2) the measurements of one or more other variables in the hypothesis lack validity. The logic of construct validation thus depends on solid theoretical predictions and well-measured external variables. And we become increasingly confident in the validity of a measure as repeated tests of theoretical hypotheses are confirmed.

SUMMARY

One criterion by which the quality of an operational definition is assessed is reliability, which refers to the consistency or stability of a measurement. The three major forms of reliability assessment are test-retest reliability, internal consistency, and inter-rater (or inter-coder) reliability. Another criterion by which the quality of an operational definition is assessed is validity, which refers to whether the operational definition is accurately measuring the concept in question. Compared to reliability assessment, validity assessment is more difficult and is often indirect. Two major forms of validity assessment are convergent and construct validation. Both reliability and validity can be improved through repeated tests and by refining operational definitions through data analysis as discussed next. See Box 6.9 to assess your understanding of concepts learned within this section.

BOX 6.9

CHECKING YOUR UNDERSTANDING

Matching Definitions

1. Match the term to the appropriate definition.

Term	Response	Definition
Reliability		a. The extent to which different observers or coders get equivalent results when applying the same measure
Measurement validity		b. Measurement validation based on an accumulation of research evidence indicating that a measure is related to other variables as theoretically expected
Scale		c. The stability or consistency of an operational definition
Inter-rater reliability		d. A composite measure of a concept constructed by combining separate indicators according to procedures designed to ensure unidimensionality or other desirable qualities
Construct validation		e. The goodness of fit between an operational definition and the concept it is purported to measure

Answers: c; e; d; a; b

2. Stacey is conducting a study examining the effects of depression on criminal behavior. She gives a sample of offenders the depression inventory at time 1, and one week later gives the same sample the same depression inventory. This is an example of:
   a. Inter-rater reliability
   b. Convergent validation
   c. Test-retest reliability
   d. Construct validation

3. The terms index and scale are synonymous (i.e., they represent the same thing).
   a. True
   b. False

4. The strongest evidence of convergent validity occurs when independent measures of the same concept are associated with one another, particularly if one of the measures is a well-established direct measure of the concept.
   a. True
   b. False

Answers: 2. c, 3. b, 4. a

6.7 THE FEEDBACK LOOP: FROM DATA BACK TO CONCEPTS AND MEASUREMENT

The measurement process we have outlined so far follows the deductive model of inquiry, providing the critical link between theory and data. In this model, data analysis represents the last stage in answering our research questions and providing evidence of the validity of our operational definitions. But, as we have emphasized, social science is inevitably cyclical, with data also informing theory. In this way, data analysis may contribute to the measurement process by leading to the development of concepts and by refining operational definitions.

In inductive inquiry, researchers do not necessarily decide in advance what concepts to study and how to measure them; rather, they use data from observations and in-depth interviews to develop or refine important concepts. One well-known field researcher in criminology and criminal justice is James Marquart who spent 19 months, June 1981–January 1983, as a guard in a Texas maximum security facility. In one of his published works, he investigated unofficial physical force among guards as a way of informal social control. He collected data through direct observation, records, interviews, and informants. Based on these data, he found that a small yet significant number of correctional officers, many with low-ranking positions, used force in order to control inmates, even when they were not provoked. Further, he observed that this behavior was often learned from their peers and rewarded via promotions. This research helped to refine what behaviors constitute social control within a prison setting. The study also brought light to the prison guard subculture, which later studies have continued to explore.

Another study shows how in-depth interviews may be used to explore the meaning of questions used in the US Census and other government surveys to measure the concept of race. In the 2020 census, respondents were asked the following question: "What is this person's race? Mark one or more boxes." The options are "White," "Black or African American," "American Indian or Alaska Native," seven different choices of Asian, Native Hawaiian or Pacific Islander, and "Some other race." In addition, a separate question asked if the respondent is of "Hispanic, Latino, or Spanish origin." The validity of the race question has been challenged, however, especially as it applies to Hispanic Americans. For many Hispanics, who identify racially with their ethnic group (e.g., Puerto Rican or Mexican) or identify as Hispanic or Latino, the question does not seem to capture how they think about race (Roth, 2010). The 2020 census expanded the question regarding Hispanic origins in order to better measure the diversity of race and ethnicity.

To explore Hispanics' understanding of race and how they answer questions about race, Wendy Roth (2010) conducted in-depth interviews with 60 Dominican and Puerto Rican migrants in the New York metropolitan area. During the course of the interviews, she asked several questions, including the US Census question, designed to measure different aspects of racial identity, including the 2010 Census question that differed slightly from the 2020 question above. Many of her respondents found the census question ambiguous, leading them to answer it in varying ways. For example, a Dominican remarked, "This question is very interesting because, one, I'm not totally Black, and then I'm not White. So I'm in the middle. And I'm not Indigenous. So in this case I have to put Hispanic . . ." (Roth, 2010, p. 1299). Similarly, a Puerto Rican identified his race as *trigueño,* a term meaning wheat-colored or brown skin. Yet, he believed that most Americans saw him as non-White, so he checked "White" on the census question, explaining:

> *Yes, I am Puerto Rican but I don't consider myself White. Obviously, the options that the questionnaire gives don't have anything like mixed. Don't have anything like trigueño, which is what I consider myself. And the options that are given me make me fill out what is closer to what I consider myself...* (Roth, 2010, p. 1299)

Roth also found that the respondents' answers to the census question often did not reflect a person's "observed race," which she classified as White, Black, or Hispanic based on her impression of each individual's appearance. For Hispanics, in short, answers to the census question had a variety of meanings, making it difficult to discern exactly what it is measuring and how it should be used in social research.

Researchers may also use quantitative analysis to refine operational definitions. Some statistical techniques are specifically designed to do this by helping to identify the underlying dimensions of a set of indicators, such as the items making up the Rosenberg Self-Esteem Scale. For example, despite the evidence supporting the validity of the self-esteem scale, researchers have debated whether the set of items represents one or two dimensions (Owens, 1993, 1994). One position is that Rosenberg's scale measures "global self-esteem," or a generally positive or negative attitude toward the self. The other position is that the scale actually consists of two subscales, one measuring self-deprecation and the other measuring positive self-worth. Applying a method called "factor analysis," Timothy Owens (1993) found support for the two-dimensional interpretation. His research also showed that the use of these two dimensions revealed "nuances previously overlooked" when the self-esteem scale was treated as unidimensional (Owens, 1994, p. 403). For example, self-deprecation was much more strongly related to depression than either positive self-worth or global self-esteem, and positive self-worth had a bigger impact on school grades than negative self-feelings.

SUMMARY

Whereas the first major steps in the measurement process, conceptualization and operationalization, largely follow the deductive logic of inquiry, concepts and operational definitions may emerge and be refined through data analysis, reflective of the inductive logic of inquiry. Researchers may develop concepts from data, assess the quality of measures by using in-depth interviews, and modify operational definitions and refine their meaning through statistical analysis. To assess your understanding of the topics discussed within this section, check out Box 6.10.

BOX 6.10

CHECKING YOUR UNDERSTANDING

Models of Inquiry

1. Concepts and operational definitions may emerge and be refined through data analysis, which represents the deductive logic of inquiry.
    a. True
    b. False

2. In the _____ model of inquiry, data analysis represents the last stage in answering research questions and providing evidence of the validity of our operational definitions.
    a. Deductive
    b. Inductive
    c. Reductive
    d. Constructive

3. Factor analysis represents a quantitative technique used to refine operational definitions.
    a. True
    b. False

continues

continued

4. James Marquart's research on prison guards' use of force as a form of social control represents which type of scientific inquiry.
   a. Inductive
   b. Constructive
   c. Reductive
   d. Deductive

Answers: 1. b, 2. a, 3. a, 4. a

KEY TERMS

archival records, p. 141
conceptual (or theoretical) definition, p. 132
conceptualization, p. 131
construct validation, p. 163
convergent validation, p. 162
Cronbach's alpha, p. 160
empirical indicator, p. 134
exhaustive, p. 145
index, p. 135
inter-rater reliability (inter-coder reliability), p. 160
internal consistency, p. 159
interval measurement, p. 147
measurement error, p. 163
measurement validity, p. 155
mutual exclusivity, p. 146
nominal measurement, p. 145
operational definition, p. 136
operationalization, p. 132
ordinal measurement, p. 146
ratio measurement, p. 148
reliability, p. 154
scale, p. 157
social desirability effect, p. 163
test-retest reliability, p. 158
unidimensionality, p. 157
verbal report (self-report), p. 139

KEY POINTS

- The measurement process may follow the deductive logic of inquiry in which theory informs data collection and analysis, but there may be "feedback loops" in this process, which reflect an inductive logic of inquiry.
- In research addressing quantitative questions, the measurement process begins with conceptualization, in which the meaning of a concept is defined and refined based on a careful review of the scientific literature.
- Following conceptualization, concepts are operationalized by specifying empirical indicators and spelling out the procedures to gather data.
- To measure a concept, a researcher may use manipulation operations, which are by definition experimental, or measured operations, which include verbal reports, observation, and the use of archival records.

- An important consideration in operationalization is the level of measurement. Four levels of measurement—nominal, ordinal, interval, and ratio—indicate the meaning of numbers or labels assigned to variable categories and provide progressively more information.
- Concepts are operationalized based on the data source and desired level of precision with the aim of providing the best possible fit between concept and measure.
- Operational definitions may be assessed on the basis of their reliability and validity.
- Reliability may be assessed by calculating the correlation between repeated applications of an operational definition (test-retest reliability), examining the consistency of responses across the items of a composite measure (internal consistency reliability), or observing the correspondence between different coders or raters applying the same operational definition (inter-rater reliability).
- Validity may be assessed by examining the correlation between alternative measures of a concept (convergent validation) or by examining the pattern of associations between an operational definition of a concept and other variables with which the concept should and should not be related (construct validation).
- Analyzing data and assessing the quality of measures may lead to the generation of new concepts and the refinement of operational definitions.

REVIEW QUESTIONS

1. What does it mean to say that measurement moves from the abstract to the concrete? How does this reflect the difference between conceptualization and operationalization in research addressing quantitative questions?
2. Explain the difference between manipulated and measured operational definitions. Which general research approach uses both? What are the three types of measured operational definitions?
3. Rank the four levels of measurement, from least to most, in terms of how much information they provide.
4. What is the relationship between reliability and validity? Is it possible for an operational definition to be valid but unreliable? Reliable but invalid?
5. Which of the three methods of reliability assessment discussed in the text is seldom applied in social research? Which method applies to composite measures? Which method may be used with operational definitions based on observation?
6. Explain the difference between convergent and construct validation.
7. How can data analysis lead to the development of concepts and refinement of operational definitions?

EXERCISES

1. Suppose you were conducting a campus survey on procedural justice. According to one conceptual definition, procedural justice is the fairness of processes used by those in positions of authority to reach specific outcomes or decisions. When citizens believe their encounters with authority, such as police, are procedurally fair, they tend to view the authority figure as more legitimate. Give examples of at least two empirical indicators of procedural justice.

2. Suppose you want to test the following hypotheses with data from the General Social Survey (GSS). For each hypothesis, identify the independent and dependent variables, and then find an appropriate GSS question to measure each variable. (Go to the GSS Data Explorer website and do a keyword search or filter variables by subject.)

    1. Men are more likely than women to say that they sometimes drink more than they should.
    2. People who have completed high school or the equivalent are less likely to use cannabis than those who have not.
    3. People who own a gun are more likely to support stiffer sentences for lawbreakers than people who do not own a gun.
    4. As income increases, likelihood of being arrested decreases.

3. One problem with many studies of domestic violence, including child abuse, is that they have relied upon self-reports. Because domestic abuse is socially stigmatized and can result in criminal charges, individuals may be tempted to underreport abusive conduct. What effect would this have on the reliability and/or validity of such self-report measures?

4. Suppose you want to create a composite measure of job satisfaction in which you ask correctional officers their opinions on their job during the past year (e.g., feeling stressed by work, being unable to relax at home due to work, and feeling fulfilled by their job). How would you assess the reliability and validity of your composite measure?

5. Suppose you were interested in studying juveniles' interactions with each other at a local detention center. To do so, you become an intern at a local juvenile detention center and conduct field observations in as many settings and during as many times as possible while at your internship, taking copious notes of everything you observed. You are struck by a recurring pattern in your notes: the juveniles interacted more positively with their peers than with the teachers and staff. Discuss how you might operationalize this peer/staff interaction if you were to go back into the field to see how such interaction varies across social settings. (Hint: You will need to identify and define various observational categories.)

7

Sampling
Case Selection as a Basis for Inference

LEARNING OBJECTIVES

By the end of this chapter, you should be able to

7.1 Describe the steps in the sampling process for probability and nonprobability sampling.

7.2 Identify the principles of probability sampling and explain how they form the basis for making statistical inferences from a sample to a population.

7.3 Distinguish among probability sampling designs, such as simple random sampling, stratified sampling, and cluster sampling.

7.4 Distinguish among nonprobability sampling designs, such as convenience sampling, purposive sampling, snowball sampling, and theoretical sampling.

CHAPTER OUTLINE

7.1 Overview: The Sampling Process 174

7.2 Principles of Probability Sampling 176
Probability and Random Selection 176
Probability Distribution and Sampling Error 179
Statistical Inference 180
Summary 182

7.3 Steps in Probability Sampling 183
Define Target Population 183
Construct Sampling Frame 184
Devise Sampling Design 185
Draw Sample 189
Summary 191

7.4 Nonprobability Sampling 192
Overview of Nonprobability Sampling 192
Steps in Nonprobability Sampling 193
Making Inferences from Nonprobability Samples 197
Summary 198

Inference is so common in everyday life that we hardly ever take note of it. For example, when you overhear two students saying they find a course "interesting," you might infer that you will find it interesting too. If you see a premed student studying on a Friday night, you may infer that this is the norm for premeds. If you see two students sitting close to one another in the cafeteria, you might infer that they are friends. In each of these examples, the inference is a conclusion or generalization based on an observation. The inference may be true, but it also may be refuted by additional observations.

In general, our confidence in our inferences depends on how many and what particular observations we make. Sometimes we gain confidence by increasing the number of observations; for example, knowing 10 students found a course interesting is likely to strengthen your inference that you will find it interesting. At other times, we enhance our confidence by virtue of the observational context. You probably would be more likely to believe studying on a weekend night is the norm for college students if you observed this happening in the middle of the semester rather than at the end of the semester during final exams. And, it seems safe to say, you are not likely to infer that two students are friends if you merely observed them sitting next to one another on a crowded subway.

In a similar fashion, criminal justice researchers make inferences from systematic observations of crime and the criminal justice system. Chapter 6 described methods for determining *what* to observe and *how* to carry out and record one's observations. These methods assume, however, that you have selected the cases—persons, objects, or events—to which you apply your operational definitions. Sampling is the process of selecting cases. This chapter outlines methods for selecting cases and establishing a basis for making inferences.

As with other elements of research design, sampling methods depend on the research question as well as practical considerations. To begin, we discuss the sampling process, focusing on how the research question gives rise to two broad types of sampling design: probability and nonprobability. Then we consider the principles, methods, and process of sampling within each type. In subsequent chapters we discuss sampling in relation to each of the major approaches to criminal justice research; this chapter introduces basic sampling concepts that will help you to understand our later discussions.

7.1 OVERVIEW: THE SAMPLING PROCESS

Figure 7.1 depicts the steps in the sampling process. As the figure shows, the process begins with the research question, which indicates the kind of inferences we wish to make. The research question dictates the research strategy (e.g., an experiment, survey, field research, in-depth interview, use of existing data) as well as the unit of analysis (e.g., individual people, families, nations, television programs). Together, these two choices shape whether the researcher samples cases at random or by some other means.

Sampling methods in which cases are selected randomly and have a known probability of being selected are referred to as **probability sampling**. Methods of nonrandom selection are called **nonprobability sampling**. Much of this chapter is devoted to the steps in drawing probability and nonprobability samples.

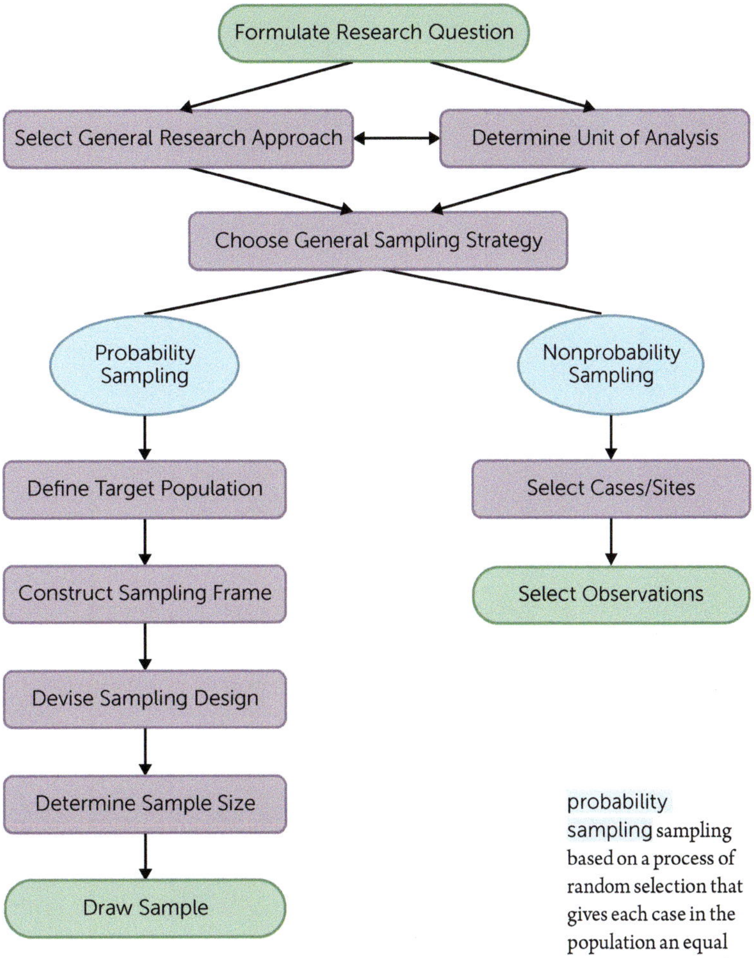

The purpose of probability sampling is to make inferences from a sample to a population (see Figure 7.2). A **population** consists of a complete set of persons, objects, or events that share some characteristic, such as all students enrolled in your methods class, all residents of the city of Chicago, or all criminal justice books published in the 21st century. A **sample** is simply a subset of a population.

For the purpose of estimating population characteristics, probability sampling offers two major advantages over nonprobability sampling. The first is that it removes the possibility that investigator biases will affect the selection of cases. The second advantage is that, by virtue of random selection, the laws of mathematical probability may be applied to estimate the accuracy of the sample. These advantages lend themselves well to certain kinds of research. Survey researchers often use probability sampling, and it is a common method in some kinds of existing data research, such as content analysis. Probability sampling works best in sampling individual people or particular artifacts such as periodicals, television programs, and songs. It also may be possible and appropriate for sampling groups or aggregates, such as married couples, organizations, and cities.

Probability sampling may not be desirable or possible, however. If you want to understand the meaning of people's actions in a particular context or explain a social movement or historically significant event, it is best to use nonprobability sampling.

FIGURE 7.1 The Sampling Process

probability sampling sampling based on a process of random selection that gives each case in the population an equal or known chance of being included in the sample

nonprobability sampling methods of case selection other than random selection

population the total membership of a defined class of people, objects, or events

sample a subset of cases selected from a population

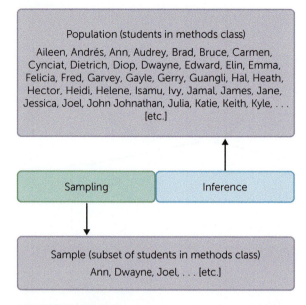

FIGURE 7.2 Making Inferences from a Sample to a Population. Drawing names from a hat is often used to convey the meaning of random selection. An analysis of the 1970 draft lottery indicated, however, that manual methods such as this might not give every case an equal chance of being selected.

These research objectives necessarily involve the intensive study of a very small number of cases or events. And as the study unfolds, selecting additional observations will depend on how these may add to one's theoretical understanding. As you will see, probability sampling is less reliable with small samples; it also is inappropriate when sampling is intended to enhance "the researcher's exposure to different understandings of what is being studied" (Schwartz-Shea & Yanow, 2012, p. 85). To gain different understandings, field researchers generally use nonprobability sampling both to select research settings and to sample events or actors within those settings. Nonprobability sampling also is the rule in research using in-depth interviews as well as historical and comparative research. Finally, nonprobability sampling may be necessary when a population is unknown or is not readily identifiable, as in many studies of deviant or criminal behavior.

7.2 PRINCIPLES OF PROBABILITY SAMPLING

Before you learn the steps in probability sampling, it is important to understand how this form of sampling enables researchers to estimate population characteristics based on the results of a single sample. This requires a discussion of the principles of probability sampling and statistical inference. As you probably (pun intended) know, whole courses are offered in statistics; however, you can gain a good intuitive grasp of the statistical principles underlying probability sampling by knowing a few key concepts. We begin with the concepts of "probability" and "random selection."

Probability and Random Selection

probability the likelihood that something will occur, which may vary from 0 to 100 percent

Probability refers to the odds or chances that something will occur. If your instructor puts the names of all 20 students in your class in a hat (with each name presumably on the same-size slip of paper) and selects one at random, the probability that you or any other student will be drawn is 1 in 20, or 5 percent. We know that this is the probability because the selection process—drawing a name from a hat—is random. Statistical inference in probability sampling is based on random selection.

Sometimes we hear students say that they "randomly" met someone; implicit in this everyday understanding of "randomness" is that the meeting occurred by *chance*.

Technically speaking, **random selection** refers to a process that gives each element in a set, such as each student in your methods class, a known and independent chance of being chosen. To begin, we need to know the chance of selection. By your instructor's method, the chance of randomly choosing one student, say James or Audrey, is 1 in 20. If there were 5 men and 15 women enrolled in the class and your instructor randomly selected one woman and one man, the chances of choosing James would be 1 in 5 and the chances of choosing Audrey would be 1 in 15. Although the chances (or probabilities) differ, selection is random because the probability of selection is *known*.

To be *independent*, the chances of choosing one student should not affect the chances of choosing another. Suppose your instructor divided the class in half and selected one student from the left side of the room and one student from the right side. If James and Audrey were seated on the same side of the room, the selection would not be random because choosing James would mean that Audrey could not be chosen.

If for any reason the selection process favors certain cases, or if the selection of one case increases or decreases the likelihood that another case will be selected, then the selection is *biased*. By this definition, your circle of friends clearly would be a biased sample of the student population at your college. So, too, would a number of other samples, including examples from criminal justice research, such as the inmates at just one correctional institution, residents who live in one neighborhood, and police officers from one agency. To satisfy the condition of randomness, researchers cannot simply pick cases haphazardly or in any hit-or-miss fashion; subtle and often unconscious bias invariably will enter into the selection process. Rather, mechanical or electronic aids should be used to ensure that chance alone dictates selection. One such aid is described in Box 7.1.

> **random selection** a selection process that gives each element in a population a known and independent chance of being selected

---

BOX 7.1

DOING CRIMINAL JUSTICE RESEARCH

How to Select Things Randomly

If your instructor put each student's name on a slip of paper, placed all the slips in a hat, stirred the slips around with her fingers, and then drew out one slip of paper, would the drawing be random? You might think so, but a well-known example of the failure of physical mixing to achieve randomness suggests that it is probably not. During the Vietnam War, a lottery was conducted, using birthdates, to determine the order in which men (women were not eligible) would be selected for the military draft. Each date was recorded on a slip of paper, each slip was placed in a cylindrical capsule, and the capsules were put first in a box and then poured into a large bowl. Although the box was shaken several times, analyses showed that the order of selection was nonrandom.

continues

continued

FIGURE 7.3 The Random Integer Generator at RANDOM.ORG

Capsules were placed in the box in order of the month of birth, beginning with January; as a consequence, those with birthdays in later months of the year had lower lottery numbers, and hence were more likely to be drafted (Fienberg, 1971).

To make sure that selection is random, you need a mechanism that eliminates physical mixing and human judgment from the selection process. Nowadays, researchers generally use a variety of computer programs that generate random numbers. If all population elements are listed in an Excel spreadsheet, for example, you can use the Excel random number generator to draw a random sample. We recommend one of the easy-to-use, free online services such as RANDOM.ORG or Research Randomizer.

Figure 7.3 is a window from RANDOM.ORG for randomly selecting whole numbers. From the RANDOM.ORG website, go to the "Numbers" drop down menu and select "Integers." You can use this program to draw a sample or hold a drawing or lottery. If you are drawing a random sample, you will first need to number all the cases in the population. In Part 1, you enter the sample size in the first box, indicate the size of the population in the third box, and choose a format—one or more columns—for listing the selected random numbers in the last box. Then you click on "Get Numbers." If you want to start over, you click "Reset Form"; and if you want to refine your choice of numerals and output format, you click "Switch to Advanced Mode."

As the note at the bottom of the RANDOM.ORG screen indicates, the numbers generated are "picked independently of each other (like rolls of a die)," which is a requirement of random selection. Consequently, the numbers may "contain duplicates." In other words, each random number is generated from the same range of numbers (the population size). The reason for this is that random selection generally assumes an equal probability of selection. If your instructor were to select two students instead of one, she would probably select one name, set it aside, and then select another. But in doing this, the probability of selection would change. For the first selection, the chances of a student being chosen are 1 in 20, or 5 percent, whereas for the second selection, the chances are 1 in 19, or 5.26 percent. The procedure of removing a case from the population once it is selected is called **sampling without replacement**. By contrast, RANDOM.ORG uses **sampling with replacement**.

In criminal justice research and in most real-life applications, we do not want duplicates. After all, we do not want to interview the same person twice! Therefore, sampling with replacement is rare. Fortunately, sampling without replacement has no practical effect on statistical estimates when the population is large and the sample is a small fraction of the population, which is most often the case in social research. If the sample size is a large fraction of the population size (say a half or more), researchers use a correction formula to increase the accuracy of the results.

sampling without replacement a sampling procedure whereby once a case is selected, it is NOT returned to the sampling frame, so that it cannot be selected again

sampling with replacement a sampling procedure whereby once a case is selected, it is returned to the sampling frame, so that it may be selected again

Probability Distribution and Sampling Error

To return to our opening example, when your instructor draws one name randomly from a hat containing 20 names, you might imagine two possible outcomes: your name either will or will not be selected. The probability that it will be selected is 1 in 20 or .05; the probability that some other name will be chosen is 19 in 20 or .95. Together, the probability of these two outcomes constitutes a **probability distribution**. Another example is flipping a fair coin. The probability distribution consists of the probabilities of flipping a head (.50) or a tail (.50).

Similarly, in criminal justice research we can construct the probability distribution for a single variable. Suppose, for instance, to measure the variable "alcohol use among students," we interviewed the entire population of 50,000 students at a university and asked them: "Have you consumed alcohol in the last 30 days?" Table 7.1 presents hypothetical data showing the distribution of responses to this question. The second column shows the number of students who answered "yes" or "no." The third column shows the percentage of students who answered "yes" or "no"; note that 43 percent said they consumed alcohol in the last 30 days. The last column is the probability distribution. We form the probability distribution by calculating the proportion of "yes" and "no" answers, dividing each number in the second column by the total number of students at University X (50,000). These proportions are equivalent

probability distribution a distribution of the probabilities for a variable, which indicates the likelihood that each category or value of the variable will occur

Table 7.1 Alcohol Consumption Among Students, University X, Hypothetical Data

Alcohol Consumption	Number	Percentage	Probability
Yes	21,500	43	.43
No	28,500	57	.57
Total	50,000	100	1.00

to probabilities; thus, if you were to draw a student at random from this university, the probability that he or she would say "yes" is .43.

It would be very expensive and time-consuming to interview everyone in this population. Just think of all the interviewers you would need to hire and the time required to track down all 50,000 students! Indeed, the cost factor is a major reason for drawing a sample.

Let us assume, then, that we obtain enough funds to draw a sample of 500. Table 7.2 shows a hypothetical distribution of responses to the same question for this sample. Notice that 45 percent of students in the sample answered "yes." Using this as an estimate of the population percentage, we would be off by 2 percent (45%–43%). This difference is called the **sampling error**. In actual research, we do not know the sampling error (i.e., how far off our estimate is) because we do not know the distribution of the population (as shown in Table 7.1). That is why we are drawing a sample. Therefore, we need some way of knowing how much sample estimates are likely to vary and how confident we can be in a single estimate based on a sample of a given size.

sampling error the difference between an actual population value (e.g., a percentage) and the population value estimated from a sample

Statistical Inference

Table 7.2 shows that 45 percent of the sample answered "yes" to a survey question asking if they had consumed alcohol in the last 30 days, but as you might imagine, other random samples of 500 students might yield estimates such as 39 or 44 or

Table 7.2 Alcohol Consumption Among Students, University X, Sample of 500

Alcohol Consumption	Number	Percentage
Yes	225	45
No	275	55
Total	500	100

48 percent. Let us use this example to see how statistical inference works in probability sampling. Our random sample is but one of the nearly infinite number of samples we could have drawn of all possible samples of 500 students. We do not know the percentage of students at University X who answered "yes" to the question about alcohol use, but we would like to estimate this percentage. Our best guess is the sample estimate of 45 percent; however, short of interviewing all 50,000 students, we cannot determine whether this is equal to the actual population percentage. To get around this problem, rather than using a single point estimate, like 45 percent, statisticians construct *interval estimates*. Knowing the sampling distribution, we can determine how confident we are that the population value lies within some range of a sample estimate. Level of confidence is a function of how many standard errors we add and subtract from the sample estimate. A **standard error** is the average distance of sample values from the population value. For example, based on the normal distribution, we are confident that 95 percent of the time, selecting a random sample of 500 students will result in a sample estimate that is within two standard errors of the population value (see Figure 7.3). The standard error for this hypothetical data is 2.2. Using the 500 student sample data to estimate the standard error, we come up with the following interval estimate for a confidence level of 95 percent:

standard error a statistical measure of the "average" sampling error for a particular sampling distribution, which indicates how much sample results will vary from sample to sample

$$45 - 2(2.2) \text{ and } 45 + 2(2.2) = 40.6 \text{ to } 49.4$$

Based on this result, called a **confidence interval**, we could conclude that we are 95 percent confident that the actual population value falls between 40.6 and 49.4 percent.

confidence interval a range (interval) within which a population value is estimated to lie at a specific level of confidence

In many surveys and opinion polling, it is common practice to select random samples, calculate statistics, and then use theoretical knowledge of sampling distributions to make inferences about population characteristics. Pollsters usually do not report the "confidence level" or make reference to "confidence intervals." Instead, they present "margins of error" that are equivalent to the 95 percent confidence interval. For example, on December 22, 2023, Gallup reported, based on telephone interviews conducted with 1,013 adults, that the percentage of Americans who approved of the job Joe Biden was doing as president was 39 percent, plus or minus 4 percentage points (Brenan, 2023). Now you know what this means. Gallup is claiming that they are 95 percent confident that Biden's approval rating among all Americans at the time was between 35 and 43 percent.

Gallup's margin of error of plus or minus 4 percentage points is smaller than the margin of error for our sample of 500 students (plus or minus 4.4) because it is based on a larger sample (1,018 vs. 500). This confirms what we inferred from Figure 7.4: the standard error decreases as the sample size increases. As you will see, how big a sample you choose to draw depends partly on how precise your sample estimates need to be. Smaller margins of error are more precise.

SUMMARY

Based on random selection and statistical inference, all probability sampling follows a unified framework for making inferences from a sample to a population. Confidence intervals can be calculated to indicate the level of confidence that a population value falls within a specified range. To check your understanding of the concepts learned within this section, please refer to Box 7.2.

BOX 7.2

CHECKING YOUR UNDERSTANDING

Probability Sampling I

1. Probability sampling is the most appropriate when
    a. studying a small number of cases.
    b. trying to understand the context of people's actions.
    c. the research objective is to estimate population characteristics.
    d. the population is unknown or not readily identifiable.

2. In order to calculate the margin of error of a sample estimate, all of the following must be known except:
    a. desired level of confidence in the margin of error.
    b. size of the sample.
    c. the population value.
    d. standard error of the sampling distribution.

3. Box 7.1 discusses the use of computer programs such as RANDOM.ORG to obtain a random sample. Computer programs for random selection such as this one typically use _____; in criminal justice research, case selection involves _____?
    a. sampling with replacement; sampling with replacement
    b. sampling with replacement; sampling without replacement
    c. sampling without replacement; sampling without replacement
    d. sampling without replacement; sampling with replacement

Answers: 1. c, 2. c, 3. b

7.3 STEPS IN PROBABILITY SAMPLING

Armed with an understanding of probability sampling theory and statistical inference, we are ready to review the steps in probability sampling. Before you draw a random sample and calculate sample estimates, you must identify the set of cases from which to draw your sample. This involves the first two steps in probability sampling: defining and then operationalizing the population to which you wish to generalize (see Figure 7.1). These steps should sound familiar to you, as they parallel the steps in defining (conceptualizing) and operationalizing concepts in the process of measurement.

Define Target Population

Probability sampling is intended "to describe or make inferences to *well-defined populations*" (Groves et al., 2009, p. 69; our emphasis). Thus, the first step in drawing a probability sample is to clearly identify the **target population**, that is, the population to which the researcher would like to generalize the results. To define the target population, the researcher must specify the criteria for determining which cases are included in the population and which cases are excluded. The relevant criteria depend on the type of unit, the research topic, and pragmatic considerations. With individual people, some combination of locale and selected demographic variables such as gender, race, employment status, and age may be used. For example, in a study on the influence of adolescent misperceptions of alcohol use, researchers utilized data collected from the National Longitudinal Study of Adolescent to Adult Health (Add Health) (Amialchuk & Sapci, 2021). Add Health includes five waves of data, beginning in 1994, when the individuals were in 7th–12th grade, to the 2016–2018 timeframe. Amialchuk and Sapci intentionally chose individuals from wave 2 who were below the legal drinking age (under 20). This group was targeted to understand the influence of the misperception of peer behavior on illegal alcohol use among adolescents. In another example, the Glaze (2019) collected data for the seventh time using a nationally representative sample of inmates from state and federal prison populations who were 18 years of age or older. Prison inmates were targeted, not because they are particularly easy to access, but because the objective was to provide national statistics on this specific population, including demographic characteristics, incident characteristics, criminal history, family background, mental and physical health and treatment, etc.

For the Monitoring the Future (MTF) study, which Baumer and colleagues (2020) used to analyze whether changes in youth offending were associated with attachment and commitment to school, community involvement, or parental supervision, the target population for their analysis (years 1991–2015) consisted of

> **target population**
> the population to which the researcher would like to generalize his or her results

students in 8th and 9th grade, intentionally avoiding 12th-grade students. The exclusion of 12th-graders was based upon several pragmatic considerations:

> We excluded twelfth graders because their observed trends in offending prevalence and other factors are more likely to be impacted by selection effects related to school drop-out and because some of the key explanatory variables were not available for the twelfth-grade sample. (Baumer et al., 2020, p. 116)

Construct Sampling Frame

The next step is to find a way of identifying all the persons or cases in the population. This involves constructing a sampling frame. The **sampling frame** denotes the set of all cases from which the sample is actually selected. Because the term can be misleading, please note that the sampling frame is *not a sample*; rather, it is an *operational definition of the population* that provides the basis for sampling.

sampling frame an operational definition of the population that provides the basis for drawing a sample; ordinarily consists of a list of cases

There are two ways of constructing a sampling frame:

1. listing all cases from which a sample may be drawn, and
2. defining population membership by a rule that provides a basis for case selection.

For example, in a city telephone survey, the sampling frame could consist of the city telephone directory (a listing) or telephone numbers with targeted telephone area codes and prefixes (a rule). In survey research, establishing a sampling frame often amounts to obtaining an adequate listing—either of the population as a whole or of subgroups of the population. But listing is not always possible or preferable. In fact, telephone directories are now generally a thing of the past. But as long as cases can be identified, a rule procedure usually can be devised for finding and selecting cases. Suppose you want to interview people attending a concert. You obviously cannot obtain a list in advance of the concert; however, the fact that everyone must arrive at (and may leave) the concert at a particular time allows you to establish a rule based on time of arrival (or departure). Thus, stationing interviewers at points of entry or exit, you could randomly select one attendee in every 10.

For relatively small populations—such as members of a local school, church, or some other institution—lists are often available. The sampling frame for a college campus survey, for example, could consist of a complete list of students from the school's registrar. For many populations, though, especially at the national level, lists are unavailable. To sample national populations, researchers generally break the target population down into natural groupings for which lists (or sampling frames) are available or can be constructed at low cost. We discuss this sampling strategy further under "Sampling Designs."

Figure 7.4 shows the relationship among the target population, sampling frame, and sample. To make accurate inferences from a sample to a target population, the sampling frame should be identical to the target population, as in Figure 7.4A. However, existing frames often are incomplete, as suggested by the imperfect overlap between the target population and sampling frame in Figure 7.4B. Although registrar data at a college or university would provide a reasonably accurate frame, it may nonetheless be flawed. Through changes in retention and mid-semester dropouts, the target population may change somewhat by the time students are recruited into the sample. This mismatch between the sampling frame and target population is called **coverage error**. It is a particular problem in telephone surveys, which we discuss in Chapter 9.

Once you have defined the target population and obtained or constructed a sampling frame, you are ready to draw a random sample. Probability sampling always involves random selection, but how random selection is implemented depends on the type of sampling design.

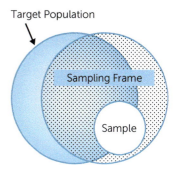

A. Perfect Correspondence between Target Population and Sampling Frame

B. Imperfect Correspondence between Target Population and Sampling Frame

FIGURE 7.4 Relationship Among Target Population, Sampling Frame, and Sample

coverage error the error that occurs when the sampling frame does not match the target population

Devise Sampling Design

The defining characteristic of a probability sample is that each case has a *known, nonzero probability* of being selected. For some types of probability samples, the chance or probability of selection is equal. But for others, it is not. Whether the probability of selection is equal is one of the ways that probability–sampling designs differ from one another. In this section, we discuss three probability–sampling designs: simple random sampling, stratified random sampling, and cluster sampling.

SIMPLE RANDOM SAMPLING

We begin with the most basic design, a **simple random sample**, in which not only does every case in the sampling frame have an equal probability of being selected, but every possible *combination* of cases has an equal chance of being included in the sample. If your instructor put every student's name in a hat and randomly selected two students, one after the other, she would produce a simple random sample because all combinations of two students would have an equal chance of being selected. But if she put female students in one hat and males in another, and randomly selected one name from each hat, she would not have a simple random sample because many combinations, such as any two females or any two males, could not be drawn.

Simple random sampling requires a complete list of the population. For example, Sarah Tahamont and her colleagues (2022) were able to draw a simple random sample for their study exploring barriers to Pell eligibility for prisoners in the Second Chance

simple random sample a probability sampling design in which every case and every possible combination of cases has an equal chance of being included in the sample

Pell pilot program in Pennsylvania prisons because they had access to the complete population of individuals incarcerated in Pennsylvania prisons. While a list of the complete population was available for Tahamont et al.'s population of interest, as we noted earlier, such a list may not always exist (and may be prohibitively expensive to construct). In addition, very often there are more effective ways of applying probability sampling than drawing a simple random sample, to which we now turn.

STRATIFIED RANDOM SAMPLING

In the study conducted by Baumer, Cundiff, and Luo (2020) data came from the MTF study, which utilizes a stratified random sampling procedure to collect data from a nationally representative sample of 8th, 10th, and 12th grade students. While the MTF sampling procedures were relatively complex and took place in three stages, one example of stratified sampling took place when researchers intentionally oversampled illicit drug users (Bachman et al., 2011). The main objective of the MTF study is to monitor drug use and, given that a relatively small portion of high school students engage in illicit drug use, oversampling this subpopulation was necessary to ensure that the sample contained enough illicit drug users for analysis. Breaking the population into groups of those who do and do not use illicit drugs would be examples of strata, from which a random subsample could be drawn.

Breaking down a sampling frame into the separate groups and drawing a random sample within each of these subpopulations creates what is called a **stratified random sample**. The word "strata" refers to the subpopulations into which the sampling frame is divided. Stratification can be based on categories of any one, or a combination of, relevant variables, but it requires that you identify the stratum of each person (or object) being sampled and that you know the size of each stratum in the population.

There are two types of stratified random samples, which differ based on whether the proportion of people sampled in each stratum is equal to the proportion of people in each stratum of the population. In **proportionate stratified sampling**, the sample proportions equal the population proportions of each stratum; by contrast, in **disproportionate stratified sampling**, the sample proportions do *not* equal the population proportions of each stratum. The MTF study's stratified sampling procedure oversampled illicit drug users, intending to have more illicit drug users in the sample than they would expect to find in the population of high school students, thereby using a disproportionate stratified sample.

Whereas a proportionate stratified sample produces a representative sample of the population on the basis of the stratifying variable, a disproportionate stratified sample does not. To obtain unbiased estimates of population characteristics, researchers therefore make a statistical adjustment, called **weighting**, which takes into account the disproportionality of the sample.

---

stratified random sample a probability sampling design in which the population is divided into strata (or variable categories) and independent random samples are drawn from each stratum

proportionate stratified sampling a sampling procedure in which strata are sampled proportionately to population composition

disproportionate stratified sampling a sampling procedure in which strata are sampled disproportionately to population composition

weighting a procedure that corrects for the unequal probability of selecting one or more segments (e.g., strata) of the population

Compared to simple random sampling, stratified random sampling can be advantageous in two ways: by (1) ensuring a sufficient number of cases in each stratum and (2) reducing the standard error. Stratified random sampling was more efficient in the MTF study because, in comparison with a simple random sample, a smaller overall sample would be needed to obtain an adequate number of illicit drug users in their sample for analysis.

By reducing the standard error of the sample, stratified random sampling also provides more precise estimates of population characteristics. In addition to sample size, the standard error depends on the amount of variation in the population: the greater the variability, the higher the standard error. Stratified sampling controls for this variability by dividing the population into strata that are relatively homogeneous on key variables. In the MTF study, for example, people in each group (i.e., illicit drug use or no illicit drug use) should be more similar to one another than to people in the other group on several variables, such as attitudes toward drug use, deviance and victimization, and personality characteristics. Consequently, the standard error for each sampled group will be lower than the overall standard error, based on a simple random sample.

Compared to simple random sampling, the only way in which stratified random sampling is less efficient is that you must divide the sampling frame into the relevant strata and draw separate samples from each stratum. The next design we discuss offers different gains in efficiency by reducing the costs of data collection.

CLUSTER SAMPLING

Both simple random sampling and stratified random sampling assume that a complete list of the population is available. What do you do, however, when your target population is so large that it is either impossible or impractical to list all its members? The only lists of the current US population—income tax forms and census forms filed every 10 years—are confidential and not available to the public. Lists of most city and all state populations simply do not exist, and it would be too expensive to compile lists of these and other very large populations. In such instances, researchers often are able to obtain a sample in stages, using a method called **cluster sampling**.

In cluster sampling, the population is broken down into groups of cases, called "clusters." Clusters consist of natural groupings, such as colleges and churches, or geographic areas like states, counties, cities, and blocks. The first step in drawing a cluster sample is to randomly select a sample of clusters. The second step is to obtain a list of all cases within each selected cluster. If all the cases in each sampled cluster are included in the sample, the design is called a *single-stage cluster sample* in that sampling occurs once—at the cluster level.

More frequently, cluster sampling involves sampling at two or more steps or stages, hence the term **multistage cluster sampling** (see Figure 7.5). An example of a two-stage cluster sample comes from the Add Health data discussed earlier in the chapter

cluster sampling a probability sampling design in which the population is broken down into natural groupings or areas, called clusters, and a random sample of clusters is drawn

multistage cluster sampling a sampling design in which sampling occurs at two or more steps or stages

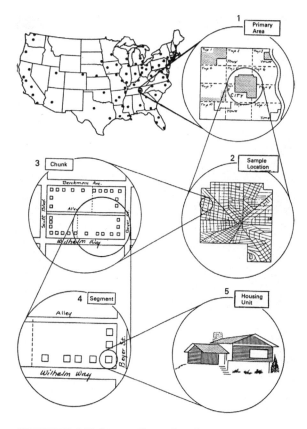

FIGURE 7.5 A Multistage Cluster Sample

(Chen & Chantala, 2014). Although a single list of all 7th-12th grade students in the United States does not exist and would be difficult and extremely costly to compile, all 7th-12th-graders (except for the homeschooled) attend schools. Therefore, the Add Health used a complete and accurate list of public and private *schools* in the United States maintained by Quality Education Data, Inc. From the nearly 26,666 schools nationwide in this database during the 1994–1995 school year, the researchers selected a random sample of 132 schools (first stage); then, from each participating school, they obtained enrollment rosters and randomly selected approximately 200 students from each school community (may have been one school or a pair of junior and high schools) (second stage).

Cluster samples differ from stratified random samples in a few important ways. First, in terms of population breakdown, strata consist of *variable* categories, whereas clusters are geographical units or natural groupings formed by existing social arrangements, such as schools, churches, and city blocks. Second, in a stratified sample, every stratum is included in the sample because sampling occurs within every stratum; in a cluster sample, however, not all clusters are included in the sample because clusters are randomly selected. Third, while stratified random sampling is used either to increase sample precision or to provide a sufficient number of cases in small strata, the principal reason for cluster sampling is to reduce the costs of data collection. In face-to-face interview studies of large, widely scattered populations, two major costs are interviewer travel and the listing of population elements. Compared to simple random and stratified random sampling methods, clustering concentrates interviews within fewer and smaller geographical areas, thereby spreading the travel costs over several cases and reducing the costs of any one interview. Moreover, since the listing of population elements is a prerequisite for simple random and stratified random methods, clustering also can reduce costs by limiting the compilation of lists of cases to selected clusters rather than compiling a list of the entire population.

Multistage sample designs may involve either simple random or stratified random sampling at each stage of the design. In other words, we can stratify clusters just as we stratify individual units. The Add Health stratified clusters, dividing schools into several strata according to five variables: region, urbanicity, school type (public, private, parochial), ethnic mix, and size. A number of schools were then selected within each stratum.

One main problem with cluster samples is that, even though they are more *cost-efficient*, they are less precise, size for size, than either simple random or stratified random samples. The main reason for this is that variation within clusters tends to be much smaller than variation between clusters. For example, people who live on the same block tend to have similar incomes and other socioeconomic characteristics; those who live on one block may differ markedly on these same characteristics from those who live on another block. Consequently, because we select a random sample of clusters, the variability across clusters can be relatively large, which increases the standard error. In addition, sampling errors are associated with each stage of a multistage cluster sample. So, the sampling error (or standard error) in the total sample is compounded and can be quite large relative to the error produced by one simple random selection. One way to reduce the standard error is to stratify clusters. Indeed, most large-scale surveys, such as the Add Health, use complex sampling designs combining both cluster and stratified sampling.

Having carefully defined the target population, obtained a good sampling frame, and come up with a sampling design, the researcher finally must determine an appropriate sample size.

Draw Sample

The final step in the sampling process is to draw the sample. Like the assessment of reliability and validity in measurement, samples should be evaluated for their accuracy following data collection. Up to this point, we have limited ourselves to one kind of error produced by random selection: sampling error, or the difference between a sample estimate and the true population value. This error can be estimated and can be reduced by increasing the size or efficiency of one's sample. But there are other sources of *nonrandom* sampling error present in surveys, where probability sampling is the norm: coverage error and nonresponse error.

Coverage error, which we mentioned earlier in the chapter, is due to incomplete sampling frames; **nonresponse error or bias** is due to incomplete data collection. The problem of nonresponse bias arises when, through refusals to cooperate, unreturned questionnaires, missing records, or some other means, the sample turns out to be a fraction of the number of cases originally selected for observation. The crux of this problem is that nonobservations may differ in systematic ways from observations. For example, in face-to-face interview surveys, respondents who live in densely populated urban areas are less likely to cooperate than respondents in less densely populated areas (Groves & Couper, 1998). Also, those who feel most strongly about the topics or issues of a study are more likely to respond than those in the middle (Groves et al., 2004).

nonresponse error in survey sampling, the error that occurs when nonrespondents (sampled individuals who do not respond or cannot be contacted) differ systematically from respondents (also called *nonresponse bias*)

Of these two sources of error, the problem of coverage error tends to be addressed prior to data collection, when additional sampling frames may be used to provide more complete coverage (see Chapter 9). Nonresponse error may be reduced by improving the process of data collection, but survey nonresponse is always present to some degree, and various methods have been used to assess its impact on sample quality. A few of these methods are briefly described in Box 7.3.

> **BOX 7.3**
>
> **READING CRIMINAL JUSTICE RESEARCH**
>
> ## Assessing Nonresponse Bias and Overall Sample Quality
>
> The most frequently cited indicator of nonresponse bias is the *response rate* (Dixon & Tucker, 2010), which refers to the proportion of cases sampled from whom data are collected. The conventional wisdom has been that nonresponse bias declines as the response rate increases. It seems plausible, for example, that a sample with a 95 percent rate of response would be more representative of the population than a sample with a 10 percent response. Evidence suggests, however, that the response rate may not be the best indicator of sample representativeness (Groves, 2006; Groves & Peytcheva, 2008; Sturgis et al., 2017), and researchers have devised other means for assessing the quality of a sample.
>
> In relatively rare instances, it may be possible to assess survey nonresponse bias by obtaining data from the pool of nonrespondents. For example, in a mail survey of "binge" drinking among college students, the researchers sent a short form of the questionnaire to students who failed to return their questionnaires (Wechsler et al., 1994). They found that "the rate of binge drinking among these nonresponders did not differ from that of respondents to the original survey" (pp. 1673–1674).
>
> Another method, also applied in the alcohol survey, is to use late responders to a survey (say, the last 5 percent) to approximate noncontacts (Dixon & Tucker, 2010). The assumption is that these late respondents would have been noncontacts if a concerted effort were not made to convince them to participate. For example, arguing against nonresponse bias, the alcohol researchers found no significant differences between early and late responders in the percent of nondrinkers, non-binge drinkers, and binge drinkers (Wechsler et al., 1994).
>
> A common method of assessing nonresponse bias and the general representativeness of a sample is to compare the composition of the sample on key variables with other surveys, known population characteristics, or existing administrative data. For example, we discussed earlier in the text a study conducted by Bolin, Pate, and McClintock (2017) which involved the collection of self-report data from undergraduate students on the topics of alcohol use, cannabis use, and academic achievement. The survey was sent to the entire population of students listed in the sampling frame for one university, approximately 8,500 students. Yet they received responses from only 1,104 students. Given that their response rate was low, 13%, it would be important to determine if the sample of individuals who responded was representative of the overall

population. Their population consisted of undergraduate students from one university, giving them the ability to compare their sample characteristics to the characteristics of the overall population. They concluded that the sample was significantly different from the university population leading to potential limitations in the interpretation of their conclusions; students who were female, White, older, upperclassmen, and Greek-affiliated were overrepresented in the sample.

SUMMARY

Probability sampling should begin with a careful definition of the population to which inferences are to be made. The second step is to construct a sampling frame, usually by locating one or more available lists. If a complete list is available, it is possible to draw a simple random sample or, to increase sampling efficiency, draw a stratified random sample. When a complete list is unavailable, multistage cluster sampling may be used. Besides the measurable error produced by random selection, probability sampling is subject to coverage error and nonresponse error. Assess your understanding of the information within this section in Box 7.4.

BOX 7.4

CHECKING YOUR UNDERSTANDING

Probability Sampling II

1. Probability sampling procedures typically utilize a sampling frame from which they can randomly select participants. What occurs when the sampling frame does not match the target population?
    a. Sampling error
    b. Coverage error
    c. Faulty frame
    d. Sampling frame error
2. In a study looking at citizens' perceptions of the police, researchers need to make sure they have a decent number of participants from diverse racial backgrounds. To do so, they break the population up into four strata based upon race and select

continues

continued

> 25% of their sample from each strata even though the population is not equally distributed by race. This would be an example of:
> a. proportionate stratified sampling
> b. nonprobability sampling
> c. cluster sampling
> d. disproportionate stratified sampling
>
> 3. If a researcher were to list all public or private high schools in their state, randomly select 10, and interview all students within each of the 10 schools, what would the schools be called?
>   a. Strata
>   b. Populations
>   c. Clusters
>   d. Frames
>
> **Answers: 1. b, 2. d, 3. c**

7.4 NONPROBABILITY SAMPLING

In contrast to probability sampling, nonprobability sampling involves methods of selecting cases other than random selection. Before we examine various methods of nonrandom case selection, let us examine how nonprobability sampling is integral to criminal justice research. As we point out, not only is it often a practical necessity, it also complements probability sampling in important ways.

Overview of Nonprobability Sampling

Probability sampling assumes a great deal of knowledge about the target population and the variables to be measured, but researchers may lack the necessary information to draw a probability sample. For example, when studying past events, the archaeologist or historian often finds only a fraction of relevant materials available. Similarly, in contemporary societies, certain individuals or institutions may be inaccessible. Under these circumstances, the researcher must adopt a nonprobability method of case selection or abandon the study altogether. Nonprobability sampling also is a necessity if an adequate sampling frame cannot be obtained or constructed. If the target population is unknown or hidden, such as undocumented immigrants, illegal weapons dealers, or intravenous drug users, only nonprobability methods of selection are possible. Likewise, if the population is rare (e.g., individuals who are exonerated of a crime or gang members) it may be too costly to compile a list or to use probability sampling to screen for members of the target population.

Yet, nonprobability sampling is not dictated by practical necessity alone. The decision to use nonprobability sampling, like probability sampling, depends on the research question, units of analysis, and methods of data collection. Nonprobability sampling is commonly used when the aim is to develop a holistic understanding of complex social units, such as a fraternity, nursing home, or ethnic community. To arrive at a comprehensive understanding, researchers usually elect to study a single unit or a small sample of units, in which case probability sampling is inappropriate and it is better to leave the selection of cases to expert judgment (in other words, nonrandom selection). Similarly in field research, once the researcher is in the field, the choice of whom to observe and interview is usually based on how likely the people are to enhance the researcher's insight and understanding. "Choosing someone at random," as Martin Marshall (1996) writes, "would be analogous to randomly asking a passerby how to repair a broken-down car, rather than asking a garage mechanic." Asking the mechanic "is likely to be more productive" (p. 523).

Steps in Nonprobability Sampling

In field research and in some other studies addressing qualitative research questions, the researcher may select a single case or research site in which to carry out observations, and then choose what to observe within the site. Therefore, we begin by discussing the selection of cases or research sites; then we turn our attention to nonrandom methods of selecting units of observation within sites. Note, however, that it is possible for researchers, especially those using in-depth interviews as a stand-alone method, to only complete the second step in this process.

SELECT CASES OR RESEARCH SITES

Researchers seeking an in-depth knowledge of social patterns and processes may conduct case studies or select a single setting in which to carry out their research. A **case study** consists of the holistic analysis of a single person, group, or event by one or more methods (Thomas, 2011). Cases and research sites may be selected for several reasons. They may (1) be conveniently located, (2) fit the research topic, (3) provide relevant theoretical comparisons, or (4) represent extreme or deviant cases.

> **case study** the holistic analysis of a single person, group, or event by one or more research methods

For example, William Foote Whyte (1993) chose an Italian neighborhood for his classic study *Street Corner Society* partly because of its convenience—it was located in the city where he lived—but also because it was a good example of what he wanted to study. Whyte's classic study revealed important insights into poor, urban communities and street gangs. Researchers continue to rely upon this model of "urban ethnography" today.

In addition to being convenient to the researcher and fitting the research topic, cases may be chosen for the purpose of comparison. All criminological research involves some form of comparison (Lieberson, 1985). As an example, research has established that placing prisoners in solitary confinement (disciplinary segregation) for prolonged periods of time can have detrimental impacts on prisoners' mental health (Wildeman & Andersen, 2020). However, little research has looked at the long-term consequences of disciplinary segregation for prisoners, extending beyond their release from prison. In studying the long-term consequences of this type of punishment, it is not enough to look only at inmates who have experienced disciplinary segregation. Rather, one needs to compare a group of those who have experienced disciplinary segregation to inmates who have not experienced disciplinary segregation to determine differences.

Wildeman and Andersen's (2020) study illustrates comparison through the selection of three distinct groups of participants for comparative purposes: inmates who were never officially punished while incarcerated, inmates who were officially punished but not through disciplinary segregation, and inmates who were officially punished through the use of disciplinary segregation. Comparing different groups of inmates helps the researchers determine if there are inherent differences between those who are and are not officially sanctioned in prison that might impact the offenders post-release, regardless of disciplinary segregation. It is also necessary to compare those who have experienced disciplinary segregation to those who have not to conclude whether disciplinary segregation has long-term impacts. Wildeman and Andersen's use of official data on the inmates in their study made it possible to analyze data for *individual* offenders.

In historical and field research, researchers analyze larger social units, such as organizations, neighborhoods, or nations as whole entities. To understand historical processes, they are interested in identifying similarities and differences among these units (Ragin, 1987); so, they select cases that provide important bases of theoretical comparison. In the Comparative Neighborhood Study, for example, William Julius Wilson and Richard Taub (2006) investigated the reactions of urban neighborhoods in Chicago to looming changes, such as the increase in Latino residents in the 1990s. For over two years, they conducted field research in selected neighborhoods to understand how racial and ethnic tensions affect neighborhood social organization and stability. To capture the ethnic diversity of the city, they chose four working- and middle-class neighborhoods: a White neighborhood, a neighborhood in transition from White to Mexican, a predominantly Mexican neighborhood, and an African-American neighborhood.

Finally, a time-honored strategy throughout the sciences is to analyze cases that are extreme or special in some way, such as persons who survived ordinarily terminal illnesses, unusually successful businesses, or schools in low socioeconomic areas with high graduation rates. Such "deviant" cases may provide evidence that challenges or extends existing theory. For example, studies of juvenile delinquency show that juvenile confinement is reserved for the most extreme cases of juveniles. Similarly, most individuals engaged in delinquency at a young age will stop offending into adulthood, leaving a small proportion of individuals who go on to become "career criminals." Delisi and colleagues (2011) chose to study adult career criminals and determine the impact of juvenile confinement on homicide offending in adulthood, an extreme and unique subset of the criminal justice population.

SELECT OBSERVATIONS

For many researchers, the selection of a research site is the first step in the sampling process. The next step concerns who or what to observe within the site. This step may involve probability sampling, such as randomly choosing places and times to record observations. In many observational or interview studies, however, deciding what to observe or whom to interview involves one or more methods of nonprobability sampling. In this section, we consider three of the most common methods: convenience, purposive, and snowball.

CONVENIENCE SAMPLING As the name implies, **convenience sampling** consists of selecting a requisite number of conveniently accessible cases. If you were doing a brief survey for your methods class, for example, you might seek volunteers to interview among students who are exiting the cafeteria, who live in your residence hall, or who are studying in the library. Many online surveys are directed to whoever visits a particular website; television stations sometimes tap public opinion by providing a telephone number to call; newspaper reporters may interview conveniently available commuters or shoppers. Wildeman and Andersen (2020) utilized a convenience sample in their study by using inmate data available to them through official records.

> **convenience sampling** the selection of cases that are conveniently available

Convenience samples are easy, quick, and inexpensive, and they may be perfectly appropriate for some research purposes. For practical reasons, field research and in-depth interview studies often begin with a convenience sample of observations or interviewees; however, these are usually followed up by a more controlled or theoretically based selection. Convenience samples are also a useful tool for pretesting survey questions, which we discuss in Chapter 9, and for conducting a pilot study to assess the feasibility of a bigger data-collection project. But they should be used with caution, as they provide no sound basis for statistical generalization.

Despite this limitation, over the past decade, as more and more social research has been conducted online, nonprobability sampling, including convenience sampling, has become common. This development is described in Box 7.5.

PURPOSIVE SAMPLING Researchers may also rely on their expert judgment to select cases. Known as **purposive** or **judgmental sampling**, this method applies to the selection of research sites as well as other units of observation. DeLisi et al.'s (2011) selection of career criminals from an adult, urban jail in the western United States is an example of purposive sampling; they recruited offenders labeled "frequent offenders," whose criminal histories had on average 30 arrests to be a part of the study. Purposive sampling has its broadest application in field research and in-depth interviews, in which observations and interviews are necessarily limited. In this kind of research, it is

> **purposive sampling** sampling that involves the careful and informed selection of typical cases or of cases that represent relevant dimensions of the population. Also called *judgmental sampling*

BOX 7.5

READING CRIMINAL JUSTICE RESEARCH

Methodological Issues Related to Sampling via Crowdsourcing and Online Panels

As we discuss in later chapters, the internet has become an increasingly important site for the conduct of criminal justice research. This research has given rise to two new sampling methods that are now widely used: crowdsourcing and online panels (Thompson & Pickett, 2020).

Crowdsourcing combines the words crowd and outsourcing to convey the process of asking a large group of people to perform a task. The "crowd" consists of an online labor force; "requestors" who wish to use these "workers" post a task on the platform. Currently, the most popular platform, Amazon Mechanical Turk (MTurk), has a workforce of over 500,000 self-recruited workers. Requestors post tasks, and workers decide whether to perform them. Besides research participation, other possible tasks include data entry, transcription of audio tapes, and text editing. **Online panels** (also called opt-in panels) consist of samples of volunteers who are recruited and paid by vendors for the specific task of participating in online "surveys." Vendors invite the panelists to participate in surveys commissioned by researchers.

Like convenience samples, crowdsourcing and online panels are easily accessible and relatively low cost. Hundreds of workers on MTurk can participate per day at a cost of 10 to 25 cents per minute of participant time (Chandler et al., 2019). Online panels are generally more expensive than crowdsourced samples but still cost much less than probability-based surveys. For experimenters, such as criminologists or psychologists, who often rely on convenience samples, crowdsourcing platforms also offer more diverse research participants than the college student samples that have traditionally been used.

Despite these advantages, the main drawback to these methods is their potential bias in drawing inferences beyond the sample itself. Strictly speaking, only a random sample is truly representative of the target population and can be used to statistically estimate its characteristics within a range of sampling error. MTurk workers who participate in a study are a self-selected convenience sample, which is inherently biased and bears little resemblance to the United States or any other population. Studies have found that MTurk workers based in the United States tend to be younger, female, somewhat better educated, more liberal politically, and less religious compared to the US population as a whole (Casey et al., 2017; Hitlin, 2016; Levay et al., 2016). Thus, crowdsourcing samples are not appropriate when the research aims to generalize to a clearly defined target population.

Online panels also may be poorly representative of the larger population. However, they often apply one of two strategies to enhance sample representativeness (AAPOR, 2020; Couper, 2017). In the first strategy, applied during sample recruitment, panel members who are invited to participate "are carefully selected to match the makeup of the intended population on" demographic variables such as age, sex, and education level (AAPOR, 2020). The second strategy, which occurs during the data analysis, makes statistical adjustments that assign weights to match the population on key study variables.

The challenge with online panels is to identify which variables to control in sample selection and/or estimation. Relying on the appropriate selection of such variables poses greater risk of biased results than the use of probability sampling (Baker et al., 2013). Thus far, the evidence shows that online panels are less accurate than probability samples (AAPOR, 2020). Does this mean that researchers should not use online panels? We agree with Andrew Thompson and Justin Pickett's (2020) conclusion: Researchers should "exercise caution when making inferences" and perform various checks on the generalizability of their findings (pp. 926–927).

important to carefully select informants and interviewees who can best help to answer the research question. To decide whom to select, researchers may use their developing knowledge of the research setting as well as a variety of sources of information.

SNOWBALL SAMPLING Another set of sampling methods has been developed specifically for sampling target populations that make up small subgroups of the larger population (Sudman & Kalton, 1986; Sudman et al., 1988). In criminal justice research, these subgroups may be hidden populations who choose to stay under the radar (e.g., gang members, persons using or dealing illicit substances, or homeless individuals). A common method of reaching these populations is **snowball sampling**, which uses a process of chain referral: when members of the target population are located, they are asked to provide names and addresses of other members of the target population, who are then contacted and asked to name others, and so on.

A basic assumption of snowball sampling is that members of the target population often know each other. Snowball sampling is particularly applicable to studies of deviant behavior, where "moral, legal, or social sensitivities surrounding the behavior in question . . . pose some serious problems for locating and contacting potential respondents" (Biernacki & Waldorf, 1981, p. 144). In these studies, members of the population are usually socially invisible by virtue of their illicit, clandestine activities. Their characteristics, therefore, are unknown, and drawing a probability sample is virtually impossible. Often the best that one can do is to use all available means to find eligible respondents and start referral chains. The quality of the sample ultimately depends on the researcher's ability to develop initial contacts and referral chains that represent a range of characteristics in the target population.

> **crowdsourcing** as applied to sampling in online studies, the practice of hiring a group of paid workers to participate in a study, usually accomplished through requests on a crowdsourcing platform
>
> **online panel** a sample of people who have agreed to participate in online surveys upon request
>
> **snowball sampling** a sampling procedure that uses a process of chain referral, whereby each contact is asked to identify additional members of the target population, who are asked to name others, and so on

Making Inferences from Nonprobability Samples

As we noted, sampling is about selection and inference. Researchers select cases and observations that will provide reasonable inferences pertinent to their research question. But different sampling methods allow for different inferences, and we must be careful about the kind of inferences we can make.

Unlike probability samples, nonprobability samples provide no basis for making *statistical inferences* from a sample to a well-defined population. Based on a purposive sample, such as DeLisi's, for example, we cannot estimate the percentage of individuals who experienced juvenile confinement and went on to become repeat offenders who committed homicide. As with all criminal justice research, it remains for subsequent studies to expand and test theory.

The tentative conclusions researchers draw from nonprobability samples are consistent with all scientific inquiry, for criminal justice researchers ultimately want to make *theoretical inferences* about the social world. They are not interested merely in students enrolled at University X, older residents of a midsize North American city, or US voters; rather, they want to understand humankind. To make universal generalizations, no single probability sample, bound by place and time, is adequate. In this sense—within the context of societies around the world—a single probability sample is a nonprobability sample of the theoretical population (Sjoberg et al., 1991).

Finally, determining an appropriate sample size is based on very different criteria when making statistical vs. theoretical inferences. The impact of sample size on statistical inference can be estimated mathematically in probability sampling; and so, as discussed earlier, researchers determine sample size based on how many cases they need to achieve a desired level of precision, given finite resources. There are few guidelines, however, for determining appropriate sample sizes for theoretical inferences. According to the most common guideline, sample sizes in purposive sampling should be determined inductively, based on the concept of **saturation** (Charmaz, 2006; Glaser & Strauss, 1967; Guest et al., 2006). That is, researchers should continue to sample cases until little or no new information can be extracted from the data. Based on an empirical analysis of 60 in-depth interviews, Guest, Bunce, and Johnson (2006) found that 70 percent of the variability in the data set was identified within six interviews, and 88 percent was identified after 12 interviews. Therefore, they recommend six to 12 interviews per subgroup as minimally adequate.

saturation in purposive sampling, the point at which new data cease to yield new information or theoretical insights

SUMMARY

Nonprobability sampling involves nonrandom selection. It is useful for studying populations to which researchers have limited access or cannot construct sampling frames, and it is appropriate for studying a small number of cases or deciding what to observe and whom to interview within a research setting. Nonprobability sampling typically occurs in two stages: selecting cases or research sites and selecting observations within selected sites. Three common methods of selecting units of observation within sites are convenience sampling, purposive sampling, and snowball sampling. Although nonprobability samples should not be used to make precise statistical inferences, they can be used effectively for developing and generalizing theories. Check your understanding of sampling in Box 7.6.

Key Terms

> **BOX 7.6**
> **CHECKING YOUR UNDERSTANDING**
>
> ## Matching Exercise: Sampling
>
> Match the example provided on the left to the nonprobability sampling method on the right.
>
> | | | | |
> |---|---|---|---|
> | 1. | To study drug sales on college campuses, researchers use an informant who has a knowledge of this subgroup to collect a sample of known dealers. | a. | Convenience sampling |
> | 2. | To study the differences between male and female property offenders, researchers go to several probation agencies seeking data on property offenders only. | b. | Purposive sampling |
> | 3. | To study obstacles that victims of intimate personal violence may face when bringing charges against their batterers, qualitative researchers seek to interview victims. In the process, they determine they need to sample more women with children in order to develop conclusions for this study. | c. | Snowball sampling |
> | 4. | To study the effectiveness of a cognitive behavioral training program on inmates, a program supervisor at a correctional institution uses his class of inmates as his study sample. | d. | Theoretical sampling |
>
> Answers: 1. c, 2. b, 3. d, 4. a

KEY TERMS

case study, p. 193
cluster sampling, p. 187
confidence interval, p. 181
convenience sampling, p. 195
coverage error, p. 185
crowdsourcing, p. 196
disproportionate stratified sampling, p. 186
multistage cluster sampling, p. 187

nonprobability sampling, p. 175
nonresponse error (nonresponse bias), p. 189
online panel, p. 196
population, p. 175
probability, p. 176
probability distribution, p. 179
probability sampling, p. 175

proportionate stratified sampling, p. 186
purposive sampling (judgmental sampling), p. 195
random selection, p. 177
sample, p. 175
sampling error, p. 180
sampling frame, p. 184
sampling with replacement, p. 179

sampling without replacement, p. 179
saturation, p. 198
simple random sample, p. 185
snowball sampling, p. 197
standard error, p. 181
stratified random sample, p. 186
target population, p. 183
weighting, p. 186

KEY POINTS

- The two general strategies for selecting cases or observations are probability sampling and nonprobability sampling.
- Based on random selection, probability sampling is used to make precise statistical inferences from a sample to a population.
- The steps in probability sampling consist of defining the target population, constructing a sampling frame, devising the sampling design, and drawing the sample.
- The most basic probability sampling design, simple random sampling, gives each case in a sampling frame an equal chance of being selected.
- Stratified random sampling divides the frame into strata (variable categories) and samples within each stratum; multistage cluster sampling divides the population into a succession of clusters (natural or geographic groupings), first sampling across clusters and then within each selected cluster.
- Surveys using probability sampling may be subject to two sources of sample bias: coverage error and nonresponse error.
- Based on nonrandom selection, nonprobability sampling may be used when the target population cannot be readily identified, a sampling frame cannot be obtained or easily constructed, and research goals seek a holistic or in-depth understanding of a small number of cases.
- Nonprobability sampling may occur at two stages: when choosing one or a few cases or research sites and when choosing whom or what to observe within selected sites.
- Cases and research sites may be selected because they are conveniently located, fit the research topic, provide theoretical comparisons, or represent deviant cases.
- Nonprobability methods of selecting interviewees or observations consist of convenience sampling, purposive sampling, and snowball sampling.
- Probability sampling provides a basis for statistical inference; nonprobability sampling generally is intended to provide a basis for theoretical inference.

REVIEW QUESTIONS
1. Explain the difference between probability and nonprobability sampling. When is it appropriate to use each of these sampling strategies?
2. Explain the difference between a sample and a sampling frame. Which of these concepts is associated with coverage error? Which is associated with nonresponse error?
3. Explain how simple random sampling is incorporated into both stratified random sampling and multistage cluster sampling.
4. Give an example from the textbook of the purposive sampling method.
5. What kind of inferences may be drawn from probability and nonprobability sampling?

EXERCISES
1. This exercise will help familiarize you with some types of probability sampling. First, using the "A" section of the latest issue of your campus directory as a starting point, draw up a sampling frame composed of the first 50 names listed.

    a. *Simple random sample.* Select a random sample of 10 names using the Random Integer Generator in RANDOM.ORG. (See Box 7.1 for instructions on how to use this site.) List all the random numbers you select, and then list the 10 names in your sample. Repeat this procedure in drawing a random sample of five names.
    b. *Stratified random sample.* Divide the names in your sampling frame into strata on the basis of an identifiable characteristic, such as class year. Now, using RANDOM.ORG again, select a sample of five names within each stratum. List the names that you obtain. Is your sample proportionate or disproportionate? Explain.

2. Each election year, the media rely on exit polls to forecast and analyze election outcomes. Exit polls are surveys of voters immediately after they have cast their votes at their polling places. The polling places (or precincts) are randomly selected to represent each state and, for national polls, the nation as a whole. Interviewers usually give selected voters a questionnaire that takes only a couple minutes to complete. It asks for whom they voted, about important issues, and about demographics such as gender, age, and race. Participation is voluntary and anonymous. Interviewing starts when the polls open and continues throughout the day until about an hour before they close at night.

In one national election exit poll, voters were selected in the following way. Within each state, a complete list of precincts was obtained. The precincts were divided up into counties, and within each county, precincts were selected randomly so that the odds of being selected were proportionate to the number of people who typically voted in that precinct. At each selected precinct, one or two interviewers stood outside and randomly selected roughly one hundred voters during the day as they exited from voting. The interviewers accomplished this task by counting voters as they left the polling place and selecting every voter at a specific interval (say, every third or fifth voter). The interval was chosen so that the approximately 100 interviews were spread evenly over the course of the day. (Note that the selection of voters at polling places approximates simple random sampling.)

    a. What is the overall sampling design? (Be specific. This is a complex design, involving more than one sampling method.)
    b. What sampling frame was used in the design?
    c. Is stratification incorporated into the design? If so, what was the stratifying variable?
    d. Some journalists and commentators would like to obtain midday numbers or estimates from the exit polls. Why would the midday numbers have a much larger margin of error than the numbers compiled when the polls are closed at the end of the day? Give *two* possible reasons, one involving random sampling error and the other involving sampling bias.
    e. Evaluate the sampling strategy with respect to coverage error, assuming that the target population is all voters in the national election.

3. Suppose that you want to draw a sample from each of the following populations. Devise a sampling plan for each by (1) indicating the unit of analysis, (2) clearly defining the target population, (3) constructing the sampling frame, and (4) selecting and justifying an appropriate sampling design (e.g., simple random sampling, stratified random sampling, purposive sampling).

    a. Students enrolled in US colleges and universities (to study alcohol use).
    b. Residents of Chicago who work night shifts (to study their lifestyles).
    c. Conversations in public places on campus (to study what people talk about in various social settings).
    d. Campus substance use (to study gender differences).
    e. College employees at a specific college (for a study of factors—pay, hours, working conditions, and so forth—that affect job satisfaction).

8

Experiments
What Causes What?

CHAPTER OUTLINE

8.1 Introductory Example: Misconduct in Criminal Prosecution 204

8.2 The Logic of Experimentation 206
Summary 210

8.3 Variations on the Experimental Method 211
Variations in Experimental Design 211
Variations in Experimental Context 213
Summary 216

8.4 The Process of Conducting Experiments 217
Pretesting 218
Participant Recruitment and Informed Consent 219
Introduction to the Experiment 219
Experimental Manipulation and Random Assignment 221
Manipulation Checks 221
Measurement of the Dependent Variable 223
Debriefing 224
Summary 225

8.5 Strengths and Weaknesses of Experiments 226
Internal Validity 226
External Validity 229
Reactive Measurement Effects 231
Content Restrictions 233
Summary 233

LEARNING OBJECTIVES

By the end of this chapter, you should be able to

8.1 Explain the logic of experimentation with respect to how experiments effectively meet the criteria for establishing causality.

8.2 Describe variations in experimental design related to the timing and measurement of the dependent variable as well as the number of independent variables manipulated.

8.3 Describe variations in experimental context by distinguishing among laboratory, field, and survey-based experiments.

8.4 Describe the steps in the process of planning and conducting an experiment and apply them to a research topic.

8.5 Evaluate experiments as a method of data collection, identifying their strengths and weaknesses.

If you are like us, you have conducted "experiments" of your own in everyday life. For example, you may have intentionally broken a social norm and observed people's reactions. In fact, whole websites are devoted to this. Type "50 fun things to do in an elevator" into your search engine, and you will see what we are talking about. A classic elevator norm-breaking "experiment" is to stand very close to people who enter the elevator and observe their reactions. Most likely, they will move away because in mainstream North American culture people tend to prefer at least a few feet of personal space between a stranger and themselves.

Criminal justice experiments are conducted in a similar but more systematic way. Researchers observe people's behavior under different conditions, such as a *control* condition in which people act "normally," and an *experimental* condition, in which a norm is broken. With the exception of the manipulated factor (acting normally or elevator norm-breaking), everything else is the same. Consequently, if we observe a change in people's behavior, such as moving away from a person who stands too close to them in the elevator, we can be pretty sure that the manipulated factor caused the change.

More than any other methodological approach, experiments help researchers to understand whether one factor *caused* a change in another. Because they provide the strongest possible evidence of cause and effect, experiments are an ideal model for answering quantitative research questions. Even when it is impractical or impossible to do an experiment and some other approach must be used, the logic of experimentation serves as a standard by which other research strategies are judged.

We begin this chapter by describing a typical laboratory experiment as found in criminal justice research. Using this example, we introduce the essential features and causal logic of experiments. Then, we discuss variants of the experimental approach, including designs that manipulate two or more variables and experiments conducted outside the laboratory. Again, using our introductory example, we outline the process of conducting or "staging" an experiment. Finally, we discuss the strengths and limitations of the experimental approach.

8.1 INTRODUCTORY EXAMPLE: MISCONDUCT IN CRIMINAL PROSECUTION

The basic features of an experiment are nicely illustrated by a study of the impact of crime severity on prosecutorial misconduct (Lucas et al., 2006). In criminal trials in the United States, prosecuting attorneys are supposed to turn over to the defense any evidence that might pertain to a defendant's guilt or innocence. Not to do so is illegal and is defined as misconduct. Scholars have noted that cases involving serious crimes, such as rape and murder, are more likely to result in erroneous convictions than other kinds of cases. To account for these findings, Jeffrey Lucas, Corina Graif, and Michael Lovaglia (2006) theorized that prosecutorial misconduct might be more likely in serious cases because "prosecutors succumb to increased pressure to convict" (p. 97; See Photos 8.1, 8.2, & 8.3). Feeling pressure, they use their belief in the defendant's guilt as justification for misconduct by withholding evidence that may help prove the defendant's *innocence*. Based on this theory, Lucas and associates derived three hypotheses. One hypothesis was that misconduct will be more likely to occur in cases involving more severe crimes than less severe crimes.

To test this hypothesis and others, the researchers carried out a laboratory experiment at a Midwestern university. The study design called for research participants to play the role of prosecutor in a criminal case, read a "Police Report" and other materials describing either a murder or an assault, and perform duties in preparation for a trial.

▲ PHOTO 8.1 Jeffrey Lucas

After setting up the experiment, the researchers recruited undergraduate students to participate and paid them $10 for their participation. Before the volunteers arrived at the laboratory, they were randomly assigned to either a "murder" or an "assault" condition (described further below). When they arrived, each participant was told that

> he or she would be acting as a defense attorney, a prosecuting attorney, or a judge in a contrived criminal trial. The participant then was asked to draw one of three slips of paper from a hat to determine his or her role in the study. All of the slips, however, contained the word prosecutor, so participants always acted as prosecuting attorneys. (Lucas et al., 2006, p. 100)

▲ PHOTO 8.2 Corina Graif

All participants were then asked to read the police report, which described a crime in which police responded to a report of a missing person. When police arrived at the residence of the person reported as missing, they found a man's body in the front hallway and immediately called emergency medical personnel. Depending on the condition to which they were assigned in the experiment, participants then read that either

a) the victim was pronounced dead at the scene (murder condition) or
b) the victim fully recovered from his injuries (assault condition).

The report further revealed that the police had apprehended a male ex-felon, who was indicted for either (a) murder or (b) assault, depending again on the experimental condition.

After reading the police report, participants read two forms. The first form contained detailed information about the case, most of which implied the guilt of the defendant. The second form carefully explained the duties of the prosecuting attorney. The form describing the prosecutor's job

▲ PHOTO 8.3 Michael Lovaglia

emphasized the responsibility to present the case against the defendant, but also the legal obligation to "turn over to the defense all materials that might point to the defendant's guilt or innocence" (Lucas et al., 2006, p. 101).

Finally, participants were asked to perform several tasks. The first of these was to read a set of interviews obtained by police officers that contained a total of 60 questions, and then "compile a list of questions from the interviews to turn over to the defense." Although the interview information "generally pointed to the defendant's guilt," four questions contained "information identifying the victim's wife as a potential suspect" (Lucas et al., 2006, p. 101). The measure of misconduct consisted of the number of these four questions that participants withheld from the defense. As hypothesized, participants in the murder condition (average = 2.15) withheld more questions than participants in the assault condition (average = 1.50).

Using this study as an illustration, we focus on the logic of experimentation in the next section. First, we identify those essential features that make experiments a model for testing causal relationships; then, we relate these features to the criteria for inferring causality.

8.2 THE LOGIC OF EXPERIMENTATION

What basic features of an experimental design are illustrated in the foregoing experiment? Notice, first, that Lucas and associates' hypothesis concerns the relationship between two variables: crime severity and prosecutorial misconduct. In an experiment, a *manipulated* independent variable (the severity of the crime) is *followed by* a measured dependent variable (prosecutorial misconduct). There are at least two groups or conditions, represented by the categories of the independent variable (murder vs. assault). And except for this experimental manipulation, all groups are treated *exactly alike*. Finally, participants are *randomly* assigned to one group or the other.

How do these features meet the requirements of causal inference? Although we can never prove beyond all doubt that two variables (say, X and Y) are causally related, recall from Chapter 5 that certain types of empirical evidence are regarded as essential for causal statements:

1. association (i.e., evidence that X and Y vary together in a way predicted by the hypothesis);
2. direction of influence (i.e., evidence that X affected Y rather than Y affected X); and
3. the elimination of plausible rival explanations (i.e., evidence that one or more variables other than X did not cause the observed change in Y).

The first two kinds of evidence show that X could have affected Y; the third kind shows that the relationship between X and Y is nonspurious—that other variables are not responsible for the observed effects. Let us refer back to Lucas and associates' experiment to see how these types of evidence were provided.

1. *Association.* It was found, as hypothesized, that the independent variable, severity of the crime, was associated with the dependent variable, misconduct, as measured by the number of questions pointing to another suspect that were withheld from the defense. That is, participants in the murder condition withheld more questions than participants in the assault condition.
2. *Direction of influence.* Evidence that the independent variable (X) influenced the dependent variable (Y) and not the other way around is based on time order in experiments: Y cannot be the cause of X if it occurred after X. In the experiment, we know that misconduct could not have caused the severity of the crime because participants were told first either that the victim died (murder) or survived his injuries (assault).
3. *Elimination of rival explanations.* What might be plausible reasons why participants in the murder condition withheld more questions than those in the assault condition? One possibility is that participants in the two conditions differ systematically in terms of personal qualities such as honesty, intelligence, or attention to detail. For example, if participants in the murder condition were less careful in performing their duties, they may simply have supplied fewer questions, irrespective of their content, to the defense. Such extraneous variables are controlled, however, by randomly assigning participants to the two conditions. **Random assignment** means that the procedure by which participants are assigned (in this case, tossing a coin) ensures that each participant has an equal chance of being in either group. By virtue of random assignment, individual characteristics or experiences that might confound the results theoretically should be evenly distributed between the two groups. Thus, there should be just about as many participants who are honest or dishonest, motivated or unmotivated, and so forth, in one condition as in the other. To clarify an important point about random assignment, see Box 8.1.

random assignment the assignment of research participants to experimental conditions by means of a random device, such as a coin toss

In addition to controlling preexperimental, individual differences through random assignment, the researcher makes every attempt to treat both groups exactly alike during the experiment except for the experimental manipulation. Lucas and colleagues took care to ensure that the laboratory where the research took place, all of the instructions and materials, and the tasks that participants were asked to perform were the same for both groups. An example of a violation of this principle would have been if participants in the assault condition had additional information provided by the victim after he recovered. Such information (which is often included in real criminal trials) obviously would not be available if the victim is deceased.

In an airtight experimental design, there is only one rival explanation: the results could have occurred by chance. This would mean that the process of randomly assigning

> **BOX 8.1**
>
> ## DOING CRIMINAL JUSTICE RESEARCH
>
> ## The Difference Between Random Sampling and Random Assignment
>
> As we pointed out in Chapter 7, researchers apply the word *random* to processes that give each element in a set, such as all students at your college or university, a known and independent chance of being selected. Probability sampling, also called "random sampling," is based on random processes of selection. So, too, is random assignment of participants in an experiment. It is important to note, however, that random sampling and random assignment refer to distinct methods that occur at different points in the research process and serve different purposes (see Figure A).
>
> Sampling occurs first when you select the participants for your study. Surveys often use random sampling to select respondents, thus giving every person in the target population a known and independent chance of being selected. This allows researchers to make statistical estimates of population characteristics. Did Lucas and colleagues use random sampling to select their sample of participants? No, they did not. As is typical of laboratory experiments, they selected a convenience sample of students who volunteered to participate.
>
> But once they had their sample of participants, the experimenters randomly assigned each participant to one of the two experimental conditions, murder or assault. In this way, participants had an equal chance of being in either condition, which ensured that the groups were approximately equal on all uncontrolled variables. As we discuss below, this enabled the researchers to use a test of statistical significance to determine whether there was a difference between the two groups.
>
>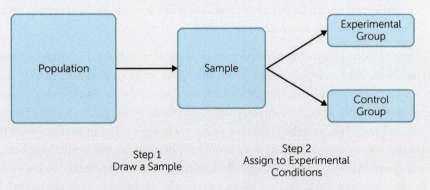
>
> **FIGURE A** The Two-Step Process of Drawing a Sample and Assigning Participants to Experimental Conditions

8.2 The Logic of Experimentation

Table 8.1 Lucas and Associates' Experimental Results

	Mean (SD)	t	p
Number of Exculpatory Questions Withheld from Defense			
Murder condition	2.15 (1.51)		
Assault condition	1.50 (1.45)		
Hypothesis: Murder condition > Assault condition		1.96	.027

Source: Adapted from Table 1 in Lucas et al. (2006, p. 103).

persons to the experimental and control groups resulted, by chance, in an unequal distribution between the groups on variables such as honesty, intelligence, or how carefully they attended to instructions—variables that could affect their performance on the tasks they were given. As we noted, for example, participants in the murder condition might have supplied fewer questions to the defense than participants in the assault condition because they generally were less careful in performing their duties.

To assess the likelihood that the results of an experiment occurred by chance, experimenters use a test of statistical significance. Recall from Chapter 5 that significance tests indicate the likelihood or probability that an association is due to random processes. Such tests express this probability in decimal form. So, when you read that the results of an experiment were found to be significant at the .05 level, this means that only about 5 percent of the time, or 5 times in 100, would differences this large between the experimental conditions occur by chance when the experimental variable actually has no effect. With such a low probability, it would be reasonable to rule out prior differences uncontrolled by the randomization process as a plausible explanation of the experimental results. To illustrate, Table 8.1 presents results from Lucas and associates' experiment. Consistent with their hypothesis, participants in the murder condition withheld more "exculpatory" questions (questions that may help prove the defendant's innocence) from the defense, on average, than participants in the assault condition. And according to the t-test statistic, the probability ("p" in the table) that this difference is due to chance is less than .05 (.027 to be exact).

On the other hand, if the results were not found to be statistically significant, it would not be reasonable to rule out differences due to random assignment, and we could not have much confidence that the experimental manipulation caused the effects. In short, a statistical test of significance assesses the likelihood that the observed difference between the groups is real (significant) and not of a magnitude that would occur frequently by chance.

SUMMARY

Experiments provide the ideal model for testing hypotheses and inferring causal relationships. To determine association, experiments compare outcomes in two or more groups or conditions, representing categories of the independent variable. To establish direction of influence, the *manipulated* independent variable (the cause) always precedes the *measured* dependent variable (the effect). To control for variables that might produce a spurious association, participants are *randomly assigned* to conditions, and everything except the experimental manipulation remains the same throughout the experiment. Check your understanding of the concepts learned within this section in Box 8.2.

BOX 8.2

CHECKING YOUR UNDERSTANDING

Experimental Design Review I

1. All of the following are an essential feature of a true experiment, except:
   a. measurement of the dependent variables
   b. at least one comparison or control group
   c. random assignment
   d. manipulation of the independent variable
   e. laboratory setting

2. The causal criterion _____ is supported in an experiment by random assignment.
   a. nonspuriousness
   b. association
   c. direction of influence

3. The purpose of tests of statistical significance in an experiment is to:
   a. determine if chance is a reasonable explanation of experimental results
   b. determine if random assignment created similar experimental and control groups
   c. establish direction of influence
   d. determine the generalizability of the findings

Answers: 1. e, 2. a, 3. a

8.3 VARIATIONS ON THE EXPERIMENTAL METHOD

Now that you have learned the essential features of experiments and have seen how experiments offer strong evidence of cause and effect, let us examine additional research examples that illustrate how these features may be extended to more complex study designs and to contexts outside the laboratory.

Variations in Experimental Design

As you can see, scientific experiments, such as the misconduct study, contain certain basic requirements. Studies that meet these basic requirements are sometimes called "true experiments." If we let "X" represent the independent variable, "Y" the dependent variable, and "R" random assignment, we can diagram the basic elements of an experimental design as follows:

$$R \begin{cases} X_1 \quad Y \\ X_2 \quad Y \end{cases}$$

Thus, in the misconduct study, each participant was randomly assigned (R) to one of two conditions, murder (X_1) or assault (X_2), after which participants' level of misconduct (Y) was measured. Within these baseline requirements, however, experimental designs may vary in two principal ways: the timing and measurement of the dependent variable and the number of independent variables that are manipulated.[1] As we review these variations, notice that each variant contains the basic design elements as diagrammed above.

TIMING AND MEASUREMENT OF THE DEPENDENT VARIABLE

The misconduct study is called a **posttest-only control group design** because the dependent variable was measured (or "tested") *after* the manipulation of the independent variable. In some experiments, however, the dependent variable is measured *both* before *and* after the manipulation. As diagrammed below, this is called a **pretest-posttest control group design**.

$$R \begin{cases} Y_1 \quad X_1 \quad Y_2 \\ Y_1 \quad X_2 \quad Y_2 \end{cases}$$

Aside from pretests, experiments may apply multiple operational definitions of the dependent variable, such as more than one measure of misconduct. In order to

posttest-only control group design an experimental design in which the dependent variable is measured both before and after the experimental manipulation

pretest-posttest control group design the most basic experimental design in which the dependent variable is measured after the experimental manipulation

---

[1] Another variation is the within-subjects design in which research participants receive both treatments X_1 and X_2. This design is not discussed in this chapter, but the interested reader can learn more about it in Singleton and Straits (2018, pp. 235–237).

determine when and how long an effect occurs, experiments also may contain multiple posttests at varying points in time. Or, they may test the impact of the independent variable on more than one dependent variable. In the misconduct study, for example, Lucas and associates administered a questionnaire to participants after they had prepared their case. Included among the questions were measures of two other dependent variables: how strongly participants believed that the defendant was guilty and how important it was to them to attain a conviction. These variables provided a test of two additional hypotheses that were part of the researchers' theory: participants would feel greater pressure to attain a conviction and would be more likely to believe in the defendant's guilt when the crime was more serious.

NUMBER OF INDEPENDENT VARIABLES MANIPULATED

A second variation in the basic design is to manipulate more than one independent variable. Given that social events often are caused by a number of variables, it makes sense to study several possible causes, or independent variables, at the same time. When two or more independent variables are studied in a single experiment, they are referred to as *factors*, and the designs are called **factorial designs**. Let us examine an experiment that manipulated two factors.

factorial design an experiment in which two or more variables (factors) are manipulated

Andrew Smith and colleagues (2019) were interested in exploring how witnessing or testing conditions impact eyewitness identification. They hypothesized that providing witnesses with a weak recognition experience would have a negative impact on their ability to accurately identify a culprit. To test this hypothesis, they conducted a series of experiments in which they manipulated participants' recognition experience.

In one experiment, Smith and colleagues randomly assigned participants "to watch either a clear or degraded culprit video and then viewed either a culprit-present or culprit-removed lineup identification procedure" (Smith et al., 2019, p. 358). After viewing the lineup, participants were asked to indicate whether the culprit was present in the lineup. Participants were told that the actual culprit might not be present in the lineup and were given the option to not identify any of the individuals if they believed the culprit was not pictured. The measurement of the dependent variable consisted of whether the participant identification (or lack thereof) was accurate.

The overall design of this study thus manipulated two factors, "video quality" and "culprit-presence," each with two categories or levels (i.e., high quality, low quality, culprit-present, or culprit-removed). When a design has two independent variables, each having two levels, it is called a 2 × 2 (two by two) factorial design. A design that has three levels of one variable and two levels of another variable would be a 3 × 2 factorial design having six conditions. Following the notation we introduced, we could diagram this experiment as follows, where each subscript represents a variable (view of culprit in video or lineup type) and the number (1 or 2) of the subscript represents the level (high quality or low quality; culprit-present or culprit-removed). (Thus, X_{11} signifies that in this condition, participants were exposed to a high-quality video and a culprit-present lineup.)

Factorial designs such as this provide evidence of the impact of each factor as well as the joint effect of the factors. In the eyewitness identification experiment, the researchers found that while the interaction between video quality and culprit presence did not significantly predict identification accuracy, they did find that the degraded encoding conditions (video quality) did decrease accuracy in both culprit-present and culprit-absent identifications. Specifically, they found that "when the culprit was present, the odds ratio for accurate-identification decisions was 8.34 times greater for the clear versus degraded video" (Smith et al., 2019, p. 363). When the culprit was absent from the lineup, the odds ratio for accurate-identification decisions was 5.07 times greater for the high quality vs. low quality video.

Like the misconduct study, the eyewitness identification experiment took place in a laboratory. Experimental design methodology also may be applied in settings outside the laboratory, to which we now turn.

Variations in Experimental Context

Laboratory experiments have a long tradition in scientific research. However, in criminal justice research, many experiments occur outside of the lab. Below we discuss two variations in experiments outside of the traditional lab context: field experiments and survey-based experiments.

laboratory experiment an experiment conducted in a controlled environment

FIELD EXPERIMENTS

A study that has all the features of a true experiment (manipulation of independent variable, random assignment, etc.) but is carried out in a natural, real-world setting is called a **field experiment**. A good example is Devah Pager's (2003) study of job discrimination. Let us take a closer look at this study to examine the unique advantages and disadvantages of doing experiments "in the field."

field experiment an experiment conducted in a natural setting

To examine job discrimination, Pager conducted a special type of field experiment, known as an **audit study**, in which matched pairs of confederates ("testers") applied for real job openings. The testers were similar in physical appearance and job qualifications, but differed in other characteristics. Pager varied two characteristics: race and criminal record. She manipulated race by having two pairs, one Black and one White; and within each same-race pair, one tester presented himself as having a criminal record and the other did not (see Figure 8.1). Thus, this is a 2 × 2 factorial design. As the testers applied

audit study a study that examines racial and other forms of discrimination by sending matched pairs of individuals to apply for jobs, purchase a car, rent an apartment, and so on

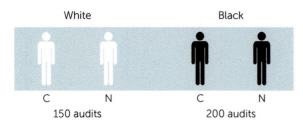

FIGURE 8.1 Pager's Study Design. "C" refers to criminal record; "N" refers to no criminal record.

for jobs, employment opportunity was measured by recording whether an applicant received a callback for an interview. Pager found evidence of discrimination on both counts: Black people received fewer callbacks than White people, and men with criminal records received fewer callbacks than their counterparts without criminal records.

One advantage of a field experiment over a lab experiment is that behavior is observed in a real-life setting in which the individuals—employers in this case—are unaware that they are participants in a study. As a consequence, their behavior should be more "natural." In addition, a field experiment more closely mirrors reality. For example, unlike role-playing "prosecutors" in the misconduct study, individuals in the audit study applied for real jobs with real employers.

On the other hand, field experiments afford less control in design and implementation. In the laboratory, for example, it would be relatively straightforward to manipulate whether a job applicant has a criminal record; but in the field, an applicant's criminal status is more difficult to convey. Pager used various means to draw attention to an applicant's criminal record, including direct responses on application forms, reporting work experience obtained in a correctional facility, and listing a parole officer as a reference. Field experiments also raise ethical and legal issues, as the ordinary means of protecting participants' rights, such as informed consent and debriefing, are usually impossible to implement.

SURVEY-BASED EXPERIMENTS

In addition to natural settings, experiments may be incorporated in surveys. For example, numerous **survey-based experiments** have investigated the effects of slight changes in the wording of a question in a survey. For instance, Applegate and Sanborn (2011) examined the impact of question wording on people's reported opinions on the harshness of their local courts using one of three possible versions of the General Social Survey (GSS) question about the harshness of local courts. The original version of the GSS question asked the following: "In general, do you think the courts in this area deal too harshly or not harshly enough with criminals?" A later version focused on leniency rather than harshness asking, "In general, do you think the courts in this area are not lenient enough or too lenient with criminals?" An additional version replaced the word *deal* with *punish* and asked, "In general, do you think the courts in this area punish criminals too harshly or not harshly enough?" The experiment found that question wording mattered, with fewer respondents expressing a desire for increased harshness with the alternative questions.

> **survey-based experiment** an experiment embedded in a survey in which respondents are given different, randomly assigned versions of survey questions

For many years, experiments embedded in surveys tended to focus on methodological topics such as question order and wording; however, innovations in survey design, in particular computer-assisted interviewing, have stimulated experiments on broader substantive issues (Sniderman, 2018; Sniderman & Grob, 1996). Survey experiments have proven particularly useful for investigating determinants of public opinion on social policies, such as sanctioning offenders (Norris & Mullinix, 2020; Schutten et al., 2020), the US war on drugs (Bobo & Johnson, 2004), and police officers' use of force (Salerno & Sanchez, 2020).

For example, several incidents in 2020 sparked controversy and protest over White police officers' excessive use of force against African Americans. Historically, the lack of objective evidence regarding interactions between the police and the public resulted in divergent views of such incidents. In recent years, police body cameras and private citizens' cell phones have produced video evidence that can resolve these divergent views. Jessica Salerno and Justin Sanchez (2020) point out, however, that the efficacy of video evidence may be mitigated by biased and stereotypical perceptions of "seemingly objective evidence" (p. 98). To examine this possibility, they conducted a survey in which they tested whether a police officer's gender and race affected people's perception and interpretation of an officer's use of force.

Survey participants were recruited from Amazon MTurk, an online crowdsourcing platform, which we described in Chapter 7. All participants viewed a video of a police–civilian encounter in which a police officer responded "to a call about a person acting disorderly" (Salerno & Sanchez, 2020, p. 102). The study consisted of a 2 × 2 × 2 factorial design with three independent variables:

1. whether the officer used force by throwing or not throwing the civilian to the ground;
2. officer gender, male or female; and
3. officer race, White or Black.

The use of force was clearly visible in the film, but the officer's gender and race were obscured. To manipulate gender and race, Salerno and Sanchez showed participants a photograph of the officer (revealing race and gender) before they saw the video and then before they completed several dependent measures. Here we focus of one of these measures: participants' trust in the officer, which consisted of the average ratings on five items (e.g., "I trust the police officer in the video can make decisions that are good for everyone in the city"). Participants indicated their level of agreement with each item on a 7-point scale ranging from strongly disagree (=1) to strongly agree (=7).

Salerno and Sanchez found a strong overall negative reaction to officers who used force. They also found that the officer's race had no effect on participants' perceptions

Table 8.2 Ratings of Trust by Officer's Use of Force and Gender

	Male	Female
Did not use force	5.41	5.29
Used force	3.43	3.89

Source: Adapted from Figure 1 in Salerno and Sanchez (2020, p. 104).

of trust, but that the officer's gender did. Table 8.2 presents the average ratings of trust broken down by gender and use of force. The results show no difference in trust by gender when the officers *did not use force*; however, when force was used, participants trusted female officers significantly more than male officers. Thus, as the researchers note, the negative reaction to use of force was "buffered somewhat" for female officers. This finding suggests a "gender contrast effect," given that the exertion of force is a traditionally masculine behavior, and women often "are penalized for violating gender stereotypes in the workplace" (Salerno & Sanchez, 2020, p. 107). More generally, it shows how ostensibly "objective" video evidence may be interpreted differently depending on gender stereotypes.

One advantage of embedding experiments in surveys is that the study can be carried out with a much larger and generally more diverse set of respondents than in laboratory experiments. Salerno and Sanchez's online survey was based on 452 participants. Although not nationally representative, their sample was much larger and far more diverse than the 80 undergraduate students who participated in the misconduct experiment.

SUMMARY

Experiments vary in design and context. Experimental designs may measure the dependent variable after the manipulation of an independent variable (in a posttest-only control group design) or both before and after the manipulation (in a pretest-posttest control group design); and they may measure more than one dependent variable. Designs also may include two or more independent variables (called factors) in a factorial design. Finally, experiments may be conducted outside the traditional lab context, such as "in the field" (field experiments) or embedded in surveys. Test your understanding of the concepts covered in this section in Box 8.3.

> **BOX 8.3**
>
> **CHECKING YOUR UNDERSTANDING**
>
> ## Experimental Design Review II
>
> 1. An experiment conducted in a natural setting is referred to as a:
>   a. laboratory experiment
>   b. survey-based experiment
>   c. natural experiment
>   d. field experiment
>
> 2. The prosecutorial misconduct study utilized which type of experimental design?
>   a. Pretest-posttest control group design
>   b. Posttest-only control group design
>   c. 2 × 4 factorial design
>   d. 2 × 2 factorial design
>
> 3. An experimental design in which the dependent variable is measured both before and after the experimental manipulation is called a:
>   a. 2 × 2 factorial design
>   b. posttest-only control group design
>   c. pretest-posttest control group design
>   d. audit design
>
> 4. An advantage of survey-based experiments in comparison with laboratory and field experiments is that survey-based experiments
>   a. use a larger and more diverse sample of research participants
>   b. focus on what people say rather than how they act or behave
>   c. assign participants to experimental conditions
>   d. control the conditions of observation
>
> Answers: 1. d, 2. b, 3. c, 4. a

8.4 THE PROCESS OF CONDUCTING EXPERIMENTS

Now that you know the logic of, and key variations in, the experimental approach, let us examine more closely how experiments are carried out. As with all criminal justice research, the process of conducting a study begins with the formulation of a research question. Thereafter, however, the process of designing research and collecting data vary depending on the unique features of each major approach.

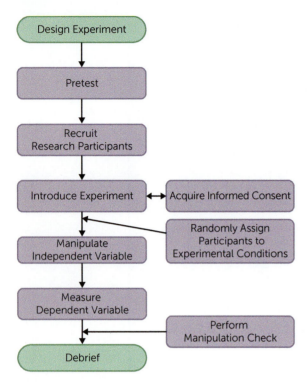

FIGURE 8.2 The Process of Planning and Conducting an Experiment

pretest a trial run of an experiment or survey instrument to evaluate and rehearse study procedures and personnel

Figure 8.2 shows the key points in planning and conducting an experiment. The first stage consists of designing the experiment, or deciding on the context and principal elements of the design, such as the number of manipulated variables. Based on this overall plan, the ensuing steps are much like producing a play. There are "scripts" to write and rewrite; a sequence of "scenes," each contributing something vital to the production; a "cast" of experimental assistants to recruit and train; "props" and "special effects"; and "rehearsals." And once the stage is set, the experimenter must publicize the experiment and sell potential participants, for without an audience there can be no play. We make reference to this metaphor as we describe in greater detail how Lucas and colleagues (2006) carried out the misconduct experiment.[2]

Pretesting

Like the script of a play, the production of an experiment follows a set of procedures that implement the overall experimental design. After the development of a preliminary "script" of experimental procedures, the next step is to conduct a **pretest** in which the procedures are applied to a few participants, preferably similar to those who will participate in the final production of the experiment, to see how well the "script" is working. Feedback from pretest participants is often used to modify procedures.

In the misconduct experiment, Lucas and associates made several changes as a result of pretesting (Lucas, personal communication, February 2013). One change involved enhancing participants' motivation. During pretesting, participants were told that they would earn $10 for participating in the experiment. However, when the pretest showed that participants were not very invested in "winning" the case, the researchers decided to tell them that they would receive $10 if they lost the case and $15 if they won. They also made an important change in the language of the script of the study in an effort to make attaining a conviction more important to participants.

---

[2] The discussion of the misconduct experiment in this section relies on additional information graciously provided to us by its principal investigator Jeff Lucas (personal communication, February 2013).

Participant Recruitment and Informed Consent

Before the start of the "production," participants must be recruited, and the investigator must obtain the participants' informed consent to participate. Lucas and associates' participants were a convenience sample of college students who were recruited from introductory sociology classes. Participants had two incentives to sign up: they would receive extra credit from their sociology instructor, which is a common practice, and they would be paid.

Once participants signed up, they received an e-mail briefly describing the nature of the study, how long it would take, and available times. Then, when participants arrived at the laboratory, the experimenter repeated the brief study description—that they were doing a study on how people reach decisions on legal matters—and immediately asked them to sign an informed consent form. For an abridged copy of the form used in the Lucas and associates' study, see Box 8.4.

Introduction to the Experiment

Continuing the theatrical production metaphor, we might say that the first "scene" of an experiment consists of some sort of introduction to the study. Basically, this involves an explanation of the purpose or nature of the research, together with instructions to the participant. As we noted, the researchers initially told participants that they were interested in how people reach legal decisions. After signing the informed consent agreement, participants were informed that there would be three people completing the study as part of the participant's group—a defense attorney, a prosecuting attorney, and a judge—and that the three people might complete the study at different times. Then they were asked to draw one of three slips of paper to determine their role—but, as explained earlier in our description of the experiment, they were actually all given the role of prosecutor (i.e., without their knowledge, all three slips of paper indicated

---

BOX 8.4

DOING CRIMINAL JUSTICE RESEARCH

Informed Consent Form for an Experiment

Figure A is an abridged copy of the informed consent form used by Lucas and colleagues (2006). This form contains key elements of informed consent that we outlined in Chapter 4. In particular, it (1) explains the experimental procedures and potential risks and benefits to the participants or to others and (2) informs them that their participation is voluntary and that they have the right to leave the experiment at any time without penalty.

continues

continued

Project Title: Criminal Prosecution and Defense
Project Investigator: Jeffrey W. Lucas, PhD

This study involves research. The purpose of the research is to examine the procedures followed in using evidence to build cases in criminal trials. You are here today because you indicated interest in participating in this study. If you agree to participate in the study, you will be reading a pamphlet of materials and playing an imaginary role in a court case.

Foreseeable risks, discomforts, or inconveniences to you include (1) the time commitment (should you elect to participate, the study takes about an hour and a half to complete), (2) potential anxiety (you will have to read through material describing a violent crime and make decisions about how the criminal case should be handled), and (3) possible frustration (all of the information that you might like to have in making your decisions will not be available to you).

There may be no personal benefit to you for participating in the study, aside from pay. However, we will learn a great deal about the factors that affect the decisions people make in assembling and evaluating criminal cases. This may help researchers better understand individual behavior.

A record of your participation in this research will be maintained, but it will be kept completely confidential. The records of your participation will be in the form of an identification number and your name will not be retained in the record of your participation.

Questions about this research are encouraged and will be answered by:

[Jeff Lucas and the Director of the Office of Research]*

Your participation is voluntary. No penalty or loss of benefits to which you are entitled will occur if you decide not to participate. You may discontinue participation at any time without penalty or loss of benefits to which you are entitled. You will be compensated for time and inconvenience involved in participating in the research in the amount of $10.00. This payment will be in addition to any extra credit you may receive for participation. Compensation will be pro-rated if you withdraw before the research is completed.

Subject's Name (please print):_____

_____   _____
(signature of subject)   (date)

I have discussed the above points with the research participant, using a translator when necessary. It is my opinion that the subject understands the risks, benefits, and obligations involved in participation in this project.

_____   _____
(signature of investigator)   (date)

*This information has been modified and abridged by the book authors for reasons of confidentiality. The latter's name is not displayed and contact information for both parties has been redacted.

FIGURE A An Abridged Copy of the Informed Consent form Used by Lucas and Colleagues (2006)

"prosecutor," so it did not matter which slip they chose). Next, they received the police report and other materials and were instructed to prepare a list of questions for the defense and to write a one-page closing argument that would be read by the judge.

All research participants are likely to want to understand what the study is about, and they will expect to be given some sort of explanation. But this explanation is especially important in a laboratory experiment. More so than in a survey or in field research, participants are acutely aware that they are participating in a scientific study, that they are being observed, and that certain behaviors are expected of them. Thus, they are in a sense "on stage" and will be very sensitive to any cues about how they should perform. If participants are told the actual hypothesis, then instead of behaving as they ordinarily would, they may behave as they think they should to fulfill the researchers' expectations. On the other hand, participants need to be given some explanation; otherwise, they may try to guess the hypothesis and "help" the experimenter by behaving in a way that confirms whatever they guess the hypothesis may be.

The challenge, then, is to provide a believable explanation that will encourage participants to behave naturally. Therefore, a false explanation, or **cover story**, such as Lucas and associates offered, is thought to be necessary to prevent preoccupation with the true purpose of the study. A good cover story must make sense to participants; that is, it must be understandable and believable. The first scene, including the cover story, should also have enough impact on the participant to arouse interest. For if the participant is not paying attention to the directions or to the events being staged, experimental "findings" will be worthless.

cover story an introduction presented to research participants to obtain their cooperation while disguising the research hypothesis

Experimental Manipulation and Random Assignment

The "second scene" of the experiment is the manipulation of the independent variable. This is the point when some stimulus or set of stimuli is introduced, which serves as an operational definition of the independent variable. The major independent variable in the misconduct study was the severity of the crime, assault vs. murder. To randomly assign participants to these conditions, the experimenter flipped a coin before each participant arrived (Lucas, personal communication, February 2013). (Random assignment may occur at any time before the experimental manipulation.) As we described earlier, crime severity was manipulated by indicating in the police report that (1) the victim either died and the defendant was indicted for murder or (2) the victim recovered from his injuries and the defendant was indicted for assault.

Manipulation Checks

To obtain evidence that the manipulation of the independent variable was experienced or interpreted by participants in the intended way, the experimenter may incorporate some sort of **manipulation check** into the experiment. This might involve asking participants, either directly or by means of a written instrument, what they felt or thought

manipulation check procedure used to provide evidence that participants interpreted the manipulation of the independent variable in the way intended during or immediately after the experimental manipulation. A manipulation check also may be used to determine whether participants understood or recalled essential directions or facts related to the manipulation.

As we noted earlier, Lucas and associates asked participants to complete a brief questionnaire after the study ostensibly was over. Because they hypothesized that the severity of the crime would affect degree of misconduct, it was important to know if participants perceived murder as a more serious crime than assault. To check the validity of this manipulation, therefore, the post-study questionnaire included an item that asked participants to rate the severity of the crime on a scale from 1 (very severe) to 7 (not at all severe). As expected, the average rating of participants in the murder condition (1.28) was significantly lower than the average rating of participants in the assault condition (3.03). Similarly, in their online survey experiment, Salerno and Sanchez (2020) performed manipulation checks by asking participants to identify the race and gender of the police officer and to indicate how much force was used on a scale ranging from 1 (no force) to 7 (extremely excessive force). Of the 637 MTurk workers who were recruited, the researchers ended up excluding 158 participants who failed the manipulation checks of gender and/or race. The average rating of the no-force video (1.45) was significantly lower than the average rating of the force video (5.59).

Researchers may assess the validity of a manipulation at varying points in an experiment. Whereas Lucas et al. and Salerno and Sanchez performed their manipulation checks *after* the experiment ostensibly was over, a manipulation check might be performed after the independent variable is manipulated but before the dependent variable is measured. The advantage here is that the manipulation is still fresh and the participant's memory of it has not been distorted by later events. At this point, however, it may not be feasible and it could alter participants' subsequent behavior (the dependent variable) by calling attention to or emphasizing the manipulation.

Alternatively, researchers may establish the validity of an experimental manipulation through pretesting. For example, numerous studies of racial discrimination have manipulated the race of target persons by using racially connected names, such as Emily and Greg for White people and Lakisha and Jamal for Black people. In an oft-cited study, Marianne Bertrand and Sendhil Mullainathan (2004) established a set of racially unique names by calculating the frequency of names by race in birth certificates of all babies born in Massachusetts between 1974 and 1979. After compiling a list of "racial" names, they conducted a pretest in which they asked 30 respondents to identify each name as either "White," "African-American," "Other," or "Cannot Tell." Only names perceived as distinctively "White" or "African-American" were used. Thus, the researchers eliminated Maurice and Jerome, which were not *perceived* as racially distinct despite being identified as such by the frequency data. We hasten to add that despite such validity checks, questions have been raised about the use of names to signify race (Gaddis, 2017).[3]

Measurement of the Dependent Variable

The dependent variable, which always follows the introduction of the independent variable, is measured in experiments with either self-reports or observations of behavior. Lucas and associates used observation to measure their dependent variable, level of misconduct. Their operationalization consisted of the number of questions forwarded to the defense attorney that pointed to the possible guilt of the victim's wife (and thus the possible innocence of the defendant). In the Pager study of employment discrimination, a behavioral measure of the dependent variable—number of callbacks for an interview—also was used.

In addition to their observational measure of misconduct, Lucas and associates included a self-report measure of whether participants withheld relevant information from the defense. Specifically, participants were asked on the post-study questionnaire to rate the extent to which they believed that they had "turned over all the relevant evidence to the defense" (1 = definitely turned over all relevant facts; 7 = definitely did not turn over all relevant facts). Consistent with the results for the observational measure, participants in the murder condition had a higher average rating (2.70) than participants in the assault condition (1.93), which suggests that "participants in the murder condition made conscious decisions to withhold exculpatory evidence" (Lucas et al., 2006, p. 104).

The use of verbal vs. observational measures of the dependent variable is a controversial point among experimenters. Our examples notwithstanding, verbal reports are common, even though they often contain serious weaknesses. Verbal measures have the advantage of being easy to devise, allowing for more numerous and varied assessments of the dependent variable. There are two major problems with such self-reports, however. First, participants may censor their responses, especially when they construe the "truth" to reflect negatively on themselves. Second, research consistently has shown differences between what people do and what they think and say they will do (e.g., Deutscher et al., 1993; Pager & Quillian, 2005).

With observations of behavior, on the other hand, participants tend to be less aware or even unaware of the measure. Behavioral measures also can be more precise, as in counting the number of questions submitted to the defense or the number of callbacks for interviews. Finally, when a specific behavior (e.g., misconduct or discrimination) is of interest, it is better to get a direct measure of that behavior than an indirect measure of how participants *say* they will behave.

---

[3] As S. Michael Gaddis (2017) has pointed out, fewer than one in five Blacks are given names that are distinctively Black; the most distinctively Black names are not used exclusively by Blacks; racially distinct names may be correlated with perceived socioeconomic status; and the use of last names also may affect study outcomes.

Debriefing

The closing scene of the experiment is a debriefing session in which the experimenter discusses with the participant what has taken place. When participants have been deceived, it is ethically imperative that they be told at this point about the nature of and reasons for the deception and that their feelings about being deceived be explored fully (see Chapter 4). The experimenter also may try to learn what the participant experienced throughout the experiment:

- Did the participant understand the directions?
- If a cover story was used, did the participant believe it?
- Why did the participant respond as they did to the experimental manipulation?
- Did the participant experience psychological stress or discomfort?
- How does the participant feel about the experiment as a whole?

The experimenter should be aware that the manner in which the debriefing session is conducted may make a great deal of difference in the feelings of the participant about being deceived (if the participant has been deceived), about this research and researcher, and about criminal justice research in general. Thus, the experimenter should explain the real purpose of the research and why it is of importance. If deception has been used, they should inform the participant of this in a sensitive manner and carefully explain the reasons it was necessary. If the deception aroused the participant's emotions, the experimenter should further justify these feelings and make every effort to relieve a participant's discomfort. In general, participants should be encouraged to ask questions and to share any negative feelings toward the study, so that these questions and feelings can be openly discussed.

The debriefing protocol in Lucas and associates' study began with a series of questions that asked participants how they felt about the case and their experiences during the study. The experimenter asked participants what they thought the purpose of the study was. Then he told them its true purpose and carefully explained why deception was necessary to test their hypothesis. To ascertain that participants had positive feelings about their participation, the experimenter asked if they were satisfied with this explanation and had any further questions. Finally, he asked them not to talk to other potential participants about the study (Lucas, personal communication, February 2013).

This final request in the debriefing session is important because potential participants frequently are acquainted with one another. Certainly, experiments requiring deception will not yield valid results if participants coming to the experiment have been informed of its true purpose. Even experiments not requiring deception will usually suffer if participants previously have been told the hypothesis or what the experimental manipulation is. If the debriefing process has been an open, satisfying experience for the participant up to this point, they are very likely to respect the researcher's wishes in regard to secrecy.

SUMMARY

The process of conducting a laboratory experiment generally involves all of the steps we have just described: pretesting, recruiting participants and acquiring informed consent, introducing the experiment, randomly assigning participants to conditions/groups and manipulating the independent variable, checking the manipulation of the variable, measuring the dependent variable, and debriefing participants. In a series of similar experiments, though, later experiments may not be pretested; and if the validity of the experimental manipulation is well established, an experiment may not contain a manipulation check.

In experiments outside the laboratory, some steps routinely are eliminated. Because participants in a field experiment are unaware that they are actually in an experiment, it is not possible to acquire their informed consent, to provide an introduction to the study, and to debrief them. These stages also are excluded in surveys that incorporate experiments. Excluding some stages, such as informed consent and debriefing, can raise ethical issues, which is a weakness of some field experiments. As we now turn our attention to the strengths and weaknesses of experiments relative to other approaches to criminal justice research, we will note how these strengths and weaknesses may depend on the experimental context. See Box 8.5 to check your understanding of the process of conducting experiments.

BOX 8.5

CHECKING YOUR UNDERSTANDING

Experimental Process

1. Identify the correct sequence in which an experiment should be conducted.
    a. randomly assign participants to conditions → acquire informed consent → measure dependent variable → manipulate independent variable
    b. debrief → acquire informed consent → randomly assign participants to conditions → perform manipulation check
    c. introduce experiment → manipulate independent variable → measure dependent variable → debrief
    d. introduce experiment → perform manipulation check → debrief → measure dependent variable
    e. acquire informed consent → perform manipulation check → randomly assign participants to conditions → measure dependent variable

continues

2. All of the following are an advantage of behavioral measures of the dependent variable in comparison with verbal reports, except:
   a. measuring what people do is better than measuring what they say they will do
   b. easy to devise
   c. greater precision
   d. lower participant awareness being measured

3. A trial run of an experiment or survey instrument to evaluate and rehearse study procedures and personnel is known as a:
   a. pretest
   b. manipulation check
   c. quasi-experiment
   d. debriefing

4. The closing scene of an experiment in which the experimenter discusses with the participant what has taken place is known as a(n) _____ _____ session.
   a. ending
   b. posttest
   c. manipulation
   d. debriefing

Answers: 1. c, 2. b, 3. a, 4. d

8.5 STRENGTHS AND WEAKNESSES OF EXPERIMENTS

Besides knowing *how* to conduct an experiment, you also need to know *when* it is appropriate to use experimentation as opposed to some other research strategy. Understanding the unique strengths and weaknesses of the experimental approach will enable you to answer the *when* question. It also will help you to evaluate experiments, which is in keeping with our twin goals of making you both an informed consumer and producer of research evidence.

Internal Validity

The main reason to conduct an experiment is based on its principal strength. More so than other approaches, experiments provide sound evidence of a causal relationship. As you will see, most scientific studies offer evidence of an *association* between variables, and some nonexperimental studies can clearly establish *direction of influence*. But only experiments effectively rule out the possibility that extraneous variables, rather than the manipulated independent variable, are responsible for observed changes in the dependent variable. Studies that provide such evidence are said to be high in **internal validity**; studies that fail to control adequately for extraneous variables lack internal validity.

The strength of experiments in testing causal hypotheses extends to their use in evaluating research designs more generally. To determine how well a study tests a causal hypothesis, criminal justice researchers often compare its design to that of an experiment. Study designs that are deficient suffer from one or more common **threats to internal validity**. Such threats refer to uncontrolled extraneous variables that may account for study results. For example, the threat of **selection** is present in any study that has all the ingredients of an experiment except for random assignment. Without random assignment, it is possible that the comparison groups will differ in ways that affect the outcome of the study; in other words, the "selection" of the groups may be biased. Suppose, for example, that participants in the misconduct study were told that they could *choose* whether to prosecute a defendant indicted for murder or assault. This raises the possibility that participants in the two conditions differ systematically. For instance, perhaps participants choosing the "murder condition" are more inclined to commit misconduct than participants choosing the "assault condition."

Knowing the elements of experimental design can be a powerful tool in helping you to evaluate the trustworthiness of research evidence. Indeed, now that you understand *how* experiments provide sound evidence of cause and effect, you can apply this knowledge to assess the internal validity of almost any study. To test your understanding of these ideas, see Box 8.6.

internal validity evidence that rules out the possibility that factors other than the manipulated independent variable are responsible for the measured outcome

threats to internal validity a threat to internal validity that is present whenever participants are not randomly assigned to experimental conditions

selection types of extraneous variables that pose alternative explanations of an experimental outcome, thereby threatening the validity of the experimental manipulation

---

BOX 8.6

READING CRIMINAL JUSTICE RESEARCH

Thinking Critically About Research Designs and Threats to Internal Validity

Assessing internal validity is particularly suitable for studies designed to evaluate the effectiveness of a criminal justice program, as they often incorporate elements of experimental methodology. The first step is to identify the study design; the second step is to consider alternative explanations to the researcher's causal inference (threats to internal validity) that are posed by inadequate designs.

To understand how this works, consider research on Drug Abuse Resistance Education (D.A.R.E), a school-based program designed to increase students' knowledge of drugs and their resistance to drug use and violence. Taught by a police officer who visits the classroom, D.A.R.E is intended for children in their last year of elementary school (fifth or sixth grade), although it has been used with children

continues

continued

in kindergarten through 12th grade. This program depends on public support and receives millions of dollars annually in public funding (Rosenbaum, 2007). Its effectiveness has been extensively evaluated, but many of the earliest studies were inadequate. Below are two types of studies that can be found in the literature. As you read these, begin by identifying the study design; then, consider alternative explanations to the causal inference (threats to internal validity) that are posed by inadequate designs.

> Knowing that D.A.R.E is being administered in all sixth-grade classes in the local school district, a researcher randomly selects 10 classes. At the beginning of the school year, he measures attitudes toward drug use among all students in the ten randomly chosen classes. Then, at the end of the year, after the children have been exposed to the D.A.R.E program, he measures their attitudes toward drug use again. The data show that students have more negative attitudes toward drug use at the end of the year than they did at the beginning.

Were you able to identify the study design? The investigator has measured the dependent variable, attitude toward drug use, before and after students participated in the D.A.R.E program. Using the notation we introduced earlier in the chapter, we could represent the study as follows, where Y is the measurement of the dependent variable, attitude toward drug use, at times 1 and 2, and X stands for D.A.R.E:

$Y_1 \quad X \quad Y_2$

This is called a "pretest-posttest design." One problem with this design is that it lacks a comparison group, such as sixth-grade students who did not go through the D.A.R.E program (recall the pretest-posttest *control group* design). And, without a comparison group, there can be no random assignment to experimental conditions. (Beware that randomly selecting classes from the local school district is a way of drawing the sample; it has nothing to do with randomly assigning research participants to experimental conditions. See Box 8.1.)

Now that you know how this design is inadequate, can you come up with alternative explanations of the study results? That is, what else besides the D.A.R.E program could account for the more negative attitudes toward drug use at the end of the year? The problem with this design is that children's attitude toward drugs may change between the pretest and posttest even if they were not exposed to D.A.R.E. Methodologists have identified two principal threats to the internal validity of studies with this design.

The first threat is called **maturation**, which refers to psychological or physical changes taking place within participants over time. Maturation may account for the results insofar as the children develop psychologically, becoming more aware of their bodies and of the unhealthy effects of ingesting drugs. A second threat is **history**; this refers to events in the participants' environment other than the experimental manipulation. Perhaps events outside the D.A.R.E program, in the school or community, influenced the children's attitude toward drugs. For example, a fellow student may have been arrested or suffered serious effects from drug use or an anti-drug campaign may have been undertaken in the media.

Now, let us turn to the second example:

> A researcher discovers that the D.A.R.E program is administered in the local school district but that it is not administered in an adjacent school district. So,

with the permission of school administrators and parents, at the end of the school year she has students in all sixth-grade classes in the two districts complete a survey that asks them about their attitudes toward drug use. The data show that students exposed to the D.A.R.E program have more negative attitudes toward drug use than those who were not exposed to the program.

Is this study design internally valid? First, let us consider its design. We could represent the design as follows, where Y is the dependent variable, attitude toward drug use, X_1 represents exposure to D.A.R.E, and X_2 represents no exposure to D.A.R.E:

X_1 Y
X_2 Y

This design, called a "static group comparison," lacks an essential feature for establishing a causal connection between X and Y: random assignment. Without it, we cannot be sure that students exposed to D.A.R.E are similar in all respects to students who were not exposed to D.A.R.E. In fact, we bet you can think of many possible differences between students in the two districts that may affect students' attitude toward drugs. Any one of these differences signifies the internal validity threat of selection.

There are many other threats to internal validity in addition to selection, maturation, and history. You can learn more about these in the classic treatment by Donald Campbell and Julian Stanley (1963). For a briefer treatment, also see Singleton and Straits (2018, pp. 226–230).

External Validity

Although the primary concern in designing experiments is to make sure that they provide a sound test of a causal hypothesis, criminal justice researchers have the broader scientific goal of applying their findings beyond the specific situations they study. In addition to internal validity, therefore, researchers are also concerned with **external validity**. External validity refers to the question of generalizability, or what the experimental results mean outside the particular context of the experiment.

The researchers in the experiment on prosecutorial misconduct were careful to acknowledge that generalizing the results of their laboratory experiment "to naturally occurring situations is not advisable" (Lucas et al., 2006, p. 104). They simply could not assume that working prosecutors handling actual criminal cases would behave similarly to undergraduate students performing the role of prosecutor in a contrived court case. The laboratory and real-world situations differ in numerous ways, including many other factors that may influence a prosecutor's wrongdoing. For example, as Lucas and associates point out, prosecutors who engage in misconduct may be punished, so

> . . . fear of punishment may make misconduct less likely in cases involving more severe crime. The opposite effect also could occur: the greater rewards and opportunities for advancement earned by obtaining convictions in serious, high-profile cases may increase pressure to engage in wrongdoing. (Lucas et al., 2006, p. 105)

external validity the extent to which experimental findings may be generalized to other settings, measurements, populations, and time periods

maturation a threat to internal validity that refers to events other than the manipulation of the independent variable

history a threat to internal validity that refers to psychological or physiological changes taking place within participants

How, then, can we apply the results of this experiment—or any other experiment—to the real world? In other words, how can we enhance external validity? Let us examine four answers to this question that are pertinent not only to experiments but also to other research strategies.

1. Because the least generalizable experiments take place in the artificial environment of the laboratory, one way to enhance external validity is to conduct field experiments. By carrying out a study in a natural social setting, the events in the experiment are more similar to everyday experiences. We are relatively more certain, for example, about the applicability of research findings when we send out testers to apply for real jobs with real employers, as in Pager's field experiment on job discrimination, than when we ask undergraduate students to play the role of prosecutor in a contrived court case.
2. All experiments—indeed, all criminal justice studies—involve a particular group of participants and take place at a specific time and setting with a certain set of procedures and researchers. Because all these aspects limit external validity, the best strategy for increasing the generalizability of findings often is replication, or repetition of the experiment. Replication may be carried out by the same investigator or by another investigator, who conducts the research in a different setting, with slightly different procedures, or with a different sample of participants. In fact, the strongest argument for generality is that widely varying experimental tests, or replications, have produced similar results.

    One limitation to the external validity of Pager's field experiment, for example, was that it was carried out in a single city, Milwaukee. Although similar to many other US metropolitan areas, Milwaukee had two unique features at the time of the study that may have limited its representativeness: it was the second most segregated city in the country, and it had the third largest growth in incarceration rates (and highest rate of incarceration for Blacks). Pager speculates that a high level of segregation may strain race relations and that statewide incarceration rates may reflect a punitive approach to crime, which could affect employers' openness to hiring Blacks and ex-offenders. As she further notes, "the only way to directly address these issues is through replication in additional areas" (Pager, 2003, p. 966). When Pager replicated her audit study in other cities (Pager, Western, & Bonikowski, 2009; Pager, Western, & Sugie, 2009), she found similar results, which enhanced the external validity of her findings.
3. A third way to increase external validity is through research design. The best examples of this apply to sample selection. One of the most persistent criticisms of experiments is that they are short on external validity because they tend to rely on convenience samples of college students (Henry, 2008; Sears, 1986). Because experimental manipulation often involves a laboratory setting and/or elaborate

staging, it is usually impractical either to sample participants over wide areas or to utilize a large number of participants. As a consequence, experimenters tend to use small samples drawn from readily available populations. And because most experimentation is done in universities, the participants often are college students.

College students have been described as the "weirdest people in the world," comprised of samples drawn from Western, educated, industrialized, rich, and democratic societies (Henrich et al., 2010). They also differ from people in general on several other dimensions, including age, occupational goals, and interests. Given such differences, it is important to broaden the participant population (Sears, 1986). By embedding experiments in surveys, criminal justice researchers can use much larger and more diverse samples, as we saw in the study of police officers' use of force. The sample in that study was recruited from the crowdsourcing service MTurk. As we noted in Chapter 7, MTurk participants are a convenience sample; they are not representative of any particular population. But when they are used in hypothesis-testing research, and not intended for application or generalization to a specific target population, they offer a much more diverse sample than undergraduate students.[4]

4. Finally, a fourth means of increasing external validity (as well as internal validity) is to extend the methods of replication and improved design by using different research strategies to test the same hypothesis or study the same phenomenon. As is true in experiments as much as other forms of research, each approach to criminal justice research has unique strengths and weaknesses. By combining them and using them in complementary ways, the strengths of one approach may offset the weaknesses of another. In testing causal hypotheses, for example, surveys provide weaker evidence of cause and effect than do experiments. On the other hand, surveys are almost always based on larger and more diverse samples than experiments. We discuss the use of multiple methods in Chapter 13, where we describe a study that combined an experiment and a survey.

In the end, all studies are limited to some extent with regard to external validity. The value of an experiment therefore rests largely on how well it validates the underlying theory that is being tested. If it offers strong support, then it provides a useful guide for future research.

Reactive Measurement Effects

Another weakness of laboratory experiments, specifically, is related to the process of measurement. As we noted earlier, participants in an experiment are acutely aware that they are being observed. When this awareness affects how participants behave, it

---

[4] Evidence is mixed on the reliability and validity of data from MTurk. Several studies indicate that data quality is just as high and sometimes superior to undergraduate data collection (Casler et al., 2013; Hauser & Schwarz, 2016; Thomas & Clifford, 2017). One recent study showed, however, that MTurk workers were more likely to fail validity checks than college students (Aruguete et al., 2019).

reactive measurement effect an effect in which participants' awareness of being studied produces changes in how they ordinarily would respond

is called a **reactive measurement effect**. Just as people behave differently alone than in front of an audience, or with friends than with strangers, they may react differently when in a research setting. For example, survey respondents who are asked about socially approved behavior may over-report how much they engage in the behavior to project a favorable image. This sort of self-censoring is present to varying degrees in survey and field research, but it is most problematic in laboratory experiments.

Reactive effects tend to occur in experiments for one of two reasons. First, knowing that they are taking part in a scientific study, many participants are determined to be helpful by acting in accord with the experimenter's hypothesis. Secondly, participants are very likely to want to project a favorable image of themselves. Although they know it is normative not to be told the true nature of the experiment, they nonetheless will look for cues about the study's hypothesis and about how they should act to "help" the experimenter and/or to "look good." This is why it is important in an experiment to divert participants' attention from the actual hypothesis by presenting a convincing cover story. Imagine, for example, that participants in the misconduct study had known or guessed that the real purpose of the experiment was to observe their level of misconduct. We can be sure that, with this knowledge, participants would have forwarded *all* the questions implicating another suspect to the defense attorney.

It is often difficult for experimenters to gauge the extent to which participants are reacting to cues about how they should respond or are acting as they would ordinarily. One place to try to learn this is the debriefing session. In fact, it is not unusual for experimenters to eliminate from their results the data pertaining to participants who correctly guessed the hypothesis.

One way in which participants may learn how they should respond is through their interaction with the experimenter. When experimenters know which experimental condition a participant is in, they may unconsciously and subtly communicate how the participant should act. Medical researchers have long known that a physician's belief in the efficacy of a drug or treatment may have as much to do with a patient's recovery as the treatment itself. Similarly, in criminal justice research, it is possible, especially in evaluating a new criminal justice program, that staff members may convey their enthusiasm to participants. An effective way to control for such effects is to keep experimenters *blind* to the participants' condition. This would have been possible in the misconduct study, for example, if the research assistant had not known whether participants were in the murder or assault condition. An even more effective control, commonly used in medical research, is a **double-blind experiment**, in which neither the participants nor the experimenter know which experimental condition a participant is in.

double-blind experiment an experiment in which neither research participants nor research personnel know participants' treatment condition during the running of an experiment

Finally, a different sort of "reactivity" may occur outside the laboratory in experiments conducted online. Whereas in the laboratory, participants' awareness of being tested and observed is heightened by the experimenter's presence, in online surveys, participants' anonymity may make them less attentive to important experimental details.

This may be especially true of MTurk workers, who are motivated to participate by financial incentives. In fact, it is now common practice to embed validity checks in MTurk surveys to identify inattentive participants. Salerno and Sanchez performed "attention checks" at several points in their survey by asking respondents the following question: "This question is designed to make sure survey respondents are paying attention. Please choose 'somewhat agree' to answer this question." Response categories consisted of "strongly disagree," "somewhat disagree," "neither agree nor disagree," "somewhat agree," and "strongly agree" (Salerno, personal communication 2020). Eighty-one respondents who chose an answer other than "somewhat agree" were excluded.

Content Restrictions

Experiments provide an ideal model for testing causal hypotheses. Yet, despite the scientific goal of establishing causal explanations, criminal justice researchers often choose some other research strategy. The primary reason is that the requirements for an experiment limit what is feasible and practical to study. Many of the variables of interest to criminal justice researchers, such as race, gender, age, and socioeconomic status, cannot be manipulated. It often is impossible to randomly assign people to different conditions. And, criminal justice researchers often study units of analysis (e.g., neighborhoods, cities, and whole nations), institutions (e.g., police, courts, prisons), and social and historical processes (e.g., immigration, desegregation, social movements) that simply are not amenable to experimentation or must be studied in their entirety.

SUMMARY

The primary strength of an experiment lies in its ability to establish causal relationships; well-conducted experiments tend to be high in internal validity by ruling out extraneous variables that may produce a spurious association between the independent and dependent variables. One weakness of laboratory experiments, in particular, is that they tend to be low in external validity, but external validity may be increased through replication, by doing a field experiment, by selecting a broader range of participants, and/or by combining different approaches. Experiments are also subject to reactive measurement effects, although researchers may check for such effects by performing attention checks and asking probing questions during debriefings, and they may control for them through double-blind experiments. Despite their strengths and the flexibility that different experimental designs offer in overcoming weaknesses, experiments are nevertheless limited by content restrictions, as it is not possible to manipulate many phenomena in social life. See Box 8.7 to assess your understanding of the strengths and weaknesses of experimentation.

> **BOX 8.7**
>
> **CHECKING YOUR UNDERSTANDING**
>
> ## Internal and External Validity
>
> 1. Experiments tend to be _____ in external validity and _____ in internal validity.
>   a. low; low
>   b. low; high
>   c. high; low
>   d. high; high
>
> 2. Testing and confirming a hypothesis in both laboratory and field experiments, among a variety of populations in a wide range of situations enhances the _____ of an experiment.
>   a. internal validity
>   b. external validity
>   c. measurement reliability
>   d. reactivity
>
> 3. By randomly assigning research participants to experimental conditions, researchers are able to control which threat to internal validity?
>   a. Selection
>   b. History
>   c. Maturation
>
> Answers: 1. b, 2. b, 3. a

KEY TERMS

audit study, p. 213
cover story, p. 221
double-blind experiment, p. 232
external validity, p. 229
factorial design, p. 212
field experiment, p. 213
history, p. 228
internal validity, p. 227
laboratory experiment, p. 213
manipulation check, p. 221
maturation, p. 228
posttest-only control group design, p. 211
pretest, p. 218
pretest-posttest control group design, p. 211
random assignment, p. 207
reactive measurement effect, p. 232
selection, p. 227
survey-based experiment, p. 214
threats to internal validity, p. 227

KEY POINTS

- The primary features of an experiment are two or more groups or conditions to which participants are randomly assigned, manipulation of the independent variable(s), measurement of the dependent variable(s), and keeping conditions the same except for the manipulation.
- Experiments meet all three requirements for inferring cause and effect: association, direction of influence, and nonspuriousness.
- Experimental designs vary in whether the dependent variable is measured before or both before and after an experimental manipulation, and whether one or more independent variables is manipulated.
- Although traditionally carried out in a laboratory setting, experiments also may be performed "in the field" (field experiments) or embedded in surveys.
- Similar to the steps in producing a play, the process of conducting experiments often begins with pretesting to see how well the "script" of the experiment works.
- The researcher "gets an audience" by recruiting participants and acquiring informed consent.
- The "opening act" is the introduction of the experiment, which is intended to pique participants' interest through a compelling cover story.
- The "second scene" includes the random assignment of participants and experimental manipulation.
- Following the manipulation of the independent variable, the next "scene" consists of the measurement of the dependent variable(s) and, sometimes, a manipulation check.
- The "closing act" is the debriefing, which informs participants of the true nature of the study and attempts to minimize any discomfort that may have resulted from deception.
- Whereas the principal strength of experiments is high internal validity, experiments may be less generalizable than other studies, are subject to reactive measurement effects, and are limited in the topics that they can address.

REVIEW QUESTIONS

1. Explain how experiments offer sound evidence of cause and effect.
2. Explain two ways in which experimental designs may differ from one another.
3. What are the relative advantages and disadvantages of laboratory experiments compared with experiments conducted outside the laboratory?
4. Explain the purpose(s) of the following experimental procedures: (a) cover story; (b) manipulation check; and (c) debriefing.
5. Briefly distinguish between internal and external validity. Identify two threats to internal validity.
6. What are the major strengths and limitations of experiments in social research?

EXERCISES

1. Similar to Pager's field experiment on the mark of a criminal record, Agan and Starr (2018) conducted a study examining the impact of race and criminal record on hiring decisions both before and after the implementation of the Ban The Box policy. Ban the Box policies prohibit employers from requiring applicants to "check the box" that indicates whether or not they have ever been convicted of a crime. The intent of the policy is to reduce discrimination among Black men who are more likely to have a criminal record. Rather than use "live" auditors, the investigators submitted online job applications for fake applicants to entry-level openings both prior to and after these policies were implemented in New Jersey and New York City. Researchers completed online applications in pairs for each job posting with one applicant being randomly assigned either a White- or Black-sounding name. In addition, applications were randomly assigned to report a criminal conviction. Then, they recorded whether an applicant received a phone or e-mail callback for an interview.

   a. Does this study have all the features of a true experiment? Carefully explain.
   b. What are the independent variables in this study? How are they manipulated?
   c. What is the dependent variable?

2. In our brief description of the study in Question 1, we omitted one feature of the study design. In addition to the names and criminal record assigned to each résumé, the investigators varied whether the applicant had a GED or high school diploma as well as the length of employment gap, with either a 0–2 month gap or a one-year employment gap between the past two jobs.

   a. What type of experimental design is this? Be specific.
   b. In discussing the weaknesses of the study, the investigators note that (1) they focused only on chain employers (e.g., restaurant and retail businesses) and (2) they only studied callbacks rather than actual hiring decisions. Explain whether these criticisms pertain to the *internal validity* or *external validity* of the study.

3. Suppose you want to test the hypothesis that individuals will find use of force to be more justified with male suspects than female suspects. How would you test this hypothesis in a *laboratory* experiment? As you develop your study design, address each of the following questions:

   a. How will you manipulate the independent variable?
   b. What will your dependent variable be and how will you measure it?

    c. How will you recruit research participants and obtain their informed consent?

    d. What will you say to research participants during the debriefing?

4. Suppose you want to test whether a new drug rehabilitation program for drug offenders is effective in reducing the offender's likelihood of engaging in new drug offenses. Design a *field* experiment to assess the effectiveness of the program.

    a. How will you manipulate the independent variable?

    b. What will your dependent variable be and how will you measure it?

    c. How will you recruit research participants and obtain their informed consent?

    d. Why would it be better to conduct your study in the field than in the laboratory?

9

Surveys
Questioning and Sampling

CHAPTER OUTLINE

9.1 General Features of Survey Research 239
- Large-Scale Probability Sampling 240
- Structured Interviews or Questionnaires 240
- Quantitative Data Analysis 242
- Summary 242

9.2 Variations in Survey Designs and Modes 243
- Survey Research Designs 243
- Data-Collection Modes 245
- Summary 253

9.3 The Process of Planning and Conducting a Survey 254
- Choose Mode of Data Collection 255
- Construct and Pretest Questionnaire 255
- Choose Sampling Frame/Design and Select Sample 261
- Recruit Sample and Collect Data 261
- Code and Edit Data 262
- Summary 263

9.4 Strengths and Weaknesses of Surveys 264
- Generalization to Populations 265
- Versatility 265
- Efficiency 265
- Establishing Causal Relationships 265
- Measurement Issues 266
- Summary 266

LEARNING OBJECTIVES

By the end of this chapter, you should be able to

9.1 Describe the three general features of surveys.

9.2 Explain variations in survey designs by distinguishing between cross-sectional and longitudinal designs.

9.3 Compare the strengths and weaknesses of face-to-face, telephone, paper-and-pencil, computer-assisted, and mixed modes of data collection. Describe the steps in the process of planning and conducting a survey and apply them to a research topic.

9.4 Evaluate surveys as a method of data collection, identifying their strengths and weaknesses.

You probably know what surveys are. Maybe you have called to get customer service for some product only to be asked by an automated recording if you would be willing to participate in a survey after the call. Perhaps you have had e-mail requests to participate in online surveys on your health or political views, sometimes with an incentive—such as a gift card for coffee or music downloads—to encourage you to participate. Opening your "snail mail" one day, you may have received a questionnaire from a political organization or from the US Census Bureau.

Even if you have never participated in a survey, you almost certainly have heard or read news headlines about survey results:

- "AP-NORC Poll: Nearly all in US Back Criminal Justice Reform" (Long & Fingerhut, 2020)
- "ACLU Poll Shows Wide-Ranging Support for Releasing Vulnerable People from Jails and Prisons" (ACLU, 2020)
- "Gallup: Support in U.S. for Death Penalty at Lowest Point in Decades" (Hughes, 2020).

These examples contain the essential elements of survey research: asking a sample of people a predetermined set of questions in order to estimate characteristics of the population from which the sample was drawn. As you saw in Chapter 7, such estimates are often based on random sampling. And if you have taken a survey, you may have been told that you were randomly selected to participate. At their best, surveys produce accurate quantitative data that not only describe the attitudes, opinions, and behavior of a target population but also reveal how social characteristics, such as gender, race/ethnicity, class, and age, are related to people's responses. As such, surveys are widely used in criminal justice and criminological research addressing quantitative questions (Wright & Marsden, 2010).

We begin this chapter by using the National Crime Victimization Survey (NCVS), a national household survey conducted annually by the Census Bureau that collects information on criminal victimization (Bureau of Justice Statistics (BJS), 2021) to discuss the primary features of survey research. Next, we describe major variations in surveys, including designs that gather data at more than one point in time and different modes of collecting data such as face-to-face interviews, telephone interviews, and self-administered questionnaires. We then outline the process of conducting a survey. Finally, we discuss the strengths and weaknesses of survey research.

9.1 GENERAL FEATURES OF SURVEY RESEARCH

The NCVS illustrates three features that surveys have to varying degrees:

1. A large number of respondents chosen to represent a population of interest.
2. Structured questionnaire or interview procedures that ask a predetermined set of questions.
3. The quantitative analysis of survey responses.

Let us examine more carefully each of these features with reference to the NCVS and to other studies that illustrate variations in the general rule for each feature.

Large-Scale Probability Sampling

Professional surveys generally make use of large samples chosen through scientific sampling procedures to ensure accurate estimates of population characteristics. For instance, the NCVS collects data annually from a sample of approximately 240,000 interviews, involving 160,000 individuals from around 95,000 households (BJS, 2021). Not all surveys make use of such large samples, however. National opinion polls typically number around 1,000 respondents, and the General Social Survey (GSS) has had sample sizes ranging from 1,372 (in 1990) to 4,510 (in 2006).

Sample accuracy is a function of two factors: sample design and sample size. Probability samples, which involve random selection, provide the most precise and accurate estimates of population characteristics; and when cases are chosen randomly, the larger the sample, the more accurate the sample estimates. Both of these factors, however, require considerable resources—time, money, and personnel—that may be beyond the capacity of independent researchers or small research teams. Many surveys, therefore, involve smaller samples drawn from state or local populations.

There are legitimate reasons for doing a small-scale survey, particularly if you have a low budget or some specialized or applied research purpose. In fact, you can conduct your own low-budget research if you have a research problem that can be studied appropriately with a brief questionnaire survey of the home campus or a telephone survey of the local dialing area. Some surveys also involve nonprobability sampling. For example, the Boston Reentry Study, a study carried out by researchers at Harvard University in collaboration with the Massachusetts Department of Correction (DOC) to explore the reentry experiences of men and women recently released from state prisons in Massachusetts, relied on DOC officials to recruit participants into the study based on certain criteria (see Western et al., 2017). Further, as we noted in Chapter 7 (Box 7.3), surveys conducted online increasingly are using opt-in panels consisting of volunteers who are paid for their participation. Although these panels often select respondents or make statistical adjustments to match the target population, they are less accurate than probability sampling, which is still much preferred by survey researchers.

Structured Interviews or Questionnaires

structured interview a type of interview with highly specific objectives in which all questions are written beforehand and asked in the same order for all respondents, and the interviewer's remarks are standardized

Surveys gather data by asking people predetermined questions following standardized procedures that are designed to enhance the reliability of the data. This epitomizes the **structured interviews** that were used in the NCVS: the survey objectives were very specific; all the questions were written beforehand and asked in the same order for all respondents; and interviewers were highly restricted in the use of introductory and closing remarks, transitions or "bridges" from topic to topic, as well as supplementary questions to gain a more complete response (probes).

9.1 General Features of Survey Research

Surveys can contain many types of questions and question formats, but they almost always include **closed-ended questions**, which require respondents to choose a response from those provided, much like a multiple-choice test. For example, NCVS respondents who indicated that they had been a victim of crime are asked a number of questions about the incident such as: Did this incident happen

1) in your home or lodging,
2) near your home,
3) at, in, or near a friend's/relative's/neighbor's home;
4) at a commercial place,
5) in a parking lot or garage,
6) at school,
7) in open areas, on the street, or on public transportation;
8) somewhere else?

Was the offender male or female?

1. Male
2. Female
3. Don't know

How old would you say the offender was?

1. Under 12
2. 12–14
3. 15–17
4. 18–20
5. 21–29
6. 30 or older
7. Don't know

> **closed-ended question** survey question that requires respondents to choose responses from those provided

One reason that survey researchers prefer closed-ended questions is that they produce data that lend themselves well to the kinds of quantitative analysis that drives survey research. In contrast, **open-ended questions** are adopted when the research purpose is not to derive precise quantitative descriptions but to understand respondents' interpretations and experiences, as in qualitative research. In these approaches, open-ended questions provide flexibility in meeting broad research objectives and in developing theory.

> **open-ended question** a survey question that requires respondents to answer in their own words

The NCVS also included some open-ended questions. For example, a closed-ended question asked respondents to indicate whether or not they experienced a range of physical problems associated with being a victim of crime, such as high blood pressure, fatigue, muscle tension, or back pain. One response option was "some other physical problem." Respondents who selected that they had experienced "some other physical problem" were asked to describe the other physical problems they had experienced in their own words.

Open-ended questions provide a wealth of information that can clarify and deepen the researcher's understanding of a topic. However, open-ended questions pose several problems that limit their use in survey research. Summarizing and analyzing rich and varied (and sometimes irrelevant and vague) responses is a time-consuming and costly process. Respondents may be reluctant to reveal detailed information or socially unacceptable opinions or behavior. And open-ended questions require more effort to answer; indeed, they often are left blank—and therefore should be used sparingly—in self-administered questionnaires or online surveys, where respondents must write or type rather than speak.

Quantitative Data Analysis

Data-analysis techniques depend on whether the survey's purpose is descriptive, explanatory, or a combination of the two. Surveys that are primarily **descriptive**, such as many opinion polls, make use of simpler forms of data analysis to describe the distribution of certain characteristics, attitudes, or experiences within a population. **Explanatory surveys**, on the other hand, require more sophisticated data-analysis techniques to investigate relationships between two or more variables.

descriptive survey a survey that investigates relationships between two or more variables, often attempting to explain them in cause-and-effect terms

explanatory survey a survey undertaken to provide estimates of the characteristics of a population

SUMMARY

There are three general features of surveys. First, a large number of respondents are chosen, usually through probability sampling, to represent a population of interest. Second, surveys tend to use structured questionnaire or interview procedures that ask a predetermined set of closed-ended rather than open-ended questions. Third, surveys involve quantitative analysis of responses, which may be descriptive (to describe a population), explanatory (to test hypotheses), or both. Check out Box 9.1 to assess your understanding of the concepts discussed within this section.

BOX 9.1

CHECKING YOUR UNDERSTANDING

Survey Research and Questions

1. All of the following are general features of survey research except:
    a. quantitative data analysis
    b. direct observation of behavior
    c. structured questionnaires and/or interviews
    d. large probability samples

> 2. The Gallup Poll, which provides estimates of the characteristics of a population, utilizes which type of survey?
>   a. Descriptive
>   b. Open-ended
>   c. Explanatory
>   d. Probability
>
> 3. Which of the following is true of closed-ended questions?
>   a. They are more time consuming to analyze than open-ended questions.
>   b. They require respondents to answer in their own words.
>   c. They produce data that lend themselves well to quantitative analysis.
>   d. They can provide in-depth understanding.
>
> Answers: 1. b, 2. a, 3. c

9.2 VARIATIONS IN SURVEY DESIGNS AND MODES

Like experiments, surveys vary in research design and context. The research design specifies the overall structure or plan by which a study will address the research question(s). The context refers to the setting in which the data are collected. Let us take a closer look now at the NCVS and other research examples to understand variations in survey design and the mode of data collection.

Survey Research Designs

The basic idea of a survey is to measure variables by asking people questions and then to describe the distribution of responses to single questions or examine the relationships among responses to multiple items. The major design decision is whether to ask the questions just once or to repeat the questions over time.

CROSS-SECTIONAL DESIGNS

The most commonly used survey design by far is the **cross-sectional design**, which involves a sample or "cross-section" of respondents chosen to represent a particular target population. Cross-sectional data are gathered at essentially one point in time. By "one point in time" we do not mean that respondents are interviewed or that self-administered questionnaires are collected simultaneously (although this might be the case with some questionnaire studies). Rather, the data are collected in as short a time as is feasible. The 2018 Family History of Incarceration survey, which sought to determine the percentage of Americans who had ever had a family member incarcerated,

cross-sectional design the most common survey design, in which data are gathered from a sample of respondents at essentially one point in time

employed a cross-sectional design. During the summer of 2018, data were collected from 2,815 respondents (Enns et al., 2019).

LONGITUDINAL DESIGNS

Because cross-sectional designs call for collection of data at one point in time, they do not always clearly show the direction of causal relationships. Moreover, they are not well suited to the study of process and change. To provide stronger inferences about causal direction and patterns of change, survey researchers have developed **longitudinal designs**, in which the same questions are asked at two or more points in time. The questions may be asked repeatedly of either independently selected samples of the same general population or the same individuals. This results in two main types of longitudinal designs: trend studies and panel studies.

A **trend study** consists of a repeated cross-sectional design in which each survey collects data on the same items or variables with a new, independent sample of the same target population. This allows for the study of trends or changes in the population as a whole. The National Survey on Drug Use and Health (NSDUH) represents a trend study. Data are collected annually in order to estimate substance use and mental health in the United States. Other common examples include the monthly government surveys used to estimate unemployment in the United States (target population) and repeated preelection public-opinion polls of candidate preferences among registered voters (target population).

Whereas a trend study identifies which *variables* are changing over time, a **panel study** can reveal which *individuals* are changing over time because the same respondents are surveyed again and again. Panel studies of any duration were a rarity in the social sciences until the late 1960s, when the federal government began conducting large-scale longitudinal studies. The NCVS is an example of a panel study. For the NCVS, households are randomly selected to participate in the study. Every six months, households are interviewed, totaling seven surveys over a three-year period. Once the three-year period is up, that household is removed from the study and a new one is randomly selected to replace it. The longest-running household panel survey in the world is the Panel Study of Income Dynamics (PSID), conducted by the Survey Research Center in the Institute for Social Research at the University of Michigan. The PSID has collected data on a sample of US households annually from 1968 to 1997 and biennially beginning in 1999. As of 2009, nearly 6,000 of the original participants from 1968 were still living and had participated in every survey (McGonagle et al., 2012). "Through its 2017 survey wave," the PSID has collected data from more than 80,000 individuals and "on nearly as many variables" (Pfeffer et al., 2020, p. 99). See Table 9.1 for the similarities and differences between trend and panel studies.

Two drawbacks to panel studies of this magnitude are that they are very expensive and take considerable time. Therefore, cross-sectional and trend designs are far more

9.2 Variations in Survey Designs and Modes

Table 9.1 Similarities and Differences Between Trend and Panel Studies

Trend Study	Panel Study
Survey questions are repeated to understand change over time	Survey questions are repeated to understand change over time
A different independent sample of respondents, representative of the same target population (e.g., US adults), is asked the same questions in each survey	The initial sample of respondents is asked the same questions each time the survey is administered
Data show how *the population* changes over time	Data show how *individuals* change over time

common. But irrespective of the survey design, surveys also differ in how the data are collected.

Data-Collection Modes

A critical aspect of survey research is the mode of asking questions: interviewer-administered (face-to-face or telephone surveys), self-administered (paper-and-pencil or computer-assisted questionnaires), or some combination of these modes. Figure 9.1 lists the four basic data-collection modes along with typical computer-based variations. The modes may be conceptualized as falling along a continuum from the most to the least interactive. At one end of the continuum, involving all channels of communication, is the face-to-face interview; this is followed, in turn, by telephone interviews, various digital self-interviews, and autonomous self-administered questionnaires. Each mode, as you will see, has its distinctive advantages and disadvantages; the choice depends on many considerations, including research objectives, quality of measurement, and available resources, such as time and money. Although we focus primarily on the four basic modes, recent technological developments have rapidly expanded the options and encouraged the use of multiple modes of data collection within the same study, which we discuss at the end of this section.

face-to-face (FTF) interview a software program, usually on a portable computer, that aids interviewers by providing appropriate instructions, question wording, and data-entry supervision

FACE-TO-FACE INTERVIEWS

The oldest and most highly regarded method of survey research is the **face-to-face (FTF) interview**, which involves direct, in-person contact between an interviewer and interviewee. The GSS is primarily an FTF interview survey, although it

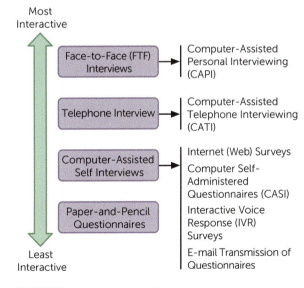

FIGURE 9.1 Survey Data-Collection Modes

▲ PHOTO 9.1 Computer-assisted personal interviewing (CAPI) is now the standard for conducting large-scale face-to-face interview surveys, nationally and internationally, as shown in this photo from the Yemen Polling Center.

shifted to other modes in 2020. From 1972 until 2002, GSS interviewers circled or recorded answers in writing on questionnaires, but in 2002, the GSS shifted to **computer-assisted personal interviewing (CAPI)**. With CAPI, interviewers carry out the survey through a laptop computer, which they bring to the respondent's home. The computer screen prompts the interviewer with instructions and questions; the interviewer reads the questions and then enters the respondent's answers. CAPI makes the interviewer's job easier, reduces mistakes, and saves time and cost since the data are entered directly into a computer file and do not have to be entered manually. For an example, see the photo from the Yemen Polling Center.

computer-assisted personal interviewing (CAPI) a type of interview in which the interviewer interacts face-to-face with the respondent

response rate in a survey, the proportion of people in the sample from whom completed interviews or questionnaires are obtained

FTF interview surveys offer many advantages. The presence of an interviewer permits a great deal more flexibility than is possible with a self-administered questionnaire. If the research objectives call for open-ended questions, interviewers can probe for more complete responses; they can also clarify or restate questions that the respondent does not understand. The **response rate**, the proportion of people in the sample who completed interviews (or questionnaires), is typically higher than in comparable telephone or mail surveys (de Leeuw, 2008, pp. 128–129), although response rates in all three modes have been declining in recent years. Between 1975 and 1998, the average response rate for the GSS was 77 percent; the GSS rate dipped to 70–71 percent between 2000 and 2012 and has fallen below 70 percent since then, with a low of 59.5 percent in 2018 (Smith et al., 2019, Appendix A, Table A.8).

For sustaining respondents' attention and motivation, the FTF mode is generally the best choice when long interviews are necessary. In fact, FTF interviews of one hour's length are common, and they sometimes go much longer. GSS interviews take about 90 minutes for completion of some 400 questions. With the FTF technique, one can use visual aids such as photographs and drawings in presenting the questions, as well as cards that show response options (see Figure 9.2). The cards may be useful when response options are difficult to remember or when it is face-saving for respondents to select the option or category on the card rather than to say the answer aloud.

1. In open country but not on a farm
2. On a farm
3. In a small city or town (under 50,000)
4. In a medium-size city (50,000–250,000)
5. In a suburb near a large city
6. In a large city (over 250,000)

FIGURE 9.2 FTF Visual Aid. GSS interviewers hand respondents a card similar to this one when they ask, "Which of the categories on this card come closest to the type of place you were living in when you were 16 years old?"

The greatest disadvantage to the FTF method is cost. Compared to telephone interviews, the research budget for an FTF survey must provide not only for recruiting, training, and supervising personnel but also for interviewer wages and travel expenses, including lodging and meals in some cases. Moreover, it takes much longer to complete each interview in an FTF survey; therefore, the cost per interview is much greater. Robert Groves and associates (2009) estimate that national FTF surveys cost 5 to 10 times as much as telephone surveys. The full cost of the 2014 GSS, from sampling through release of the data to the public, was about $1,350 per completed interview (T. W. Smith, personal communication, 2016).

For financial or other reasons, however, it may not always be possible to conduct an FTF survey. This was dramatically illustrated in the United States during the COVID-19 pandemic, when the Centers for Disease Control (CDC) promoted social distancing to protect public health. Consequently, the GSS shifted to a telephone and "mixed-mode web" survey in 2020 (GSS, 2020).

TELEPHONE INTERVIEWS

In the last quarter of the 20th century, **telephone interviews** became the most popular survey method in the United States and western Europe. The primary reason for the increasing popularity of the telephone survey was its substantial savings in cost and time. In addition, survey research organizations like the Center for Survey Research, which have a permanent staff, can complete a telephone survey very rapidly. Even those researchers who must hire and train interviewers can complete a telephone survey in less billable time than one requiring FTF interviews or mailed questionnaires.

Besides savings in cost and time, another major advantage of telephone interviewing is the opportunity for centralized quality control over all aspects of data collection (Lavrakas, 2010), including question development and pretesting, interviewer training and supervision, sampling and callbacks, and data entry. Also, administration and staff supervision for a telephone survey are much simpler than for an FTF interview survey.

Still, telephone surveys have their limitations. Without the benefit of visual aids, the questions in a telephone survey must be simpler, with fewer response options, than in an FTF interview. And without face-to-face contact, it is more difficult for interviewers to establish trust and rapport with respondents, which may lead to higher rates of nonresponse for some questions and underreporting of sensitive or socially undesirable behavior (Aquilino, 1994; Groves et al., 2009; Holbrook et al., 2003). Overall response rates also tend to be lower than in FTF interview surveys; and conducting a telephone interview longer than 20 to 30 minutes increases the risk of nonresponse and mid-interview termination (de Leeuw, 2008).

You may need to look no farther than your hand, your pocket, or your purse to guess the most serious problems facing telephone surveys. The rapid proliferation of mobile telephones in the 2000s and the growth of the cell phone-only population has made it difficult to reach respondents (Lavrakas et al., 2007). As Mick Couper (2017) points

telephone interview a type of interview in which interviewers interact with respondents by telephone

out, "the declines in survey response rates have affected telephone surveys more than any other mode" (p. 125). Response rates for many federal telephone surveys declined from around 70 percent in the 1990s to 50 percent by 2005 (Dixon & Tucker, 2010), and rates for private US survey organizations are even lower, with most telephone surveys between 20 and 50 percent (Holbrook et al., 2008). One private US-based survey organization, the Pew Research Center, indicates that the response rates for its telephone surveys have dropped from 36% in 1997 to 6% in 2018 (Kennedy & Hartig, 2019). Factors contributing to the plunging telephone response rates include the growth of caller ID call-screening and call-blocking technologies, heightened privacy concerns in the face of increased telemarketing calls and robocalls, as well as the increase in cell phone-only households (Couper, 2017; Curtin et al., 2005; Deane et al., 2019; Dixon & Tucker, 2010). In short, many people do not answer their phone unless they recognize and wish to speak to the caller. Moreover, these declining response rates make telephone surveys "more difficult and expensive to conduct" (Deane et al., 2019), mitigating their advantages over other survey modes. In light of these mounting obstacles to telephone surveys, some foresee an increasing reliance on self-administered questionnaires (Couper, 2011; Deane et al., 2019; Dillman, 2007), which we discuss next.

PAPER-AND-PENCIL QUESTIONNAIRE

paper-and-pencil questionnaire survey a survey form filled out by respondents

Occasionally, the site of a **paper-and-pencil-questionnaire survey** is a school or organization, where the questionnaire may be hand-delivered and filled out in a group or individually. Most often, however, the setting is the home or a workplace, to which a self-administered questionnaire is mailed to respondents. An interesting example of a *mail survey* is the College Alcohol Study (CAS; Wechsler & Nelson, 2008), a widely cited national survey of American college students' drinking habits and other health issues. The CAS was conducted four times: in 1993, 1997, 1999, and 2001. In each of the four surveys, the researchers found that two in five students who responded were binge drinkers, operationally defined as the consumption of five or more drinks in a row for men and four or more drinks in a row for women during the two weeks prior to the survey. Binge drinkers, especially those who frequently binged, were far more likely than non-binge drinkers to experience a variety of alcohol-related and other health problems, such as engaging in unprotected and unplanned sex, getting in trouble with campus police, damaging property, and getting hurt or injured.

There are several advantages to using a mail survey. A mail survey is less expensive than interview surveys, with costs estimated at 20 to 70 percent less than telephone surveys (Groves et al., 2009, p. 173). No interviewers or interviewer supervisors are needed; there are no travel or telephone expenses; and very little office space is required. The time needed to complete the data-collection phase of the survey is greater than that for telephone surveys but usually less than that for FTF surveys. The sample size may be very large, and geographical dispersion is not a problem. The 1993 CAS, for example, surveyed a random sample of 17,592 students at 140 colleges in 39 states and the District of Columbia (Wechsler et al., 1994). There also is greater accessibility to respondents with this method since those who cannot be reached by telephone or who are infrequently at home usually receive mail. Finally, in contrast to interview surveys, mail surveys can provide respondents with anonymity, which is important in investigating sensitive or threatening topics, such as college drinking or illicit drug use. Anonymity protects respondents' privacy, and research has shown that respondents are more likely to admit to undesirable behavior with self-administered than with interview-administered surveys (Groves et al., 2009, p. 170; Tourangeau & Yan, 2007; see Krumpal, 2013 for a review).

Despite these advantages, especially its lower cost, the mail questionnaire survey method is inferior to FTF and telephone interview surveys in several ways. Although the response rate for the 1993 CAS was 69 percent, the response rate for mail surveys tends to be much lower, with rates of 50 percent or lower common (Shih & Fan, 2008). Certain groups of people, such as those with little writing ability and those not interested in the topic, are less likely to respond to a mailed questionnaire than to a personal interview request. More questions are left unanswered with self-administered questionnaires than with interview methods. And without an interviewer, there is no opportunity to clarify questions, probe for more adequate answers, or control the conditions under which the questionnaire is completed or even who completes it.

Still, the mail survey may serve the research purposes well with specialized target groups who are likely to have high response rates, when very large samples are desired, costs must be kept low, ease of administration is necessary, and moderate response rates are considered satisfactory.

COMPUTER-ASSISTED SELF-INTERVIEWS

Researchers have developed a variety of digital surveys that are self-administered. In **computer-assisted self-administered interviewing (CASI)**, the questionnaire is transmitted to respondents using a digital program (e.g., as a link in an e-mail) or provided by the researcher on a laptop. Whereas **computer-assisted personal and telephone interviewing** (CAPI and CATI) make the interviewer's job easier, CASI replaces the interviewer. Examples of CASI include emailed questionnaires, interactive voice response (IVR) surveys, digital self-administered questionnaires, and online surveys (Figure 9.1). E-mail and online surveys are conducted over the internet. Both involve digital transmission of a questionnaire; in e-mail surveys, the questions are sent as the text of an e-mail message or in an attached file, whereas in online surveys, the questionnaire is accessed on specially designed webpages. IVR surveys are conducted by telephone as respondents listen to prerecorded, voice-read questions and then use touch-tone data entry or give verbal answers, which are recorded (Steiger & Conroy, 2008). Of these methods, we focus here on online surveys, which have had the broadest

computer-assisted self-administered interviewing (CASI) an electronic survey in which a questionnaire is transmitted using a digital program or on digital equipment provided by the researcher

computer-assisted telephone interviewing (CATI) a set of digital tools that aid telephone interviewers and supervisors by automating various data-collection tasks

application and have increased dramatically in recent years (Couper, 2017; Dillman et al., 2009).

An example of an online survey is Wozniak, Drakulich, and Calfano's (2021) exploratory study of public opinion regarding the use of various police weapons and equipment during interactions with citizens. To examine this topic, the researchers conducted an online survey through the use of a Qualtrics national online panel. Individuals who were part of the panel were able to "opt-in" to take the survey. A total of 1,100 responses were obtained. The researchers concluded that there is no clear distinction in public opinion of militarized vs. routine equipment; thus, one should be cautious of the polls that indicate that most Americans oppose police use of military weapons and gear. Additionally, they found a number of perceptions to be predictive of support or opposition including police efficacy, frequency of physical assaults on police officers, police misconduct, and bias.

Among the advantages of online surveys such as this one, the greatest is reduced cost. Compared to self-administered questionnaires, the cheapest of the traditional modes, internet surveys eliminate the costs of paper, postage, assembly of the mailout package, and data entry (Dillman, 2007). The principal costs are computer equipment and programming support, questionnaire development and testing, and internet service provider fees. For faculty and students, some of these costs are eliminated. And for all researchers, the development of online survey software questionnaire tools such as SurveyMonkey®, Survs, Qualtrics®, and QuestionPro™ has facilitated questionnaire construction and delivery. A related advantage is time savings. Online surveys require much less time to implement than other survey modes; compared to mail surveys, which may take weeks or months for questionnaires to be delivered and returned, online surveys may be completed in only a few days. Finally, online surveys can substantially reduce the cost of increasing sample size because once the digital questionnaire has been developed, the cost of surveying each additional person is far less than in an interview or mail survey (Dillman, 2007).

Another advantage of online surveys, one they share with other digital methods, is flexibility in questionnaire design. As Don Dillman (2007) points out, the questionnaire can be designed "to provide a more dynamic interaction between respondent and questionnaire" than is possible in a paper-and-pencil survey (p. 354). Online questionnaires can incorporate pop-up instructions for individual questions, drop-down boxes with lists of answer choices, feedback on possibly incorrect answers (e.g., birth date "1839"), pop-up word definition screens, and automatic fill-ins for later answers. They can use a great variety of shapes and colors and can add pictures, animation, video clips, and sound (p. 458). When designed carefully, online survey options and features may be used to motivate and assist respondents and otherwise substitute for the role that an interviewer plays (Couper et al., 2001; Manfreda & Vehovar, 2008, pp. 276–281).

At this point, the great practical advantages and enormous design potential of online surveys for criminal justice research are offset by some major weaknesses. Response rates to online surveys tend to be lower than other modes—generally about 11–12 percent less than other modes of surveys (Daikeler et al., 2021). Another issue is coverage error, the error produced when the sampling frame does not include all members of the population. This error derives from two related problems: the proportion of the general population who are internet users and the lack of a sampling frame to sample users. By 2022, 91.2 percent of US households had internet (US Census Bureau, 2022). However, a "digital divide" remains, with nonusers being more likely to be Black or Hispanic, older, and with less income than those with internet access (Remaley, 2020). The second problem is the absence of a good frame for sampling internet users. For example, no list is available, nor is it possible, to generate a list of all US households with internet service. Researchers often address this problem by limiting their online surveys to special populations having membership lists and internet access, such as college students, certain professionals, or employees of an organization. Finally, as we pointed out, many online surveys use nonprobability samples consisting of online panels, which are further biased as samples of internet users.

To summarize our discussion of modes thus far, Table 9.2 compares the principal survey modes on five criteria. It is important to know the relative strengths and weaknesses of these modes before we consider the final option: how modes can be combined effectively in a single survey.

MIXED-MODE SURVEYS

Choosing a data-collection mode is difficult when none of the primary modes seems optimal for the intended research. An alternative solution is to design a **mixed-mode survey**, which uses more than one mode, either sequentially or concurrently, to sample and/or collect the data. In this way, the weaknesses of one mode may be offset by the strengths of another mode. For example, since 1970, the US decennial census has combined less expensive mail surveys followed by more expensive in-person interviews

mixed-mode survey a survey that uses more than one mode of data collection, either sequentially or concurrently, to sample and/or collect the data

Table 9.2 Comparison of Survey Modes on Five Criteria

	Cost	Time	Response rate	Population coverage	Quality of measurement
Best	Online	Online	FTF	FTF	FTF
	Mail	Telephone	Mail	Mail	Telephone
	Telephone	Mail	Telephone	Telephone	Online
Worst	FTF	FTF	Online	Online	Mail

with people who do not return the mail questionnaires. In addition, the 2020 Census allowed people to respond by phone or online.

The proliferation of modes, among other developments, has fueled a marked increase in mixed-mode designs in the 21st century (Couper, 2011; Dillman et al., 2009). Modes may be combined in many different ways for a variety of reasons. Here we briefly mention three of the most common ways of mixing survey modes (de Leeuw, 2005; Dillman et al., 2009).

1. Use one mode to recruit, screen, or contact respondents and another mode to administer the survey. For example, to increase response to an online survey, Royce Singleton initially contacted respondents with a letter sent by mail. The letter explained the purpose of the survey, provided a link to the webpage where respondents could complete the survey, and included a $2 incentive to respond. As another example, a researcher might use an inexpensive telephone survey to screen and locate specialized populations, such as people with an incarcerated family member, for a study requiring expensive FTF interviews.
2. Use a second mode to collect data on a subset of questions from the same respondents. A mode shift to self-administered questionnaires—paper-and-pencil or CASI—often is used in FTF surveys to increase privacy in the collection of sensitive information. Typically, an interviewer administers the largest part of the interview but then provides the respondent with either a paper questionnaire to be sealed in an envelope or a CASI laptop to complete the self-administered portion that requests the most sensitive information. In this way, respondents are less susceptible to social desirability biases, which are more likely when questions are administered by an interviewer. An early application of this strategy occurred in the 1992 National Health Interview Survey–Youth Risk Behavior Supplement, which used an audio questionnaire to collect sensitive information from adolescents about drug use, sexual intercourse, cigarette smoking, and other unhealthy behaviors (Willard & Schoenborn, 1995). Teens listened to the questions on a portable audio headset and recorded their answers on an answer sheet that did not contain any information by which parents or other household members would know the questions being answered.
3. Use different modes to survey different respondents. One solution to the coverage problem in online surveys, for example, is a respondent-specific approach whereby those without internet access are surveyed in person or by mail. Another example would be increasing the response rate of the sampled population by conducting telephone or FTF interviews with those who did not respond to an initial mail questionnaire, as in the decennial census.

The first two mixed-mode designs have been common practice for some time; their advantages in reducing cost, increasing response rates, and improving data quality are well established. The recent surge of interest in mixed-mode surveys is due mainly to the third design, in which different modes are used with different respondents during the data-collection process (Couper, 2011). The major weakness of this design is the uncertainty as to whether the data from respondents surveyed by different modes are comparable. As the various modes may differ in coverage, sampling, nonresponse, and measurement quality, merging the mode subsamples to statistically estimate the target population is a difficult and uncertain undertaking.

SUMMARY

Surveys vary in their design and modes of data collection. Surveys using a cross-sectional design ask a sample of people questions at one point in time, while surveys using a longitudinal design ask people questions at two or more points in time. Of the two major types of longitudinal designs, a trend study asks the same questions of independent samples of people, whereas a panel study asks the same questions of the same sample of people at multiple points in time. Surveys collect data through face-to-face interviews, telephone interviews, paper-and-pencil questionnaires including mail surveys, digital self-interviews, or some combination of these modes (mixed-mode surveys). Each mode has strengths and limitations related to its costs, the time it takes to administer the survey, the response rate, the population coverage, and its quality of measurement. Face-to-face interviewing is considered to be the best (and most interactive) mode, but its costs and time investment can be prohibitive. See Box 9.2 to assess your understanding of this section.

BOX 9.2

CHECKING YOUR UNDERSTANDING

Types of Data Collection

1. The National Crime Victimization Survey (NCVS), described within the chapter,
    a. is a panel survey.
    b. uses only open-ended questions.
    c. has a target population consisting of all undergraduate students in the United States.
    d. is an online survey.

continues

continued

2. Suppose you hypothesize that the more criminal justice courses a student takes, the more sensitive they become to discrimination within the criminal justice system. You then ask a random sample of students at your college how many criminal justice courses they have taken and also ask them a set of questions measuring perceptions of discrimination within criminal justice. Finally, you calculate the association between the two variables. This is an example of a:
   a. laboratory experiment.
   b. cross-sectional survey.
   c. longitudinal survey.
   d. panel study.

3. Compared with face-to-face interview studies, telephone interview studies
   a. take more time to complete.
   b. have a higher response rate.
   c. cost more.
   d. demand less attention to staff supervision.

4. Which survey mode is <u>most costly</u> and takes the <u>most amount of time</u>?
   a. Face-to-face interview
   b. Telephone interview
   c. Mailed questionnaire
   d. Online survey

Answers: 1. a, 2. b, 3. d, 4. a

9.3 THE PROCESS OF PLANNING AND CONDUCTING A SURVEY

Once you have decided to do a survey, your research purposes (e.g., descriptive or explanatory) and available resources will determine two key decisions: the measurement of variables (shown on the left side of Figure 9.3) and the selection of the sample (on the right side of Figure 9.3). Survey measurement occurs by asking questions, and the wording and complexity of the questions will depend, first, on the survey mode. Having selected the mode, you must then construct and pretest the survey questionnaire. Drawing a sample involves finding or creating an appropriate sampling frame, and then selecting cases based on the sampling design. With the survey instrument ready and the sample drawn, the process of conducting the survey converges by contacting eligible respondents and administering the questionnaire. The data then must be coded and edited before they are analyzed to answer the research questions.

As we examine the steps of planning and conducting a survey in Figure 9.3, we will discuss a number of studies that have used various modes of data collection in the survey process.

Choose Mode of Data Collection

The first step in the process of planning and conducting a survey is to choose a mode of data collection, considering the strengths and limitations of each. This choice depends on the goals of the research and the resources available.

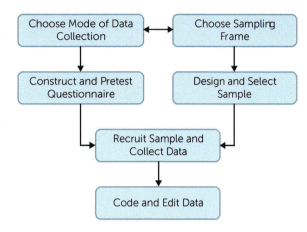

FIGURE 9.3 The Process of Planning and Conducting a Survey

If you are doing a small-scale survey, say, for a class project, it is unlikely you will have the resources available to large research firms. As we noted earlier, an online survey is the least costly mode of data collection in terms of both time and money. Therefore, we recommend that you consider this mode, provided that it meets your research goals.

Construct and Pretest Questionnaire

To construct the survey instrument, the researcher should first outline the question topics to be covered in the interview or questionnaire. When addressing quantitative research questions with the purpose of explanation or hypothesis-testing, these topics should cover your independent and dependent variables as well as extraneous variables that may affect the hypothesized relationships.

There are many advantages to this well-established practice: it shortcuts the measurement process, capitalizes on others' expertise (assuming the questions are from credible sources), and enables researchers to compare results across studies. Lest you be concerned about the ethics of using another person's questions, the norms "of social science in general and survey research in particular not only permit but encourage the repetition of questions" (Sudman & Bradburn, 1982, p. 14).

Writing questions is a challenge. How questions are written depends on the question topic and whether you are asking about factual events and behaviors or subjective states, such as knowledge, perceptions, feelings, and judgments (Fowler, 1995). The survey researcher must choose between question forms, such as open and closed, and the number and type of response categories.

As you are designing a survey, you need to pay particular attention to language, as even slight changes in the wording of a question can greatly affect responses. For example, a question might be written, "What is your annual income?" or "What is your total annual income from all sources?" A person answering the first item might neglect to consider income from such sources as interest on stocks or savings, sale of stocks, and rental income. As Jean Converse and Stanley Presser (1986) note, "writing sufficiently clear and 'simple' questions is hard-won, heavy-duty work for survey researchers" (p. 10). Part of the work involves carefully examining the language of the items. In general, you want to use questions that

(1) respondents understand in a consistent way, so that they would give the same answer if they were asked the same question again (AAPOR, 2020),
(2) mean the same thing to all respondents, and
(3) have the same meaning for respondents as they do for the researcher.

For more specific tips on how to write good survey questions, see Box 9.3.

> **BOX 9.3**
>
> **DOING CRIMINAL JUSTICE RESEARCH**
>
> ## Writing Survey Questions
>
> Through research and experience, researchers have developed guidelines for designing survey questions. These guidelines are so numerous that we cannot review them adequately here (for a more extensive discussion, see Singleton and Straits (2018, Chapter 10)). An excellent resource is Floyd Fowler's (1995) *Improving Survey Questions: Design and Evaluation*; another is Jon Krosnick and Stanley Presser's (2010) chapter, "Question and Questionnaire Design," in *Handbook of Survey Research*, 2nd ed. In addition, there are many useful guides to survey design online. Based on these and other sources (AAPOR, 2020; Krosnick & Presser, 2010; Schaeffer & Dykema, 2020) as well as our own experience, we offer the following brief tips for writing good survey questions. After reviewing the tips, utilize Box 9.4 to assess your understanding of this section.
>
> *Avoid ambiguous or imprecise words.* Clarity and precision are essential qualities of well-worded items. At times, an item that appears perfectly clear to the designer may be very confusing or carry a different meaning to someone with a different background and point of view. The point is easily illustrated by the question, "How many years have you been living here?" To one respondent, "here" may mean the present house or apartment; to another, the city; and to another, the country.
>
> Especially troublesome are indefinite words such as *usually, seldom, many, few, here,* and *there*; these will have different meanings to different respondents. Following are two alternative items illustrating the problem. The second item is an improvement over

the first because the responses are specific and thereby have the same precise meaning for both researcher and respondent.

How often do you attend religious services? Would you say:

- ( ) often
- ( ) occasionally
- ( ) seldom, or
- ( ) never

How often do you attend religious services? Would you say:

- ( ) every day
- ( ) more than once a week
- ( ) once a week
- ( ) two or three times a month
- ( ) once a month
- ( ) a few times a year, or
- ( ) once a year or less

Use "not" or "non" sparingly. Items should be easy to read or hear accurately. Some respondents will skip over or tune out the negative word in an item and respond the opposite of the way the question is actually intended, so it is best to avoid the use of negative words such as *not*. And it is generally not advisable to have two negatives in the question (AAPOR, 2020).

Use simple, familiar words, not technical jargon. It is important to keep vocabulary extremely simple in surveys. Designers can evaluate whether their survey questions are clear and nontechnical using an online tool called the Question Understanding Aid (QUAID, Graesser et al., 2006). Other online tools and programs also can facilitate question writing (see Schaeffer & Dykema, 2020). Finally, if you are using an online survey program, it may give you question wording and response category suggestions.

Limit the question to a single idea, not two or more issues at once. A **double-barreled question** is one in which two separate ideas are presented together as a unit. An example might be, "What factors contributed to your decision to drink and engage in crime?" The researcher seems to assume that drinking and engaging in crime is a single act or decision, whereas in fact there are two questions being asked here. It is a good idea for the survey designer to examine all questions with the words "and" or "or" in them to be sure that they are not double-barreled.

---

double-barreled question a question in which two separate ideas are presented together as a unit

continues

continued

leading question
a question in which a possible answer is suggested, or some answers are presented as more acceptable than others

Avoid emotionally loaded words and other sources of bias. Emotionally loaded words and phrases, such as *racial preferences, pro-life, cops,* or *liberal* may evoke responses that have little to do with the real attitudes or opinion of the respondent regarding the issue the researcher is attempting to address. In general, try to word questions in a neutral way, and avoid identifying a statement or position with any controversial or prestigious person or group. Notice the loaded words (*union czars, forcing, knuckle under*) in the following question (Sudman & Bradburn, 1982, p. 2):

> *Are you in favor of allowing construction union czars the power to shut down an entire construction site because of a dispute with a single contractor, thus forcing even more workers to knuckle under to union agencies?*

Another source of bias is **leading questions**. Leading questions suggest a possible answer or make some responses seem more acceptable than others. The question "How often do you smoke cannabis?" may seem to imply that everyone indulges at least occasionally. A question that begins "Do you agree . . ." may suggest to some persons that they ought to agree. The generally accepted practice is to balance attitudinal questions by using such phrases as *agree or disagree, favor or oppose,* and *satisfied or dissatisfied* (Sudman & Bradburn, 1982). In asking about attitudes toward the harshness of courts, for example, Burton and associates (2020) utilized a question that has been used by the GSS for decades. The question asked, "In general, do you think the courts in this area deal too harshly or not harshly enough with criminals?"

Ensure that response options are exhaustive and mutually exclusive. In our experience as survey respondents, we find it very frustrating to read a question that we cannot answer because none of the possible answers applies to us or because more than one answer applies. Questions like this, moreover, are almost impossible to interpret. Therefore, when a question is closed-ended, (1) the list of response options should include all reasonable responses so that every person is capable of answering it (the list is exhaustive), and (2) the response options should provide clear choices so that only one answer is possible (the options are mutually exclusive).

Recall from Chapter 6 that exhaustive and mutually exclusive are requirements of all levels of measurement. An example of a closed-ended question, with ordinal level measurement, that is not exhaustive is the following:

What is your grade-point average (GPA)?
1. 2.00–2.33
2. 2.34–2.66

> 3. 2.67–3.00
> 4. 3.01–3.33
> 5. 3.34–3.66
> 6. 3.67–4.00
>
> Can you tell what is missing? The set of categories omits GPAs below 2.00. In addition, if you are answering this question and happen to be in your first semester in college, even this additional category would not apply to you. Therefore, if a question like this is directed to students without an established GPA, it also should have a category such as "Does not apply." Below is a question, also directed to college students, that violates the principle of mutual exclusivity:
>
> What is your age?
> 1. Less than 18 years old
> 2. 18–20
> 3. 20–22
> 4. 22–24
> 5. Greater than 24 years old
>
> Did you catch the error? What category would you circle if you were 20 or 22 years old?

ORGANIZING THE QUESTIONS

Once researchers have developed the questions, the next steps are to decide the order in which to ask them and to write an introductory statement as well as appropriate transitions from topic to topic. The introduction used in the NCVS was fairly standard: the interviewer gave their name, identified the survey sponsor, and briefly stated the general purpose of the study—to determine "how often people are victims of crime." Deciding how to order the questions after the introduction involves several considerations.

First, the opening question should be relatively easy to answer. Starting with a difficult question may discourage respondents and make them feel inadequate to fulfill their role as respondents. Imagine yourself taking an exam that starts out with a really difficult question—it might make you feel so intimidated and anxious that you have a hard time with the rest of the exam, even if the other questions are easier!

> **BOX 9.4**
>
> ## PRACTICE WHAT YOU LEARNED
>
> # Wording Questions
>
> 1. What is the major wording problem with the following question: "Do you approve of the irresponsible person who would drive after having several drinks?"
>   a. Double-barreled question
>   b. Inappropriate vocabulary
>   c. Leading question
>   d. Lack of precision
>
> 2. What is the major wording problem with the following question (asked of respondents who say they drink beer): "When you drink beer, how much, on the average, do you usually drink at any one time? [ ] quite a bit, [ ] a moderate amount, [ ] very little"?
>   a. Double-barreled question
>   b. Inappropriate vocabulary
>   c. Leading question
>   d. Lack of precision
>
> 3. What is the major wording problem with the following question: "How satisfied are you with the number and fairness of the tests in this course?"
>   a. Double-barreled question
>   b. Inappropriate vocabulary
>   c. Leading question
>   d. Lack of precision
>
> **Answers: 1. c, 2. d, 3. a**

A second consideration is the placement of background questions. Although we have seen many surveys that begin with background items such as gender, age, religious preference, and so on, it is much better to place such uninteresting routine questions at the end of the survey. A good strategy is to start with an interesting question at the beginning that is in line with respondents' expectations: it should be a question they might reasonably expect to be asked, on the basis of what they have been told by the interviewer about the study.

A third consideration is the placement of sensitive questions. Asking sensitive questions prematurely may embarrass or upset respondents, possibly leading them to terminate the interview or question the researcher's motives.

To improve the flow of the interview and enhance respondent understanding and motivation, it is advisable to include several transitions indicating that one topic has been completed and another topic is about to be discussed. Transitions focus the respondent's attention on the new topic, and may be used to explain briefly why the new topic will be discussed or how it relates to the research purposes.

PRETESTING

It is important to pretest the instrument by trying it out and evaluating its effectiveness before the main survey. Experience has shown that pretesting can greatly improve the ease with which data may be analyzed and the quality of results. For no matter how carefully a researcher may follow guidelines for best practices, it is still possible that a large number of respondents misunderstand the meaning of a question or resist answering some questions. And once the study has been conducted, it is too late to benefit from this information.

Survey pretesting may involve a variety of methods. The survey researcher may ask colleagues or experts in the field to critique the questions, apply formal schemes or computer software to identify question-wording problems, or administer the survey to a small sample of respondents (Krosnick & Presser, 2010). The federal government and many survey organizations often pretest specific items in a laboratory setting, where respondents are asked in various ways to reveal their thought processes in answering survey questions. The usual method, however, is **field pretesting**, which involves trying out the survey instrument on a small sample of persons having characteristics similar to those of the target group of respondents.

field pretesting an evaluation of a survey instrument that involves trying it out on a small sample of persons

Choose Sampling Frame/Design and Select Sample

Recall from Chapter 7 that a sampling frame denotes the set of all cases from which the sample is actually selected. For most surveys, the sampling frame consists of an available listing of all units in the target population. As Figure 9.3 indicates, the selection of the survey mode and the sampling frame are interdependent. Face-to-face interviews require a listing of residences, mail surveys need mailing addresses, telephone surveys need telephone numbers, and online surveys need e-mail addresses. If a sampling frame fails to provide adequate coverage of the target population, a researcher may switch modes or resort to a mixed-mode strategy.

Recruit Sample and Collect Data

Collecting the data in a survey is itself a multistep process. In an interview survey, if mailing addresses are known, the process may begin by sending respondents a cover letter in advance of being contacted. Then, the interviewer must contact a household member, select an eligible person to interview, obtain their agreement to participate, and conduct the interview. And if no one answers a doorbell or dialed telephone number, the interviewer must make additional attempts to reach someone at that address or number.

A concerted effort is made in all surveys to gain the cooperation of nonrespondents. In FTF interview surveys, interviewers may leave notes or ask neighbors when people are usually at home. In mail surveys, respondents are sent follow-up mailings. For example, respondents in the CAS—the alcohol mail survey discussed earlier—received four separate mailings, approximately 10 days apart: the initial mailing of the questionnaire, a postcard thanking those who had completed the questionnaire and urging those who had not to do so, a mailing with another copy of the questionnaire again appealing for its return, and a second reminder postcard (Wechsler et al., 1994).

For telephone and FTF surveys, the major problem is dealing with refusals to participate. In many surveys, more experienced interviewers or supervisors are used to trying to gain the respondent's cooperation on the second try. In response to a clear refusal, however, one follow-up call or visit should be the limit.

The process of recruiting respondents is simpler in computer-assisted self-interviews, such as online surveys, which is one of the reasons for their appeal. If the survey is of individuals, the researcher only needs to send out separate e-mails to potential respondents once a sampling frame of e-mails has been created; the researcher does not need to select individuals within households or families. Further, it is easy to follow up with e-mail reminders.

Code and Edit Data

Like the analysis of experiments, virtually all surveys involve quantitative analysis, with the results presented in numerical form. But survey data require much more extensive preparation (or processing) for data analysis. Survey respondents' answers must be coded (transformed into numbers), entered into a datafile, and checked and corrected for errors. Some correcting for errors, called editing, occurs during survey data collection. We briefly describe coding and editing here, although we have more to say about them in Chapters 14 and 15, where we cover quantitative and qualitative analysis.

coding the sorting of data into numbered or textual categories

Coding answers for closed-ended questions is straightforward. You simply assign unique numbers to each response category. For example, in the NCVS, the respondent's sex at birth was coded as 1 for male and 2 for female. The particular codes were arbitrary and were specified directly on the **interview schedule**. The coding of textual responses to open-ended questions, on the other hand, is much more complicated. Because the number of unique responses may number in the hundreds, the researcher must develop a coding scheme that does not require a separate code for each response but that adequately reflects the full range of responses. This is typically done with digital software, such as Atlas.ti.

interview schedule a survey form used by interviewers that consists of instructions, the questions to be asked, and, if they are used, response options

Editing a survey involves checking for errors and inconsistencies in responses. Examples of errors would be multiple responses to a single item or a response with a code outside the range of numbers allowed (e.g., a code of "3" for respondent's sex). Inconsistencies occur when responses to certain questions are not related in plausible ways to particular other items. For example, it would be unreasonable, and therefore an indication of an error, to find a respondent who is married and age five or a medical doctor with three years of formal schooling.

Researchers edit and, when possible, correct responses to mail surveys manually by going over completed questionnaires; however, most editing is programmed into digital interviewing and online surveys. For example, the CATI program used in some surveys will flag responses that are outside the acceptable limits and prompt interviewers with follow-up questions to address apparent inconsistencies. Thus, in many surveys, editing (as well as coding and data entry) occurs during the process of data collection.

> **editing** checking data and correcting for errors in completed interviews or questionnaires

SUMMARY

The process of planning and conducting a survey involves choosing a mode of data collection, constructing and pretesting the questionnaire, choosing a sampling frame, designing and selecting the sample, recruiting the sample and collecting data, and coding and editing data, which are then analyzed. Each of these steps involves additional steps or considerations. Choosing a mode of data collection depends on the researcher's goals and the resources available. Constructing and pretesting the questionnaire depends on the mode of data collection, and researchers should strive to write unambiguous and neutral questions, present them in a logical order, and get feedback on question drafts. Likewise, choosing a sampling frame, selecting and recruiting a sample, and collecting data depend on the mode of data collection. At the minimum, this involves ensuring that the sampling frame is as close to the target population as is possible; selecting respondents randomly; clearly explaining the purposes of the survey to potential respondents and their rights; and attempting to gain their cooperation. Once the data are collected, they need to be coded and edited before being analyzed. See Box 9.5 to assess your understanding of the information within this section.

> **BOX 9.5**
>
> **CHECKING YOUR UNDERSTANDING**
>
> ## Question and Survey Framing
>
> 1. Which of the following questions would serve best as the opening question for a questionnaire study of campus alcohol use?
>   a. Do you presently drink beer, liquor, or wine?
>   b. Would your father approve of your present drinking habits?
>   c. Do you ever drink alone?
>   d. What is your major?
>
> 2. Which of the following questions should be placed toward the end of a questionnaire or interview in a survey study of campus alcohol use?
>   a. Do you presently drink beer, liquor, or wine?
>   b. Would your father approve of your present drinking habits?
>   c. Do you ever drink alone?
>   d. What is your major?
>
> 3. To gain the cooperation of nonrespondents, survey researchers
>   a. use follow-ups in telephone surveys, but not in FTF or mail surveys.
>   b. may make numerous follow-up attempts to reach them.
>   c. never attempt to convert clear refusals to participate.
>   d. have found that more than one follow-up is not cost effective.
>
> **Answers: 1. a, 2. d, 3. b**

9.4 STRENGTHS AND WEAKNESSES OF SURVEYS

Surveys are the "method of choice for much data collection in the [social sciences]" (Wright & Marsden, 2010, p. 10), especially in criminology and criminal justice. Yet, the use of surveys outside the scientific community is even more extensive. Media opinion polls, marketing research, and government surveys shape major decisions by politicians, businesspeople, and government officials. Reported survey results inform much of our knowledge about society. For example, we know from surveys that nationally registered Democrats outnumber Republicans (Blake, 2020; Pew Research Center, 2020); the majority (58%) of Americans support stricter gun laws, and there is bipartisan support for preventing people with mental illnesses from purchasing guns (Schaeffer, 2023). Because surveys carry so much weight in our knowledge and decision-making, we all need to know something about their strengths and weaknesses. What can surveys tell us better than other methods of criminal justice research? And what are their limitations?

Generalization to Populations

Whereas experiments are used for explanatory, hypothesis-testing research, surveys are used extensively for both descriptive and explanatory purposes. Among all approaches to criminal justice research, surveys offer the most effective means of social description. By using probability sampling, survey researchers can be certain, within known limits of sampling error, of how accurately the responses to a sample survey can be generalized to the larger target population. However, this does not apply to surveys collected through nonrandom selection.

Versatility

The effectiveness of surveys is also reflected in their versatility. The topics covered and the questions that may be included in surveys are wide-ranging. Topics of studies cited in this chapter range from crime victimization to alcohol consumption and the consequences thereof to the experience of having a family member incarcerated. Many surveys, such as the GSS, cover numerous topics in the same survey.

Efficiency

Their versatility makes surveys, in some ways, a very efficient data-gathering approach. While an experiment usually will address only one research hypothesis, numerous research questions can be covered by a single large-scale survey. Furthermore, the wealth of data typically contained in a survey may yield unanticipated findings or lead to new hypotheses. Adding to their cost effectiveness, data from many large-scale surveys such as the GSS are made available to the public. Such data are usually of high quality, and the cost of obtaining the data for analysis is a small fraction of the cost of collecting the data. It is common practice, called **secondary analysis**, for criminal justice researchers to analyze publicly accessible survey data.

secondary analysis analysis of survey or other data originally collected by another researcher, ordinarily for a different purpose

Establishing Causal Relationships

A major disadvantage of surveys relates to their use in explanatory research. Beyond association between variables, the criteria for inferring cause-and-effect relationships cannot be established as easily in surveys as in experiments. For example, the criterion of directionality—that a cause must influence its effect—is predetermined in experiments by first manipulating the independent (or causal) variable and then observing variation in the dependent (or effect) variable. But in most surveys (i.e., cross-sectional designs) this is often a matter of interpretation since variables are measured at a single point in time. Although a longitudinal design may address this limitation, surveys are also problematic in meeting the criterion of eliminating plausible rival explanations. Whether using cross-sectional or longitudinal designs, surveys must first anticipate and measure relevant extraneous variables in the interviews or questionnaires and then exercise statistical control over these variables in the data analysis. Thus, the causal inferences from survey research generally are made with less confidence than inferences from experimental research.

Measurement Issues

Another inherent weakness of surveys is their reliance almost exclusively on self-reports of behavior rather than observations of behavior. As a consequence, validity and reliability may be undermined by respondents' lack of truthfulness, misunderstanding of questions, inability to recall past events accurately, and instability of opinions and attitudes. Like experiments, surveys also are susceptible to reactive measurement effects produced by participants' awareness of being studied. A good example of this, noted in Chapter 6, is the tendency of respondents to give socially desirable answers to sensitive questions; this is particularly likely to occur in interview surveys. Because of this and other limitations of surveys, researchers sometimes turn to the analysis of existing data (see Chapter 11), including "big" data (see Couper, 2017). Finally, a brief encounter for the purpose of administering a survey does not provide a very good understanding of the impact of the context on behavior. For that understanding, criminal justice researchers turn to field research, which we discuss in Chapter 10.

SUMMARY

The major strengths of surveys lie in their ability to provide reasonably accurate estimations of population characteristics, their versatility in speaking to a wide range of topics, and their efficiency. However, surveys are limited in their ability to establish causal relationships and in their reliance on self-reports of human behavior and in the quality of measurement. Finally, it is important to note several problems that have surfaced in the past quarter-century, which are making it increasingly difficult and costly to conduct surveys. These include access impediments such as "walled subdivisions, locked apartment buildings, telephone answering machines, [and] telephone caller ID," declining response rates, increasing costs due to "increased effort to contact and interview the public," and telephone survey coverage issues created by the increase in mobile phones (Groves, 2011, p. 866). These and other challenges have led researchers increasingly to conduct surveys online, with online panels (Deane et al., 2019), and in some cases abandon them in favor of alternative approaches to social research (Couper, 2017). Refer to Box 9.6 to assess your understanding of this section.

> **BOX 9.6**
>
> **CHECKING YOUR UNDERSTANDING**
>
> ## Survey Review
>
> 1. Of the following, which is a weakness of survey research?
>   a. Reliance of self-reports
>   b. Sample size
>   c. Cost effectiveness
>   d. Range of possible topics
>
> 2. Compared with experiments, surveys are generally
>   a. less economical
>   b. lower in generalizability
>   c. less effective in testing causal relationships
>   d. less susceptible to reactive measurement effects
>
> Answers: 1. a, 2. c

KEY TERMS

closed-ended question, p. 241
coding, p. 262
computer-assisted personal interviewing (CAPI), p. 246
computer-assisted self-administered interviewing (CASI), p. 249
computer-assisted telephone interviewing (CATI), p. 249
cross-sectional design, p. 243
descriptive survey, p. 242
double-barreled question, p. 257
editing, p. 263
explanatory survey, p. 242
face-to-face (FTF) interview, p. 245
field pretesting, p. 261
interview schedule, p. 262
leading question, p. 258
longitudinal design, p. 244
mixed-mode survey, p. 251
open-ended question, p. 241
panel study, p. 244
paper-and-pencil questionnaire survey, p. 248
response rate, p. 246
secondary analysis, p. 265
structured interview, p. 240
telephone interview, p. 247
trend study, p. 244

KEY POINTS

- The primary features of surveys are relatively large probability samples, structured questioning, and quantitative analysis.
- Structured interviews address specific objectives with mostly closed-ended questions.

- Quantitative analysis of surveys may be descriptive and/or explanatory.
- Survey designs may ask questions at one point in time (cross-sectional) or may repeat the same questions at multiple points in time (longitudinal).
- Survey data-collection modes include face-to-face interviews, telephone interviews, paper-and-pencil questionnaires, computer-assisted self-interviews, as well as combinations of these modes (i.e., "mixed mode" surveys).
- Survey data-collection modes vary in their costs, the time they take to complete, their response rates, their population coverage, and their quality of measurement.
- The process of planning and conducting a survey involves key decisions about how to measure variables and how to select a sample.
- Measuring variables entails choosing a mode of data collection and constructing and pretesting a questionnaire.
- Selecting a sample involves choosing an appropriate sampling frame, drawing a probability sample, and, in interview surveys, randomly selecting respondents within households.
- Following recruitment of respondents and administration of the questionnaire, survey responses are coded, edited, and analyzed.
- The strengths of surveys are their versatility, efficiency, and ability to produce accurate generalizations about targeted populations, but surveys offer relatively weak inferences about causality, are limited to self-reports, and are susceptible to reactive measurement effects.

REVIEW QUESTIONS

1. What are the three general features of survey research?
2. What is the difference between (a) cross-sectional and longitudinal survey designs and (b) trend and panel surveys?
3. Compare FTF interviews, telephone interviews, and mail questionnaires with respect to (a) time and cost, (b) complexity and sensitivity of questions asked, and (c) quality of sample (coverage and response rate).
4. Give two examples of how researchers may use more than one survey mode in the same study.
5. Explain how the choice of a survey mode affects the choice of a sampling frame.
6. What is the purpose of field pretesting a survey instrument?
7. What are the principal strengths and weaknesses of surveys?

EXERCISES

1. Exercise 2 in Chapter 5 introduced you to a website for analyzing data from the General Social Survey (GSS). Return to this website to answer the following questions.

a. Examine the distribution of responses to an item in the 2018 GSS. Using the shaded column on the left, click on "PERSONAL AND FAMILY INFORMATION," click on a variable, and then click on a GSS questionnaire item. Now click "Copy to: Row" to examine the distribution of responses to this item; move to the right side of the page and type "Year (2018)" opposite "Selection Filter(s)"; opposite "Weight:" choose "No weight"; click on "Output Options" and check Percentaging "Column" (if it is not already checked) and "Confidence intervals" just below that; and then click "Run the Table." Report the percentage of respondents in the first variable category and the confidence interval for this percentage.

b. Examine the *relationship* between two questionnaire items in the GSS. Begin again on the left side of the web page. Select the same GSS item as you did in Question (a), but this time "Copy to: Column" rather than "Row." Now select a question from the category "CONTROVERSIAL SOCIAL ISSUES." Copy to Row, delete "Year (2018)" from the "Selection Filter(s)" box you put in as part (a) of the exercise, check Percentaging "Column" if it is not already checked, and then click "Run the Table." Carefully describe the relationship between the two items (or variables) by comparing percentages across each row of the table.

c. Perform a trend analysis of a "controversial social issue." Select the same GSS item that you inserted as the "Row" variable in Question (b) and select "Copy to: Row." Now type "year" as your "Column" variable. Check Percentaging "Column" and click "Run the Table." Reading across the table, report how the percentage has changed over time. If the controversial social issue in which you are interested has only been asked in one year, repeat the process with another selection.

2. Box 9.3 identifies several common wording problems in constructing survey questions. Using the box as a guide, identify the wording problem(s) in each of the following questions and then rewrite the questions to make them more satisfactory.

a. How often do you drink alcohol?
( ) Often
( ) Occasionally
( ) Seldom
( ) Never

b. Do you agree or disagree that incarcerated individuals who fail to complete any educational program during their incarceration should not be released?
( ) Strongly agree
( ) Agree
( ) Neither agree nor disagree

( ) Disagree
( ) Strongly disagree

    c. Have you ever smoked cigarettes and cannabis?
    d. Are you in favor of supporting the liberal agenda of defunding the police?
    e. Since turning 18, how many times have you been arrested?
       ( ) 1–2 times
       ( ) 3–4 times
       ( ) 5–6 times
       ( ) More than 7 times

3. Suppose you are constructing a questionnaire for the purpose of conducting a survey of attitudes toward and interactions with the police. What would be the best placement (beginning, middle, end) of the following questions?

    a. How old are you?
    b. How often do you see police officers in your neighborhood?
    c. Have you ever been arrested?

4. Imagine that you want to conduct a campus survey on extracurricular participation. Specifically, you are interested in who participates in extracurricular activities, what kind of extracurricular activities they participate in, how often they participate, and why they choose to participate. To reduce costs, assume you choose to do either a mail questionnaire survey or an online survey and you need to construct a survey instrument.

    a. Outline the question topics to be covered.
    b. Write at least one question or find an existing question for each topic.
    c. Give an example of a good opening question.
    d. Identify possible sensitive questions. Where will you place them in the questionnaire?

5. Once you have developed questions for your campus survey (Exercise 4), field pretest your questions on a small sample of potential respondents.

10

Field Research and In-Depth Interviews

Systematic People-Watching and Listening

LEARNING OBJECTIVES

By the end of this chapter, you should be able to

10.1 Describe the six general features of qualitative research.

10.2 Explain variations in qualitative research with respect to how observations and interviews are conducted.

10.3 Describe the steps in the process of planning and conducting field research and apply them to a research topic.

10.4 Describe the steps in the process of planning and conducting in-depth interviews and apply them to a research topic.

10.5 Evaluate qualitative research, identifying its strengths and weaknesses.

CHAPTER OUTLINE

Introduction: Prisonization and the Problems of Reentry 273

10.1 General Features of Qualitative Research 274
Observation 274
Interviews 275
Supplementary Archival and Other Data 277
Nonprobability Sampling 277
Qualitative Data Analysis 278
Reflexivity 278
Summary 280

10.2 Variations in Qualitative Research Methods 280
Degrees of Participation and Observation 280
Overt vs. Covert Observation 282
Between Overt and Covert Observation 284
Interview Structure 285
Individual vs. Group Interviews 286
Impact of Technological Developments on Observations and Interviews 287
Summary 289

10.3 The Process of Conducting Field Research 290
Select Setting/Group 291
Gain Access 291
Establish Roles and Relationships 294
Decide What to Observe/Whom to Interview 295
Gather and Analyze Data 296
Leave the Field 297
Write the Report 298
Summary 298

10.4 The Process of Conducting In-Depth Interviews 300
Select and Recruit Interviewees 300
Develop an Interview Guide 301
Gather Data 303
Analyze Data 304
Summary 305

10.5 Strengths and Limitations of Qualitative Research 306
Naturalistic Approach 306
Subjective and Contextual Understanding 307
Flexible Research Design 307
Generalizability 308
Reliability and Validity 308
Efficiency 309
Summary 309

Think back to the first day of your first-ever college course. You probably entered the classroom with some trepidation, not knowing what to expect. You may have checked to make sure you were in the right location. As you entered the classroom, you probably scoped it out: Was it a big lecture hall, a smaller classroom, or a more intimate seminar room? Who was in the class? Did you know anyone? Maybe you asked a friend or a stranger: "Is this Introduction to Criminal Justice?" "What have you heard about this professor?" You also might have wondered what others were thinking and feeling: Are the other students as nervous as I am? Is the professor nervous too? In watching and questioning others, you better understood what was going on.

This example captures the essence of qualitative research as discussed in this chapter: to make sense of our surroundings by keenly observing others, interacting with them, posing questions, and analyzing people's experiences, including our own. This is not to say that everyone is a researcher or that common sense is all there is to it. The ultimate goal of qualitative research is not personal but scientific—to build a general, abstract understanding of social phenomena. To gain this understanding, qualitative researchers have developed special skills and techniques for observing and asking questions as well as describing and analyzing everyday life and culture.

In Chapter 5 we identified methodological approaches designed to address qualitative research questions, which focus on social context, cultural meanings, and processes. In this chapter, we discuss two of these approaches: field research and in-depth interviews. (The qualitative analysis of existing data is discussed in Chapter 11.)

While the first approach, field research, can be conducted on a variety of topics and in many settings, it has one distinguishing characteristic: It is carried out "in the field"—in a social setting familiar to the people being observed—with the goal of not disturbing the naturalness of the setting. When it focuses on the culture of a group of people, whether near or afar, field research is often referred to as **ethnography**, a term derived from cultural anthropology. The second approach, in-depth interviewing, may be used to complement observations in field research or as a stand-alone method of data collection. In contrast to survey interviews, in-depth interviews provide a deeper, more comprehensive understanding of interviewees' experiences and interpretations, as reported in their own words.

We begin the chapter by describing two contemporary research examples: a field research study and an in-depth interview study. Based on these examples, we discuss the general features of qualitative research, followed by a discussion of its variations. We then outline the separate processes of conducting field research and in-depth interviews. We conclude by discussing the strengths and weaknesses of qualitative research.

> **ethnography**
> an alternate word, derived from cultural anthropology, to describe field research, especially when it focuses on the culture of a group of people

INTRODUCTION: PRISONIZATION AND THE PROBLEMS OF REENTRY

Based upon his ethnographic research, Donald Clemmer (1940) introduced the term *prisonization* in his book titled, *The Prison Community*. Prisonization refers to the changes an individual undergoes during their time in prison. Clemmer argued that there are universal elements of prisonization that take place for all inmates, including new habit development, eating and sleeping patterns, and speaking in the "local language." A large body of research has explored the factors that affect individuals' development and extent of prisonization, such as their sentence length and the type of institution in which they are incarcerated. Less research has focused on the influence of prisonization *after* an inmate has been released into society. Recognizing this gap in the literature, Liam Martin, a lecturer in criminology at the Victoria University of Wellington in New Zealand, set out to explore this understudied area. Martin utilized Pierre Bourdieu's (1990) concept of habitus as a framework for his study, the idea that individuals are socialized to meet the expectations of an environment and over time behaviors or habits that are socially acceptable become natural and unconscious. According to Martin (2018), "these imprints of experience remain with people and guide their practice as they enter new institutional arenas" (p. 674). However, as individuals are reentering society, their communities will likely have significantly different expectations of them than prison, which may lead the habitus to produce behaviors or habits that seem bizarre and out of place in the "real world." Examples of this can include the use of tattoos. In prison, tattoos provide an artistic outlet and help prisoners connect with a group or their own identity. Post release, however, the tattoos can brand individuals as former convicts who may be perceived as dangerous. Wanting to gain an insider's perspective on the social process of transitioning out of prison and the impacts of prisonization post-release, Martin began a two-year field research study on prisoner reentry.

To address his research questions, Martin lived in a halfway house for three months each year (June–August) from 2012 to 2014 in an urban area in central Massachusetts. During this time he engaged in observation and interviews of former prisoners. Martin was provided access by the director of the halfway house and his identity as a researcher was known by the men living in the home (approximately 15 at a time). However, Martin assimilated to their culture in order to gain trust, sharing a room with a resident, being assigned a chore and dish night, and smoking cigarettes with the residents.

While Martin's observations mainly took place in the halfway house, for the most part, he chose to interview participants who did not live in the home and were not part of a reentry program in order to understand reentry more generally. He gained access to these individuals via snowball sampling (discussed in depth in Chapter 7). In addition,

Martin recruited a resident from the home to assist as a co-researcher with interviews; this likely increased trust between the researcher and the interviewees, as they saw one of their own involved in the research. Martin did feel that the men were open and transparent with him, providing lengthy responses to questions that may have been perceived as obvious, perceiving him as an "empathetic outsider." The life history interviews were quite in-depth and lasted approximately three hours each. Martin's interviews tended to be less structured and more flexible, while his co-researcher Joe tended to stick to the script and conducted more structured interviews. However, all interviews were conducted in an informal setting, such as in the park, over food, and without the script present to create a relaxed atmosphere.

Martin found the men's reflections could be categorized into three major themes: the physical habits formed and carried through to post-release (Martin called these "corporeal after-effects"), the culture shock of the social transition, and adaptation to life outside of prison.

10.1 GENERAL FEATURES OF QUALITATIVE RESEARCH

Qualitative research lends itself best to understanding the social context of people's lives, people's interpretations of their experiences, and social processes. Martin's questions addressed this kind of understanding. Martin's study contained several of the six features common to qualitative research:

1. observation,
2. interviews,
3. supplementary archival and other data,
4. nonprobability sampling,
5. qualitative data analysis, and
6. reflexivity.

Observation

Observation in qualitative research generally differs from observation in other forms of social research in two ways. First, it is direct, usually with the naked eye, rather than the sort of indirect observation that characterizes respondents' reports in questionnaires or interviews. Second, in field research especially, it takes place in a natural setting, not a laboratory or other contrived situation.

Field researchers, for whom observation is the primary method of data collection, record their observations in notes. Observations are often accompanied by the researcher's direct experience (Lofland et al., 2006). Unlike experiments and surveys, this experience is an integral part of field research and other qualitative research designs.

Observation and direct experience may also enrich the interpretation of data drawn mainly from interviews. Martin's study provides an example of how his observations at the halfway house helped corroborate information from his interviews. Martin found, "the most common enduring prison trait described by participants was a fixation on cleanliness" (p. 681). One interviewee, named Ricky for the interviews, elaborated on this lasting effect of prison, identifying these adaptations to prison as ways to both maximize space (could not have clutter in a 6x8 foot cell with two people) and occupy time to avoid boredom ("What else is there to do but clean and fix your books?" (p. 682)). Martin also observed this while living in the halfway house; he noticed that the house was always clean and clutter free, yet cleanliness was often a point of contention during the weekly house meetings. The men were hyper aware of cleanliness and tidiness due to both an adaption to prison as well as "the sanctions and rewards of the particular situation: a halfway house emphasizing individual responsibility and clean living" (p. 682).

Interviews

A second general characteristic of qualitative research is interviewing. As Johnny Saldaña (2011) explains, "observation is primarily the researcher's take on social action, whereas the interview is the participant's take" (p. 46). Most interviewing in field research occurs informally, in ordinary conversations and as a natural extension of observation. Field interviewing may begin with questions that orient the researcher to the setting or group, such as:

- "Where can I find this?"
- "What is that?"
- "Who is she?"
- "What does she do?"

Eventually, questions are aimed at expanding information about specific actions and events as well as probing their deeper meanings. Indeed, field researchers devote much of their time to asking questions such as:

- "What do you think she meant by that?"
- "What are they supposed to do?"
- "Why did she do that?"
- "Why is that done?" (Lofland & Lofland, 1995, p. 70).

After researchers have been in the field for a while and have begun to develop an understanding of the setting, they may conduct formal interviews to secure more detailed information on individuals and to round out and check information already obtained. Unlike spontaneous informal questioning, researchers schedule and prepare questions in advance of formal interviews. This was the primary method of data collection in Martin's study. While Martin prepared and scheduled formal interviews, he tried his best to keep the atmosphere casual for his unique population. Characteristically, Martin's interviews lasted around three hours. Interviews of such length are typically audio recorded and transcribed; however, Martin did not provide this detail in his publication.

Formal qualitative interviews, particularly when used as a stand-alone method, are synonymous with in-depth interviews, sometimes called "intensive" interviews (Lofland et al., 2006). According to Rubin and Rubin (2012), **in-depth interviews** share three characteristics:

1. they are intended to yield rich and detailed information on participants' experiences and interpretations;
2. they primarily make use of open-ended questions, which require interviewees to answer in their own words (see Chapter 10); and
3. they are generally flexible (p. 29).

in-depth interview a type of formal interview intended to yield deep responses through open-ended questions and a flexible format

In order to yield "deep" responses characteristic of in-depth interviews, it is centrally important that the researcher establish rapport and trust with the interviewee (Johnson & Rowlands, 2012, p.101). The interviewer and interviewee are said to be "conversational partners" (Rubin & Rubin, 2012), responsible for the "co-generation of data" (Schwartz-Shea & Yanow, 2012). The interpersonal nature of in-depth interviews also makes face-to-face interviewing by far the primary mode of data collection.

In final reports of in-depth interview research, the data take the form of interviewees' verbatim statements, vividly describing their thoughts, feelings, or experiences. Consider, for example, Louie Bell's response to Martin's question about the disorienting nature of culture shock upon reentry:

> You ever have those nightmares where you're trying to scream and trying to wake up but you can't? I didn't know which way to go. I didn't know what to say to anybody. All I wanted to do was ball up, just ball up in a corner and hide. I didn't know what to do. . . . People out here, people are disrespectful. It's not like that in prison. You know not to cross certain lines. Out here people didn't have to live by those codes. So it was culture shock. The way I was living in there, I couldn't live out here like that, because the rules are different out here. I didn't know what the rules were, or how to go about them. All I wanted to do was just hide. (Martin, 2018, p. 684)

Just as interviews may serve as a cross-check on observations and vice versa, so too may interviews with different individuals serve as a cross-check of one another. An important feature of Martin's research design, for instance, was his decision to interview different groups of ex-inmates, those living in the halfway house and those not living in one, who provided different perspectives. One man, Matt, who transitioned from prison directly to his parents' house, for example, reported being filled with anxiety and fear, "it almost like the fear of the unknown again. Now all it did was flip [from the earlier fear entering prison]. Because there I had no responsibilities, I didn't have to pay bills, I didn't have to worry about where I was going to live, I was fed three times a day. I didn't have to deal with society. That's what they call institutionalized" (p. 684). Matt was at his parents' house for only one week when he decided to go to a halfway house so he could be with people who understood him. In this case, Matt's culture shock may have been more pronounced than someone who immediately transitioned to a halfway house with familiar structure and people who understand.

Supplementary Archival and Other Data

Qualitative researchers may also make use of a variety of supplementary data, such as archival records and documents. While some of these data—for example, time diaries and logs—may be generated by participants, researchers also tend to use publicly accessible information, such as governmental records (Bailey, 1996; Lofland et al., 2006; Saldaña, 2011). The usefulness and choice of supplementary data depend on the understanding that the researcher wants to achieve and the setting, group, or participants being studied. Documents and archival records may further establish the context of a study and serve as a cross-check of other data.

There are a variety of other supplementary data that researchers may use. When studying a group or organization, for example, researchers may examine organizational charts, brochures, electronic communications, and official records. Photos, videos, and visual materials can also be used to facilitate a researcher's understanding (Lofland et al., 2006).

Nonprobability Sampling

Qualitative research is also characterized by nonprobability sampling involving the nonrandom selection of settings or groups of people. Furthermore, the time required to carry out observations and interviews tends to restrict the possible sample size to a small number of cases. Martin (2018) used a combination of both convenience sampling and snowball sampling to recruit participants; both sampling methods are considered nonprobability. Martin recruited several participants using the convenience method by interviewing those who lived in the halfway house with him. In addition, he recruited a majority of the participants using the snowball sampling method, where interviewees who trusted him helped him recruit other former prisoners to participate in the study.

Beyond the selection of a setting or group of people, qualitative researchers must decide what to observe. In field research, the delicate operation of entering the field tends to necessitate the nonrandom selection of observation sites. Martin conducted his observations at one halfway house in central Massachusetts, where he observed people, interactions, and events. He chose this halfway house for observation given its relevance to the topic of observing life post-prison, but he was also given the necessary access by the director, who saw the research as an opportunity to promote reintegration. It would likely have been challenging for Martin to observe this specific population any other way or for Martin to move between multiple halfway houses given the difficulties of getting access to this special population.

Qualitative Data Analysis

In qualitative research, data generally consist of written text from field notes and interview transcriptions, which require qualitative methods of analysis. Unlike researchers conducting experiments or surveys, qualitative researchers do not necessarily wait until all of the data have been collected to begin analysis. Rather, the hallmark of qualitative data analysis is an ongoing, iterative process in which data are compared across cases, time, and other relevant dimensions.

Martin (2018) describes his process of analyzing the qualitative data he received via interviews. He engaged in multiple rounds of "coding" the data for themes. In the first round, Martin used codes that were similar to the words the men used to describe their experience; he chose not to come up with codes prior to the first round of coding in order to avoid trying to make the data fit into his own pre-identified groupings. After this process, Martin went back through the data and used theoretically derived codes, such as the term "prisonized habitus" to group similar experiences together. Martin describes the process of developing theoretical concepts as codes here:

> *For example, my first round of coding revealed connected themes in the narratives of imprisonment: the code becoming comfortable labeled instances of imprisonment becoming easier over time as people got used to the experience, and when many participants used the term institutionalization to describe adjusting to imprisonment so much that living outside became difficult—that term itself became a code. Finally, the code little things was used to describe habits and rituals that former prisoners learned in prison and reproduced outside. The goal in choosing theoretical concepts was capturing relationships between these specific codes, and I found that the three codes—becoming comfortable, institutionalization, and little things—tended to cluster together. This relationship became the basis for the theoretical code prisonized habitus.* (p. 678)

We will have more to say about the process of analyzing qualitative data later in this chapter, and we devote the entirety of Chapter 15 to qualitative analysis.

Reflexivity

As discussed in Chapter 2, qualitative research relies on a different way of knowing than quantitative research. The qualitative researcher is an "instrument" of the research itself (Saldaña, 2011, p. 22). The researcher's understandings are greatly shaped by their relationships with the people being studied, which themselves are a product of the researcher's experiences and personal characteristics, such as race, class, gender, and sexuality. **Reflexivity** refers to the researcher's reflections on how these factors influence their knowledge of what is being studied. Reflexivity occurs throughout the research process, and in final reports of the study, researchers' reflections are intended to promote transparency and help the reader evaluate findings (Schwartz-Shea & Yanow, 2012).

reflexivity
a common practice in qualitative research, whereby a researcher reflects on how their characteristics and presence shape the research process

Qualitative researchers often reflect on their status as an *insider* or *outsider* in the setting or group being studied and how this shapes what they know. An insider is someone who, by virtue of their personal characteristics or experiences, is similar to the people being studied; an outsider is dissimilar (Collins, 1986; Merton, 1972). Martin identified himself as an outsider, someone who is not part of the population. However, over the course of interviews he grew empathetic to their frustrations. Martin also recruited Joe Badillo, a resident at the house, as an interviewer and researcher. Utilizing an insider as a researcher helped provide legitimacy to the research and a different perspective than Martin.

These reflections are integrally important for the kind of understanding qualitative researchers hope to achieve. To practice this yourself, see Box 10.1.

BOX 10.1

CHECKING YOUR UNDERSTANDING

Reflexivity in Criminological Research

In the edited book, *Reflexivity in Criminological Research*, editors Lumsden and Winter (2014) begin by encouraging criminologists engaging in research on crime to, "reflect on the relationship between 'deviance' not only as a label, but also as it relates to wider issues of social power" (p. 4). And they also caution researchers who may be conducting research on behalf of the *powerful* (i.e., prisons, courts, police, etc.) to be mindful not to become complicit in the mechanism of power that would continue to apply labels further stigmatizing and marginalizing the *powerless* (i.e., those engaging in deviance). Reflexive criminological researchers must consider the way that their own background may impact the way they observe and perceive the subjects being studied. Consider the following question as it relates to reflexivity:

1. How do you believe your cultural background would shape your response to those engaged in criminal activity that you might study as a qualitative researcher?

2. Do you believe the type of criminal activity would matter to your response?

SUMMARY

Qualitative research is directed toward answering research questions focused on understanding social context, cultural meanings, and processes. It is characterized by six general features:

1. observation (and, often, direct experience) in natural settings;
2. interviews, which may be informal or formal and in-depth;
3. use of supplementary archival and other data;
4. small nonprobability samples of cases, settings, and people;
5. the iterative and often inductive analysis of qualitative data; and
6. reflexivity, which refers to researchers reflecting on how their characteristics and other factors shape the research.

10.2 VARIATIONS IN QUALITATIVE RESEARCH METHODS

Our description of the general features of qualitative research glosses over variations in how these methods are applied. The most significant variations involve the primary methods of data collection: observation and interviews. Observation differs in the extent to which the researcher (1) participates in the social setting and (2) reveals their identity as a researcher. In addition to the level of formality, qualitative interviews vary in (1) structure and (2) whether research participants are interviewed individually or as a group. Moreover, technological developments crosscutting observation and interviews parallel the move to cyberspace in experiments and surveys. Let us examine Martin's study, as well as other research examples, to understand these important variations.

Degrees of Participation and Observation

Traditionally, in field research, a distinction is made between **participant** and **nonparticipant observation**. The participant observer is actively and intentionally involved in the phenomena being observed; the nonparticipant is a passive and intentionally unobtrusive observer. It is more accurate, however, to think of the two types of observation as poles of a continuum.

PARTICIPANT OBSERVATION

A primary goal of field research is to gain an insider's view of reality. Often the best way to do this, as the old adage says, is to walk a mile in another person's shoes—in other words, to participate actively, for an extended period of time, in the daily lives of the

---

participant observation
a form of observation in which the field researcher participates to some degree in the activity or group being studied

nonparticipant observation
a form of observation in which the field researcher does not participate in the activity or group being studied

people and situations under study. This may require that the observer live or work in an area; it clearly assumes that the observer will become an accepted member of the group or community, able to speak informally with the people—to "joke with them, empathize with them, and share their concerns and experiences" (Bogdan & Taylor, 1975, p. 5). Martin certainly participated at least to this degree: throughout the several months he studied the ex-prisoners, he was living with several of the men. He was as much a resident as the men, sharing a room with a resident and being assigned a chore and dish night.

Becoming a participant observer carries some risks. It can be an emotionally stressful experience for the researcher. In the early days in the field, before learning the ropes, researchers are likely to experience awkward and embarrassing encounters. Balancing the requirements of both participating and observing can be challenging. To gain an insider's view, you need to gain the acceptance of those you are studying; to be accepted, you need to become actively involved in others' activities. However, it often is difficult to know where to draw the line. In fact, it is not unusual for fieldworkers to witness and to be pressured to participate in physically dangerous or morally and legally questionable activities. In a field study of a Chicago gang, Sudhir Venkatesh (2008) observed violence and other illegal activities such as the distribution of crack cocaine. He also participated in gang violence directed toward a man, who allegedly had beaten a woman, by kicking him (Venkatesh, 2008, pp. 65–77). Although this example is extreme, it illustrates the difficulties of observing and participating, particularly when studying a deviant group.

NONPARTICIPANT OBSERVATION

The nonparticipant observer is, in effect, an eavesdropper, someone who attempts to observe people without interacting with them and, typically, without their knowing that they are being observed. A good example of nonparticipant observation is Townsley and Grimshaw's (2013) study of alcohol-related violence, specifically looking at how crowding in entertainment precincts can increase instances of aggression. Townsley and Grimshaw's study was based on over 96 hours of observations. They recruited and trained 14 undergraduate students to be observers and conducted the observations in Fortitude Valley in Brisbane (Australia). This area was purposefully chosen because of its notoriety as an entertainment hub with up to 50,000 individuals in the area on a Saturday night yet only a residential community of approximately 5,000. In coordination with the Brisbane City Council, Queensland Police Service, and the Valley Liquor Accord, the researchers identified six "block faces" known to be "hot spots" for violence where large crowds gathered and included public space outside of licensed (for alcohol) businesses or late-night transportation lines. The sites were each visited four times on Friday and Saturday nights for two hours each, across four weeks. All observations took place in pairs for safety and reliability of the observations. Six pairs went out for observation each night. Observers dressed and acted as if they were part of the crowd in order to observe unobtrusively and inconspicuously. They also recorded their observations of crowding, low-level aggression, high-level aggression, the physical and social environment, the street population, and the characteristics of queues (people waiting in line).

As a separate, inclusive method, nonparticipant observation is comparatively used less often in research to address qualitative research questions. Rather, it is often combined with some degree of participation.

BETWEEN PARTICIPATION AND OBSERVATION

Despite the tidiness of the descriptions of participant and nonparticipant observation, there is a rather fine line—or a fuzzy one—between the two. Indeed, some would argue that even a relatively unobtrusive observer sitting at a table in a restaurant taking notes influences the situation by virtue of their mere presence; thus, however unwittingly, such an observer is also a participant. This argument could be made about the observers in Townsley and Grimshaw's (2013) study as they were dressed similarly to those for a "night on the town" in order to blend in. Furthermore, one's role may vary across sites and situations within the research field. During his research, Martin participated in the halfway house experiences, having conversations over cigarettes and staying with a roommate, but he was also an observer. It is thus useful to view participation as a matter of degree.

Overt vs. Covert Observation

Another variation in field observation concerns whether the researcher reveals or conceals their identity as a researcher to those who are being observed. In **overt observation**, the researcher's status as a researcher is made known to others; in **covert observation**, it is not. (To help remember the difference, think of it like this: **o**vert = **o**pen; **c**overt = **c**losed.)

OVERT OBSERVATION

Most field research involves overt observation. In many cases, assuming an overt observer role may be a prerequisite for gaining access to a setting or group (Lofland et al., 2006). It also may be necessary to let participants know they are being observed when the researcher's presence would elicit questions or arouse suspicion. Martin's (2018) study is an example of overt observation. Martin identified himself as a researcher to the director of the halfway house. His identity as a researcher was also known by the men in the home. Martin wrote, "my identity as a researcher was front and center from the outset. I worked to gain trust among the men organically, letting them see what I was about by being present and participating as fully as possible in the daily rounds . . ." (p. 676).

---

overt observation
a form of observation in which the researcher identifies themselves as a researcher to those who are being observed

covert observation
a form of observation in which the researcher conceals their identity as a researcher

A limitation of overt observation is that participants may change their behavior when they know they are being observed, just as in laboratory experiments (see Chapter 8). It is important that researchers consider these *reactivity effects* in their studies. Such reactivity may be mitigated as field researchers establish trust and rapport with the participants. With time, participants can become habituated to the researcher's presence.

COVERT OBSERVATION

The major strength of covert observation is that it overcomes the problem of reactivity effects in overt observation. When people do not know they are being observed, they may act more "naturally." This strength, however, can be offset by a serious ethical weakness: covert observations may invade privacy and, by definition, prevent the observed from providing their informed consent. The extent to which this is ethically questionable depends on the nature of the research setting and the researcher's role in the setting. For example, nonparticipant, covert observation in public settings, such as a restaurant, rarely is a problem. However, when the researcher gains access to a private setting such as home, private office, or closed meeting, without divulging their role as a researcher, this is clearly an invasion of privacy. Laud Humphreys' (1970/2009) field research on sexual behavior in public restrooms was considered ethically questionable (see Chapter 4), largely because he misrepresented himself as a voyeur and gained access to observational data as a result of this misrepresentation. Another example of ethically questionable covert observation is presented in Box 10.2.

BOX 10.2

READING CRIMINAL JUSTICE RESEARCH

Parts Unknown: Undercover Ethnography of the Organs-Trafficking Underworld

Perhaps you have heard a story, an urban legend, of children being kidnapped for their organs or the clientele of prostitutes waking up from a drugged stupor to find they are missing a kidney. The concept of human trafficking for exchange of organs on the black market is actually a reality in today's world. Ethnographer Nancy Scheper-Hughes (2004) took on an extensive, multiyear project exploring this taboo underworld that is the global trafficking of human organs. Through her fieldwork, she learned of multiple organ-trade circuits and discovered an extensive network of illicit trafficking of organs and tissues taken from individuals in vulnerable populations, some dead, some "dead/not quite dead," and some alive. Her study is important, as it brings to light a trade that has taken place in secret, due in part to the "great social trust invested in transplant medicine as unquestioned social and moral good" and the professional loyalties and secrets held by the medical elite (p. 37). In addition, this trade, that has taken advantage of the marginalized, brings into question bioethics and human rights. However, the study also raises ethical concerns related to its use of covert observation.

Wanting to provide a naturalistic account of what took place in the world of medical transplants, Scheper-Hughes collaborated with many individuals, including doctors and journalists. Data collection involved interviews with kidney sellers in multiple countries, as well as the gathering of transplant statistics from medical facilities. She also utilized more covert methods to gather information on illegal and highly stigmatized activities, the kinds of activities individuals would not openly discuss in an interview. Her covert methods included posing as a patient or a patient's relative hoping to purchase a kidney, visiting medical units unannounced and, if asked, posing as a confused visitor searching for a different part of the hospital, or introducing herself to transplant facility medical staff as a doctor conducting a study on transplants without specifically identifying what kind of doctor.

At the time of her research, limited covert research had been conducted, and such deceptions were more closely regulated by human subjects review committees. Given the restrictions that approval from the University of California's Human Subjects Protection Committee would pose on her research, Scheper-Hughes applied for an exception to traditional human subjects approval. Instead, she requested that she be afforded the flexibility of a human rights investigative reporter, with similar rights as her colleagues in the school of journalism. She was granted permission by the committee to conduct research as an investigative reporter.

At times the information she uncovered led her to share information with necessary authorities so something could be done about the atrocities she witnessed. In one specific example, she worked with the South African Police to help them capture organ traffickers. These traffickers were stripping organs from poor individuals' bodies in an academic hospital mortuary. From there, the organs were sent to Korea for "processing" and then sold to biotech companies in the United States.

While covert ethnographic research may be disregarded by some researchers, such as an attender at the Social Science Research Council workshop in Prague in May 2002 who told the audience that "ethnography was dead," or those who question the ethicality of undercover research, Scheper-Hughes's study brought to light many illegal medical practices throughout the Middle East, Southeast Asia, and Africa showing the value of such a research methodology. These medical practices disproportionately affect the poor and the marginalized and leave the trafficked with future medical problems and shame from their local community. In addition, her research allowed illegal practices to be exposed and reported to police and government agencies so that changes could be made.

Between Overt and Covert Observation

Just as the "participant" and "nonparticipant" observers are ideal descriptions of a researcher's role, so too are descriptions of the overt and covert observer. Even under the most overt form of observation, the emergent and flexible nature of field research often results in the researcher being in settings, situations, or groups when *not all* participants know they are being observed. Similarly, it may not be possible to completely conceal one's identity, for practical and ethical reasons. In Scheper-Hughes's study (Box 10.2), she revealed her true identity to some individuals, such as journalists and some medical personnel, in order to gain valuable data and observations.

At any given moment, a field researcher's level of participation and overtness can be located in the two-dimensional space shown in Figure 10.1. The figure represents the extent to which the researcher (1) acts as a scientific observer or participant and (2) conceals their identity as a researcher. Most criminal justice research is overt or located above the line, with varying degrees of participation. Martin's fieldwork can be placed in the upper right quadrant. Nonparticipation observation studies in public spaces, such as Townsley and Grimshaw, can be placed in the lower left corner of the figure. Studies such as Scheper-Hughes's fall in the lower right quadrant.

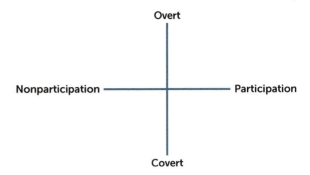

FIGURE 10.1 Levels of Participation and Overtness in Field Research

A researcher's level of participation and overtness is also related to the functional role they may assume in a group. We will discuss this when we outline the process of conducting field research. For now, we turn to variations in qualitative interviews.

Interview Structure

One of the ways qualitative interviews vary is in their structure. *Structured interviews* have very specific objectives, the same questions are asked in the same order for all interviewees, and interviewers have very little freedom in how the interview is conducted. Surveys use structured interviews, whereas interviews in qualitative research are usually unstructured or semi-structured. An **unstructured interview** has broad research objectives and involves a wide-ranging discussion in which individual questions are developed spontaneously in the course of the interview. Between the two extremes, the **semi-structured interview** has specific objectives, but the interviewer has some freedom in meeting those objectives. In both unstructured and semi-structured interviews, rather than follow a pre-established script, the interviewer is free to adapt the interview to capitalize on the special knowledge, experience, or insights of respondents. In either case, topics and questions may be covered in a different order for interviewees and may be skipped for some interviewees but not others (Rubin & Rubin, 2012).

The informal, casual conversations typical of field research are examples of unstructured interviews. In-depth interviews may be semi-structured or unstructured. Martin (2018) describes his life history interviews as semi-structured. Each interview was guided by a list of topics with specific, open-ended questions. However, interviews were conducted in a flexible way, and a script was not read.

There are strengths and weaknesses related to each type of interview. The primary advantage of unstructured interviews is their spontaneity. In fact, as Vasquez (2011, p. 251)

unstructured interview a type of interview guided by broad objectives in which questions are developed as the interview proceeds

semi-structured interview a type of interview that, while having specific objectives, permits the interviewer some freedom in meeting them

suggests, researchers may inadvertently limit interviewees' responses by interrupting with questions and being overly concerned with following a script. The advantage of a more structured interview is that it helps keep the researcher and interviewee on topic. This is particularly important for novice researchers, as we discuss later.

Individual vs. Group Interviews

Interviews also vary in the number of participants. Researchers may decide to interview family members, students, or inmates together as a group as opposed to individually. One special type of group interview is a **focus group**, defined as "a research technique that collects data through group interaction on a topic determined by the researcher" (Morgan, 1996, p.130). In focus groups, the researcher typically takes the role of "facilitator" or "moderator" by posing questions and encouraging discussion from members of the group. Focus groups are conducted with people who may or may not already know one another, and may range in size from as few as four or five participants to as many as 10 or 12. The participants in a focus group respond not only to the interviewer's questions, but also to one another's responses. The data thus consist of participants' verbatim statements and their interactions with one another, which are recorded in notes, audio files, and/or on video. Focus groups may be used as a sole data collection method or in combination with other methods, such as individual, in-depth interviews (King & Horrocks, 2010; Krueger & Casey, 2015; Morgan, 1996, 2012).

A group of researchers from the Rochester Institute of Technology used focus group interviews in a study on perceptions of the justice system and police–community relationships locally (Smith et al., 2017). Focus groups were asked questions about their interactions with the police, their perceptions of safety in their neighborhoods, trust in the police, belief that police treat people with dignity, respect, and fairness, and their view of body-worn cameras. Participants were able to answer structured questions using a clicker and live-polling software known as Turning Point, followed by a group discussion.

An advantage of a group interview, as opposed to an individual one, is that it allows the researcher to observe social interaction among participants (King & Horrocks, 2010; Morgan, 1996, 2012). A practical benefit is that a researcher can gather information from a greater number of participants at one time. Methodologically, the biggest limitation of group interviews is that they add an extra layer of reactivity. Interviewees may provide responses that are not only socially desirable to the interviewer, but also to the other participants in the interview; similarly, participants may tend to go along with what others say. A final limitation concerns ethics; one ethical challenge is that group interviews, by their nature, do not protect participants' confidentiality. As such, researchers can ask participants to sign a disclosure statement asking them to protect one another's confidentiality (King & Horrocks, 2010). Other ethical challenges are

---

focus group an interview method in which a researcher collects data from a group by moderating a group discussion on a particular topic

simultaneously related to the flexibility of qualitative research and the unpredictability of the group context. For instance, it is difficult to know beforehand what participants will say in focus groups and how it will affect each individual participant, which may pose potential risks (and benefits) (Sim & Waterfield, 2019). Finally, technological developments may affect the way observation and interview data are collected. We discuss these in the next section.

Impact of Technological Developments on Observations and Interviews

Just as some experiments (Chapter 8) and surveys (Chapter 9) have moved online, so too has qualitative research. Sometimes online research complements field observations and/or in-depth interviews. Consider the study conducted by Stuart (2020) that examined how gangs challenge one another on social media. The primary data were direct observations and interviews of gang members, but the investigator also observed online gang activity. At other times, online observation may be the sole or primary data source, as in studies of communities on the internet, or in-depth interviews may be conducted exclusively online. Qualitative research can be very time intensive and may require (costly) travel, so a major advantage of doing online research is that it can save time and money. Yet, online research has its own set of considerations and limitations.

The online parallel to field research or ethnography is sometimes called **netnography**, which denotes the study of internet-based forums where people discuss particular topics by posting messages (Kozinets, 1998, 2020). Netnography has been used by marketing researchers to understand consumers' behaviors and opinions, as in an early study of coffee culture on online newsgroups (Kozinets, 2002). Netnography also lends itself well to the study of sensitive topics or illegal acts, which individuals may be reluctant to discuss offline but are willing to discuss anonymously in online communities (Costello et al., 2017). Netnography is similar to ethnography in that researchers formulate one or more research questions and consider such issues as their degree of participation and how to present themselves. But in addition to being conducted primarily online, netnography departs from ethnography in other ways: ethnography involves the observation of all forms of human communication, whereas netnography usually is limited to textual communication; data collection requires ethnographers to be physically present in the research setting and to record observations in field jottings and notes, whereas netnographers are able to download online communications directly at any time, so the research is less obtrusive as well as faster and cheaper (Kozinets, 1998, 2002). So far, much of what passes as netnography has been restricted to nonparticipant or passive monitoring (Costello et al., 2017). But this lacks the active personal experience and reflexivity that characterize field research and contribute to in-depth understanding.

netnography
a research method used to study internet-based forums where people discuss particular topics by posting messages

One of the ethical challenges in conducting netnography revolves around whether the forums that are investigated are public or private sites. Some researchers maintain that the study of public forums does not require informed consent. Others contend that the line between public and private is less clear in cyberspace, and people may be confused about the public nature of their communications (King, 1996); therefore, measures should be taken to protect privacy no matter how "public" the online community appears to be.

Increasingly, in-depth interviews are also being conducted online. In fact, as the COVID-19 pandemic took hold and social distancing guidelines were put in place, qualitative researchers had "limited options such as telephonic or online interviews or other technologically mediated modes of interaction [e.g., email]"—if they were even able to carry out their research at all (Fine et al., 2020, p. 8). The closest online approximation to a face-to-face interview is a video call. Assuming a good connection, it is possible that a researcher can pick up on the nonverbal and other aspects of face-to-face interviews mentioned earlier. Still, compared to a landline phone call, the extent to which researchers can assure participants the confidentiality and security of a video call may depend on the provider's terms and conditions and is an issue best addressed by an IRB.

An interesting example of the use of netnography and different modes of collecting data is a study of gang-associated youth and young adults in Chicago. As part of the fieldwork, Stuart (2020) examined gang-associated participants' social media activity including their posts and private messages. Social media has become popular among gang-associated youth as a way to establish and enhance their reputation. Stuart found that social media allowed the gang-associated youth to validate a violent reputation through menacing images. The youth also used social media to contradict or tear down their challengers' online image. In one example, a gang member found a four-year-old prom photo of a rival member (Will) on their Facebook page prior to his gang activity. He posted the old photo of Will next to a more recent photo Will posted of himself standing menacingly on a street corner with the caption, "sweet bruford say he a savage" (Stuart, 2020, p. 198). In addition to the social media data collected in his fieldwork, Stuart interviewed the gang-associated youth and received consent to shadow them, spending approximately 20–50 hours each week on direct observation.

Although technological developments have made qualitative research more time efficient and less costly, as with experiments and surveys, the jury is still out on the quality of data collected online. Moreover, researchers need to consider the security and ethical challenges of the online environment. Whether researchers should use netnography and other such methods partly depends on the research question. In the case of the study of gang members, it made sense to do so, albeit with the necessary precautions, as young individuals' worlds are increasingly moving online.

SUMMARY

Qualitative research varies in how observations and interviews are conducted. In observational research, researchers may participate in what they are observing (participant observation), merely observe without participating (nonparticipant observation), or participate to some degree in between. Furthermore, observation may be overt (open), covert (closed), or somewhere in between. Interviews may be more or less formal and structured; they may also be conducted individually or with groups of different sizes. Finally, technological developments provide different means of gathering data. Check your understanding of this section in Box 10.3.

BOX 10.3

CHECKING YOUR UNDERSTANDING

Qualitative Research Review I

1. What are the differences in types of observations a qualitative field researcher might engage in?
    a. Discreet and open observation
    b. Open and closed observation
    c. Participant and nonparticipant observation
    d. Identified and non-identified observation

2. Studies such as the one conducted by Martin living in the halfway home or Stuart shadowing gang-associated youth involve researchers who are engaged in the activities of the individuals they are studying. These examples would fall under which type of observation?
    a. Discreet observation
    b. Participant observation
    c. Open observation
    d. Nonparticipant observation

3. When researchers conceal their identity as a researcher during their observation and study of subjects, such as Scheper-Hughes did in the study of organ trafficking, this is known as which of the following?
    a. Covert observation
    b. Overt observation

continues

> *continued*
>
> c. Discreet observation
> d. Closed observation
>
> 4. If researchers decide to interview a group of people at the same time, acting as a moderator, and allowing group discussion, this is which form of qualitative data collection?
>   a. Structured interview
>   b. Focus group
>   c. Nonparticipant observation
>   d. Survey
>
> **Answers: 1. c, 2. b, 3. a, 4. b**

10.3 THE PROCESS OF CONDUCTING FIELD RESEARCH

Now that you know the general features of qualitative research and its major variations, are you ready to "go get the seat of your pants dirty in real research?" as University of Chicago Professor Robert Park reportedly told his students (McKinney, 1966, p. 71). Before you begin, remember that the general process for answering qualitative research questions is different than the process for answering quantitative research questions. The research questions themselves tend to be broader—sometimes called **guiding questions**—than those posed in surveys and experiments. In addition, these guiding questions are usually accompanied by a set of more focused research questions, which may emerge during the course of research. Recall, for example, that Martin's guiding question concerned the experiences of men postprisonization, while his more focused questions concentrated on physical habits carried out by men from prison to post-release, the social transition, and adaptation to life outside of prison.

Initially, qualitative researchers may rely on a literature review to a lesser extent than researchers working from a deductive logic of inquiry. Because preconceived images can be very misleading, researchers may attempt to avoid preset hypotheses and instead let their observations and interviews guide the course of the research.

As outlined in Figure 10.2, the major steps in conducting field research are to select a research setting/group, gain access, establish roles and relationships, decide what to observe/whom to interview, gather and analyze data, leave the field, and write the report. Note that many of the arrows in the figure are bidirectional. This is because the steps in field research are interrelated; they may not be completed in the same order; and the researcher may move back and forth between them (Bailey 1996, p. xiv). As an example, a researcher may select a setting or group to study and then gain access; alternatively, he or she may gain access first and then choose to conduct a study.

guiding question
a relatively broad research question that guides the initial stages of qualitative research

Select Setting/Group

The most important considerations in selecting a setting or group are that it should speak to the research question at hand and should allow the researcher to better understand meaning, process, and/or actors' points of views (Lofland et al., 2006). Martin, for example, intending to study prison release and the problems of reentry, selected a halfway house likely due to the ability to interact with several men recently released from prison more conveniently than finding individual, recently released men in society. From the men at the halfway house, Martin was introduced to other individuals also working through reentry outside of the halfway house via snowball sampling. The group of men he studied, and the setting of the halfway house, were logical choices to assist Martin in exploring his research topic.

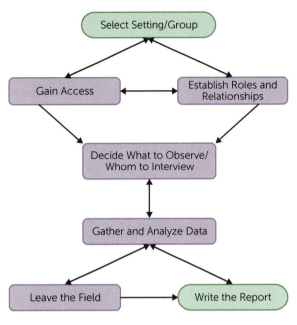

FIGURE 10.2 **The Process of Conducting Field Research**

Researchers have different opinions on where to start in selecting a setting or group. On the one hand, Lofland and colleagues (2006) recommend "starting where you are"—that is, in a setting with which you are familiar. The advantage of starting where you are is that it facilitates entry. For our student readers, examples of starting where you are might include your college or university, where you live or work, student groups with which you are involved, or a place where you volunteer.

On the other hand, Saldaña (2011) advises against "starting where you are," at least for novices who want to study their friends. For one thing, according to Saldaña (2011), you may lose valuable insight into the process of "gaining entry" (p. 34). In familiar settings, especially where researchers have a direct personal or professional stake, they may also experience problems in overcoming their own particular views of reality and of holding their feelings in abeyance (Taylor & Bogdan, 1998).

Wherever you start, you need to evaluate sites for their appropriateness, access, risks, and ethics (Lofland et al., 2006). You should also document why you selected a particular setting or group (Bailey, 1996, p. 37).

Gain Access

An important consideration in selecting a setting or group may be your ability to gain access to it. A number of factors shape a researcher's ability to gain access, including personal characteristics, the nature of the setting, and gatekeepers and others from whom permission may be needed.

PERSONAL CHARACTERISTICS

A researcher's personal characteristics, such as gender, class, race/ethnicity, religion, sexuality, and disability status, may shape her or his ability to access certain settings and groups. The most obvious instance is when a setting or a group is explicitly closed to certain people. The public bathrooms for men studied by Laud Humphreys (1970) were closed to women. Some groups and institutions also are largely closed to outsiders. For example, it may not be possible to study recently released prisoners in a halfway house in the manner Martin did, without being part of the corrections community, due to confidentiality or liability issues.

Martin's personal characteristics, such as being a university professor, also shaped his ability to gain access because the director wanted to promote reintegration of the men by connecting them with a university-educated individual outside the justice system. His gender as a male also likely made it possible for the men to open up to him. However, Martin's status as a university professor, rather than ex-prisoner, posed challenges in gaining access to other released prisoners outside the halfway home. In this instance, utilizing other men in the halfway home as recruits helped him gain access to a wider net of participants.

As you prepare to conduct your own study, it is worth reflecting on how your personal or other characteristics may shape your access. Yet, these characteristics do not necessarily *determine* access, as Lofland and colleagues (2006) advise: "Just because you do not share certain characteristics with the persons you wish to study, you should not automatically conclude that such research is impossible or even unusually difficult" (p. 24). Although one may seem an "outsider" to the group, they may be able to gain access because those being studied want their stories told, which is typical of some marginalized groups.

NATURE OF THE SETTING

A researcher's ability to gain access to a setting varies according to whether the setting is public, private, or something in between. A *public setting* is one that is open to everyone, such as a park, street corner, or a public restroom, thus making entry relatively easy (Lofland et al., 2006). Observations in public settings typically do not require formal permission, although it can be a good idea to inform relevant authorities of the study. As an example, David Snow negotiated and legitimated access to a number of settings for his partner Leon Anderson in a study of the homeless in Austin, Texas. Letting police know proved useful later, as Anderson was arrested and jailed for violation of an open-container ordinance with two homeless men one evening. He was bailed out the same night, and as a result of prior negotiations with the local police, "his arrest record was subsequently expunged from the police file and the arresting officer was reprimanded" (Snow et al., 1986, p. 395).

Examples of *semi-public settings* include movie theaters, stores, and for adults, bars. A semi-public setting is open to the public, but there is generally an expectation that people in these settings will purchase an item or "do" something. Conducting observations in a movie theater's lobby for an extended period of time, for example, may arouse suspicion about the researcher, who also may be accused of loitering. As such, it is generally a good idea to speak with the owner or manager before you begin your research. Formal permission may also be required.

Private settings, such as a person's home or a private club deny access to all but acknowledged members and invited guests; others may be considered intruders (Lofland, 1973, p. 19). These settings typically require formal permissions and may be the most challenging to access. If a researcher wished to conduct field research in the field of criminal justice, many settings may be considered private, such as the halfway house Martin was granted access to, and difficult to enter as a researcher.

GATEKEEPERS AND OTHER PERMISSIONS

The process of gaining access, according to Peregrine Schwartz-Shea and Dvora Yanow (2012, p. 58), is like negotiating passage through "gates of various sorts." "Gates" refer to authorities in charge of a setting or group—traditionally called **gatekeepers** in field research—who can grant or deny permissions for entry. Some examples of gatekeepers include the family members living in a home to be visited and owners or managers of movie theaters. In Martin's study, the director of the halfway house, from whom he sought permission to conduct his research, was the gatekeeper. The concept of "gates" also refers to institutions or organizations from which permission may be needed to gain access (Schwartz-Shea & Yanow, 2012). For example, depending on the topic of research, legal permissions may be required, or at least sought, as in Snow's contact with the local police in the homeless study.

gatekeeper relevant authority whose permission is needed to gain access to a setting or group

Researchers may need multiple permissions, as illustrated in a study by visual ethnographer Luigi Gariglio (2014). His photographic work inside prisons was intended to portray the prisoner as an individual to overcome the representation of prisoners from popular media. In a post about his experience as a photographic ethnographer, he discusses the challenges of gaining access to an Italian prison. Luigi had already been inside the prison to take photos as a photographer over the previous two years, however, labeling his new role as a researcher was met with skepticism. As a photographer, Luigi was granted access by the Italian Prison Service's press office. However, as a researcher he sought permission from the prison director. The negotiations with the director took approximately five months, and then after hearing no news for an additional five months, he was finally given permission to enter the prison as a researcher. However, he was only allowed to take photographs, he could not engage in field research with the inmates (his main research objective).

Obtaining formal permission from gatekeepers, however, does not guarantee interpersonal access (Schwartz-Shea & Yanow, 2012, p. 60). In Gariglio's (2014) study, he had received formal access to the prison via the director, yet he found, "once I was inside, I learned that informal access had to be negotiated and renegotiated on a day-to-day basis with participants on the wing" (para. 6).

Gaining access is a process that requires negotiation and *renegotiation* throughout the time one spends in the field (Bailey, 1996). Gatekeepers and other actors change; so do you and your research. This can be seen in Gariglio's work described previously in this section. In the process of gaining access to the prison, a dangerous inmate also escaped which required that he renegotiate access. In his post, he describes this process:

> As a consequence of this episode, I was 'locked out' from prison and everything had to be renegotiated. The pressure of public opinion and all the journalists waiting outside the prison wall made things difficult. I still remember the wrath and anxiety I experienced when the prison officer at the gate of the prison laughed at me when I told him I had permission to start my research and I was there, ready to begin. The officer knew my face and hilariously asked me if I had read the newspapers in recent days. I did not understand his comment nor why everything seemed to be so slow and complicated. Then the officer simply told me something like: all visitors must renegotiate all their access and that's it. This renegotiation took around another seven months. When I finally entered my first time in prison as a visual researcher, it was 2000. I was already exhausted. The lead up made it clear that formal access should not be taken for granted. (para. 7)

Establish Roles and Relationships

When field research involves a degree of participation, the researcher must balance the requirements of the roles of *scientific observer* and *participant* in a group or community. In addition, as a participant, the researcher must work out how he or she will relate to those in the field, which often amounts to assuming a particular role in the group or setting being observed. Forming relationships is important, as this will determine the level of rapport and trust that can be developed with others and the extent and type of information that can be gathered.

You are likely to have the broadest access to information if you can become a fully accepted member of the group or community. This would be possible if you could join the group you were studying. For instance, if you were studying a charitable organization, you could become a volunteer member of that organization. At other times, you might assume a functional role in the setting. As an outsider, Martin could not become a full member of the halfway house community. But he thoroughly immersed himself in the community, living in the home and accepting the same responsibilities as the other men so that he formed close relationships. Martin (2018) writes, "I worked to gain trust among the men organically, letting them see what I was about by being present and participating as fully as possible in the daily rounds" (p. 676). In this way, he was able to relate to and better understand the men in the halfway house.

In general, the more immersed you are in the setting and the closer you are to attaining full-member status, the greater the acceptance by others, and the more likely the opportunity to gather data on the most personal and intimate matters. In addition, gaining full membership in a group or community enables researchers "to supplement the data they gather with the greatest degree of their own subjective insight" (Adler & Adler, 1987, p. 81). On the other hand, full membership is intense and time-consuming, may have profound personal consequences, and can create a conflict between the member and researcher roles.

The role you assume in your research may be shaped by a self-conscious decision about how much you want to participate. However, it also can be influenced by personal characteristics and your ability to access certain settings and group members.

Decide What to Observe/Whom to Interview

Field researchers' decisions about what to observe or whom to interview are partly influenced by practical considerations. It can be challenging to locate suitable observation sites, make fruitful contacts, and access records. Convenience, accessibility, and happenstance shape where researchers can begin to make observations, whom they will meet there, and whom they will find most informative.

Research questions also influence what field researchers observe. Broader, guiding questions may lead researchers to simply observe as much as they can. More focused questions may direct researchers to particular types of observation. Scheper-Hughes explicitly selected transplant units and hospital wards for observation, given its relevance to the organ trafficking process in which she was interested. Similarly, your research question may focus on dimensions of the setting or particular actors, events, or processes (Miles & Huberman, 1994; Schwartz-Shea & Yanow, 2012).

Traditionally, field researchers also have relied on information provided by **key informants**—also called key actors or insiders (Bailey, 1996)—who are selected on the basis of their knowledge, expertise, or status within the group. For Scheper-Hughes, it was important to gather information from people with knowledge of the local organ trafficking processes in which she was interested. Hence, many of her key informants were individuals who were labeled as "kidney-sellers" themselves. The informants provided firsthand accounts of being taken advantage of or kidnapped in exchange for their kidneys, such as one kidney-seller who told her how a hotel manager/organbroker "promises illegal immigrants freshly minted counterfeit passports in exchange for a freshly extracted 'spare' kidney" (p. 33). As often occurs in field research, researchers may select many of the individuals they interview through a process of "serial selection" (Lincoln & Guba, 1985) similar to snowball sampling (see Chapter 7), in which initial informants introduced him to others.

key informant a person from whom field researchers acquire information who is selected on the basis of knowledge, expertise, or status within the group

Gather and Analyze Data

> **field jottings** brief quotes, phrases, and key words that are recorded by field researchers while in the field

The data that a field researcher collects are vast and varied, consisting of direct observations and experiences, interviews, and supplementary archival data. Observations, the primary data in field research, are recorded in a variety of ways. To begin, a researcher may try to remember significant details of what is observed. Although these "mental notes" may serve as one source of the "record," memory is a poor substitute for a written record. During the course of observation, therefore, field researchers usually take **field jottings**—"little phrases, quotes, key words, and the like" (Lofland et al., 2006, p.109). As a general rule, jottings should be made as inconspicuously as possible, which may require that the researcher wait until participants are out of sight. Based on these jottings, field researchers then write a more complete set of **field notes**—that is, detailed written accounts of field observations—at the end of each day or as soon after the observations as possible (Lofland et al., 2006). Above all, these notes are intended to be descriptive of what the researcher observed. In addition, they may include what the researcher thought or felt at the time as well as some preliminary analysis of the situation or setting (Saldaña, 2011).

> **field notes** detailed written accounts of field observations, which may also include a researcher's reflections and preliminary analyses

To show you what field jottings look like and how they can be transformed to notes, examine the partial example of field jottings below. These are from observations of a trial court proceeding in which the claimant, Marcia Snow, is pursuing a temporary restraining order (TRO) from two landlords, Robert Thomas and Mike Murphy, the latter of whom is not in court due to illness (Emerson et al., 2011, pp. 30–31). The jottings mainly capture quotes and phrases, albeit with the speakers unidentified and unclear statements indicated in parentheses. Much of the dialogue concerns the health of the codefendant.

[case number]
Snow, Marcia
Thomas

           atty— AIDS Mike
               Murphy
               legal guardian

are you prepared to proceed against
the one individual—(both)
massive doses of chemother(apy)
I don't think he's ever going to come in here
I know he's well enough to walk—
came in (returned heater)—when?
you can call his doctor at UCLA and
he can verify all this
I just don't call people on the
telephone—courts don't operate that way—it has to be on paper or (in person)
(Emerson et al., 2011, p. 54)

An abbreviated example of the field notes based on the previously presented jottings and the researcher's memory is presented below (Emerson et al., 2011, p. 55). They describe the claimant (Marcia Snow (MS)), one of the codefendants (Robert Thomas (RT)), and parts of the court proceedings, especially concerning the health of the other codefendant, Mike Murphy (MM):

> *Marcia Snow has longish, curly, dark brown hair, in her 20s, dressed informally in blue blouse and pants. No wedding ring, but with a youngish looking guy with glasses. Robert Thomas is in his 40s, light brown hair, shaggy mustache, jacket with red-black checked lining. Judge begins by asking RT if he has an atty; he does, but he is not here. He explains that his business partner, Mike Murphy, who is also named in the TRO, is not here today; he has AIDS and is very ill. "I'm his legal guardian," so I can represent his concerns. J asks MS: "Are you prepared to proceed against this one individual?" MS answers that she wants the order against both of them. RT then explains that MM has had AIDS for three years, has had "massive doses of chemotherapy," and adds: "I don't think he's ever going to come in here." J asks MS if from what she knows that MM is this sick. MS hesitates, then says: "I know he's well enough to walk." I saw him walking when he returned the heaters that they stole. J: When was this? (I can't hear her answer.) RT: He's had his AIDS for three years. He's very sick. "You can call his doctor at UCLA, and he can verify this." J: "I just don't call people on the telephone. Courts don't operate that way. It has to be on paper" or testified in person. RT repeats that MM is very ill, that he has to take care of him, and he is not getting better . . .*

Data analysis usually begins in field notes. As field notes are recorded or reviewed, analysis may be aided by writing **analytic memos**, which Saldaña (2013) vividly describes as "somewhat comparable to research journal entries or blogs—a place to 'dump your brain' about the participants, phenomenon, or process under investigation by thinking and thus writing and thus thinking even more about them" (p. 41). Analytic memo writing is intended to help the researcher identify emergent empirical patterns and concepts in the data. Qualitative analytic techniques, further discussed in Chapter 15, are used throughout the process of field research, both during and after one has left the field.

analytic memo an adjunct to field notes, observations, and interviews that consists of recorded analyses that come to mind in going over data

Leave the Field

Except in rare cases in which the researcher decides to permanently live in the setting or among the group being studied, he or she must leave the field at some point. Given that field researchers often develop close relationships, this can be an emotionally difficult step. Nevertheless, according to Lofland and colleagues (2006, p. 78), the process is similar to saying good-byes in everyday life, and the same advice for how to do so applies to field research as well:

> Most generally, don't burn your bridges. And, more specifically in keeping with the etiquette of departures: inform people of your plans ahead of time; explain why and where you are going; say your good-byes personally insofar as it is possible; and, if appropriate, promise to stay in touch.

Throughout the research—and especially when the researcher leaves—an important question of reciprocity arises: Given that participants have shared their lives with the researcher, what is his or her responsibility to them? Answers to this question vary; so, too, do researchers' strategies.

Just as gaining access to a setting or group involves considering how people will relate to your presence as a researcher, leaving the field involves considering how people will relate to your absence. Consistent with the ethical principles outlined in Chapter 4, it is important to be careful and deliberate in relating your plans to leave and to think about what happens afterward.

Write the Report

The last step is to write the report. In final reports of field research, data take the form of vivid descriptions and verbatim statements as well as analytic summaries. The former are intended to provide the reader with an understanding of what it feels like to be in the setting or among the people being studied.

Writing is important as a way of clarifying analysis and deepening thoughts. Writing occurs throughout the research process, both in and out of the field. As you embark on field research, do not underestimate the power of writing at all stages of your study.

SUMMARY

The process of conducting field research involves selecting a setting or group, gaining access, establishing roles and relationships, deciding what to observe/whom to interview, gathering and analyzing data, leaving the field, and writing the report. This process is nonlinear; researchers may move back and forth between steps. For example, a researcher may first gain access to a setting or group and then decide to study it; data analysis may affect subsequent decisions about what to observe and whom to interview. Gaining access is shaped by the researcher's personal characteristics, the nature of the setting, and gatekeepers and others from whom permission may be needed. Given that field research often involves some degree of participation, an important consideration is establishing relationships with others, which may be facilitated by assuming a functional role within the group or setting. Analysis begins in the field and continues afterward, resulting in a final written report that includes vivid descriptions of the setting/group and analytic summaries. To check your understanding of the concepts discussed within this section, refer to Box 10.4.

> **BOX 10.4**
>
> **CHECKING YOUR UNDERSTANDING**
>
> # Field Research
>
> 1. Which of the following factors may impact a researcher's ability to gain access to a setting or group?
>   a. Personal characteristics
>   b. Nature of the setting
>   c. Gatekeepers
>   d. All of the above
>
> 2. In Martin's study of the halfway house, who did he identify as the main gatekeeper he needed to seek approval from in order to gain access to the setting?
>   a. Director of the home
>   b. Department of Corrections
>   c. The chair of his department
>   d. He did not need permission from a gatekeeper
>
> 3. During the course of observation, field researchers usually take _____ which are little notes, phrases, key words, etc. and at the end of the day or observations, they write _____ which are descriptive, detailed written accounts of the observations.
>   a. field scribbles; field narrative
>   b. field notes; field jottings
>   c. field jottings; field notes
>   d. field narrative; field scribbles
>
> 4. Given that field researchers often develop close relationships, which step of the field research process can be emotionally difficult?
>   a. Writing the report
>   b. Gaining access
>   c. Gathering and analyzing data
>   d. Leaving the field
>
> **Answers: 1. d, 2. a, 3. c, 4. d**

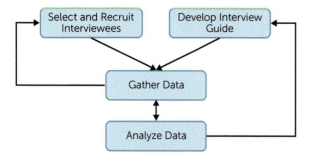

FIGURE 10.3 The Process of Conducting In-Depth Interviews

10.4 THE PROCESS OF CONDUCTING IN-DEPTH INTERVIEWS

The process of conducting in-depth interviews is outlined in Figure 10.3. This process parallels field research and involves the following steps: select and recruit interviewees, develop an interview guide, gather data, and analyze data. The process may also be nonlinear, with the researcher moving back and forth between steps. To illustrate this process, we will frequently rely on Jackson and colleagues' (2021) study of exonerees. The guiding question explored the impact of a wrongful conviction on the convicted; more focused questions concentrated on the innocent inmates' experience in prison, adaptation to prison, and life post-release.

Select and Recruit Interviewees

The first step is to select and recruit interviewees, which Jackson et al.'s (2021) study illustrates. The identification of potential interviewees began with the research question, which focused on exonerees, those who have "been wrongfully arrested, convicted, and incarcerated then exonerated through the courts and/or had their conviction vacated" (p. 6). The focus on the exoneree experience was a response to a "hole" in the literature. Previous research had examined the causes of wrongful conviction, but had largely neglected the voices of the exonerees themselves. Interviews were conducted over the phone so that invited potential participants were not limited to a specific location or region of the country (COVID-19 had also limited the ability for researchers to meet interviewees in person).

To recruit interviewees who met the research profile, Jackson began by contacting exonerees known personally to her through her work with innocence organizations and through the Willie T. Donald Exoneration Advisory Coalition, a board she founded to advocate for the wrongfully convicted by examining wrongful conviction cases, connecting exonerees to local resources, and advocating for reform in her state of Indiana.

From the initial contacts known to Jackson, she utilized snowball sampling to recruit additional participants:

> *An exoneree known to the lead author posted on an exoneree social media page that researchers were looking for volunteers to be interviewed about prison experiences. Contact information was provided and all participants were self-selected.* (Jackson et al., 2021, p. 6)

The process of snowball sampling led to a sample 23 exonerees.

Just as personal characteristics shape access in field research, they also shape recruitment efforts in interview research. Exonerees may have been drawn to the solicitation to be part of the research study because it was an opportunity for their voices to be heard, and they likely trusted Dr. Jackson given her previous advocacy work for the wrongfully convicted.

As you embark on your own in-depth interview study, your research question will likely provide general guidance about whom to interview. For reasons of convenience and accessibility, however, you may need to limit your focus. Vasquez, a qualitative researcher, gives the following advice to novice researchers: "[D]on't be scared of your project. Understand that your project may morph as you proceed—you might sharpen your research question or revise your interview schedule—and that is *part* of the research process" (personal communication, 2014).

Develop an Interview Guide

The next step involves developing interview questions. As noted earlier, most in-depth interviews tend to be conducted individually (as well as face-to-face), using a semi-structured or unstructured format with almost exclusively open-ended questions. We suggest that novice interviewers begin with semi-structured interviews, making use of an **interview guide**. An interview guide, sometimes called an *interview protocol*, includes at least a list of topics but also, depending on the planned structure of the interview, specific questions.

To the extent that the interview guide includes specific questions, this requires writing out the questions beforehand. To draft an interview guide, first consider the two primary types of questions asked in in-depth interviews: main questions and probes. The main questions are those most directly related to the research question. They are shaped by a researcher's knowledge or experience, the literature, or preliminary research (Rubin & Rubin, 2012, pp. 134–135). In Jackson et al.'s study, the main questions concerned exonerees' experiences in prison and post-release. **Probes** are follow-up questions used to gather additional detail and clarify responses. They may be written into an interview guide and/or asked spontaneously. In Jackson et al.'s interview guide, one of the main questions asked whether the exoneree expressed that they were innocent to the guards and inmates. A probe following this question asked for more information about sharing innocence by asking whether the inmates and guards believed their claims of innocence.

As you write drafts of questions, you should carefully consider their wording. Some of the tips for writing survey questions, discussed in Chapter 9, apply to in-depth interview questions as well. For example, the questions should be clear and unbiased, contain familiar words, and avoid technical jargon. Yet, in-depth interviews allow researchers greater freedom in constructing questions because you need not specify response options, as in closed-ended questions, and you can make liberal use of probes to clarify and amplify the meaning of answers. Ordinarily, for example, it is not a good idea to ask too many either/or questions or questions that elicit one-word or brief responses; however, these can effectively set up probing follow-up questions, as in the

interview guide a list of topics and specific questions to be asked in a qualitative interview

probes follow-up questions used in surveys and in-depth interviews to gather more information about a respondent's answer

example shared earlier in this section when Jackson and colleagues asked whether exonerees shared their claims of innocence with inmates and guards.

As in surveys, question order is also important. However, the more flexible nature of in-depth interviews makes the exact placement of questions less important than the overall "rhythm" of the interview. Ideally, the interview should begin with questions that are easy to answer and end on a neutral or positive note (Charmaz, 2006; Rubin & Rubin, 2012). Opening questions may include a few background questions or a **grand tour** (or simply, **tour**) **question**. A tour question asks interviewees for a broad description of the people, processes, or events being studied (Rubin & Rubin, 2012). As the name implies, a tour question gives the interviewee an opportunity to "walk the interviewer around" the topic. Jackson et al. began the interview with demographic information about the exoneree and the crime for which they were wrongfully convicted in order to establish rapport and increase the participant's comfortability answering questions. Also consistent with guidelines for survey interviews, Jackson and colleagues placed the potentially sensitive questions on the topic of violence in prison and negative experiences in the middle of the interview. Finally, in wrapping-up an interview, it was important for Jackson et al. to ask if interviewees wanted to add or clarify anything.

For many qualitative researchers, the interview guide and questions may be refined throughout the process of conducting several interviews. A great way to refine a guide is by posing the question at the end of an interview: "Is there anything I did not ask but that I should have?" Preparing for the interview involves other considerations beyond the construction of an interview guide. Some of these are discussed in Box 10.5.

> **grand tour question** a broad opening question in in-depth interviews that asks for a general description of the people, processes, or events being studied (also called a tour question)

BOX 10.5

DOING CRIMINAL JUSTICE RESEARCH

Preparing for an In-Depth Interview

In final reports, researchers rarely recount every single step they take in carrying out research, and interview preparation is an area that often receives little or no attention. Yet the amount and type of preparation can have a major impact on the quality of the interview.

Unlike surveys, in which interviews begin immediately after interviewers contact and gain the cooperation of respondents, in-depth interviews are almost always scheduled in advance, after the successful recruitment of the person to be interviewed. So, to begin, you need to contact the person to schedule a time and place for the interview. Saldaña (2011) recommends scheduling the interview on a day and in a time block "in which the participant will not feel fatigued or rushed, if possible"; moreover, the location of the interview should be as comfortable, private, and free of distractions as is possible (pp. 34–35). If you are scheduling multiple interviews on the same day, you should give yourself ample time to rest in between (Rubin & Rubin, 2012).

> Prior to the scheduled date and time, you should remind the participant(s) of the interview. You also should prepare an informed consent form and be prepared to answer questions about how you will protect confidentiality.
>
> On the day of the interview, it is a good idea to arrive early, make sure that the location is still well suited for interviewing, and check audio or video equipment, if used, for proper functioning. Some researchers may bring water to the interview for participants and themselves to prevent dry mouth; researchers may also provide candy or lozenges (Rubin & Rubin, 2012; Saldaña, 2011).

Gather Data

The next step is to gather data. In qualitative interviews, the quality and depth of the data partly depend on the rapport that the interviewer establishes with the interviewee. Although there is no recipe for establishing rapport (King & Horrocks, 2010), you can do a few things to make the interviewee feel comfortable. For example, you should "enter the interview with an attitude of courtesy and respect," treating interviewees "as if they are important invited guests to [your] home" (Saldaña, 2011, p. 39). You also may "chitchat" with interviewees before the interview starts as a way of establishing a more relaxed atmosphere (Rubin & Rubin, 2012).

Prior to beginning the formal interview, you should explain the nature of the study and acquire verbal or written consent; you also should ask permission to use an audio or tape recorder if that is part of the research. Here you might want to follow the procedure that Robert Weiss (2004, p. 46) uses:

> *I bring two copies of consent forms describing the study to my interviewees, both copies bearing my signature. After briefly explaining the study, I give both forms to the respondent, ask him or her to read one and, if comfortable with it, to sign one of the copies and keep the other. I usually have a tape recorder and ask if it is all right to turn it on.*

As you begin to ask questions, recall that the purpose of the interview is often to obtain *in-depth* responses. Though probes may be written into an interview guide, you will likely need to ask for more information on the basis of people's responses. Weiss (2004) provides a good example of a spontaneous probe: "If a respondent says, 'We got along fine,' the interviewer should ask something like, 'When you say that, what are you thinking of?' or 'Can you tell me the last time that happened?' or 'Can you think of a time that really showed that happening?'" (p. 47).

The rest of the interview process largely depends on the type of interview being conducted—its focus, level of structure, and the number of participants. As is typical with in-depth interviews, Jackson and colleagues' questions were not rigid, and each interview was "unique." As stated by Vasquez (2011), "Even with an interview schedule, some questions were covered in depth while others were briefly touched on. Depending on interviewer-interviewee dynamic and rapport, an interviewee's life history, and personal style, the interview takes on its own form" (pp. 251–252). Jackson et al. (2021) found that while "interviews focused on the exoneree's prison experience rather than details of the crime and exoneration. Some exonerees expressed the desire to discuss the nature of the case against them, which contributed to longer interview times" (p. 7). With time, you may rely on your guide/schedule to a lesser extent, as Vasquez (p. 251) did:

> In the course of an interview, I would juggle peering down periodically at my interview schedule while at the same time listening to the interviewee's narrative for thematic leads to follow. As I became comfortable with interviewing and my interview schedule became seared into my memory, I realized that I was conversationally delivering my questions.

Regardless of the type of interview, the interview typically ends with the researcher thanking the participant, exchanging contact information, and assessing the participant's feelings. As Rubin and Rubin (2012) state, "Your interviewees should be no worse off, and ideally should be better off, for having taken the time to talk to you" (p. 89). According to Vasquez (2011), "While some [of her] respondents found the interview difficult to the extent that it brought up sensitive topics, most ended their encounter with me with an expression of neutral or positive emotion" (p. 245). One of her interviewees found the interview particularly beneficial, as he said, "Wow, this is like therapy. I haven't been this open with anyone besides my close friends in a long time" (p. 245). At the same time, researchers need to be particularly sensitive to potential risks to interviewees such as discomfort; they also should remind interviewees that they are not therapists and provide them with necessary resources after the interview is completed (Johnson & Rowlands, 2012; Rubin & Rubin, 2012).

Like observational data, interview data may be recorded in jottings and more detailed notes, but it is recommended to use audio or video devices, either alone or in combination with jottings and notes. Jackson et al., for example, recorded interviews via an app that can record phone calls in addition to taking notes. This gave her a complete verbatim record to which she could return again and again. On the other hand, interviews need to be transcribed, and in some cases translated. And this can take a great deal of time.

Analyze Data

Once interview data are transcribed, they need to be analyzed. A primary means of analysis is coding, or sorting data into categories, as was defined in Chapter 9. Qualitative interview data are sorted into categories represented by *words*, not *numbers* as in survey research. Moreover, codes are not usually predefined as in survey research, but rather emerge through an inductive analytic process. As further discussed in Chapter 15, the analyst often attempts to identify broader themes and patterns and discern how they relate to one another. Jackson and colleagues note that they followed this general approach, identifying the process as conceptual content analysis where:

> Each researcher examined the transcriptions, drew inferences, and categorized data into themes; words and phrases frequently used by participants were coded. Through coding, researchers were able to make inferences regarding the exonerees' prison experiences. (p. 7)

In the final research reports, the product of data analysis can take the form of rich description, as in field research, and theoretical conclusions.

SUMMARY

The process of conducting in-depth interviews involves selecting and recruiting interviewees, developing an interview guide, gathering data, and analyzing data. Like the process of conducting field research, the steps may be completed in different orders. Selecting and recruiting interviewees is guided by the research question and ease of access. Developing an interview guide involves selecting good main questions and appropriate probes and paying attention to question wording and order. Gathering data involves establishing rapport with interviewees, listening carefully, taking notes, and recording and transcribing interviewees' responses. Data analysis begins with coding in an attempt to find emergent patterns and themes as well as to understand how patterns and themes are related to one another. See Box 10.6 to assess your understanding of this section.

BOX 10.6

CHECKING YOUR UNDERSTANDING

In-Depth Interviews

1. In order to recruit participants who were unique to the research question, Jackson and colleagues utilized a sampling method often seen in qualitative work which involves the current participants recruiting additional participants for the study. This is known as:
    a. qualitative sampling
    b. snowball sampling

continues

continued

    c. informant sampling
    d. none of the above

2. Either written into an interview guide or asked spontaneously, researchers may ask follow-up questions to gather more information about a respondent's answer. These are known as:
    a. unstructured interviews
    b. interview guides
    c. probes
    d. contingencies

3. Which of the following is a primary means of analyzing qualitative data?
    a. Statistical tests
    b. Coding, or sorting data into categories
    c. Equations
    d. Listing

Answers: 1. b, 2. c, 3. b

10.5 STRENGTHS AND LIMITATIONS OF QUALITATIVE RESEARCH

Many social scientists favor qualitative research because they believe it addresses some of the limitations of experiments, surveys, and other quantitative methods. Of course, like all research methods, it has its own set of weaknesses. Understanding these strengths and limitations will help you not only to evaluate qualitative research but also to decide if this is an appropriate method to use in your own research.

Naturalistic Approach

On balance, qualitative research is considered to be a more "naturalistic" approach than methods of quantitative data collection. Whereas experiments involve observing people in a lab or other contrived situations, field research involves observing people in their natural settings—in their homes, their places of work, where they volunteer, and so forth. Whereas surveys ask people to answer questions according to preconstructed categories, qualitative interviews allow people to describe their feelings and experiences in their own words, similar to everyday conversation. In these ways, qualitative research better captures the naturally occurring elements of an individual's life.

Subjective and Contextual Understanding

Another strength of qualitative research is that it can provide an in-depth understanding of social–cultural meanings, processes, and contexts. To a greater extent than other methods, this understanding is achieved through the development of relationships and interactions, which, as Robert Smith (2006) suggests, enable the researcher "to see social processes that might otherwise remain hidden" (p. 351). By participating in the activities of people being studied, field researchers especially can gain an insider's view of people's worlds that quantitative methods do not allow. Qualitative interviews can provide in-depth insights into people's thoughts, feelings, and experiences that may not be possible without establishing the kind of rapport and trust with participants characteristic of this method.

Furthermore, as researchers know all too well, it is difficult to disentangle the effects of people's social context from their experiences. Experiments attempt to standardize the setting, while survey research sometimes employs statistical controls to capture some aspects of the context. By studying people *within* their sociocultural contexts, field research provides a view of people embedded within their environments.

Flexible Research Design

A final strength of qualitative research is its flexible research design. Because of its flexibility, qualitative research lends itself well to studies of dynamic situations and settings as well as to studies of populations that otherwise may be difficult to access. Suppose, for example, you are interested in how people cope with the aftermath of being a crime victim. People's responses are likely to depend on the severity of the crime and the length of time which they endured victimization. To determine the immediate impact of a criminal event, you would have to act quickly to get to the victim, observe, and interview; otherwise, the opportunity to understand certain reactions may be lost. Drafting a questionnaire or designing a probability sample of households would result in the loss of valuable time and information. Similarly, there are many groups and sub-populations for which there is no sampling frame, which is the basis of probability sampling. Among them are homeless people (Snow & Anderson, 1993), women in the hate movement (Blee, 2002), and members of a gang (Venkatesh, 2008). The nonprobability sampling techniques characteristic of qualitative research design afford researchers the flexibility to find these populations "where they are."

Another important strength of the flexibility inherent in qualitative research design is well stated by Kathy Charmaz (2006): "Qualitative researchers have one great advantage over our quantitative colleagues. We can add new pieces to the research puzzle or conjure entire new puzzles—*while we gather data*—and that can even occur late in the analysis" (p. 14). Once beyond the pretesting stage of an experiment or survey, for example, quantitative researchers are fairly locked into their design. The standardization requisite of experiments and surveys does not afford quantitative researchers the opportunity to significantly change their data collection methods midcourse, although they may (and often do) conduct post-hoc statistical analyses to explore unanticipated findings.

Generalizability

Compared to surveys, which are characterized by probability sampling, qualitative research shares with experiments a similar weakness: an inability to generalize findings to a specific population. Qualitative research is particularly adept at providing *theoretical* generalizations, but the strength of these inferences is contingent upon the care and judgment of researchers in selecting cases. One way to improve theoretical generalizations is to select cases based on their similarities with and differences from other cases. Another strategy is to sample in a way that maximizes variation in the settings and groups observed (Schwartz-Shea & Yanow, 2012, p. 85–89). David Snow and Leon Anderson (1991) used this strategy in their study of the homeless by spending "time with as many homeless as possible in the range of settings most relevant to their daily lives" (p. 155).

Reliability and Validity

Another limitation that is the object of some debate concerns the quality of the data. On the one hand, as we noted above, qualitative research can yield an insider's view of reality and an in-depth, holistic understanding that is beyond the reach of quantitative approaches. In this sense, qualitative researchers argue, their data have greater validity. Because of the depth of the relationships that qualitative researchers establish, they observe more honest behavior and get more truthful responses to their questions than the experimenter or survey researcher.

On the other hand, most qualitative research is carried out by a single observer or interviewer. The reliability and validity of the data, therefore, are highly dependent on the observational, interactive, and interpretive skills of the researcher; without the usual controls found in experiments and surveys, findings may be influenced more by the researcher's personal biases; and it is easy to imagine how another observer may see things quite differently. Furthermore, despite investigators' best efforts to blend into the setting and establish rapport as a way of encouraging participants to act and speak as they would "naturally," qualitative research may still be susceptible to reactive measurement effects. As discussed in Chapter 11, only some forms of existing/available data analysis are immune to this problem. Finally, just as surveys may not yield honest and accurate answers to questions, in-depth interviews may not either.

Researchers can effectively address some of these concerns. One of the simplest ways to enhance reliability is to conduct team research with two or more investigators. This was the approach taken by Snow and Anderson (1993) in their field research on the homeless in Austin, Texas. Smith also used this approach at times, conducting observations and interviews with students and other researchers. Qualitative researchers may also improve the quality of their data by comparing findings across different data sources: observations, interviews, and supplementary archival data. Cross-checking interviewees' accounts with other data, for instance, can assess the presence of reactivity effects as well as the tendency for interviewees to forget or misremember. This is the general model followed by field researchers, although it may not be used to the same extent in in-depth interviews as a stand-alone method. In both field research and qualitative interviews, however, interviewees' accounts of events sometimes can be crosschecked against one another.

Efficiency

Efficiency is an important consideration as you prepare to embark on your own research, likely with limited time and resources. So, it is important to realize that qualitative research can be labor-intensive and very time-consuming. To gain the kind of in-depth understanding that field research seeks to achieve, researchers must establish an accepted presence and develop relationships in the field, which can take a great deal of time and effort. And while in-depth interviews take considerably less time than field research to conduct, they tend to take longer than surveys because of the greater difficulty in selecting and recruiting interviewees and because of the greater investment made in each interview. Moreover, the amount and the form of the data often make qualitative analysis far more time-consuming than the analysis of quantitative data. On the other hand, if conducted at some nearby location, field research can be the least expensive approach. It does not require elaborate tools or equipment and, since it is typically conducted entirely by a single investigator, requires no additional personnel or training beyond the preparation of the investigator. Conducting research online can be more efficient, but this must be balanced against other costs and potential ethical concerns.

SUMMARY

The greatest strengths of qualitative research are its naturalistic approach, ability to provide subjective and contextual understandings, and flexible research design. However, qualitative research may have limited generalizability; the quality of the data depends heavily on the observational and interpretive skills of individual researchers; and it can be a relatively inefficient approach to gathering and analyzing data. Among the strategies that can strengthen field research are purposive case selection and sampling for maximum variation, employing a team approach, and comparing findings across different data sources and/or participants. Check Box 10.7 to assess your understanding of this section.

> **BOX 10.7**
>
> ## CHECKING YOUR UNDERSTANDING
>
> # Qualitative Research Review II
>
> 1. Which of the following are strengths of qualitative research?
>   a. Naturalistic approach
>   b. Generalizability
>   c. Reliability
>   d. Efficiency
>
> 2. Conducting research as a team, as Snow and Anderson did, rather than alone as individual investigators, can help qualitative researchers overcome the challenge of _____ in qualitative research.
>   a. generalizability
>   b. naturalistic approach
>   c. validity
>   d. reliability
>
> 3. Qualitative research can yield an insider's view of reality and an in-depth understanding that is beyond quantitative research; however, despite a researcher's best efforts to establish rapport and blend into the setting, qualitative research may still be susceptible to reactive measurement effects, which may impact which of the following?
>   a. Efficiency
>   b. Generalizability
>   c. Validity
>   d. Contextual understanding
>
> **Answers: 1. a, 2. d, 3. c**

KEY TERMS

analytic memo, p. 297
covert observation, p. 282
ethnography, p. 272
field jottings, p. 296
field notes, p. 296
focus group, p. 286
gatekeeper, p. 293
grand tour question, p. 302
guiding question, p. 290
in-depth interview, p. 276
interview guide, p. 301
key informant, p. 295
netnography, p. 287
nonparticipant observation, p. 280
overt observation, p. 282
participant observation, p. 280
probes, p. 301
reflexivity, p. 279
semi-structured interview, p. 285
unstructured interview, p. 285

KEY POINTS

- The two principal methods of qualitative research are field research, which is based primarily on observation, and in-depth interviewing.
- In addition to observations and interviews, qualitative researchers tend to use supplementary archival data, nonprobability sampling, and qualitative data analysis.
- A unique feature of qualitative research is reflexivity, or researchers' reflections on how their experiences and personal characteristics influence the acquisition of knowledge.
- Observations in field research vary in the researcher's level of participation in the groups and settings under observation and the extent to which the researcher reveals their identity as a researcher.
- Interviews vary in structure, ranging from unstructured conversations to semi-structured in-depth interviews, and in number of interviewees.
- In focus group interviews, the researcher acts as a moderator or facilitator of group discussion and observes interaction among participants.
- The nonlinear process of conducting field research includes selecting a setting/group, gaining access, establishing roles and relationships, deciding what to observe/whom to interview, gathering and analyzing data, exiting the field, and writing a report.
- The nonlinear process of conducting qualitative interviews includes selecting and recruiting interviewees, developing an interview guide, gathering data, and analyzing data.
- The strengths of qualitative research include its naturalistic approach, ability to provide subjective and contextual understandings, and flexible research design.
- Qualitative research is highly dependent on the interpersonal and interpretive skills of the researcher, may be subject to reactive measurement effects, tends to be limited in generalizability, and is usually labor-intensive and time-consuming.

REVIEW QUESTIONS

1. What are the six general features of qualitative research?
2. How can observations and interviews complement one another in qualitative research?
3. Using Figure 10.2 as a reference, describe the ways in which observations in field research vary.
4. What are the relative advantages and disadvantages of group interviews as compared to individual interviews?
5. Give an example of how a researcher's personal characteristics may affect (a) field research and (b) in-depth interviews.

6. How and when do field researchers record their observations?
7. Describe how the processes of conducting (a) field research and (b) in-depth interviews are "nonlinear."
8. What are the major strengths and limitations of qualitative research?

EXERCISES

1. In final reports of quantitative and qualitative research, authors rarely report all the details of their studies, especially problems they encountered or mistakes they made. A special issue of the *Journal of Contemporary Ethnography* (39, no. 5 [2010]) includes some of these "seldom told tales from the field." Read this issue and identify some of the challenges that qualitative researchers face.
2. In the May 2020 issue of *Social Problems* (67, no. 2, 191–207), Forrest Stuart describes a field research study in which he studied the lives of gang-associated youth. Read this article and then answer the following questions.

    a. What is the main research question?
    b. What are three means of data collection that Stuart used?
    c. Why was the addition of the netnography of the youth's social media an important element in this study?
    d. How do the interviews complement the data obtained from participant observation?
    e. Provide one example of how data from observation, interviews, or social media corresponded to one another.
    f. How is this research impactful for the real world?

3. A maxim of field research is that there is more to observation than meets the eye. To better understand this, select a public setting, such as a cafeteria, coffee shop, library, or student lounge where you can unobtrusively observe others without anyone questioning your presence. Your research objective is to describe as fully as possible how people use this space. Are they alone or with others? In what sort of activities are they engaged? How long are they in the setting? And so forth. Before entering the field, you should consider what to observe and record: think about dimensions of the setting, actors, events, and processes. Plan to observe for at least an hour during a relatively busy time of the day and focus on a clearly delimited area such as a set of tables. Record your field notes as soon after leaving the field as possible, then go over your notes and develop a coding scheme for organizing the information.
4. Suppose you want to gain valuable qualitative interview practice by interviewing members of your class about their decision to pursue a criminal justice degree. Develop an interview guide that would be useful for this topic.

5. One of the best ways of learning is by doing—and, sometimes, making mistakes. To learn about some common challenges that students experienced in conducting in-depth interviews, read Kathryn Roulston, Kathleen deMarrais, and Jamie B. Lewis's "Learning to Interview in the Social Sciences" (*Qualitative Inquiry*, 9, no. 4 [2003], pp. 643–668). Then, with the appropriate permissions, conduct a recorded interview yourself and analyze it, preferably with a seasoned researcher (as these authors analyze their students' interviews), to determine how you can improve your interviewing skills.

11

Existing Data Analysis

Using Data from Secondhand Sources

CHAPTER OUTLINE

11.1 Sources and Examples of Existing Data 315
- Public Documents and Official Records 316
- Private Documents 318
- Mass Media 318
- Physical, Nonverbal Evidence 320
- Criminal Justice Data Archives 321
- Summary 321

11.2 Content Analysis 322
- Content Analysis Example: Portrayal of Mental Illness in US Crime Dramas 323
- The Process of Content Analysis 324
- Summary 331

11.3 Comparative Historical Analysis 332
- An Example of Comparative Historical Analysis: The Emergence of Mass Imprisonment 332
- The Process of Comparative Historical Analysis 335
- Summary 339

11.4 Strengths and Limitations of Existing Data Analysis 340
- Studying Social Structure, History, and Social Change 340
- Nonreactive Measurement 341
- Cost Efficiency 341
- Data Limitations 341
- Summary 342

LEARNING OBJECTIVES

By the end of this chapter, you should be able to

11.1 Give examples of the range and potential uses of existing data.

11.2 Describe the steps in content analysis and apply them to a research topic.

11.3 Describe the steps in comparative historical analysis and apply them to a research topic.

11.4 Evaluate existing data analysis as a general approach to criminal justice research, identifying its strengths and limitations.

In this chapter we explore the analysis of existing data. What does existing data analysis have to do with you? You may have made a very important life decision on the basis of it. As you considered what college or university to attend, you might have examined the *US News and World Report* Best Colleges rankings. For the most part, *US News* does not collect original data; rather, it relies on data that schools routinely collect and provide, which it supplements with information from other sources. *US News* then compiles and analyzes these data to produce the numerical rankings, which are determined by several factors, including students' graduation rates, alumni giving, faculty resources, and overall financial resources.

This example captures the essence of *existing data analysis*. Existing data analysis departs from experiments, surveys, field research, and in-depth interviews in that it makes use of data produced by others, regardless of whether these data were intended for the purposes of research. Data can be found everywhere—death certificates, business personnel records, newspaper articles, Google trends, and even garbage. The sources are limited only by the researcher's imagination.

We begin the chapter by describing the diversity of data available to the imaginative researcher. Some existing data, such as statistics on births, deaths, marriages, and the like, are inherently quantitative; other data, such as letters and diaries, are best analyzed qualitatively. Thus, the diverse sources of existing data give rise to very different forms of analysis, with distinct research purposes. To illustrate the analysis of existing data, we consider three major methods: analysis of existing statistical data, content analysis, and comparative historical analysis. In each case, we present a research example that addresses a contemporary criminal justice issue and describe the general process of carrying out the research. We conclude by discussing general strengths and limitations of existing data analysis.

11.1 SOURCES AND EXAMPLES OF EXISTING DATA

The sources of existing data may be placed in five broad categories:

1. public documents and official records, including the extensive archives of the Census Bureau;
2. private documents;
3. mass media;
4. physical, nonverbal materials; and
5. criminal justice data archives.

Table 11.1 presents a short, partial list of *official* data sources and the kinds of statistics they provide. These statistics are the primary data sources for many studies. They also are used as supplementary information. Although these categories provide a useful summary of data sources, keep in mind that they overlap and that analysts may draw on more than one data source in any given study.

Table 11.1 Some Sources of Existing Official Statistics

Source	Sample Statistics
US Census Bureau	National, state, and local populations by age, sex, race, foreign-born, education, income
National Center for Education Statistics	Enrollment, racial/ethnic composition, dropout rate, expenditures from prekindergarten through graduate school
Bureau of Justice Statistics	Crime, criminal offenders, victims of crime
Centers for Disease Control and Prevention	Births, deaths, injuries, obesity, smoking, various diseases
World Health Organization	Life expectancy, infant mortality, causes of death, infectious diseases, physicians, hospitals
Federal Bureau of Investigations	Crime, law enforcement officer deaths, hate crimes, use of force, police employment
National Institute on Drug Abuse	Adolescent drug use, substance use trends
Federal Bureau of Prisons	Inmates, prison population, prison staff

Public Documents and Official Records

Exemplifying the existing data approach is the historian who searches the written record for traces of events and processes from the past. A great deal of this record is public and can be found in **archives**—document collections located in physical and digital libraries. In addition, documents created to ensure the normal functioning of offices and departments are maintained at every level of government in every society throughout the world. These include the proceedings of government bodies, court records, state laws, and city ordinances. Many government agencies also maintain numerous volumes of official statistics. Add to this directories, almanacs, and publication indexes such as the *New York Times Index* and *Reader's Guide to Periodical Literature*, and one can imagine the massive information available from public records.

archive a physical or digital library that contains a collection of historical documents or records

An especially rich data source is **vital statistics**: data on births, deaths, marriages, divorces, and the like. By state law, all births must be recorded, and death records must be filed before burial permits can be obtained. Birth records provide information not only on the child born but also on the parents, including their full names, address(es), ages, and usual occupations. Similarly, death records may contain, in addition to the usual biographical information, data on cause of death; length of illness (where applicable); whether injuries were accidental, homicidal, or self-inflicted; and the time and place of death. Ordinarily, the researcher obtains these records from an agency such

vital statistics data collected from the registration of "vital" life events, such as births, deaths, marriages, and divorces

as the Centers for Disease Control and Prevention (CDC), which compiles data for the nation as a whole, or from international organizations such as the United Nations, which compile such statistics for the world.

In a recent study, researchers used death records obtained from the CDC to calculate homicide rates for Black people and White people, which they linked to residential segregation (Light & Thomas, 2019). The data showed that racial segregation increases the risk of homicide for Black people, but decreases the risk of homicide for White people. Consequently, the decline in segregation since 1970 has substantially reduced the gap between Black and White homicides.

Perhaps the most widely used public storehouse of data is that collected and maintained by the US Bureau of the Census. According to the Constitution, every person in the nation must be counted at least once every 10 years. The censuses of population and housing gather information on the composition of every household in the country. In 2020, this included data on the age, gender, and race of each person, number of household members, and whether the residence was a house, apartment, or mobile home. Data from these decennial censuses, which began in 1790, are made available in two different forms: aggregate and individual. Aggregate data are released within months of their collection and describe various characteristics of the population of the states, counties, metropolitan areas, cities and towns, neighborhood tracts, and blocks.

Criminal justice researchers have used these data to study how the ecology of cities, residential mobility, and racial segregation impact crime. As an example, the aforementioned study on homicide rates and residential segregation used aggregate level data from US censuses of the population. Specifically, data regarding poverty, unemployment, single-parent families, residential instability, and foreign-born population were obtained from the US Census.

Beginning with the 1960 census, the bureau also has made available individual-level data (actual census responses) on a sample of the population, called the Public Use Microdata Sample (PUMS). A 1 percent PUMS sample is available for 1960 and 1970 and both 1 percent and 5 percent samples are available for subsequent censuses. To ensure confidentiality, the bureau removes names, addresses, and all other personal identifying information from these sample files. A project called IPUMS (the "I" is for "Integrated") is extending this series to other years and integrating the data over time by creating uniform codes for variables (IPUMS USA, 2020). All IPUMS data are available free online. In addition to the variables available through the Census, the IPUMS data include information such as people's wages, country of birth, and citizenship status. Nattahicha Chairassamee (2018) used these data to examine the impact that crime has on an individual's decision to move to another state. Among their findings were that the ratio of crimes between one's current state and the state of consideration is associated with one's decision to move. However, crime type tends to influence the decision, with people being less likely to move if the rate of violent crime is higher, but still willing to move if property crimes are higher. Demographic factors such as age, education, and income level were not found to influence interstate migrants' concerns about crime.

Private Documents

A less accessible but no less important data source is private documents: information produced by individuals or organizations about their own activities that is not intended for public consumption. Diaries and letters long have been a favorite data source for the historian; other examples would be businesses' personnel and sales records, inventories, and tax reports; hospital patient records; and college transcripts.

An example of the use of private documents is Robert J. Kane and Michael D. White's (2009) study exploring correlates of police misconduct, which drew upon confidential New York City Police Department personnel files. The study compared personnel and career histories of all NYPD officers who had been dismissed for cause between 1975 and 1996 with a randomly selected sample of peer officers who had served with honor. Through their research, a number of significant predictors of misconduct were identified, including race of the officer, level of education, lack of advancement with the agency, and a history of prior criminality, poor employment, and/or citizen complaints.

Institutional records also have been used to supplement survey data. For example, Lahm (2016) used official prison misconduct reports to explore whether certain characteristics of female inmates predicted either the likelihood of perpetrating an offense or becoming a victim.

Mass Media

Also constituting part of the written record (as well as an oral and nonverbal record) are the media—books, newspapers, magazines, television, radio, films, and the internet. The internet contains numerous links to online data archives as well as the public's online search habits (Google Trends). Moreover, social network analysis programs, such as NodeXL have been developed that allow researchers to extract data from various social media outlets to identify public sentiment, communication activity, key influencers, etc. (For a description of these new online and other digitized data sources, see Box 11.1.) By analyzing the content of these various sources, criminal justice researchers have addressed a variety of issues, from what online media reports reveal about regional differences in police-related fatalities (Schwartz & Jahn, 2020) to the portrayal of offenders and victims of fatal family violence in US national news media coverage (Grau, 2021) to how newspaper reports framed the depiction of the opioid crisis in North America (Webster et al., 2020).

BOX 11.1

READING CRIMINAL JUSTICE RESEARCH

The Big Data Revolution

Around 2000, "very few people were using the term 'big data'" (Kitchin, 2014, p. 67). Since then, it has become a buzzword in industry and academia. The term first appeared in academic publications in 2011 (Jenkins et al., 2016). Now, big data is used extensively in criminal justice research and even within the criminal justice system, as datafication (the quantifying of social life) becomes more common (Lavorgna & Ugwudike, 2021).

The term *big data* refers to unusually large data sets that are generated digitally and require sophisticated computational methods (Lewis, 2015, p. 1). It is a product of the movement of organizations toward digital records (McFarland et al., 2016, p. 15) and the "digitization of social life" (Lazer & Radford, 2017, p. 19). You can appreciate the enormous growth in the digitization of social life when you realize that "we generate data whenever we go online, when we carry our GPS-equipped smartphones, when we communicate with our friends through social media or chat applications, and when we shop. You could say we leave digital footprints with everything we do that involves a digital transaction, which is almost everything" (Marr, 2017).

A few examples illustrate the scope and variety of research using big data:

- Crime data analysis is used to predict concentrations of crime at specific times and in specific locations in order to inform policing strategies and allow police to more proactively prevent crime from happening (Rummens et al., 2021). Typical crime rates are calculated using a residential population, a static measure of the number of people who live in a particular area. However, Rummens and colleagues argue that crime rates should be calculated using the ambient population, the number of people present in a particular area at a given time. To determine which measure of population performed better as a predictor for crime events, they utilized 9,397,473 mobile phone data points. They found that the ambient population measure was more strongly correlated with crime, and should be used for predictive policing.

- Oh, Zhang, and Greenleaf (2022) utilized Twitter messages to examine public sentiment of policing in different geographical locations. For data, they collected 3,917,894 tweet text messages that included the word *police* from October 2018 to June 2019. Additional data were pulled from the 2017 Uniform Crime Report as well as the 2017 American Community Survey. The results revealed a number of correlates of public sentiment. Twitter users who lived in areas with higher violent crime rates and greater racial heterogeneity were more likely to post negative messages about the police.

As these examples show, big data present opportunities for criminal justice research. At this early stage, a primary source of big data for criminal justice researchers is social media, especially Facebook and X (formerly Twitter). Researchers have viewed these platforms in two ways: as a generalizable microcosm of society and a distinctive realm of human

continues

continued

> experience (Lazer & Radford, 2017). In either case, it is important to remember that "big data are almost always convenience samples" (Lazer & Radford, 2017). In reality, "certain kinds of people are more likely than others to turn up in certain digital data sets"; even if the data set contains "every phone call, every message, or every friendship," not everyone owns a cell phone, is on X (formerly Twitter), or has a Facebook account (Lewis, 2015, pp. 1–2).
>
> The analysis of big data poses methodological challenges. One challenge is the varied and complex structure of the data. Unlike a simple subject × variable matrix of data (see Chapter 14), which can be analyzed with standard computer software and statistics, big data often have a different structure (e.g., with Facebook data, subject × subject) or format (narrative text and photos) that are not easily combined or analyzed. The analysis of data of such variety (and scale) requires advanced technical training, which is why "the first wave of studies" of big data "has been dominated by physical, computer, and information scientists" (Golder & Macy, 2014, p. 145).
>
> There also are major ethical issues regarding the use of big data. For example, ordinarily, obtaining informed consent and anonymizing data protect privacy. But both of these processes may be inadequate in the age of big data. Aside from typically unread use agreements, there are no protections for human participants on the internet. Further, several examples of big-data research that attempted to anonymize the data failed to prevent the identification of individuals (Zook et al., 2017). According to federal regulations, research using public data sets is exempt from IRB review, with the assumption being that "public" data are inherently low risk. But big data are forcing scientists to reconsider the ethical rules. Combining big data sets and other publicly available data, for example, can pose risks to individuals by revealing sensitive information such as political views, annual income, and sexual orientation (Metcalf & Crawford, 2016).
>
> Criminal justice is just beginning to take advantage of the opportunities afforded by big data; however, many challenges lie ahead (Brady, 2019).

big data unusually large data sets that are collected digitally and, because of their variety and structure, may require sophisticated computational methods

Physical, Nonverbal Evidence

Although seldom used in criminal justice, nonverbal materials such as graffiti, trash, and abandoned cars have been used as a source of data. One example of the use of physical evidence can be seen in studies testing the broken windows thesis, such as Keuschnigg and Wolbring's (2014) study discussed previously in Chapter 6. Recall that broken windows theory asserts that minor signs of physical and social disorder within a neighborhood will lead to increased signs of disorder, as it sends the message that "nobody cares" about the area (Wilson & Kelling, 1982). To measure the consequences of physical disorder, Keuschniig and Wolbring placed fliers on bicycles outside of dorm rooms in two different settings: a clean setting of the dorm parking area and a heavily littered setting of the dorm parking area. To measure the consequences of disorder (i.e., heavily littered area), they counted the number of fliers that were thrown on the ground. Others have measured physical disorder via the presence or absence of a series of items within a given area such as graffiti, beer or liquor cans or bottles, cigarette butts, litter or broken glass, abandoned cars, condoms, drug paraphernalia, etc. (Quinn et al., 2016; Sampson & Raudenbush, 1999).

Criminal Justice Data Archives

Over the last 50 years, the field of criminal justice has seen a tremendous proliferation of **data archives**, repositories of data collected by various agencies and researchers that are accessible to the public. Most of these archives contain survey data, but archives also exist for collections of ethnographies and in-depth interviews. Thus, the use of data archives is an extension of survey research, field research, and in-depth interviews.

We already mentioned the analysis of existing survey data, called *secondary analysis*, in Chapter 9. A noteworthy example is the General Social Survey (GSS), whose data are deposited in several archives, including the ICPSR (Inter-University Consortium for Political and Social Research) and the Survey Documentation and Analysis Archive. Through these archives, you can find other survey data sets, such as the Survey of Prison Inmates (SPI), which provides "national statistics on prisoner characteristics across a variety of domains, such as current offense and sentence, incident characteristics, firearm possession and sources, criminal history, demographic and socioeconomic characteristics, family background, drug and alcohol use and treatment, mental and physical health and treatment, and facility programs and rules violations" (Bureau of Justice Statistics, 2021, para. 1), as well as the Monitoring the Future Survey, which collects substance use information annually from 8th, 10th, and 12th grade students.

> **data archives** repositories of survey, ethnographic, or qualitative interview data collected by various agencies and researchers that are accessible to the public

SUMMARY

As you can see, there is an abundance of existing data that may be used to address a wide range of research questions. Sources of these data include public documents and official statistics maintained by virtually every society throughout the world; private and personal records; mass media; physical, nonverbal materials; and criminal justice data archives. In the remainder of the chapter, we focus on publicly accessible data and mass media, which comprise much of existing data research. Check Box 11.2 to assess your understanding of this section.

> **BOX 11.2**
>
> **CHECKING YOUR UNDERSTANDING**
>
> ## Data Sources
>
> 1. Vital statistics refer to data on
>   a. births, deaths, and marriages
>   b. economic indicators such as GNP and GDP
>   c. sex and race of US residents counted in the census
>   d. individual physical attributes, such as height and weight
>
> 2. Private documents as data sources would include all but which one of the following?
>   a. Hospital patient records
>   b. City directories
>   c. Personal letters
>   d. College transcripts
>
> 3. All of the following are a form in which census data are made available to the public, except
>   a. aggregate data on states and counties
>   b. aggregate data on cities and towns
>   c. individual census records, 10 years after the census
>   d. a sample of individual-level data with names and other identifying information removed
>
> Answers: 1. a, 2. b, 3. d

11.2 CONTENT ANALYSIS

content analysis systematic analysis of the symbolic content of communications in which the content is reduced to a set of coded variables or categories

The second analytic technique, **content analysis**, is not a single method but a set of procedures for systematically analyzing the symbolic content of recorded communications. In all communications, a sender conveys a message to an audience. The aim of content analysis is to make valid inferences about the sender, the message itself, or the intended audience (Weber, 1990). Although the inferences depend on the research question, the basic approach is the same: to reduce the total content of a communication (e.g., all of the words or all of the visual imagery) to a set of coded variables, categories, or themes. This approach differs from the analysis of existing statistics in two important ways: it generates its own statistics and it analyzes the *content* of communications.

Content analysis encompasses a great deal. First, the "data" or "content" of the analysis may include printed matter and oral recordings as well as visual communications and works of art. Second, content analysis is not limited to existing data; it also may be applied to the analysis of responses to open-ended questions in survey research and to the coding of field notes in field research. Third, content analysis may be either qualitative or quantitative. In this chapter, we focus on content analysis of existing data as a form of deductive, quantitative research.

Content analysis may involve either manual or computer coding of message content. (Recall from Chapter 9 that *coding* is the assignment of a number or label to a piece of textual data.) Manual coding is more common and may be applied to a broader range of content than computer coding, which is used almost exclusively to analyze transcribed verbal materials. Therefore, we focus on manual coding. We begin by describing one study in detail. Then, as we discuss the process of content analysis, we introduce additional examples, including one that uses computer coding.

Content Analysis Example: Portrayal of Mental Illness in US Crime Dramas

Television shows consistently portray inaccurate stereotypes of the mentally ill. For example, many crime shows portray mentally ill suspects as unpredictable, chaotic, and violent (Link & Phelan, 2014). These negative, inaccurate portrayals have contributed to society's stigma of the mentally ill (Wahl, 2003), and resulted in devastating effects for those who struggle with a mental illness including discrimination across a variety of areas such as housing, health, employment, etc. (Corrigan, 2004). Recognizing the role that the media plays in public perceptions of the mentally ill, Parrott and Parrott (2015) sought to examine how popular fictional crime-based dramas portrayed those with mental illness. The study had a number of objectives. First, the researchers noted that much of the research examining media's portrayal of the mentally ill was data. Thus, they aimed to see whether television continued to portray the mentally ill in an inaccurate and stereotypical fashion. Consistent with prior research they hypothesized that:

1) Characters who were labeled mentally ill would be more likely to be associated with violence as (a) victims of violence and (b) perpetrators of violence than characters in the general character population of crime-based television dramas from 2010–2013.
2) Characters who were labeled mentally ill would also be more likely to be (a) victims of crime and (b) perpetrators of crime. (p. 644)

To test these hypotheses, Parrott and Parrott analyzed 983 characters from 65 randomly selected television episodes of US fictional crime-based dramas that aired during the 2010–2013 seasons. Sample selection occurred in a few stages. First, the researchers consulted websites for the major US television networks as well as viewership information from industry websites to determine which shows to include. They then indexed all episodes of the selected crime-shows that aired during the 2010–2013 season. Examples of the selected shows include *Blue Bloods, Bones, CSI, Law and Order: Special Victims Unit,* and *NCIS*. The researchers numbered the episodes from each show and then utilized a random generator to determine which 65 episodes to code.

Once the episodes were selected, Parrott and Parrott developed a coding scheme, which two coders applied. To test their hypotheses, the coders rated each focal character, "people who appeared on screen for 10 seconds or more (throughout the episode) and whose facial features were clearly discernible at least once during that period" (pp. 646–647), on 80 items, including demographic information, the character's role in the episode, mental illness labels, violence victimization and perpetration, crime victimization and perpetration, physical appearance, and social standing (for a more thorough discussion of the coding scheme, refer to the article). The independent variable consisted of whether a character was either self-labeled or labeled by another character as mentally ill. The dependent variables consisted of whether the character was a victim and/or perpetrator of either explicit and/or implied violence and whether the character was a victim and/or perpetrator of crime. Violence referred to "the use or verbal threat of physical force such as hitting, kicking, punching, slapping, stabbing, and shooting, regardless of whether physical harm occurred" (pp. 647–648). A character was coded as a victim of crime if they "experienced harm or negative consequences through the illegal actions of another individual or group" (p. 648). Those characters who actually committed an illegal action, on the other hand, were coded as crime perpetrators. Eighteen different crimes were coded, ranging from murder and rape/sexual assault to verbal dispute and driving under the influence.

The analyses consistently supported Parrott and Parrott's hypotheses. They found that the mentally ill characters were significantly more likely to be both victims and perpetrators of violence. Approximately 50% of the mentally ill characters were presented as committing or being a victim of violence, compared to approximately 20% and 30% of characters from the television general population, respectively. A similar result was found when exploring mental illness and crime perpetration. Characters with a mental illness were significantly more likely to be a perpetrator of a crime. Interestingly, however, no significant difference was found for crime victimization.

The Process of Content Analysis

Now that you are familiar with a research example, let us take a closer look at the steps in carrying out a content analysis. Figure 11.1 shows the major steps. Some of the steps may be skipped, depending on whether human or computer coding is used. For example, without the need for human coders, computer coding does not entail coder training or checks for reliability. In addition, although we present the steps as separate methodological decisions, some steps may be interdependent, depending on the type of communication—for example, text or visual images—being analyzed.

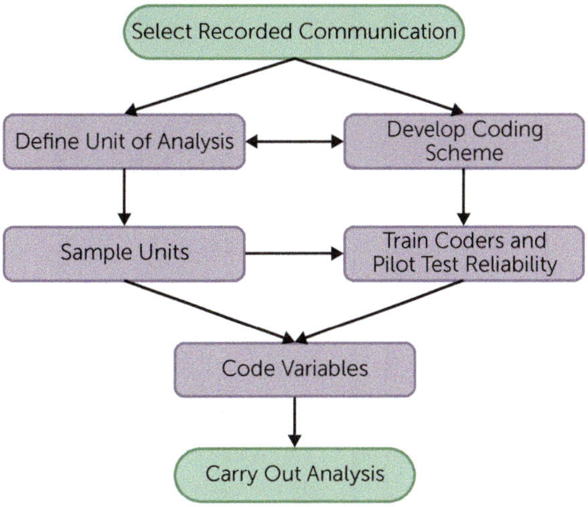

SELECT RECORDED COMMUNICATION

As in all forms of criminal justice research, the initial steps in content analysis depend on the research question, which determines what content will be examined and why (Neuendorf, 2002). Content analysis also may be applied to describe patterns and trends in content and to examine the association between communication content and social behavior. The sources of analyzable content include print and broadcast media, websites, tweets, photos, videos, music, interviews, and any other communication that has been or can be recorded.

DEFINE UNITS OF ANALYSIS

FIGURE 11.1 The Process of Content Analysis

In much criminal justice research, the units of analysis are whole elements that cannot be subdivided. Each individual interviewed in survey research, for example, is an integral unit, and in sampling, collecting, and analyzing survey data, the unit is the same. By contrast, the units of content analysis often can be segmented and may differ for purposes of sampling, coding, and analysis. For example, the text of a news article can be broken down into words, sentences, paragraphs, or some other grammatical unit.

The segmentation of units gives rise to two primary types of units in content analysis: sampling units and recording units. Sampling units serve as the basis for identifying and sampling the target population (Neuendorf, 2002). Parrott and Parrott's (2015) target population consisted of all episodes from "fictional crime-based dramas from the 2010–2013 seasons of US basic cable television programming" (p. 646). Their sampling unit, therefore, was the whole episode. **Recording units** (also called **coding units**) refer to that part of a communication that is the basis for coding; in an analysis of text, it is that element of the text described by the coded variables. Parrott and Parrott's recording unit was the same as their sampling unit: the episode. By comparison, in a content analysis of race and gender images in introductory criminal justice and criminology textbooks, the sampling unit was introductory criminology and criminal justice textbooks and the recording unit was images that featured White and minority men and women (Eigenberg & Park, 2016). To further clarify this distinction, see Box 11.3.

recording units the units of analysis in content analysis, such as words, sentences, paragraphs, and whole articles (also called coding units)

DEVELOP CODING SCHEME

Developing a coding scheme is a matter of operationalizing the variables in the researcher's hypothesis. The key variables in Parrott and Parrot's hypotheses were mental illness labels, violence (victim and/or perpetrator), and crime (victim and/or perpetrator). They operationalized mental illness based on whether characters

> **BOX 11.3**
>
> ## CHECKING YOUR UNDERSTANDING
>
> ### Identifying Units of Analysis
>
> Prior to this chapter, we have restricted ourselves almost exclusively to individuals as the units of analysis. As you will recall, units of analysis are the cases or entities you study; they are the things that variables describe. In nearly all experiments and surveys, the unit of analysis is the individual. But in much research using existing data, the unit is a social aggregate such as a small group, formal organization, or nation, or a social artifact such as a news report, book, or magazine. Now we have added another distinction among units that often occurs in content analysis: sampling units, which are the basis of sampling, and recording units, which are the basis for analyzing content. To check your understanding of these concepts, we ask you to identify the relevant units in the following study.
>
> The media plays a significant role in shaping public opinion about crime. How reporters craft their stories along with the images they choose to include has the ability to provide an unbalanced understanding of crime. Interested in exploring whether differences exist in the portrayals of minorities in print media in comparison to White people, Alayna Colburn and Lisa Melander (2018) conducted an ethnographic content analysis of newspaper crime stories and accompanying images. Crime articles were selected from five widely circulated newspapers published between August 1, 2014 and October 31, 2014. To explore whether racialized text was used in the reporter's writing, a text analysis was conducted on all 292 crime articles. A detailed visual analysis was conducted on 112 crime articles that included an accompanying photo.
>
> a. What is the sampling unit in this study?
>
> b. There are two recording units. What are they?
>
> **Answers: a. Crime article is the sampling unit. b. One recording unit is the text of the article; the other recording unit consists of the image(s) accompanying the article.**

were given a label of mentally ill by either the character themselves (e.g., "I have schizophrenia") or another character within the show (e.g., "He has schizophrenia") (p. 647). Then they identified a set of variables that represented one being a victim and/or perpetrator of violence, either implicit or explicit, as well as a victim and/

or perpetrator of crime. A number of other variables not included in their primary analysis were also coded for including social standing, physical characteristics, criminal history, extent of inflicted harm, the relationship between the perpetrator and victim, and the weapon used.

All variables to be coded are included within the coding scheme along with the codes for each variable. To the extent that human coders are used, selecting and coding the variables in content analysis is analogous to deciding on a set of closed-ended questions in survey research. Instead of giving the questions to respondents who provide the answers, the content analyst applies them to a document or image. The "questions" applied to the document should be adequate for the research purpose, and the codes should be clearly defined, exhaustive, and mutually exclusive.

The way researchers code variables determines *how* the data may be quantified. Below is a list of the most common ways of measuring and quantifying the data:

1. *Appearance.* The simplest method is to code the presence or absence of message content. Parrott and Parrott applied this method: they recorded whether specific labels or actions, as defined by their variables, *appeared* for each character. Although appearance measures tend to be rather imprecise, they can be applied to a large range of content.
2. *Intensity.* When attitudes and values are the objects of the research, the content analyst may use measures of intensity. An example would be the coding of the "valence" of drug and alcohol references in song lyrics—whether the lyrics presented substance use as negative, neutral, or positive.
3. *Time–space measures.* Early content analysts of (physical) newspapers often measured the space devoted to certain topics. Analogously, television content has been measured in time (e.g., the number of hours of televised violence). Space–time measures may appropriately describe gross characteristics of the media, but they are too imprecise to serve as indicators of most verbal content.
4. *Frequency.* In computer analyses of textual content, variables often are defined and measured in terms of the frequency with which a given category of words appears. In an analysis of tweets from the Toronto Police Service and citizens, Kudla and Parnaby (2018) used text mining software to identify the number of tweets that contained words associated with specific categories such as *crime, missing persons, praise for police, critical of police*, etc. We will tell you more about this study, including the main findings, next.

Once key variables have been identified and operationalized, the content analyst constructs either a codebook (for manual coding) or dictionary (for computer coding). A content analysis **codebook** consists of a list of the variables to be coded together with definitions, codes, and guidelines for applying the codes. Codebooks guide coders in locating and coding variables. Figure 11.2 presents the codebook for Everhart and

codebook a guide for coding that consists of a list of the variables together with definitions, codes, and instructions for applying the codes

> Code Book
> 1. <u>Film title</u>: List the name of the Disney film.
> 2. <u>Total Running Time</u>: List the amount of minutes the film runs.
> 3. <u>Coding Sheet#</u>: Record the number of the coding sheet. Begin with number one, and prepare one coding sheet for each violent incident per film. For instance, if there are five violent incidents, there should be five coding sheets, numbered one through five.
> 4. <u>Film Release Date</u>: List the year the film was released.
> 5. <u>Coder</u>: List the name of the coder.
> 6. <u>Date</u>: Record the date the coding is performed.
> 7. <u>Violence</u>: Circle the type of violence used in the film. More than one type of violence may be circled during one incident: (a) Character's body part, (b) Sword, (c) Gun, (d) Magic, (e) Explosives, (f) Poison, (g) Other (i.e., this includes any item, which does not fit in categories a-f).
> 8. <u>Demographics</u>: (a) Circle the character's role (i.e., Protagonist, Antagonist, or Supporting Character), (b) Circle the character's type (i.e., Human or NonHuman), and circle the character's gender (i.e., Male or Female), (c) Circle the character's age (i.e., Child, Teen, or Adult).
> 9. <u>Name of character</u>: List the name of the character or characters involved in the violent incident.
> 10. <u>Context</u>: Circle the context of the violence (i.e., Accepted, Rejected, or Unknown).

FIGURE 11.2 The Codebook for Everhart and Aust's Content Analysis of Violence in Animated Disney Films

Aust's (2006) content analysis of violence in animated Disney films. Other codebooks may contain more elaborate information and guidelines.

dictionary
in computerized content analysis, the set of words, phrases, or other word-based indicators (e.g., word length) that is the basis for a search of texts

A **dictionary** for computer text analysis "is a set of words, phrases, parts of speech, or other word-based indicators (e.g., word length, number of syllables) that is used as the basis for a search of texts" (Neuendorf, 2002, p. 127). Studies usually have several dictionaries, each representing the measurement of a variable. To analyze the content of tweets, Kudla and Parnaby (2018) created a dictionary to identify words representing specific categories. For example, in order for a tweet to be categorized as "missing person," the tweet had to include words such as *looking for*, *missing*, and mention of a man/woman/boy/girl (see Table 11.2). Like codebooks, a set of content analysis dictionaries generally contains variable or category names, rules for assigning text, and the specific text (e.g., words) to be assigned. Researchers may construct their own dictionaries, use standard dictionaries that accompany the computer program being used, or use dictionaries developed for specific content areas.

SAMPLE UNITS

Because content analysis is a labor-intensive activity for human coders, it is seldom possible to analyze all of the typically large volume of available texts and images. Yet, sampling is complicated for several reasons: there may be more than one unit to sample; not

Table 11.2 Kudla and Parnaby's Dictionary for Missing Persons

Rule	Category	Notes
@torontopolice & looking for & missing & (man|woman|boy|girl)	Missing Person	Looks for the first three concepts and at least one of man, woman, boy, or girl
@torontopolice & (great work|good job|nicely done)	Praise for Police	Looks for the first concept and at least one of great work, good job, or nicely done
@torontopolice & investigating &! (collision)	Crime	The first two concepts must be present but excludes tweets that *also* make reference to a collision

all text and images may be equally relevant to the research question; and, unlike survey researchers, content analysts are seldom interested in making precise statistical inferences about the population of texts or images (Krippendorff, 2004). In general, when sampling in content analysis, you should aim to select a manageable amount of content-analyzable material that provides a valid answer to the research question. Parrott and Parrott, for example, randomly selected 65 episodes from 15 different fictional crime-based television dramas that aired during the 2010–2013 seasons to examine how mental illness was portrayed in US crime dramas.

Many content analyses of the media *do focus* on text and images that are most likely to reach the consumer. Some of these studies purposefully select units to address the research question. For example, to study portrayals of alcohol and drugs in popular songs, Peter Christenson, Donald Roberts, and Nicholas Bjork (2012) aimed "to examine the songs most likely to reach the ears of young listeners over an extended period of time" (p. 126). Therefore, they selected the top 100 *Billboard* songs from each of the years 1968, 1978, 1988, 1998, and 2008. Other studies use probability sampling to provide statistically accurate estimates of media content. The National Television Violence Study (Wilson et al., 1997), which measured the amount of violence on television, constructed a sampling frame consisting of all television programs aired between 6 a.m. and 11 p.m. for 20 weeks between October 1994 and June 1995 in the Los Angeles market. Then the researchers randomly selected two half-hour time slots for each channel during each week that the sampling covered.

One development that has facilitated content analysis is the creation of a wide array of message archives, many available online, which can serve as sampling frames for selecting content. Parrott and Parrott used several online sources, including websites for major US television networks (ABC, CBS, FOX, NBC) and industry websites that document television viewership (Deadline, TV by the Numbers), to compile a list of fictional crime-based television dramas. Christenson and colleagues (2012) used several lyric websites to compile lyrics for the top 100 *Billboard* songs they analyzed. Other content analysts may draw on archives of television news and programs, political ads, and films.

TRAIN CODERS AND PILOT-TEST RELIABILITY

Although content analysis may be undertaken by a sole researcher, most often it involves multiple coders. To assure reliable and valid measurement, it is important to train coders. In Parrott and Parrott's study, the lead investigator trained the second coder by "reviewing the coding protocol and answering questions" (p. 649). Parrott and Parrot's training protocol involved the lead investigator discussing the coding protocol with the second coder and answering any questions, followed by both coders independently coding an episode. After coding the episode, notes were compared and interrater reliability was assessed. Following an additional discussion of the coding scheme and addressing any items of confusion, official coding began. Optimally, content analysis should involve two checks for reliability, each based on separate subsamples (Neuendorf, 2002). The first check serves as a pilot test of reliability before full coding of the data; the second provides a final check on the reliability of the coding scheme.

CODE VARIABLES AND CARRY OUT ANALYSIS

The final two steps are to code the sampled material and analyze the message content. With human coding, the coders often use a coding form that corresponds to the codebook. The form typically lists variables with codes to check and/or space to enter the data. Parrott and Parrott used a coding form to take notes during the episode and then entered the data into an online questionnaire. Several computer programs are available for content analysis, and most include pre-set dictionaries (Neuendorf, 2011). Myers and colleagues (2018), for example, used the program Linguistic Inquiry Word Count (LIWC) to examine emotional language used in 192 capital trial victim impact statement transcripts, focusing specifically on anger words and sadness words.

Finally, the content analyst summarizes the message content and may relate content variables to one another or to some other variable. As you may recall, Parrott and Parrott found that crime-based television dramas associated mental illness with violent and criminal behavior. This study and other quantitative content analyses apply statistical methods that we discuss in Chapter 14. It is also possible to conduct content analyses using the qualitative data analysis techniques that are the topic of Chapter 15.

Now that you know the steps in content analysis, Box 11.4 will guide you through an analysis that will help you learn something about yourself.

> **BOX 11.4**
>
> **DOING CRIMINAL JUSTICE RESEARCH**
>
> ## Analyzing the Content of Cell Phone Use
>
> Cell phones have become an integral part of our daily lives. For most people, they are the primary means of communicating with others. How you use your cell phone reveals much about yourself: With whom do you communicate? What do you communicate about? What is important enough to put in a phone message? We propose that you conduct a content analysis of your own cell phone use. What makes this possible is that cell phones store communications, so that you can analyze the stored data. To guide your analysis, we have identified a series of decisions that you will need to make:
>
> 1. What specific messages will you analyze? Text messages, voice messages, social media messages, or something else? Will you analyze sent and/or received messages? How will you decide?
> 2. Whatever type of communication you analyze, we suggest that you obtain a sample of at least 100 communications. What is your sampling unit? How will you select your sample? What is your recording unit?
> 3. What will you code? You probably ought to code the date and time of each message. But then think about characteristics of the sender/receiver and of the communication content. How will you decide what to code? Once you have decided, develop a coding scheme or form.
> 4. How will you summarize the communication content? Will you relate communication content to other variables?

SUMMARY

Content analysis consists of a set of procedures for summarizing the content of recorded human communications, including both printed matter and visual imagery. After selecting a particular communication, researchers define the unit of sampling and coding and develop an appropriate coding scheme. They then select a sample and, in human coding, train coders and pilot test the reliability of the coding scheme. Finally, the communication content is coded and analyzed.

11.3 COMPARATIVE HISTORICAL ANALYSIS

The third method of analyzing existing data originates with many of the founders of modern social science. In an effort to understand large-scale social processes, such as industrialization and modernization, scholars such as Alexis de Tocqueville, Karl Marx, and Max Weber combined the systematic comparison of a small set of cases with in-depth historical analysis.

comparative historical analysis the development of causal explanations of social change by describing and comparing historical processes within and across cases

Comparative historical analysis is comparative insofar as it involves a comparison of the similarities and differences between cases and between historical periods; it is historical in that it "considers events that occurred in the past" (Arthur, 2011, p. 175). In this section, we consider comparative historical studies that follow in the tradition of Marx and Weber. In addition to using existing data, these studies have three distinct features (Mahoney & Rueschemeyer, 2003; also see Lange, 2013). First, they are concerned with developing causal explanations. Second, they analyze historical sequences to understand how events unfold over an extended period of time. Third, they systematically compare a small number of similar and contrasting cases. Comparative historical analysis is like quantitative criminal justice research in its emphasis on causal explanations. On the other hand, the systematic comparison of in-depth historical narratives generally limits this approach to the qualitative analysis of a small number of carefully selected cases (Lange, 2013). As you will see, case selection is of critical importance, and the tools for establishing causality differ from experimental and survey methods.

Although comparative historical research most often uses existing data, we should note that it might utilize oral history and interviewing as data sources (Arthur, 2011). It also is not used exclusively to study large-scale social change; for example, it can be used to study organizations. Finally, comparative historical research is not limited to the study of a small number of cases (sometimes called "small-N" studies); in recent years it has been applied increasingly to large-N studies.

We begin with the description of a study that examined a major transformation in America's criminal justice system in the last quarter of the 20th century.

An Example of Comparative Historical Analysis: The Emergence of Mass Imprisonment

For 100 years, incarceration rates in the United States hovered around 100 inmates imprisoned per 100,000 population. Then, in the last quarter of the 20th century, there was a sudden and massive increase. By 2000, the incarceration rate had more than doubled in every state in the union, with an average increase of 285 percent (Campbell & Schoenfeld, 2013). Moreover, this punitive turn was unique to the United States; no other Western democracy experienced a similar increase in imprisonment. What accounts for this extreme shift? Given that both the United States and other Western democracies experienced the same broad socioeconomic changes, sociologists Michael Campbell and Heather Schoenfeld (2013) believe that the answer lies in the US political system, or, more specifically, in the "interaction between national politics and policy and state-level politics and policy" (p. 1383).

To develop a detailed explanation of widespread transformation in the US penal system, Campbell and Schoenfeld conducted a comparative historical analysis of penal development and politics from 1960 to 2001 in a sample of eight states: Arizona, California, Florida, Oregon, Minnesota, New York, Texas, and Washington. In addition, they examined national-level politics and penal policy during the same period.

As a general analytic strategy, Campbell and Schoenfeld followed a three-step process that they call "inductive periodization." The first step was to simplify the historical analysis by breaking down the 41-year history into three distinct periods. Their second step was to analyze the state and national data to explain the underlying causes of dominant patterns and policy outcomes within each period. The third step was to explain how politics and policy solutions in one period influenced changes that occurred in subsequent periods.

Table 11.3 identifies the three historical periods: *destabilization* (~1960–1975), *contestation* (~1975–1992), and *reconstruction* (~1992–2001). The table also shows the key defining characteristics of each period as indicated by "type of crime politics" (the political use of crime control), "definition of policy problem" (how policymakers defined the crime problem), and "policy outcome" (the types of penal policies that were formulated). Campbell and Schoenfeld's explanation of dominant patterns within each period and of changes over time is complex and detailed, and we cannot hope to do

Table 11.3 Periodization in the Transformation of the Penal Order

	Destabilization	Contestation	Reconstruction
Dates	~1960–1975	~1975–1992	~1992–2001
Description	Questioning and challenges to the penal status quo	Political contestation over the direction of penal policy	Solidification of a new penal order
Type of crime politics	Emergent crime politics	High crime politics	Captured crime politics
Definition of policy problem	Ineffective criminal justice response	Crisis in confidence	Leniency
Policy outcome	Capacity-building/Reform	Constrain discretion/Build prisons	Lengthen sentences/Equip law enforcement

Source: Table 3 in Campbell and Schoenfeld (2013, p. 1389).

justice to their analysis here. What we will do is highlight some of the major developments that led to mass imprisonment so that you can understand how national and state-level politics influenced penal policy.

During the destabilization period, crime entered the national spotlight partly in reaction to the civil rights movement and other social unrest in the 1960s, as presidential candidates, including Richard Nixon and George Wallace, introduced "law-and-order" rhetoric to appeal to anti-Black sentiment. Congress passed an omnibus crime act in 1968, which established a federal agency to make grants to states for crime control. Meanwhile, the federal courts focused on the rights of defendants and prisoners, which became a matter of concern to the states. At the state level, California gubernatorial candidate Ronald Reagan emphasized the link between social protest and crime to overwhelmingly defeat his opponent in 1966. In many states, new federal funding was used to hire and train police and helped to create victims' rights groups and law enforcement associations, and reformers advocated new sentencing guidelines and other changes to strengthen the criminal justice system. In short, this period was characterized by "questioning and challenges to the penal status quo" at both the national and state level (Campbell & Schoenfeld, 2013, p. 1389).

Events in the first period opened up a period of "contestation" in which policymakers had to figure out how to reform their penal systems. The key national event ushering in mass incarceration during this period was the 1980 election of Ronald Reagan as president. Not only did the Reagan presidency emphasize crime (even though serious crime rates were stable or falling), it also launched the "war on drugs," which led to anti-drug abuse laws in 1986 and 1988. These laws established lengthy mandatory prison terms for drug sales and possession and provided generous funds that "increased the incentives for the state and local enforcement of drug laws" (Campbell & Schoenfeld, 2013, p. 1396). Another important consequence of Reagan's election was that Republican gubernatorial candidates in the 1980s, especially in the South, also adopted his "law and order" rhetoric to win elections. In the short run, the crime politics of this period resulted in debates over penal policy; in the long run, states tended to expand prison capacity and introduce mandatory minimum sentences that limited judges' power to decide the length of imprisonment. Playing a key role in these developments were law enforcement and victims' interest groups, which helped frame the crime problem in the media as a need to keep violent criminals off the streets.

The developments in the first two periods, according to Campbell and Schoenfeld, helped establish a "new penal order" between about 1992 and 2001. The final period, reconstruction, is characterized "by relentless political pressure to toughen criminal sanctions and a dominance of ideas and politics that demonized offenders and privileged victims and law enforcement" (Campbell & Schoenfeld, 2013, p. 1401). During this period, state initiatives influenced federal policy. For example, provisions of the Violent Crime Control and Law Enforcement Act of 1994 included stricter liability for juveniles, "three strikes and you're out," and "truth in sentencing," all of which began at the state level. "Three strikes and you're out" statutes impose harsher sentences for repeat offenders convicted of three or more serious crimes; "truth in sentencing" refers to policies designed to maximize sentence terms and eliminate or restrict parole. Also, by this time, the federal courts upheld lengthy sentences for minor crimes and generally gave state legislatures free rein in establishing penal policy regulations. Both Democrats and Republicans aggressively supported punitive anti-crime policies. As Campbell and Schoenfeld note, "a new political culture" had evolved "where 'law and order' politics became sacred pillars of state government, consuming a growing share of state resources, regardless of their effectiveness and relative utility in an era of declining crime and fiscal crisis" (p. 1408).

The Process of Comparative Historical Analysis

Characteristic of comparative historical analysis, Campbell and Schoenfeld's study explains the development of mass imprisonment as a complex interaction of multiple causal factors operating at the national and state levels. Also characteristic, the research process is less apparent than in content analysis and the analysis of existing statistics. This is due partly to the dynamic interplay between theory and data as researchers apply both inductive and deductive logics to arrive at a configuration of factors that interact to produce particular outcomes (Ragin, 1987). Figure 11.3 captures the general process of comparative historical research. The process combines two complementary sets of methods: within-case methods for analyzing individual cases and comparative methods to systematically compare cases (Lange, 2013).[1]

SPECIFY ANALYTIC FRAMEWORK

Comparative historical research begins by establishing an analytic or theoretical framework for addressing the research question. To understand real-world transformations, for example, scholars invariably theorize about the causes of such transformations, and it is to this literature that comparative researchers turn to guide their research.

Campbell and Schoenfeld examined several theoretical explanations for mass incarceration. For example, socioeconomic changes in the late 20th century increased crime and "produced

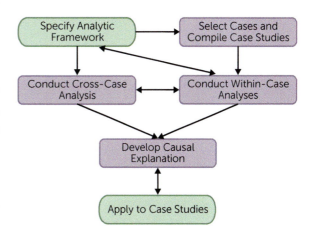

FIGURE 11.3 The Process of Comparative Historical Analysis

---

[1] The discussion of the mass incarceration study in this section relies on additional information graciously provided to us by Michael Campbell and Heather Schoenfeld (personal communication, June 7, 2014).

public anxiety that caused a dramatic shift in society's approach to crime control" (Campbell & Schoenfeld, 2013, p. 1376); "politicians, aided by the media, created and exploited crime as a proxy for a more explicit politics of race" (pp. 1376–1377); and "the nature of the political system and the policy-making process in the United States create[d] incentives for tough-on-crime politics and policy" (p. 1377). None of these explanations, however, accounts for a central paradox of mass incarceration in the United States: "If incarceration rates are first and foremost the result of decisions at the local level (arrests, prosecutions, and sentencing) and state level (sentencing policy, prison capacity), how is it that imprisonment grew in every state during roughly the same time period?" (p. 1376).

In light of this paradox, Campbell and Schoenfeld (personal communication, 2014) used a combination of existing theories and data from state cases to create their analytic framework, as outlined in Table 11.3. The literature pointed to politics as a source of incarceration growth, but the meaning of "politics" was not always clear. Since they "knew from examining [their] cases that politicians used crime control differently at different points in time," they first named the type of crime politics they observed in the cases: emergent crime politics, high crime politics, and captured crime politics (second row of Table 11.3). Second, to link politics with policies that increased imprisonment, they needed to have "policy outcomes" in their framework (last row of Table 11.3). Third, to incorporate a problem-solving model in which policy changes were a response to recurring problems, they decided to examine policymakers' definitions of the crime problem (third row of Table 11.3).

SELECT CASES AND COMPILE CASE STUDIES

The object of case selection varies by approach. Quantitative methods often assume that the "primary goal is to explain variation in dependent variables" (Ragin, 2006, p. 637). Therefore, the researcher wants cases to vary on the dependent variable; otherwise, there is nothing to explain. By contrast, comparative researchers tend to ask why particular transformations occur, which focuses attention on the presence of an outcome. Consequently, they often start by *selecting on the dependent variable*—by studying cases with the same outcome to "search for causally relevant commonalities" (Ragin, 2006, p. 638). This is essentially what Campbell and Schoenfeld did insofar as all of the states they selected had undergone, to varying degrees, a marked increase in the number of people imprisoned in the late 20th century. To strengthen inferences about "causally relevant commonalities" that produced this shift, they also selected cases that varied in size by region and by political and penal history. In short, their case selection was driven by the research topic (or outcome of interest) and analytic framework.

As Charles Ragin (2006) points out, sometimes researchers, like Campbell and Schoenfeld, limit their search to "positive cases to identify potential necessary [causal] conditions" (p. 638). But "[m]ore often, the identification of *relevant* negative cases follows from the study of positive cases, and researchers use these cases to validate the findings from the positive cases" (p. 638). Ultimately, this second phase of case selection is crucial for testing theories. For although studying cases selected on the dependent variable can generate insights into causal processes and can contribute to theory building, it also can bias the conclusions (Geddes, 1990).

Campbell and Schoenfeld's choice of states was theory-driven but was also a practical matter of the availability of case studies. For each state selected, they needed detailed historical data on key actors and events in politics and penal policy from 1960 to 2001. Constructing in-depth case studies of this type, however, is an arduous task requiring extensive archival research. Consequently, comparative researchers frequently use the historical narratives of others, especially historians (Lange, 2013). Campbell and Schoenfeld drew upon one or more data sources for each of the eight states. Three of the case studies were written by one of the coauthors based largely on original data such as "legislative bill files, internal communications between various actors in the penal and political field . . . , constituent letters, press releases, public testimonies, legal files . . . , and news articles pertaining to crime, prisons, and politics" (Campbell and Schoenfeld, 2013, p. 1384). The remaining case studies were secondary sources, which were drawn from similarly in-depth archival research.

CONDUCT WITHIN-CASE ANALYSES

The first analytic step in comparative historical analysis is to analyze sequences of events *within each case*. If you were studying countries, for example, you would begin by effectively creating a timeline, or narrative, for each country based on your case studies.

Having compiled narratives for eight states, Campbell and Schoenfeld proceeded to analyze them case by case. As they read the cases, they report (personal communication, 2014), "we created a shared Google document where we kept a running narrative for each state that we could each add to, comment on, and code for relevant information." Each narrative provided a chronological account or story of the events and processes that led to changes in penal policy. Following their general framework, they coded national-level factors that seemed relevant for each state, and they coded state developments that seemed to be changing policy. Based on their coding, they uncovered similarities across cases that generated the three time periods identified in Table 11.3 (personal communication, 2014). They then used two primary methods to identify causal sequences within cases: inductive periodization, which we described earlier, and process analysis.

Process analysis (also called **process tracing**) examines the specific mechanisms through which one phenomenon has an effect on another (Mahoney, 2004). In general,

process analysis
a within-case method of comparative historical analysis that examines possible intervening mechanisms that link an observed or theoretical association between events (also called *process tracing*)

the analyst starts with an observed or theoretical association between events and then looks for intervening mechanisms linking these events within each case. This is analogous to identifying and testing the effects of intervening variables in a statistical association, discussed in Chapter 5. And like the quantitative analysis of intervening variables, it strengthens the inference that a relationship is causal (Mahoney, 2004). Campbell and Schoenfeld's general framework theorized an association between politics and penal policy. Through process analysis, they uncovered recurring intervening links between national politics and state policy. One of these was interest group activity. The election of tough-on-crime politicians like President Reagan facilitated the organizational strength and activism of crime-related interest groups, such as prosecutor's associations, correctional officers' unions, and victims' organizations, which influenced crime policy.

CONDUCT CROSS-CASE ANALYSIS/DEVELOP CAUSAL EXPLANATION/ APPLY TO CASE STUDIES

The comparison of cases actually begins with the analysis of each case study, as investigators make note of similarities and differences. However, comparative historical analysts have developed more formal methods of cross-case analysis. We briefly discuss the method used by Campbell and Schoenfeld below. For overviews of other methods, see James Mahoney (2004) and Matthew Lange (2013).

Campbell and Schoenfeld developed a general causal understanding of mass incarceration that applied to all states, using a technique that Matthew Lange (2013) calls **narrative comparison** (also see Mahoney, 2000; Rueschemeyer & Stephens, 1997). With this approach, the analyst compares sequences of events across cases to determine if the cases follow a similar causal process. Campbell and Schoenfeld's comparison of historical sequences across states revealed the general causal pattern shown in Figure 11.4. They arrived at this model through an inductive, iterative process of data analysis and interpretation, as they describe (personal communication, 2014):

> In our first round of analysis of the cases, we coded for national factors that seemed to influence the states and state

narrative comparison a method of causal inference in which historical narratives of cases are analyzed to develop a general cross-case causal pattern and to validate it within each case

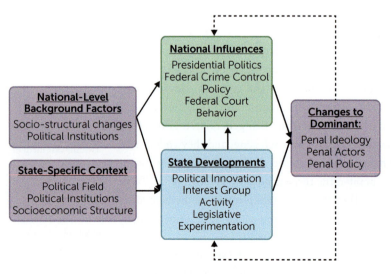

FIGURE 11.4 General Causal Model of Penal Transformation

factors that seemed to change politics and policies on the ground. We then went back to the data to try to determine what common national influences the cases shared and what exactly was changing at the state-level (the center boxes [Figure 11.4]). *Here we found broad similarity across the cases . . . [However,] we had cases that were not entirely consistent. That is, while all states trended toward mass incarceration, it happened at slightly different speeds and intensities. So we went back to the data a third time to code for state-level factors that may have influenced this process* (the bottom left box).

Thus, Campbell and Schoenfeld worked back and forth between their evolving model and the case studies, developing a general model of the causal process that produced mass imprisonment and checking it against the case studies. By considering each case as a whole, they could attend to causal complexity and determine the combinations of conditions, as presented in Figure 11.3, which led to increasingly punitive crime policy across all eight states.

SUMMARY

Traditionally, comparative historical analysis has consisted of the in-depth study of a small number of cases to determine the causes of historical change. Working from a theoretical framework that drives the search for causes, the analyst applies two complementary sets of methods: one set entails the construction and analysis of detailed historical narratives; the other involves the systematic comparison of cases. Both methods are strategic in developing explanations that identify configurations of causes of particular outcomes. Check Box 11.5 to assess your understanding of this section.

BOX 11.5

CHECKING YOUR UNDERSTANDING

Comparative Historical Analysis

1. Comparative historical research is most like quantitative social research in that:
    a. it analyzes numerical data.
    b. it emphasizes causal explanation.
    c. interviewing is one possible source of data.
    d. it studies a sample of cases.

continues

continued

2. Comparative historical research usually involves the analysis of a large number of cases.
   a. True
   b. False

3. Comparative historical researchers often analyze existing historical narratives rather than conduct their own case studies.
   a. True
   b. False

Answers: 1. a, 2. b, 3. a

11.4 STRENGTHS AND LIMITATIONS OF EXISTING DATA ANALYSIS

Although existing data analysis makes use of a diversity of data sources and methods, most analyses share certain advantages and limitations. Like other approaches, existing data analysis is better suited to some research questions than others, and provides benefits and challenges for data collection and analysis.

Studying Social Structure, History, and Social Change

Despite the benefits to criminal justice research of focusing on the impact that properties and changes in social structure have on criminal behavior and the justice system, much of criminal justice research focuses on individual attitudes and behavior. Surveys are of individuals, and very few surveys provide direct measures of social relations; experiments rarely study the group as the unit of analysis; qualitative research often is based on interviews or observation of individual behavior. Existing data, however, often enable the researcher to analyze larger social units. You can see this most clearly in comparative historical research, with its emphasis on global and national transformations.

Similarly, existing data provide the best and often the only opportunity to study the past. To study some aspect of American society 50 or more years ago, it might be possible to conduct a survey of people who were alive at the time. But to do so presents several methodological problems, from the inaccuracy of respondents' memories to survivor bias in the sample. To study periods before the 20th century necessitates the search for existing data.

Most other approaches are also ill-equipped to study social changes. Experiments, qualitative interviews, and field research have limited time spans, and longitudinal surveys rarely were undertaken until the last quarter of the 20th century. The analysis of existing data, however, is well suited to studies of social and cultural change. In fact, the sole object of comparative historical research is the study of social change.

Nonreactive Measurement

A major problem in much criminal justice research is *reactive measurement*: changes in behavior that occur because of research participants' awareness that they are being studied or observed. Research with existing data also encounters this problem to the extent that the data sources are surveys or documents like autobiographies in which the author is clearly aware that the public will have access to what is said. Still, many existing data sources are nonreactive. With physical evidence and many other existing data sources, there is simply no reasonable connection between a researcher's use of the material and the producer's knowledge of such use.

Cost Efficiency

Insofar as research using existing data bypasses the stage of data collection, it can economize greatly on cost, time, and personnel. This is most apparent in the secondary analysis of survey data, but other existing data sources also tend to be less costly than experiments, surveys, qualitative interviews, and field research. These costs vary depending on the nature of the data source and the time, money, and personnel required to obtain and to analyze the data. The tasks of the researcher using existing data, such as searching for and coding relevant information, often are tedious and time-consuming. Imagine, for example, the efforts of Parrott and Parrott in watching and coding numerous variables for 65 television episodes. Yet, the cost per case in such studies is generally quite small compared with the cost of interviewing a respondent or running a single participant through an experiment.

Data Limitations

A major challenge that we noted about the analysis of existing statistics applies to all forms of existing data: finding data appropriate to answer a research question. This obstacle may seem less apparent to you than it is because of the numerous studies cited in this chapter that address a wide range of research questions. Using existing data, however, is a bit like wearing someone else's shoes. They may fit perfectly well. But more likely they will either be too small, pinching your toes, or too large, causing you to stumble. Data to address a research question simply may not exist. If available, the data may not be ideally suited to the researcher's purposes, may provide only indirect measurement, or may not be complete.

selective survival incompleteness of existing historical data due to the fact that some objects survive longer than others

selective deposit systematic biases in the content of existing historical data due to actions such as selective destruction or editing of written records

The completeness or representativeness of the data is especially problematic for researchers studying the remote past. Often, they must rely on whatever traces of information they can find, which are almost certain to be incomplete and are probably biased. Physical evidence is invariably subject to selective survival and selective deposit. **Selective survival** refers to the fact that some objects survive longer than others. The fact that pottery and bone survive the elements better than wood and paper has long been a problem for the archaeologist. A more serious problem for users of the written record is **selective deposit**—systematic biases in the content of the evidence that is available. Records may be selectively destroyed; other information may be edited.

SUMMARY

Compared with other approaches to criminal justice research, existing data analysis is better suited for studying social structure, history, and social change; much of existing data tends to be less subject to reactive measurement effects; and using existing data tends to be more cost effective. On the other hand, it may be difficult to find data that fit a research question, the data may provide only approximate and indirect indicators of variables, and the data may be incomplete and unrepresentative of actions and events. See Box 11.6 to check your understanding of this section.

BOX 11.6

CHECKING YOUR UNDERSTANDING

Data Analysis Review

1. Which of the following data sources are most likely to be reactive?
    a. Autobiographies
    b. Physical materials
    c. Mass media
    d. Birth records

2. The analysis of existing data generally is superior to other approaches for all but which one of the following research objectives?
    a. Studying the past
    b. Understanding social change
    c. Studying individual attitudes and behavior
    d. Studying properties of social structure

3. One problem with existing data analysis is finding data that adequately measure variables relevant to the research question.
    a. True
    b. False

Answers: 1. a, 2. c, 3. a

KEY TERMS

archive, p. 316
big data, p. 319
codebook, p. 327
comparative historical analysis, p. 332
content analysis, p. 322
data archives, p. 321
dictionary, p. 328
narrative comparison, p. 338
process analysis, p. 337
recording units, p. 325
selective deposit, p. 342
selective survival, p. 342
vital statistics, p. 316

KEY POINTS

- Existing data analysis encompasses a variety of methods in which researchers make use of data produced by some other person or organization.
- Existing data are everywhere; they may be found in public documents and official statistics; private and personal records; mass media; physical, nonverbal materials; and criminal justice data archives.
- A huge volume of statistical data is readily available from the official statistics of government agencies and international organizations and from the internet.
- The biggest challenge to using existing statistics for criminal justice research is locating data that can adequately address a research question.
- Content analysis involves the analysis of verbal or visual communications by systematically summarizing their symbolic content.
- Content analysts develop coding schemes to record the content of a sample of communications.
- Traditionally, comparative historical analysis has addressed large-scale social transformations by systematically comparing the historical narratives of a small number of cases.
- To infer complex causal configurations, comparative historical researchers develop or use existing historical narratives of cases, and then use both within- and cross-case methods of analysis.

- Existing data analysis is the best approach for studying social structure, history, and social change; it tends to be more cost effective than other approaches; and much of existing data is nonreactive.
- It is often a challenge, however, to find data that fit a research question, the data may provide only indirect evidence of variables, and may be incomplete or a biased sample.

REVIEW QUESTIONS

1. Give an example of criminal justice research that uses each of the following data sources: (1) public documents, (2) private documents, (3) media, and (4) physical artifacts.
2. In what forms does the Census Bureau release information from the decennial census?
3. What do the authors mean when they say that "the use of data archives is an extension of survey research, field research, and in-depth interviews"?
4. Name two sources of *official* statistics and give examples of the data they provide.
5. Identify common units of analysis in the content analysis of textual data. What is the difference between a recording unit and a sampling unit?
6. What are the three defining characteristics of traditional comparative historical research?
7. What are the principal advantages of using existing data?

EXERCISES

1. Visit the US Census Bureau website to familiarize yourself with the data sources and tools available online. Using this site as a point of departure, find the table or data that will answer the following questions (unless otherwise indicated, provide the most recent estimates and specify the date):

    a. What percentage of the US population has income below the poverty level?
    b. What percentage of the US population is foreign born?
    c. Which states have the highest and lowest median household incomes?
    d. What is the average price of new single-family homes?
    e. What percentage of the US population who commute to work drive alone?
    f. What percentage of the population in your state are college graduates?
    g. What was the growth rate of the world population in 1969–1970? What is it estimated to be in 2024–2025?

2. In the Fall 2006 issue of *The Kentucky Journal of Communication*, Kimberly Everhart and Phillip J. Aust report a content analysis of violence depicted in Disney animated films. The study focused on G-rated films from 1937 to 2000.

A number of Disney movies have been released since this time. To practice conducting a content analysis, locate a more recently released Disney movie (post 2000) and use the coding sheet and codebook found in Appendices A and B of their article. After analyzing the film, write a brief response detailing your findings as well as how they compare to those of Everhart and Aust.

3. An advantage of much existing data is the ability to measure social change. Often you can measure change by replicating previous research. Older content analyses in particular are well suited to this task. Find a study using content analysis that was published in the 1970s or 1980s and replicate it by extending the period of observation from the end date in the original study until the present. Examples of studies that could be replicated are Drew Humphries (1981) study of the coverage of serious crime by the *New York Post*, Neil Malamuth and Barry Spinner's (1980) analysis of sexual violence in best-selling erotic magazines (*Playboy* and *Penthouse*), and Joseph R. Dominick's (1973) analysis of the portrayal of crime, criminals, victims, and law enforcement on prime-time network programming available on New York television.

12

Evaluation Research

Assessing Program Need and Impact

with contributions from Danielle Fenimore

CHAPTER OUTLINE

12.1 Overview of Evaluation Research 348
- Evaluation Research Defined 348
- Components of Evaluation Research 349
- Summary 351

12.2 Types of Evaluation Research 352
- Needs Assessment 352
- Evaluability Assessment 355
- Process Evaluations 358
- Outcome Evaluations 360
- Efficiency Evaluations 363
- Summary 364

12.3 Conducting Evaluation Research 365
- Program Theory 365
- Orientation of Research 366
- Feasibility 368
- Quantitative, Qualitative, or Mixed Methods 369
- Summary 370

12.4 Experimental, Quasi-, and Nonexperimental Designs 371
- Experimental Designs 371
- Quasi-Experimental Designs 371
- Nonexperimental Designs 373
- Summary 373

LEARNING OBJECTIVES

By the end of this chapter, you should be able to

12.1 Identify the basic components of evaluation research.

12.2 Identify, define, and describe the main purpose(s) for conducting each of the different types of evaluation research commonly used in criminal justice.

12.3 Explain the importance of program theory for evaluation research.

12.4 Compare and contrast experimental, quasi-experimental, and nonexperimental research designs used in evaluation research.

As humans, we are naturally curious, with some of us more curious than others. We may be told, for example, that a stove is hot. Regardless, we may choose to touch the stove to determine for ourselves whether this is true, and thus suffer the outcome of a burned hand. Perhaps you have seen a viral video on social media of a "hack" that will "change your life" and your curiosity inspires you to test it out to see whether it is truly as effective as the influencer claims. As a student learning about criminal justice, perhaps you have read about programs or policies that have specific goals like reducing drug use among adolescents, preventing violent gun crime, or improving police–community relations. Hopefully, as a curious human and critically thinking student, you wonder whether these programs and policies are effective at achieving their stated goals. You might not realize it, but questions regarding the effectiveness of a program to achieve its intended goals is a type of research known as evaluation research.

Evaluation research has become so prominent in the last several decades that there are entire books devoted to the topic. In fact, there now exists a national organization and annual conferences dedicated to evaluation research, and peer-reviewed journals that focus specifically on implementation science and evaluation research. This chapter will introduce you to a number of different types of evaluation research utilized in criminal justice and will help you learn how to use the research design elements discussed thus far in the textbook for the purposes of evaluating criminal justice policies and programs. To begin, we will illustrate the process of one type of evaluation research, an outcome evaluation, used to assess the effect of de-escalation training on police officer behavior.

The year 2020 will live in infamy for people around the world as the year that most countries went into lockdown due to the novel coronavirus (COVID-19). In the United States, 2020 was also a year marked by social unrest as a result of multiple police-involved killings of Black individuals. While criticism over police practices and use-of-force policies—especially those that targeted young, Black men—was not new in 2020, public outcry for police reform increased. One approach law enforcement agencies across the country have utilized to address citizen concerns regarding the number of use-of-force incidents is the implementation of electronic devices, such as body-worn cameras, to hold officers accountable for their actions and to have evidence of police–citizen interactions. A study on the effectiveness of body-worn cameras was discussed in Chapter 6 (see Ariel, Farrar, & Sutherland, 2015). In addition to the implementation of technological devices, "de-escalation" policies and trainings aimed at reducing use of force have also become widely adopted and supported by policymakers, legislatures, and experts in policing. A curious individual may ask, what are the goals of "de-escalation" trainings and are "de-escalation" trainings effective in achieving these goals?

While legislatures and agencies jumped on the initiative to adopt "de-escalation" training, at the time, there was no empirical evidence to support the effectiveness or potential risks of such training. Utilizing the Integrating Communications, Assessment, and Tactics (ICAT) de-escalation training developed by the Police Executive Research Forum

(PERF), Engel and colleagues (2022) in collaboration with the Louisville Metro Police Department (LMPD) in Louisville, Kentucky, began to systematically evaluate the impact of training on use of force, defined by the researchers as "the number of individuals who had force used against them during a single encounter" (p. 211). The study investigated the effect that "de-escalation" training had on officers' behavior, focusing specifically on the frequency, severity, and type of force used, as well as officer and citizen injuries. To determine the effect of the training itself, these outcomes were measured before the training, immediately following the training, and again four to six months after the training.

To assess the effect of the training on the specified outcomes, the researchers randomly assigned officers to receive and implement the training, with some groups receiving the training sooner than others (stepped-wedge randomized controlled trial (RCT) design) (Engel et al., 2022). This allowed the researchers to compare those who had received the training (treatment group) with those who had not yet received the training (control group), while still providing the treatment with a potential benefit to all officers by the end of the study. The experimental design was carefully controlled so that changes in the outcomes could be attributed to the training alone rather than contamination by extraneous variables (i.e., officer experience, demographics of officers or citizens, officer attitudes, etc.).

Comparing the outcomes pre- and post-training, as well as comparing the treatment groups (trained divisions) to the control groups (untrained divisions), Engel and colleagues (2022) found a significant decrease in the total count of uses of force. Additionally, officer and citizen injuries were both significantly reduced post-training. Through their robust analyses, the researchers were able to determine that changes in use of force and citizen and officer injuries were most likely due to the training rather than other factors, such as changes in arrest patterns in general, department policies, and police practices. Despite regular limitations of research projects that continue to warrant further empirical study, the evaluation of the ICAT training concluded that such training is effective in reaching the goal of de-escalating officer–citizen interactions to reduce use of force. Therefore, legislatures and policing agencies can move forward with relative confidence when recommending or implementing ICAT de-escalation training in the future, though evaluation would be warranted to ensure the training was achieving its intended outcomes in the newly implemented locations.

12.1 OVERVIEW OF EVALUATION RESEARCH

Evaluation Research Defined

Systematically assessing the effectiveness of a program, policy, or practice, as Engel and colleagues (2022) did with the ICAT de-escalation training in Louisville, Kentucky, is an example of just one type of **evaluation research**. In this chapter on evaluation research, we will explore five different types of evaluation research conducted in the field

---

evaluation research a systematic assessment of a program, practice, policy, or system to determine the need and merit of investing time, money, and resources to achieve a goal as well as the effectiveness of achieving the stated goals

of criminal justice, although this is not an exhaustive list of the types of evaluation research conducted in the field! In addition, we will discuss the application of different research designs learned about in previous chapters for the purpose of evaluation research.

The great thing about evaluation research is that it is an **applied research method**; we are *applying* everything we have already learned about research methods and research design to programs being designed and implemented in the world of criminal justice through law enforcement, corrections, courts, and more. Evaluation research is not a specific method for collecting data, nor is it itself a specific type of research design. Rather, evaluation research is more of a *purpose* for conducting research than a specific *method* of conducting research.

In addition, the findings of such research can be *applied* to real-world problems. Results from evaluation research can have immediate impacts on policies, programs, and practices to reduce crime and help victims. The applied method separates evaluation research as unique to traditional, basic research whose purpose is to create more scientific knowledge, either through generalizations that can be applied to multiple people, groups, or scenarios or in-depth understanding of a limited number of peoples' lived experiences. A large portion of criminal justice research is evaluative in nature because of the need to resolve significant real-world problems that impact society at large, and the need to determine the worth of investing billions of dollars from the public into criminal justice programs, policies, and practices.

Given that the government, rather than researchers, is responsible for implementing criminal justice programs and policies, evaluation research is also unique in that it requires criminal justice researchers to work alongside various stakeholders with different goals and interests, providing empirical evidence and recommendations that can impact society. This requires researchers to remain objective and systematic in their approach to evaluation research and to provide empirical evidence rather than opinions that may feed a political agenda. In fact, policymakers have moved toward more evidence-based policymaking, and criminal justice agencies have sought to implement more **evidence-based practices**.

applied research methods using evidence to find solutions to specific real-world problems faced by society, individuals, or organizations/businesses

evidence-based practices programs, practices, and policies that are considered effective as supported through systematic, rigorous, and empirical research

Components of Evaluation Research

Evaluation research is also unique because of the close involvement researchers have with criminal justice professionals and clients. For example, Engel et al.'s study of de-escalation would not have been possible without the cooperation of the LMPD as a whole. The individuals implementing the programs or individuals on the receiving end of treatment from a program are the first part of evaluation research, referred to as **inputs**. Any resources, clients, or staff that are required to run a program are included as inputs. To evaluate the effectiveness of the ICAT training on use of force, there were many inputs, including training resources and staff as well as officers implementing the training during interactions with citizens.

inputs resources, materials, clients, or staff required for the program

program process the steps required for the delivery of the treatment or implementation of the service

outputs direct products or services delivered from the program process

outcomes the direct impact of the program process on the cases who underwent treatment

feedback the process of providing information about program process, outputs, or outcomes that can further program development

Evaluation research projects systematically study the way in which the program, treatment, or service is carried out, called the **program process** or activities, essentially asking the question, what is being done with the inputs? Program implementation may be simple and easy, or complicated and lengthy with many moving parts. Ultimately, the program process is meant to have an impact on the individuals involved, such as the officers of LMPD in Engel et al.'s (2022) evaluation research. The direct result of the program process on the cases that have undergone the treatment or received a service is called an **output**. An output is not a measure of the *impact* or *effectiveness* of the program; rather it is a simple measure indicating the program is running. For Engel and colleagues, this would simply be the number of officers trained under the ICAT model. If another researcher were to evaluate juvenile drug courts, their output would be the juveniles served by the drug courts, and yet another may evaluate trauma-informed care of crime victims with their outputs being the victims treated under the trauma-informed model.

The outputs usually lead to a program **outcome**, the impact on the cases that have undergone the treatment or service. The hope is that these outcomes align with program goals and address the need for which the program was originally implemented. There are typically multiple outcomes measured in evaluation research. Published in their article in *Criminology & Public Policy*, Engel et al. identified three main outcomes measured: uses of force, officer injuries, and citizen injuries. Yet, in their expanded report published in Fall 2020, they also include outcomes such as changes to officer attitudes, officers' self-reported behavior, and supervisor perceptions (Engel et al., 2020). For further examples, consider the hypothetical studies previously mentioned on juvenile drug courts and trauma-informed care for crime victims. Potential outcomes for the juvenile drug courts may be measures of self-reported drug use or arrests for drug-related offenses after involvement with the drug court, and for trauma-informed care, outcomes may include measures of victims' self-reported satisfaction with the system, or post-traumatic stress, depression, and/or anxiety symptoms following care.

Important in evaluation research is the process of **feedback**, which can in turn impact future inputs. Feedback allows agencies to determine whether they should keep as is, modify, or terminate the existing program processes to continue to provide positive outcomes that align with program goals and needs. Feedback is vital for continued program development. See the entire process in Figure 12.1.

For all programs, policies, and practices evaluated, researchers have many individuals and groups who care about the program and the outcomes or who are directly involved in the operations of the program;

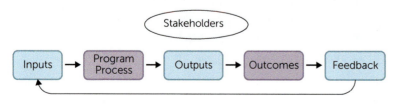

FIGURE 12.1 Evaluation Research Process

this group of individuals is called **stakeholders**. Stakeholders can include staff implementing the program, clients receiving the program, funders, policymakers, executive boards, and the list goes on. The role that these stakeholders play in program implementation and their attitudes toward the evaluation research can have a significant impact on the research process.

During an evaluation project, stakeholder relationships are incredibly important, and maintaining good rapport is crucial for objective, systematic assessment and effective feedback processes post-evaluation. However, some stakeholders may not be cooperative with researchers. Hostile stakeholder relationships can lead to researchers being denied access to facilities that they were once authorized to access, having important documents go missing or having funding removed or changed midway through a project. The need to consider many other peoples' or groups' interests while objectively and empirically conducting criminal justice research is a unique component of evaluation research that those engaging in basic research may not have to consider.

stakeholders any individual or group who is involved with or has an interest in a program, or who may be affected by the outcomes of the evaluation of the program

SUMMARY

There is no shortage of demand for evaluation research in the field of criminal justice. As evidence-based practices become the gold standard across law enforcement, courts, and corrections, researchers will be called upon to systematically evaluate needs, outcomes, and impacts. Now that we have reviewed the basics of evaluation research and the unique components that differentiate evaluation from basic criminal justice research, in the next section we will discuss various types of evaluation research. Thus far, much of the discussion has centered around the effectiveness of programs and outcomes, yet criminal justice researchers engaging in evaluation research explore more than outcomes alone. See Box 12.1 to check your understanding of this section.

> **BOX 12.1**
>
> **CHECKING YOUR UNDERSTANDING**
>
> ### Research and People Involved in Research
>
> 1. Evaluation research is a
>   a. data collection method
>   b. data analysis procedure
>   c. purpose for conducting research
>   d. research design

continues

> *continued*
>
> 2. Research that can be used to find solutions to immediate, real-world problems is called
>   a. needs research
>   b. applied research
>   c. basic research
>   d. good research
>
> 3. Researchers conducting an evaluation of the Drug Abuse Resistance Education (D.A.R.E.) program may have to take into consideration the concerns of the parents of the students participating in the program during their research study. These parents would be identified as which of the following?
>   a. Inputs
>   b. Outputs
>   c. Feedback
>   d. Stakeholders
>
> Answers: 1. c, 2. b, 3. d

12.2 TYPES OF EVALUATION RESEARCH

formative evaluation a type of evaluation research conducted in the beginning stages of program development to determine whether a program is needed and to help improve the program prior to full implementation

summative evaluation a type of evaluation research conducted after full program implementation to determine the overall effectiveness of the program

needs assessment a type of evaluation research that collects objective data or information to determine the needs of a specified population that might be served by the implementation of a program or policy

Many types of evaluation research exist. However, generally speaking, they can be grouped into two categories: formative evaluation and summative evaluation. **Formative evaluation** is a type of evaluation research that occurs in the beginning stages of program development. This type of evaluation aims to determine whether a program is needed and to help improve the program before it is fully implemented. **Summative evaluation**, on the other hand, occurs after a program has been fully implemented. The purpose of this type of evaluation is to assess the program's overall effectiveness. Within each category of evaluation research, there are a number of subcategories. Our focus is on five common forms of evaluation research, three of which fall under formative evaluation—needs assessment, evaluability assessment, and process evaluation—and two which fall under summative evaluation—outcome evaluation and cost-efficiency evaluation. The type of evaluation conducted depends upon the question(s) the researchers are attempting to address about the program or practice of interest (see Table 12.1). The section below provides a brief overview of each form of evaluation research along with illustrative examples.

Needs Assessment

A common type of evaluation research is a **needs assessment**. Soriano (2013) defines a needs assessment as "a well-thought-out and impartial systematic effort to collect objective data or information that brings to light or enhances understanding of the need

Table 12.1 Types of Evaluation Research

	Evaluation Type	Questions Addressed	What It Shows	Why It Is Useful
Formative	Needs Assessment	Is the program needed?	Whether the proposed program elements are likely to be needed, understood, and accepted by the target population	It allows for modifications to be made to the plan before full implementation begins
	Evaluability Assessment	Is the program able to be evaluated?	The extent to which an evaluation is possible, based on the goals and objectives	Determines whether a program has been planned and implemented well enough to be formally evaluated
	Process Evaluation	Is the program being implemented as intended?	The extent to which the program is being implemented as designed. Whether the program is accessible and acceptable to its target population.	Provides an early warning for any problems that may occur. Allows programs to monitor how well program plans and activities are working.
Summative	Outcome and Impact Evaluations	Is the program producing its intended outcomes?	The degree to which the program is achieving its intended outcomes for the target population and overall.	Provides evidence for use in policy and funding decisions.
	Efficiency Evaluations (e.g., cost–benefit analysis; cost–effectiveness analysis)	Is the program cost effective?	Whether the benefits of a program offset the program's costs and whether the same benefits might be achieved at a lower cost with an alternative program.	Provides program managers and funders a way to assess cost relative to effects.

Source: Adapted from Salabarría-Peña, Apt, & Walsh (2007)

for services or programs" (p. 5). Simply stated, a needs assessment involves collecting data to determine the needs of a targeted population and how those needs may best be met. Such assessments are typically conducted for several reasons, including determining potential gaps in service delivery, informing decision-making and resource allocation, evaluating the target population's perceptions of whether a program would be beneficial, exploring stakeholder interest in a program, and assisting with prioritizing program planning. This type of evaluation is often the first step in developing a new program or restructuring a current, established program.

There are a number of steps in conducting a needs assessment (see Figure 12.2). A broad overview of the steps follows; for a more thorough discussion, refer to Soriano (2013). A needs assessment begins with determining the purpose and scope of the evaluation. Within this first step, researchers define the problem and identify the target population that the program or policy will address. For example, suppose a community is conducting a needs assessment in order to determine whether there is a need for a program aimed at reducing offender recidivism. In that case, the research team must first define the problem. The researchers might ask questions such as:

- Why are the individuals reoffending?
- Are they experiencing barriers to reintegration? If so, what are those barriers?
- Are they obtaining jobs?
- Do they know how to get a government-issued ID?

Answers to these questions help to inform the program that could be implemented (i.e., job skills, reintegration strategies, etc.).

In addition to defining recidivism, the team would need to define their target population. Would the target population for the program be first-time offenders? Nonviolent offenders? Previously incarcerated offenders? After the problem is clearly defined, the next step is assessing the extent of the problem through the collection of data. Both qualitative and quantitative data are often collected from a variety of sources including surveys, focus groups, interviews, and secondary data such as police reports; court records; or data from local, state, and federal agencies (e.g., Census Bureau, Federal Bureau of Investigation, National Institute of Drug Abuse, etc.) to determine the needs of the targeted population and possible solutions. After identifying needs and possible solutions, recommendations for actions are developed and communicated to the key stakeholders.

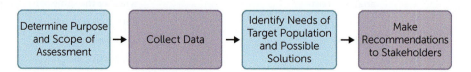

FIGURE 12.2 Steps in a Needs Assessment

Within criminal justice, it is not uncommon for there to be calls to action for various issues to be addressed such as police use of force, gun violence, juvenile drug abuse, etc. Often the response to such calls is the development of a policy or program. Without a needs assessment first being conducted to fully understand the population in need of the intervention and objective information on the nature and scope of the issue, inappropriate or unneeded policies or services may be implemented, leading to wasted time, money, and, ultimately, failed efforts. The implementation of legislation banning the sale of handguns to felons is one example of failed legislation that may have been thwarted if a suitable needs assessment had first been conducted (Rossi et al., 2004). While legislatures believed that the use of guns in the commission of crime would be reduced by banning gun sales to felons, it turned out that most criminals were not purchasing their weapons legally, but rather through the "black market" or theft, and thus the legislation was ineffective in reducing gun-related crime.

An example of a needs assessment is Sussman and colleagues (2008) assessment of a social service referral telephone program for high risk youth. The study assessed whether there was interest in a potential social service referral telephone program (SSRTP) for youth at high risk of drug abuse that would provide participants with resources and referral information in a variety of areas including vocational, recreational, educational, transportation, and mental health and drug counseling. Study participants and the target population were former students in California alternative high schools. Through telephone interviews, the researchers assessed participants' perceptions of the usefulness and helpfulness of such a program as well as overall interest and likelihood of utilizing the services. The results indicated participants had a strong interest in the telephone referral program and "provided feedback on how to better structure and tailor such a prevention intervention program" (p. 2071).

Evaluability Assessment

Evaluability assessment is a type of exploratory evaluation study that assesses whether programs or interventions are ready for useful evaluation. It serves as a preliminary step to a formal outcome evaluation helping researchers to determine whether it is worth committing the resources to actually do an evaluation as well as whether decision-makers are likely to use the information produced. Stated simply, evaluability assessment "helps to determine whether a program has been planned and implemented well enough to be evaluated" (Van Voorhis & Brown, 1996, p. 4). Given the expansive number of criminal justice programs and interventions along with the limited financial resources available for conducting evaluations, evaluability assessments are one way to determine what programs are ready and able to be successfully evaluated. For a more detailed discussion of the purpose of evaluability assessments and their value, see Table 12.2.

evaluability assessment a type of exploratory evaluation study that assesses whether programs or interventions are ready for useful evaluation

A number of frameworks for conducting evaluability assessments have been proposed within the literature (see Chen, 1990; Rutman, 1980; Welsh, 2006). While there

Table 12.2 The Purposes of Evaluability Assessments and Their Value to Program Administrators and Practitioners

- Clarifying a program's goals and objectives.
- Diagnosing goal confusion among stakeholders and preventing staff, clients, administrators, funders, and others from working at cross purposes.
- Assessing the feasibility of the program's goals and objectives and determining which program objectives are most attainable.
- Identifying program priorities. Which objectives are most important?
- Maximizing programs, use of research monies by discouraging a costly comprehensive evaluation until ready.
- Diagnosing a program's strengths and weaknesses.
- Improving program performance.
- Examining the logical consistency between program components. Is there an explicit theory which links needs to program procedures in a logical manner and is reflective of cause–effect solutions? If not, the EA may suggest one where problems are linked to objectives and specific activities/services for achieving the objectives.
- Assessing the extent to which the program design fits the knowledge base of the discipline (e.g., whether interventions are being used that have been known to fail in the past).
- Making recommendation for the larger evaluation or determining if an outcome evaluation is possible.
- Determining the information needs of stakeholders, thereby assuring that a larger evaluation will obtain the appropriate information needs of the stakeholders.
- Saving agency resources by making improvements in a timely manner and forestalling expensive but unwarranted evaluations of a program that is not ready to be evaluated.
- Facilitating the development of a "learning organization," where agencies and programs plan futures according to accurate diagnostic information regarding present-day operations. Evaluability assessments then serve as aids to program development and planning.

Source: Adapted from P. Van Voorhis and K. Brown (1996)

is some variation, most include the following components (see Figure 12.3 for visualization of the steps):

1. Review available documents to prepare a description of the program. This includes program history, goals and objectives of the program, theory guiding the program, program design, how the program operates in practice, etc.

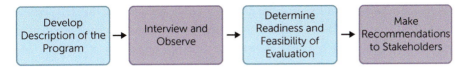

FIGURE 12.3 Steps in an Evaluability Assessment

2. Interview and observe. During this step, evaluators interview program managers and key stakeholders to determine their understanding of the program. Additionally, evaluators go into the field to observe how the program is being implemented in practice. This step allows evaluators to see if there are inconsistencies between what is "on paper" and what is happening "in practice."
3. Determine readiness and feasibility for evaluation. Utilizing the information obtained in steps one and two, a number of questions regarding program design, research design, data availability, context and environment, and cost should be considered to determine whether an evaluation is feasible. Example questions include: Is it likely that the program as currently implemented would achieve the desired results? Is there currently sufficient reliable and valid data available to answer key evaluation questions? If not, can the data be collected? Is the operating environment favorable to conducting the evaluation? Are there enough available funds to conduct an adequate evaluation study? Are the results of the study likely to be accepted and used by stakeholders? Will program staff be open to having their program evaluated?
4. Make recommendations. After completing the evaluability assessment, the evaluator should develop a final report making a recommendation regarding whether conducting an evaluation is viable and would produce meaningful results. Suppose the recommendation is that an evaluation of the program is not currently feasible. In that case, the evaluator should provide recommendations on how to increase program readiness for evaluation. Suggestions could entail expanding or clarifying definitions of program goals and objectives, improving program implementation, improving data collection efforts, or strengthening stakeholder commitment to evaluation.

To illustrate the steps in an evaluability assessment, we reference Finckenauer and colleagues (2005) evaluability assessment of three juvenile justice programs in New Jersey. They began their assessment by collecting and analyzing program documents, including funding proposals, published brochures, administrative manuals, annual reports, minutes, and any existing completed program evaluations to see how the programs were described on paper (Step 1). Next, the researchers moved on to observe program implementation and interview program personnel (Step 2). Program personnel were asked to describe the program in detail to determine whether there was consistency between what the program documents indicate and what the staff persons believe they are doing. The researchers also conducted site visits to each program to determine the actual size and characteristics of the target population as well as to observe the intervention activities in action. To determine feasibility, the research team assessed the available data to see whether additional data collection would be needed (Step 3). The last step (Step 4) involved a joint meeting with all the program stakeholders and program representatives where the researchers recommended an impact evaluation of one program, a process evaluation of another program, and not to undertake a formal evaluation of the third program.

Process Evaluations

Process evaluations are a type of evaluation research that focuses on assessing program or intervention implementation and delivery. They seek to address whether the program or intervention is reaching the appropriate target population, whether service delivery and support are consistent with the original program design, and whether problems (if any) are occurring. Additionally, the process evaluation may gauge satisfaction of program participants' or staff's perception of how well the program was delivered. When process evaluations are conducted repeatedly over time, they are referred to as program monitoring. Process evaluations may attempt to answer a number of questions, such as the following:

- Are the intended targets receiving the program services?
- Are the intended targets receiving the proper amount, type, and quality of services?
- Are the program functions being performed adequately?
- Are resources adequate to support important program functions?
- Are participants satisfied with program services? (Rossi et al., 2004)

> **process evaluation** a type of evaluation research that focuses on assessing program or intervention implementation and delivery. When the evaluation is conducted repeatedly over time, it is referred to as program monitoring

Through extensive data collection, process evaluations can identify inefficiencies and problems in program implementation that can then be addressed prior to time and effort being invested in evaluating the program's effectiveness. Process evaluations are thus valuable as they help avoid wasting resources evaluating a program's effectiveness if it is not properly implemented.

To determine whether a program is being implemented as intended, process evaluations must obtain a detailed description of program operations and their implementation (Vito & Higgins, 2014). This information can be drawn from various quantitative and qualitative data, including direct observations, focus groups, satisfaction surveys, and interviews. Table 12.3 provides a detailed description of the types of process evaluation information and why they are important to process evaluation. Once a detailed description of current program operations and implementation is collected, a comparison with the original program design should be conducted to determine program

fidelity, and the extent to which program delivery adheres to the program as originally designed. A detailed report should be developed and then presented to key stakeholders.

You may have noticed that there are some similarities between evaluability assessments and process evaluations. For a more detailed comparison of the two types of evaluation research, see Box 12.2.

Densley and colleagues (2017) conducted a qualitative process evaluation of Growing Against Gangs and Violence (GAGV), a gang prevention program in the United Kingdom aimed at reducing gang involvement, delinquency, and violent offending among youth, as well as improving youth's confidence in police. The evaluation was originally intended to assess "whether the curriculum met its criminological intentions and was being delivered with fidelity" (p. 244). To conduct the process evaluation, the research team reviewed all syllabi, handbooks, and supporting materials in terms of their content and accessibility. Additional data were collected via eight observations conducted in three different schools. Following data collection, the findings were presented to GAGV. The GAGV then revised the program as a result of the recommendations prior to the final outcome evaluation of the program.

fidelity the extent to which program delivery adheres to the program as originally designed

---

BOX 12.2

DOING CRIMINAL JUSTICE RESEARCH

Comparing and Contrasting Evaluability Assessments and Process Evaluation

There is a degree of overlap between evaluability assessments and process evaluation. Specifically, some definitions note that evaluability assessments can be used to determine how well a program was planned and implemented (Van Voorhis & Brown, 1996). Process evaluations are similarly used to determine how well a program was planned and implemented, to ensure the validity of a program's implementation. Evaluability assessments are often conducted prior to beginning the evaluation to ensure that resources are available but also to determine if the evaluation of a program will contribute to improving the program. Process evaluations are most often conducted at the end of an evaluation to ensure that the program was implemented as planned. The Justice Research and Statistics Association summarizes the difference between the two, noting that "[an evaluability assessment] . . . determines whether a program has the basic foundation for an evaluation to take place (data collection, program model, adequate staffing, etc.), while process evaluation takes the components that make up the foundation and assesses whether and how they are utilized" (JRSA, 2003, p. 5).

Table 12.3 Types of Process Evaluation Data and Their Importance

Data Type	Description	Importance
Participant	Specific information about participants, such as age, gender, race/ethnicity, education level, and household income	Allows for the determination of whether the program is serving the targeted population and whether program outreach efforts are working to engage the participants planned to be reached
Focus groups	Focus groups are facilitator-led discussions on a specific topic with a group of no more than 6–12 participants brought together to share their opinions on that topic.	Focus groups are an excellent way to learn what people think about a program and get suggestions about the program. Listening as people share and compare their different points of view provides a wealth of information—not just about what they think but also why they think the way they do.
Satisfaction surveys	Information about whether the participants enjoyed the program, whether they got something out of it, and whether the program met their needs or expectations	Provides information on whether participants feel good about the program and can help identify ways to improve participant satisfaction, which would be likely to improve retention in the program
Staff perception data (collected via focus groups, surveys, or interviews)	Staff perceptions about what worked and what did not during the implementation of a program. Staff perceptions about training and supervision quality may also be collected.	Program staff are often in an excellent position to comment on how well a program is being implemented and may have ideas for improvement.
Program adherence monitoring	Systematically tracking how closely each intervention activity was implemented as laid out in the final work plan. This includes how much of a program was administered ("dose") and whether it was administered according to the program developer's intentions.	The closer a program is implemented as it was intended, the better chance the program has of achieving its goals and outcomes.

Source: Adapted from Ebener et al. (2017) and Hannah et al. (2011)

Outcome Evaluations

Once it has been determined that a program is being administered as intended, an evaluator can conduct an evaluation to determine whether the program is meeting its intended short- and long-term goals. There are two commonly used evaluations that measure whether a program "worked": outcome evaluations and impact evaluations. **Outcome evaluations** measure whether the program achieved its intended outcomes for the *target population*. For example, researchers are looking to determine if the program they're evaluating had an effect on the group it was intended for. **Impact evaluations**, on the other hand, measure whether a program is broadly meeting program goals. In other words, they help to assess the program's overall impact beyond the immediate benefits (if any) received by the target population. The results of an impact evaluation illustrate the extent to which a program has met its *ultimate* goal (e.g., What has been the overall impact of the program beyond the study population?).

> **outcome evaluation** a type of evaluation research that measures whether a program achieved its intended outcomes on the *target population*

> **impact evaluation** a type of evaluation research that measures whether a program is broadly meeting its stated goals

For example, an outcome evaluation of the Drug Abuse Resistance Education (DARE) program may seek to answer how youth substance use was impacted by program participation. As such, the focus of an outcome evaluation for the DARE program examines if there was a change in substance use among youth (the *target population*). What were the short-term impacts of the program? Did the program increase student knowledge about substances and the abuse of them? What were the long-term impacts? Was there a reduction in substance use among program participants? An impact evaluation, however, might seek to answer the broader question of how implementation of the DARE program impacted the broader community. Did the overall rate of substance use within the community decline? In the outcome evaluation, the program's success on the participant is evaluated; in the impact evaluation, the program's success is evaluated more broadly.

To conduct both types of evaluations, quantitative data are primarily used including surveys, existing data, and experiments (for a discussion of the use of RCTs to evaluate program impacts, see Box 12.3). However, impact evaluations may also rely on qualitative data stemming from focus groups and interviews to assess the program's broader impact on the community. If a program is found to be ineffective in achieving program goals, the program should be revised or terminated. Figure 12.4 presents the general steps involved in impact and outcome evaluations.

The introductory example represents an impact evaluation. Recall that Engel and colleagues (2022) evaluated the outcome of the ICAT de-escalation training developed by the PERF with the LMPD in 2019. The goal of ICAT training is to teach law enforcement officers the tactics and skills needed to de-escalate hostile officer–citizen interactions— involving a citizen who is behaving erratically and either unarmed or

FIGURE 12.4 Steps in Outcome and Impact Evaluations

> **BOX 12.3**
>
> **DOING CRIMINAL JUSTICE RESEARCH**
>
> ## Randomized Controlled Trials
>
> True experimental designs are the gold standard in research to establish causal relationships between a treatment and an outcome. One type of experimental design that is often proposed in evaluation studies is an RCT to determine the impact of a particular intervention or treatment. For example, Engel and colleagues evaluated the use of a de-escalation training program called Integrating Communications, Assessment, and Tactics (ICAT) in Louisville, Kentucky. Using a stepped-wedge RCT design (a specific type of RCT), to evaluate the impact of ICAT training on reducing officer use of force, Dr. Engel and her colleagues were able to isolate the effect of the treatment on the outcomes, much like you would in a true experiment. This particular design allowed for random allocation of police beats to a training schedule that ultimately allowed the department to be its own control without losing the rigorousness of the design. This design helped establish causality, provided the researchers with as much control over the treatment as possible, and established a randomized treatment and control group, each of which are components of a true experimental design.

armed with anything less than a firearm—with the intent to enhance officer and citizen safety. With this goal in mind, the specific and measurable program outcomes identified in the 2022 study of the ICAT training were uses of force, officer injuries, and citizen injuries. The next step in the process involved the development of the design that would allow them to collect data systematically from officers who had been trained and those who had not (control group for comparison purposes). Data were collected through official LMPD use of force data; each time force is used, commanding officers are required to complete Administrative Incident Reports which include information on injuries. Once the stepped-wedge RCT was completed and all official data collected, researchers analyzed the data through a series of univariate analyses that allowed them to display patterns in use of force over time, as well as the frequency of officer and citizens injuries reported in these incidents. In addition, a multivariate analysis was conducted to determine the impact of the training (independent variable) on the dependent measures (i.e., program outcomes) including uses of force, officer injuries, and citizen injuries. Engel and colleagues' results aligned with anticipated goals for the ICAT training; however, regardless of whether evaluation results are positive or negative, reporting to key stakeholders is of utmost importance. For Engel et al., some key stakeholders to share reports with include the LMPD, the City of Louisville, the PERF, and the research funders, as well as large-scale agencies with an interest in de-escalation training, such as the Department of Justice, the Office of Community Oriented Policing Services, and the National Institute of Justice.

Efficiency Evaluations

Another type of evaluation research becoming more important in criminal justice as government budgets continue to shrink is **efficiency analysis**. This type of evaluation compares program costs to program outcomes. Questions addressed by efficiency analyses include whether the benefits of a program offset the program's costs and whether the same benefits might be achieved at a lower cost with an alternative program. Based on the results of an efficiency analysis, program changes or even elimination may be instituted.

There are two commonly utilized types of efficiency evaluations: cost–benefit analysis and cost-effectiveness analysis. **Cost–benefit analysis** "identifies and places monetary values on the costs of programs and weighing these against the benefits of the programs" (Vito & Higgins, 2014, p. 103). Simply stated, a cost–benefit analysis compares monetary program costs to the monetary program benefits to obtain the net benefits (or net costs). **Cost-effectiveness analysis**, on the other hand, seeks to link "the cost of a program to specific measures of program effectiveness" (Vito & Higgins, 2014, p. 104), such as reducing recidivism and increasing the number of days between failed drug tests and the number of individuals diverted from being formally processed. The specific program outcomes are quantified and compared to program costs in these evaluations. For example, a cost-effectiveness analysis of a juvenile diversion program might report an estimate of how much it costs the program for each juvenile diverted from being formally processed in the juvenile court system. In other words, the results would be presented as "dollars per juvenile diverted."

Farrington and Kogel (2015) conducted a cost–benefit analysis of the Stop Now and Plan-Under 12 Outreach Project (SNAP-ORP), a cognitive-behavioral skills training and self-control program aimed at preventing involvement in criminal offending. To conduct their analysis, they first estimated the number of crimes prevented by the program. Next, they estimated the cost savings per program participant based on the cost of each type of crime and then compared that with program costs. The results indicated that the monetary benefits of the program exceeded the monetary costs of the program. Specifically, they found savings estimates between $2.05 and $3.75 for every $1 spent on the program when relying on conviction data. The estimate was even higher when using data estimating undetected offenses; these results produced estimates between $17.33 and $31.77 savings for every $1 spent on the program.

efficiency analysis a type of evaluation research that compares program costs to program outcomes

cost–benefit analysis a type of evaluation research that seeks to compare the monetary costs of a program to the monetary benefits of the program

cost-effectiveness analysis a type of evaluation research that compares program costs to specific measures of program effectiveness

SUMMARY

As stated in the previous section, a plethora of evaluation research types exist (Assess your understanding through the cases presented in Box 12.4). The types discussed simply represent some that are commonly used within criminal justice. Determining the type of evaluation research that best meets your goals is the first step in conducting evaluation research. The next step is to decide the most appropriate evaluation method.

BOX 12.4

CHECKING YOUR UNDERSTANDING

Types of Evaluation Research

1. Stacey is the program coordinator for Project A, a program designed to reduce recidivism among those newly released from prison. She wants to assess whether her program is achieving its intended outcomes on the target population. Which type of evaluation should she perform?
    a. Needs assessment
    b. Evaluability assessment
    c. Impact evaluation
    d. Outcome evaluation

2. John is the creator of Project Y, a program implemented in police departments designed to reduce the number of citizen complaints against police officers. Before investing time and resources into assessing the effectiveness of his program, he wants to make sure that his program is being implemented according to the original plan. Which type of evaluation is John interested in conducting?
    a. Needs assessment
    b. Process evaluation
    c. Cost–benefit analysis
    d. Outcome evaluation

3. Riley has applied for a grant that would allow her to create a program aimed at reducing gang membership among youth. Part of the grant application requires that she prove that there is a need for the program in the intended community. Which

> type of evaluation could Riley perform to assess whether a gang prevention program was needed?
> a. Needs assessment
> b. Cost-effectiveness analysis
> c. Evaluability assessment
> d. Impact evaluation
>
> Answers: 1. d, 2. b, 3. a

12.3 CONDUCTING EVALUATION RESEARCH

Thus far, you have learned about the basic components of evaluation research, as well as the various types of evaluation research commonly used and their purposes. This section identifies research design considerations that you need to make as an evaluation researcher, including if the program theory will be clearly stated, if the project is feasible, if you would like to evaluate the project from a researcher or stakeholder orientation, and if you want to use quantitative or qualitative research methods. The discussion should not be considered a complete list, but rather a guide for starting your journey in evaluation research. We will conclude this section with a review of experimental research designs, and some of the other design choices available when a true experiment is not possible.

Program Theory

One consideration that must be made when designing an evaluation project is whether you are interested in *how* the program works (program theory) or simply whether the program works ("black box"). In evaluation research, **program theory** provides a map for the evaluator to follow, with the end goal of identifying a relationship between the program (the independent variable) being evaluated and the outcome(s) of interest (the dependent variable). This map also allows the researcher to keep track of what happened along the way. When evaluators opt to base their research on program theories, there are two key elements present: an explicitly stated model and an evaluation guided by this model (Rogers, 2000). In using program theory, understanding why a program achieves its intended outcome is much easier to identify.

Pawson and Tilley (1997) highlight the importance of the **mechanism** and **context** (Pawson & Tilley, 1997) in program theory, noting that programs are only effective, *given a specific mechanism and context*. They state that this is key to realistic evaluation in criminal justice and that "the careful enunciation of program theory is the prerequisite

program theory an explicitly stated explanation of why a social program should have the intended outcome

mechanism ideas and opportunities relative to a social program that help effect change

context the social and cultural conditions surrounding the implementation of a social program

to sound evaluation" (pp. 56–57), but that successful social programs are only so if they introduce the proper mechanisms in the appropriate context. However, Rogers (2000) notes that this is both the greatest strength and the greatest weakness of program theory: these projects are often empirically strong but also often have a narrow focus on outcomes.

In contrast, **"black box" evaluation** research is when the program theory is not explicitly stated. This is more evident in evaluation research when a program works, but there is little done to explain why. This is simply an input–output model, in which we know that someone was exposed to a program, the desired outcome was achieved, and there are no further attempts to explore the program process and really get a sense of *why* it worked. Simpson and Fraser (1993) state that black box evaluation metrics "assume that the internal workings of a system are invisible to the evaluator" (p. 1424). In other words, projects that choose to use a "black box" evaluation approach rely heavily on, and reflect, the quality of data that are collected during the implementation period. As such, it is important to recall discussions on measurement validity and the importance of conceptualization when deciding how to collect data in these projects.

black box evaluation evaluating a program without understanding or knowing the nature of the program

Orientation of Research

Another consideration that needs to be made when designing your evaluation project is whether the orientation of your research is simply identifying whether the project is stakeholder-driven or researcher-driven. More specifically, whose goals are going to be driving the project the most? This is a deviation from the typical approach to research in which the scientific method guides the research questions and the goals of the project, and the primary audience is other researchers. However, because program sponsors and key stakeholders are often included in the design of the program and the ensuing evaluation, and because nonacademics, practitioners, and laypersons are the intended audience for the findings, the outcomes of interest and the research goals and questions may often be more reflective of the people who are involved in the program.

That said, the researcher holds the responsibility to develop and clarify the key stakeholders' program theory. There are several approaches to stakeholder-driven evaluation research, including utilization-focused evaluations, action-researcher partnerships (see Box 12.5 for more information on this type of stakeholder-driven research), participatory action research, and appreciative inquiry. Under researcher-oriented research, the researcher is left with a degree of autonomy. This freedom allows them to be able to develop rigorous, unbiased studies to evaluate social programs.

However, there are also integrated approaches for research orientation that allows for leveraging the researcher's expertise and the standards of the scientific community, while also taking into consideration the concerns of key stakeholders. Shirk and colleagues (2012) have identified five models through which researchers and stakeholders can participate in evaluation research, based on the level of participation from the

> **BOX 12.5**
>
> ## DOING CRIMINAL JUSTICE RESEARCH
>
> ## Action-Research Partnerships
>
> Evaluations can be used to implement and improve existing practices, and this is especially important in criminal justice. Participatory action research/action research partnerships are super important to the improvement of the system since it allows for feedback in real time and for addressing emerging issues that were not anticipated in the planning phase.
>
> It is important to note that there is a difference between action-research partnerships and participatory action research. Though they both involve collaborations with key stakeholders, participatory action research engages with stakeholders as the research participants (i.e., research subjects), while action-research partnerships engage stakeholders as partners in the evaluation/research process.
>
> Stephens (2022) notes that effective police–researcher partnerships are rare among policing agencies and are most likely to be concentrated in large (more than 500 sworn officers) agencies. These partnerships often end when grant funding has expired and often fail to be maintained at the end of a project. Though there are several examples that could be mentioned, he highlights two examples of long-standing police–researcher partnerships that exemplify successful partnerships between the University of Cincinnati and the Cincinnati Police Department (CPD), and between Arizona State University and Phoenix Police Department (PPD). In Cincinnati, he notes that credibility and respect were developed when researchers asked tough questions and offered candid feedback. Through their work, researchers at the university "have developed relationships at every level of the department ... [and] have demonstrated a commitment to the community and the department through the contributions they have made to addressing [policing] problems" (p. 348). In Phoenix, the relationship has proven to be mutually beneficial; this partnership provided PPD with the resources they required to address complex policing issues in their community, and PPD acts as "a living laboratory for researchers to test their ideas and to learn while making important contributions to their community" (p. 350).

stakeholders: contract (evaluators are asked to conduct and report on a specific investigation), contribute (evaluators collect and contribute data), collaborate (stakeholders assist evaluators throughout the research process, including collecting and analyzing data), cocreate (stakeholders, guided by evaluators, develop their own study), and colleagues (stakeholders conduct independent research to advance the field).

An example of an integrated research-orientation approach can be seen in Stokes and Clare's evaluation of a burglary prevention initiative developed by the Western Australian Police. Stokes and Clare (2019) were asked to conduct a *post hoc* evaluation of this burglary prevention initiative. Police developed the research design, and implementation included distributing pamphlets with crime prevention information to burglary victims and their neighbors to reduce the likelihood of near repeat victimization patterns. Though the project was designed by the primary stakeholders (Western Australia Police), the researchers were able to employ a pre-post study design to determine if the program was effective, following the standards of the scientific community. Though there were issues with data management during the implementation period, the researchers were able to provide recommendations for improving the delivery of the treatment.

Feasibility

feasibility the ability to complete a project within the available timeframe and with the available resources

Feasibility is an important consideration in all research designs, but it becomes much more prominent in evaluation research due to the public nature of evaluation research. In other words, evaluation research can often be required for social programs where resources and time may be in short supply. For example, a city that used federal funding to implement a co-response model within their police department may be required to hire an external researcher to evaluate the program. Co-response models have law enforcement and mental health clinicians jointly responding to specific calls for service for people experiencing mental crises. However, the funding source may have a quick deadline for the evaluation of the program and the researcher, who did not participate in implementation, does not know what resources are available. The researcher may feel that this project is *not* feasible, given the timeline and the unknown status of evaluation resources, including the amount of funding that remains in the original budget or the data that were collected as part of the newly implemented program. As such, evaluation researchers must consider whether a rigorous study can be completed given the limited knowledge of resources and the short timeline.

Feasibility can be partially determined through an evaluability assessment, which determines if a program *can* be evaluated, though there are more considerations about feasibility than just whether the program was designed to collect relevant data for evaluation. Researchers can conduct feasibility studies, which largely investigate the viability of a proposed project. Feasibility studies are typically used by businesses to help identify whether a company possesses the needed resources and if the return on investment is worth the risk. The concept can be extended to apply to criminal justice evaluations. For example, a researcher might want to assess if the timeline being requested by the funding agency and the funding amount is sufficient to conduct a rigorous study and provide useful results for the key stakeholders.

Quantitative, Qualitative, or Mixed Methods

One of the more obvious considerations of evaluation design is what sort of methods are most appropriate for evaluating your program. Recall again that evaluation research is simply an *applied* research design, and a solid understanding of research methods will help inform which is the most appropriate methods. There has been a drive for an increase in empiricism in criminal justice over the last several decades (Garrett, 2018). As such, many **requests for proposals** have often emphasized a desire for proposals that include quantitative methodologies that will provide strong statistical support for a program to help develop reliable evidence-based practices.

However, that does not mean that quantitative research always provides the most appropriate approach to evaluating a social program. Because qualitative research designs rely on in-depth observational strategies, qualitative evaluation provides the researcher more flexibility over the course of the evaluation and a richer dataset than what may be expected from quantitative data. For example, Pear and colleagues (2021) used a qualitative evaluation approach to evaluate key issues related to the implementation process and perceived effectiveness of California's gun violence restraining orders (GVROs). To evaluate these laws using a qualitative approach, Pear and colleagues interviewed 27 key informants using a semi-structured interview strategy and analyzed the resulting transcript data using **grounded theory** and the **Consolidated Framework for Implementation Research** (Damschroder et al., 2009). Given the findings from this evaluation, the authors developed a set of recommendations for states to consider before passing their own GVRO laws.

There are pros and cons to each type of research design. Specifically for evaluation research, the feasibility of the research design may contribute significantly to the design choices that are made with regard to whether an evaluation researcher chooses to use qualitative, quantitative, or even mixed research methods to evaluate the program of interest. For example, one of the largest drawbacks to qualitative research designs is that they are often time-consuming and can become extremely costly, depending on the type of funding the researcher is receiving to complete the project. However, quantitative research designs, such as a nationally representative survey of law enforcement agencies, can also become costly. Though a survey can be a much less time-consuming design choice, the costs that are associated with surveys can add up very quickly; if the survey is mailed, this requires printing services (e.g., paper, ink, and letterhead design), mailing materials (e.g., envelopes), and postage costs. Further, in order to gain a higher response rate, researchers may be required to follow up with mailed reminders to participate, which will include the same sorts of costs, and can continue to increase, depending on the number of reminder mailings the researcher chooses to send.

Multiple methods designs, sometimes known as mixed methods designs, provide a way to integrate quantitative and qualitative methods in a way that allows for

---

request for proposal a document that solicits proposals for research, often found through funders' websites (the National Institute of Justice posts requests for proposals for criminal justice research on an annual basis)

grounded theory the systematic and inductive approach to identifying ideas and concepts as they emerge the iterative review of qualitative data

Consolidated Framework for Implementation Research a set of tools and guides for formative evaluation developed by Laura Damschroder and colleagues in 2009, to help build implementation knowledge, such that constructs remain consistent across multiple projects combining the best aspects of each design approach. When methods are combined, the findings are much more robust. For example, evaluation researchers may choose to quantitatively investigate changes in the rates of residential burglaries, comparing pre-implementation rates to post-implementation rates to see if the intervention had a significant impact on the outcome. In a mixed methods study, they may also opt to conduct in-depth, semi-structured interviews with those officers that were responsible for implementing the intervention to better understand why or why not an effect was observed in the burglary data.

SUMMARY

In this section, we have emphasized several key design considerations that an evaluation researcher makes when determining which research design is best suited to address evaluation research questions. In evaluation research, it is important to determine if the program or policy is effective at changing the outcome of interest and, as such, we need to make sure that we can definitively state that the program or policy in question had an impact on the outcome of interest (To check your research terminology understanding, see Box 12.6).

BOX 12.6

CHECKING YOUR UNDERSTANDING

Research Terminology

1. Jack is asked to design a project to evaluate an arrest diversion program that was implemented by his city's police department for repeat drug offenders. The city puts out a request for proposals that includes details about funding and the expected turnaround for a completed evaluation. Jack notes that the timeline is extremely tight, and that he may not be able to conduct a rigorous evaluation in that time. This program is not:
    a. fundable
    b. feasible
    c. evaluable
    d. probable

Answer: b

12.4 EXPERIMENTAL, QUASI-, AND NONEXPERIMENTAL DESIGNS

Recall the beginning of this chapter where we discussed that evaluation is an *applied* research method. That said, the design choices that you have available when designing an evaluation research project are no different than those that are available for research projects that do not have an evaluation element. However, because evaluation projects can often be conducted in social environments or other, less-controlled environments, we may not always have access to all elements of experimental designs. The following section provides a review of experimental designs, and why these are often considered the gold standard in research. After revisiting true experiments, we provide guidance on the type of research designs that are available when some, or even all, elements of a true experiment are missing. There are two alternative design types that are commonly discussed in conjunction with evaluation research: quasi-experimental designs and nonexperimental designs.

Experimental Designs

Experimental designs are the gold standard for research, as they increase the validity and reliability of results to the utmost extent. Recall our discussion about the logic of experimentation and causality in Chapter 8 and Chapter 5, respectively. When conducting an experiment, the relationship between two variables is being explored to determine whether a causal statement between them can be made. As such, the researcher manipulates the independent variable and measures the response in the dependent variable. Except for the manipulation of the independent variable, both groups are treated exactly the same, and participants are randomly assigned to one group or the other. By doing so, it can be established that X and Y are *associated*, that X directly influences Y (precedes in time), and that the relationship between X and Y is **non-spurious** and, in turn, can unequivocally be stated that the independent variable caused the dependent variable. This is ultimately the goal of evaluation research—determining the extent to which a social program impacts a particular outcome—and so the underlying logic of causality still applies. However, in evaluation research, and social research in general, true experimental designs may not always be possible, and so some design accommodations may need to be made to ensure that the studies remain as rigorous as possible and support the causal relationship between treatment and outcome.

Quasi-Experimental Designs

Working with social groups and social programs introduces a variety of issues related to perfectly randomized samples, like what is expected in a true experimental design. Recall that in a true experiment, assignment to the treatment or control groups requires randomization. For this reason, we must employ designs that are meant to approximate

non-spurious if introducing a control variable (an alternative explanation to the dependent variable) into the model, the relationship between X and Y would become nonexistent

quasi-experimental designs research designs where at least one element, typically random assignment to treatment and control groups, of a true experiment is not present, or not included in the evaluation design

FIGURE 12.5 An Illustration of Nonequivalent Control Group Designs

true experiments to the extent that we are still achieving the most validity in the design as possible. The following examples of **quasi-experimental designs** are not an exhaustive list of quasi-experimental designs; there are many different quasi-experimental designs. Instead, we will focus on two commonly used examples: nonequivalent control group designs and before-and-after designs.

NONEQUIVALENT CONTROL GROUP DESIGNS

The first type of, and most commonly used, quasi-experimental design that we will be discussing is **nonequivalent control group designs**. These designs are often used when both a treatment and control group exist, but random assignment is not possible, which is the primary advantage of this type of quasi-experimental design. The groups that are generated are expected to be similar, but researchers are unable to control for selection bias in the sample. This threatens the internal validity of the research, though external validity remains acceptable under these conditions, given that this design occurs in a natural setting (Rennison & Hart, 2018). Collins, Lonczak, and Clifasefi (2019) utilized a nonequivalent control group design to determine the effects that a law enforcement assisted diversion (LEAD) program had on the justice and legal system costs related to low-level drug and prostitution offending. Because random assignment of the LEAD program to these types of offenders was not possible for this impact assessment, the authors randomized strategies used by particular officer shifts. Those that were on day or night bike patrol and anti-crime squads who made the most drug arrests in a particular police beat were required to enter arrestees into the diversion program. The authors found that incarceration was reduced significantly by 88% for participants in the LEAD program, compared to those that did not participate in the program (see a diagram of a nonequivalent control group design in Figure 12.5).

nonequivalent control group designs quasi-experimental designs that have predesignated treatment and control groups, but assignment to these groups is not randomized

before-and-after designs quasi-experimental designs that consist of analyzing data from the outcome before and after treatment, following a pretest/posttest design (random assignment and control groups are absent from these designs)

BEFORE-AND-AFTER DESIGNS

The second most common design for evaluations of social programs is **before-and-after designs** (see Figure 12.6 for an illustration). Sometimes these designs are known as pre-test-posttest designs, or a pre-post design. These designs are fairly straightforward and are characterized by an absence of both random assignment and a control group. These designs rely on calculating the difference in the outcome before and after treatment. Typically, research that employs a pre-post design is examining changes in the trends of a particular outcome over time. For example, Hodgkinson and colleagues (2023) investigated whether the presence of a warning sticker noting that a panic alarm

Pretest → Treatment → Posttest

FIGURE 12.6 An Illustration of Before-and-After Designs

system was installed on the premises of domestic violence (DV) victims' homes would deter DV recidivism. Pretest and posttest rates of criminal charges for DV offending were compared across two treatment groups, those with standard panic alarms and those with audio-recoding abilities. Though the authors were able to note a reduction in reoffending between the pre- and post-time periods, there was an observed difference between the use of audio-recording alarms and standard panic alarms; those homes with audio-recording saw a 57% *increase* in the number of charges compared to the standard panic alarm.

Nonexperimental Designs

The least rigorous designs are nonexperimental designs, which rely on designs in which random assignment is not possible, manipulation of the treatment is not done by the researcher, and little effort is made to control for threats to internal validity (Lobmeier, 2010). As such, statements of causal relationships between the treatment or intervention and the outcome cannot be made. One such example of a nonexperimental design is an ex post facto control group design. These designs are employed when the treatment was implemented without interference or influence from the researcher. For example, Braga and colleagues (2011) utilized an **ex post facto design** to evaluate place-based interventions being used by Boston Police Department. The authors note that Safe Street Teams in Boston were rolled out in response to precipitous increases in violence without significant consideration given to how to evaluate the impact that these programs had, leaving evaluators with limited options to evaluate the program after it had been implemented. As such, the authors needed to utilize a design that allowed them to evaluate the impact of this program without having the ability to manipulate or randomly assign treatment for comparison. The authors note that ex post facto designs are incredibly useful designs when evaluations are not planned into program implementation strategies.

ex post facto control group designs
a nonexperimental design in which evaluation of a program begins after it has already been implemented (also called an after-the-fact design)

SUMMARY

This section describes and compares true experiments, the gold standard in research, to quasi-experimental and nonexperimental designs, as these often are the best research designs for a particular evaluation project. These designs are available to maximize the researcher's ability to establish causality when not all components of a true experiment are possible (see Box 12.7 to assess your understanding of this section).

> **BOX 12.7**
>
> ### CHECKING YOUR UNDERSTANDING
>
> ## Research Design
>
> 1. Ashley is asked to conduct an experiment to reduce residential burglaries using a targeted crime prevention effort. The impact of this project is best evaluated by determining if there was a change in the number of residential burglaries that occurred. She examines the average number of residential burglaries that occurred prior to treatment implementation and compares this to the average number of residential burglaries that occurred once the implementation period ended. What type of design is this?
>   a. Feasibility design
>   b. Ex post facto design
>   c. Before-and-after design
>   d. Nonequivalent control group design
>
> 2. Chuck estimates a statistical model to measure the impact of a work-release program for low-level offenders at the jail in his county. He introduces a demographic variable and notes that the impact from the work-release program on his recidivism outcome becomes nonsignificant. This breaks down his causal model because the relationship between the program (independent variable) and the outcome (dependent variable) is:
>   a. non-spurious
>   b. extraneous
>   c. correlational
>   d. ordered
>
> **Answers: 1. c, 2. a**

KEY TERMS

applied research methods, p. 349
before-and-after designs, p. 372
black box evaluation, p. 366
Consolidated Framework for Implementation Research, p. 369
context, p. 365
cost–benefit analysis, p. 363
cost-effectiveness analysis, p. 363
efficiency analysis, p. 363
evaluability assessment, p. 355
evaluation research, p. 348
evidence-based practice, p. 349
ex post facto control group designs, p. 373
feasibility, p. 368
feedback, p. 350
fidelity, p. 359
formative evaluation, p. 352

grounded theory, p. 369
impact evaluation, p. 361
inputs, p. 349
mechanism, p. 365
needs assessment, p. 352
nonequivalent control group designs, p. 372
non-spurious, p. 371
outcome evaluation, p. 361
outcomes, p. 350
outputs, p. 350
process evaluation, p. 358
program process, p. 350
program theory, p. 365
quasi-experimental designs, p. 372
request for proposal, p. 369
stakeholders, p. 351
summative evaluation, p. 352

KEY POINTS

- Evaluation research is an applied research method, utilizing the data collection methods and research designs learned in previous chapters to find solutions to real-world problems.
- Programs and practices that are supported by empirical research, also known as evidence-based practices, have become more popular in the field of criminal justice.
- The basic components of evaluation research include inputs, program process, outputs, outcomes, feedback, and stakeholders.
- Evaluation research can be grouped into two categories: formative evaluation and summative evaluation.
- There are five types of evaluation research commonly used in criminal justice: needs assessment, evaluability assessment, process evaluation, outcome evaluation, and efficiency evaluation.
- The type of evaluation research conducted depends upon the question(s) researchers are attempting to address about the program or practice of interest.
- There are many considerations to make about research design, including if the project is feasible, whether we are interested in an explicit statement of why a program works, who the primary audience is, and whether the design will be quantitative or qualitative.
- True experiments are not always possible in evaluation research, but establishing causality is still equally important.
- Quasi-experimental and nonexperimental designs are available for when at least one component of a true experiment is not available.

REVIEW QUESTIONS

1. What is evaluation research? What are applied research methods?
2. What are the components of evaluation research and at what stage in the process are they identified?

3. Explain the difference between formative and summative evaluation.
4. Compare and contrast the five common types of evaluation research used in criminal justice.
5. Describe the differences between true experiments, quasi-experiments, and non-experimental designs.
6. Why is mechanism and context important to the program theory?
7. Describe the strengths and weaknesses of mixed methods designs.

EXERCISES

1. Go to the National Institute of Justice and identify a program of interest to you. Explore the details provided under the collapsible headings: Program Summary, Program Description, Evaluation Outcomes, Evaluation Methodology, and Cost. Provide a short write-up identifying the purpose of the program, expected program outcomes, the research design used to evaluate the program, and the results of the evaluation research.
2. Considering the same program that you identified for the previous question, identify the weaknesses in the design that may cause issues with causality and/or generalizability. Describe how you would redesign the study to improve it.

Multiple Methods

Two or More Approaches Are Better Than One

13

CHAPTER OUTLINE

13.1 A Comparison of Four Basic Approaches to Criminal Justice Research 379
Summary 382

13.2 Examples of Mixed Methods Research 383
Bullying and Victimization During Childhood and Adolescence 383
What Employers Say vs. What They Do 385
Explaining Discrimination in a Low-Wage Labor Market 388

13.3 Purposes of Mixed Methods Research 390
Triangulation 390
Complementarity 391
Development 391
Expansion 392
Summary 392

13.4 Mixed Methods Research Designs 393
Sequential Designs 395
Concurrent Designs 395
Component Designs 395
Integrated Designs 396
Summary 396

LEARNING OBJECTIVES

By the end of this chapter, you should be able to

13.1 Identify the relative strengths and weaknesses of major approaches to criminal justice research.

13.2 Explain the value of using multiple approaches to address a research question.

13.3 Describe the four main purposes of conducting mixed methods research.

13.4 Describe how mixed methods research designs vary in terms of timing and integration.

The preceding chapters have described a variety of approaches to criminal justice research. Much of the time, investigators use only one of these approaches. In the long run, though, the best strategy is to address a research question with multiple methods. Indeed, people often adopt this strategy to solve problems in their everyday lives.

Consider, for example, the simple problem of waking up early to catch a flight. Let us say you normally awaken by means of an electric clock radio set for 7:30 a.m. To make sure that you are awake by 6:00 a.m., you might employ several methods. You might set the clock radio for 5:55 a.m., set your cell phone alarm for 6:00 a.m., and ask an early-rising friend to phone you at 6:05 a.m. You would then have three independent and somewhat dissimilar methods for solving the problem. If the electricity should go off, the cell phone alarm would work. If your cell phone battery dies, the friend should come through. If the friend proves unreliable, one of the other methods should work. By using multiple methods that do not share the same inherent weaknesses, we enhance our chances of solving the problem.

triangulation addressing a research question with multiple methods or measures that do not share the same methodological weaknesses

The value of using multiple methods is conveyed by the concept of **triangulation**, a term borrowed from the field of navigation. To understand its conventional usage, imagine that you are lost deep in the woods of Maine and need to pinpoint your location for the local rescue team. Assume you have an old cell phone *without* GPS. Using your phone, you could call members of the team stationed at two different places, A and B. The team member at each position would then use a directional antenna to get a bearing on your location, which is represented by each of the dashed lines running from A and B in Figure 13.1. Neither direction by itself would provide enough information because you could be located anywhere along the A or B lines. But the point where the lines intersect would pin down your location. (Incidentally, GPS is based on a more sophisticated form of triangulation from satellites.)

Triangulation in criminal justice research refers to the use of two or more dissimilar methods to address the same research question. Each method is analogous to the different vantage points in Figure 13.1. As you have seen, all research procedures are subject to limitations and biases; however, dissimilar methods are not likely to share the same weaknesses. Therefore, we become more confident when different methods separately zero in on the same findings. In effect, the strengths of one method offset the weaknesses of the other.

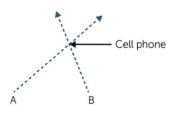

FIGURE 13.1 Triangulating the Location of a Cell Phone from Two Points, A and B

The logic of triangulation applies to many different research activities, some of which we have described in previous chapters. These activities include the use of multiple measures of the same underlying concept: construct validation, in which researchers consider a variety of evidence to assess the validity of measurement; experimental replications to enhance external validity; and the use of two or more observers to record observations in field research.

This chapter extends these examples of multi-method research in two ways. First, we focus here on the use of different approaches (e.g., surveys and field observation) or kinds of data (e.g., field notes and statistical records). Combining different approaches or data, especially quantitative and qualitative, is known as **mixed methods research**; it has emerged as a new field in the social sciences, with a distinct history and methodology (Greene, 2007; Pearce, 2012; Small, 2011; Timans et al., 2019).[1] Second, multiple methods may be applied to achieve purposes other than the convergence or confirmation of findings, which is the principal aim of triangulation. As we show, different approaches may be used to address complementary questions that clarify or deepen our understanding about a phenomenon; one research approach may be used to develop another approach; or different research approaches may be combined to expand the breadth or range of the research.

> **mixed methods research** a research study that combines two or more approaches to data collection and analysis

To begin, we compare the relative strengths and weaknesses of four basic approaches to criminal justice research. Next, we present four examples of mixed methods research, which involve different combinations of approaches and serve different purposes. Then, we outline the basic purposes and designs for conducting mixed methods research.

13.1 A COMPARISON OF FOUR BASIC APPROACHES TO CRIMINAL JUSTICE RESEARCH

The principle of triangulation emphasizes the value of testing hypotheses with different methods that do not share the same methodological weaknesses. In this way, we build confidence in our assertions. An important implication of triangulation is that researchers need to know the relative strengths and weaknesses of each approach in order to decide which methods to select and how best to combine them when possible.

In the concluding sections of Chapters 8–11, we discussed the strengths and weaknesses of each of the major approaches to criminal justice research. Table 13.1 summarizes these discussions by identifying the strengths and weaknesses of four main approaches on eight dimensions. To simplify the comparisons, the table focuses attention on specific ideal forms of these four strategies: laboratory experiments, surveys, field research, and analysis of existing statistics. It is important to recall, however, the variations within each basic strategy. Experiments may be conducted in the field as well as in the laboratory; surveys vary in mode (e.g., telephone interviews and mail questionnaires); field research may involve varying degrees of participation in the research setting as well as in-depth interviewing (which also serves as a stand-alone method); and existing data come in many forms that may be analyzed in markedly different ways.

---

[1] The term "mixed methods" generally refers to research that combines quantitative and qualitative methods or data; the term "multi-methods" refers more broadly to the combined use of different methods, whether exclusively quantitative, exclusively qualitative, or mixed. This chapter focuses on research that involves any possible combination of approaches or methods of data collection; however, we prefer to call this "mixed-methods research" and to use the literature on mixed methods as a guide to thinking about how methods may be combined.

Table 13.1 Strengths and Weaknesses of Approaches on Eight Study Dimensions

	Relative Strength*			
DIMENSIONS OF ASSESSMENT	Lab Experiment	Survey	Field Research	Existing Data
Content restrictions: What is and is not feasible or practical to study	W	M	M	W
Internal validity: Control over extraneous variables	S	M	W	M
Ease of measurement: Ability to measure or perform checks on reliability and validity	S	S	W	M
Nonreactive measurement: Control for effects of awareness of being observed	W	W	M	S
Contextual understanding: Ability to study actions in relation to the social context	W	W	S	M
Control for investigator bias: Control for effects of researcher characteristics and behavior	W	W	M	S
External validity: Ability to generalize from sample results	W	S	W	M
Ability to replicate	S	S	W	M

*W, weak; M, medium; S, strong.

Furthermore, there are other research strategies that do not fit neatly into this fourfold typology, which we ignore or touch on only lightly in this book, such as structured observation, life history interviews, ethnomethodology, and conversation analysis.

The entries in the table summarize the relative strength of each approach on each of eight dimensions. "W" means that the approach is relatively weak; "M" means that it is of "medium" strength or weakness; and "S" indicates that the dimension is a strength of the approach. As the first row of the table shows, none of the basic strategies is highly flexible with regard to the topics or research questions that it may address. The relative inflexibility of experiments and existing data analysis stems from analogous limitations: experimentation depends on what it is practically and ethically possible to manipulate; existing data research depends on the availability of the data. Beyond its general accessibility to research questions, each approach is uniquely suited to obtaining particular kinds of information. Thus, surveys are best for estimating population characteristics and describing the distribution of attitudes and opinions; field research affords access to people's definitions of complex situations and events; and the analysis of existing data often provides the best and/or only means of studying the past and larger social units.

Experiments are strong in establishing internal validity because they provide the strongest inferences about cause and effect. Statistical controls possible in surveys and some existing data research allow for partial control of extraneous variables (hence the "M" in the table); however, the absence of such formal controls generally makes field research least acceptable for testing causal hypotheses.

Although it is easier to create measures and assess reliability and validity in experiments and surveys, these approaches are most vulnerable to methodological artifacts stemming from participants' awareness of being tested and experimenter or interviewer effects. Nonreactive measurement is a major strength of much existing data research. On the other hand, the extent to which field research is vulnerable to these artifacts depends on how well the investigator becomes accepted by others in the field setting and on how well they are able to perform simultaneously the roles of participant and observer. The greater the trust the investigator is able to develop, the less the likelihood of reactive measurement; the more adept they are at managing the participant and observer roles, the less the likelihood of investigator bias.

By observing social life in naturalistic settings, field research is best able to provide a holistic and contextual understanding of social actions. By comparison, experiments—whether in the laboratory or the field—isolate one or a few variables at a time, making it difficult to study complex interactions; surveys study what people say in the unique context of an interview or questionnaire, which may not indicate how they will act and feel in everyday life; and available data may provide limited contextual information.

Survey research affords the greatest control over error and bias associated with sampling and therefore provides strong sample generalization. The susceptibility of some existing data to selective deposit (i.e., the researcher(s) choice to omit things not wanting to be shared with others) makes this approach moderate on sampling generalization. By contrast, external validity is a major weakness of experiments insofar as they typically take place in highly restricted settings with small, nonrandom samples of research participants. And while the quality of sampling is generally better in field research than in experiments, field studies are nonetheless based on isolated settings and nonrandom sampling procedures.

Experiments and survey studies are the easiest to replicate. Indeed, replication is fairly common in experiments, and surveys such as the General Social Survey and various polls repeatedly ask the same questions to measure trends. The time-consuming nature of and lack of standardization in field research make this approach very difficult to replicate. Replication with alternative measures or with respect to different time periods is sometimes possible with existing data research, but this depends again on the availability of the data.

As Table 13.1 shows, patterns vary across the four main approaches, and no two research strategies share the same strengths and weaknesses. As our mixed methods examples will show, this is what makes the approaches complementary and strengthens inferences based on a triangulation of methods.

SUMMARY

The principle of triangulation implies that researchers should weigh the strengths and weaknesses of each approach to determine the best approach or best combination of approaches to address a research question. That no two approaches share the same strengths and weaknesses underscores the value of using a combination of approaches. Use Box 13.1 to assess your understanding of this section.

BOX 13.1

CHECKING YOUR UNDERSTANDING

Approaches to Criminal Justice Research

1. Which of the following is not an example of triangulation?
    a. Using three different questions to measure the same concept
    b. Replicating an experiment with a different manipulation of the independent variable
    c. Asking the same question to a large sample of respondents
    d. Using both experimentation and the analysis of existing data to test the same hypothesis

2. Which basic approach to social research is most effective in providing a holistic and contextual understanding of social actions?
    a. Field research
    b. Experimentation
    c. Survey research
    d. Analysis of existing data

3. Which basic approach to social research is best for obtaining precise estimates of population characteristics?
    a. Field research
    b. Experimentation
    c. Survey research
    d. Analysis of existing data

4. Which basic approach to social research produces the strongest inferences about causal relationships?

   a. Field research
   b. Experimentation
   c. Survey research
   d. Analysis of existing data

Answers: 1. c, 2. a, 3. c, 4. b

13.2 EXAMPLES OF MIXED METHODS RESEARCH

Mixed methods research may occur with many different combinations of approaches. In the following examples, researchers mixed a survey with focus groups, a field experiment with a survey, and a field experiment with field observation.

Bullying and Victimization During Childhood and Adolescence

Nancy C. Guerra and colleagues (2011) utilized surveys and focus groups to assess the impact of various individual and contextual factors on bullying and victimization using a sample of elementary, middle, and high school students. They also examined how the relationships varied based on gender and age. The researchers carried out their two-pronged study in 59 elementary, middle, and high schools in the state of Colorado between 2005 and 2008. Survey data were collected in Year 1 of the study with the older age groups at each school level, elementary (Grade 5), middle (Grade 8), and high school students (Grade 11). All children in all classrooms for the grade level at each school were invited to participate. A small number of 10th and 12th grade high school students were also included when the survey was administered in mixed grade classrooms. During the fall of 2005, 2,678 elementary, middle, and high school students completed surveys which included questions regarding bullying perpetration and victimization, self-esteem, normative beliefs about bullying, and school climate. Eighty-four percent of the pretest sample (2,261) completed the posttest survey in the spring of 2006.

Students who attended the schools participating in the study but did not complete the survey were recruited nonrandomly to participate in focus groups. The focus groups were utilized as a way to "further corroborate, contextualize, and expand findings from the surveys" (Guerra et al., 2011, p. 298). Students were selected by the school counselor or bullying prevention coordinator at each school. The counselors were instructed to "select a diverse group of youth who had varying degrees of experience with bullying and victimization and were explicitly told not to select extreme bullies or victims" (p. 300). Fourteen focus groups consisting of six to nine students per group were conducted with approximately equal numbers from elementary school (three schools, six groups), middle school (two schools, four groups), and high school (two schools, four groups). The total sample size was 115. Focus group participants were told that they were considered "experts" at understanding the bullying situation within their school and that their insight would help to establish effective prevention programming. Through a series of open-ended questions, students were asked their input on bullying and specific factors that they believe contribute to bullying and victimization among boys and girls.

Prior research led the investigators to predict that, for both boys and girls at each grade level, low self-esteem, normative beliefs supporting bullying, and negative perceptions of school climate would predict both bullying and victimization. As predicted, a negative relationship was found between self-esteem and both bullying and victimization; specifically, decreases in self-esteem were related to increases in both bullying and victimization. Comments from the focus groups acknowledge the role that low self-esteem may play in bullying and victimization. However, focus group participants also noted that bullying behavior can come from those with normal or high levels of self-esteem, especially if the "bully" is powerful within the peer context and uses the power to maintain this power and/or dominate others. In regard to the impact of normative beliefs on bullying, a positive relationship was found; increases in normative beliefs supporting bullying led to increases in bullying behavior; this variable was the strongest predictor of increases in bullying. Though not explicitly stating that children bullied because it was acceptable to do so, there was a consensus among focus group participants that some level of bullying was a normal part of peer interactions. This finding led the authors to call for future research exploring "whether increasing normalization of bullying within a specific setting translates into increasing acceptability of the behavior" (Guerra et al., 2011, p. 307). Further, given their finding that at least some levels of bullying are viewed as normative across the school years, the researchers called for future research to examine the functions of bullying in the peer and school context. Within the survey data, school climate, defined as individuals' perceptions that school was a good place to be, was also found to be a significant predictor of bullying and victimization. It was found that positive perceptions of school climate led to a decrease in bullying and victimization. Within the focus groups, mentions of school climate were not brought up as a contributing factor to bullying.

Recall that the study was also interested in exploring how the relationship between the predictor variables and bullying and victimization varied based on gender or age. Few significant interaction effects were identified. For age, behavioral stability was found to be slightly greater in high school compared to elementary and middle school. Additionally, compared to high school, changes in self-esteem were found to have a significantly higher estimated effect on changes in victimization than in elementary and middle school. For gender, the estimated effects of changes in perceived school climate on changes in bullying and the estimated effects of changes in self-esteem on changes in victimization were greater for males compared to females. No additional significant interaction effects were found.

A benefit of conducting qualitative research (i.e., focus groups) in conjunction with quantitative research (i.e., survey) is that in addition to clarifying issues raised with the quantitative data, new themes may be identified and suggest areas for future research. Such was the case in this study. From the focus groups, two themes not typically considered in prior research on bullying and victimization emerged: 1) bullying as fun and entertaining and 2) bullying as related to sexuality. Bullying as a form of fun and entertainment was noted by focus group participants of all grades; though it was more clearly articulated by older youth. Several older students indicated excitement when watching a good fight at school or learning about the latest student drama on the Internet. The authors noted that little research has focused on this function of bullying, as most prior research has viewed bullying as a pathology.

In the middle and high school focus groups, bullying was also linked to popularity and sexuality. For boys, bullying was used as a way to elevate their status through demonstrations of physical force against other boys, and by insulting girls by calling them "sluts" or posting lewd comments about them online. Girls, on the other hand, used bullying as a way to enhance their physical and sexual appeal through the use of rumors, gossip, and exclusion. In conjunction with their limited findings for gender differences in their specified predictors and bullying or victimization, the authors concluded that "the etiology of bullying and victimization may be relatively comparable between boys and girls although the specific form (type of bullying) and function may differ" (Guerra et al., 2011, p. 308).

What Employers Say vs. What They Do

Surveys are a very good strategy for measuring what people think and how they feel about something; however, they are less effective in measuring actual behavior. Still, researchers continue to use verbal reports of what people say they would do as indicators of what they actually do. To determine whether this is appropriate, Devah Pager (see Photo 13.1) and Lincoln Quillian (2005) compared a field experiment with a survey. Their findings show that using verbal reports of what people say they would do may be particularly problematic in studies of discriminatory behavior.

We described the field experiment (referred to as an "audit study") in Chapter 8. Recall that Pager (2003) sent matched pairs of confederates,

▲ PHOTO 13.1 Devah Pager

called testers, to apply for real job openings in Milwaukee, Wisconsin. To test for hiring discrimination, the testers were similar except for two characteristics: race and criminal record. Pager manipulated race by having one White pair, which applied for 150 jobs, and one Black pair, which applied for 200 jobs. All of the testers were men, and within each same-race pair one tester presented himself as having a criminal record and the other did not. Pager measured employment opportunity by whether the applicant received a callback for an interview, finding evidence of discrimination on the basis of both race and criminal record: Black people received fewer callbacks than White people, and men with criminal records received fewer callbacks than their counterpart without criminal records.

The second study, a telephone survey, was conducted several months after the field experiment. Each of the 350 employers who had been contacted in the field experiment was called and asked to participate in an interview about hiring preferences and practices. During the survey, interviewers read a "vignette describing a job applicant with characteristics" that closely matched the profile of the testers in the field experiment who indicated that they had a criminal record (Pager & Quillian, 2005, p. 362). Thus, if the tester had been White, the vignette described a hypothetical White applicant, and if the tester had been Black, the hypothetical applicant in the vignette was Black. Below is the wording of the vignette (Pager & Quillian, 2005, p. 362):

> *Chad is a 23-year-old [Black/White] male. He finished high school and has steady work experience in entry-level jobs. He has good references and interacts well with people. About a year ago, Chad was convicted of a drug felony and served 12 months in prison. Chad was released last month and is now looking for a job. How likely would you be to hire Chad for an entry-level opening in your company?*

To answer the question in the vignette, employers were asked whether they would be "very likely, somewhat likely, somewhat unlikely, or very unlikely" to hire the applicant.

In almost every way, the vignette presented in the survey corresponded to the profile of the tester whom the employer encountered in the field experiment. The hypothetical applicant Chad had similar levels of education, experience, and personal qualities, and the type of crime was identical. And so, Pager and Quillian were able to compare employers' self-reported willingness to hire with how they actually responded to an applicant with nearly identical characteristics. Of the 350 employers contacted in the field experiment, 199, or 58 percent, responded to the survey. The results of the survey were not at all comparable to the field experiment. In the survey, irrespective of an applicant's race, slightly more than 60 percent of employers said they would be "somewhat likely" or "very likely" to hire a drug offender. In the field experiment, the callback rate was 17 percent for White testers with a criminal record and 5 percent for Black testers with a criminal record.

To take into account the fact that some testers may not receive a callback for reasons unrelated to race or criminal record, Pager and Quillian (2005) calculated "the likelihood that a tester with a criminal record will receive a callback *relative to* a White tester without a criminal record" (p. 365). Thus, since 34 percent of White applicants with no criminal record received a callback and 17 percent of White applicants with a criminal record received callbacks, the adjusted percentage of the latter group was 17/34 or 50 percent. Figure 13.2 presents the results of this calculation, comparing the employers' self-reported likelihood of hiring with the adjusted percentage of testers with criminal records who received callbacks. The figure shows a marginally significant difference between survey and audit results for White applicants ($p < .06$) and a significant difference for Black applicants ($p < .05$). As Pager and Quillian (2005) point out, "the callback rate for Black ex-offenders (14.7) [is] far short of the survey estimates of hiring likelihoods (61.7)" (p. 365).

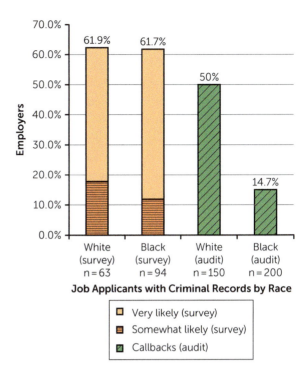

FIGURE 13.2 **Expressed Willingness to Hire a Drug Offender According to Employer Survey and Field Experiment (Audit Study).**

Why the large disparity between what employers say they would do in a survey and what they actually did in the field experiment? Pager and Quillian (2005) provide several possible methodological explanations. One possibility is that attitude measures are susceptible to the *social desirability effect*, a problem we discussed in Box 6.2. This refers to the tendency of respondents to conceal their true feelings by giving answers that project a more favorable image of themselves. Thus, if employers perceive that racial discrimination will not be viewed favorably, they may consciously suppress their negative reaction to a Black applicant by falsely reporting their feelings.

A second possibility is that employers may be indicating their "genuine willingness to consider hiring an applicant with a criminal record *in the abstract*" (Pager & Quillian, 2005, p. 371), as in response to the hypothetical applicant in the survey. However, in real hiring situations, many factors may come into play, and "the presence of a criminal record may become a salient criterion by which to weed out less-qualified applicants" (p. 371). Thirdly, the "priming" of characteristics such as race and criminal record may not elicit the same intensity of response in a phone interview as they do in person. Of course, it is possible that all of these processes as well as others may have produced the observed discrepancy.

Explaining Discrimination in a Low-Wage Labor Market

Devah Pager, Bruce Western, and Bart Bonikowski (2009) conducted a second audit study in New York City. Whereas the Milwaukee study examined the impact of a criminal record on job discrimination, controlling for race, the New York study focused directly on racial discrimination. In addition, the new study examined the experiences of three racial/ethnic groups: Black, Latino, and White. Thus, the researchers formed two teams, each consisting of a Black, Latino, and White tester, who were men of similar ages and height, carefully matched in verbal skills, and underwent rigorous training. In one of the teams, the White tester had a criminal record and in the other team he did not; therefore, unlike the Milwaukee study, the impact of race could be compared directly with the impact of a criminal record. Finally, all testers took extensive field notes of their interactions with employers, which enabled the researchers to explore the process of discrimination.

To select job openings, each week over a period of nine months, the researchers drew a simple random sample of job listings from the classified sections of major New York newspapers and the website, Craigslist. Sampled job listings were limited to "entry-level positions, defined as jobs requiring little previous experience and no more than a high school degree. Job titles included restaurant jobs, retail sales, warehouse workers, couriers, telemarketers . . . and a wide range of other low-wage positions" (Pager et al., 2009, p. 782). Testers were assigned fictitious résumés and presented themselves "as high school graduates with steady work experience in entry-level jobs" (p. 781). The dependent variable was measured as any positive response consisting of either a callback for a second interview or a job offer.

Each team performed a separate experiment, so there are two sets of results. Figure 13.3 shows the positive response rates for the first team, consisting of equally qualified White, Latino, and Black male applicants. Based on applications to 171 employers, White testers received a callback or job offer 31 percent of the time, compared with 25.1 percent for Latino testers and 15.2 percent for Black testers. Statistical tests indicate that the positive response rate for Black testers is significantly lower than the rates for both White and Latino testers, but there is no significant difference between Whites and Latino testers. Figure 13.4 shows the positive response rates for the second team, in which the White tester was assigned a criminal record. In this case, White testers received a callback or job offer for 17.2 percent of 169 job applications, compared with 15.4 percent for Latino testers and

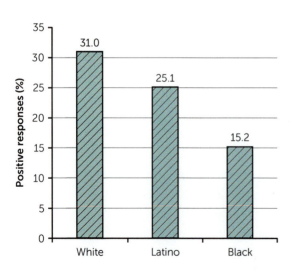

FIGURE 13.3 Percent of Callbacks or Job Offers by Race/Ethnicity

13.0 for Black testers. These positive response rates do not differ significantly, essentially replicating the results of the Milwaukee study. That is, New York employers treated Black and Latino applicants as equivalent to White applicants with a criminal record.

Together, the Milwaukee and New York audit studies provide clear evidence of "the continuing significance of race" in hiring decisions. These data do not tell us, however, the processes through which racial discrimination takes place. To uncover differential treatment, the researchers turned to testers' field notes to determine how interactions with employers differed by race/ethnicity. Although in many cases the discrimination was so subtle that differential treatment was difficult to detect, the researchers were able to identify three consistent patterns of discrimination in employers' behavior, which generally occurred at different points in the hiring process.

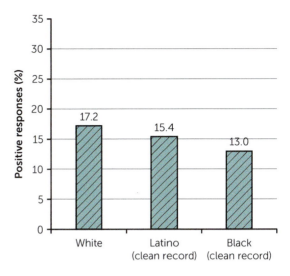

FIGURE 13.4 Percent of Callbacks or Job Offers by Race/Ethnicity and Criminal Record

The first type of discrimination, which occurred at the initial point of contact, was "categorical exclusion": "an immediate or automatic rejection of the Black (or minority) candidate in favor of a White applicant" (Pager et al., 2009, p. 787). This pattern was revealed in several cases when minority applicants were told that the "position has already been filled," but the White tester, who applied later, was offered the job.

The second pattern of discrimination, labeled "shifting standards," occurred after initial contact as employers assessed the qualifications of applicants. In these cases, "similar qualifications or deficits" took on "varying relevance depending on the applicant's race" (Pager et al., 2009, p. 787). For example, in the case of a job at a moving company, identical qualifications were evaluated differently for minority and White applicants. All three candidates pointed out their prior experience as stockpersons (albeit in different companies). But whereas both the Black and Latino testers were told that they were looking for someone with moving experience, the employer told the White tester: "To be honest, we're looking for someone with specific moving experience. But because you've worked for [a storage company], that has a little to do with moving" (p. 789). The tester was then asked "to come in tomorrow."

The third pattern of discrimination, "race-coded job channeling," occurred at the stage of job placement. This pattern "represents a process by which minority applicants are steered toward particular job types, often those characterized by greater physical demands and reduced customer contact" (Pager et al., 2009, p. 787). For example, the Black tester described the following interaction when he applied for a sales position at a lighting store:

> When she asked what position I was looking for I said I was open, but that since they were looking for a salesperson I would be interested in that. She smiled, put her head in her hand and her elbow on the table and said, "I need a stock boy. Can you do stock boy?" (Pager et al., 2009, p. 790)

The Latino and White testers, by contrast, were able to apply for the advertised sales position.

Testers' field notes revealed 53 cases of job channeling. When these cases were coded as downward (e.g., from sales to stock boy) or upward (e.g., dishwasher to waitstaff), the researchers found in the majority of cases that all testers on a team were channeled in the same direction. In the remaining 23 cases, however, channeling was strongly related to race. When channeling varied across testers, nine Black testers, five Latino testers, and one White tester (who presented a criminal record) were channeled into lower positions; and no Black testers, two Latino testers, and six White testers were channeled up.

13.3 PURPOSES OF MIXED METHODS RESEARCH

As our examples show, researchers may conduct mixed methods research for various purposes. This begs the question: When should you use multiple approaches? In the broadest sense, you should consider choosing mixed methods when this is likely to result in "a *better understanding* of the phenomenon being studied" (Greene, 2007, p. 98). While a variety of more specific purposes have been proposed (e.g., Greene et al., 1989; Mark, 2015; Mark & Shotland, 1987), four categories seem to capture most of mixed methods research: triangulation, complementarity, development, and expansion. We now discuss each of these purposes.

Triangulation

Research for the purpose of triangulation seeks to use one approach to verify or confirm the findings of another approach. Pager and Quillian's comparison of experimental audit results with those of a survey of employers contacted in the audit study was an attempt to triangulate. Although this study failed to cross-validate results from different approaches, its conflicting results further demonstrate the value of mixed methods designs with the aim of triangulation. On the one hand, the study shows the importance of applying methods that will provide the most valid answers to a research question. It clearly demonstrates that self-reports in surveys may not be appropriate to address questions about discriminatory *behavior*; more generally, it alerts us to the limitations in drawing inferences about behavior from what people say they will do. On the other hand, the discrepant findings led the researchers to theorize about why people may not always do what they say they will do. By producing discrepant results, mixed methods research thus can create empirical puzzles that raise new questions and prompt new insights and interpretations (Mark, 2015).

Complementarity

Whereas triangulation designs use different approaches to address the same research question, complementary mixed methods designs address different but related research questions. The approaches are "complementary" in the sense that they "serve to elaborate, enhance, deepen, or broaden the overall interpretations and inferences from the study" (Greene, 2007, p. 101). Most complementary designs either use qualitative data to interpret the results of a quantitative study or quantitative data to test hypotheses derived from a qualitative study (Small, 2011, p. 65). A good example of the former purpose is Pager, Western, and Bonikowski's (2009) audit study in which the auditors recorded extensive field notes. The field experiment addressed the question, "Is there racial discrimination in the low-wage labor market in New York City?" However, the experimental data alone, which showed discrimination based on whether applicants received a callback or job offer, could not answer the question, "When and how did racial bias occur in the hiring process?" To address this question and provide a deeper, more comprehensive understanding, the researchers relied on the auditors' field observations.

In this mixed methods design, the methods are complementary insofar as one method fills in a gap or makes up for the weaknesses of another. Audit studies provide evidence of racial discrimination but fail to reveal the processes by which discrimination occurs. This gap was filled in the New York audit study through field observations that showed how employer–applicant interactions differed by race/ethnicity.

Development

A mix of methods also may be used for the purpose of development, wherein one method helps in the development or implementation of another method. You have encountered this process in previous chapters even though we did not apply the term "mixed methods." For example, pretests of experiments and survey instruments usually involve qualitative observation or interviews with a small number of participants. Experimenters may interview pretest participants to probe their interpretation of procedures; survey researchers may use focus groups to create or check the wording of survey items, and they may conduct preliminary interviews to identify problematic questions and instructions. Survey pretests also may include open-ended questions to develop closed questions. These are just a few examples of how qualitative research informs the design of quantitative research (experiments and surveys). Other combinations also are possible for developmental purposes.

Expansion

The fourth purpose for mixed methods research is to expand the scope and range of the study (Greene, 2007). Although the methods in the bullying study were often complementary, Guerra et al. (2011) chose to use focus groups in addition to survey data as a way to expand upon the findings from the survey data. The survey data allowed for the examination of individual and contextual predictors of bullying and victimization. The focus group data, in addition to providing further insights into the relationship between individual and contextual factors and bullying, also brought to light new themes that were traditionally not considered in bullying research.

SUMMARY

Mixed methods may fulfill various purposes, both planned and unplanned. One methodological approach may verify or confirm the findings of another approach (triangulation); enhance the interpretation or inferences of another approach (complementarity); and facilitate the development or implementation of the methods of another approach (development); or different approaches may be used to examine different but related phenomena (expansion). While "theory suggests simplistic mixing of two or more methods for one purpose" (Greene, 2007, p. 129), in practice a mixed methods study may satisfy multiple purposes as in the study of bullying. Check your understanding of this section in Box 13.2.

BOX 13.2

CHECKING YOUR UNDERSTANDING

Mixed Methods Research

1. The comparison of experimental audit and survey results in the Pager and Quillian study is an examples of which purpose of using mixed methods?
    a. Triangulation
    b. Complementarity
    c. Development
    d. Expansion

2. Using qualitative observation and interviews to pretest experiments and survey questions serves which purpose of using mixed methods research?
   a. Triangulation
   b. Complementarity
   c. Development
   d. Expansion

3. Using different approaches to examine different but related phenomena is an example of which purpose of using mixed methods research?
   a. Triangulation
   b. Complementarity
   c. Development
   d. Expansion

Answers: 1. a, 2. c, 3. d

13.4 MIXED METHODS RESEARCH DESIGNS

In addition to research purpose, mixed methods research may be classified in terms of various design features (Creswell & Plano Clark, 2017; Greene, 2007; Tashakkori & Teddlie, 2010). Here we discuss two of the most important design decisions: timing and integration. Timing refers to whether the approaches are implemented sequentially or concurrently; integration pertains to whether they are carried out independently of one another or integrated throughout the process of data collection and analysis. Our examples above illustrate each of these design choices. (See Box 13.3 for a discussion of the limitations of mixed methods designs.)

BOX 13.3

DOING CRIMINAL JUSTICE RESEARCH

Limitations and Guidelines for Doing Mixed Methods Research

This chapter emphasizes the benefits of mixed methods research, but we would be remiss if we did not point out the obstacles and limitations in using mixed methods. With these in mind, you should be in a better position to decide if a mix of methods provides the best means, considering your resources, of addressing your research question.

continues

continued

One obstacle is that using mixed methods is more time-consuming and expensive than a single approach. It requires more resources and places more demands on the researcher, who must be knowledgeable about a range of approaches as well as how to mix them effectively. Given the training necessary to develop expertise and remain up to date in one research method, most researchers specialize. To overcome this problem, some scholars (Pearce, 2012; Yoshikawa et al., 2008) recommend a team approach for mixed methods research that brings together researchers with different methodological training and expertise.

Not only may the use of mixed methods be more difficult for researchers, but it also can be more burdensome for participants, especially with regard to time. Mixed methods invariably create a greater burden when the same participants are involved in more than one method of data collection, such as when survey respondents are asked to participate in in-depth interviews.

Besides the additional burden placed on research participants, mixed methods designs that begin with a survey and follow up with qualitative research present other problems (Leahey, 2007). For the follow-up to be possible, researchers must have access to identifying information to do fieldwork in the area of the original research site or to recontact participants. But to protect privacy, this kind of information is generally removed after data collection and is always stripped from surveys available for secondary analysis. Therefore, a practical limitation of this type of mixed methods research is that the researchers must have conducted the surveys themselves and must have the foresight to obtain the information necessary to contact respondents and get IRB approval to do so.

Finally, similar to the use of big data (see Box 11.1), mixed methods research may pose a threat to invasion of privacy whenever data from different sources are linked (Brewer & Hunter, 1989). This was an ethical issue in Laud Humphreys' classic study, in which he observed homosexual acts and then, in disguise, later contacted and interviewed the participants.

Now that you are aware of both the benefits and limitations of mixed methods research, we offer a few guidelines for doing your own research. For the novice researcher, who may be undertaking a small-scale project, we recommend:

1. Determine whether a mix of approaches can best address your research question.
2. Take a team approach by having different people carry out each method.
3. If time is short (say, less than a semester), use a concurrent mixed methods design.
4. Limit integration to a comparison of basic findings.
5. Obtain informed consent and protect privacy for each method of data collection.

Sequential Designs

In **sequential designs**, the collection and analysis of data by one approach precedes the collection and analysis of data by another. Pager and Quillian's (2005) study was sequential in design: the telephone survey of employers was carried out several months after the field experiment in which the same employers were first contacted. Only a sequential design could provide a direct comparison between what employers did (in the field experiment) and what they said they would do (in the survey) in terms of hiring job applicants. Guerra et al.'s (2011) study also entailed a sequential design as the survey was administered during Year 1 of the three-year study, and the focus groups were conducted during the second and third years of the study with students who had not completed the survey during Year 1.

Sequential designs are implicit in mixed methods research that is conducted for the explicit purpose of development, and they often are used when one method is intended to complement another. In addition to using quantitative data to test ideas derived inductively from qualitative research, Mario Small (2011) cites several studies that followed up surveys with in-depth interviews to interpret and understand the mechanisms behind statistical associations. Thus, the strength of sequential designs lies in "their ability to resolve specific questions that emerge in the process of data collection with additional data collection" (Small, 2011, p. 68).

sequential design a mixed methods design in which data collection and analysis with one approach precedes data collection and analysis with another approach

Concurrent Designs

In **concurrent designs**, data collection with different approaches is carried out more or less simultaneously. The New York audit study of discrimination in the low-wage labor market were concurrent. This type of design may be used for practical reasons or when the order of the data collection is not relevant to the research question, as in many triangulation studies. As Small (2011) points out, whether you decide on a concurrent or sequential design may depend, in part, on whether you must determine the nature of the design before you begin a study. Many qualitative researchers, especially those in the grounded theory tradition, believe that the type of data collected at any point should be based on what is being continuously discovered.

concurrent design a mixed methods design in which data collection with different approaches is carried out at the same time

Component Designs

By definition, the approaches chosen in mixed methods designs are connected or "mixed" in some way. An important distinction can be made, however, between designs in which the approaches are connected only at the concluding stage, when comparing findings, and designs in which the approaches are integrated at prior stages of data collection and analysis (Caracelli & Greene, 1997; Greene, 2007). In the former, called **component designs**, the approaches are implemented relatively independently

component design a mixed methods design in which findings from different approaches are compared after each approach is carried out independently without having one inform the other except to compare findings. Pager and Quillian's research could be considered a component design insofar as the field experiment and telephone survey were carried out and analyzed separately before connections were made between the two sets of results.

Integrated Designs

Mixed methods may be integrated in many ways during the stages of data collection and analysis. The Milwaukee audit study comparing the results of a survey and field experiment was an **integrated design** because employers in the survey were the same employers who were contacted in the field experiment.

Many integrated designs involve **nesting**, in which data collection with one approach is embedded within another approach, so that different kinds of data are collected from the same actors, organizations, or entities (Lieberman, 2005; Small, 2011). The inferential power of nesting (and integration) can be seen in the New York audit study, in which the collection of qualitative data on employer–applicant interactions was nested within the field experiment. Without this nested design, it is doubtful that the various patterns of differential treatment could have been identified. Carefully matched testers in the field experiment provided clear evidence of discrimination when they applied for entry-level positions. But these data revealed nothing directly about how and why one applicant received a callback or job offer and another did not. As Pager and colleagues (2009) point out, their testers "rarely perceived any signs of clear prejudice" (p. 793). It was only by comparing field observations of employer interactions with Black, Latino, and White applicants that patterns of differential treatment were revealed.

integrated design a mixed methods design in which different approaches are connected or merged during the process of data collection and analysis

nesting a process in mixed methods research whereby different kinds of data are collected from the same individuals or groups by embedding one approach within another

SUMMARY

The timing and level of integration of different methods creates four different types of mixed methods designs. In sequential designs, data collection and analysis with one approach precedes that of another approach; whereas in concurrent designs, data collection and analysis with different approaches occur simultaneously. In component designs, different approaches are linked only after each approach is independently implemented; whereas in integrated designs, there is a blending of approaches during the process of data collection and analysis. Neither of these distinctions is hard and fast, however, as mixed methods may involve both sequential and concurrent methodological components, and integration is a matter of degree. (Check your understanding of this section in Box 13.4.)

BOX 13.4 CHECKING YOUR UNDERSTANDING

Mixed Methods Research Design

1. Pager and Quillian used a _____ design in conducting an audit study and survey of the same employers; Pager, Western, and Bonikowski used a _____ design in combining field observations with their audit study.
   a. concurrent; component
   b. sequential; component
   c. sequential; concurrent
   d. integrated; sequential
   e. concurrent; integrated

2. Suppose you decide to conduct a campus survey and then do follow-up qualitative interviews with a small subsample of survey participants. This is an example of a(n)
   a. concurrent design
   b. developmental design
   c. expanded design
   d. nested design

3. Concurrent designs are implicit in mixed methods research that is conducted for the explicit purpose of development.
   a. True
   b. False

4. An example of nesting is conducting in-depth interviews with a sample of respondents who participate in a survey.
   a. True
   b. False

Answers: 1. d, 2. d, 3. a, 4. a

KEY TERMS

component design, p. 395
concurrent design, p. 395
integrated design, p. 396
mixed methods research, p. 379
nesting, p. 396
sequential design, p. 395
triangulation, p. 378

KEY POINTS

- Triangulating, or applying different methods and research strategies to address the same research question, enhances the validity of study results.
- In selecting a research approach and in combining approaches, researchers should carefully consider the strengths and weaknesses of alternative research strategies.
- Mixed methods research combines more than one method of data collection or analysis in the same investigation.
- Methods of data collection may be combined to examine the convergence of research findings (triangulation), to interpret or test the knowledge gained from one method with data from another method (complementarity), to facilitate the development or implementation of the methods of data collection (development), or to broaden the scope and range of a study (expansion).
- Mixed methods designs vary along two main dimensions: timing and integration.
- Sequential designs gather data from one approach before or after another approach; in concurrent designs, data collection occurs at the same time.
- Component designs gather data independently from different approaches and compare findings; integrated designs blend the methods during data collection and analysis.

REVIEW QUESTIONS

1. Explain how the principle of triangulation applies to convergent validity assessment, discussed in Chapter 6.
2. Each approach to social research applies the principle of triangulation in different ways. Explain how triangulation typically is applied in experiments, surveys, field research, and the analysis of existing data.
3. Describe the relative strengths and weakness of the four basic approaches with respect to: (a) internal validity (or the ability to determine cause and effect); (b) nonreactive measurement; and (c) external validity.
4. What are the two principal ways of combining methods for the purpose of complementarity?
5. Give two examples of how mixed methods may be used for the purpose of development.
6. What are two basic dimensions of mixed methods research designs?
7. Identify the purposes and designs of (a) Pager and Quillian's Milwaukee audit study ("What Employers Say Versus What They Do") and (b) Pager, Western, and Bonikowski's New York audit study ("Explaining Discrimination in a Low-Wage Labor Market").

EXERCISES

1. What basic approach to social research would you use to address each of the following research objectives? In each case, explain the advantages of this approach over others.

    a. Pay It Forward, 2000 film, popularized the idea that people who are the beneficiaries of a favor or good deed should "pay it forward" by doing a favor for others rather than paying back the original benefactor. Suppose you want to test the more general proposition that experiencing success or good fortune increases a person's willingness to help others. For example, will someone who receives an award or, say, happens to find a dollar bill in the street, be more likely to help others than someone who does not experience such good fortune?

    b. Suppose a student task force is asked to document the current state of formal volunteering on a college campus: How many students volunteer? Where do current students volunteer? What kinds of volunteer work do they do?

    c. Prison reading programs are offered by nonprofit organizations across the country to increase prison literacy rates and reduce recidivism among inmates. What do these programs entail? Are the programs effective in reaching their goals?

2. In an article in the September 2020 issue of *Criminal Justice and Behavior* (47:1190–1208), Shannon Dodd, Emma Antrobus, and Michelle Sydes examined correctional officer support for the use of body-worn cameras (BWCs) in prison. Read this article and answer the following questions.

    a. What two methods of data collection did the researchers use?
    b. Identify the type of mixed methods research design.
    c. How did the researchers select respondents for in-depth interviews?
    d. Table 3 reports survey results showing that correctional officers generally supported the use of BWCs in corrections. How did the in-depth interviews elaborate this finding?
    e. Table 3 also shows that correctional officers agreed that the advantages of BWCs outweigh the disadvantages. What did the in-depth interviews reveal regarding the advantages and disadvantages of BWCs?
    f. What general purpose was served by this mixed methods research?

14

Quantitative Data Analysis

Using Statistics for Description and Inference

CHAPTER OUTLINE

14.1 Introductory Overview: The Process of Quantitative Analysis 403

14.2 Prepare Data for Computerized Analysis: Data Processing 404
Coding 404
Editing 404
Entering the Data 405
Cleaning 408
Summary 408

14.3 Inspect and Modify Data 409
Nominal- and Ordinal-Scale Variables 410
Interval- and Ratio-Scale Variables 412
Summary 416

14.4 Carry Out Preliminary Hypothesis Testing 417
Nominal- and Ordinal-Scale Variables 418
Interval- and Ratio-Scale Variables 423
Summary 428

14.5 Conduct Multivariate Testing 429
Elaboration of Contingency Tables 430
Multiple Regression 433
Summary 438

LEARNING OBJECTIVES

By the end of the chapter, you should be able to

14.1 Identify the steps in quantitative data analysis.

14.2 Describe and apply the steps in processing survey data.

14.3 Explain how to read tables and graphs depicting univariate and bivariate distributions.

14.4 Differentiate tests of statistical significance from measures of association.

14.5 Explain how multivariate testing is used to statistically control for extraneous variables.

In previous chapters covering methods of measurement, sampling, and data collection, we have presented many research findings. Here is a sampling from quantitative research:

- Baumer, Cundiff, and Luo (2021) tested whether there was a statistically significant association between school commitment and changes in youth offending (Chapter 5).
- Ariel, Farrar, and Sutherland (2015) found a significant reduction in the number of use of force incidents when officers utilized body-worn cameras (Chapter 6).
- As hypothesized, Lucas, Graif, and Lovaglia (2006) found that participants in the murder condition withheld more questions, on average, than participants in the assault condition (Chapter 8).

Although we have not always presented the data in detail, all of these findings are based on statistics. What you have not yet learned, and what we want to show you in this chapter, is how these statistics are produced and what they mean.

The analysis and interpretation of data is often the final step in the research process. As we illustrated in Chapter 2, however, data analysis is part of a cycle of inquiry that takes place whenever theory and data are compared. This comparison occurs continually in qualitative research when investigators attempt to bring order to, or make sense of, their observations and interviews. In quantitative research, such as surveys and experiments, researchers typically bring theory and data together when testing a hypothesis once the data have been gathered and processed. Thus, data analysis consists of the "dynamic interplay between theory and data" (Rosenberg, 1968, p. 217): theory guides the analysis of data, and data analysis contributes to the development of theory.

This chapter covers quantitative data analysis; Chapter 15 is devoted to qualitative data analysis. By quantitative data, we mean observations that have been transformed into counts or numbers. These are the data most typically generated in experiments, surveys, and some forms of research using existing data. Quantitative analysis is synonymous with statistical analysis. A *statistic* is a summary statement about a set of data; statistics as a discipline provides techniques for organizing and analyzing data.

Researchers draw upon two broad types of statistics: descriptive and inferential. **Descriptive statistics** organize and summarize data to make them more intelligible. The high and low scores and average score on an exam are descriptive statistics that readily summarize a class's performance. **Inferential statistics** are used to estimate population characteristics from sample data (discussed in Chapter 6) and to test hypotheses. In this chapter, we describe these different types of statistics and elaborate on the logic underlying their application in quantitative analysis.

Because much of quantitative research follows the deductive model of inquiry, we focus on the process by which investigators perform statistical tests of hypotheses. The most elaborate forms of analysis are done with survey data and with some forms of existing (quantitative) data. Given the widespread use of surveys in criminal justice

descriptive statistics procedures for organizing and summarizing data

inferential statistics procedures for determining the extent to which one may generalize beyond the data at hand

research, we concentrate on survey data in this chapter. We begin with a description of a survey. Using data from this survey and the General Social Survey (GSS), we then describe the key steps in quantitative data analysis.

In Chapter 7 we discussed a study conducted by Amialchuk and Sapci (2021), which utilized data collected from the National Longitudinal Study of Adolescent to Adult Health (Add Health) on the influence of adolescent misperceptions of alcohol use. Add Health survey responses are collected across multiple years from individuals in 7th–12th grades via in-home interviews. In Amialchuk and Sapci's (2021) study of underage alcohol use, they focused on data collected in wave 2 (1996).

Like many large-scale surveys, the Add Health survey yielded data enabling researchers to address numerous research questions. For purposes of illustration, we will consider the one posed by Amialchuk and Sapci (2021): What is "the effect of misperception about friends' alcohol use on adolescents' alcohol consumption behaviors and alcohol-related problems?" (p. 453). This study added to the previous research because they utilized a nationally representative sample and were able to actually measure misperceptions of friends' drinking behaviors: when responding about the perceptions of their friends' consumption, participants identified the friend, and researchers followed up with the friend to measure their actual behaviors to be able to identify whether individuals correctly perceive their friends' behaviors.

Multiple self-reported outcome (dependent) variables were tested in this study, including three measures of alcohol consumption and 11 measures of alcohol-related problems. The survey contained many background variables that might influence alcohol consumption and alcohol-related problems, including but not limited to age, gender, race, family income, whether the adolescent lived with both biological parents, attendance at religious services, and whether alcohol, cigarettes, or illegal drugs were easily available at home.

To measure the main independent variable, alcohol use misperception, the researchers created a score by taking the difference between the perceived and the actual proportions of friends who use alcohol. To measure perception, participants were asked, "Of your 3 best friends, how many drink alcohol at least once a month?" To measure actual proportion of friends who consumed alcohol, the participants' nominated friends provided responses. "The resulting alcohol misperception score ranges between –1 and 1, where negative values indicate underestimation and positive numbers indicate overestimation of the proportion of friend drinkers, and the score of zero indicates correct estimation (no perceptual bias)" (Amialchuk & Sapci, 2021, p. 460).

Amialchuk and Sapci's (2021) quantitative analysis of data from the Add Health data showed that higher misperception scores led to an increased probability of all three alcohol consumption outcomes: respondent's drinking in general, binge drinking, and getting drunk more than once a month in the previous year. In addition, when the participants' perceptual biases increased, so did the severity of all 11 alcohol-related problems, such as driving while drunk, getting into a physical fight because of drinking, getting into a regrettable sexual situation after drinking, and having problems at school or with schoolwork because of drinking.

In this chapter, we describe in detail how researchers have analyzed data to reach their conclusions as Amialchuk and Sapci were able to. But first we provide an overview of the steps involved in quantitative analysis.

14.1 INTRODUCTORY OVERVIEW: THE PROCESS OF QUANTITATIVE ANALYSIS

Figure 14.1 outlines the steps involved in analyzing quantitative data. While some of these steps apply to all forms of quantitative analysis, the process as a whole is most applicable to the analysis of survey and existing (quantitative) data. These steps vary depending on the data collection approach; moreover, there are sub steps within each step.

The first step of preparing data for computerized analysis, called **data processing**, overlaps with data collection. To conduct quantitative analyses, the information gathered in a survey, for example, must be quantified and transcribed to a computer-readable datafile. In addition, the datafile should be as error-free as possible.

data processing the preparation of data for analysis

Researchers analyzing existing data—whether from a survey, such as the Add Health study, or another source—begin their analysis at the second step: data inspection and data modification. The goal of inspection is to get a clear picture of the data in order to determine appropriate statistical analyses and necessary data modifications. The reasons for data modification are many: for example, a researcher may want to combine the responses to several items in order to create an index or scale (see Chapter 6), change one or more of the values for a variable, or combine categories for purposes of analysis. As we described above, Amialchuk and Sapci (2021) combined answers to two survey questions to create a measure of alcohol use misperception.

The analysis then turns to empirical testing of the hypothesized relationships. For simple two-variable (bivariate) hypotheses, the analyst determines whether the association between the independent and dependent variables confirms theoretical expectations. For example, a researcher may test a bivariate hypothesis such as: alcohol consumption is negatively associated with GPA. In a true experiment, assessing the relationship between the independent and dependent variables is often the final analysis step because an adequate design effectively controls extraneous variables.

In nonexperimental designs, some extraneous variables may affect a hypothesized bivariate relationship. Therefore, the quantitative analyst conducts multivariate testing as a final step by statistically controlling for extraneous variables. If preliminary hypothesis testing supports theoretical expectations, the analyst formulates and tests multivariate models to rule out, to the extent possible, that the initial results are a spurious consequence of uncontrolled

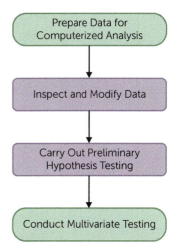

FIGURE 14.1 The Process of Quantitative Data Analysis

antecedent variables. Amialchuk and Sapci had to examine the possibility, for example, that students' access to substances (alcohol, cigarettes, or illegal drugs) creates a spurious association between misperceptions of friends' drinking and their own alcohol consumption. Conversely, if hypothesized relationships are not supported in preliminary testing, the researcher designs multivariate models to determine if uncontrolled extraneous variables are blocking or distorting the initial results. While quantitative data analysis often proceeds from the deductive logic of inquiry, as in the above examples, it may also follow the inductive logic of inquiry. For example, the preliminary testing step may reveal unanticipated (serendipitous) findings that suggest alternative multivariate models.

14.2 PREPARE DATA FOR COMPUTERIZED ANALYSIS: DATA PROCESSING

According to James Davis and Tom Smith (1992), data preparation is the "least glorious" step of survey research (p. 60). But, as they also note, the quality of the data rests largely on data processing: many errors may be introduced into the data, and many checks and safeguards should be incorporated to avoid such errors. To make this step more manageable, data processing can be broken down into four smaller steps: coding, editing, entering data into a datafile, and checking data for errors (cleaning). The accomplishment of each data-processing task depends on the type of data and how they were collected.

Coding

In quantitative research, coding consists of transforming data into numbers, if it is not already in this form. As we described in Chapter 9, coding survey responses generally occurs as part of the process of data collection. Actually, most surveys are precoded; that is, prior to data collection, each response category of closed-ended questions is assigned a number, which may be specified directly on the interview schedule. In conducting the survey, interviewers either circle the numbered response or, in computer-assisted interviewing, enter the numbered response directly into a datafile.

Coding answers to closed-ended survey questions is straightforward: there are relatively few categories, and you simply assign a different code to each category. However, the coding of responses to open-ended survey questions with large numbers of unique responses and textual data more generally, as in in-depth interviews and some forms of content analysis, is much more complicated. We will have more to say about this type of coding in Chapter 15 on qualitative analysis.

Editing

Editing involves checking for errors and inconsistencies in the data. An error in a survey asking for birth date, for example, would be the recording of a student's birth date as 4/11/1899; an inconsistency in the Add Health data would have occurred if a respondent reported "never" when asked, "During the past 12 months, on how many days did you drink alcohol?" but also reported "three to 12 times in the past 12 months" when asked, "Over the past 12 months, on how many days did you drink five or more drinks in a row?" Most editing is programmed into digital and online surveys; for instance, if an interviewer entered "0" ("never") on the question regarding general drinking, the program would likely prompt the interviewer to skip the additional alcohol consumption questions.

Entering the Data

Once data are coded and edited, they need to be entered into a digital datafile. As with editing, data entry into a digital file occurs automatically in digital interviews. For some paper-and-pencil surveys, data may be entered using software programmed to detect some kinds of erroneous entries; this is called computer-assisted data entry (CADE). The software, originally named Statistical Package for the Social Sciences and known today by the acronym SPSS, is widely used by criminal justice researchers. (Other popular statistical software packages are Stata, SAS, and R, the latter of which is free. In addition, programs such as Microsoft Excel and Google Sheets, which is also free, may be used for data entry and some forms of analysis.)

When data are entered, they are stored in a **data matrix** or spreadsheet, with observations as rows and variables as columns. Figure 14.2 presents a partial data matrix for a 2003 campus survey on alcohol consumption. The figure shows the typical form of data storage. The rows represent respondents, who are identified by unique ID codes (first column). The remaining columns contain the coded responses to each question or variable. Carefully look over the matrix. As you review the figure, take note of the following:

data matrix the form of a computer datafile, with rows as cases and columns as variables; each cell represents the value of a particular variable (column) for a particular case (row)

- Notice that the columns are headed by abbreviated variable names. To facilitate data analysis, the campus survey used mnemonic labels. For example, the labels FREQALC and NUMDRNKS, stand for "frequency of alcohol consumption" and "number of drinks consumed."
- Numerical codes in the matrix cells identify question responses or variable categories. For respondent's sex (sixth column), a code of 1 was used for males and 2 for females. Thus, the first four listed respondents are females, and the next two are males.
- Distinct codes are used to identify respondents to whom the question does not apply or missing data. The term **missing data** refers to the absence of substantive information on a variable for a respondent. In the campus survey, "don't know" responses and refusals to answer the question were treated as missing data. Thus, the code "9" in column 3 (FREQALC) and the code "97" in column 4 (NUMDRNKS) opposite ID 005 indicate that these questions were skipped and did not apply to this respondent (because a code of "1" [for "abstain"] was entered in column 2 [ALCCONS]). The code "99" in column 8 (CUMGPA) for IDs 005 and 007 indicates that these data are missing (because these respondents did not grant permission to have their GPAs obtained from the Registrar).

missing data the absence of information on a variable for a given case

ID	ALCCONS	FREQALC	NUMDRNKS	RACE	SEX	CLASS	CUMGPA
001	2	6	3	1	2	1	2.34
002	2	4	7	1	2	3	3.31
003	4	2	12	5	2	2	3.33
004	3	3	6	1	2	2	3.03
005	1	9	97	3	1	4	99
006	3	3	10	1	1	3	3.37
007	2	3	3	1	2	3	99
008	2	6	2	1	1	4	3.23
009	3	2	8	1	1	4	2.47
010	3	3	10	1	1	1	2.61

FIGURE 14.2 Partial Data Matrix for a 2003 Campus Survey

In addition to the datafile, most researchers create a codebook. Like a codebook for content analysis, described in Chapter 11, a survey codebook serves as a guide for coding and data entry and as a detailed record of the electronic layout of the data. Codebooks are essential to researchers who are analyzing available survey data such as the Add Health data. Whether you are analyzing one of the numerous data sets available online or creating a codebook for your own survey, Box 14.1 will familiarize you with the information contained in a codebook.

BOX 14.1

DOING CRIMINAL JUSTICE RESEARCH

Codebook Documentation

A survey codebook is like a dictionary in that it defines the meaning of the numerical codes for each named variable, such as the codes for sex in the campus survey. Codebooks also may contain question wording, interviewer directions, and coding and editing decision rules. Examining a codebook and other study documentation, such as information about the sample and data collection procedures, should help you decide if a given data set will be useful for your research.

Figure A is a codebook entry from the GSS Cumulative Data file 1972–2018 (Smith et al. 2019). Look over this entry and see if you can find the following information:

GUNLAW	FAVOR OR OPPOSE GUN PERMITS

Description of the Variable

86. Would you favor or oppose a law which would require a person to obtain a police permit before he or she could buy a gun?

Percent	N	Value	Label
76.3	32,038	1	FAVOR
23.7	9,975	2	OPPOSE
	21,939	0	IAP
	748	8	DK
	114	9	NA
100.0	64,814		Total

Properties	
Data type:	numeric
Missing-data codes:	0,8,9
Mean:	1.24
Std Dev:	.43
Record/column:	1/576

FIGURE A Codebook Entry from GSS Cumulative Data File, 1972–2018

1. variable name and label,
2. exact wording of the survey question,
3. values and value labels (i.e., numerical and textual response options) for valid or legitimate responses,
4. codes for missing data, and
5. record and column locations (i.e., the electronic location of these data in the datafile).

Answers: 1. GUNLAW, FAVOR OR OPPOSE GUN PERMITS. 2. Would you favor or oppose a law which would require a person to obtain a police permit before he or she could buy a gun? 3. 1 = FAVOR; 2 = OPPOSE. 4. 0 = IAP (Inapplicable); 8 = DK (Don't know); 9 = NA (No answer). 5. Record = 1; column = 576.

Cleaning

After the data have been entered into a digital file, the researcher "cleans" the data. **Data cleaning** refers to detecting and resolving errors in coding and digital transmittal.

Data entry can introduce errors when entry operators misread codes, transpose numbers, skip over or repeat responses to survey questions, and so on. The first step in data cleaning is to check for these kinds of errors by verifying data entries whenever feasible. One procedure is to have two persons independently enter the information into separate digital files and then use a software program to compare the two files for noncomparable entries. Another procedure, which we recommend for small-scale student projects, is to have one person enter the information and then have another person compare on-screen data entries with the completed survey.

Beyond verification, two cleaning techniques generally are applied. These techniques check for the same kinds of errors that could occur during data collection, except that they screen data entries in a digital file rather than responses recorded on a questionnaire or interview schedule. The first of these, called **wild-code checking**, consists of examining the values entered for each item to see whether there are any out-of-range codes. In the campus survey responses from Figure 14.2, for example, any code other than 1 ("male") or 2 ("female") for the variable "sex" is out of the range for this variable. The second cleaning technique, used in most large-scale surveys, is called **consistency checking**. The idea here is to see whether responses to certain questions are related in reasonable ways to responses to particular other questions. Checks for consistency thus require comparisons across variables, such as comparing data entries for ALCCONS and FREQALC to see if respondents who "abstain" from drinking are correctly coded as "9" (for "not applicable") on the frequency of consumption item.

Once you have entered and cleaned the data, you are ready to inspect, modify, and analyze them.

> **data cleaning** the detection and correction of errors in a computer datafile that may have occurred during data collection, coding, and/or data entry
>
> **wild-code checking** a data-cleaning procedure involving checking for out-of-range and other "illegal" codes among the values recorded for each variable
>
> **consistency checking** a data-cleaning procedure involving checking for unreasonable patterns of responses, such as a 12-year-old who voted in the last US presidential election

SUMMARY

Preparing data for quantitative analysis entails four steps: coding, editing, data entry, and cleaning. Coding consists of assigning numbers to the categories of each variable. Editing is designed to ensure that the data to be digitally transmitted are as complete, error-free, and readable as possible. When data are transmitted and stored in a digital datafile, they are organized as a matrix or spreadsheet, with observations as rows and variables as columns. After entry, the data are cleaned for errors in coding and transmission to the computer. This is a multistep process, usually beginning with a verification procedure and continuing with checks for out-of-range codes (wild-code checking) and inconsistent patterns (consistency checking). (See Box 14.2 to assess your understanding of quantitative data analysis.)

> **BOX 14.2**
> **CHECKING YOUR UNDERSTANDING**
>
> ## Quantitative Data Analysis
>
> 1. Quantitative data analysis most often involves the analysis of textual data retrieved through observations and interviews.
>   a. True
>   b. False
>
> 2. These types of statistics allow researchers to estimate population characteristics from sample data and test hypotheses:
>   a. descriptive statistics
>   b. bivariate statistics
>   c. inferential statistics
>   d. complicated statistics
>
> 3. After the data have been digitized, the researcher must go through the process of detecting and resolving errors in coding and digital transmission, this process is known as:
>   a. editing
>   b. cleaning
>   c. coding
>   d. entering the data
>
> **Answers: 1. b, 2. c, 3. b**

14.3 INSPECT AND MODIFY DATA

Starting with a cleaned data set, the next analysis step is to inspect the data to decide on subsequent data modifications and statistical analyses. The goal of inspection is to get a clear picture of the data by examining one variable at a time. The data "pictures" generated by **univariate analysis** come in various forms—tables, graphs, charts, and statistical measures. These pictures allow us to see how much the data vary and where they are mainly concentrated or clustered. The nature of the techniques depends on whether the *level of measurement* of the variables you are analyzing is nominal/ordinal or interval/ratio. Recall from Chapter 6 that we cannot add, subtract, multiply, or divide the numbers assigned to the categories of nominal and ordinal variables, whereas we can perform basic mathematical operations on the values of interval and ratio variables.

univariate analysis the statistical analysis of one variable at a time

Consequently, different forms of analysis and statistics are applied to variables measured at different levels. Following data inspection, the researcher may want to change one or more variable codes, rearrange the numerical order of variable codes, combine variable categories, estimate values for missing data, add together the codes for several variables to create an index or scale, and otherwise modify the data for analysis.

Nominal- and Ordinal-Scale Variables

At first, Amialchuk and Sapci performed univariate analyses to observe the amount of variation in the variables to be analyzed. It is generally a good idea, for example, to see if there is sufficient variation in responses to warrant including the variable in the analysis. As a rule, the less variation, the more difficult it is to detect how differences in one variable are related to differences in another variable. To take an extreme example, if almost all of the students in the Add Health survey identified their race as White, it would be impossible to determine how *differences* in race were related to differences in misperceptions of friends' alcohol consumption or their own alcohol consumption.

Suppose we wanted to inspect the responses to the question on "race" in the Add Health survey. To measure "race," interviewers were instructed to code the race of the respondent from observation alone. The questionnaire contained five response categories (White, Black/African American, Asian/Pacific Islander, American Indian/Native American, and other), yet Amialchuk and Sapci collapsed responses to just three race categories for their analysis: White, Black, and Other.

One means of data inspection is to organize responses into a table called a **frequency distribution**. A frequency distribution is created by adding up the number of cases that occur for each coded category. Utilizing SPSS to do a frequency distribution for the race question from Amialchuk and Sapci, our output looked like that in Table 14.1.

As you can see from the table, the number of participants identified as White in the sample is 3,781. This is important information; however, this number by itself is meaningless unless we provide a standard or reference point with which to interpret it.

frequency distribution a tabulation of the number of cases falling into each category of a variable

Table 14.1 Frequency Distribution of Race*

Code	Label	Frequency
1	White	3,781
2	Black	853
3	Other	52
Total		4,686

*Estimates based upon Table 1 from Amialchuk and Sapci (2021)

Table 14.2 Percentage Distribution of Race

Response	%
White	80.7
Black	18.2
Other	1.1
Total	100.0
(Number of responses)	(4,686)

To provide an explicit comparative framework for interpreting distributions, researchers often create **percentage distributions**, which show the size of a category relative to the size of the sample. To create a percentage distribution, you divide the number of cases in each category (White, Black, Other) by the total number of cases overall and multiply by 100. This is what we have done in Table 14.2. Now you can see more clearly the relative difference in responses. For example, we see that White participants constitute 81 percent of the sample, compared to Black participants who made up approximately 18 percent of the sample. Additionally, less than 2 percent of the respondents were identified as a different race group ("Other").

In Table 14.2, the percentages are based on the total number of responses, *excluding* missing data—those in the "no answer" category. Amialchuk and Sapci only utilized participants in their final sample who did not have missing data, so we do not have a category in either table to indicate total number or percentage of missing responses. In a typical analysis where a researcher may have missing data, this category would not be a meaningful variable category, and it would be misleading to include it in the percentage distribution. The total number of missing responses is important information. If this information is not placed in the main body of a table, then it at least should be reported in a footnote to the relevant table or in the text of the research report. Also notice that the base number for computing percentages, 4,686, is given in parentheses below the percentage total of 100 percent. It is customary to indicate in tables the total number of observations from which the statistics are computed. This information may be found elsewhere—at the end of the table title (this was true for Amialchuk and Sapci) or in a headnote or footnote to the table; often it is signified with the letter *N*.

Univariate analysis is seldom an end in itself. One important function mentioned earlier is to determine how to combine or recode categories for further analysis. The decision to combine (or collapse) categories may be based on theoretical criteria and/or may hinge on the empirical variation in responses. Thus, years of education might

percentage distribution a norming operation that facilitates interpreting and comparing frequency distributions by transforming each frequency to a common yardstick of 100 units (percentage points) in length; the number of cases in each category is divided by the total and multiplied by 100

N an abbreviation representing the number of observations on which a statistic is based (e.g., $N = 753$)

be collapsed into "theoretically" meaningful categories (grade 8 or lower, some high school, high school graduate, some college, college graduate) based on the schooling deemed appropriate for qualifying for certain occupations in the United States. Alternatively, one might collapse categories according to how many respondents fall into each category. If the sample contains only a handful of respondents with less than a college education, these respondents may be placed in one category for purposes of analysis.

One problem with the race data from the Add Health survey is that there are too few respondents in several categories to provide reliable bases of comparison. To resolve this problem, Amialchuk and Sapci likely applied both theoretical and practical criteria in their decision to collapse the categories. Prior research and theory indicate that there is an association between being White and heavy alcohol use among US adolescents. While Amialchuk and Sapci do not provide the breakdown of the original Add Health race variable for their participants, we can assume that some racial identities such as American Indian/Native American or Asian/Pacific Islander had too few respondents for meaningful analysis. Therefore, Amialchuk and Sapci created a "new" variable by collapsing the categories for race/ethnicity with three categories: White, Black, and Other.

Interval- and Ratio-Scale Variables

Creating frequency or percentage distributions is about as far as the univariate analysis of nominal- and ordinal-scale variables usually goes. On the other hand, data on interval and ratio variables may be summarized not only in tables or graphs but also in terms of various statistics. Consider an open-ended question from the Add Health study that asks respondents, "During the period when you drank the most, how many drinks did you usually have each time?" Since respondents' answers are recorded in number of drinks, this variable may be considered a ratio-scale measure. We could get a picture of the number of drinks consumed, as we did with the race/ethnicity variable, by generating a distribution of the responses. Table 14.3 presents a computer-like output for the number of drinks participants reported consuming. Notice that Table 14.3 presents two kinds of distributions: frequency and percentage. Notice also that some individuals refused to answer (coded as "96") or legitimately skipped the question because it was not relevant for them (coded as "97"). Can you tell from the table what percentage of respondents reported that they typically consumed *one drink* at a time during the period when they drank the most?

We also can get a picture of a distribution by looking at its various statistical properties. Three properties may be examined. The first consists of measures of central tendency—the mean, median, and mode. These indicate various "averages" or points of concentration in a set of values. The **mean** is the arithmetic average, calculated by adding up all of the responses and dividing by the total number of respondents.

mean the average value of a data set, calculated by adding up the individual values and dividing by the total number of cases

Table 14.3 Number of Drinks Consumed at One Time During Period When You Drank the Most*

Code	Label	Frequency	Percent
01	1 drink	142	2.1
02	2 drinks	468	6.8
03	3 drinks	935	13.6
04	4 drinks	1057	15.3
05	5 drinks	1097	15.9
06–16	6–16 drinks	3015	43.8
18	18 drinks	174	2.5
96	Refused	6	Missing
97	Not applicable (legitimate skip)	8,723	Missing
98	Don't know	81	Missing
Total		15,701	100.0
(Valid cases) (6,891)			
(Missing cases) (8,810)			

*Data taken from Add Health Codebook Explorer (https://addhealth.cpc.unc.edu/documentation/codebook-explorer/#/)

It is the "balancing" point in a distribution because the sum of the differences of all values from the mean is exactly equal to zero. The **median** is the midpoint in a distribution—the value of the middle response; half of the responses are above it and half are below. You find the median by ordering the values from low to high and then counting up until you find the middle value. In an odd-numbered data set with $N = 3$, the second ordered value would be the median. For example, if we had a data set with three respondents who respectively say they consume 7, 10, and 12 drinks at a time, the median would be 10. In an even-numbered data set with $N = 4$, the median would be the average of the second and third ordered values. For instance, if we had a data set of four respondents who respectively say they consume 7, 10, 12, and 15 drinks at a time, the median would be 11 ($= [10 + 12]/2$). The **mode** is the value or category with the highest frequency.

A second property that we can summarize statistically is the degree of variability or dispersion among a set of values. The simplest dispersion measure is the **range**. Statistically, this is the difference between the lowest and highest values, but it is usually reported by identifying these end points, such as "the number of drinks consumed

median the midpoint in a distribution of interval- or ratio-scale data; indicates the point below and above which 50 percent of the values fall

mode the value or category of a frequency distribution having the highest frequency; the most typical value

range the difference between the lowest and highest values in a distribution, which is usually reported by identifying these two extreme values

standard deviation a measure of variability or dispersion that indicates the average "spread" of observations about the mean

histogram a graphic display in which the height of a vertical bar represents the frequency or percentage of cases in each category of an interval/ratio variable

outliers unusual or suspicious values that are far removed from the preponderance of observations for a variable

ranged from 1 to 18." Of several other measures of dispersion, the most commonly reported is the **standard deviation**; this is a measure of the "average" spread of observations around the mean.

With respect to the variable of number of drinks consumed, the standard deviation could be used to compare the degree of variability in drinks consumed among different subgroups or in samples from different populations. While we do not have standard deviation for the data displayed in Table 14.3, imagine that the standard deviation of number of drinks consumed at one time during the period the respondents drank was 3.68. Then, hypothetically among male respondents, the standard deviation was 3.97, revealing more variability among men than women, for whom the standard deviation was 2.23. As a further example, the ages of Add Health respondents ($N = 89,712$) in general ranged from 10 to 19, with a standard deviation of 1.72 years. By comparison, the standard deviation for age in Amialchuk and Sapci's study, which had significantly fewer respondents, was 1.55 years. The two samples had relatively similar variability in age.

A third statistical property of univariate distributions is their shape. This property is most readily apparent from a graphic presentation called a **histogram**. Figure 14.3 presents a histogram for the data in Table 14.3. The figure reveals that the distribution has a cluster of high points (6–16 drinks), with the data lopsided or "skewed" mostly to the right. Superimposed on the histogram is a "bell-shaped" distribution, so called because it has the general shape of a bell. In a bell-shaped distribution, the three measures of central tendency (mean, median, and mode) are identical. In a positively skewed distribution like Figure 14.3, the mean has a higher value than the mode and median. One particular type of bell-shaped distribution is the *normal distribution*, which we described in Chapter 7. The normal distribution describes the shape of many variables and statistics, such as the sampling distribution of the mean.

Collectively, these three statistical properties—central tendency, dispersion, and shape—provide a good picture of quantitative data. Many investigators, in fact, describe their data in terms of a mean or median, an index of dispersion, and occasionally the overall form (for which there are also statistical indices).

Inspecting the frequency distribution also enables you to spot extreme values or **outliers** that can adversely affect some

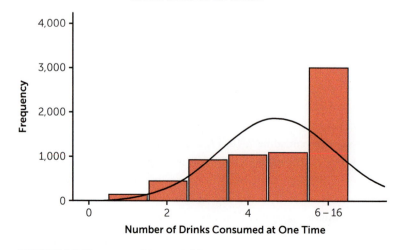

FIGURE 14.3 Histogram of Data in Table 14.3

statistical procedures. For the data in Table 14.3 and Figure 14.3, for example, participants who may have reported 30 drinks at a time would be considered an outlier. Various analytic procedures, which are beyond the scope of this book, exist for identifying outliers. Researchers can use the "Explore" function in SPSS, to detect data points that are outliers in the distribution. If such outliers are the product of interviewer errors, it is probably best to exclude these data from the analysis.

Data inspection can also reveal the prevalence of missing values. The simplest way to handle cases with missing values is to remove them from the statistical calculations. This method, called **listwise deletion**, often is used when there are relatively few missing cases. Excluding cases with missing data on *any* of the variables in a planned multivariate analysis, however, can lead to a much smaller, biased sample that is unrepresentative of the target population. To avoid limitations of listwise deletion, researchers may use various procedures for replacing or otherwise handling missing data.

In a research study on the correlates of violent political extremism, LaFree and colleagues (2018) utilized a database titled Profiles of Individual Radicalization in the United States which included background and incident information for 1,473 individuals who had been radicalized in the United States from 1948 to 2013. Because the data were retrieved through publicly available sources and includes relatively private information, such as whether the radicalized individual experienced mental illness, there is understandably a lot of missing information (more than 80% of cases were missing data for the mental illness variable). Because eliminating these cases would produce a smaller and less representative sample, LaFree et al. (2018) did not apply listwise deletion. Instead, they used formal statistical solutions, called **imputation**, that have been devised to replace missing values with a typical value calculated from the available ("nonmissing") data. For example, one procedure they utilized was the process of simple imputation using means of non-missing values to replace the missing values. Another procedure, which LaFree et al. (2018) applied predicts missing values from known values of other variables. For a thorough discussion of imputation procedures, which are beyond the scope of this textbook, see McKnight et al. (2007).

Another important function of data modification is to reduce data complexity by combining variables into indexes, scales, or other composite measures. For instance, in Chapter 6 we discussed the use of scales and indexes, such as the Rosenberg Self-Esteem Scale, a 10-item scale made up of individual statements, to which respondents are asked to indicate their level of agreement. Participants indicate their agreement with the statements on a scale of 1 to 4, with a 4 representing strong agreement with a positive statement about the self (or, conversely, strong disagreement with a negative statement). Responses to the individual items are averaged together to create a self-esteem scale which provides each individual a self-esteem score. This reduces data complexity by developing one comprehensive variable from 10 separate indicators.

listwise deletion a common procedure for handling missing values in multivariate analysis that excludes cases which have missing values on any of the variables in the analysis

imputation a procedure for handling missing data in which missing values are assigned based on other information, such as the sample mean or known values of other variables

SUMMARY

Having entered and cleaned the data, the researcher is ready to inspect and modify the data for the planned analysis. The goal of inspection is to get a clear picture of the data by examining each variable singly (univariate analysis). At first, the categories or values of each variable are organized into frequency and percentage distributions. If the data constitute interval-level measurement, the researcher will also compute statistics that define various properties of the distribution. Statistical measures of central tendency include the most typical value (mode), the middle value (median), and the average (mean). Common measures of dispersion are the difference between the lowest and highest values (range) and an index of the spread of the values around the mean (standard deviation). Distributions also may be described in terms of their shape. Data modifications include changing one or more variable codes, collapsing variable categories, imputing estimated values for missing data, and adding together the codes for several variables to create an index or scale. (Check Box 14.3 to assess your understanding of quantitative data concepts.)

> **BOX 14.3**
>
> ### CHECKING YOUR UNDERSTANDING
>
> ## Quantitative Data Concepts
>
> Consider the following set of numbers: [18 12 13 13 14 19 17 20 5]
>
> 1. What is the mean, median, and mode of this set of numbers?
>   a. Mean: 14; Median: 14; Mode: 14
>   b. Mean: 14; Median: 14.56; Mode: 13
>   c. Mean: 13; Median: 14; Mode: 13
>   d. Mean: 14.56; Median: 14; Mode: 13
>
> 2. Which of the following is a measure of central tendency?
>   a. Range
>   b. Univariate
>   c. Frequency
>   d. Mean

3. Which of the following is a measure of dispersion?
    a. Median
    b. Percentage
    c. Standard deviation
    d. Mode

4. Which level of measurement is needed to create a histogram for a variable?
    a. Nominal
    b. Ordinal
    c. Interval/ratio
    d. All of the above can be used

Imagine you developed a survey asking individuals in your community to report how many times in the last month they interacted with police in their neighborhood.

5. If response options to this question included categories such as "often", "sometimes", "rarely", or "never", which type of univariate statistics would be appropriate?
    a. Frequency distribution
    b. Measures of central tendency
    c. Measures of dispersion
    d. All of the above

6. If this question were open-ended and individuals could write in the specific number of times they had interacted with the police in the last month (i.e., 1, 2, 3, 4, etc.), which type of univariate statistics would be appropriate?
    a. Frequency distribution
    b. Measures of central tendency
    c. Measures of dispersion
    d. All of the above

Answers: 1. d, 2. d, 3. c, 4. c, 5. a, 6. d

14.4 CARRY OUT PRELIMINARY HYPOTHESIS TESTING

Having collected, processed, inspected, and modified the data, a researcher is finally in position to carry out preliminary hypothesis testing. For novice researchers, this can be an exciting—but also potentially disappointing—stage in the research process.

This is because whenever we formulate a hypothesis, it is possible that the hypothesis is "wrong" (and it is hard not to take this personally!).

The object of **bivariate analysis** is to assess the relationship between two variables, such as between the independent and dependent variable in a hypothesis. As in the previous section, we begin by showing how tables and figures can be used to depict the joint *distribution* of two variables. "Eyeballing" the data helps, but there are more precise ways of assessing bivariate relationships. And so, we also introduce two types of statistics for determining whether one variable is associated with the other: tests of statistical significance and measures of association. In general, this amounts to determining, first, whether the relationship is likely to exist (or whether it might be a product of random error) and, second, the strength of the relationship between the variables. Finally, as with univariate analysis, the way in which bivariate analysis is done depends on the level of measurement.

> **bivariate analysis**
> the statistical analysis of the relationship between two variables

Nominal- and Ordinal-Scale Variables

When the variables analyzed have only a few categories, as in most nominal- and ordinal-scale measurement, bivariate data are presented in tables. The tables constructed are known as *cross-tabulations* or *contingency tables*. A cross-tabulation requires a table with rows representing the categories of one variable and columns representing the categories of another. When a dependent variable can be identified, it is customary to make this the row variable and to treat the independent variable as the column variable.

Let us first consider the cross-tabulation of two nominal-scale variables from the 2018 GSS shown in Table 14.4. The row variable consists of "attitude toward gun control" or, more precisely, whether the respondent favors or opposes a law that would require a person to obtain a police permit before they could buy a gun (see Box 14.1). The column variable is "sex." Sex is clearly the independent variable in this relationship.

What sort of information does this table convey? First, notice that the last column and the bottom row, each labeled "Total," show the total number of respondents with

Table 14.4 Attitude Toward Gun Control by Sex, 2018 General Social Survey

ATTITUDE TOWARD GUN CONTROL*	Sex		Total
	Male	Female	
Favor	453	649	1,102
Oppose	235	204	439
Total	688	853	1,541

*Would you favor or oppose a law which would require a person to obtain a police permit before he or she can buy a gun?

each single characteristic, for example, 688 males. Because these four numbers (1,102; 439; 688; 853) are along the right side and the bottom margin of the table, they are called **marginal frequencies**, or *marginals*. The row marginals (1,102; 439) are the univariate frequency distribution for the variable "attitude toward gun control"; the column marginals (688, 853) are the univariate frequency distribution for the variable "sex." Also, the number at the lower right-hand corner (1,541) is N, the total sample size excluding missing cases. N equals either the sum of the row or column marginals or the sum of the four numbers (453 + 649 + 235 + 204) in the body of the table.

The body of the table where the categories of the two variables intersect contains the bivariate frequency distribution. Each intersection is called a *cell*, and the number in each cell is called a **cell frequency**. Cell frequencies in a *bivariate* table indicate the numbers of cases with each possible combination of *two* characteristics; for example, there were 453 *males* who *favored gun control*. Because Table 14.4 has two rows and two columns, it is referred to as a 2 × 2 table.

Now that we know the meaning of the numbers in a cross-tabulation, how do we analyze these numbers to assess the relationship between the variables? With sex as the independent variable in Table 14.4, we can assess the relationship by examining whether males or females are more likely to favor (or oppose) gun control. To determine the "likelihood" that a male or female either supports or opposes gun control, we need to create separate percentage distributions for males and females. Doing this converts each column "total" to 100 percent, so that the cell values are based on the same total. The result is a *bivariate percentage distribution*, presented as Table 14.5. Now when we compare responses across sex, we see clearly that males are less likely to favor gun control by a percentage of 65.8 to 76.1 and, conversely, are more likely to oppose (34.2 percent to 23.9 percent).

A bivariate percentage distribution enables one to compare the distribution of one variable across the categories of the other. In Table 14.5, we created such a distribution by percentaging *down* so that the column totals, corresponding to the categories of the independent variable, equaled 100 percent (also called "column percentages"). The rule

marginal frequencies row and column totals in a contingency table (cross-tabulation) that represent the univariate frequency distributions for the row and column variables

cell frequency the number of cases in a cell of a cross-tabulation (contingency table)

Table 14.5 Attitude Toward Gun Control by Sex, 2018 General Social Survey

	Sex	
ATTITUDE TOWARD GUN CONTROL	Male	Female
Favor	65.8%	76.1%
Oppose	34.2%	23.9%
Total	100.0%	100.0%
(N)	(688)	(853)

that we followed in deriving this table is to *compute percentages in the direction of the independent variable* (i.e., based on the categories of the independent variable). If sex had been the row variable and attitude toward gun control the column variable, we would have run the percentages in the other direction—across rather than down (i.e., "row percentages").

To interpret the relationship in Table 14.5, we compared percentages by reading *across* the table. In so doing, we followed a second rule: *Make comparisons in the opposite direction from the way percentages are run.* Having percentaged down, we compared across; had we percentaged across, we would have compared down. These are extremely important rules to follow because cross-tabulations may be percentaged in either direction and are easily misinterpreted.

As you read across Table 14.5, you see that there is a difference of 10.3 percent (76.1–65.8) in females relative to males who favor gun control. This "percentage difference" indicates that a relationship exists for these data; if there were no difference between the percentages, we would conclude that no relationship exists. Remember, however, that these are *sample* data. The important question is not whether a relationship exists in the sample; rather, do the observed cell frequencies reveal a true relationship between the variables in the *population*, or are they simply the result of sampling and other random error? To answer this question, you need to understand the logic of tests of statistical significance.

TESTS OF STATISTICAL SIGNIFICANCE

To determine whether a relationship is due to chance factors, researchers use **tests of statistical significance**, which you read about in Chapter 5 (see Box 5.3). The way that such tests work is that we first assume what the data would look like if there were *no relationship* between the variables—that is, if the distribution were completely random. The assumption of no relationship or complete randomness is called the **null hypothesis**. The null hypothesis in Amialchuk and Sapci's research is that there is *no* relationship between misperception of friends' alcohol use and an adolescent's alcohol consumption. Based on the null hypothesis, we calculate the likelihood that the observed data could have occurred at random. If the relationship is unlikely to have occurred randomly, we reject the null hypothesis of no relationship between the variables. In such cases, researchers generally interpret this as supporting the hypothesis that there *is* a relationship.

Psychologist David Lane (2014) provides an interesting example of this logic based on James Bond's insistence that he could tell whether a martini has been shaken or stirred:

> *Suppose we gave Mr. Bond a series of 16 taste tests. In each test, we flipped a fair coin to determine whether to stir or shake the martini. Then we presented the martini to Mr. Bond and asked him to decide whether it was shaken or stirred. Let's say Mr. Bond was correct on 13 of the 16 taste tests.*

---

test of statistical significance a statistical procedure used to assess the likelihood that the results of a study could have occurred by chance

null hypothesis the hypothesis, associated with tests of statistical significance, that an observed relationship is due to chance; a test that is significant rejects the null hypothesis at a specified level of probability

Does this prove that Mr. Bond has at least some ability to tell whether the martini was shaken or stirred?

This result does not prove that he does; it could be he was just lucky and guessed right 13 out of 16 times. But how plausible is the explanation that he was just lucky? To assess its plausibility, we determine the probability that someone who was just guessing would be correct 13/16 times or more.

According to the probability distribution of random guessing, the probability of being correct 13 of 16 times is very low: 0.0106. "So, either Mr. Bond was very lucky, or he can tell whether the drink was shaken or stirred" (Lane, 2014). Given the low probability of his being lucky, we would conclude that Mr. Bond can tell the difference between a stirred and a shaken martini.

Which statistics can be used to determine the probability that a relationship does not exist? For cross-tabulations, the most commonly used statistic is the **chi-square ($or \chi^2$) test for independence**. The chi-square test is based on a comparison of the observed cell frequencies with the cell frequencies one would expect if there were no relationship between the variables. Table 14.6 shows the expected cell frequencies, assuming no relationship, and the derived bivariate percentage distribution for the data in Table 14.4. Notice that the cell percentages in Table 14.6 (reading across) are the same as the marginals; this indicates that knowing whether a respondent is male or female is of no help in predicting attitude toward gun control, precisely the meaning of the null hypothesis of "no relationship" between the variables. The larger the differences between the actual cell frequencies and those expected assuming no relationship, the larger the value of chi-square, the less likely the relationship occurred randomly, and the more likely that it exists in the population.

The chi-square value $(17.79)^1$ for the data in Table 14.4 is statistically significant ($p < .01$), which indicates that there is a significant difference between the observed cell

> **chi-square test for independence ($\chi 2$)** a test of statistical significance used to assess the likelihood that an observed association between two variables could have occurred by chance

Table 14.6 Attitude Toward Gun Control by Sex, Assuming No Relationship (Expected Frequencies), 2018 General Social Survey

ATTITUDE TOWARD GUN CONTROL	Frequencies			Percentages		
	Male	Female	Total	Male	Female	Total
Favor	492	610	1,102	71.5%	71.5%	71.5%
Oppose	196	243	439	28.5	28.5	28.5
Total	688	853	1,541	100.0%	100.0%	100.0%
(N)				(688)	(853)	(1,541)

[1] The chi-squared tests of GSS data in this chapter are based on the Rao-Scott-P statistic.

frequencies in Table 14.4 and the cell frequencies one would expect if there were no relationship between the variables (Table 14.6). Recall from Chapter 5 that the lowercase *p* stands for "probability"; for example, "$p < .01$" means that the probability is less than .01, or 1 in 100, that the association could have occurred randomly, assuming there is no relationship in the larger population from which the sample was drawn. With odds this low, we can be confident that the result would not have occurred by chance. Therefore, we can conclude that in the American adult population, females are more likely than males to favor gun control.

Knowing that this relationship is likely to exist in the population, however, does not tell us the strength of the relationship between the independent variable and the dependent variable. It is possible for a relationship to exist when changes in one variable correspond only slightly to changes in the other. The degree of this correspondence, or association, is a second measurable property of bivariate distributions.

MEASURES OF ASSOCIATION

In a 2 × 2 table, the percentage difference provides one indicator, albeit a poor one, of the strength of the relationship: the larger the difference, the stronger the relationship. However, researchers prefer to use one of several other statistics to measure relationship strength. These **measures of association** are standardized to vary between 0 (no association) and plus or minus 1.0 (perfect association). One such measure, which can be used for 2 × 2 tables, is the phi coefficient, which varies from 0 to 1; this equals .11 for the data in Table 14.4. Although the choice of labels is somewhat arbitrary, this magnitude suggests a "low" association between sex and attitude toward gun control (Davis, 1971, p. 49).

measures of association descriptive statistics used to measure the strength and direction of a bivariate relationship

Although some measures of association may vary from –1 to +1, for variables with nominal categories, the sign, – or +, does not reveal anything meaningful about the nature of the relationship. However, when both variables have at least ordinal-level measurement, the sign indicates the direction of the relationship. Statistically, *direction* refers to the tendency for increases in the values of one variable to be associated with systematic increases or decreases in the values of another variable. Both variables may change in the same direction (a positive relationship) or in opposite directions (a negative relationship).

In a positive relationship, lower values of one variable tend to be associated with lower values of the other variable, and higher values of one variable tend to go along with higher values of the other. For example, from Amialchuk and Sapci's study, we would likely expect a positive relationship between responses on the ordinal variables measuring how often a respondent drank five or more drinks in a row and how often they were drunk or very, very high on alcohol.

In a negative (inverse) relationship, there is a tendency for *lower* values of one variable to be associated with *higher* values of the other variable. Looking at the sociodemographic controls that were included in Amialchuk and Sapci's study, one might hypothesize a negative relationship between attendance at religious services and an adolescent's likelihood to engage in alcohol consumption. This hypothesis would expect that the more often an adolescent attends religious services, the less likely they would be to engage in drinking behaviors.

One ordinal measure of the strength of association is the statistic *gamma*. If, hypothetically, the value of gamma is .84 for two measures of alcohol consumption, we would consider this is a high positive association between the two variables. Likewise, say we find the value of gamma to be –.24 for the relationship between attendance at religious services and alcohol consumption, this would suggest a moderate negative association between the two. The statistical significance of a relationship between two ordinal-scale variables also may be tested with the chi-square statistic.

So far we have restricted ourselves to variables having only 2 to 5 categories and to tables with 4 to 15 cells. This is not unusual because most cross-tabulation analyses in criminal justice research are limited to variables with relatively few categories. There are three important reasons for this. First, the size of the table increases geometrically as the number of categories for each variable increases. And the larger the table, the more difficult it is to discern the pattern of the relationship, which can be much more complex than the positive or negative relationships we have described. Second, the finer the breakdown of one's sample into various categories, the fewer cases there will be for any given breakdown (or cell of the table). Hence, larger tables may require impractically large samples for reliable assessments. Finally, variables with a relatively large number of categories either constitute or tend to approximate interval-scale measurement. With interval-scale variables, we can use a more precise and more powerful form of statistical analysis known as "correlation" and "regression."

Interval- and Ratio-Scale Variables

The analysis of the relationship between two interval/ratio variables begins by plotting the values of each variable in a graphic coordinate system, which may take you back to high school geometry. Researchers then use a statistical method called **regression analysis** to determine the mathematical equation that most closely describes the data. Through this equation, they identify statistics that show the relationship between two variables. For the purposes of illustration, we begin here using data from Pate and Bolin's (2019) study examining the relationship between strain and the use of nonmedical prescription drugs. A quick overview: Pate and Bolin conducted this study with the criminological theory of general strain as the framework. Their overall tests were a pathway model of the relationship between stress, a negative emotional state (i.e., depression), and the use of nonmedical prescription drugs. With this data, we will perform a regression analysis on two variables that we expect to have a strong relationship: an index of stress and depression. Then, we will apply the same analysis to test the hypothesis that students who experience more depression will use nonmedical prescription drugs more often.

regression analysis
a statistical method for analyzing bivariate (simple regression) and multivariate (multiple regression) relationships among interval- or ratio-scale variables

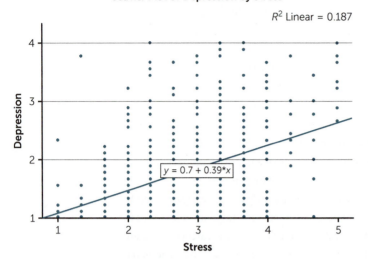

FIGURE 14.4 Scatterplot of Depression by Stress

Let us begin our analysis by looking at a **scatterplot** of data from Pate and Bolin's survey of college students on stress felt from college, friends, and significant others and a depression index of nine items (Figure 14.4). Each plot or point in the graph represents the values of one of the students for whom we have data on both of these variables. With the vertical axis as our reference, we can read the value of the dependent variable (depression index); and with the horizontal axis as our reference, we can read the value of the independent variable (stress index).

The scatterplot gives the researcher a rough sense of the form of the relationship: whether it is best characterized with a straight or a curved line and whether it is positive or negative. This is crucial information because regression analysis assumes that the data have a particular form. If a straight line provides the best fit with the data, we should do linear regression; if a curve provides the best fit, we should use special techniques for fitting curvilinear relationships (which are beyond the scope of this book). The overall form of the data in Figure 14.4 clearly shows a linear trend from the lower left corner to the upper right corner. The trend of the data also shows, as expected, that scores on the depression index increase as overall stress increases.

Having decided to fit a straight line to the data, and therefore to do *linear* regression analysis, we need to know two things: (1) the mathematical equation for a straight line and (2) the criterion for selecting a line to represent the data.

The general form of the equation for a straight line is $\hat{Y} = a + bX$, where $\hat{Y}$ is the predicted value of the dependent variable and X is the corresponding value of the independent variable. Thus, an equation for a straight line, relating depression as the dependent variable and stress as the independent variable, is:

$$\text{Despression} = a + b(\text{Stress})$$

The value a, called the **Y-intercept**, is the point where the line crosses the vertical axis (where Stress = 0). The value b, called the **slope** or **regression coefficient**, indicates how much $\hat{Y}$ increases (or decreases) for every change of one unit in X. In our example, the slope indicates how much increase (or decrease) occurs in depression for every 1 unit change of the stress score. To get the line of best fit, then, we could simply

scatterplot a graph plotting the values of two variables for each observation

Y-intercept the predicted value of the dependent variable in regression when the independent variable or variables have a value of zero; graphically, the point at which the regression line crosses the Y-axis

slope/regression coefficient a bivariate regression statistic indicating how much the dependent variable increases (or decreases) for every unit change in the independent variable; the slope of a regression line

draw a line on the scatterplot that seems to best reflect the trend in the data and then determine the values of *a* and *b* from the graph. Of course, there are many lines that we could draw—*a* and *b* can take on an infinite number of values. How, then, do we know when we have obtained the best fit?

Regression analysis uses the method of least squares as the criterion for selecting the line that best describes the data. According to this method, the best-fitting line *minimizes* the sum of the *squared* vertical distances from the data points to the line. We have drawn the **regression line**, also called the least squares line, on the scatterplot. Now imagine a dashed line showing the vertical distance, as measured by depression, between a specific data point and the regression line. The regression line represents the equation for predicting *Y* from *X*; the vertical distances between data points and this line represent prediction errors (also called **residuals**). Thus, by finding the line that minimizes the sum of the squared distances from it, we are, in effect, finding the best linear predictor of the depression score from knowledge of a student's stress score.

The precise equation generated by the method of least squares can be found via a mathematical formula with the aid of a computer program. When we applied this formula to the data in Figure 14.4, we got the following equation:

$$\text{Depression} = .701 + .385(\text{Stress})$$

This equation indicates that students with a hypothetical 0.0 stress score would be predicted to have an average depression score of 0.701 (i.e., .701 + [.385 × 0] =.701). For every one-unit increase in stress score, an increase of just over one-third of a point (.385) is expected in the depression score. The regression equation gives the best linear prediction of the dependent variable based on the data at hand.

The strength of the association between two interval/ratio variables is frequently measured by the **correlation coefficient** (symbolized as *r*), which may vary between −1 and +1. The sign of the coefficient, which is always the same as the sign of the regression coefficient, indicates the direction of the relationship. The magnitude of its value depends on two factors: (1) the steepness of the regression line and (2) the variation or scatter of the data points around this line. If the line is not very steep, so that it is nearly parallel to the *X*-axis, then we might as well predict the same value of *Y* for every unit change in *X*; in other words, there is very little change in our prediction (as indicated by *b* in the equation) for every unit change in the independent variable. By the same token, the greater the spread of values about the regression line (regardless of the steepness of the slope), the less accurate are predictions based on the linear regression. The scatterplot for the regression of depression on stress shows that the line is moderately steep in relation to the horizontal axis and that the data points do not cluster close to the line. Not surprisingly, therefore, the correlation coefficient indicates a moderate positive association of .43.

> **regression line** a geometric representation of a bivariate regression equation that provides the best linear fit to the observed data by virtue of minimizing the sum of the squared deviations from the line; also called the *least squares line*
>
> **residuals** the difference between observed values of the dependent variable and those predicted by a regression equation
>
> **correlation coefficient** a measure of the strength and direction of a linear relationship between two variables; it may vary from −1 to 0 to +1

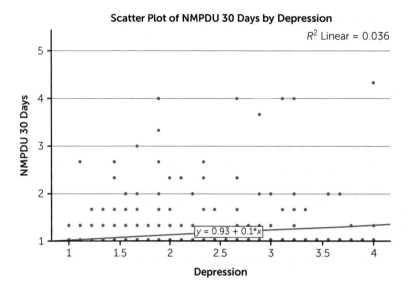

FIGURE 14.5 Scatterplot of Nonmedical Prescription Drug Use by Depression

Statistics also exist for testing whether the correlation coefficient and the regression coefficient are significantly different from zero. These may be found in most statistics textbooks. Both of these coefficients are significant ($p < .001$) for the data in Figure 14.4.

Now that we have illustrated regression analysis and introduced its key concepts, let us examine the bivariate relationship between the depression index scores and nonmedical prescription drug use (NMPDU) reported within the last 30 days. NMPDU is an index of three items: participants' reported occasions of using (1) pain relievers, (2) tranquilizers, and (3) stimulants without a prescription within 30 days of the survey administration. Figure 14.5 shows the scatterplot for these variables. How would you describe the form of the relationship? Does it seem to show a positive or negative association? Would a straight or curved line best fit the data? The overall pattern is somewhat difficult to discern; however, the trend seems to indicate that as depression scores increase, so does the number of occasions participants' used nonmedical prescription drugs. Also, since the relationship does not appear to be sharply curvilinear, we can assume that a straight line offers as good a fit as a curved line.

When we applied the method of least squares to the data in Figure 14.5, we obtained the following regression equation:

$$\text{NMPDU} = 0.931 + .103(\text{Despression})$$

The equation thus shows that a student's NMPDU score increases by .103 for every one-unit increase in the depression score. For students who reported having no depression symptoms (coded as 1), the average predicted NMPDU is 1.034 (between 0 occasions and 1–2 occasions) $(0.931 + [.103 \times 1])$; by comparison, students who experienced all depression symptoms "nearly every day" (coded 4) would have an average predicted NMPDU score of 1.343 $(0.931 + [.103 \times 4])$. The correlation between NMPDU and depression was .19, which was statistically significant at $p < .001$. Thus, a preliminary test of the bivariate relationship supports the hypothesis that students who experience higher levels of depression also use nonmedical prescription drugs more often. Before you read further, be sure to read Box 14.4.

BOX 14.4

CHECKING YOUR UNDERSTANDING

The Meaning of Statistical Significance and Strength of Association

As you have seen, two types of statistics can be used to assess bivariate relationships: tests of statistical significance and measures of strength of association. Each of these statistics provides different information, and even seasoned researchers sometimes misinterpret what they can and cannot tell us about the relationship between two variables (Shaver, 1993). So, let us consider each statistic as it relates to tests of the hypothesis that nonmedical prescription drug use is associated with depression.

Suppose researchers at three other colleges conduct surveys in which they use the same questions on NMPDU and depression. Each survey is based on a random sample of the undergraduate student population; however, because of different resources, the surveys have markedly different sample sizes. Below are hypothetical findings.

College A:	$r = .28$	$p < .10$	$N = 30$
College B:	$r = .11$	$p < .001$	$N = 795$
College C:	$r = .20$	$p < .01$	$N = 196$

1. At which college is the relationship between NMPDU and depression strongest?
2. Is the association statistically significant at all three colleges?
3. What do these data tell us about the theoretical and practical importance of the association between NMPDU and depression?

To answer the first question, we use the correlation coefficient r. This is a *descriptive* statistic that indicates strength of association, or how well we can predict one variable from knowledge of another. The absolute value of r (ignoring the plus or minus sign) is the measure of strength. The coefficient is largest, and therefore the relationship is strongest, for College A.

To answer the second question, we need to examine the p-values, which are based on tests of statistical significance. Tests of significance are *inferential* statistics that determine the probability (at some specified level p) of a particular result, assuming the null hypothesis is true. The null hypothesis here is $r = 0$. If the null hypothesis is rejected, we can be reasonably confident that there is a relationship between NMPDU and depression in the population from which the sample was drawn. Using the traditional level of significance of .05, the association is significant at College B and College C, but not at College A.

continues

continued

Comparing the findings, you can see that the association is strongest ($r = .28$) at College A, whereas the association is least likely to occur by chance ($p < .001$) at College B. This suggests that the level of statistical significance (or p-value) tells us nothing about strength of an association. The reason is that p-values depend not only on the magnitude of the correlation coefficient but also on the size of the sample. If the sample is big enough, even very weak correlations are unlikely to occur by chance and, therefore, are likely to differ from 0 in the population from which the sample was drawn. For example, given the sample size of 795 at College B, a correlation of .06 (or –.06) would be significant; and with a sample size of 10,000, a correlation of .02 (or –.02) would be significant.

Just as statistical significance tells us nothing about strength of association, or the magnitude of a result, it also reveals nothing about its theoretical or practical importance. In fact, neither of these judgments can be based on statistics alone. For example, statistical significance is insufficient to establish causality, which often determines whether a finding is theoretically important. Further, practical importance depends on the magnitude of the result as well as an assessment of human values and costs (Shaver, 1993).

If we were to replicate the survey and produce the above results, this would enhance the theoretical importance of the association between NMPDU and depression. Although the size of the coefficient varies, it is consistently a negative nonzero correlation. How important this result is theoretically depends on subsequent multivariate analysis. As for practical importance, we will let you be the judge.

SUMMARY

Bivariate analysis examines the relationship between two variables. For relationships involving exclusively nominal- or ordinal-scale variables, such analysis begins with the construction of cross-tabulations. Tests of statistical significance and measures of association are then applied to determine, respectively, whether the relationship is likely to have occurred by chance and the strength of the association. For relationships involving interval- or ratio-scale variables, the data are plotted in a scatterplot and characterized in terms of a mathematical equation. Linear regression analysis identifies the straight-line equation that provides the best fit with the data by virtue of minimizing the sum of the squared deviations from the line. The slope of the line reveals the predicted change in the dependent variable per unit change in the independent variable, and the correlation coefficient indicates the strength of the association.

14.5 CONDUCT MULTIVARIATE TESTING

Once you have conducted bivariate analyses on nonexperimental data, all is not said and done. If you have found a statistically significant relationship, there is reason to hold your excitement. The regression analysis in the previous section shows that there is a bivariate *association* between NMPDU and depression. However, if the goal is to test the causal hypothesis that depression increases the use of nonmedical prescription drugs, our analysis cannot end here. As we have emphasized repeatedly, causal inferences are based not only on association but also theoretical assumptions and empirical evidence about *direction of influence* and *nonspuriousness*.

In a cross-sectional survey such as the campus survey by Pate and Bolin (2019), for example, a correlation between X and Y may imply that X causes Y, Y causes X, and X and Y mutually cause each other or that X and Y are causally unrelated (spurious association). Multivariate analysis can help the researcher to choose among such possible interpretations. But it is important to realize that *statistical analyses by themselves do not provide a basis for inferring causal relationships*. Instead, a researcher starts with a theoretical model of the causal process linking X and Y and then determines if the data are consistent with the theory.

The theoretical model (or hypothesis) linking depression and NMPDU can be summarized simply in an arrow diagram with a line connecting the variables, as shown in Figure 14.6A. This model assumes that the direction of influence is from depression to NMPDU. It is possible, however, that the reverse direction holds—using nonmedical prescription drugs leads to depression—or that these variables mutually cause each other (not shown in the figure). In this section, we use data from Pate and Bolin's study to test Model A, leaving tests of alternative directional models to future research.

Another shortcoming of Model A is that there are many other, extraneous variables that may be a cause of drinking or NMPDU or both. Of the many possible alternative models, we will briefly

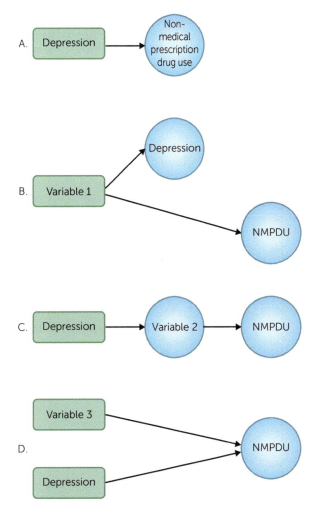

FIGURE 14.6 Arrow Diagrams for Different Causal Models of the Relationship Between Drinking and GPA

describe three. Model B in Figure 14.6 illustrates an outcome in which the original relationship is spurious. Notice that an antecedent variable (variable 1) is a cause of both depression and NMPDU and there is no direct causal link (arrow) between these variables. Model C presents a second alternative in which an intervening variable (variable 2) is causally positioned between depression and NMPDU; that is, depression influences variable 2, which in turn influences NMPDU. Finally, Model D represents an outcome in which an extraneous variable is neither antecedent nor intervening but rather has an independent effect on NMPDU.

The figure represents models with generic extraneous variables. Which variables are actually in the data? Data from Pate and Bolin's survey include several antecedent variables: sex, race, GPA, class standing, whether a student is part of Greek life, and living arrangements. Any one of these variables might create a spurious association between depression and NMPDU (Model B) or be an independent cause of NMPDU (Model D). To test for spuriousness (Model B) as well as independent effects on NMPDU (Model D), we now introduce two of the several strategies for multivariate analysis: elaboration of contingency tables and multiple regression. Furthermore, to show how these strategies are based on the same logic of analysis, we use the same data, albeit in different forms.

Elaboration of Contingency Tables

The multivariate analysis of contingency tables introduces a third control variable (and sometimes additional variables) into the analysis to enhance or "elaborate" our understanding of a bivariate relationship. To illustrate the logic of this elaboration, we first created a contingency table of the *bivariate* relationship between NMPDU and depression by dichotomizing each of these variables. That is, for each variable, we collapsed all the values into two categories with an approximately equal proportion of cases in each category. For NMPDU, the split occurred at a score of 1 (abstained) and any score greater than 1; for depression, the split occurred at a score of 1.56 or less and 1.67 or greater.

Table 14.7 shows the bivariate relationship between the dichotomized variables NMPDU and depression. The data indicate an association by a difference of 8.0

Table 14.7 NMPDU by Depression (Pate & Bolin 2019)

NMPDU	Depression	
	Score of 1.56 or Less	Score of 1.67 or More
1 (Abstained)	89.1%	81.1%
Greater than 1 (used at least once)	10.9%	18.9%
Total	100.0%	100.0%
(N)	(366)	(291)

percent; that is, students who had depression scores over 1.67 are more likely to use nonmedical prescription drugs than are students who had depression scores less than 1.56. Moreover, the chi-square test is significant at $p < .01$; so, an association is likely to exist among all students at the college from which this sample was drawn.

The objective of elaboration is to examine the impact of additional "third" variables on a bivariate relationship. We are especially interested in understanding the impact of antecedent variables that might create a spurious relationship, as in theoretical Model B. For example, the association between depression and drug use might be spurious due to factors such as academic performance. That is, students with a relatively low GPA might be likely to use nonmedical prescription drugs more *and* struggle with depression more than students with a relatively high academic performance. To explore this possibility, we introduce a measure of respondents' academic performance—self-reported GPA—into the analysis by holding it constant. In contingency table elaboration, third variables are held constant by means of subgroup classification. Each category of the third variable constitutes a distinct subgroup, and the original two-variable relationship is recomputed separately for each subgroup. Table 14.8 does this for the variables of NMPDU, depression, and dichotomized GPA.

Notice that we now have two "tables," one for each category of the variable "GPA." These are called **partial tables** or **partials** because each shows the association between depression and NMPDU for part of the total number of observations. GPA is held constant because in each partial table all respondents are alike with respect to their GPA. Look over the partial tables carefully. What do they reveal about the relationship between depression and NMPDU when GPA is controlled?

Reading across each partial table, we see that individuals with lower depression scores are more likely to abstain from NMPDU in both GPA groupings. Thus, the original relationship shown in Table 14.7, has remained when GPA is controlled. These data do not support Model B in Figure 14.6. The relationship is not spurious, meaning the

partial table a table in elaboration analysis which displays the original two-variable relationship for a single category of the control variable, thereby holding the control variable constant

Table 14.8 NMPDU by Depression and GPA (Pate & Bolin 2019)

	GPA less than 2		GPA greater than 2	
NMPDU	Dep. < 1.56	Dep. > 1.67	Dep. < 1.56	Dep. > 1.67
1 (Abstained)	60.0%	45.5%	90.7%	85.8%
Greater than 1 (used at least once)	40.0%	54.5%	9.3%	14.2%
Total	100.0%	100.0%	100.0%	100.0%
(N)	(5)	(11)	(270)	(183)

relationship was not produced by a common association with GPA. GPA seems to enhance the relationship seen between depression and NMPDU, with a greater majority of individuals with higher GPAs abstaining from NMPDU.

Showing that the relationship between depression and NMPDU is maintained when controlling for GPA eliminates the possibility that GPA produced a spurious relationship. This conclusion is limited, however, and it is subject to three criticisms that pertain to much analysis of contingency tables:

1. Collapsing variables such as NMPDU, depression, and GPA into two categories may eliminate important information and distort the results;
2. Several other variables (e.g., sex, race, stress) might produce a spurious association between depression and NMPDU; and
3. Controlling for one variable at a time ignores the possibility that spuriousness may be created by the simultaneous action of two or more extraneous variables.

Another possibility can be seen with the hypothetical data in Table 14.9, which are hypothetical. Reading across each partial table, we find no association between depression and NMPDU (e.g., in the first partial, 62.3 – 62.3 = 0). Thus, the original relationship (shown in Table 14.7), which indicated that those with higher depression scores utilized nonmedical prescription drugs more often than those with lower depression scores, has disappeared when GPA is controlled. These hypothetical data, therefore, support Model B in Figure 14.6. The relationship is spurious, produced by a common association with GPA, an indicator of academic performance.

We can never be absolutely certain that depression increases NMPDU. Ultimately, our confidence in this causal relationship depends on our holding constant all antecedent variables that might reasonably be expected to produce a spurious relationship. Multiple regression, described in the next section, is generally better when we want to analyze the simultaneous effects of several independent variables on a dependent variable.

Table 14.9 NMPDU by Depression and GPA, Hypothetical Data

NMPDU	GPA less than 2		GPA greater than 2	
	Dep. < 1.56	Dep. > 1.67	Dep. < 1.56	Dep. > 1.67
1 (Abstained)	62.3%	62.3%	36.1%	36.1%
Greater than 1 (used at least once)	37.7%	37.7%	63.9%	63.9%
Total	100.0%	100.0%	100.0%	100.0%
(N)	(5)	(11)	(270)	(183)

Multiple Regression

Multiple regression is simply an extension of bivariate regression to include two or more independent variables. Like the partial tables of elaboration analysis, it provides information about the relationship between an independent variable and a dependent variable while controlling for the effects of other independent variables. Unlike partial tables, control is not limited to a few variables nor is information lost from collapsing variables into fewer categories.

The general formula for a multiple-regression equation is like the formula for the linear equation in bivariate regression except that it includes additional independent variables:

$$\hat{Y} = a + b_1 X_1 + b_2 X_2 + b_3 X_3 + \ldots$$

In this equation, $\hat{Y}$ is the predicted value of the dependent variable, each X represents an independent variable, the b values are **partial regression coefficients** or **partial slopes**, and a is the Y-intercept (the predicted value of the dependent variable when all of the X values are equal to zero). The slopes in this equation differ from those in bivariate regression in that each represents the impact of the independent variable when *all other variables in the equation are held constant*. This tells us the effect of a given variable beyond the effects of all the other variables included in the analysis.

When researchers report the results of multiple regression, they present the intercept and the regression coefficient for each variable in a table. Table 14.10 shows the outcome for Pate and Bolin's data after completing a regression of nonmedical prescription drug use on selected independent variables. Model 1 includes seven independent variables; Model 2 adds an eighth: scores on the depression index, which is the independent variable of theoretical interest. To interpret the results of this analysis, we need to explain several features of the variables and the statistics presented in the table.

- Three of the variables—"male," "White," and "Greek life"—represent dummy variables. A **dummy variable** is a variable that is recoded into two categories that are assigned the values of 1 and 0. Dummy coding enables the researcher to manipulate the variable numerically, as in multiple regression. Thus, for the campus survey data, 1 = male and 0 = female; 1 = White and 0 = nonwhite; 1 = involved in Greek life and 0 = not involved in Greek life.
- All other independent variables are treated as interval/ratio level measures.
- The statistics opposite each independent variable in the first and third columns are *unstandardized* regression coefficients. The second and fourth columns display estimated standard errors, which are used to compute significance tests.
- The last row of the table contains a statistic, R^2, which indicates how well the data fit the model or how well we can predict the dependent variable based on this set of independent variables. R^2 may vary from 0 to 1. It is particularly

---

multiple regression a statistical method for determining the simultaneous effects of several independent variables on a dependent variable

partial regression coefficient/partial slope coefficients in a multiple-regression equation that estimate the effects of each independent variable on the dependent variable when all other variables in the equation are held constant

dummy variable a variable or set of variable categories recoded to have values of 0 and 1. Dummy coding may be applied to nominal- or ordinal-scale variables for the purpose of regression or other numerical analysis

R^2 a measure of fit in multiple regression that indicates approximately the proportion of the variation in the dependent variable predicted or "explained" by the independent variables

Table 14.10 Regression of Nonmedical Prescription Drug Use on Selected Independent Variables (Pate & Bolin 2019)

INDEPENDENT VARIABLES	Model 1		Model 2	
	Coefficient Estimate	Standard Error	Coefficient Estimate	Standard Error
GPA	−.033	.025	−.027	.025
Male	.096*	.030	.083*	.030
White	−.012	.034	−.003	.035
Greek life	.012	.032	.010	.033
Age	−.009	.009	−.009	.009
Stress index	.038*	.017	.022	.019
Other drug/alcohol use	.116**	.012	.114**	.012
Depression index			.060*	.021
Intercept	1.030	.216	.958	.217
Adjusted R^2	.155		.157	

Model 1 N = 691; Model 2 N = 661; *p < .05; **p < .001

useful for comparing models containing the same dependent variable but different sets of independent variables, such as Models 1 and 2 in Table 14.10.

- Asterisks (*,**) next to the coefficients indicate which independent variables are significantly related to NMPDU. The levels of significance are specified in a footnote to the table.
- In addition to levels of significance, the footnote shows the number of cases upon which the statistics are based. It also indicates that values of "0" in the table mean that the statistic has been rounded to 0.

Now that you know the meaning of the statistics reported in Table 14.10, let us examine the outcome of the multiple regression. To begin, we will pose some questions:

1. Is depression significantly related to NMPDU when controlling for all of the other independent variables in the equation?
2. Which variables in Model 2 have a significant impact on NMPDU?
3. In Model 1, what does the coefficient for "male" mean?
4. What happens to the regression coefficient for male when depression is added to the equation (Model 2)? What does this imply about the relationship among sex, depression, and NMPDU?
5. In both models, which variable has the biggest impact on NMPDU?

Now, on to the answers:

1. To answer the first question, the coefficient for depression is statistically significant when controlling for all the other independent variables in the model. The coefficient (.060) is not identical to the regression coefficient we obtained in the bivariate regression (.103). So, the relationship between depression and NMPDU does appear to be affected by these other variables; however, the data support the hypothesis that depression is associated with NMPDU.
2. In addition to depression, two other variables in Model 2 are significant predictors of NMPDU: sex ("male"), and other past 30-day drug/alcohol use (alcohol, cannabis, and cocaine).
3. The coefficient of .096 for "male" in Model 1 means that, on average, when controlling for all other variables in the model, males have an NMPDU score that is .096 higher than females. (To control the other variables, just assign each variable a value of 0.)
4. When number of drinks is added to the equation, the coefficient for sex reduces in absolute magnitude from .096 to .083. This difference shows the effect of depression on the *relationship* between sex and NMPDU. It suggests that depression may be an intervening variable between sex and NMPDU: sex affects depression (at least willingness to report), which in turn affects NMPDU. In other words, one of the reasons males have higher levels of NMPDU than females is that they report experiencing more symptoms of depression. This relationship should be further explored in the literature on depression symptoms across gender.
5. To determine which variable has the greatest impact on NMPDU, we need to compare the coefficients. There is a problem, however, in comparing the unstandardized slope coefficients in Table 14.10. As you may recall, regression coefficients (or slopes) indicate the amount of change in Y that is associated with each change of one unit in X. For example, the *unstandardized* regression coefficient of .060 for depression means that NMPDU increases by .060 with each increase in the depression index score. The problem with unstandardized regression coefficients, however, is that the units differ for each independent variable. For GPA, it is a point; for income, the unit is dollars; for a basic question about the amount of alcohol consumed, it is a single drink; and so on. Because the units differ, you cannot compare the slopes to determine their relative impact on the dependent variable. After all, what sense does it make to compare the impact of a single point on GPA with a single drink of alcohol? To compare slopes, they should be "standardized" in a way that expresses the effects in terms of a common unit; a standard deviation is a unit common to both independent variables and the dependent variable. One way of calculating a standardized regression coefficient is to multiply the unstandardized regression coefficient (presented in Table 14.10) by the ratio of the standard deviation of the independent variable to the standard deviation of the dependent variable. This is what we have done in creating the coefficients in Table 14.11.

Table 14.11 Standardized Regression Coefficients for Regression of NMPDU on Selected Independent Variables (Pate & Bolin 2019)

Independent Variables	Model 1	Model 2
GPA	−.048	−.040
Male	.116**	.102*
White	−.013	−.003
Greek life	.013	.011
Age	−.035	−.037
Stress index	.077*	.045
Other drug/alcohol use	.350**	.342**
Depression index		.112*

*$p < .05$; **$p < .001$

standardized regression coefficients coefficients obtained from a norming operation that puts partial-regression coefficients on common footing by converting them to the same metric of standard deviation units

The statistics opposite each independent variable in Table 14.11 are **standardized regression coefficients**. Notice that we have not included the Y-intercept in this table. The reason is that, when standardizing the coefficients, the Y-intercept is set to 0. Notice also that the *standardized* regression coefficient for depression in Model 2 is .112. This means that for every increase of one standard deviation in depression, there is an increase of .112 standard deviation in NMPDU. With each variable now standardized, we can compare coefficients to see which has the biggest impact. The variable with the biggest impact is other past 30-day drug and alcohol use, followed by depression index scores.

Now that you see how we could use multivariate analysis to test theoretical models, we hasten to add that we have barely scratched the surface of multivariate modeling. What we have tried to do is give you a sense of the logic of statistical control and the kinds of inferences that can be made from various statistics. But there are many methods of multivariate analysis other than elaboration and multiple regression. For example, there are special techniques for modeling different types of dependent variables (e.g., dichotomous, nominal, and ordinal measures), for straightening or transforming nonlinear relationships into a form suitable for linear modeling, for modeling mutual causation, processes occurring over time, and so forth. In addition, we have ignored the process of model testing, which usually involves the consideration of a series of models of varying complexity. In short, our presentation is quite superficial and cannot be substituted for formal coursework in statistics.

Finally, we also should point out that our presentation generally ignores the assumptions that underlie multiple regression as well as other forms of statistical analysis. Box 14.5 alerts you to a few of the more important assumptions.

BOX 14.5

READING CRIMINAL JUSTICE RESEARCH

The Impact of Statistical Assumptions in Quantitative Data Analysis

All statistics make certain assumptions about the data, and researchers often apply these statistics even though the assumptions are not met. Fully understanding how the violation of assumptions may affect an analysis requires an advanced knowledge of statistics. Still, it is important to understand the critical role of a few basic assumptions in the interpretation of quantitative data analysis.

The most fundamental assumption of inferential statistics is that the data are based on a random process—either random sampling or random assignment. As we saw in Chapter 7, the ability to estimate the margin of error in a sample depends on a known sampling distribution, which is produced by repeated random sampling. Similarly, in tests of statistical significance, we compare results from a random sample against a randomly generated statistical distribution, such as chi-square, to determine the likelihood that the result occurred by chance. If the sample is nonrandom, the test statistic does not apply because there is no basis for estimating the chance occurrence of the result.

Another important assumption in linear regression and correlation analysis is that a straight line provides the best fit for the data. As we pointed out, researchers often make this determination by examining a scatterplot. This method is far from foolproof, however, and if the best-fitting straight line is calculated for data that are nonlinearly related, statistical predictions based on the sample data may be seriously in error.

Multiple regression makes an additional assumption about the correlations among independent variables: a regression equation should not contain two or more variables that are highly correlated. If two variables are highly correlated, then we cannot estimate the independent effects of the variables, and the inclusion of both variables in the equation can distort estimates of coefficients. If two highly correlated variables (e.g., academic class and age in Pate and Bolin's (2019) study) are found, then the easy solution is to drop one from the regression equation. A far more difficult problem is *multicollinearity*, which arises when combinations of two or more variables are highly related with each other.

Finally, all forms of regression analysis are subject to what is called a *specification error*. All regression analysis involves the specification of a model containing a set of variables. A specification error occurs when the equation leaves out important variables. For example, if an equation fails to contain an antecedent variable that is a common cause of a bivariate relationship, the results of a bivariate analysis may be misleading because the relationship is spurious. To the extent that a model is misspecified, a regression analysis will produce biased estimates of coefficients.

SUMMARY

We introduced two methods of model testing that are used to examine the effects of an independent variable on a dependent variable while controlling for other relevant independent variables. In elaboration of contingency tables, we begin with a two-variable relationship and then systematically reassess this relationship when controls are introduced for a third variable (and sometimes additional ones). Variables are controlled, or held constant, by computing partial tables, which examine the original two-variable relationship separately for each category of the control variable. Of the numerous possible outcomes, one is of particular interest: if the model specifies the control variable as causally antecedent to the other two variables and the original relationship disappears in each partial table, then the original relationship is spurious. A better technique for analyzing the simultaneous effects of several independent variables on a dependent variable is multiple regression. The partial-regression coefficients in a multiple-regression equation show the effects of each independent variable on the dependent variable when all other variables in the equation are held constant. Comparison of partial regression coefficients may be facilitated by standardizing them to the same metric of standard deviation units. (See Box 14.6 to assess your understanding of multivariate testing.)

BOX 14.6

CHECKING YOUR UNDERSTANDING

Multivariate Testing

1. Which of the following would be an appropriate analysis to run to test the impact of multiple variables at once?
    a. Correlation
    b. Bivariate regression
    c. Descriptive statistics
    d. Elaboration of contingency tables

2. Why are multivariate analyses an important part of quantitative research?
    a. To establish an association between two variables
    b. To describe multiple variables
    c. To establish a nonspurious association between two variables
    d. They are not important

3. Which of the following statistics can be used to determine approximately the proportion of the variation in the dependent variable predicted or "explained" by the independent variables, telling us the overall "fit" of the regression?
   a. The intercept
   b. The standardized regression coefficient
   c. Adjusted R^2
   d. The unstandardized regression coefficient

4. Which of the following statistics can be used to determine the independent variable that has the most significant impact on the dependent variable in a multiple regression?
   a. The intercept
   b. The standardized regression coefficient
   c. Adjusted R^2
   d. The unstandardized regression coefficient

Answers: 1. d, 2. c, 3. c, 4. b

KEY TERMS

bivariate analysis, p. 418
cell frequency, p. 419
chi-square test for independence (χ^2), p. 421
consistency checking, p. 408
correlation coefficient, p. 425
data cleaning, p. 408
data matrix, p. 405
data processing, p. 403
descriptive statistics, p. 401
dummy variable, p. 433
frequency distribution, p. 410
histogram, p. 414
imputation, p. 415
inferential statistics, p. 401
listwise deletion, p. 415

marginal frequencies, p. 419
mean, p. 412
measures of association, p. 422
median, p. 413
missing data, p. 405
mode, p. 413
multiple regression, p. 433
N, p. 411
null hypothesis, p. 420
outliers, p. 414
partial regression coefficient/partial slope, p. 433
partial table, p. 431
percentage distribution, p. 411

R^2, p. 433
range, p. 413
regression analysis, p. 423
regression line, p. 425
residuals, p. 425
scatterplot, p. 424
slope/regression coefficient, p. 424
standard deviation, p. 414
standardized regression coefficients, p. 436
tests of statistical significance, p. 420
univariate analysis, p. 409
wild-code checking, p. 408
Y-intercept, p. 424

KEY POINTS

- To prepare quantitative data for computerized analysis, the data must be processed by coding and editing the data, entering them into an electronic datafile, and cleaning for errors.
- Once processed, the data are inspected by examining the univariate distribution of each variable.
- Data inspection is facilitated by creating percentage distributions and, for interval/ratio variables, by calculating statistics that describe the central tendency, variation, and shape of a distribution.
- Data inspection may lead to data modification, such as imputing missing values and combining data from two or more variables.
- After univariate analysis comes bivariate analysis, in which the statistical significance and degree of association between two variables are examined.
- Bivariate relationships of nominal/ordinal variables are depicted in contingency tables.
- Examining the relationship of two interval/ratio variables often involves regression analysis: plotting the variables in a graph and then determining the best-fitting line.
- Various statistics are available to test for significance (e.g., chi-square for contingency tables) and to measure degree of association (e.g., the correlation coefficient).
- The analysis of three or more variables involves applying statistical procedures that test specified theoretical models.
- Elaboration of contingency tables systematically controls for third variables by creating partial tables in which categories of the third variable are held constant.
- Multiple regression can examine the effect of an independent variable by controlling simultaneously for several other variables.

REVIEW QUESTIONS

1. What is the purpose of editing and data cleaning? When does editing occur? When does data cleaning occur?
2. What are some reasons for inspecting the data prior to analysis?
3. Explain the difference between descriptive and inferential statistics by providing examples of each.
4. What are the rules for percentaging and reading contingency tables to determine the relationship between variables?
5. What does the chi-square test for independence tell you about the association between variables?
6. Consider the following regression equation based on hypothetical data. In this model, Offender Risk Score ranges from 1 to 5 with 5 being highest risk:

    Sentence length in years = 10.27 + .32 (Offender Risk Score)

a) How much change in respondent's sentence length is associated with each increase of one point in their Offender Risk Score?
b) What is the predicted sentence length (in years) of a respondent whose Offender Risk Score is a 4?

7. Describe the difference between a regression coefficient and a correlation coefficient.
8. Explain the difference between the regression coefficient in bivariate regression and the partial regression coefficients in multiple regression.

EXERCISES

1. In Chapter 5, Exercise 2, we asked you to examine a contingency table and a correlation based on data from the GSS. In accessing and analyzing the GSS data, you used a website maintained by the University of California Berkeley. Now we want you to repeat these analyses, but answer additional questions about various statistics. The GSS data may be accessed and analyzed by searching online for "SDA GSS 1972–2018" (this data is published by the University of California at Berkeley). Click on the data set, generate the statistics specified below, and answer the following questions.

   a. First, opposite "Row:" enter DRUNK; opposite "Column:" enter SEX; opposite "Selection Filter(s):" enter YEAR (1994), and opposite "Weight:" use the dropdown menu to find and click "No weight." Now click on the "Output Options" tab and under "Cell Contents," you will see "Percentaging:" check "Column." Below that you will see "Other options," where you should check "Summary Statistics" and "Question text." Finally, click "Run the Table." Compare the percentages in the first row of the table. Who is more likely to say that they sometimes drink more than they think they should? What is the value of gamma (a measure of association that may vary from −1 to +1)? What is the significance of the first Rao-Scott test (which is a modified version of the chi-square test)? What does each of these statistics tell you about the relationship between DRUNK and SEX?

   b. At the top of the page, click the "Regression" Tab. Opposite "Dependent" enter REALRINC (which stands for respondent's income in constant dollars); below "Independent," enter EDUC; opposite "Selection Filter(s)," enter YEAR (2018), and opposite "Weight:" use the dropdown menu to find and click "No weight." Now click "Run Regression." Write out the regression equation. (Note that the "constant" is the Y-intercept, which in this case is negative because it is an estimate for someone with 0 years of education—a highly unlikely occurrence in the contemporary United States.) What is the value of the *un*standardized regression coefficient (B)? What does it tell you about the relationship between years of education and annual income? In a bivariate regression, the correlation is the same as the standardized regression coefficient (Beta). What is the correlation between highest year of education completed and annual income?

2. Now that you know how to use the Berkeley website, go to the website and test a bivariate hypothesis using GSS data. First, formulate a hypothesis by selecting one independent variable and one dependent variable from the following lists. (Note that all variables have nominal- or ordinal-level measurement.)

Independent Variable	Mnemonic Label
Respondent's sex (male/female)	SEX
Respondent's race (White/nonwhite)	RACE(1,2)
Level of education (high school or less/ > high school)	DEGREE(r:0–1;2–4)

Dependent Variable	Mnemonic Label
Support for legalization of marijuana (should/should not be legal)	GRASS
Attitude toward homosexuality (sexual relations between same-sex adults is always or almost always wrong/sometimes wrong or not wrong at all)	HOMOSEX(r:1–2;3–4)
Whether or not one has seen an X-rated movie	XMOVIE

3. Conduct an elaboration analysis by repeating the test of your hypothesis in Exercise 2 using either SEX or RACE(1, 2) as a control variable. (Note: If SEX is the independent variable in your hypothesis, then use RACE; if RACE is the independent variable, then use SEX.) Carefully explain what happens to the original relationship in each of the partial tables.

4. Surveys typically report that residents of large cities are more tolerant of deviant behavior than are residents of smaller cities and rural areas. Suppose that data are available for three variables: (1) respondent's tolerance of deviant behavior (let's label this TOLERANCE), (2) size of current place of residence (CURRENT RESIDENCE), and (3) size of place in which the respondent was living at age 16 (AGE16 RESIDENCE). For each of the following hypotheses, draw arrow diagrams to specify an appropriate causal model: (a) the social environment of the current residence renders people more or less tolerant; (b) tolerance is learned during adolescence and remains relatively constant thereafter; (c) both AGE16 and CURRENT residential environments affect tolerance of deviant behavior.

5. Repeat the steps in Exercise 1(b) with REALRINC as the dependent variable and EDUC as an independent variable, and then add the following independent variables to the equation: RACE(d:1), a dummy variable with "White" = 1; and SEX(d:1), a dummy variable with "male" = 1. Recall that B = unstandardized regression coefficient and Beta = standardized regression coefficient.

   a. Write out the multiple regression equation using the *unstandardized* partial regression coefficients. Based on this equation, what is the estimated income, on average, of a White male with a bachelor's degree (i.e., 16 years of education)? How much less, on average, does a White female with the same education earn?
   b. Which variable—EDUC, RACE, or SEX—has the biggest impact on income? Which variable is not statistically significant?

15

CHAPTER OUTLINE

15.1 Overview: A Process of Analyzing Qualitative Data 446

15.2 Prepare Data 447
  Transform the Data to Readable Text 447
  Check for and Resolve Errors 448
  Manage the Data 449
  Summary 451

15.3 Identify Concepts, Patterns, and Relationships 452
  Coding 452
  Memo Writing 455
  Data Displays 455
  Summary 459

15.4 Draw and Evaluate Conclusions 460
  Summary 461

15.5 Variations in Qualitative Data Analysis 462
  Grounded Theory Methods 462
  Narrative Analysis 464
  Conversation Analysis 465
  Summary 467

Qualitative Data Analysis

Searching for Meaning

LEARNING OBJECTIVES

By the end of this chapter, you should be able to

15.1 Identify and apply the steps in qualitative data analysis.

15.2 Describe how textual data are prepared for analysis.

15.3 Explain the purposes of different types of coding, memo writing, and data displays.

15.4 Explain how researchers may draw and evaluate conclusions from qualitative data.

15.5 Give examples of major variations in qualitative data analysis.

What do the following findings have in common?

- Based on observations and interviews with men living in a halfway house post-release, Liam Martin (2018) found a common theme among the men was a disorienting culture shock upon being released from prison (Chapter 10).
- Through in-depth interviews and covert participation, Nancy Scheper-Hughes (2004) uncovered illegal medical practices were being conducted throughout the Middle East, Southeast Asia, and Africa (Chapter 10).
- Ida Johnson's (2015) in-depth interview study found familial ties post-release to be important for female parolees' success (Chapter 5).

If you answered that these findings are based on qualitative research designs, you are correct. Now note the process by which you came to this conclusion: you read the text of the examples and made comparisons. This is similar to the process of analyzing qualitative data, the subject of this chapter. Qualitative analysis is largely an inductive process that involves grouping together specific pieces of usually nonnumerical data, such as text, that share similarities to formulate more general and abstract conclusions. As we have mentioned before, the inferences generated through this process are subject to *multiple interpretations* and *vary in strength*. Hence, if you answered that the above findings are similar in that they are all reported in this book, you would also be correct. And while this and the previous inference may be strong, a weaker inference, as you will see, would be that these studies followed the same qualitative analysis techniques.

In this chapter, we outline a general process by which qualitative data can be analyzed. But note the tentative nature of this statement: "a general process by which qualitative data *can be* analyzed." There are few agreed-upon standards about how researchers *should* analyze qualitative data, as numerous authors suggest (Charmaz, 2014; Corbin & Strauss, 2015; Emerson et al., 2011; Gibbs, 2018; Lofland et al., 2006; Miles et al., 2020; Saldaña, 2013). Drawing on these authors' work, we present a process model that integrates common features of qualitative data analysis. We then illustrate the steps in this model with data from multiple research studies. We conclude with a discussion of some of the major variations in qualitative data analysis.

Millions of children in the United States have experienced the incarceration of at least one parent at some point in their childhood. Research on the effects of parental incarceration has found many negative, long-term impacts that children must cope with into adulthood. This area of research tends to study children of incarcerated parents as one general population, without considerations for the unique experiences one may face due to gender, race, and ethnicity. Noting this gap in research on parental incarceration, Melissa Noel Monde and Cherrell Green (2022) interviewed Black and Latina women to understand their experiences with and coping strategies for managing parental incarceration.

Data were collected through the use of semi-structured interviews conducted over a six-month period, from November 2019 to April 2020 (Noel Monde & Green, 2022). Interviews were conducted privately either in-person, via telephone, or Zoom. The questions asked participants how they viewed their experience with parental incarceration, ways in which they compartmentalized this portion of their life, and the coping strategies employed to deal with their experience. Participants consented to their interviews being audio-recorded to preserve the data. In addition, all interviews were transcribed verbatim by an online transcription service.

Noel Monde and Green (2022) found the experience of parental incarceration to be a complex process that impacts the women well into young adulthood. One woman, who chose to disassociate herself with her abusive, incarcerated father due to the strain of witnessing domestic violence and navigating prison visits, was still struggling with the anticipation of his release in the near future. Another woman described her experience of becoming an adult quickly as she became the primary caregiver to her siblings at a young age due to parental incarceration. In addition, she never knew her father outside of prison and had to relearn his role in her life as a parent upon his release when she had become accustomed to being the "parent." Finally, she described the tension of dealing with her own psychological distress as well as adjusting to his mental state post-release.

To help them remain resilient despite their experiences with parental incarceration, coping mechanisms were employed by the women. Specifically, Noel Monde and Green (2022) identified four coping mechanisms utilized by the women: "(a) acknowledging their incarcerated parent's decisions and accepting the reality of their circumstances, (b) keeping themselves occupied with tasks and activities, (c) relying on their social support groups or mental health services, (d) reconstructing their social identity" (p. 395).

15.1 OVERVIEW: A PROCESS OF ANALYZING QUALITATIVE DATA

The qualitative methods discussed in this book—field research, in-depth and focus group interviews, and comparative historical analysis—use different kinds of data. Field research, for example, prizes observational data; interviews primarily yield verbal reports; existing data may come in the form of text and visual imagery. In this chapter, we focus on the analysis of textual data based on field notes and interviews. Figure 15.1 outlines a general process of analyzing these data. As the figure indicates, the steps in this process overlap with one another and are not linear, reflecting the iterative nature of qualitative research.

In much qualitative research, data analysis begins during data collection. The next step, *preparing the data*, is similar to quantitative analysis, except the data to be prepared are primarily text, which need to be transformed into a more readable form, checked for errors and corrected, and organized and managed using a physical filing system or an electronic database.

Analysis incorporates the inductive process of measurement, discussed in Chapter 6, whereby researchers *identify concepts, patterns,* and *relationships* in the data through operationally defining the phenomena they are studying. This is facilitated by coding, memo writing, and other analytic strategies.

The *conclusions researchers draw* from their analysis range from the descriptive to the theoretical and need to be *evaluated* for their strength and quality. This is a back-and-forth process in which inferences from an early stage of the analysis may be discarded, modified, or replaced through additional analysis or data collection.

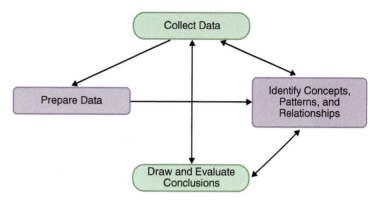

FIGURE 15.1 A Process of Analyzing Qualitative Data

We now elaborate on each of these steps using the parental incarceration study and other research examples. We caution, however, that these studies do not always follow the process in the order in which we present their analysis.

15.2 PREPARE DATA

An initial step is to prepare the data. To do so, researchers transform the data into readable form, edit and clean, and manage or store the data. These are not just "mechanical" processes; they also involve analysis (Gibbs, 2018, p. 19).

Transform the Data to Readable Text

Field jottings alone may not provide the necessary detail for analysis, and as you might imagine, starting and stopping an audio or video device in order to analyze its content may prove difficult. As such, these data are typically prepared by transforming them into more readable text.

Field jottings, as you will recall from Chapter 10, are brief quotes, phrases, and key words that are recorded by researchers in the field. After researchers leave the site or are otherwise inconspicuous to the participants, they expand upon the jottings to form a more complete set of field notes. Field researchers today most often enter their notes directly into word-processing programs.

To prepare interview data, researchers often transcribe interviewees' words into text. There are many questions to consider about *how* to transcribe interview data (Gibbs, 2018). For example, should you transcribe the data yourself or hire someone

```
1  BARRY
2  Well, the only thing that we've really given up is—well we used to
3  go dancing. Well she can't do it now so I have to go on my own,
4  that's the only thing really. And then we used to go indoor bowling
5  at the sports centre. But of course, that's gone by the board now. So
6  we don't go there. But I manage to get her down to works club, just
7  down the road on the occasional Saturdays, to the dances. She'll sit
8  and listen to the music, like, stay a couple of hours and then she's
9  had enough. And then, if it's a nice weekend I take her out in the
10 car.
```

FIGURE 15.2 Partial Transcript from a Qualitative Interview

to do so (assuming you have resources)? Should you use a digital voice recorder or voice recognition software to transcribe your data? Should you correct any grammatically incorrect remarks by your interviewees? Should the transcribed data include every utterance, pause, or "filler" (e.g., "uh," "um")? We address some of these questions below. For other questions that are beyond the scope of this chapter, you may want to consult Graham Gibbs's (2018) *Analyzing Qualitative Data* for guidance.

The transcript often appears as a series of numbered lines, with an interviewee's pseudonym or identification number noted somewhere on the transcript. An example of a partial transcript is presented in Figure 15.2, in which "Barry"—who looks after his wife with Alzheimer's disease—is asked, "Have you had to give anything up that you enjoyed doing that was important to you?" (Gibbs, 2018, p. 57).

Check for and Resolve Errors

Transformations of data in any form—numerical or textual—may introduce errors. Although field researchers strive to accurately capture observed reality, recorded observations involve interpretations that can vary from one observer to another. Therefore, researchers may check their field notes with participants and other sources to identify and resolve errors. When research is conducted in a team, observers may compare notes. As you conduct your research, it is a good idea to have someone else look over your notes, provided that ethical considerations allow for this. A common "error" that novices make is simply one of omission—that is, they do not include pertinent information or enough detail in their notes (Emerson et al., 2011; Rossman & Rallis, 2003).

Errors are especially likely to occur in the transcription of interview data. Regardless of whether you transcribe the data yourself, have someone else transcribe it, or use voice recognition software, it is possible that what the interviewee said will not be accurately recorded. This could occur because the interviewee was simply misheard, because the quality of the recording was poor, or for some other reason (Gibbs, 2018, pp. 26–27). To get an idea of how easy it would be to make a mistake, look at Table 15.1 for examples of transcription errors provided by Carl Cuneo in a study of trade union activities (quoted in Gibbs, 2018, p. 27).

Some errors, such as those in Table 15.1, can be detected by comparing the audio/video recording to the transcription. Other errors, such as typos and misspelled words, can be detected by reading over the transcript or using a word processing spellchecking function. While it is important to correct these and other such "input" errors, researchers generally are not advised to correct an interviewee's grammar (Gibbs, 2018).

Table 15.1 Examples of Transcription Errors

Transcriber's Typed Phrase	What Interviewee Actually Said
DIFFERENT INTERPRETATIONS	
reflective bargaining	collective bargaining
certain kinds of ways of understanding	surface kinds of ways of understanding
and our	and/or
mixed service	lip service
denying neglect	benign neglect
OPPOSITE MEANINGS	
ever meant to	never meant to
it just makes sense	it doesn't make sense
formal	informal
there's one thing I can add	there's nothing I can add
there's more discernible actions	there aren't discernible factions

Source: Adapted from Table 2.1 in Gibbs (2018, p. 27)

Manage the Data

Field notes can fill a book, especially if they encompass years of research; interview transcripts can run several pages just for a single interview; and pages of archival records may number in the thousands. It is thus important to find a means of managing your data, which involves organizing and storing it.

A basic strategy as you begin to organize qualitative data is to label it. Called **attribute coding**, this differs from the coding discussed later in that its primary intent is to manage the data by labeling characteristics of fieldwork settings, participants, and so forth at the top of a set of field notes or interview transcript, or by typing them into a word-processing or **Computer-Assisted Qualitative Data Analysis Software (CAQDAS)** program (Saldaña, 2013, pp. 69–70). Below is an example of attribute-coded field notes (Saldaña, 2013, p. 71), which identifies primary features of the participants, setting, and activities observed:

PARTICIPANTS: 5TH GRADE CHILDREN
DATA FORMAT: P.O. FIELD NOTES/SET 14 OF 22
SITE: WILSON ELEMENTARY SCHOOL, PLAYGROUND
DATE: 6 OCTOBER 2010

attribute coding a method of coding that identifies the characteristics of participants, settings, and other phenomena of interest, largely as a means of managing the data

Computer-Assisted Qualitative Data Analysis Software (CAQDAS) software packages that aid in the management and analysis of data

```
TIME: 11:45 a.m.–12:05 p.m.
ACTIVITIES INDEX [a list of the field notes' major contents]:
    RECESS
    BOYS PLAYING SOCCER
    BOYS ARGUING
    GIRLS IN CONVERSATION
    GIRLS PLAYING FOUR-SQUARE
    TEACHER MONITORING
    DISCIPLINE
```

When applied to transcribed interviews, this method resembles the coding of variables in survey research, as evidenced in another example from Saldaña (2013, pp. 70–71):

```
PARTICIPANT (PSEUDONYM): BARRY
AGE: 18
GRADE LEVEL 12
GPA: 3.84
GENDER: MALE
ETHNICITY: WHITE
SEXUAL ORIENTATION: HETEROSEXUAL
SOCIAL CLASS: LOWER-MIDDLE
RELIGION: METHODIST
DATA FORMAT: INTERVIEW 4 OF 5
TIME FRAME: MARCH 2011
```

In addition, John Lofland, David Snow, Leon Anderson, and Lyn Lofland (2006) recommend creating "coding files" into which data can be categorized. In the case of fieldwork, they advise, "Initially, you should develop coding files for every actor you encounter, every major setting-relevant activity and/or event, and the range of places in which the actors have been encountered and the activities/events observed . . ." (Lofland et al., 2006, p. 206). Noel Monde and Green (2022) created coding files for each of the 11 women interviewed for their parental incarceration study. In these files, they were able to line-by-line code for themes.

To store qualitative data, you need to decide whether to use a physical filing system, electronic system, or some combination. This decision has implications for the rest of your analysis. On the one hand, the physical filing system helps novice researchers to gain intimate familiarity with the data. Moreover, software programs cannot do all the work of the researcher. On the other hand, basic and more specialized software programs can increase efficiency (Gibbs, 2018; Lofland et al., 2006; Miles et al., 2020; Saldaña, 2013).

With data today invariably in electronic form, researchers use word-processing and spreadsheet programs for organizing and storing data (Miles et al., 2020; Saldaña, 2013). These programs allow one to save different files; place comments, notes, and labels within a file; and cut and paste text. In addition, several CAQDAS programs allow researchers to manage, code, and display their data. In their study of parental incarceration, Noel Monde and Green (2022) utilized a qualitative analysis software, NVivo, as an organizational tool. Based on their use of the software, we can assume many of their files were electronic in nature.

SUMMARY

Data preparation involves transforming the data into more readable text, usually in electronic form. An important function of data preparation is to check for and correct errors. To manage the potentially vast amount and array of textual data, you need to organize it and decide whether to use a physical filing system, an electronic system, or some combination for storage. Qualitative data may be organized through attribute coding and by creating coding files for every actor, activity/event, and field setting. Assess your understanding of working with data in Box 15.1.

BOX 15.1
CHECKING YOUR UNDERSTANDING

Working with Data

1. All of the following sequences are possible in qualitative analysis, except:
   a. collect data → prepare data → identify patterns and relationships → draw conclusions
   b. collect data → identify patterns and relationships → prepare data → draw conclusions
   c. prepare data → identify patterns and relationships → collect data → draw conclusions
   d. prepare data → identify patterns and relationships → draw conclusions → collect data

2. Identify the sequence that most accurately describes *data preparation* in qualitative analysis.
   a. transform data to readable text → edit and clean data → manage data

continues

continued

    b. manage data → transform data to readable text → edit and clean data
    c. edit and clean data → transform data to readable text → manage data
    d. manage data → edit and clean data → transform data to readable text

3. The primary objective of attribute coding is to manage the data.
    a. True
    b. False

Answers: 1. b, 2. a, 3. a

15.3 IDENTIFY CONCEPTS, PATTERNS, AND RELATIONSHIPS

If you are sitting in front of pages of field notes or interview transcripts, you are likely wondering how to move from the bits and pieces of data to the kinds of inferences you read in research reports. Coding, memo writing, and creating data displays are different ways of doing so. Coding emerged as part of the grounded theory tradition, as its founders Barney Glaser and Anselm Strauss (1967, p. 102) sought to develop strategies that would enhance theoretical development. Coding is often accompanied by memo writing (see Chapter 10). While contemporary versions of grounded theory inform our discussion of coding and memo writing in this section (Charmaz, 2014; Corbin & Strauss, 2015), we describe these strategies in more general terms and reserve our discussion of grounded theory methods for a later section.

Coding

Coding begins with the selection of a unit of textual data, which is shaped by the specific form of data collection. A researcher may derive their textual data from field notes, with each note considered a "data entry." Field notes may vary from a single sentence to several pages. In semi- and unstructured interviews, such as the ones conducted by Noel Monde and Green, data can span many transcript pages, sometimes without any discernible "break." Kathy Charmaz (2014) suggests initially selecting transcript lines as units. Whatever unit you choose, it is important that you document your decision. When there are more than two coders, it is also essential that they agree on the standard unit in order to achieve *inter-coder reliability* (Campbell et al., 2013).

Beyond organizing/managing the data, coding is used to summarize and condense the data as well as raise it to a more conceptual and abstract level. Many types of coding are applied for these purposes (Saldaña, 2013); Johnny Saldaña's *The Coding Manual for Qualitative Researchers* (2013) profiles more than 30 such methods. What researchers code depends on their research question, the form (and units) of their data, and other considerations. Emerson and colleagues (2011, p. 177) recommend asking the following questions of field notes:

- What are people doing? What are they trying to accomplish?
- How, exactly, do they do this? What specific means and/or strategies do they use?
- How do members [participants] talk about, characterize, and understand what is going on?

These and similar questions may be asked of different kinds of data, including transcripts. To illustrate the coding process, let us return to Noel Monde and Green's study. They conducted line-by-line coding to identify themes. Four themes emerged regarding respondents' ability to cope and remain resilient:

a) acknowledging their incarcerated parent's decisions and accepting the reality of the circumstances,
b) keeping themselves occupied with tasks and activities,
c) relying on social support groups or mental health services, and
d) reconstructing their social identity (Noel Monde & Green, 2022, p. 16). The statements below represent different data entries for each theme.

- Accepting the reality of the circumstances: "I'm still dealing with it and now I'm asking more questions, because before I was not comfortable with making him uncomfortable. But I think in a—in a way for me to, to start that process of forgiveness and moving forward I would like to know . . . kind of what his mentality was during all of that, because I never really got that conversation with him of 'what was going through your head when all of this happened?' And, how he feels moving forward" (p. 16).
- Keeping themselves busy: "So if I had to like guess my coping mechanism, it would be like, I really started taking care of the house and of my mom and of my sisters. Um, in order to like keep myself distracted from like dealing with it myself. Or, it wasn't even intentional to keep myself distracted. I think that was just, if I didn't take that role . . . I don't know the house is going to fall apart. My mom was gonna be a lot worse. Um, and so I think that's [pause] I'm guessing that's just the way that I coped with like distracting myself and keeping my mind busy. Um, by taking care of my mom. Taking care of the house and things like that" (p. 18).
- Relying on support: "Definitely my [adoptive] parents. I don't know. I would not be anywhere near like, as far as I am today. If I did not have my parents. Like biggest support. [And] like my best friend from middle school. She's like, my soul sister, and she's always a phone call away. Yeah, even the people at my job.

My bosses like, then we have like a little family there. Those are like . . . [pause]. It's nice" (p. 20).

- Reconstructing their identity: "Once I wrote the essay, and this is gonna sound like cold, but, once I wrote the entrance essay to college, I realized I have a leveraging tool here. You know? You are gonna become the source by which I push through my education. I further my education, by way of telling, this, story. You know? People are amazed by it. It's intriguing. So as much as it was like a total selfish reason, it did make me put it in a positive light by being like, 'I can use this to help me, in a positive way um [pause] and so it's not embarrassing, anymore.' You know?" (p. 22).

This gives you an idea of how Noel Monde and Green coded a portion of their data. To apply what you have learned regarding coding textual data, see Box 15.2.

BOX 15.2

DOING CRIMINAL JUSTICE RESEARCH

Coding Textual Data

Now that you are familiar with coding textual data, try your hand at it. At the beginning of this chapter, we presented findings and asked what they had in common. Let us consider the "findings" as the sentence-length units to be coded (which are also demarcated by bullet points). To refresh your memory, they are:

- Based on observation and interviews with men living in a halfway house post-release, Liam Martin (2018) found a common theme among the men was a disorienting culture shock upon being released from prison (Chapter 10).
- Through in-depth interviews and covert participation, Nancy Scheper-Hughes (2004) uncovered illegal medical practices were being conducted throughout the Middle East, Southeast Asia, and Africa (Chapter 10).
- Ida Johnson's (2015) in-depth interview study found familial ties post-release to be important for female parolees' success (Chapter 5).

If we assume that the answer mentioned at the outset is a commonality—the findings are all based on qualitative research designs—then how do they *differ*?

One way to code these data is to ask what *kind* or *type* of qualitative research design each finding is based on. For example, you might code Martin's as "field research," Scheper-Hughes's as "field research," and Johnson's as "in-depth interviews." Note that these codes "stick closely" to the data (and are also quite literal), which is a practice

> Charmaz (2014, p. 112) recommends. If you coded this way, the preliminary outcome would look like this:
> - Qualitative research design
>   - Field research
>   - In-depth interviews
>
> This should help you to understand the basics of coding textual data. We will see a similar outcome/data display later.

Memo Writing

In Chapter 10 we noted that researchers write analytic memos as a way of "dumping their brains" about their research (Saldaña, 2013). Memos may include personal reflections on the research experience, a discussion of methodological issues, or thoughts about what is going on in the data. Memo writing is often used in conjunction with coding. Saldaña (2011) writes, "think of codes and their consequent categories as separate picture puzzle pieces, and their integration into an analytic memo as the assembly of the picture" (p. 99).

There are many different types of memos; here we highlight what Lofland and colleagues (2006, p. 210) call a **code memo** (also called a **code note** [Strauss & Corbin, 1990]). Code memos are written as a means of elaborating the basis of coding categories and have a form similar to a *codebook* (see Chapters 10 and 14); they are effectively the *operational definitions* of a concept.

Noel Monde and Green (2022) utilized memo writing in their analysis of how young women compartmentalized parental incarceration. Short analytic memos were completed following an interview that contained observation notes and reflective thoughts. For example, "conceptualizing parental incarceration" was a note written in the margin for the following participant quote: "I've put it in the back of my mind, but I don't think I'm ever gonna be able to get over the fact that he was in prison" (Noel Monde & Green, 2022, pp. 12–13).

code memo a type of memo written explicitly for describing the basis of one's operational definitions (also called a *code note*)

Data Displays

Qualitative analysts need to summarize the vast amount of text with which they are working. To do so, they may create different "data displays" (Miles et al., 2020) or "diagrams" (Lofland et al., 2006). Displays help researchers differentiate among concepts and identify patterns or relationships in the data. In this section, we focus on taxonomies, data matrices, typologies, and flowcharts.

TAXONOMIES

A **taxonomy** is a system of classification in which objects are placed into ordered categories, which may be arranged hierarchically. Examples of taxonomies are the table of contents of a book and the outline of a book chapter (Saldaña, 2013, p. 157).

taxonomy a system of classification that is usually ordered in some way

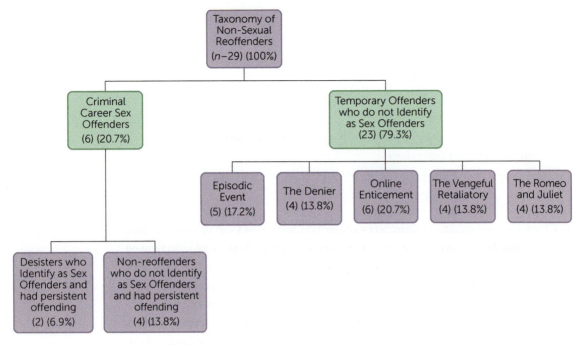

FIGURE 15.3 Taxonomy of Contact Sex Offenders

The outcome of coding presented in Box 15.2 is an example of a preliminary taxonomy in which "field research" and "in-depth interviews" were classified as components of "qualitative research designs."

An example of a taxonomy can be found in Brooke N. Cooley's (2022) study on desistance among sexual offenders. She conducted qualitative conversational interviews with 29 contact sex offenders. She generated taxonomies by asking what kinds or types of phenomena are represented in the data. Figure 15.3 illustrates a taxonomy derived from her data on desistance among contact sex offenders (Cooley, 2022).

DATA MATRICES

You are familiar with the notion of a data matrix from Chapter 14. Data matrices are particularly effective in helping researchers to understand relationships. They may be populated with numbers or text. Kennedy, Meier, and Prock (2021) utilized semi-structured interviews to qualitatively study women's experiences with intimate partner violence (IPV) in abusive first relationships as well as the process that led to disclosure of the abuse. In their analysis, Kennedy and colleagues developed two data matrices to organize interview data. First, a preliminary data matrix was developed by the lead author after researchers coded the first 11 interviews. This allowed the research team to fill in the matrix with summarized data from each interview. For example, the code "disclosure" was included in the preliminary matrix, and in the cell researchers would provide details about disclosure from individual participants such as how, when, and to whom.

As researchers continued their coding process and categories were refined, a second data matrix was developed with the following categories:

1. different types of IPV and their characteristics,
2. victim's social location (e.g., race/ethnicity, public assistance and ACEs, homelessness),
3. prior victimization and violence exposure,
4. developmental context,
5. situational context (e.g., ages, age difference, pregnancy or baby, live together, community or neighborhood factors, family and peers), and
6. the disclosure process.

The second matrix allowed researchers to discover connections between categories and patterns across participants' experiences. See Table 15.2 for a hypothetical example of a data matrix based upon Kennedy, Meier, and Prock's study. This matrix should give you a sense of the importance of displaying data to draw inferences. In a complete data matrix, researchers can see how text or numbers cluster together, the latter of which can be facilitated by quantitative data analysis.

Table 15.2 Hypothetical Partial Data Matrix

	Participant #1	Participant #2	Participant #3	Participant #4
IPV type and characteristics				
Social location				
Prior victimization and violence exposure				
Developmental context				
Situational context				
Disclosure process				

TYPOLOGIES

typology a representation of findings based on the cross-classification of two or more concepts, variables, or ideas

Typologies are displays "based on the cross-classification of two or more ideas, concepts, or variables" (Lofland et al., 2006, p. 214). A typology differs from a taxonomy, which distinguishes among categories of "ideas, concepts, or variables," but not their interrelationships. As an example, Cathy Murray (2009) created a typology of teenage resisters (those who never offended) and desisters (those who offended and then stopped) of delinquent behavior (See Table 15.3). Resisters were classified into two types: "innocents" and "streetwise resisters." Murray described innocents as experiencing "limited, if any, exposure to offending, had not contemplated offending themselves and refrained from engaging in antisocial behavior" (p. 121). These individuals had a good upbringing, with little exposure to family or friends who engaged in offending behavior.

Streetwise resisters differed from innocents in that while they did not report involvement in offending, they did report engagement in various types of antisocial behavior. Also in contrast to the innocents, streetwise resisters indicated having at least one family member, friend, or neighbor who had offended, with many having a mix of offender and non-offender friends (p. 122).

Murray classified desisters into three major types: "reformed characters," "quasi-resisters," and "on the margins." Reformed characters were described as those who offend and then "go straight." Most expressed regret for their behavior and had developed strategies to help them desist from offending behavior, such as changing their peer group. Reformed characters are distinguished from the other two desister types as they have a desistance tale, "a coherent explanation for a shift from offending to non-offending" (p. 119).

Quasi-resisters are distinct in that they retain a resister identity, despite self-reported involvement in offending. As they never identified themselves as "offenders," they told no desistance tale as was characteristic of the reformed characters (pp. 119–120).

The third type of desisters, those "on the margins" expressed "a weak resolve to cease offending," appearing as though desistance may be more of a pause rather than complete cessation. These desisters were also distinct in that they "reported more offending among friends and family than other desisters and came from neighbourhoods with high rates of offending" (p. 120).

Murray's typology aids in understanding youth who resist or desist from offending behavior in two towns in Scotland.

Table 15.3 Murray's Typology of Resisters and Desisters

Resisters		Desisters		
Innocents	Streetwise resisters	Reformed characters	Quasi-resisters	On the margins

SUMMARY

To identify concepts, patterns, and relationships in their data, researchers may use coding, memo writing, and/or other analytic techniques. Coding begins with the selection of a textual unit and involves comparing units to identify commonalities, which may be facilitated by writing memos about coded material and other aspects of the research. Creating visual displays or diagrams, including taxonomies, data matrices, and typologies may then be used to summarize the data as well as identify patterns and relationships. Challenge your understanding of coding terms in Box 15.3.

BOX 15.3

CHECKING YOUR UNDERSTANDING

Coding Terms

1. A _____ memo is a type of memo written explicitly for describing the basis of one's operational definitions.
   a. data
   b. code
   c. action
   d. operation

2. The table of contents of a book is similar to a taxonomy.
   a. True
   b. False

3. Which way of summarizing textual data represents findings based on the cross-classification of two or more concepts, variables, or ideas?
   a. Taxonomy
   b. Typology
   c. Flow chart
   d. Data matrix

Answers: 1. b, 2. a, 3. b

15.4 DRAW AND EVALUATE CONCLUSIONS

Matthew Miles, A. Michael Huberman, and Johnny Saldaña (2020) suggest that the "final" step is to draw and verify conclusions, which we give a slightly different name: draw and *evaluate* conclusions. Researchers' conclusions range from the descriptive to the more theoretical. Description is fundamental to qualitative research. Researchers may also infer *themes*, which are recurring threads or patterns that "summarize the manifest (apparent) and latent (underlying) meanings of data" (Saldaña, 2011, p. 108). An example is Noel Monde and Green's theme that the Black and Latina women use various strategies to cope with having experienced parental incarceration. Inferences that are more theoretical attempt to connect patterns, themes, and concepts to develop propositions, which—as you will recall from Chapter 2—are characteristic of theory (Miles et al., 2020). It is important to note, however, that qualitative research may modify or extend existing theory (Lofland et al., 2006) or develop it from "the ground up" (known as *grounded theory*, discussed below).

Noel Monde and Green's study shows the variety of conclusions one may draw from data. They described how Black and Latina women interpreted and coped with experiencing parental incarceration. They identified numerous patterns and themes in the data, including that "the effect of parental incarceration continues to work as an ongoing process within their lives as they emerge into adulthood" (p. 23). Additionally, they found that participants developed coping strategies which consisted of four distinct themes, which were previously discussed. In conducting their analysis, they defined concepts, differentiated their dimensions and types, and showed relationships among concepts, including from previous research. They state that their research on coping with parental incarceration suggests a need for programs that "are not only geared towards early development states, but young adulthood as issues with parental incarceration continue to emerge within the lives of Black and Latina women" (p. 28). Such programs, they argue, should focus on "developing cultural knowledge, building rapport and trust, and examining strategies that will enable successful outcomes and resiliency" (p. 28).

But how can you evaluate—and perhaps even strengthen—the conclusions you draw? In Chapter 10 we discussed means of evaluating reliability, validity, and generalizability mainly as they pertain to aspects of research design. Some of the strategies we mentioned as means of strengthening conclusions were to use a team approach, multiple sources of data, and different sampling strategies.

Beyond elements of research design, there are other ways of evaluating, or "verifying," conclusions (see Miles et al., 2020 for a complete discussion). One is to look for *exceptions* to patterns in the data. Analyzing "exceptional" data may provide unique insight into the area under study. McPherson and Thorne (2006) note that "thoughtful attention to contradictory or challenging observations can deepen our expectations about the kinds of knowledge products that qualitative research ought to yield, thereby helping us advance the credibility of our findings and the ultimate utility of our empirical conclusions" (p. 73).

You may also check with participants in your research. **Member checking** refers to asking participants if the findings make sense to them, which Kelly and Ward (2020), discussed later in the chapter, did in their research on gang disengagement. Thus, they might be asked to read one's research report or portions thereof. Similarly, findings that make use of participants' own words are sometimes said to be more valid accounts of their experiences, especially from the perspective of grounded theory (Charmaz, 2006).

While some of the strategies for evaluating conclusions differ for qualitative and quantitative research, they ultimately serve the same overall goal: to see if the model "fits." In assessing fit, researchers move between data and theory, characteristic of the scientific process.

member checking a method of evaluating qualitative data in which researchers share their results with participants and ask them to comment on their accuracy and completeness

SUMMARY

Conclusions that may be drawn from qualitative analysis range from the descriptive to the more theoretical. They may be strengthened by aspects of research design and further evaluated by looking for exceptions to patterns, checking with members, and ensuring that they are grounded in participants' voices and experiences. Test your understanding of data evaluation in Box 15.4.

BOX 15.4

CHECKING YOUR UNDERSTANDING

Evaluating Data

1. One way to increase the reliability of field research is to use multiple sources of data.
    a. True
    b. False

2. Like outliers in quantitative data analysis, exceptions to patterns in qualitative data are treated as errors that can be ignored.
    a. True
    b. False

continues

> *continued*

3. Member checking in the gang disengagement study would have involved
   a. verifying that individuals classified as having disengaged from a gang are indeed disengaged from a gang.
   b. asking individuals who had disengaged from a gang for permission to be identified in the study.
   c. verifying personal information on individuals who had disengaged from a gang by checking institutional records.
   d. asking individuals who had disengaged from a gang if the study findings make sense to them.

Answers 1. a, 2. b, 3. d

15.5 VARIATIONS IN QUALITATIVE DATA ANALYSIS

While we have presented a general process of qualitative data analysis, researchers vary in how they approach the data. This variation is partly a function of the form of the data and partly a reflection of different philosophical orientations to analysis. Below we discuss three variations in qualitative data analysis: grounded theory methods, narrative analysis, and conversation analysis.

Grounded Theory Methods

In its original form, as advanced by Glaser and Strauss (1967), grounded theory best epitomizes the inductive logic of inquiry, emphasizing the *discovery* of theory through data analysis. A strict interpretation of grounded theory suggests that the analysis should be made without reference to existing research. Researchers are advised, "at first, literally to ignore the literature of theory and fact on the area under study, in order to assure that the emergence of categories will not be contaminated by concepts more suited to different areas" (Glaser & Strauss, 1967, p. 37). Although this interpretation has been called into question and opinion is divided (Charmaz, 2014; Corbin & Strauss, 2015; Glaser, 1978; Strauss & Corbin, 1990), grounded theory retains at its core an emphasis on theoretical development and places a premium on research participants' voices and actions as sources of data in which a theory is rooted.

The primary grounded theory analytic technique is the **constant-comparative method**, by which the researcher makes comparisons throughout the process of analysis until theoretical *saturation* has occurred; theoretical sampling is part of this process (see Chapter 7). Comparisons are made through coding and memo writing, which occur in *at least* two phases or steps (Charmaz, 2014, p. 113; Charmaz & Belgrave, 2012, p. 356): the *initial/open* phase and the *focused/selective* phase. The following discussion

---

constant-comparative method the general analytic strategy of grounded theory methods, which involves making comparisons at increasingly higher levels of abstraction through coding, memo writing, and theoretical sampling

identifies some specific types of coding and memos used by those working in grounded theory traditions (Saldaña, 2013).

In the initial/open phase, units of data are compared with each other to develop codes. Common units of analysis in grounded theory are lines (for interview transcripts) and incidents (for field research). **In vivo coding**, which uses people's own words as codes, may be employed in this stage (Charmaz, 2014; Corbin & Strauss, 2015). This form of coding reflects grounded theory's emphasis on participants' voices. It can help the analyst understand the extent to which people are expressing their thoughts and feelings in the same language.

> **in vivo coding** a form of coding that uses participants' own words as labels

Another form that may be used in the initial phase is called **action coding** or **process coding**. This technique uses gerunds (*-ing* words) to refer to processes or action in the data (Charmaz & Belgrave, 2012, pp. 356–357; Saldaña, 2013, p. 96). Both action/process coding and in vivo coding can be used in combination with other forms of coding (Saldaña, 2013). The key to this phase is to "remain open," as Charmaz (2014, p. 113) suggests.

> **action coding** a form of coding that uses gerunds (*-ing* words) to signal activity in the data (also called *process coding*)

The focused/selected phase of the analysis uses "the most significant and/or frequent earlier codes to sift through and analyze large amounts of data" (Charmaz, 2014, p. 138). Here the analyst applies the constant-comparative method by: comparing selected codes and their associated data developed during the initial/open phase to data collected later (e.g., through theoretical sampling); comparing codes to one another to develop concepts and their dimensions and properties; and integrating concepts into a theory (Charmaz, 2014; Corbin & Strauss, 2015; Glaser & Strauss, 1967).

Much of advanced grounded theory methods is facilitated by memo writing, which is done throughout the process (Saldaña, 2013, pp. 52–53). As Juliet Corbin and Anselm Strauss (2015, p. 117) note, there are memos for:

1. open . . . data exploration,
2. identifying or developing the properties and dimensions [of] concepts . . . or categories,
3. making comparisons and asking questions,
4. exploring relationships among conditions, actions-interactions, and consequences, and
5. developing the story line.

As ordered, these memos roughly reflect the progression from data to theory, characteristic of grounded theory methods. In open data exploration, researchers write memos about the data. They also write memos that identify properties and dimensions, similar to the code memos described earlier; write memos that ask questions about the data; and so on.

This gives you an idea of some specific techniques used in the grounded theory tradition, which may be adopted more widely. Researchers working in this tradition may use still other techniques, such as data displays/diagrams discussed earlier. For more in-depth guidance in using grounded theory methods for analysis, we recommend Kathy Charmaz's (2014) *Constructing Grounding Theory* and Juliet Corbin and Anselm Strauss's (2015) *Basics of Qualitative Research*. For an advanced discussion of how researchers can use computational methods for grounded theory and other forms of qualitative analysis, see Nelson (2020).

Narrative Analysis

A narrative is essentially a story, which often has an internal structure. The stories we tell about ourselves, for example, may be organized chronologically or topically. They may be told for a variety of reasons: to recount events, to affirm our identity, and so forth (Gibbs, 2018). **Narrative analysis** examines the structure and meaning of stories. It may be used to analyze literary works, interviews, and other data (Franzosi, 1999; Gibbs, 2018; Riessman, 2012; Wertz et al., 2011). The primary focus of this section will be on interview data.

Narrative analysis begins in a similar way to the analysis of other interview data: interviews are transcribed and read. But in narrative analysis it is the narrative, or story line, that constitutes the primary focus. Narratives are compared to one another within a case (i.e., a single interview participant telling multiple stories), across cases (i.e., multiple interviewees), or both. The analytic techniques vary depending on whether the relative emphasis is on structure, meaning, or other considerations. One of these considerations concerns whether narratives should be analyzed as a whole or broken down into parts, as you do when you code text (Wertz et al., 2011, p. 226).

A traditional way of analyzing the structure of narratives is to classify the parts of the story as follows (Saldaña, 2013, p. 133, citing Patterson, 2008, p. 25):

1. ABSTRACT—what is the story about?
2. ORIENTATION—who, when, where?
3. COMPLICATING ACTION—then what happened?
4. EVALUATION—so what?
5. RESULT—what finally happened?
6. CODA—a "sign off" of the narrative

Although this may seem complicated, you would probably recognize the structural elements of a narrative event in your daily life. "Let me tell about this one time . . ." might signal an abstract. "That's all I have to say about that," a phrase uttered by actor Tom Hanks in the title role of the 1994 movie *Forrest Gump*, is an explicit coda or "sign off." The "essential" element of a narrative is the "complicating action," according to William Labov, who developed this classification scheme (Franzosi, 1998, p. 522, citing Labov, 1972, p. 370). You are likely familiar with "complicating actions" from movies: this is what happens to set up plots and subplots. To return to

narrative analysis
the qualitative analysis of narratives, including literary texts and stories derived from interviews and other sources, which examines their structure, meaning, and other characteristics

Forrest Gump, which is especially appropriate given that the film is told as a series of biographical narratives, a complicating action in Forrest's childhood narrative is that he is not able to run. Similarly, one may analyze narratives by classifying their parts into scenes (Riessman, 2012).

Another way of analyzing narratives is to focus on meaning. To do so, researchers may identify *themes*. Common themes in people's biographies are related to their trajectories in life (where they have been and where they are now), their careers, and their relationships with others (Gibbs 2018, pp. 79–82). The interview questions asked by researchers may also help to identify themes (Rubin & Rubin, 2012, p. 195).

An example of narrative analysis comes from Jane Kelly and Catherine Ward's (2020) study of gang disengagement among former South African gang members. To understand how former gang members in South Africa understand their gang disengagement, Kelly and Ward conducted two *life history interviews* with 12 former gang members. Typical of life history interviews, the first interview began in an open-ended way by asking the former gang members to tell their life stories "focusing on the transitions and trajectories they saw as being important in their lives" (p. 1513). The second interview was spent clarifying and gathering more detail on points made in the previous interview. Additionally, it provided participants with an opportunity to share details of their lives that they may have previously forgotten or did not feel comfortable sharing in the initial interview.

Kelly and Ward analyzed the interview data using thematic narrative analysis. Both inductive and deductive methods were used to code the data. A comparison of the codes was then conducted to look for patterns and commonalities and organized into potential themes. Mind-mapping and listing were used to help determine how codes were best grouped together thematically. Findings revealed that key to gang disengagement is personal agency along with access to appropriate resources.

Conversation Analysis

Stop for a moment and think about a conversation you have recently had: How was it organized? Did you and your conversational partner take turns talking, responding in sequence to one another? If your conversation was with your professor in a college/university setting, how might that differ from one with your friends? Which words did you choose and why? Conversations—the focus of **conversation analysis**—are social interactions consisting of language, other "utterances," and nonverbal behavior. Conversation analysis is partly rooted in a tradition in sociology called ethnomethodology (Garfinkel, 1967), the study of the methods people use to make sense out of everyday life, which posits that social life is patterned by norms that people may not recognize and take for granted. It is also grounded in Erving Goffman's work, which highlights the importance of roles and identity in shaping interactions. Conversation analysts have sought to understand the structure and sequence of a conversation,

conversation analysis the qualitative analysis of conversations, which are typically recorded, transcribed, and analyzed in terms of their structure, sequencing, word choice, and other characteristics including how people take turns talking (Sacks et al., 1974) and the strategies people employ to achieve goals (Heritage, 2004; Maynard & Clayman, 1991; Rapley, 2018).

Analyzing conversations is a somewhat different process than the general process of analyzing qualitative data outlined earlier. These differences begin with data collection: conversation analysis is especially likely to be used with (field) observational data. When video is used to record conversations—for example, to capture important nonverbal interaction—narrative accounts may be added to the transcription. Regardless of whether video or audio recordings are used, transcriptions tend to be quite detailed (Rapley, 2018; Ten Have, 2006).

Data may be transcribed using the Jeffersonian method, named after Gale Jefferson (Jefferson, 2004; Sacks et al., 1974), which consists of a shorthand notation to indicate speakers' pauses, their length, and other such details. Below are a few examples of Jeffersonian transcribing conventions (Rapley, 2018, p. 64, based on Jefferson, 2004):

0.6	Length of silence measured in tenths of a second
(.)	A micro-pause of less than two-tenths of a second
:::	Two or more colons indicate sound-stretching of the immediately prior sound
WORD	All capital letters convey a marked increase in volume

Based on these examples of the conventions, you can imagine how time-consuming transcription may be: the length of pauses is counted; overlaps are noted; and attention is paid to volume. As such, samples of conversations tend to be small. For more in-depth guidance on performing conversation analysis, we recommend Tim Rapley's (2018) *Doing Conversation, Discourse, and Content Analysis*.

The analysis of conversational data partly depends on its context. Whereas some research focuses on ordinary everyday conversations, other research focuses on "institutional talk," or how people converse and interact in formal settings, such as when making 911 calls, in their doctors' offices, and so forth (Heritage, 2004). John Heritage (2004, p. 120) cites Don Zimmerman's (1984) research on emergency calls as an example of institutional talk. Zimmerman's analysis identified five phases:

1. an opening,
2. request,
3. interrogative series,
4. response, and
5. closing.

Figure 15.4 identifies these phases by number in an example of an emergency call transcript. The phases indicated in the transcript are effectively patterns repeated across data.

In an analysis of calls from three dispatch centers, including observation at two of them, Zimmerman (1992, pp. 434–435) found that the structure of emergency calls is different from ordinary calls in that the callers and call takers are usually anonymous and the traditional "How are you?" opening is skipped. The conversation moves along certain sequences, similar to those noted above, but not without variation and "work" on the part of the caller and call taker, as callers may give frantic or incomprehensible descriptions of what the problem is, which the call taker then needs to discern and respond to (p. 461). In instances where the caller is distraught, for example, "this may involve such things as [issuing] directives ('stop shouting' or 'answer my questions') or reassurances ('help is on the way')" (p. 430).

These examples represent some ways to analyze conversational data in terms of its structure and sequencing. Yet, there are many more strategies for analyzing conversations (see Heritage, (2004) for a discussion), some of which are similar to the strategies used for analyzing narratives.

```
1    911:   Midcity Emergency::,
2           (.)                                      1
3    C:     U::m yeah (.)
- - - - - - - - - - - - - - - - - - - - - -
4           somebody just vandalized my car,         2
5           (0.3)
- - - - - - - - - - - - - - - - - - - - - -
6    911:   What's your address.
7    C:     three oh one six maple
8    911:   Is this a house or an apartment.
9    C:     I::t's a house                           3
10   911:   (Uh-) your last name.
11   C:     Minsky
12   911:   How do you spell it?
13   C:     M I N S K Y
- - - - - - - - - - - - - - - - - - - - - -
14   911:   We'll send someone out to see you.
15   C:     Thank you.=                              4
16   911:   =Mmhm=
- - - - - - - - - - - - - - - - - - - - - -
17   911:   =bye.=
18   C:     =Bye.                                    5
```

FIGURE 15.4 An Emergency Call Transcript with Phases Identified

SUMMARY

Among major variations in qualitative data analysis, grounded theory follows the general strategy of the constant-comparative method and uses various types of coding and memo writing in different phases of the analysis to generate theory "grounded" in data. Narrative analysis focuses on narratives, or stories, to examine the structure and/or meaning of existing textual data and interviews. Conversation analysis focuses on conversations, which are usually transcribed in detail and analyzed in terms of their structure, sequencing, word choice, and other characteristics. (Assess your understanding of data analysis in Box 15.5.)

BOX 15.5

CHECKING YOUR UNDERSTANDING

Qualitative Data Analysis

1. The object of narrative analysis is to
    a. use reflexivity to create a chronologically accurate analysis.
    b. use observations and interviews to create a narrative of a group or event.

continues

continued

    c. examine the structure and meaning of stories derived from interviews and other sources.

    d. create a single story line from divergent accounts of the same event.

2. _____coding is a form of coding that uses participant's own words as labels.

    a. In vivo
    b. Action
    c. Realistic
    d. Mimic

3. The constant-comparative method is a general analytic strategy of

    a. grounded theory methods
    b. narrative analysis
    c. conversation analysis
    d. historical analysis

4. Conversation analysis emphasizes the meaning of the written word.

    a. True
    b. False

Answers: 1. c, 2. a, 3. a, 4. b

KEY TERMS

action coding, p. 463
attribute coding, p. 449
code memo, p. 455
Computer-Assisted Qualitative Data Analysis Software (CAQDAS), p. 449
constant-comparative method, p. 462
conversation analysis, p. 465
in vivo coding, p. 463
member checking, p. 461
narrative analysis, p. 464
taxonomy, p. 455
typology, p. 458

KEY POINTS

- Beyond data collection, qualitative data analysis entails preparing the data; identifying patterns, relationships, and concepts; and drawing and evaluating conclusions.
- Data preparation involves transforming the data into readable text, checking for and correcting errors, and managing or organizing the data into physical and/or computer files.

- Qualitative analysts discover patterns in the data and develop concepts by means of coding, memo writing, and data displays.
- Coding summarizes the data and invites comparison; memo writing helps researchers record their thoughts about codes or other issues; and data displays create more abstract summaries that facilitate concept and theory development.
- The conclusions researchers draw range from the descriptive to the more theoretical. Evaluating them amounts to assessing their strength and quality, such as by checking for exceptions and member checking.
- Grounded theory methods stress the discovery of theory largely through the constant-comparative method, which involves making comparisons at increasingly higher levels of abstraction through coding, memo writing, and theoretical sampling.
- Narrative analysis is applied to stories, from literary works or from interviews, which may be analyzed in terms of their structure, meaning, type, and other characteristics.
- Conversation analysis focuses on conversations, usually from observations, which are recorded, transcribed in detail, and analyzed in terms of their structure, sequencing, word choice, and other characteristics.

REVIEW QUESTIONS

1. List some ways in which errors can occur in the transcription of interview data. How can interview transcripts be checked and corrected?
2. What are the two major forms of storing data? What are their relative advantages and disadvantages?
3. What is attribute coding, and when does it occur in the process of qualitative analysis?
4. What is the general purpose of analytic memo writing? In what ways may it be used?
5. Give an example of a (a) taxonomy, (b) typology, and (c) data matrix.
6. Compare and contrast in vivo and action/process coding. What purpose does each serve, and how are the codes generated?
7. Explain the difference between narrative analysis and conversation analysis.

EXERCISES

1. In Box 15.2, we asked you to practice coding data. What were you thinking as you considered how to code the data? Did you jot down any notes? Now that you understand memo writing, return to the box and, using any notes you may have taken, write a memo. Ideally, of course, this should be completed as you are making the coding decisions, but this will help you to understand one of the purposes of memo writing.

2. We want to give you some practice in constructing a typology based on the text of this chapter. To give you some direction, below we present a data display with the different approaches as the columns and two of the major steps in qualitative analysis as the rows. Filling out this data matrix should help you learn how to construct a typology (and study for the test!).

	"General"	Grounded Theory	Narrative Analysis	Conversation Analysis
Data preparation				
Analytic strategies for identifying concepts and patterns				

3. The best way of understanding qualitative data analysis is to analyze your own data. If you do not have any at this point, complete Exercise 3 in Chapter 10 by applying the steps outlined in this chapter. For example, transform your field jottings to notes and write a memo about your coding. You will likely find that this process differs depending on whether you recorded observations, dialogue, or both.

4. To understand variations in qualitative data analysis, read *Five Ways of Doing Qualitative Analysis: Phenomenological Psychology, Grounded Theory, Discourse Analysis, Narrative Research, and Intuitive Inquiry* (Wertz et al., 2011), in which the authors analyze the same text from different perspectives. If you have collected interview data, you may want to try each approach on a segment of it just to see what you come up with.

Glossary

abstract a capsule version of a research report that briefly describes the research question or hypothesis, data and methods, and the major findings or results

action coding a form of coding that uses gerunds (*-ing* words) to signal activity in the data (also called *process coding*)

analytic memo an adjunct to field notes, observations, and interviews that consists of recorded analyses that come to mind in going over data

anonymity ethical safeguard against invasion of privacy in which data cannot be identified with particular research participants

antecedent variable a variable that occurs before, and may be a cause of, both the independent and dependent variables in a causal relationship

applied research methods using evidence to find solutions to specific real-world problems faced by society, individuals, or organizations/businesses

archival records a source of operational definitions that consists of existing documents and institutional records

archive a physical or digital library that contains a collection of historical documents or records

attribute coding a method of coding that identifies the characteristics of participants, settings, and other phenomena of interest, largely as a means of managing the data

before-and-after designs quasi-experimental designs that consist of analyzing data from the outcome before and after treatment, following a pretest/posttest design (random assignment and control groups are absent from these designs)

beneficence the Belmont principle that researchers have an obligation to secure the well-being of participants by maximizing possible benefits and minimizing possible harms

big data unusually large data sets that are collected digitally and, because of their variety and structure, may require sophisticated computational methods

bivariate analysis the statistical analysis of the relationship between two variables

black box evaluation evaluating a program without understanding or knowing the nature of the program

case study the holistic analysis of a single person, group, or event by one or more research methods

causal relationship a relationship in which it is theorized that changes in one variable produce or bring about changes in another variable

cell frequency the number of cases in a cell of a cross-tabulation (contingency table)

chi-square test for independence ($\chi 2$) a test of statistical significance used to assess the likelihood that an observed association between two variables could have occurred by chance

closed-ended question survey question that requires respondents to choose responses from those provided

cluster sampling a probability sampling design in which the population is broken down into natural groupings or areas, called clusters, and a random sample of clusters is drawn

code memo a type of memo written explicitly for describing the basis of one's operational definitions (also called a *code note*)

codebook a guide for coding that consists of a list of the variables together with definitions, codes, and instructions for applying the codes

coding the sorting of data into numbered or textual categories

Common Rule label given to the federal policy for the protection of human subjects

comparative historical analysis the development of causal explanations of social change by describing and comparing historical processes within and across cases

component design a mixed methods design in which findings from different approaches are compared after each approach is carried out independently

Computer-Assisted Qualitative Data Analysis Software (CAQDAS) software packages that aid in the management and analysis of data

computer-assisted self-administered interviewing (CASI) an electronic survey in which a questionnaire is transmitted using a digital program or on digital equipment provided by the researcher

computer-assisted telephone interviewing (CATI) a set of digital tools that aid telephone interviewers and supervisors by automating various data-collection tasks

concept a term scientists use to group together phenomena that have important things in common

conceptual definition the meaning of a concept expressed in words that is derived from theory and/or observation (also called *theoretical definition*)

conceptualization defining and clarifying the meaning of concepts

concurrent design a mixed methods design in which data collection with different approaches is carried out at the same time

confidence interval a range (interval) within which a population value is estimated to lie at a specific level of confidence

confidentiality ethical safeguard against invasion of privacy by which data obtained from participants are not shared with others without their permission

consistency checking a data-cleaning procedure involving checking for unreasonable patterns of responses, such as a 12-year-old who voted in the last US presidential election

Consolidated Framework for Implementation Research a set of tools and guides for formative evaluation developed by Laura Damschroder and colleagues in 2009, to help build implementation knowledge, such that constructs remain consistent across multiple projects

constant-comparative method the general analytic strategy of grounded theory methods, which involves making comparisons at increasingly higher levels of abstraction through coding, memo writing, and theoretical sampling

construct validation measurement validation based on an accumulation of research evidence indicating that a measure is related to other variables as theoretically expected

content analysis systematic analysis of the symbolic content of communications in which the content is reduced to a set of coded variables or categories

context the social and cultural conditions surrounding the implementation of a social program

control variable a variable that is not allowed to vary or otherwise held constant during the course of data collection or analysis

convenience sampling the selection of cases that are conveniently available

convergent validation measurement validation based on an accumulation of research evidence indicating that a measure is related to other variables as theoretically expected

conversation analysis the qualitative analysis of conversations, which are typically recorded, transcribed, and analyzed in terms of their structure, sequencing, word choice, and other characteristics

correlation coefficient a measure of the strength and direction of a linear relationship between two variables; it may vary from −1 to 0 to +1

cost–benefit analysis a type of evaluation research that seeks to compare the monetary costs of a program to the monetary benefits of the program

cost-effectiveness analysis a type of evaluation research that compares program costs to specific measures of program effectiveness

cover story an introduction presented to research participants to obtain their cooperation while disguising the research hypothesis

coverage error the error that occurs when the sampling frame does not match the target population

covert observation a form of observation in which the researcher conceals their identity as a researcher

Cronbach's alpha a statistical index of internal consistency reliability that ranges from 0 (unreliable) to 1 (perfectly reliable)

cross-sectional design the most common survey design, in which data are gathered from a sample of respondents at essentially one point in time

crowdsourcing as applied to sampling in online studies, the practice of hiring a group of paid workers to participate in a study, usually accomplished through requests on a crowdsourcing platform

data information recorded from observation; may be in numerical or nonnumerical form

data archives repositories of survey, ethnographic, or qualitative interview data collected by various agencies and researchers that are accessible to the public

data cleaning the detection and correction of errors in a computer datafile that may have occurred during data collection, coding, and/or data entry

data matrix the form of a computer datafile, with rows as cases and columns as variables; each cell represents the value of a particular variable (column) for a particular case (row)

data processing the preparation of data for analysis

debriefing a session at the end of a study in which an investigator meets with a participant to impart information about the study, including its real purpose and the nature and purpose of deception (if used), and to respond to questions and concerns

deductive logic reasoning in which the conclusion necessarily follows if the evidence is true

dependent variable the variable that the researcher tries to explain or predict; the presumed effect in a causal relationship

descriptive statistics procedures for organizing and summarizing data

dictionary in computerized content analysis, the set of words, phrases, or other word-based indicators (e.g., word length) that is the basis for a search of texts

disproportionate stratified sampling a sampling procedure in which strata are sampled disproportionately to population composition

double-barreled question a question in which two separate ideas are presented together as a unit

double-blind experiment an experiment in which neither research participants nor research personnel know participants' treatment condition during the running of an experiment

dummy variable a variable or set of variable categories recoded to have values of 0 and 1. Dummy coding may be applied to nominal- or ordinal-scale variables for the purpose of regression or other numerical analysis

ecological fallacy erroneous use of data describing an aggregate unit (e.g., organizations) to draw inferences about the units of analysis that make up the aggregate (e.g., individual members of organizations)

editing checking data and correcting for errors in completed interviews or questionnaires

efficiency analysis a type of evaluation research that compares program costs to program outcomes

empirical indicator a single, concrete proxy for a concept such as a questionnaire item in a survey

empirical pattern a relationship among phenomena usually inferred from data

ethics Standards of moral conduct that distinguish right from wrong

ethnography an alternate word, derived from cultural anthropology, to describe field research, especially when it focuses on the culture of a group of people

evaluability assessment a type of exploratory evaluation study that assesses whether programs or interventions are ready for useful evaluation

evaluation research a systematic assessment of a program, practice, policy, or system to determine the need and merit of investing time, money, and resources to achieve a goal as well as the effectiveness of achieving the stated goals

evidence-based practices programs, practices, and policies that are considered effective as supported through systematic, rigorous, and empirical research

exhaustive the measurement requirement that a measure includes all possible values or categories of a variable so that every case can be classified

existing data analysis analysis of data from existing sources of information that were not produced directly by the researcher who uses them

experiment basic approach to social research that entails manipulating an aspect of the environment to observe behavior under different, controlled conditions

ex post facto control group designs a nonexperimental design in which evaluation of a program begins after it has already been implemented (also called an after-the-fact design)

external validity the extent to which experimental findings may be generalized to other settings, measurements, populations, and time periods

extraneous variable a variable that is not part of a hypothesized relationship

factorial design an experiment in which two or more variables (factors) are manipulated

feasibility the ability to complete a project within the available timeframe and with the available resources

feedback the process of providing information about program process, outputs, or outcomes that can further program development

fidelity the extent to which program delivery adheres to the program as originally designed

field experiment an experiment conducted in a natural setting

field jottings brief quotes, phrases, and key words that are recorded by field researchers while in the field

field notes detailed written accounts of field observations, which may also include a researcher's reflections and preliminary analyses

field pretesting an evaluation of a survey instrument that involves trying it out on a small sample of persons

field research basic approach to social research that involves directly observing and often interviewing others to produce nonnumerical data

focus group an interview method in which a researcher collects data from a group by moderating a group discussion on a particular topic

formative evaluation a type of evaluation research conducted in the beginning stages of program development to determine whether a program is needed and to help improve the program prior to full implementation

free writing an exercise to overcome the difficulty in beginning to write by quickly recording thoughts, without regard to grammar and punctuation or reference to notes, data, books, and other information

frequency distribution a tabulation of the number of cases falling into each category of a variable

gatekeeper relevant authority whose permission is needed to gain access to a setting or group

grand tour question a broad opening question in in-depth interviews that asks for a general description of the people, processes, or events being studied (also called a tour question)

grounded theory the systematic and inductive approach to identifying ideas and concepts as they emerge the iterative review of qualitative data

guiding question a relatively broad research question that guides the initial stages of qualitative research

Hawthorne effect a change in behavior, such as an improvement in performance, that occurs when research participants know they are being studied

histogram a graphic display in which the height of a vertical bar represents the frequency or percentage of cases in each category of an interval/ratio variable

history a threat to internal validity that refers to events other than the manipulation of the independent variable

hypothesis an expected but unconfirmed relationship among two or more phenomena

impact evaluation a type of evaluation research that measures whether a program is broadly meeting its stated goals

imputation a procedure for handling missing data in which missing values are assigned based on other information, such as the sample mean or known values of other variables

in vivo coding a form of coding that uses participants' own words as labels

independent variable a presumed influence or cause of a dependent variable

in-depth interview a type of formal interview intended to yield deep responses through open-ended questions and a flexible format

index a composite measure of a concept constructed by adding or averaging the scores of separate indicators; differs from a scale, which uses less arbitrary procedures for combining indicators

inductive logic reasoning in which the conclusion is implied by, but goes beyond, the evidence at hand and, hence, may or may not be true

inferential statistics procedures for determining the extent to which one may generalize beyond the data at hand

informed consent the ethical principle that individuals should be given enough information about a study, especially its potential risks, to make an informed decision about whether to participate

inputs resources, materials, clients, or staff required for the program

Institutional Review Board (IRB) a committee formed at nearly all colleges and universities that is responsible for reviewing research proposals to assess provisions for the treatment of human (and animal) subjects

integrated design a mixed methods design in which different approaches are connected or merged during the process of data collection and analysis

internal consistency a form of reliability assessment; the consistency of "scores" across all the items of a composite measure (i.e., index or scale)

internal validity evidence that rules out the possibility that factors other than the manipulated independent variable are responsible for the measured outcome

inter-rater reliability the extent to which different observers or coders get equivalent results when applying the same measure (also called *inter-coder reliability*)

interval measurement a level of measurement that has the qualities of the ordinal level plus equal distances (intervals) between assigned numbers

intervening variable a variable that is intermediate between two other variables in a causal relationship; it is an effect of one and a cause of the other

interview guide a list of topics and specific questions to be asked in a qualitative interview

interview schedule a survey form used by interviewers that consists of instructions, the questions to be asked, and, if they are used, response options

justice the Belmont principle that the benefits and burdens of research should be fairly distributed so that the group selected for research also may benefit from its application

key informant a person from whom field researchers acquire information who is selected on the basis of knowledge, expertise, or status within the group

laboratory experiment an experiment conducted in a controlled environment

leading question a question in which a possible answer is suggested, or some answers are presented as more acceptable than others

listwise deletion a common procedure for handling missing values in multivariate analysis that excludes cases which have missing values on any of the variables in the analysis

longitudinal design survey design in which data are collected at more than one point in time

manipulation check procedure used to provide evidence that participants interpreted the manipulation of the independent variable in the way intended

marginal frequencies row and column totals in a contingency table (cross-tabulation) that represent the univariate frequency distributions for the row and column variables

maturation a threat to internal validity that refers to psychological or physiological changes taking place within participants

mean the average value of a data set, calculated by adding up the individual values and dividing by the total number of cases

measurement validity the goodness of fit between an operational definition and the concept it is purported to measure

measures of association descriptive statistics used to measure the strength and direction of a bivariate relationship

mechanism ideas and opportunities relative to a social program that help effect change

median the midpoint in a distribution of interval- or ratio-scale data; indicates the point below and above which 50 percent of the values fall

member checking a method of evaluating qualitative data in which researchers share their results with participants and ask them to comment on their accuracy and completeness

missing data the absence of information on a variable for a given case

mixed methods research a research study that combines two or more approaches to data collection and analysis

mixed-mode survey a survey that uses more than one mode of data collection, either sequentially or concurrently, to sample and/or collect the data

mode the value or category of a frequency distribution having the highest frequency; the most typical value

multiple regression a statistical method for determining the simultaneous effects of several independent variables on a dependent variable

multistage cluster sampling a sampling design in which sampling occurs at two or more steps or stages

mutual exclusivity the measurement requirement that each case can be placed in one and only one category of a variable

N an abbreviation representing the number of observations on which a statistic is based (e.g., $N = 753$)

narrative analysis the qualitative analysis of narratives, including literary texts and stories derived from interviews and other sources, which examines their structure, meaning, and other characteristics

narrative comparison a method of causal inference in which historical narratives of cases are analyzed to develop a general cross-case causal pattern and to validate it within each case

needs assessment a type of evaluation research that collects objective data or information to determine the needs of a specified population that might be served by the implementation of a program or policy

nesting a process in mixed methods research whereby different kinds of data are collected from the same individuals or groups by embedding one approach within another

nominal measurement a level of measurement in which numbers serve only to label categories of a variable

nonequivalent control group designs quasi-experimental designs that have predesignated treatment and control groups, but assignment to these groups is not randomized

nonparticipant observation a form of observation in which the field researcher does not participate in the activity or group being studied

nonprobability sampling methods of case selection other than random selection

nonresponse error in survey sampling, the error that occurs when nonrespondents (sampled individuals who do not respond or cannot be contacted) differ systematically from respondents (also called *nonresponse bias*)

non-spurious if introducing a control variable (an alternative explanation to the dependent variable) into the model, the relationship between X and Y would become nonexistent

null hypothesis the hypothesis, associated with tests of statistical significance, that an observed relationship is due to chance; a test that is significant rejects the null hypothesis at a specified level of probability

online panel a sample of people who have agreed to participate in online surveys upon request

operational definition a detailed description of the research procedures necessary to assign units of analysis to variable categories

operationalization the process of identifying empirical indicators and the procedures for applying them to measure a concept

ordinal measurement a level of measurement in which different numbers indicate rank order of cases on a variable

outcome evaluation a type of evaluation research that measures whether a program achieved its intended outcomes on the *target population*

outcomes the direct impact of the program process on the cases who underwent treatment

outliers unusual or suspicious values that are far removed from the preponderance of observations for a variable

outputs direct products or services delivered from the program process

overt observation a form of observation in which the researcher identifies themselves as a researcher to those who are being observed

panel study a longitudinal design in which the same individuals are surveyed more than once, permitting the study of individual and group change

paper-and-pencil questionnaire survey a survey form filled out by respondents

partial regression coefficient/partial slope coefficients in a multiple-regression equation that estimate the effects of each independent variable on the dependent variable when all other variables in the equation are held constant

partial table a table in elaboration analysis which displays the original two-variable relationship for a single category of the control variable, thereby holding the control variable constant

participant observation a form of observation in which the field researcher participates to some degree in the activity or group being studied

peer review a system in which researchers' reports are evaluated by fellow academics and researchers

percentage distribution a norming operation that facilitates interpreting and comparing frequency distributions by transforming each frequency to a common yardstick of 100 units (percentage points) in length; the number of cases in each category is divided by the total and multiplied by 100

population the total membership of a defined class of people, objects, or events

posttest-only control group design the most basic experimental design in which the dependent variable is measured after the experimental manipulation

pretest a trial run of an experiment or survey instrument to evaluate and rehearse study procedures and personnel

pretest-posttest control group design an experimental design in which the dependent variable is measured both before and after the experimental manipulation

probability the likelihood that something will occur, which may vary from 0 to 100 percent

probability distribution a distribution of the probabilities for a variable, which indicates the likelihood that each category or value of the variable will occur

probability sampling sampling based on a process of random selection that gives each case in the population an equal or known chance of being included in the sample

probes follow-up questions used in surveys and in-depth interviews to gather more information about a respondent's answer

process analysis a within-case method of comparative historical analysis that examines possible intervening mechanisms that link an observed or theoretical association between events (also called *process tracing*)

process evaluation a type of evaluation research that focuses on assessing program or intervention implementation and delivery. When the evaluation is conducted repeatedly over time, it is referred to as program monitoring

program process the steps required for the delivery of the treatment or implementation of the service

program theory an explicitly stated explanation of why a social program should have the intended outcome

proportionate stratified sampling a sampling procedure in which strata are sampled proportionately to population composition

purposive sampling sampling that involves the careful and informed selection of typical cases or of cases that represent relevant dimensions of the population. Also called *judgmental sampling*

qualitative research basic approach to social research that involves directly observing and often interviewing others to produce nonnumerical data

qualitative research question a question that asks about social processes or the meaning and cultural significance of people's actions

quantitative research question a question that asks about the relationship between two or more variables

R^2 a measure of fit in multiple regression that indicates approximately the proportion of the variation in the dependent variable predicted or "explained" by the independent variables

random assignment the assignment of research participants to experimental conditions by means of a random device, such as a coin toss

random selection a selection process that gives each element in a population a known and independent chance of being selected

range the difference between the lowest and highest values in a distribution, which is usually reported by identifying these two extreme values

ratio measurement the highest level of measurement, which has the features of the other levels plus an absolute (nonarbitrary) zero point

reactive measurement effect an effect in which participants' awareness of being studied produces changes in how they ordinarily would respond

recording units the units of analysis in content analysis, such as words, sentences, paragraphs, and whole articles (also called coding units)

reflexivity a common practice in qualitative research, whereby a researcher reflects on how their characteristics and presence shape the research process

regression analysis a statistical method for analyzing bivariate (simple regression) and multivariate (multiple regression) relationships among interval- or ratio-scale variables

regression line a geometric representation of a bivariate regression equation that provides the best linear fit to the observed data by virtue of minimizing the sum of the squared deviations from the line; also called the *least squares line*

reliability the stability or consistency of an operational definition

replication the repetition of a study

request for proposal a document that solicits proposals for research, often found through funders' websites

research design the overall plan of a study for collecting data

residuals the difference between observed values of the dependent variable and those predicted by a regression equation

respect for persons the Belmont principle that individuals must be treated as autonomous agents who have the freedom and capacity to decide what happens to them, and researchers must protect those with diminished autonomy

response rate in a survey, the proportion of people in the sample from whom completed interviews or questionnaires are obtained

sample a subset of cases selected from a population

sampling error the difference between an actual population value (e.g., a percentage) and the population value estimated from a sample

sampling frame an operational definition of the population that provides the basis for drawing a sample; ordinarily consists of a list of cases

sampling with replacement a sampling procedure whereby once a case is selected, it is returned to the sampling frame, so that it may be selected again

sampling without replacement a sampling procedure whereby once a case is selected, it is NOT returned to the sampling frame, so that it cannot be selected again

saturation in purposive sampling, the point at which new data cease to yield new information or theoretical insights

scale the combination of several indicators to measure a single dimension of a concept

scatterplot a graph plotting the values of two variables for each observation

secondary analysis analysis of survey or other data originally collected by another researcher, ordinarily for a different purpose

selection a threat to internal validity that is present whenever participants are not randomly assigned to experimental conditions

selective deposit systematic biases in the content of existing historical data due to actions such as selective destruction or editing of written records

selective survival incompleteness of existing historical data due to the fact that some objects survive longer than others

semi-structured interview a type of interview that, while having specific objectives, permits the interviewer some freedom in meeting them

sequential design a mixed methods design in which data collection and analysis with one approach precedes data collection and analysis with another approach

serendipity pattern unanticipated findings that cannot be interpreted meaningfully in terms of prevailing theories and, therefore, give rise to new theories

simple random sample a probability sampling design in which every case and every possible combination of cases has an equal chance of being included in the sample

slope/regression coefficient a bivariate regression statistic indicating how much the dependent variable increases (or decreases) for every unit change in the independent variable; the slope of a regression line

snowball sampling a sampling procedure that uses a process of chain referral, whereby each contact is asked to identify additional members of the target population, who are asked to name others, and so on

social desirability a tendency of respondents to answer self-report measures in a manner that they believe will be viewed as socially desirable by others

spurious relationship noncausal statistical association between two variables produced by a common cause, that is, an antecedent variable

stakeholders any individual or group who is involved with or has an interest in a program, or who may be affected by the outcomes of the evaluation of the program

standard deviation a measure of variability or dispersion that indicates the average "spread" of observations about the mean

standard error a statistical measure of the "average" sampling error for a particular sampling distribution, which indicates how much sample results will vary from sample to sample

standardized regression coefficients coefficients obtained from a norming operation that puts partial-regression coefficients on common footing by converting them to the same metric of standard deviation units

statistical significance the likelihood that the results of a study, such as an association between variables, could have occurred by chance

stratified random sample a probability sampling design in which the population is divided into strata (or variable categories) and independent random samples are drawn from each stratum

structured interview a type of interview with highly specific objectives in which all questions are written beforehand and asked in the same order for all respondents, and the interviewer's remarks are standardized

summative evaluation a type of evaluation research conducted after full program implementation to determine the overall effectiveness of the program

survey basic approach to social research that involves asking a relatively large sample of people direct questions through interviews or questionnaires

survey-based experiment an experiment embedded in a survey in which respondents are given different, randomly assigned versions of survey questions

target population the population to which the researcher would like to generalize his or her results

taxonomy a system of classification that is usually ordered in some way

telephone interview a type of interview in which interviewers interact with respondents by telephone

test of statistical significance a statistical procedure used to assess the likelihood that the results of a study could have occurred by chance

test-retest reliability the association between repeated applications of an operational definition

theory an interconnected set of propositions that shows how or why something occurs

threats to internal validity types of extraneous variables that pose alternative explanations of an experimental outcome, thereby threatening the validity of the experimental manipulation

triangulation addressing a research question with multiple methods or measures that do not share the same methodological weaknesses

typology a representation of findings based on the cross-classification of two or more concepts, variables, or ideas

unidimensionality a concept that measures just one dimension

units of analysis the entities such as people, nations, and artifacts that are studied, which are described and compared in terms of variables

univariate analysis the statistical analysis of one variable at a time

unstructured interview a type of interview guided by broad objectives in which questions are developed as the interview proceeds

variable a measured concept that may vary across cases or across time

verbal reports an operational definition based on respondents' answers to questions in an interview or questionnaire (also called *self-report*)

vital statistics data collected from the registration of "vital" life events, such as births, deaths, marriages, and divorces

weighting a procedure that corrects for the unequal probability of selecting one or more segments (e.g., strata) of the population

wild-code checking a data-cleaning procedure involving checking for out-of-range and other "illegal" codes among the values recorded for each variable

Y-intercept the predicted value of the dependent variable in regression when the independent variable or variables have a value of zero; graphically, the point at which the regression line crosses the Y-axis

References

CHAPTER 1

Auxier, B., & Anderson, M. (2021). *Social media use in 2021.* Pew Research Center. https://www.pewresearch.org/internet/2021/04/07/social-media-use-in-2021/

Burton, A. L., Cullen, F. T., Jr., Burton, V. S., Graham, A., Butler, L. C., & Thielo, A. (2020). Belief in redeemability and punitive public opinion: "Once a criminal, always a criminal" revisited. *Criminal Justice and Behavior, 47*(6), 712–732. https://doi.org/10.1177/0093854820913585

Gottfredson, D. C., Najaka, S. S., & Kearley, B. (2003). Effectiveness of drug treatment courts: Evidence from a randomized trial. *Criminology & Public Policy, 2*(2), 171–196. doi: 10.1111/j.1745-9133.2003.tb00117.x

Hart Research Associates. (2018). *Fulfilling the American dream: Liberal education and the future of work.* AACU. https://www.aacu.org/sites/default/files/files/LEAP/2018EmployerResearchReport.pdf

Hong, M., & Kleck, G. (2018). The short-term deterrent effect of executions: An analysis of daily homicide counts. *Crime & Delinquency, 64*(7), 939–970. doi: 10.1177/0011128717719514

Karpinski, A. C., & Duberstein, A. (2009). *A description of Facebook use and academic performance among undergraduate and graduate students* [Poster presentation]. Annual Meeting of the American Educational Research Association, San Diego.

Kigotho, W. (2023, May 18). *Social media addiction takes toll on academic performance.* University World News: Africa Edition. https://www.universityworldnews.com/post.php?story=20230514192452245

Kimball, T., & Alexander, A. (2019, March 2). *Sheriff says "Scared Straight" program helps troubled kids. Experts say it's child abuse.* Charlotte Observer. https://www.charlotteobserver.com/news/local/article226325665.html

Mitchell, O., Wilson, D. B., Eggers, A., & MacKenzie, D. L. (2012). Assessing the effectiveness of drug courts on recidivism: A meta-analytic review of traditional and non-traditional drug courts. *Journal of Criminal Justice, 40*(1), 60–71. doi: 10.1016/j.jcrimjus.2011.11.009

Murray, D., Boothby, C., Zhao, H., Minik, V., Bérubé, N., Larivière, V., & Sugimoto, C. R. (2020). Exploring the personal and professional factors associated with student evaluations of tenure-track faculty. *PLoS One, 15*(6): e0233515. https://doi.org/10.1371/journal.pone.0233515

Newswise. (2023, August 2). *Social media usage negatively impacts the schoolwork of students from adolescence to college research suggests.* https://www.newswise.com/articles/social-media-usage-negatively-impacts-the-schoolwork-of-students-from-adolescence-to-college-research-suggests

Pasek, J., more, e., & Hargittai, E. (2009). Facebook and academic performance: Reconciling a media sensation with data. *First Monday, 14*(5). https://doi.org/10.5210/fm.v14i5.2498

Petrosino, A., Turpin-Petrosino, C., Hollis-Peel, M. E., & Lavenberg, J. G. (2013). "Scared Straight" and other juvenile awareness programs for preventing juvenile delinquency. *Cochrane Systematic Review—Intervention, 4.* doi: 10.1002/14651858.CD002796.pub2

Rosen, A. (2018). Correlations, trends and potential biases among publicly accessible web-based student evaluations of teaching: A large-scale study of RateMyProfessors.com data. *Assessment & Evaluation in Higher Education, 43*(1), 31–44.

Shen, N. (2023, May 6). *Teachers say B.C. school teens showed improved grades and social skills after a ban on phones.* Canadian Press. https://www.cbc.ca/news/canada/british-columbia/bc-school-cellphone-ban-1.6834914

Stuart, F. (2020). Code of the tweet: Urban gang violence in the social media age. *Social Problems, 67*(2), 191–207.

van der Put, C. E., Boekhout van Solinge, N. F., Stams, G. J., Hoeve, M., & Assink, M. (2021). Effects of awareness programs on juvenile delinquency: A three-level meta-analysis. *International Journal of Offender Therapy and Comparative Criminology, 65*(1), 68–91. https://doi.org/10.1177/0306624X20909239

WBTV. *Chester County Sheriff's Dept featured on the Steve Harvey Show.* (2016a, April 12). https://www.wbtv.com/story/31707433/chester-county-sheriffs-dept-featured-on-the-steve-harvey-show/

WBTV. *Parents volunteer kids for night in jail in hopes of behavior turnaround.* (2016b, November 22). https://www.wbtv.com/story/33769052/parents-volunteer-kids-for-night-in-jail-in-hopes-of-behavior-turnaround/

Whelan, E., & Golden, W. (2023, January 4). *Why social media diminishes student performance and wellbeing.* RTE. https://www.rte.ie/brainstorm/2023/0104/1344863-why-social-media-diminishes-student-performance-and-wellbeing/

Zgoba, K. M., & Mitchell, M. M. (2023). The effectiveness of sex offender registration and notification: A meta-analysis of 25 years of findings. *Journal of Experimental Criminology, 19*, 71–96. https://doi.org/10.1007/s11292-021-09480-z

CHAPTER 2

Academy of Criminal Justice Sciences. (2024). About ACJS. https://www.acjs.org/page/AboutACJS

American Psychological Association. (2024). About APA. https://www.apa.org/about

American Society of Criminology (2023). About us. https://asc41.org/about-asc/

Back, S., Soor, S., & LaPrade, J. (2018). Juvenile hackers: An empirical test of self-control theory and social bonding theory. *International Journal of Cybersecurity Intelligence and Cybercrime, 1*(1), 40–55.

Berger, P. (1963). *Invitation to sociology: A humanistic perspective.* Doubleday.

Berk, R. A., Campbell, A., Klap, R., & Western, B. (1992). A Bayesian analysis of the Colorado Springs Spouse Abuse Experiment. *Journal of Criminal Law and Criminology, 83*(1), 170–200.

Carey, A. (1967). The Hawthorne studies: A radical criticism. *American Sociological Review, 32*, 403–416.

Criminology. (2020). Retraction statement: Ethnic threat and social control: Examining public support for judicial use of ethnicity in punishment. *Criminology, 58*, 190. doi: 10.1111/1745-9125.12235

Ditton, P. M., & Wilson, D. J. (1999). Truth in sentencing in state prisons. *Bureau of Justice Statistics.* https://bjs.ojp.gov/content/pub/pdf/tssp.pdf

Doyle, A. C. (1894). *The memoirs of Sherlock Holmes.* Harper and Brothers.

Dunford, F., Huizinga, D., & Elliott, D. S. (1990). The role of arrest in domestic assault: The Omaha experiment. *Criminology, 28*, 183–206.

Freese, J., & Peterson, D. (2017). Replication in social science. *Annual Review of Sociology, 43*, 147–165.

Gieryn, T. (1999). *Cultural boundaries of science: Credibility on the line.* University of Chicago Press.

Glaser, B. G., & Strauss, A. L. (1967). *The discovery of grounded theory: Strategies for qualitative research.* Aldine.

Gottfredson, M. R., & Hirschi, T. (1990). *A general theory of crime.* Stanford University Press.

Hirschi, T. (1969). *Causes of delinquency.* University of California Press.

Hoppe, S. J., Zhang, Y., Hayes, B. E., & Bills, M. A. (2020). Mandatory arrest for domestic violence and repeat offending: A meta-analysis. *Aggression and Violent Behavior, 53.* doi: 10.1016/j.avb.2020.101430

Kuhn, T. (1970). *The nature of scientific revolutions* (2nd ed.). University of Chicago Press.

Law School Admissions Council (2020). *Logical reasoning.* https://www.lsac.org/lsat/taking-lsat/test-format/logical-reasoning

Lieberson, S. (1985). *Making it count: The improvement of social research and theory.* University of California Press.

Meisenhelder, T. (1977). An exploratory study of exiting from criminal careers. *Criminology, 15*(3), 319–334.

Merton, R. K. (1996). *On social structure and science.* University of Chicago Press.

Milgram, S. (1974). *Obedience to authority: An experimental view.* Harper and Row.

Molina, M., & Garip, F. (2019). Machine learning for sociology. *Annual Review of Sociology, 45*, 27–45.

Pate, A. M., & Hamilton, E. E. (1992). Formal and informal deterrents to domestic violence: The Dade County Spouse Assault Experiment. *American Sociological Review, 57*(5), 691–697.

Popper, K. R. 1992. *The logic of scientific discovery.* Routledge. (Original published 1959)

Roethlisberger, F. J., & Dickson, W. J. (1939). *Management and the worker: An account of a research program conducted by the Western Electric Co. Hawthorne Works, Chicago.* Harvard University Press.

Sherman, L. W., & Berk, R. A. (1984). The specific deterrent effects of arrest for domestic assault. *American Sociological Review, 49*(2), 261–272.

Sherman, L. W., Schmidt, J. D., Rogan, D. P., Gartin, P. R., Cohn, E. G., Collins, D. J., & Bacich, A.R. (1991). From initial deterrence to long-term escalation: Short-custody arrest for poverty ghetto domestic violence. *Criminology*, 29, 821–850.

Sherman, L. W., Smith, D. A., Schmidt, J. D., & Rogan, D. P. (1992). Crime, punishment, and stake in conformity: Legal and informal control of domestic violence. *American Sociological Review*, 57(5), 680–690.

Singleton, R. A., Jr. (1998). *Is sociology a science? A classroom exercise for promoting discussion* [paper presentation]. Annual Meeting of the American Sociological Association, San Francisco.

Smith, T. W., Darven, M., Freese, J., & Morgan, S. L. (2019). *General Social Surveys, 1972–2018: Cumulative codebook*. National Opinion Research Center.

Sterling, B. (1994). *The hacker crackdown: Law and disorder on the electronic frontier*. Penguin.

Wray, M., Colen, C., & Pescosolido, B. (2011). The sociology of suicide. *Annual Review of Sociology*, 37, 505–528.

Yar, M. (2005). Computer hacking: Just another case of juvenile delinquency? *Howard Journal of Criminal Justice*, 44(4), 387–399. doi: 10.1111/j.1468-2311.2005.00383.x

Zorza, J. (1992). Criminal law of misdemeanor domestic violence, 1970–1990. *Journal of Criminal Law and Criminology*, 83(1), 46–72.

Zuberi, T. (2003). *Thicker than blood: How racial statistics lie*. University of Minnesota Press.

Zuberi, T., & Bonilla-Silva, E. (eds.). (2008). *White logic, white methods: Racism & methodology*. Rowman and Littlefield.

CHAPTER 3

Alexander, M. (2010). *The New Jim Crow: Mass incarceration in the age of colorblindness*. The New Press.

American Psychological Association. (2020). *Publication manual of the American Psychological Association* (7th ed.). American Psychological Association.

Back, S., Soor, S., & LaPrade, J. (2018). Juvenile hackers: An empirical test of self-control theory and social bonding theory. *International Journal of Cybersecurity Intelligence and Cybercrime*, 1(1), 40–55. https://www.doi.org/10.52306/01010518VMDC9371

Becker, H. S. (2007). *Writing for social scientists: How to start and finish your thesis, book, or article* (2nd ed.). University of Chicago Press.

Demir, M., & Park, S. (2022). The effect of COVID-19 on domestic violence assaults. *Criminal Justice Review*, 47(4), 445–463. https://doi.org/10.1177/07340168211061160

Edwards, M. (2012). *Writing in sociology*. Sage.

Gottfredson, M. R., & Hirschi, T. (1990). *A general theory of crime*. Stanford University Press.

Hirschi, T. (1969). *Causes of delinquency*. University of California Press.

Katzer, J., Cook, K. H., & Crouch, W. W. (1998). *Evaluating information: A guide for users of social science research* (4th ed). McGraw-Hill.

Rosen, L. J., & Behrens, L. (1992). *The Allyn & Bacon handbook*. Allyn and Bacon.

Saldaña, J. (2011). *Fundamentals of qualitative research: Understanding qualitative research*. Oxford University Press.

Sherman, L. W., & Berk, R. A. (1984). The specific deterrent effects of arrest for domestic assault. *American Sociological Review*, 49(2), 261–272. https://doi.org/10.2307/2095575

Steneck, N. H. (2007). *ORI Introduction to the responsible conduct of research*. Government Printing Office. http://ori.hhs.gov/sites/default/files/rcrintro.pdf

Stojmenovska, D., Bol, T., & Leopold, T. (2019). Teaching replication to graduate students. *Teaching Sociology*, 47(4), 303–313.

Terrill, W., & Reisig, M. D. (2003). Neighborhood context and police use of force. *Journal of Research in Crime and Delinquency*, 40(3), 291–321. https://doi.org/10.1177/0022427803253800

CHAPTER 4

Academy of Criminal Justice Sciences (ACJS). (2000). *Code of ethics*. ACJS. https://www.acjs.org/page/Code_Of_Ethics

American Political Science Association. (2013). Senate delivers a devastating blow to the integrity of the scientific process at the National Science Foundation http://www.prnewswire.com/news-releases/senate-delivers-a-devastating-blow-to-the-integrity-of-the-scientific-process-at-the-national-science-foundation-199221111.html

American Psychological Association (APA). (2017). *Ethical principles of psychologists and code of conduct*. APA. https://www.apa.org/ethics/code/ethics-code-2017.pdf

American Society of Criminology. (2016). *Code of ethics*. ASC. https://asc41.org/wp-content/uploads/ASC_Code_of_Ethics.pdf

American Sociological Association (ASA). (2018). *Code of ethics and policies and procedures of the ASA Committee* on *Professional Ethics*. ASA. https://www.asanet.org/code-ethics

Barrera, D., & Simpson, B. (2012). Much ado about deception: Consequences of deceiving research participants in the social sciences. *Sociological Methods and Research 41*, 383–413.

Baumrind, D. (1985). Research using intentional deception: Ethical issues revisited. *American Psychologist, 40*, 165–74.

Becker, H. S. (1967). Whose side are we on? *Social Problems, 14*, 239–247.

Bolin, R. M., Pate, M., & McClintock, J. (2017). The impact of alcohol and marijuana use on academic achievement among college students. *The Social Science Journal, 54*, 430–437. doi: 10.1016/j.soscij.2017.08.003

Citro, C. F. (2010). Legal and human subjects considerations in surveys. In P. V. Marsden & J. D. Wright (Eds.), *Handbook of survey research* (pp. 59–79). Emerald Group.

Code of Federal Regulations (CFR). (2024). *Title 45—Public welfare, Part 46—Protection of human subjects*. Office of the Federal Register. Government Printing Office.

Cook, K. S., & Yamagishi, T. (2008). A defense of deception on scientific grounds. *Social Psychology Quarterly, 71*, 215–221.

Diener, E., & Crandall, R. (1978). *Ethics in social and behavioral research*. University of Chicago.

Farrell, H. (2013, March). Blogs, the conversation: Tom Coburn doesn't like political science *The Chronicle of Higher Education*. http://chronicle.com/blogs/conversation/2013/03/22/tom-coburn-doesnt-like-political-science/

Glazer, M. (2009). Impersonal sex. In L. Humphreys (Ed.), *Tearoom trade: Impersonal sex in public places*. Enlarged edition with a retrospect on ethical issues (pp. 213–222). Aldine Transaction. (Original published 1972)

Haney, C., Banks, W. C., & Zimbardo, P. (1973). Interpersonal dynamics in a simulated prison. *International Journal of Criminology and Penology, 1*, 69–97.

Hertwig, R., & Ortmann, A. (2008). Deception in social psychological experiments: Two misconceptions and a research agenda. *Social Psychology Quarterly, 71*, 222–227.

Humphreys, L. (2009). *Tearoom trade: Impersonal sex in public places*. Enlarged edition with a retrospect on ethical issues. Aldine Transaction. (Original published 1970)

Inckle, K. (2015). Debilitating times: Compulsory able-bodiedness and white privilege in theory and practice. *Feminist Review, 111*(1), 42–58.

Irvine, J. (2012). Can't ask, can't tell: How institutional review boards keep sex in the closet. *Contexts, 11*, 28–33.

Jones, J. H. (1981). *Bad blood: The scandalous story of the Tuskegee Experiment—When government doctors played God and science went mad*. Free Press.

Katz, J. (1972). *Experimentation with human beings: The authority of the investigator, subject, professions, and state in the human experimentation process*. Sage.

Kelman, H. C. (1968). *A time to speak: On human values and social research*. Jossey-Bass.

Krasnow, M. M., Howard, R. M., & Eisenbruch, A. B. (2020). The importance of being honest? Evidence that deception may not pollute social science subject pools after all. *Behavior Research Methods, 52*, 1175–1188.

Leavitt, F. (2001). *Evaluating scientific research: Separating fact from fiction*. Waveland Press.

Mervis, J. (2013, March). Congress limits NSF funding for political science. *Science, 339*, 1510–1511.

Meyer, M. N. (2020). "There oughta be a law": When does(n't) the U.S. Common Rule apply? *The Journal of Law, Medicine & Ethics, 48*(S1), 60–73.

Milgram, S. (1974). *Obedience to authority: An experimental view*. Harper and Row.

Myrent, M. (2019). *Using state criminal history records for research and evaluation*. Justice Research and Statistics Association. https://justiceresearch.dspacedirect.org/server/api/core/bitstreams/d45648c4-ee3f-4cfb-a2f7-2765a09ef778/content

National Commission for the Protection of Human Subjects of Biomedical and Behavioral Research. (1979). *The Belmont Report*. https://www.hhs.gov/ohrp/regulations-and-policy/belmont-report/index.html

National Science Foundation (NSF). (2024). *About SBE*. https://new.nsf.gov/sbe/about

Palys, T., & Lowman, J. (2012). Defending research confidentiality "to the extent the law allows:" Lessons from the Boston College subpoenas. *Journal of Academic Ethics, 10*, 271–297. doi: 10.1007/s10805-012-9172-5

Perry, G. (2013). Deception and illusion in Milgram's accounts of the obedience experiments. *Theoretical & Applied Ethics, 2*(2), 79–92. https://www.muse.jhu.edu/article/536095

Petersilia, J. (1991). Policy relevance and the future of criminology: The American Society of Criminology 1990 presidential address. *Criminology, 29*(1), 1–15.

Pielke, Jr., R. A. (2007). *The honest broker: Making sense of science in policy and politics*. Cambridge University Press.

Prewitt, K. (2013, May). Is any science safe? *Science, 340,* 525.

Ragin, C. C., & Amoroso, L. M. (2011). *Constructing social research: The unity and diversity of method* (2nd ed.). Sage.

Rahwan, Z., Fasolo, B., & Hauser, O. P. (2022). Deception about study purpose does not affect participant behavior. *Scientific Reports, 12,* 19302.

Rosnow, R. L., & Rosenthal, R. (2011). "Ethical principles in data analysis: An overview." In A. T. Panter & S. K. Sterba (Eds.), *Handbook of ethics in quantitative methodology* (pp. 37–58). Routledge.

Salt-N-Pepa. (1991). Let's talk about sex. On *Blacks' Magic.* New Plateaus Records.

Savelsberg, J. J., King, R., & Cleveland, L. (2002). Politicized scholarship? Science on crime and the state. *Social Problems, 49*(3), 327–348.

Scarce, R. (1999). Good faith, bad ethics: When scholars go the distance and scholarly associations do not. *Law and Social Inquiry, 24*(4), 977–86. https://www.jstor.org/stable/829153

Scarce, R. (2005, August). A law to protect scholars. *Chronicle of Higher Education, 51,* B24–B25.

Sell, J. (2008). Introduction to deception debate. *Social Psychology Quarterly, 71,* 213–214.

Shamoo, A. E., & Resnik, D. B. (2009). *Responsible conduct of research* (2nd ed.). Oxford University Press.

Silver, H. J. (2006). Science and politics: The uneasy relationship. *Footnotes, 34*(2), 1, 5. https://www.asanet.org/wp-content/uploads/fn_2006_02.pdf

Sjoberg, G. (1967). Introduction. In G. Sjoberg (Ed.), *Ethics, politics, and social research* (pp. xi–xvii). Schenkman.

Stratford, M. (2014, January 24). *Poli Sci victory, for now.* Inside Higher Ed. https://www.insidehighered.com/news/2014/01/24/wake-coburn-amendment-repeal-social-science-groups-plot-path-forward

US Centers for Disease Control and Prevention. (2022). *U.S. Public Health Service syphilis study at Tuskegee: The Tuskegee timeline.* CDC. http://www.cdc.gov/tuskegee/timeline.htm

Vaughan, T. R. (1967). Governmental intervention in social research: Political and ethical dimensions in the Wichita jury recordings. In G. Sjoberg (Ed.), *Ethics, politics, and social research* (pp. 50–77). Schenkman.

Von Hoffman, N. (2009). Sociological snoopers. In L. Humphreys (Ed.), *Tearoom trade: Impersonal sex in public places.* Enlarged edition with a retrospect on ethical issues (pp. 177–181). Aldine Transaction. (Original published 1970)

Warwick, D. P. (2009). Tearoom trade: Means and ends in social research. In L. Humphreys (Ed.), *Tearoom trade: Impersonal sex in public places.* Enlarged edition with a retrospect on ethical issues (pp. 177–181). Aldine Transaction. (Original published 1970)

Weber, M. (1949). *The methodology of the social sciences* (E.A. Shils & H.A. Finch, Trans.). Free Press.

Worley, R. M., Worley, V. B., & Wood, B. A. (2016). "There were ethical dilemmas all day long!": Harrowing tales of ethnographic researchers in criminology and criminal justice. *Criminal Justice Studies, 29*(4), 289–308. doi: 10.1080/1478601X.2016.1237945

Zimbardo, P. G. (1973). On the ethics of intervention in human psychological research: With special reference to the Stanford prison study. *Cognition, 2,* 243–256.

Zimbardo, P. G., Haney, C., Banks, W. C., & Jaffe, D. (1973). The mind is a formidable jailer: A Pirandellian prison. *The New York Times Magazine,* Section 6, April 8:38, ff.

CHAPTER 5

Baumer, E. P., Cundiff, K., & Luo, L. (2021). The contemporary transformation of American youth: An analysis of change in the prevalence of delinquency, 1991–2015. *Criminology, 59*(1), 109–136. https://doi.org/10.1111/1745-9125.12264

Blalock, H. M., Jr. (1964). *Causal inferences in nonexperimental research.* University of North Carolina Press.

Boas, F. (1911). *Handbook of the American Indian languages.* Government Printing Office.

Bolin, R. M., Pate, M., & McClintock, J. (2017). The impact of alcohol and marijuana use on academic achievement among college students. *The Social Science Journal, 54,* 430–437. https://doi.org/10.1016/j.soscij.2017.08.003

Bunge, M. A. (1979). *Causality and modern science* (3rd ed.). Dover.

Color of Change. (2020). *Normalizing injustice: The dangerous misrepresentations that define television's scripted crime genre.* https://hollywood.colorofchange.org/wp-content/uploads/2020/02/Normalizing-Injustice_Complete-Report-2.pdf

Erikson, K. T. (1966). *Wayward Puritans: A study in the sociology of deviance.* Wiley.

Felson, R., Savolainen, J., AAltonen, M., & Moustgaard, H. (2008). Is the association between alcohol use and delinquency causal or spurious? *Criminology, 46*(3), 785–808. https://doi.org/10.1111/j.1745-9125.2008.00120.x

Firebaugh, G. (1978). A rule for inferring individual-level relationships from aggregate data. *American Sociological Review, 43*(4), 557–572. https://doi.org/10.2307/2094779

Firebaugh, G. (2008). *Seven rules for social research*. Princeton University Press.

Gross, S. R., Jacoby, K., Matheson, D. J., Montgomery, N., & Patil, S. (2005). Exonerations in the United States, 1989 through 2003. *Journal of Criminal Law & Criminology, 95*, 523–560. https://ssrn.com/abstract=753084

Hagan, J., & Palloni, A. (1998). Immigration and crime in the United States. In J. P. Smith & D. Edmonston (Eds.), *The immigration debate: Studies on the economic, demographic, and fiscal effects of immigration* (pp. 367–387). National Academy Press.

Hirschi, T. (1969). *Causes of delinquency*. University of California Press.

Hu, X., Rodgers, K., & Lovrich, N. P. (2018). "We are more than crime fighters": Social media images of police departments. *Police Quarterly, 21*(4), 544–572. https://doi.org/10.1177/1098611118783991

Hume, D. (1951). An enquiry concerning human understanding. In D. C. Yalden-Thomson (Ed.), *Theory of knowledge* (pp. 3–176). Nelson. (Original work published 1748)

Johnson, I. M. (2015). Women parolees' perceptions of parole experiences and parole officers. *American Journal of Criminal Justice, 40*, 785–810. https://doi.org/10.1007/s12103-014-9284-0

Krupnik, I., & Müller-Willie, L. (2010). Franz Boas and Inuktitut terminology for ice and snow: From the emergence of the field to the "Great Eskimo Vocabulary Hoax." In I. Krupnik, C. Aporta, S. Gearheard, G. J. Laider, & L. K. Holm (Eds.), *SIKU: Knowing our ice* (pp. 377–400). Springer.

Kubrin, C. E., & Desmond, S. A. (2015). The power of place revisited: Why immigrant communities have lower levels of adolescent violence. *Youth, Violence and Juvenile Justice 13*(4), 345–366. https://doi.org/10.1177%2F1541204014547590

Lassiter, G. D. (2010). Psychological science and sound public policy: Video recording of custodial interrogations. *American Psychologist, 65*(8), 768–779. https://doi.org/10.1037/0003-066x.65.8.768

Lassiter, G. D., Beers, M. J., Geers, A. L., Handley, I. M., Munhall, P. J., & Weiland, P. E. (2002). Further evidence of a robust point-of-view bias in videotaped confessions. *Current Psychology, 21*, 265–288. https://doi.org/10.1007/s12144-002-1018-7

Lassiter, G. D., & Irvine, A. A. (1986). Videotaped confessions: The impact of camera point of view on judgments of coercion. *Journal of Applied Social Psychology, 16*(3), 268–276. https://doi.org/10.1111/j.1559-1816.1986.tb01139.x

Lassiter, G. D., Munhal, P. J., Geers, A. L., Weiland, P. E., & Handley, I. M. (2001). Accountability and the camera perspective bias in videotaped confessions. *Analyses of Social Issues and Public Policy, 1*(1), 53–70. https://doi.org/10.1111/1530-2415.00003

Lisuzzo, M. (2014). *Out-group salience bias against juveniles' in an equal-focus perspective videotaped interrogation* (Publication No. UFE0046485) [Doctoral dissertation, University of Florida]. University of Florida Digital Collections.

Martinez, R., Jr., & Lee, M. T. (2000). On immigration and crime. In G. LaFree (Ed.), *Criminal justice 2000. The nature of crime: Continuity and change* (Vol. 1, pp. 485–524). US Department of Justice, Office of Justice Programs, National Institute of Justice.

Meisenhelder, T. (1977). An exploratory study of exiting from criminal careers. *Criminology, 15*(3), 319–334. https://doi.org/10.1111/j.1745-9125.1977.tb00069.x

Pearl, J. (2010). The foundations of causal inference. *Sociological Methodology, 40*, 75–149. https://doi.org/10.1111/j.1467-9531.2010.01228.x

Ratcliff, J. J., Lassiter, G. D., Jager, V. M., Lindberg, M. J., Elek, J. K., & Hasinski, A. E. (2010). The hidden consequences of racial salience in videotaped interrogations and confessions. *Psychology, Public Policy, and Law, 16*(2), 200–218. https://psycnet.apa.org/doi/10.1037/a0018482

Reid, K., & Niebuhr, N. (2022). "Prison TikTok": Incarcerated life shared on social media. *Journal of Qualitative Criminal Justice & Criminology*. https://doi.org/10.21428/88de04a1.98ebdd0c

Robinson, W. S. (1950). Ecological correlations and the behavior of individuals. *American Sociological Review, 15*(3), 351–357. https://doi.org/10.1093/ije/dyn357

Robson, D. (2013, January 14). There really are 50 Eskimo words for "snow." *Washington Post*. https://www.washingtonpost.com/national/health-science/there-really-are-50-eskimo-words-for-snow/2013/01/14/e0e3f4e0-59a0-11e2-beee-6e38f5215402_story.html

Schwartz, H., & Jacobs, J. (1979). *Qualitative sociology: A method to the madness*. Free Press.

Schwartz-Shea, P., & Yanow, D. (2012). *Interpretive research design: Concepts and processes*. Routledge.

Simmel, G. (1972). *On individuality and social forms.* University of Chicago Press.

Smith, O. (2018, July 6). Mapped: The 53 places that still have the death penalty—including Japan. *The Telegraph.* https://www.telegraph.co.uk/travel/maps-and-graphics/countries-that-still-have-the-death-penalty/

Weber, M. (1998). *The Protestant ethic and the spirit of capitalism* (2nd ed.) (trans. T. Parsons). Roxbury Publishing Company. (Original work published 1905)

CHAPTER 6

Adcock, R., & Collier, D. (2001). Measurement validity: A shared standard for qualitative and quantitative research. *American Political Science Review, 95*(3), 529–546. https://www.jstor.org/stable/3118231

Akins, S. (2009). Racial segregation, concentrated disadvantage, and violent crime. *Journal of Ethnicity in Criminal Justice, 7*(1), 30–52. https://doi.org/10.1080/15377930802711771

Ariel, B. Farrar, W. A., & Sutherland, A. (2015). The effect of police body-worn cameras on use of force and citizens' complaints against the police: A randomized control trial. *Journal of Quantitative Criminology, 31,* 509–535. https://doi.org/10.1007/s10940-014-9236-3

Badr, H. S., Du, H., Marshall, M., Dong, E., Squire, M. M., & Gardner, L. M. (2020). Association between mobility patterns and COVID-19 transmission in the USA: A mathematical modelling study. *The Lancet Infectious Diseases, 20*(11), 1247–1245. https://doi.org/10.1016/S1473-3099(20)30553-3

Blascovich, J., & Tomaka, J. (1991). Measures of self-esteem. In J. P. Robinson, P. R. Shaver, & L. S. Wrightsman (Eds.), *Measures of social psychological attitudes, Vol. 1. Measures of personality and social psychological attitudes* (pp. 115–160). Academic Press. https://psycnet.apa.org/doi/10.1016/B978-0-12-590241-0.50008-3

Carmines, E. G., & Zeller, R. A. (1979). *Reliability and validity assessment.* Sage. https://dx.doi.org/10.4135/9781412985642

Cooley, C. (1912). *Human nature and the social order.* Scribners.

Davis, J. A. (1971). *Elementary survey analysis.* Prentice-Hall.

Demo, D. H. (1985). The measurement of self-esteem: Refining our methods. *Journal of Personality and Social Psychology, 48*(6), 1490–1502. https://psycnet.apa.org/doi/10.1037/0022-3514.48.6.1490

Dixon, T. L. (2017). Good guys are still always in white? Positive change and continued misrepresentation of race and crime on local television news. *Communication Research, 44*(6), 775–792. https://doi.org/10.1177/0093650215579223

Fleming, J. S., & Courtney, B. E. (1984). The dimensionality of self-esteem: II. Hierarchical facet model for revised measurement scales. *Journal of Personality and Social Psychology, 46*(2), 404–421. https://psycnet.apa.org/doi/10.1037/0022-3514.46.2.404

Fouts, G., Callan, M. J., Piasentin, K., & Lawson, A. (2006). Demonizing in children's television cartoons and Disney animated films. *Child Psychiatry and Human Development, 37*(1), 15–23. https://doi.org/10.1007/s10578-006-0016-7

Glaser, B. G., & Strauss, A. L. (1967). *The discovery of grounded theory: Strategies for qualitative research.* Aldine.

Gray-Little, B., Williams, V. S. L., & Hancock, T. D. (1997). An item response theory analysis of the Rosenberg self-esteem scale. *Personality and Social Psychology Bulletin, 23*(5), 443–451. https://doi.org/10.1177/0146167297235001

Guttman, L. (1974). The basis for scalogram analysis." In G. M. Maranell (Ed.), *Scaling: A sourcebook for behavioral scientists* (pp. 142–71). Aldine.

Harrison, L. (1997). The validity of self-reported drug use in survey research: An overview and critique of research methods. In L. Harrison & A. Hughes (Eds.), *The validity of self-reported drug use: Improving the accuracy of survey estimates* (pp. 17–36). National Institute on Drug Abuse.

Havekes, E., Bader, M., & Krysan, M. (2016). Realizing racial and ethnic neighborhood preferences? Exploring the mismatches between what people want, where they search, and where they live. *Population Research and Policy Review, 35*(1), 101–126.

Jacques, S., Lasky, N., & Fisher, B. S. (2015). Seeing the offenders' perspective through the eye-tracking device: Methodological insights from a study of shoplifters. *Journal of Contemporary Criminal Justice, 31*(4), 449–467. https://doi.org/10.1177/1043986215607258

Kadar, C., & Pletikosa, I. (2018). Mining large-scale human mobility data for long-term crime prediction. *EPJ Data Science, 7*(26). https://doi.org/10.1140/epjds/s13688-018-0150-z

Keuschnigg, M., & Wolbring, T. (2015). Disorder, social capital, and norm violation: Three field experiments on the broken windows thesis. *Rationality and Society, 27*(1), 96–126. https://doi.org/10.1177/1043463114561749

Kleck, G., Tark, J., & Bellows, J. J. (2006). What methods are most frequently used in research in criminology and criminal justice? *Journal of Criminal Justice, 34*, 147–152. https://doi.org/10.1016/j.jcrimjus.2006.01.007

Lasky, N., Jacques, S., & Fisher, B. S. (2015). Glossing over shoplifting: How thieves act normal. *Deviant Behavior, 36*(4), 293–309. https://doi.org/10.1080/01639625.2014.935651

Levine, M., Taylor, P. J., & Best, R. (2011). Third parties, violence, and conflict resolution: The role of group size and collective action in the microregulation of violence. *Psychological Science, 22*(3), 406–412. https://doi.org/10.1177/0956797611398495

Logan, J. R., & Stults, B. (2011). *The persistence of segregation in the metropolis: New findings from the 2010 Census* (Census brief). https://s4.ad.brown.edu/Projects/Diversity/data/report/report2.pdf

Maslach, C., & Jackson, S. E. (1981). The measurement of experienced burnout. *Journal of Occupational Behavior, 2*(2), 99–113. https://doi.org/10.1002/job.4030020205

Mead, G. H. (1934). *Mind, self, and society from the standpoint of a social behaviorist*. University of Chicago Press.

Meldrum, R. C., & Boman, J. H. (2013). Similarities and differences between perceptions of peer delinquency, peer self-reported delinquency, and respondent delinquency: An analysis of friendship dyads. *Journal of Criminal Justice, 41*, 395–406. https://doi.org/10.1016/j.jcrimjus.2013.07.005

Melvin, K. B., Gramling, L. K., & Gardner, W. M. (1985). A scale to measure attitudes toward prisoners. *Criminal Justice and Behavior, 12*, 241–253. https://doi.org/10.1177/0093854885012002006

Moeller, K. (2016). Temporal transaction patterns in an open-air cannabis market. *Police, Practice, and Research, 17*, 37–50. https://doi.org/10.1080/15614263.2014.994214

Oser, C. B. (2006). The criminal offending–self-esteem nexus: Which version of the self-esteem theory is supported? *The Prison Journal, 86*(3), 344–363. https://doi.org/10.1177/0032885506291024

Owens, T. J. (1993). Accentuate the positive—and the negative: Rethinking the use of self-esteem, self-deprecation, and self-confidence. *Social Psychology Quarterly, 56*(4), 288–299. https://www.jstor.org/stable/2786665

Owens, T. J. (1994). Two dimensions of self-esteem: Reciprocal effects of positive self-worth and self-deprecation on adolescent problems. *American Sociological Review, 59*(3), 391–407. https://www.jstor.org/stable/2095940

Reynolds, C. R. (1988). Putting the individual into aptitude-treatment interaction. *Exceptional Children, 54*(4), 324–331. https://doi.org/10.1177/001440298805400406

Rhineberger-Dunn, G., Mack, K. Y., & Baker, K. M. (2017). Comparing demographic factors, background characteristics, and workplace perceptions as predictors of burnout among community corrections officers. *Criminal Justice and Behavior, 44*(2), 205–225. https://doi.org/10.1177/0093854816666583

Rokkan, T., Phillips, J., Lulei, M., Poledna, S., & Kensey, A. (2015). How was your day? Exploring a day in the life of probation workers across Europe using practice diaries. *European Journal of Probation, 7*(3), 201–217. https://doi.org/10.1177/2066220315610242

Rosenberg, M. (1965). *Society and the adolescent self-image*. Princeton University Press.

Rosenberg, M. (1979). *Conceiving the self*. Basic Books.

Roth, W. D. (2010). Racial mismatch: The divergence between form and function in data for monitoring racial discrimination of Hispanics. *Social Science Quarterly, 91*(5), 1288–1311. https://doi.org/10.1111/j.1540-6237.2010.00732.x

Savin-Williams, R. C., & Jaquish, G. A. (1981). The assessment of adolescent self-esteem: A comparison of methods. *Journal of Personality, 49*(3), 324–336. https://psycnet.apa.org/doi/10.1111/j.1467-6494.1981.tb00940.x

Schaefer, L., & Williams, G. C. (2018). The impact of probation and parole officers' attitudes about offenders on professional practices. *Corrections: Policy, Practice, and Research, 5*, 1–18. https://doi.org/10.1080/23774657.2018.1538710

Simon, J. L., & Burstein, P. (1985). *Basic research methods in social science*. McGraw-Hill.

Sloan, J. J., Bodapati, M. R., & Tucker, T. A. (2004). Respondent misreporting of drug use in self-reports: Social desirability and other correlates. *Journal of Drug Issues, 34*(2), 269–292. https://doi.org/10.1177/002204260403400202

Solymosi, R., Bowers, K., & Fujiyama, T. (2015). Mapping fear of crime as a context-dependent everyday experience that varies in space and time. *Legal and Criminological Psychology, 20*, 193–211. https://doi.org/10.1111/lcrp.12076

Stacey, M. (2019). Macrostructural opportunity and violent crime: The impact of social structure on inter- and intra-racial violence. *American Journal of Criminal Justice, 44*, 125–145. https://doi.org/10.1007/s12103-018-9446-6

Steidl, C., & Werum. R. (2019). If all you have is a hammer, everything looks like a nail: Operationalization matters. *Sociology Compass, 13*(8). https://doi.org/10.1111/soc4.12727

Stevens, S. S. (1946). On the theory of scales of measurement. *Science, 103*(2684), 677–680. https://www.jstor.org/stable/1671815

Tourangeau, R., Rips, L. J., & Rasinski, K. (2000). *The psychology of survey response*. Cambridge University Press.

Voigt, R., Camp, N. P., Prabhakaran, V., Hamilton, W., Hetey, R. C., Griffiths, C. M., Jurgens, D., Jurafsky, D., & Eberhardt, J. L. (2017). Language from police body camera footage shows racial disparities in office respect. *PNAS, 114*(25), 6521–6526. https://doi.org/10.1073/pnas.1702413114

Warren, P. Y., Cochran, J., Shields, R. T., Feldmeyer, B., Bailey, C., & Stewart, E. A. (2019). Sentencing departures and female defendants: Assessing the effects of racial and ethnic threat. *Crime & Delinquency, 66*, 1–34. https://doi.org/10.1177/0011128719839394

Wilson, J. Q., & Kelling, G. L. (1982, March). Broken windows: The police and neighborhood safety. *Atlantic Monthly*. https://www.theatlantic.com/magazine/archive/1982/03/broken-windows/304465/

Wu, J., Abrar, S. M., Awasthi, N., Frias-Martinez, E., & Frias-Martinez, V. (2022). Enhancing short-term crime prediction with human mobility flows and deep learning architectures. *EPJ Data Science, 11*(53). https://doi.org/10.1140/epjds/s13688-022-00366-2

Yan, T., Curtin, R., & Jans, M. (2010). Trends in income nonresponse over two decades. *Journal of Official Statistics, 26*(1), 145–164.

CHAPTER 7

American Association for Public Opinion Research (AAPOR). (2020). Online panels. https://aapor.org/wp-content/uploads/2022/12/Online-Panels-508.pdf

Amialchuk, A., & Sapci, O. (2021). The influence of normative misperceptions on alcohol-related problems among school-age adolescents in the U.S. *Review of Economics of the Household, 19*, 453–472. https://doi.org/10.1007/s11150-020-09481-3

Bachman, J. G., O'Malley, P. M., Johnston, L.D, Schulenberg, J. E., & Wallace, Jr., J. M. (2011). Racial/ethnic differences in the relationship between parental education and substance use among U.S. 8th-, 10th-, and 12th-grade students: Findings from the Monitoring the Future Project. *Journal of Studies on Alcohol and Drugs, 72*, 279–285. https://doi.org/10.15288/jsad.2011.72.279

Baker, R., Brick, J. M., Bates, N. A., Battaglia, M., Couper, M. P., Dever, J. A., Gile, K. J., & Tourangeau, R. (2013). Summary Report of the AAPOR Task Force on non-probability sampling. *Journal of Survey Statistics and Methodology, 1*(2), 90–143. https://doi.org/10.1093/jssam/smt008

Baumer, E. P., Cundiff, K., & Luo, L. (2020). The contemporary transformation of American youth: An analysis of change in the prevalence of delinquency, 1991–2015. *Criminology, 59*, 109–136. https://doi.org/10.1111/1745-9125.12264

Biernacki, P., & Waldorf, D. (1981). Snowball sampling: Problems and techniques of chain referral sampling. *Sociological Methods and Research, 10*(2), 141–163. https://doi.org/10.1177/004912418101000205

Bolin, R. M., Pate, M., McClintock, J. (2017). The impact of alcohol and marijuana use on academic achievement among college students. *The Social Science Journal, 54*(4), 430–437. https://doi.org/10.1016/j.soscij.2017.08.003

Brenan, M. (2023, December 22). *Biden ends 2023 with 39% job approval*. Gallup. https://news.gallup.com/poll/547763/biden-ends-2023-job-approval.aspx

Casey, L. S., Chandler, J. Levine, A. S., Proctor, A., & Strolovitch, D. Z. (2017). Intertemporal differences among MTurk workers: Time-based sample variations and implications for online data collection. *SAGE Open, 7*(2), 1–15. https://doi.org/10.1177/2158244017712774

Chandler, J., Rosenzweig, C., Moss, A. J., Robinson, J., & Litman, L. (2019). Online panels in social science research: Expanding sampling methods beyond Mechanical Turk. *Behavior Research Methods, 51*(5), 2022–2038. https://doi.org/10.3758/s13428-019-01273-7

Charmaz, K. (2006). *Constructing grounded theory: A practical guide through qualitative analysis*. Sage.

Chen, P., & Chantala, K. (2014). *Guidelines for analyzing Add Health data*. Carolina Population Center at the University of North Carolina at Chapel Hill. http://cdr.lib.unc.edu/downloads/1v53k016h

Couper, M. P. (2017). New developments in survey data collection. *Annual Review of Sociology, 43*, 121–145. https://doi.org/10.1146/annurev-soc-060116-053613

DeLisi, M., Hochsettler, A., Jones-Johnson, G., Caudill, J. W., & Marquart, J. W. (2011). The road to murder: The enduring criminogenic effects of juvenile confinement among a sample of adult career criminals. *Youth*

Violence and Juvenile Justice, 9(3), 207–221. https://doi.org/10.1177/1541204010396107

Dixon, J., & Tucker, C. (2010). Survey nonresponse. In P. V. Marsden and J. D. Wright (Eds.), *Handbook of survey research* (2nd ed., pp. 593–630). Emerald Group.

Fienberg, S. E. (1971). Randomization and social affairs: The 1970 draft lottery. *Science, 171*(3968), 255–61. https://doi.org/10.1126/science.171.3968.255

Glaser, B. G., & Strauss, A. L. (1967). *The discovery of grounded theory: Strategies for qualitative research.* Aldine.

Glaze, L. (2019). *Methodology: Survey of Prison Inmates, 2016.* Bureau of Justice Statistics https://bjs.ojp.gov/content/pub/pdf/mspi16.pdf

Groves, R. M. (2006). Nonresponse rates and nonresponse bias in household surveys. *Public Opinion Quarterly, 70*(5), 646–675. https://doi.org/10.1093/poq/nfl033

Groves, R. M., & Couper, M. P. (1998). *Nonresponse in household interview surveys.* Wiley.

Groves, R. M., Fowler, Jr., F. J., Couper, M. P., Lepkowski, J. M., Singer, E., & Tourangeau, R. (2009). *Survey methodology* (2nd ed.). Wiley.

Groves, R. M., & Peytcheva, E. (2008). The impact of nonresponse rates on nonresponse bias. *Public Opinion Quarterly, 72*(2), 167–189. https://doi.org/10.1093/poq/nfn011

Groves, R. M., Presser, S., & Dipko, S. (2004). The role of topic interest in survey participation decisions. *Public Opinion Quarterly, 68*(1), 2–31. https://doi.org/10.1093/poq/nfh002

Guest, G., Bunce, A., & Johnson, L. (2006). How many interviews are enough? An experiment with data saturation and variability. *Field Methods, 18*(1), 59–82. https://doi.org/10.1177/1525822X05279903

Hitlin, P. (2016). Research in the crowdsourcing age, a case study. *Pew Research Center.* https://www.pewresearch.org/internet/2016/07/11/research-in-the-crowdsourcing-age-a-case-study/

Levay, K. E., Freese, J., & Druckman, J. N. (2016). The demographic and political composition of Mechanical Turk samples. *SAGE Open, 6*(1), 1–17. https://doi.org/10.1177/2158244016636433

Lieberson, S. (1985). *Making it count: The improvement of social research and theory.* University of California Press.

Marshall, M. N. (1996). Sampling for qualitative research. *Family Practice, 13*, 522–525. https://doi.org/10.1093/fampra/13.6.522

Ragin, C. C. (1987). *The comparative method: Moving beyond qualitative and quantitative strategies.* University of California Press.

Schwartz-Shea, P., & Yanow, D. (2012). *Interpretive research design: Concepts and processes.* Routledge.

Sjoberg, G., Williams, N., Vaughan, T. R., & Sjoberg, A. F. (1991). The case study approach in social research: Basic methodological issues. In J. R. Feagin, A. M. Orum, & G. Sjoberg (Eds.), *A case for the case study* (pp. 27–79). University of North Carolina Press.

Sturgis, P., Williams, J., Brunton-Smith, I., & Moore, J. (2017). Fieldwork effort, response rate, and the distribution of survey outcomes: A multilevel meta-analysis. *Public Opinion Quarterly, 81*(2), 523–542. https://doi.org/10.1093/poq/nfw055

Sudman, S., & Kalton, G. (1986). New developments in the sampling of rare populations. *Annual Review of Sociology, 12*, 401–429. https://www.jstor.org/stable/2083209

Sudman, S., Sirken, M. G., & Cowan, C. D. (1988). Sampling rare and elusive populations. *Science, 240*, 991–996. https://www.jstor.org/stable/1701890

Tahamont, S. Hyatt, J., Pheasant, M., Lafferty, J., Bell, N., & Sheets, M. (2022). Ineligible anyway: Evidence on the barriers to Pell eligibility for prisoners in the Second Chance Pell pilot program in Pennsylvania prisons. *Justice Quarterly, 39*(2), 402–426. https://doi.org/10.1080/07418825.2020.1853798

Thomas, G. (2011). *How to do your case study: A guide for students and researchers.* Sage.

Thompson, A. J., & Pickett, J. T. (2020). Are relational inferences from crowdsourced and opt-in samples generalizable? Comparing criminal justice attitudes in the GSS and five online samples. *Journal of Quantitative Criminology, 36*, 907–932. https://doi.org/10.1007/s10940-019-09436-7

Wechsler, H., Davenport, A., Dowdall, G., Moeykens, B., & Castillo, S. (1994). Health and behavioral consequences of binge drinking in college: A national survey of students at 140 campuses. *Journal of the American Medical Association, 272*, 1672–1677. https://doi.org/10.1001/jama.1994.03520210056032

Whyte, W. F. (1993). *Street corner society: The social structure of an Italian slum* (4th ed., rev. and enl.) University of Chicago Press.

Wildeman, C., & Andersen, L. H. (2020). Long-term consequences of being placed in disciplinary segregation. *Criminology, 58*(3), 423–453. https://doi.org/10.1111/1745-9125.12241

Wilson, W. J., & Taub, R. P. (2006). *There goes the neighborhood: Racial, ethnic, and class tensions in four Chicago neighborhoods and their meaning for America*. Alfred A. Knopf.

CHAPTER 8

Agan, A., & Starr, S. (2018). Ban the box, criminal records, and racial discrimination: A field experiment. *The Quarterly Journal of Economics*, 133(1), 191–235, https://doi.org/10.1093/qje/qjx028

Applegate, B. K., & Sanborn, J. B. (2011). Public opinion on the harshness of local courts: An experimental test of question wording effects. *Criminal Justice Review*, 36(4), 487–497. https://doi.org/10.1177/0734016811418822

Aruguete, M. S., Huynh, H., Browne, B. L., Jurs, B., Flint, E., & McCutcheon, L. E. (2019). How serious is the "carelessness" problem on Mechanical Turk. *International Journal of Social Research Methodology*, 22(5), 441–449. https://doi.org/10.1080/13645579.2018.1563966

Bertrand, M., & Mullainathan, S. (2004). "Are Emily and Greg more employable than Lakisha and Jamal? A field experiment on labor market discrimination?" *American Economic Review*, 94(4), 991–1013. https://www.jstor.org/stable/3592802

Bobo, L., & Johnson, D. (2004). A taste for punishment: Black and white Americans' views on the death penalty and the war on drugs. *Du Bois Review: Social Science Research on Race*, 1(1), 151–180. https://doi.org/10.1017/S1742058X04040081

Campbell, D. T., & Stanley, J. C. (1963). *Experimental and quasi-experimental designs for research*. Rand McNally & Company.

Casler, K., Bickel, L., & Hackett, E. (2013). Separate but equal? A comparison of participants and data gathered via MTurk, social media, and face-to-face behavioral testing. *Computers in Human Behavior*, 29(6), 2156–2160. https://doi.org/10.1016/j.chb.2013.05.009

Deutscher, I., Pestello, F. P., & Pestello, H. F. G. (1993). *Sentiments and acts*. Aldine De Gruyter.

Gaddis, S. M. (2017). How black are Lakisha and Jamal? Racial perceptions from names used in correspondence audit studies. *Sociological Science*, 4, 469–489. http://dx.doi.org/10.15195/v4.a19

Hauser, D. J., & Schwarz, N. (2016). Attentive Turkers: MTurk participants perform better on online attention checks than do subject pool participants. *Behavior Research Methods* 48(1), 400–407. https://doi.org/10.3758/s13428-015-0578-z

Henrich, J., Heine, S. J., & Norenzayan, A. (2010). The weirdest people in the world? *Behavioral and Brain Sciences*, 33(2–3), 61–83. https://doi.org/10.1017/S0140525X0999152X

Henry, P. J. (2008). College sophomores in the laboratory redux: Influences of a narrow data base on social psychology's view of the nature of prejudice. *Psychological Inquiry*, 19(2), 49–71. https://doi.org/10.1080/10478400802049936

Lucas, J. W., Graif, C., & Lovaglia, M. J. (2006). Misconduct in the prosecution of severe crimes: Theory and experimental test. *Social Psychology Quarterly*, 69(1), 97–107. https://doi.org/10.1177/019027250606900107

Norris, R. J., & Mullinix, K. J. (2020). Framing innocence: An experimental test of the effects of wrongful convictions on public opinion. *Journal of Experimental Criminology*, 16, 311–334. https://doi.org/10.1007/s11292-019-09360-7

Pager, D. (2003). The mark of a criminal record. *American Journal of Sociology*, 108(5), 937–975. https://doi.org/10.1086/374403

Pager, D., & Quillian, L. (2005). Walking the talk? What employers say versus what they do. *American Sociological Review*, 70(3), 355–380. https://doi.org/10.1177/000312240507000301

Pager, D., Western, B., & Bonikowski, B. (2009). Discrimination in a low wage labor market: A field experiment. *American Sociological Review*, 74(5), 777–799. https://doi.org/10.1177/000312240907400505

Pager, D., Western, B., & Sugie, N. (2009). Sequencing disadvantage: Barriers to employment facing young black and white men with criminal records. *Annals of the American Academy of Political and Social Sciences*, 623(1), 195–213. https://doi.org/10.1177/0002716208330793

Rosenbaum, D. P. (2007). Just say no to D.A.R.E. *Criminology & Public Policy*, 6(4), 815–824. https://doi.org/10.1111/j.1745-9133.2007.00474.x

Salerno, J. M., & Sanchez, J. (2020). Subjective interpretation of "objective" video evidence: Perceptions of male versus female police officers' use-of-force. *Law and Human Behavior*, 44(2), 97–112. https://doi.org/10.1037/lhb0000366

Schutten, N. M., Pickett, J. T., Burton, A. L., Cullen, F. T., Jonson, C. L., Burton, Jr., V. S. (2020). Punishing rampage: Public opinion on sanctions for school shooters. *Justice Quarterly*. https://doi.org/10.1080/07418825.2019.1707857

Sears, D. O. (1986). College sophomores in the laboratory: Influences of a narrow data base on social psychology's view of human nature. *Journal of Personality and Social Psychology, 51*(3), 515–530. https://doi.org/10.1037/0022-3514.51.3.515

Singleton, Jr., R. A., & Straits, B. C. (2018). *Approaches to social research* (6th ed.). Oxford University Press.

Smith, A. M., Wilford, M. M., Quigley-McBride, A., & Wells, G. L. (2019). Mistaken eyewitness identification rates increase when either witnessing or testing conditions get worse. *Law and Human Behavior, 43*(4), 358–368. https://doi.org/10.1037/lhb0000334

Sniderman, P. M. (2018). Some advances in the design of survey experiments. *Annual Review of Political Science, 21,* 259–275. https://doi.org/10.1146/annurev-polisci-042716-115726

Sniderman, P. M., & Grob, D. B. (1996). Innovations in experimental design in attitude surveys. *Annual Review of Sociology, 22,* 377–399. https://doi.org/10.1146/annurev.soc.22.1.377

Thomas, K. A., & Clifford, S. (2017). Validity and Mechanical Turk: An assessment of exclusion methods and interactive experiments. *Computers in Human Behavior, 77,* 184–197. https://doi.org/10.1016/j.chb.2017.08.038

CHAPTER 9

American Association for Public Opinion Research (AAPOR). (2020). Question wording. https://aapor.org/wp-content/uploads/2023/01/Question-Wording.pdf

American Civil Liberties Union (ACLU). (2020, March 30). ACLU poll shows wide-ranging support for releasing vulnerable people from jails and prisons. *ACLU.* https://www.aclu.org/press-releases/aclu-poll-shows-wide-ranging-support-releasing-vulnerable-people-jails-and-prisons

Aquilino, W. S. (1994). Interview mode effect in surveys of drug and alcohol use. *Public Opinion Quarterly, 58*(2), 210–240. https://doi.org/10.1086/269419

Blake, A. (2020, February 28). For the first time, there are fewer registered Republicans than independents. *The Washington Post.* https://www.washingtonpost.com/politics/2020/02/28/first-time-ever-there-are-fewer-registered-republicans-than-independents/

Bureau of Justice Statistics. (2021). Data collection: National Crime Victimization Survey (NCVS). https://bjs.ojp.gov/data-collection/ncvs

Burton, A. L., Cullen, F. T., Burton, Jr., V. S., Graham, A., Butler, L. C., & Thielo, A. J. (2020). Belief in redeemability and punitive public opinion: "Once a criminal, always a criminal" revisited. *Criminal Justice and Behavior, 47*(6), 712–732. https://doi.org/10.1177/0093854820913585

Converse, J. M., & Presser, S. (1986). *Survey questions: Handcrafting the standardized questionnaire.* Sage.

Couper, M. P. (2011). The future of modes of data collection. *Public Opinion Quarterly, 75*(5), 889–908. https://doi.org/10.1093/poq/nfr046

Couper, M. P. (2017). New developments in survey data collection. *Annual Review of Sociology, 43,* 121–145. https://doi.org/10.1146/annurev-soc-060116-053613

Couper, M. P., Traugott, M. W., & Lamias, M. J. (2001). Web survey design and administration. *Public Opinion Quarterly, 65*(2), 230–253. https://www.jstor.org/stable/3078803

Curtin, R., Presser, S., & Singer, E. (2005). Changes in telephone survey nonresponse over the past quarter century. *Public Opinion Quarterly, 69*(1), 87–98. https://doi.org/10.1093/poq/nfi002

Daikeler, J., Silber, H., & Bosnjak, M. (2021). A meta-analysis of how country level factors affect web survey response rates. *International Journal of Market Research, 64*(3), 306–333. https://doi.org/10.1177/14707853211050916

Deane, C., Kennedy, C., & Keeter, S. (2019, November 19). A field guide to polling: Election 2020 edition. *Pew Research Center, Methods.* https://www.pewresearch.org/methods/2019/11/19/a-field-guide-to-polling-election-2020-edition/

de Leeuw, E. D. (2005). To mix or not to mix data collection modes in surveys. *Journal of Official Statistics, 21*(2), 233–255.

de Leeuw, E. W. (2008). Choosing the method of data collection. In E. D. de Leeuw, J. J. Hox, & D. A. Dillman (Eds.), *International handbook of survey methodology* (pp. 113–135) Lawrence Erlbaum.

Dillman, D. A. (2007). *Mail and Internet surveys: The tailored design method* (2nd ed.). Wiley.

Dillman, D. A., Smyth, J., & Christian, L. M. (2009). *Internet, mail, and mixed-mode surveys: The tailored design method* (3rd ed.). Wiley.

Dixon, J., & Tucker, C. (2010). Survey nonresponse. In P. V. Marsden & J. D. Wright (Eds.), *Handbook of survey research* (2nd ed., pp. 593–630). Emerald Group.

Enns, P. K., Yi, Y., Comfort, M., Goldman, A. W., Lee, H., Muller, C., Wakefield, S., Wang, E. A., & Wildeman, C. (2019). What percentage of Americans have ever had a family member incarcerated? Evidence from the Family History of Incarceration Survey (FamHIS). *Socius: Sociological Research for a Dynamic World, 5*, 1–45. https://doi.org/10.1177/2378023119829332

Fowler, F. J., Jr. (1995). *Improving survey questions: Design and evaluation*. Sage.

General Social Survey (GSS). (2020). Data collection plan for GSS 2020. *NORC*. https://gss.norc.org/Documents/other/GSS_COVID_PLAN.pdf

Graesser, A. C., Cai, Z., Louwerse, M. M., & Daniel, F. (2006). Question Understanding Aid (QUAID): A web facility that helps survey methodologists improve the comprehensibility of questions. *Public Opinion Quarterly, 70*(1), 3–22. https://www.jstor.org/stable/3843968

Groves, R. M. (2011). Three eras of survey research. *Public Opinion Quarterly, 75*(5), 861–871. https://academic.oup.com/poq/article/75/5/861/1831518

Groves, R. M., Fowler, Jr., F. J., Couper, M. P., Lepkowski, J. M., Singer, E., & Tourangeau, R. (2009). *Survey methodology* (2nd ed.). Wiley.

Holbrook, A. L., Green, M. C., & Krosnick, J. A. (2003). Telephone versus face-to-face interviewing of national probability samples with long questionnaires: Comparisons of respondent satisficing and social desirability response bias. *Public Opinion Quarterly, 67*(1), 79–125. https://doi.org/10.1086/346010

Holbrook, A. L., Krosnick, J. A., & Pfent, A. (2008). The causes and consequences of response rates in surveys by news media and government contractor survey research firms. In J. M. Lepkowski, C. Tucker, J. M. Brick, E. D. de Leeuw, L. Japec, P. J. Lavrakas, M. W. Link, & R. L. Sangster (Eds.), *Advances in telephone survey methodology* (pp. 499–528). Wiley.

Hughes, C. (2020, November 19). Gallup: Support in U.S. for death penalty at lowest point in decades. *United Press International*. https://www.upi.com/Top_News/US/2020/11/19/Gallup-Support-in-US-for-death-penalty-at-lowest-point-in-decades/7701605786729/

Kennedy, C., & Hartig, H. (2019, February 27). Response rates in telephone surveys have resumed their decline. *Pew Research Center*. https://www.pewresearch.org/fact-tank/2019/02/27/response-rates-in-telephone-surveys-have-resumed-their-decline/

Krosnick, J. A., & Presser, S. (2010). Question and questionnaire design. In P. V. Marsden & J. D. Wright (Eds.), *Handbook of survey research* (2nd ed., pp. 263–313). Emerald Group.

Krumpal, I. (2013). Determinants of social desirability bias in sensitive surveys: A literature review. *Quality & Quantity, 47*(4), 2025–2047. https://doi.org/10.1007/s11135-011-9640-9

Lavrakas, P. J. (2010). Telephone surveys. In P. V. Marsden & J. D. Wright (Eds.), *Bingley handbook of survey research* (2nd ed., pp. 471–498). Emerald Group.

Lavrakas, P. J., Shuttles, C. D., Steeh, C., & Fienberg, H. (2007). The state of surveying cell phone numbers in the United States: 2007 and beyond. *Public Opinion Quarterly, 71*(5), 840–854. https://doi.org/10.1093/poq/nfm054

Long, C., & Fingerhut, H. (2020, June 23). AP-NORC poll: Nearly all in US back criminal justice reform. *AP News*. https://apnews.com/article/ffaa4bc564afcf4a90b02f455d8fdf03

Manfreda, K. L. & Vehovar, V. (2008). Internet surveys. In E. D. de Leeuw, J. J. Hox, & D. A. Dillman (Eds.), *International handbook of survey methodology* (pp. 264–284). Lawrence Erlbaum.

McGonagle, K. A., Schoeni, R. F., Sastry, N., & Freedman, V. A. (2012). The Panel Study of Income Dynamics: Overview, recent innovations, and potential for life course research. *Longitudinal and Life Course Studies, 3*(2), 268–284. https://doi.org/10.14301/llcs.v3i2.188

Pew Research Center. (2020). Democratic edge in party identification narrows slightly. https://www.pewresearch.org/politics/2020/06/02/democratic-edge-in-party-identification-narrows-slightly/

Pfeffer, F. T., Fomby, P., & Insolera, N. (2020). The longitudinal revolution: Sociological research at the 50-year milestone of the Panel Study of Income Dynamics. *Annual Review of Sociology, 46*, 83–108. https://doi.org/10.1146/annurev-soc-121919-054821

Remaley, E. (2020, June 10). NTIA data reveal shifts in technology use, persistent digital divide. *National Telecommunications and Information Administration, United States Department of Commerce*. https://www.ntia.gov/blog/2020/ntia-data-reveal-shifts-technology-use-persistent-digital-divide

Schaeffer, K. (2023). *Key facts about Americans and guns*. Pew Research Center. https://www.pewresearch.org/short-reads/2023/09/13/key-facts-about-americans-and-guns/

Schaeffer, N. C., & Dykema, J. (2020). Advances in the science of asking questions. *Annual Review of Sociology, 46*, 37–60. https://doi.org/10.1146/annurev-soc-121919-054544

Shih, T. & Fan, X. (2008). Comparing response rates from web and mail surveys: A meta-analysis. *Field Methods, 20*(3), 249–271. https://doi.org/10.1177/1525822X08317085

Singleton, R. A., Jr., and Straits, B. C. (2018). *Approaches to social research* (6th ed.). Oxford University Press.

Smith, T. W., Davern, M., Freese, J., & Morgan, S. L. (2019). *General Social Surveys, 1972–2018: Cumulative codebook* [machine-readable data file]. National Opinion Research Center. 1 data file (64,814 logical records) and 1 codebook (3,758 pp.). https://gss.norc.org/documents/codebook/gss_codebook.pdf

Steiger, D. M., & Conroy, B. (2008). IVR: Interactive voice response. In E. D. de Leeuw, J. J. Hox, & D. A. Dillman (Eds.), *International handbook of survey methodology* (pp. 285–298). Lawrence Erlbaum.

Sudman, S., & Bradburn, N. M. (1982). *Asking questions: A practical guide to questionnaire design*. Jossey-Bass.

Tourangeau, R., & Yan, T. (2007). Sensitive questions in surveys. *Psychological Bulletin, 133*(5), 859–883. https://doi.org/10.1037/0033-2909.133.5.859

US Census Bureau. (2022). *Types of computers and internet subscriptions, American Community Survey*. https://data.census.gov/table/ACSST1Y2022.S2801?q=Telephone,%20Computer,%20and%20Internet%20Access&d=ACS%201-Year%20Estimates%20Subject%20Tables

Wechsler, H., Davenport, A., Dowdall, G., Moeykens, B., & Castillo, S. (1994). Health and behavioral consequences of binge drinking in college: A national survey of students at 140 campuses. *Journal of the American Medical Association, 272*(21), 1672–1677. https://psycnet.apa.org/doi/10.1001/jama.272.21.1672

Wechsler, H., & Nelson, T. F. (2008). What we have learned from the Harvard School of Public Health College Alcohol Study: Focusing attention on college student alcohol consumption and the environmental conditions that promote it. *Journal of Studies on Alcohol and Drugs, 69*(4), 481–490. https://doi.org/10.15288/jsad.2008.69.481

Western, B., Braga, A., & Kohl, R. (2017). A longitudinal survey of newly-released prisoners: Methods and design of the Boston Reentry Study. *Federal Probation, 81*(1), 32–40.

Willard, J. C., & Schoenborn, C. A. (1995). Relationship between cigarette smoking and other unhealthy behaviors among our nation's youth: United States, 1992. Advance Data from Vital and Health Statistics, No. 263. National Center for Health Statistics.

Wozniak, K., Drakulick, K. M., & Calfano, B. R. (2021). Public opinion about police weapons and equipment: An exploratory analysis. *Criminal Justice Policy Review, 32*(9), 960–991. https://doi.org/10.1177/08874034211005005

Wright, J. D., & Marsden, P. V. (2010). Survey research and social science: History, current practice, and future prospects. In P. V. Marsden & J. D. Wright (Eds.), *Handbook of survey research* (2nd ed., pp. 3–25). Emerald Group.

CHAPTER 10

Adler, P. A., & Adler, P. (1987). *Membership roles in field research*. Sage.

Bailey, C. A. (1996). *A guide to field research*. Sage.

Blee, K. M. (2002). *Inside organized racism: Women in the hate movement*. University of California Press.

Bogdan, R., & Taylor, S. J. (1975). *Introduction to qualitative research methods: A phenomenological approach to the social sciences*. Wiley.

Bourdieu, P. (1990). *The logic of practice*. Stanford University Press.

Charmaz, K. (2006). *Constructing grounded theory: A practical guide through qualitative analysis*. Sage.

Clemmer, D. (1940). *The prison community*. Christopher Publishing.

Collins, P. H. (1986). Learning from the outsider within: The sociological significance of black feminist thought. *Social Problems, 33*(6), 14–32.

Costello, L., McDermott, M.-L., & Wallace, R. (2017). Netnography: Range of practices, misperceptions, and missed opportunities. *International Journal of Qualitative Methods, 16*(1). https://doi.org/10.1177/1609406917700647

Emerson, R. M., Fretz, R. I., & Shaw, L. L. (2011). *Writing ethnographic fieldnotes* (2nd ed.). University of Chicago Press.

Fine, G. A., Johnson, J. E., & Abramson, C. M. (2020). Ethnography in the time of COVID-19. *Footnotes, 48*(3), 8–9.

Gariglio, L. (2014, February 10). Gaining access to prison: Authority, negotiations, and flexibility in the field. *Border Criminologies*. https://www.law.ox.ac.uk/research-subject-groups/centre-criminology/centreborder-criminologies/blog/2014/02/gaining-access

Humphreys, L. (2009). *Tearoom trade: Impersonal sex in public places* (enlarged edition with a retrospect on ethical issues). Aldine Transaction. (Originally published 1970)

Jackson, N. A., Pate, M., & Campbell, K. M. (2021). Prison and post-release experiences of innocent inmates. *Journal of Aggression, Maltreatment & Trauma, 30*(10), 1347–1365. https://doi.org/10.1080/10926771.2020.1866136

Johnson, J. M., & Rowlands, T. (2012). The interpersonal dynamics of in-depth interviewing. In J. F. Gubrium, J. A. Holstein, A. B. Marvasti, & K. D. McKinney (Eds.), *The Sage handbook of interview research: The complexity of the craft* (2nd ed., pp. 99–114). Sage.

King, N., & Horrocks, C. (2010). *Interviews in qualitative research*. Sage.

King, S. A. (1996). Researching internet communities: Proposed ethical guidelines for the reporting of results. *The Information Society: An International Journal, 12*(2). https://doi.org/10.1080/713856145

Kozinets, R. (1998). On netnography: Initial reflections on consumer research investigations of cyberculture. In J. W. Alba & J. W. Hutchinson (Eds.), *Advances in Consumer Research* (Vol. 25, pp. 366–371). Association for Consumer Research.

Kozinets, R. (2002). The field behind the screen: Using netnography for marketing research in online communities. *Journal of Marketing Research, 39*(1), 61–72. https://doi.org/10.1509/jmkr.39.1.61.18935

Kozinets, R. (2020). *Netnography: The essential guide to qualitative social media research*. Sage.

Krueger, R. A., & Casey, M. A. (2015). *Focus groups: A practical guide for applied research* (5th ed.). Sage.

Lincoln, Y. S., & Guba, E. G. (1985). *Naturalistic inquiry*. Sage.

Lofland, J., & Lofland, L. H. (1995). *Analyzing social settings: A guide to qualitative observation and analysis* (3rd ed.). Wadsworth.

Lofland, J., Snow, D., Anderson, L., & Lofland, L. H. (2006). *Analyzing social settings: A guide to qualitative observation and analysis* (4th ed.). Wadsworth/Thompson Learning.

Lumsden, K., & Winter, A. (2014). Reflexivity in criminological research. In K. Lumsden & A. Winter (Eds.), *Reflexivity in criminological research* (pp. 1–19). Palgrave Macmillan.

Martin, L. (2018). "Free but still walking the yard": Prisonization and the problems of reentry. *Journal of Contemporary Ethnography, 47*(5), 671–694.

McKinney, J. C. (1966). *Constructive typology and social theory*. Appleton-Century-Crofts.

Merton, R. K. (1972). Insiders and outsiders: A chapter in the sociology of knowledge. *American Journal of Sociology, 78*(1), 9–47.

Miles, M. B., & Huberman, A. M. (1994). *Qualitative data analysis: An expanded sourcebook* (2nd ed.). Sage.

Morgan, D. (1996). Focus groups. *Annual Review of Sociology, 22*, 129–152.

Morgan, D. (2012). Focus groups and social interaction. In J. F. Gubrium, J. A. Holstein, A. B. Marvasti, & K. D. McKinney (Eds.), *The Sage handbook of interview research: The complexity of the craft* (pp. 161–176). Sage.

Rubin, H. J., & Rubin, I. S. (2012). *Qualitative interviewing: The art of hearing the data* (3rd ed.). Sage.

Saldaña, J. (2011). *Fundamentals of qualitative research: Understanding qualitative research*. Oxford University Press.

Saldaña, J. 2013. *The coding manual for qualitative researchers* (2nd ed.). Sage.

Scheper-Hughes, N. (2004). Parts unknown: Undercover ethnography of the organs-trafficking underworld. *Ethnography, 5*, 29–73. https://doi.org/10.1177/1466138104041588

Schwartz-Shea, P., & Yanow, D. (2012). *Interpretive research design: Concepts and processes*. Routledge.

Sim, J., & Waterfield, J. (2019). Focus group methodology: Some ethical challenges. *Quality & Quantity, 53*, 3003–3022. https://doi.org/10.1007/s11135-019-00914-5

Smith, C., Spinelli, M. B., & Klofas, J. (2017). Community views on criminal justice: Methodology. Rochester Institute of Technology. https://www.rit.edu/liberalarts/sites/rit.edu.liberalarts/files/documents/our-work/Comm%20Views%20-%20Methodology%20-%20final%20-%204.11.17.pdf

Smith, R. C. (2006). *Mexican New York: Transnational lives of new immigrants*. University of California Press.

Snow, D. A., & Anderson, L. (1991). Researching the homeless: The characteristic features and virtues of the case study. In J. R. Feagin, A. M. Orum, & G. Sjoberg (Eds.), *A case for the case study* (pp. 148–173). University of North Carolina Press.

Snow, D. A., & Anderson. L. (1993). *Down on their luck: A study of homeless street people*. University of California Press.

Snow, D. A., Benford, R. D., & Anderson, L. (1986). Fieldwork roles and information yield: A comparison of alternative settings and roles. *Urban Life, 14*(4), 377–408.

Stuart, F. (2020). Code of the tweet: Urban gang violence in the social media age. *Social Problems*, 67(2), 191–207. https://doi.org/10.1093/socpro/spz010

Taylor, S. J., & Bogdan, R. (1998). *Introduction to qualitative research methods: A guidebook and resource* (3rd ed.). Wiley.

Townsley, M., & Grimshaw, R. (2013). The consequences of queueing: Crowding, situation features and aggression in entertainment precincts. *Crime Prevention and Community Safety*, 15(1), 23–47.

Vasquez, J. (2011). *Mexican Americans across generations*. New York University Press.

Venkatesh, S. (2008). *Gang leader for a day: A rogue sociologist takes to the streets*. Penguin.

Weiss, R. (2004). In their own words: Making the most of qualitative interviews. *Contexts*, 3(4), 44–51.

CHAPTER 11

Arthur, M. M. L. (2011). The neglected virtues of comparative-historical methods. In I. Zake & M. DeCesare (Eds.), *New directions in sociology: Essays on theory and methodology in the 21st century* (pp. 172–192). McFarland and Company.

Brady, H. E. (2019). The challenge of big data and data science. *Annual Review of Political Science*, 22, 297–323.

Bureau of Justice Statistics. (2021). Survey of Prison Inmates, United States, 2016. *Inter-university Consortium for Political and Social Research*. https://doi.org/10.3886/ICPSR37692.v2

Campbell, M. C., & Schoenfeld, H. (2013). The transformation of America's penal order: A historical political sociology of punishment. *American Journal of Sociology* 118(5), 1375–1423.

Chairassamee, N. (2018). Crimes and moving decision in the United States: A conditional logit approach. *Applied Economics Journal*, 25(1), 1–14.

Christenson, P., Roberts, D. F., & Bjork, N. (2012). Booze, drugs, and pop music: Trends in substance portrayals in the Billboard Top 100—1968-2008. *Substance Use and Misuse* 47(2), 121–129.

Colburn, A., & Melander, L. A. (2018). Beyond black and white: An analysis of newspaper representations of alleged criminal offenders based on race and ethnicity. *Journal of Contemporary Criminal Justice*, 34(4), 383–398.

Corrigan, P. (2004). How stigma interferes with mental health care. *American Psychologist*, 59, 614–625. doi: 10.1037/0003-066X.59.7.614

Dominick, J. R., (1973). Crime and law enforcement on prime-time television. *The Public Opinion Quarterly*, 37(2), 241–250.

Eigenberg, H. M., & Park, S. (2016). Marginalization and invisibility of women of color: A content analysis of race and gender images in introductory criminal justice and criminology texts. *Race & Justice*, 6(3), 257–279.

Everhart, K., & Aust, P. J. (2006). What is your child watching? A content analysis of violence in Disney animated films: Scene 1. *The Kentucky Journal of Communication*, 25(2), 101–127.

Geddes, B. (1990). How the cases you choose affect the answers you get: Selection bias in comparative politics. *Political Analysis*, 2, 131–150.

Golder, S. A., & Macy, M. W. (2014). Digital footprints: Opportunities and challenges for online social research. *Annual Review of Sociology*, 40, 129–152.

Grau, A. B. (2021). Multifaceted offenders and minimization of victims: U.S. national news media coverage of offenders and victims in coverage of filicide. *American Journal of Qualitative Research*, 5(1), 185–205.

Humphries, D. (1981). Serious crime, news coverage, and ideology: A content analysis of crime coverage in a metropolitan paper. *Crime & Delinquency*, 27(2), 191–205. https://doi.org/10.1177/001112878102700202

IPUMS USA. (2020). IPUMS USA. https://usa.ipums.org/usa/

Jenkins, J. C., Slomczynski, K. M., & Dubrow, J. K. (2016). Political behavior and big data. *International Journal of Sociology*, 46(1), 1–7.

Kane, R. J., & White, M. D. (2009). Bad cops: A study of career-ending misconduct among New York City police officers. *Criminology & Public Policy*, 8(4), 737–769.

Keuschnigg, M., & Wolbring, T. (2015). Disorder, social capital, and norm violation: Three field experiments on the broken windows thesis. *Rationality and Society*, 27(1), 96–126.

Kitchin, R. (2014). *The data revolution: Big data, open data, data infrastructures and their consequences*. Sage.

Krippendorff, K. (2004). *Content analysis: An introduction to its methodology* (2nd ed.). Sage.

Kudla, D., & Parnaby, P. (2018). To serve and to tweet: An examination of police-related Twitter activity in Toronto. *Social Media + Society*, 4(3), 1–13.

Lahm, K. (2016). Official incidents of inmate-on-inmate misconduct at a women's prison: Using importation and deprivation theories to compare perpetrators to victims. *Criminal Justice Studies, 29*(3), 214–231.

Lange, M. (2013). *Comparative-historical methods*. Sage.

Lavorgna, A., & Ugwudike, P. (2021). The datafication revolution in criminal justice: An empirical exploration of frames portraying data-driven technologies for crime prevention and control. *Big Data & Society, 8*(2). https://doi.org/10.1177/20539517211049670

Lazer, D., & Radford, J. (2017). Data ex machina: Introduction to big data. *Annual Review of Sociology, 43*, 19–39.

Lewis, K. (2015). Three fallacies of digital footprints. *Big Data and Society, 2*(July–December), 1–4.

Light, M. T., & Thomas, J. T. (2019). Segregation and violence reconsidered: Do whites benefit from residential segregation? *American Sociological Review, 84*(4), 690–725.

Link, B. G., & Phelan, J. C. (2014). Mental illness stigma and the sociology of mental health. In R. J. Johnson, R. J. Turner, & B. G. Link (Eds.), *Sociology of mental health: Selected topics from forty years, 1970s–2010s* (pp. 75–100). Springer International Publishing.

Mahoney, J. (2000). Strategies of causal inference in small-N analysis. *Sociological Methods and Research, 28*(4), 387–424.

Mahoney, J. (2004). Comparative-historical methodology. *Annual Review of Sociology, 30*, 81–101.

Mahoney, J., & Rueschemeyer, D. (2003). Comparative historical analysis: Achievements and agendas. In J. Mahoney & D. Rueschemeyer (Eds.), *Comparative historical analysis in the social sciences* (pp. 3–38). Cambridge University Press.

Malamuth, N. M., & Spinner, B. (1980). A longitudinal content analysis of sexual violence in the best-selling erotic magazines. *Journal of Sex Research, 16*(3), 226–237. https://doi.org/10.1080/00224498009551079

Marr, B. (2017, March 14). The complete beginner's guide to big data everyone can understand. *Forbes*. https://t.co/myDvEKgwTy

McFarland, D. A., Lewis, K., & Goldberg, A. (2016). Sociology in the era of big data: The ascent of forensic social science. *American Sociologist, 47*(1), 12–35.

Metcalf, J., & Crawford, K. (2016). Where are human subjects in big data research? The emerging ethics divide. *Big Data and Society, 3*, 1–14.

Myers, B., Nuñez, N., Wilkowski, B., Kehn, A., & Dunn, K. (2018). The heterogeneity of victim impact statements: A content analysis of capital trial sentencing penalty phase transcripts. *Psychology, Public Policy, and Law, 24*(4), 474–488. https://doi.org/10.1037/law0000185

Neuendorf, K. A. (2002). *A content analysis guidebook*. Sage.

Neuendorf, K. A. (2011). Content analysis—A methodological primer for gender research. *Sex Roles: A Journal of Research, 64*(3–4), 276–289. https://doi.org/10.1007/s11199-010-9893-0

Oh, G., Zhang, Y., & Greenleaf, R. G. (2022). Measuring geographic sentiment toward police using social media data. *American Journal of Criminal Justice, 47*, 924–940. https://doi.org/10.1007/s12103-021-09614-z

Parrott, S., & Parrott, C. T. (2015). Law & disorder: The portrayal of mental illness in U.S. crime dramas. *Journal of Broadcasting and Electronic Media, 59*(4), 640–657.

Quinn, J. W., Mooney, S. J., Sheehan, D. M., Teitler, J. O., Neckerman, K. M., Kaufman, T. K., Lovasi, G. S., Bader, M. D., & Rundle, A. G. (2016). Neighborhood physical disorder in New York City. *Journal of Maps, 12*(1), 53–60.

Ragin, C. C. (1987). *The comparative method: Moving beyond qualitative and quantitative strategies*. University of California Press.

Ragin, C. C. (2006). How to lure analytic social science out of the doldrums: Some lessons from comparative research. *International Sociology, 21*(5), 633–646.

Rueschemeyer, D., & Stephens, J. (1997). Comparing social historical sequences: A powerful tool for causal analysis. *Comparative Social Research, 17*, 55–72.

Rummens, A., Snaphaan, T., Van de Weghe, N. Van den Poel, D., Pauwels, L. J. R., & Hardyns, W. (2021). Do mobile phone data provide a better denominator in crime rates and improve spatiotemporal predictions of crime? *International Journal of Geo-Information, 10*(6), 369–387. https://doi.org/10.3390/ijgi10060369

Sampson R. J., & Raudenbush, S. W. (1999). Systematic social observation of public spaces: A new look at disorder in urban neighborhoods. *American Journal of Sociology, 105*, 603–51.

Schwartz, G. L., & Jahn, J. L. (2020). Mapping fatal police violence across U.S. metropolitan areas: Overall rates and racial/ethnic inequities, 2013–2017. *PLoS One, 15*(6), 1–16.

Shelton, A. K., & Skalski, P. (2014). Blinded by the light: Illuminating the dark side of social network use through content analysis. *Computers in Human Behavior, 33*, 339–348.

Skocpol, T. (2003). Double engaged social science: The promise of comparative historical analysis. In J. Mahoney & D. Rueschemeyer (Eds.), *Comparative historical analysis in the social sciences* (pp. 407–428). Cambridge University Press.

Tiesman, H. M., Gwilliam, M., Konda, S., Rojek, J., & Marsh, S. (2018). Nonfatal injuries to law enforcement officers: A rise in assaults. *American Journal of Preventive Medicine, 54*(4), 503–509.

Wahl, O. F. (2003). *Media madness: Public images of mental illness*. Rutgers University Press.

Weber, R. P. (1990). *Basic content analysis* (2nd ed.). Sage.

Webster, F., Rice, K., & Sud, A. (2020). A critical content analysis of media reporting on opioids: The social construction of an epidemic. *Social Science & Medicine, 244*, 1–9.

Wilson, B. J., Kunkel, D., Linz, D. Potter, J., Donnerstein, E., Smith, S., Blumenthal, E., & Berry, M. (1997). *National Television Violence Study, Vol. 1, Part I: Violence in television programming overall*. Sage.

Wilson, J. Q., & Kelling, G. L. (1982, March). Broken windows: The police and neighborhood safety. *Atlantic Monthly*. https://www.theatlantic.com/magazine/archive/1982/03/broken-windows/304465/

Zook, M., Barocas, S., Boyd, D., Crawford, K., Keller, E., Gangadharan, S. P., Goodman, A., Hollander, R., Koenig, B. A., Metcalf, J., Narayanan, A., Nelson, A., & Pasquale, F. (2017). Ten simple rules for responsible big data research. *PLoS Computational Biology, 13*(3), e1005399. https://doi.org/10.1371/journal.pcbi.1005399

CHAPTER 12

Ariel, B., Farrar, W. A., & Sutherland, A. (2015). The effect of police body-worn cameras on use of force and citizens' complaints against the police: A randomized control trial. *Journal of Quantitative Criminology, 31*, 509–535. https://doi.org/10.1007/s10940-014-9236-3

Barrington, G. V., & Triana-Tremain, B. (2022). *Evaluation time*. Sage.

Braga, A. A., Hureau, D. M., & Papachristos, A. V. (2011). An ex post facto evaluation framework for place-based police interventions. *Evaluation Review, 35*(6), 592–626. https://doi.org/10.1177/0193841X11433827

Chen, H.-T. (1990). *Theory-driven evaluations*. Sage.

Collins, S. E., Lonczak, H. S., & Clifasefi, S. L. (2019). Seattle's law enforcement assisted diversion (LEAD): Program effects on criminal justice and legal system utilization and costs. *Journal of Experimental Criminology, 15*, 201–211. https://doi.org/10.1007/s11292-019-09352-7

Damschroder, L. J., Aron, D. C., Keith, R. E., Kirsh, S. R., Alexander, J. A., & Lowery, J. C. (2009). Fostering implementation of health services research findings into practice: A consolidated framework for advancing implementation science. *Implementation Science, 4*(50), 1–15. https://doi.org/10.1186/1748-5908-4-50

Densley, J. A., Adler, J. R., Zhu, L., & Lambine, M. (2017). Growing against gangs and violence: Findings from a process and outcome evaluation. *Psychology of Violence, 7*(2), 242–252. https://psycnet.apa.org/doi/10.1037/vio0000054

Ebener, P. A., Hunter, S. B, Adams, R. M., Eisenman, D., Acosta, J. D., & Chinman, M. (2017). *Getting to outcomes: Guide for community emergency preparedness*. Rand.

Engel, R. S., Corsaro, N., Isaza, G. T., & McManus, H. D. (2020). *Examining the impact of Integrating Communications, Assessment, and Tactics (ICAT) de-escalation training for the Louisville Metro Police Department: Initial findings*. International Association of Chiefs of Police.

Engel, R. S., Corsaro, N., Isaza, G. T., & McManus, H. D. (2022). Assessing the impact of de-escalation training on police behavior: Reducing police use of force in the Louisville, KY Metro Police Department. *Criminology & Public Policy, 21*, 199–233. doi: 10.1111/1745-9133.12574

Farrington, D. P., & Kogel, C. J. (2015). Monetary benefits and costs of the Stop Now and Plan program for boys aged 6–11, based on the prevention of later offending. *Journal of Quantitative Criminology, 31*, 263–287. https://doi.org/10.1007/s10940-014-9240-7

Finckenauer, J. O., Margaryan, S., & Sullivan, M. L. (2005). Evaluability assessment in juvenile justice: A case example. *Youth Violence and Juvenile Justice, 3*(3), 265–275. https://doi.org/10.1177/1541204005276267

Garrett, B. L. (2018). Evidence-informed criminal justice. *George Washington Law Review, 86*, 1490–1524. https://scholarship.law.duke.edu/faculty_scholarship/3910

Hannah, G., McCarthy, S., & Chinman, M. (2011). *Getting to outcomes in services for homeless veterans: 10 Steps for achieving accountability*. National Center on Homelessness Among Veterans.

Hodgkinson, W., Ariel, B., & Harinam, V. (2023). Comparing panic alarm systems for high-risk domestic abuse victims: A randomised controlled trial on prevention and criminal justice system outcomes. *Journal of*

Experimental Criminology, 19, 595–613. https://doi.org/10.1007/s11292-022-09505-1

Justice Research and Statistics Association (JRSA). (2003). *Evaluability assessment: Examining the readiness of a program for evaluation.* Program Evaluation Briefing Series #6. Office of Juvenile Justice and Delinquency Prevention.

Lobmeier, J. (2010). Nonexperimental designs. In N. J. Salkind (Ed.), *Encyclopedia of research design* (pp. 911–915). Sage.

Pawson, R., & Tilley, N. (1997). *Realistic evaluation.* Sage.

Pear, V. A., Schleimer, J. P., Tomsich, E., Pallin, R., Charbonneau, A., Wintemute, G. J., & Knoepke, C. E. (2021). Implementation and perceived effectiveness of gun violence restraining orders in California: A qualitative evaluation. *PLoS ONE 16*(10). https://doi.org/10.1371/journal.pone.0258547

Rennison, C. M., & Hart, T. C. (2018). *Research methods in criminal justice and criminology.* Sage.

Rogers, P. J. (2000). Program theory: Not whether programs work but how they work. In D. L. Stufflebeam, G. F. Madaus, & T. Kellaghan (Eds.), *Evaluation models* (pp. 209–232). Springer.

Rossi, P. H., Lipsey, M. W., & Freeman, H. E. (2004). *Evaluation: A systematic approach* (7th ed.). Sage.

Rutman, L. (1980). *Planning useful evaluations: Evaluability assessment.* Sage.

Salabarría-Peña, Y., Apt, B. S., & Walsh, C. M. (2007). *Practical use of program evaluation among sexually transmitted disease (STD) programs.* Centers for Disease Control and Prevention.

Shirk, J. L., Ballard, H. L., Wilderman, C. C., Phillips, T., Wiggins, A., Jordan, R., McCallie, E., Minarchek, M., Lewenstein, B. V., Krasny, M. E., & Bonnie, R. (2012). Public participation in scientific research: A framework for deliberate design. *Ecology and Society, 17*(2), 29–48.

Simpson, A., & Eraser, N. M. (1993). Black box and glass box evaluation of the SUNDIAL system. In *Proceedings of Third European Conference on Speech Communication and Technology (Eurospeech 1993).* Berlin, September (pp. 1423–1426).

Soriano, F. I. (2013). *Conducting needs assessments: A multidisciplinary approach.* Sage.

Stephens, D. W. (2022). Developing and sustaining police–researcher partnerships. *Policing: A Journal of Policy and Practice, 16*(3), 344–354. https://doi.org/10.1093/police/paac035

Stokes, N., & Clare, J. (2019). Preventing near-repeat residential burglary through cocooning: Post hoc evaluation of a targeted police-led pilot intervention. *Security Journal, 32*, 45–62. https://doi.org/10.1057/s41284-018-0144-3

Sussman, S., Skara, S., & Pumpuang, P. (2008). Project Towards No Drug Abuse (TND). Needs assessment of a social service referral telephone program for high risk youth. *Substance Use & Misuses, 43*(14), 2066–2073. https://doi.org/10.1080%2F10826080802290208

Van Voorhis, P., & Brown, K. (1996). *Evaluability assessment: A tool for program development in corrections.* National Institute for Corrections.

Vito, G. F., & Higgins, G. E. (2014). *Practical program evaluation for criminal justice.* Elsevier.

Welsh, W. N. (2006). The need for a comprehensive approach to program planning, development, and evaluation. *Criminology & Public Policy, 5*(3), 603–614.

CHAPTER 13

Brewer, J., & Hunter, A. (1989). *Multimethod research: A synthesis of styles.* Sage.

Caracelli, V. J., & Greene, J. C. (1997). Crafting mixed-method evaluation designs. *New Directions for Evaluation, 74*, 19–32. https://doi.org/10.1002/ev.1069

Creswell, J. W., & Plano Clark, V. L. (2017). *Designing and conducting mixed methods research.* Sage.

Dodd, S., Antrobus, E., & Sydes, M. (2020). Cameras in corrections: Exploring the views of correctional officers on the introduction of body-worn cameras in prisons. *Criminal Justice and Behavior, 47*(9), 1190–1208. https://doi.org/10.1177/0093854820942288

Greene, J. C. (2007). *Mixed methods in social inquiry.* Jossey-Bass.

Greene, J. C., Caracelli, V. J., & Graham, W. F. (1989). Toward a conceptual framework for mixed-method evaluation designs. *Educational Evaluation and Policy Analysis, 11*(3), 255–274. https://doi.org/10.3102%2F01623737011003255

Guerra, N. G., Williams, K. R., & Sadek, S. (2011). Understanding bullying and victimization during childhood and adolescence: A mixed methods study. *Child Development, 82*(1), 295–310. https://doi.org/10.1111/j.1467-8624.2010.01556.x

Leahey, E. (2007). Convergence and confidentiality? Limits to the interpretation of mixed methodology. *Social Science*

Research, 36(1), 149–158. https://doi.org/10.1016/j.ssresearch.2005.10.003

Lieberman, E. S. (2005). Nested analysis as a mixed-method strategy for comparative research. *American Political Science Review, 99*(3), 435–452. https://doi.org/10.1017/S0003055405051762

Mark, M. M. (2015). Mixed and multimethods in predominantly quantitative studies, especially experiments and quasi-experiments. In S. Hesse-Baber & R. B. Johnson (Eds.), *The Oxford handbook of multimethod and mixed methods research inquiry* (pp. 21–41). Oxford University Press.

Mark, M. M., & Shotland, R. L. (1987). Alternative models for the use of multiple methods. In M. M. Mark & R. L. Shotland (Eds.), *Multiple methods in program evaluation* (pp. 95–100). Jossey-Bass.

Pager, D. (2003). The mark of a criminal record. *American Journal of Sociology, 108*(5), 937–975. https://doi.org/10.1086/374403

Pager, D., & Quillian, L. (2005). Walking the talk? What employers say versus what they do. *American Sociological Review, 70*(3), 355–380. https://doi.org/10.1177/000312240507000301

Pager, D., Western, B., & Bonikowski, B. (2009). Discrimination in a low wage labor market: A field experiment. *American Sociological Review, 74*(5), 777–799. https://doi.org/10.1177/000312240907400505

Pearce, L. D. (2012). Mixed methods inquiry in sociology. *American Behavioral Scientist, 56*(6), 829–848. https://doi.org/10.1177/0002764211433798

Small, M. L. (2011). How to conduct a mixed methods study: Recent trends in a rapidly growing literature. *Annual Review of Sociology, 37*, 57–86. https://doi.org/10.1146/annurev.soc.012809.102657

Tashakkori, A., & Teddlie C. (Eds.). (2010). *Sage Handbook of mixed methods in social and behavioral research* (2nd ed.). Sage.

Timans, R., Wouters, P., & Heilbron, J. (2019). Mixed methods research: What it is and what it could be. *Theory and Society, 48*(2), 193–216. https://doi.org/10.1007/s11186-019-09345-5

Yoshikawa, H., Weisner, T. S., Kalil, A., & Way, N. (2008). Mixing qualitative and quantitative research in developmental science: Uses and methodological choices. *Developmental Psychology, 44*(2), 344–354. https://doi.org/10.1037/0012-1649.44.2.344

CHAPTER 14

Amialchuk, A., & Sapci, O. (2021). The influence of normative misperceptions on alcohol-related problems among school-age adolescents in the U.S. *Review of Economics of the Household, 19*, 453–472. https://doi.org/10.1007/s11150-020-09481-3

Ariel, B., Farrar, W. A., & Sutherland, A. (2015). The effect of police body-worn cameras on use of force and citizens' complaints against the police: A randomized control trial. *Journal of Quantitative Criminology, 31*, 509–535. https://doi.org/10.1007/s10940-014-9236-3

Baumer, E. P., Cundiff, K., & Luo, L. (2021). The contemporary transformation of American youth: An analysis of change in the prevalence of delinquency, 1991–2015. *Criminology, 59*(1), 109–136. https://doi.org/10.1111/1745-9125.12264

Davis, J. A. (1971). *Elementary survey analysis*. Prentice-Hall.

Davis, J. A., & Smith, T. W. (1992). *The NORC General Social Survey: A user's guide*. Sage.

LaFree, G., Jensen, M. A., James, P. A., & Safer-Lichtenstein, A. (2018). Correlates of violent political extremism in the United States. *Criminology, 56*(2), 233–268. https://doi.org/10.1111/1745-9125.12169

Lane, D. M. (2014). Logic of hypothesis testing. *Online statistics education: An interactive multimedia course of study*. Rice University. https://onlinestatbook.com/2/logic_of_hypothesis_testing/intro.html

Lucas, J. W., Graif, C., & Lovaglia, M. J. (2006). Misconduct in the prosecution of severe crimes: Theory and experimental test. *Social Psychology Quarterly, 69*(1), 97–107. https://www.jstor.org/stable/20141730

McKnight, P. E., McKnight, K. M., Sidani, S., & Figueredo, A. J. (2007). *Missing data: A gentle introduction*. Guilford.

Pate, M., & Bolin, R. M. (2019). Examining the relationship between strain and the use of nonmedical prescription drugs among college students. *Journal of Drug Issues, 49*(1), 163–182. https://doi.org/10.1177/0022042618812398

Rosenberg, M. (1968). *The logic of survey analysis*. Basic Books.

Shaver, J. (1993). What statistical significance testing is, and what it is not. *Journal of Experimental Education, 61*(4), 293–316. https://www.jstor.org/stable/20152383

Smith, T. W., Davern, M., Freese, J., & Morgan, S. L. (2019). *General Social Surveys, 1972–2018: Cumulative codebook* [machine-readable data file]. National Opinion

Research Center. 1 data file (64,814 logical records) and 1 codebook (3,758 pp).

CHAPTER 15

Campbell, J. L., Quincy, C., Osserman, J., & Pedersen, O. K. (2013). Coding in-depth semistructured interviews: Problems of unitization and intercoder reliability and agreement. *Sociological Methods & Research, 42*(3), 294–320. https://doi.org/10.1177/0049124113500475

Charmaz, K. (2006). *Constructing grounded theory: A practical guide through qualitative analysis.* Sage.

Charmaz, K. (2014). *Constructing grounded theory* (2nd ed.). Sage.

Charmaz, K., & Belgrave, L. L. (2012). Qualitative interviewing and grounded theory analysis. In J. F. Gubrium, J. A. Holstein, A. B. Marvasti, & K. D. McKinney (Eds.), *The Sage handbook of interview research: The complexity of the craft* (2nd ed., pp. 347–366). Sage.

Cooley, B. N. (2022). Desistance from sexual offending or not reoffending. *Criminology, Criminal Justice, Law & Society, 23*(1), 68–84. https://doi.org/10.54555/ccjls.4234.34105

Corbin, J., & Strauss, A. (2015). *Basics of qualitative research* (4th ed.). Sage.

Emerson, R. M., Fretz, R. I., & Shaw, L. L. (2011). *Writing ethnographic fieldnotes* (2nd ed.). University of Chicago Press.

Franzosi, R. (1998). Narrative analysis—or why (and how) sociologists should be interested in narrative. *Annual Review of Sociology, 24,* 517–554. http://www.jstor.org/stable/223492

Garfinkel, H. (1967). *Studies in ethnomethodology.* Prentice-Hall.

Gibbs, G. R. (2018). *Analyzing qualitative data* (2nd ed.). Sage.

Glaser, B. G. (1978). *Theoretical sensitivity.* Sociology Press.

Glaser, B. G., & Strauss, A. L. (1967). *The discovery of grounded theory: Strategies for qualitative research.* Aldine.

Heritage, J. (2004). Conversation analysis and institutional talk. In K. L. Fitch & R. E. Sanders (Eds.), *Handbook of language and social interaction* (pp. 103–147). Erlbaum.

Jefferson, G. (2004). Glossary of transcript symbols with an introduction. In G. H. Lerner (Ed.), *Conversation analysis: Studies from the first generation* (pp. 13–23). John Benjamins.

Johnson, I. M. (2015). Women parolees' perceptions of parole experiences and parole officers. *American Journal of Criminal Justice, 40,* 785–810. https://doi.org/10.1007/s12103-014-9284-0

Kelly, J. F., & Ward, C. L. (2020). Narratives of gang disengagement among former gang members in South Africa. *Criminal Justice & Behavior, 47*(11), 1509–1528. https://doi.org/10.1177/0093854820949603

Kennedy, A. C., Meier, E., & Prock, K. A. (2021). A qualitative study of young women's abusive first relationships: What factors shape their process of disclosure? *Journal of Family Violence, 36,* 849–864. https://doi.org/10.1007/s10896-021-00258-5

Labov, W. (1972). *Language in the inner city.* University of Pennsylvania Press.

Lofland, J., Snow, D., Anderson, L., & Lofland, L. H. (2006). *Analyzing social settings: A guide to qualitative observation and analysis* (4th ed.). Wadsworth/Thompson Learning.

Martin, L. (2018). "Free but still walking the yard": Prisonization and the problems of reentry. *Journal of Contemporary Ethnography, 47*(5), 671–694. https://doi.org/10.1177/0891241617737814

Maynard, D. W., & Clayman, S. E. (1991). The diversity of ethnomethodology. *Annual Review of Sociology, 17,* 385–418. https://doi.org/10.1146/annurev.so.17.080191.002125

McPherson, G., & Thorne, S. (2006). Exploiting exceptions to enhance interpretive qualitative health research: Insights from a study of cancer communication. *International Journal of Qualitative Methods, 5*(2), 73–86. https://doi.org/10.1177/160940690600500210

Miles, M. B., Huberman, A. M., & Saldaña, J. (2020). *Qualitative data analysis: An expanded sourcebook* (4th ed.). Sage.

Murray, C. (2009). Typologies of young resisters and desisters. *Youth Justice, 9*(2), 115–129. https://doi.org/10.1177/1473225409105491

Nelson, L. K. (2020). Computational grounded theory: A methodological framework. *Sociological Methods & Research, 49*(1), 3–42. https://doi.org/10.1177/0049124117729703

Noel Monde, M. E., & Green, C. (2022). "I literally roll with the punches": Black and Latina women coping through parental incarceration. *Journal of Qualitative Criminal Justice and Criminology, 11*(3), 383–415. https://doi.org/10.21428/88de04a1.a9c93b41

Patterson, W. (2008). Narratives of events: Labovian narrative analysis and its limitations. In M. Andrews, C. Squire, & M. Tamboukou (Eds.), *Doing narrative research* (pp. 22–40). Sage.

Rapley, T. (2018). *Doing conversation, discourse and document analysis* (2nd ed.). Sage.

Riessman, C. K. (2012). Analysis of personal narratives. In J. F. Gubrium, J. A. Holstein, A. B. Marvasti, & K. D. McKinney (Eds.), *The Sage handbook of interview research: The complexity of the craft* (2nd ed., pp. 367–379). Sage.

Rossman, G., & Rallis, S. F. (2003). *Learning in the field: An introduction to qualitative research*. Sage.

Rubin, H. J., & Rubin, I. S. (2012). *Qualitative interviewing: The art of hearing data* (3rd ed.). Sage.

Sacks, H., Schegloff, E. A., & Jefferson, G. (1974). A simplest systematics for the organization of turn-taking for conversation. *Language*, 50(4), 696–735. https://www.jstor.org/stable/412243

Saldaña, J. (2011). *Fundamentals of qualitative research: Understanding qualitative research*. Oxford University Press.

Saldaña, J. (2013). *The coding manual for qualitative researchers* (2nd ed.). Sage.

Scheper-Hughes, N. (2004). Parts unknown: Undercover ethnography of the organs-trafficking underworld. *Ethnography*, 5, 29–73. https://doi.org/10.1177/1466138104041588

Strauss, A., & Corbin, J. (1990). *Basics of qualitative research: Grounded theory procedures and techniques*. Sage.

Ten Have, P. (2006). Review essay: Conversation analysis versus other approaches to discourse. *Forum: Qualitative Social Research*, 7(2). https://doi.org/10.17169/fqs-7.2.100

Wertz, F. J., Charmaz, K., McMullen, L. M., Josselson, R., Anderson, R., & McSpadden, E. (2011). *Five ways of doing qualitative analysis: Phenomenological psychology, grounded theory, discourse analysis, narrative research, and intuitive inquiry*. Guilford Press.

Zimmerman, D. H. (1984). Talk and its occasion: The case of calling the police. In D. Schiffrin (Ed.), *Meaning, form and use in context: Linguistic applications Georgetown round-table on languages and linguistics* (pp. 210–228). Georgetown University Press.

Zimmerman, D. H. (1992). The interactional organization of calls for emergency assistance. In P. Drew & J. Heritage (Eds.), *Talk at work: Interaction in institutional settings* (pp. 418–469). Cambridge University Press.

Credits

PHOTO CREDITS

Chapter 1
(Photo 1.1) Katleho Seisa/Getty Images

Chapter 2
(Photo 2.1) South Agency/Getty Images; (Photo 2.2) Courtesy of AT&T Archives and History Center

Chapter 4
(Photo 4.1) Philip G. Zimbardo, Inc; c/o Jackie Wagner Permissions Administrator Philip G. Zimbardo, Inc.; (Photo 4.2) From the film OBEDIENCE © 1968; (Photo 4.3) Everett Collection Historical/Alamy Stock Photo

Chapter 5
(Photo 5.1) Jaromir Chalabala/Shutterstock

Chapter 6
(Photo 6.1) Martin Shields/Alamy Stock Photo

Chapter 8
(Photo 8.1) Photo by James Levin, The Diamondback; (Photo 8.2) Courtesy of Corina Graif; (Photo 8.3) Courtesy of Michael Lovaglia

Chapter 9
(Photo 9.1) Yemen Polling Center

Chapter 13
(Photo 13.1) Courtesy of Devah Pager

FIGURE CREDITS

Chapter 3
Figure 3.4: Demir, M., & Park, S. (2022). The effect of COVID-19 on domestic violence and assaults. *Criminal Justice Review, 47*(4), 445–463. https://doi.org/10.1177/07340168211061160.

Chapter 4
Figure 4.1: 1933 letter to "subjects" in Tuskegee Syphilis Experiment, National Archives; commentary at side from *Tuskegee Truths* (Reverby, 2000:187).

Chapter 6
Figure 6.4: Source: Krysan, M., & Farley, R. "The residential preference of Blacks: Do they explain persistent segregation?" *Social Forces, 80*(3) 937–980. Copyright © 2002 The University of North Carolina Press/Oxford University Press.

Chapter 7
Figure 7.3: https://www.random.org/integers/

Chapter 8
Figure 8.1: Source: Pager, D., "The mark of a criminal record," *American Journal of Sociology, 108*(5), Fig. 3, p. 948. Copyright © 2003 The University of Chicago Press.

Chapter 11
Figure 11.2: What is your child watching? A content analysis of violence in Disney animated films: Scene I. Source: Kentucky Journal of Communication. Fall 2006, Vol. 25 Issue 2, pp. 101–125. 25p. Author(s): Everhart, Kimberly; Aust, Philip J.

Chapter 13
Figure 13.2: Copyright © 2005 American Sociological Association; Figure 13.3: Copyright © 2009 American Sociological Association; Figure 13.4: Copyright © 2009 American Sociological Association

Chapter 14
Box 14.1 Figure A: Codebook entry from GSS Cumulative Data File, 1972–2018.

Chapter 15
Figure 15.4: Copyright 1984 by Georgetown University Press. "Example 4" from "Talk and Its Occasion: The Case of Calling the Police" by Don H. Zimmerman. From *Meaning, Form, and Use in Context: Linguistic Applications*, edited by Deborah Schiffrin, pp. 214. Reprinted with permission. www.press.georgetown.edu.

TABLE CREDITS

Chapter 5
Table 5.2: National Election Poll 2020 Presidential Election Exit Poll; data provided by Edison Research.

Chapter 8
Table 8.1: Adapted from Table 1 in Lucas et al. (2006, p.103); Table 8.2: Adapted from Figure 1 in Salerno and Sanchez (2020, p. 104).

Chapter 11
Table 11.3: Table 3 in Campbell and Schoenfeld (2013, p. 1389).

Chapter 12
Table 12.1: Adapted from Salabarría-Peña, Apt, & Walsh (2007); Table 12.2: Adapted from P. Van Voorhis and K. Brown (1996); Table 12.3 Adapted from Ebener et al. (2017) and Hannah et al. (2011)

Chapter 14
Table 14.1: Table 1 from Amialchuk and Sapci (2021); Table 14.3: Data taken from Add Health Codebook Explorer (https://addhealth.cpc.unc.edu/documentation/codebook-explorer/#/); Tables 14.4–14.6: Data taken from 2018 General Social Survey; Table 14.7–14.9; 14.10–14.11: Adapted from Pate & Bolin (2019)

Chapter 15
Table 15.1: Adapted from Table 2.1 in Gibbs (2018, p. 27); Table 15.3: Adapted from Murray (2009)

Index

Note: Tables are indicated by a *t*, Figures are indicated by a *f*, and Boxes are indicated by a *b*

AAPOR. *See* American Association of Public Opinion Research
abstracts, 18, 46*b*, 50, 50*f*, 66–67
abstract theory, 29
academic publications, 58, 62*b*, 99, 104–5, 106*b*, 107*b*
Academy of Criminal Justice Sciences (ACJS), 71, 79, 83, 88*b*
Academy Society of Criminology, 79
ACJS. *See* Academy of Criminal Justice Sciences
action coding, 463, 468
active voice, 57
administration, 356*t*
adolescence, 383–85, 458, 458*t*
African Americans, 39, 142 *See also* racism
 in prison, 230
 in surveys, 168
 in Tuskegee Syphilis study, 73–74, 78
 voting by, 115–16, 115*f*, 116*f*
Agan, A., 236
Agnew, Robert, 21
alcohol
 cannabis and, 70
 CAS, 248–49, 262
 consumption of, 402–4, 410–12, 410*t*, 411*t*, 414, 420, 422–23
 delinquency and, 118
 students and, 179–81, 180*t*, 190*b*
 studies on, 281–82, 285
Alexander, Michelle, 51, 62*b*
Alzheimer's disease, 448
Amazon Mechanical Turk (MTurk), 12, 196*b*, 215, 222, 231–33
American Association of Public Opinion Research (AAPOR), 88*b*
American Political Science Association (APSA), 94–95
American Psychological Association (APA), 62*b*, 82–83, 89
American Society of Criminology, 71, 88*b*
American Sociological Review, 58
Amialchuk, A., 402–4, 410–12, 410*t*, 411*t*, 414, 420, 422–23
Amoroso, Lisa, 95–96

analytical frameworks, 335–36, 335*f*
analytic memos, 297, 310
Analyzing Qualitative Data (Gibbs), 448, 449*t*
Andersen, L. H., 194–95
Anderson, Leon, 308–9, 450
anecdotal evidence, 4, 5*b*, 5*t*
Annual Review of Criminology, 46*b*
anonymity, 84, 86*b*, 97
antecedent variables, 112, 112*f*, 127, 129
Antrobus, Emma, 399
APA. *See* American Psychological Association
appearance, in code variables, 327
Applegate, B. K., 214
applied research designs, 369
applied research methods, 349, 374
APSA. *See* American Political Science Association
archival records, 123, 141–43, 170
archives, 316–17, 321, 343
Ariel, B., 133–36, 138–39, 144*b*, 145, 401
Arizona, 367*b*
assessment
 costs and benefits, 88–89, 88*f*
 dimensions of, 380*t*
 evaluability, 355–58, 356*t*, 357*f*, 359*b*, 374
 evaluation research and, 346–48, 364, 374–76
 of field research, 380–81, 380*t*
 ICAT de-escalation training, 347–49, 361–63, 362*b*
 needs, 352, 353*t*, 354–55, 354*f*, 375
 of operationalization, 154–57, 155*f*, 156, 157*f*
 quality of, 154–57, 155*f*, 156, 157*b*
 quantitative data and, 354
 reliability, 158–61, 159*t*, 160, 160*t*, 170
 of sampling bias, 190*b*
 scope of, 354*f*
 stakeholders and, 354, 354*f*, 357, 357*f*
 of surveys, 380–81, 380*t*
 validity, 161–65, 163*b*, 165*t*, 170
association, 115, 119
 associated variables, 371

 bivariate, 429
 measures of, 422–23, 439
 statistical, 129
 strength of, 427*b*
 between variables, 207, 226–27
attachment, 22
Attitudes toward Prisoners survey, 139–40, 146–47
Attorney General, US, 72–73
attribute coding, 449–50, 468
audit studies
 experimental method and, 213–14, 214*f*, 234
 mixed methods and, 385–90, 387*f*, 388*f*, 389*f*, 396
Aust, Phillip J., 328–29, 328*f*, 344–45
Australia, 281–82, 285, 368

Back, Sinchul, 33, 52
Bader, Michael, 140
Baltimore City Drug Treatment Court (BCDTC), 10–11
Basics of Qualitative Analysis (Corbin and Strauss), 464
Baumer, E. P.
 juvenile delinquency to, 102, 105, 108–9, 111–12, 117*b*, 118
 students to, 183–86, 401
BCDTC. *See* Baltimore City Drug Treatment Court
Becker, Howard, 56–58, 95–96
before-and-after designs, 372–73, 372*f*, 374
behavioral measures, 223
Behrens, Laurence, 65
Belfast Project, 72–73
beliefs, 22
Bell, Louie, 276
Belmont Principle of respect, 81
Belmont Report, 79, 88, 88*b*
beneficence, 79, 97
Berk, R. A., 34–35, 37, 39, 58, 62*b*
Bertrand, Marianne, 222–23
Beyond Scared Straight (TV show), 4
bias, 189–90, 190*b*, 380*t* See also *specific topics*
biased probability, 177

505

Biden, Joe, 115–16, 115f, 116f
big data, 266, 319b, 343, 393b
Billboard charts, 329–30
biology, 20
bivariate analysis, 418–26, 418t, 419t, 421t, 424f, 426f, 439
bivariate association, 429
Bjork, Nicholas, 329–30
black box evaluation, 366, 374
block quotes, 65
Blue Bloods (TV show), 324
Boas, Franz, 122, *122*
Bodapati, M. R., 163b
body-worn cameras (BWCs), 399
Bolin, Riane, 62b, 70, 119, 190b. *See also* depression
Boman, J. H., 152
Bones (TV show), 324
Bonikowski, 388–91, 388f, 389f
Boston College, 72
Boston Reentry Study, 240
Bouffard, L. A., 68
Bourdieu, Pierre, 273
Bowers, K., 141
Brady, P., 68
Braga, A. A., 373
broken windows theory, 140–41, 151–52, 320–21
Brown v. Board of Education of Topeka, 36
bullying, 383–85, 392
Bureau of Justice Statistics, 316t
Burton, A. L., 11–12, 258
Burton, V. S., 11–12, 258
BWCs. *See* body-worn cameras

CADE. *See* computer-assisted data entry
Calfano, B. R., 250
California, 143, 369
Callan, M. J., 160
Campbell, Donald, 227b
Campbell, Michael, 333–39, 333t
campus surveys, 406f
Canada, 327
cannabis, 29b, 42, 70
CAPI. *See* computer-assisted personal interviewing
capital punishment. *See* death penalty
CAQDAS. *See* Computer-Assisted Qualitative Data Analysis Software
career criminals, 31–32
carry out analysis, 325f, 330
CAS. *See* College Alcohol Study
case studies, 193–94, 200, 336–39, 338f
CASI. *See* computer-assisted self-administered interviewing

CATI. *See* computer-assisted telephone interviewing
causal relationships
 explanations of, 338–39, 338f
 General Causal Model of Penal Transformation, 338f
 in GSS, 269
 in research, 108, 114–15, 117–20, 121b, 127, 204
 statistical analysis and, 429
 in surveys, 265–66
Causes of Delinquency (Hirschi), 21
cautions, 36–40, *38*
CDC. *See* Centers for Disease Control
cell frequency, 419, 421–22, 421t, 439
cell phone use, 331b
Census, US, 167–68, 239, 315, 316t, 317, 344
Centers for Disease Control (CDC), 247, 316t, 317
Central Park Five, 104
Chairassamee, Nattahicha, 317–18
Charmaz, Kathy, 307–8, 452, 454b, 463–64
checking errors, 448, 449t
Chester County Sheriff's Office, 4, 5b, 5t
Chicago gang study, 281, 288
children, 81, 383–85
chi-square test for independence, 421–22, 421t, 439
CHRI. *See* criminal history record information
Christenson, Peter, 329–30
citations, 46b, 49f, 62b
Clare, J., 368
cleaning, in quantitative data analysis, 408
Clemmer, Donald, 273
Cleveland, L., 94, 96
closed-ended questions, 241, 267
cluster sampling, 187–89, 199
Coburn, Tom, 94–95
codebook documentation, 406b, 407f
codebooks, 327–28, 328f, 343
code memos, 455, 462–64, 468
Code of Ethics, 79, 88b
code variables, 325f, 327, 330
coding
 action, 463
 attribute, 449–50, 468
 content analysis and, 323
 data, 255f, 262–63, 278, 304–5, 469
 observations, 124–25
 process, 463
 in qualitative data analysis, 452–54, 454b

 in quantitative data analysis, 404
 research, 262, 267
 schemes, 325–28, 325f, 328f
 in surveys, 255f
 terms, 459b
 units, 325
 violence, 323–24
 in vivo, 463, 468
The Coding Manual for Qualitative Researchers (Saldaña), 452–53
coefficients
 estimation of, 437b
 partial regression, 433–34, 434t, 439
 slope/regression, 424–26, 424f, 426f, 439
 standardized regression, 435–36, 436t, 439
Colburn, Alayna, 326b
college. *See* higher education
College Alcohol Study (CAS), 248–49, 262
Color of Change, 109
combination cases, 185–86
commitment, 22
Common Rule, 79, 87b, 88, 97
communication, 331b
 active voice in, 57
 content of, 322–23
 in criminal justice research, 44–45, 45f, 65, 66b, 67–68
 human, 287
 ICAT de-escalation training, 347–49, 361–63, 362b
 recorded, 325, 325f
 in social research, 67
 strategies, 14
comparative historical analysis
 analytical framework for, 335–36, 335f
 case studies for, 336–37
 cross-case analysis in, 338–39, 338f
 of existing data, 332–39, 333t, 335f, 338f, 339b
 of mass imprisonment, 332–35, 333t
 process of, 335, 335f
 scholarship on, 339, 339b, 343
 within-case analyses and, 337–38
Comparative Neighborhood Study, 194
complementarity, 391
component designs, 395–96, 397
computer-assisted data entry (CADE), 405
computer-assisted personal interviewing (CAPI), 245f, 246, *246*, 249–51, 267
Computer-Assisted Qualitative Data Analysis Software (CAQDAS), 449–51, 468

computer-assisted self-administered interviewing (CASI), 245*f*, 249–52, 267
computer-assisted telephone interviewing (CATI), 245*f*, 249–51, 263, 267
concepts
 conceptual definition, 132–33, 170
 conceptualization, 131–34, 132*f*, 134*b*, 137, 137*b*, 170
 hypotheses and, 153*b*
 identification of, 447, 447*f*, 452–59, 454*b*, 456*f*, 457*t*, 458*t*
 operationalization and, 167–69
 in quantitative data analysis, 416*b*
 in surveys, 172
 theory and, 111
conclusions, in qualitative data analysis, 447*f*, 460–61
concrete data, 29
concurrent designs, 395, 397
conducting experiments, 217–19, 218*f*, 219*b*, 221–25, 225*b*
confidence interval, 181, 199
confidentiality, 84, 86*b*, 97
conflict of interest, 97
consistency checking, 408, 439
Consolidated Framework for Implementation Research, 369, 374
Consortium for Political and Social Research (ICPSR), 46*b*
Consortium of Social Science Associations (COSSA), 95
constant-comparative method, 462–63, 468
Constructing Grounding Theory (Charmaz), 464
construct validation, 163–65, 165*t*, 170
content, of communication, 322–23
content analysis
 of cell phone use, 331*b*
 coding schemes for, 325–28, 328*f*
 with existing data, 322–31, 325*f*, 326*b*, 328*f*, 329*t*, 331*b*
 of mental illness, 323–24
 process of, 324–25, 325*f*
 research on, 345
 sample units in, 328–30
 scholarship on, 322–23, 331, 343, 466
 units of analysis in, 325, 326*b*
content restrictions, 233, 380*t*
contestation, 333–35, 333*t*
context
 contextual understanding, 307, 380*t*
 in evaluation research, 365–66, 374
 experimental, 213–16, 214*f*, 216*t*, 218, 225

contingency tables, 418–19, 418*t*, 430–32, 430*t*, 431*t*, 432*t*
control variables, 112, 127
convenience sampling, 195, 199
convergent validation, 161–63, 170
conversation analysis, 465–68, 467*f*
Converse, Jean, 256
Cook, Karen, 75
Cook, Kenneth, 64
Cooley, Brooke N., 456
Coopersmith Self-Esteem Inventory, 162
Corbin, Juliet, 452, 463–64
correlation coefficients, 117*b*, 425–26, 426*f*, 439
COSSA. *See* Consortium of Social Science Associations
cost-benefit analysis, 363, 374
cost-effectiveness analysis, 363, 374
cost efficiency, 341
costs and benefits assessment, 88–89, 88*f*
Couper, Mick, 247–48
coverage error, 185, 199
cover stories, 221, 234
covert observation, 282–85, 285*f*, 310
COVID-19
 CDC during, 247
 data from, 143
 domestic violence in, 50–51, 50*f*
 police in, 50–51, 50*f*, 347
 social distancing in, 288
Craigslist, 388
crime data analysis, 319*b*
crime dramas, 323–27, 329–30, 341
criminal history record information (CHRI), 76
criminal justice. *See specific topics*
Criminal Justice Abstracts, 46*b*
criminal justice data, 22–23
criminal justice data archives, 321
criminal justice policies, 347
criminal justice programs, 347. See also *specific topics*
criminal justice system, 93–94
criminal prosecution, 204–6, 205
criminology. *See specific topics*
Cronbach's alpha, 160, 170
cross-case analysis, 338–39, 338*f*
cross-sectional designs, 243–44, 267
cross-tabulations, 418–19, 418*t*
Crouch, Wayne, 64
crowdsourcing, 196*b*, 199
CSI (TV show), 324
culture, 279*b*
culture shock, 276–77
cumulative scaling, 157*b*
Cundiff, K., 186, 401

DARE. *See* Drug Abuse Resistance Education
Darwin, Charles, 22, 39
data. See also *specific topics*
 from ADD Health, 402–5, 410–14, 410*t*, 411*t*, 413*t*, 420, 422–23
 archives, 321, 343
 big, 266, 319*b*, 343, 393*b*
 cleaning, 408, 439
 coding, 255*f*, 262–63, 278, 304–5
 concrete, 29
 from COVID-19, 143
 criminal justice, 22–23
 data-driven inquiry, 40*b*
 displays, 455–59, 456*f*, 457*t*, 458*t*, 470
 editing, 262–63
 electronic databases, 46*b*
 empirical patterns and, 33*f*, 34*f*
 entry, 405–6, 406*f*
 evaluating, 461*b*
 existing, 9, 15, 17, 315–18, 316*b*, 319*b*, 320–21, 322*b*, 380*t*
 eyeballing, 418
 from Family History of Incarceration survey, 243–44
 feedback loops and, 167–69
 GSS, 128, 172, 402, 441–42
 GSS Cumulative data file, 406*b*, 407*f*
 hypotheses and, 50
 hypothetical, 77*t*, 432, 432*t*
 inspection, 403*f*, 409–16, 410*t*, 411*t*, 413*t*, 414*f*
 IPUMS, 317–18
 limitations, 341–42
 management, 449–51
 matrix, 405–6, 406*f*, 439, 456–57, 457*t*
 microdata, 317–18
 missing, 405–6, 406*f*, 439
 NCJRS Abstracts Database, 46*b*, 67
 from NSDUH, 244
 observations and, 15
 official data sources, 315, 316*t*
 from operationalization, 151–53, 153*b*
 preparation, 447–51, 447*f*, 448*f*, 449*t*
 from process evaluations, 359, 360*t*
 processing, 403, 403*f*, 439
 PUMS, 317–18
 Quality Education Data, Inc., 188
 quantitative data analysis, 242
 readable text from, 447–48, 448*f*
 scholarship on, 41
 sources, 322*b*
 staff perception, 360*t*
 statistics and, 401
 strength of association, 427*b*
 supplementary archival, 277

data (cont.)
  survey, 392
  theory and, 30f, 35, 41
  theory-data relationship, 20, 20f
  from Tik Tok, 123
  validity of, 308–9
  verifiable, 22–23, 23b
data analysis. See also *specific topics*
  data gathering and, 291f, 296–97, 300f, 303–4
  for in-depth interviews, 304–5
  research and, 16, 17b, 93, 95–96
  strategy and, 122f, 266, 361f
data collection, 354f, 361f. See also data
  choice in, 255, 255f
  modes for, 245–53, 245f, 246, 246f, 251t
  observation and, 274–75
  qualitative data analysis and, 447f
  research and, 16, 30, 88f, 93, 187, 193
  research participants and, 90–91
  sample recruitment and, 261–62
  types of, 253b
data gathering. See also data
  data analysis and, 291f, 296–97, 300f, 303–4
  strategies, 108f, 110–19, 112f, 113b, 115t, 116t, 117b, 119b
Davis, James, 404
death penalty, 9b, 29b, 42, 104–5
death permits, 316–17
debriefing, 83, 97, 224–25
deception, 74–75, 75, 82–83
deductive logic
  deductive reasoning and, 26b, 29, 29b
  inductive logic and, 25–26, 33–34, 40b, 42
  of inquiry, 30–35, 30f, 33f, 34f, 41
delinquency, 102, 118
Delisi, M., 194–95, 197–98
Demir, M., 50–51
demography, 167–68, 239, 315, 316t, 317–18, 343, 344
Densley, J. A., 359
Department of Justice, 363
dependent variables, 111, 127, 210, 211–12, 223, 335, 442–43
depression
  NMPDU and, 426–32, 426f, 427b, 429–30, 429f, 430f, 431t, 432t, 436t
  research on, 423–26, 424f, 426f
descriptive research questions, 104–5
descriptive statistics, 401–2, 439
descriptive surveys, 242, 267
designs. See also *specific designs*
  applied research, 369

before-and-after, 372–73, 372f, 374
component, 395–96, 397
concurrent, 395, 397
cross-sectional, 243–44, 267
experimental, 204–7, 208b, 208f, 209–13, 209t, 210b, 218, 371
ex post facto control group, 374
factorial, 212–13, 234
flexible research, 307–8
integrated, 396–97
longitudinal, 244–45, 245t, 265–66, 267
of methodologies, 59
mixed methods research, 393, 393b, 395–96, 397b
NIJ and, 376
nonequivalent control group, 372, 372f, 375
nonexperimental, 371, 373, 403–4
posttest-only control group, 211–12, 234
pretest-posttest control group, 211–12, 227b, 234
quasi-experimental, 371–73, 372f, 375
questionnaire, 250
randomized controlled trial, 348, 361, 362b
research, 227b, 230–31, 374b
of research proposals, 54
sampling, 185–89, 188f, 254–55, 255f
sequential, 395, 397
survey, 243–53, 245f, 245t, 246, 246f, 251t, 253b
destabilization, 333–35, 333t
deterrence, 8–9, 58
developing coding schemes, 325–28, 328f
development, 391
deviant behavior, 21, 22, 281
Dickson, William J., 38
dictionaries, 328, 329t, 343
Dillman, Don, 250
direction of influence, 116–17, 207, 429
direct measurement, 162
discrimination. See also *racism*
  in low-wage labor markets, 388–90, 388f, 389f
  priming and, 387
  in US, 222–23, 389–90
discussions, 61
Disney, 344–45
disproportionate stratified sampling, 186–87, 199
District of Columbia, 249
Dixon, T. L., 142–43
documents, 316–18
Dodd, Shannon, 399

Doing Conversation, Discourse, and Content Analysis (Rapley), 466
domestic violence
  in COVID-19, 50–51, 50f
  Minneapolis Domestic Violence Experiment, 34–35, 37
  recidivism and, 372–73
  reliability and, 172
Dominick, Joseph R., 345
double-barreled questions, 256b, 267
double-blind experiments, 232–34
Doyle, Arthur Conan, 25, 26b
Drakulick, K. M., 250
draw sample, 189–90
Drug Abuse Resistance Education (DARE), 227b, 351b, 361
drug treatment courts, 10–11
dummy variables, 433–34, 434t, 439

ease of measurement, 380t
ecological fallacy, 110b, 127
Eco-Warriors (Scarce), 91
Edison Research, 115
editing, 255f, 263, 267
editing data, 262–63
education. See also *specific topics*
  to administration, 356t
  DARE, 227b, 351b, 361
  higher, 2
  National Center for Education Statistics, 316t
  Quality Education Data, Inc., 188
  social media and, 2, 2
  stakeholders in, 350f, 351, 354, 354f, 357, 357f, 361f, 366–68, 367b, 375
  studies on, 110–13, 112f
Edwards, Mark, 52, 54, 58
efficiency
  analysis, 363, 374
  cost, 341
  evaluations, 363
  in qualitative research, 309
  in surveys, 265
elaboration analysis, 442
elections, 115–16, 115f, 116f
electronic databases, 46b
elimination of rival explanations, 207
emergency calls, 466–67, 467f
emotional language, 330
empirical evidence, 5b, 5t
empirical indicators, 134–36, 170
empirical observations, 22
empirical patterns, 30f, 31, 33f, 34f, 41
employers
  low-wage labor markets and, 388–90, 388f, 389f

qualitative data to, 396
racism by, 385–87, 387f, 396
research on, 213–14, 214f
students and, 7
EndNote, 46b, 51
Engel, R. S., 348–50, 361–63, 362b
Erikson, Kai, 123
errors
  checking, 448, 449t
  coverage, 185, 199
  margin of error, 181
  measurement, 163b, 170
  nonresponse, 189–90, 190b, 199
  sampling, 179–80, 180t, 199, 265
  specification, 437b
  standard, 181, 200
ESM. *See* Experience Sampling Method
ethical decision-making
  costs and benefits assessment and, 88–89
  ethical concern and, 89
  to IRB, 89–90
  organ-trafficking and, 283b
  politics of, 87–91, 88b, 88f
  process of, 87–88, 88f
  in research, 286–87
  research proposals and, 88b
  scholarship on, 87–88, 91
ethical guidelines
  from APA, 89
  deception ground rules, 82–83
  for evaluating potential harm, 79–81
  federal, 78–84, 85b, 86, 88, 92b
  for informed consent, 81–82
  for privacy protection, 84
  review of, 92b
  scholarship on, 78–79, 86
Ethical Principles of Psychologists and Codes of Conduct, APA, 82–83
ethics
  with children, 81
  Code of Ethics, 79
  in criminal justice research, 92–93
  in field research, 84
  of human subjects training, 86b
  politics and, 69–70, 78–84, 85b, 86, 92–93, 93, 96–99
  practice, 78b, 85b
  research, 88b
  with research participants, 71–77, 72, 73f, 75, 76b, 77t, 78b
  scholarship on, 97
ethnography, 272–73, 283b, 287, 310
Europe, 247
evaluating data, 461b

evaluation research
  assessment and, 346–48, 364, 374–76
  components of, 349–51, 350f
  context in, 365–66, 374
  definitions of, 348–49
  evaluability assessment, 355–58, 356t, 357f, 359b, 374
  evaluations efficiency, 363
  experimental designs with, 371
  feasibility and, 368
  methodologies for, 369–70
  mixed methods research and, 369–70
  needs assessment for, 352, 353t, 354–55, 354f
  nonexperimental designs with, 371, 373
  orientation of, 366–68, 367b
  outcome evaluations from, 360–63, 361f, 362b, 375
  people involved in, 351b
  process evaluations and, 358–59, 359b, 360t, 375
  program theory and, 365–66, 375
  quasi-experimental designs with, 371–73, 372f
  research designs and, 374b
  research terminology, 370b
  stakeholders and, 350f, 351
  types of, 352, 353t, 364b
evaluations, from students, 76b, 77t
Everhart, Kimberly, 328–29, 328f, 344–45
evidence, 206–7
  anecdotal, 5b, 5t
  empirical, 5b, 5t
  evidence-based practice, 349, 374
  physical, nonverbal, 320–21
  research, 226
exhaustive, 145–46, 170
existing data
  analysis, 9, 15, 17, 314–15, 340–45, 342b
  assessment of, 380t
  comparative historical analysis of, 332–39, 333t, 335f, 338f, 339b
  content analysis with, 322–31, 325f, 326b, 328f, 329t, 331b
  sources of, 315–18, 316t, 319b, 320–21, 322b
exonerees, 300–302, 304–5
expansion, 392
Experience Sampling Method (ESM), 141
experiments
  with African Americans, 73–74, 78
  conducting, 217–19, 218f, 219b, 221–25, 225b
  in criminal justice research, 227b

double-blind, 232–34
experimental condition, 204
experimental context, 213–16, 214f, 216t, 218, 225
experimental designs, 204–7, 208b, 208f, 209–13, 209t, 210b, 218, 371
experimental manipulation, 221
experimental method, 211–16, 214f, 216t, 217b
experimenters, 391
external validity in, 229–31, 234
field, 212–14, 234
hypotheses and, 236–37
informed consent in, 219, 219b, 220f
internal validity in, 226–27, 234
laboratory, 213–16, 214f, 216t, 225, 234, 236–37, 380t
logic of, 204, 206–7, 208b, 208f, 209–10, 209t, 210b
Minneapolis Domestic Violence Experiment, 34–35, 37
on misconduct, 204–6, 205
prison guard, 72, 72
qualitative interviews and, 307
on racism, 213–14, 214f
reactive measurement effects of, 231–33, 234
research participants and, 204–6, 217–19, 218f, 227
sampling in, 208b, 208f
scholarship on, 9–11, 17, 17b, 203–4, 233–37, 234b
shock experiment, 74–75, 75, 83
students in, 72, 72, 74–75, 75, 83
survey-based, 214–15, 234
in US, 34–35, 37
validity and, 380–81
explanatory surveys, 242, 267
ex post facto control group designs, 374
external validity, 229–31, 234, 380t
extraneous variables, 111–12, 127

Facebook, 14, 123, 319b
face-to-face (FTF) interviews
  GSS and, 245–47, 245f, 246, 246f
  surveys and, 262
  technology and, 249–50, 251t, 252, 267
factorial designs, 212–13, 234
Family History of Incarceration survey (2018), 243–44
Farrar, W. A., 133–36, 138–39, 144b, 145, 401
Farrington, D. P., 363
FBI. *See* Federal Bureau of Investigation
feasibility, 357, 357f, 368, 374

Federal Bureau of Investigation (FBI), 23b, 43, 316t
Federal Bureau of Prisons, 316t
federal ethical guidelines, 78–84, 85b, 86, 88, 92b
feedback, 350, 350f, 355, 374
feedback loops, 167–69
female parolees, 102, 105, 123, 125
fidelity, 358–59, 374
field experiments, 212–14, 234
field jottings, 296–97, 310
field notes, 310, 390, 453
field pretesting, 261, 267
field research
  access to, 291–94, 291f
  assessment of, 380–81, 380t
  conducting, 290–99, 291f, 299b
  criminal justice research and, 15, 454b
  ethics in, 84
  in-depth interviews and, 13–14, 271–74, 310–13
  measurement in, 172
  methodologies for, 16
  permission in, 293–94
  psychology of, 297–98
  qualitative research and, 274–80, 279b, 306–9, 310b
  qualitative research methods for, 280–89, 283b, 285f, 289b
  relationships in, 291f, 294–95
  scholarship on, 17, 289
  settings for, 122f, 123, 129, 291f, 292–93
  on sexual behavior, 283
  technological developments for, 287–88
film ratings, 344–45
findings/results, 60–61
Firebaugh, Glenn, 105
first drafts, 56–61
Five Ways of Doing Qualitative Analysis (Wertz), 470
Florida, 141–42
focus groups, 286, 310, 360t, 383, 392
formative evaluation, 352, 353t, 374
Forrest Gump (film), 464–65
Fouts, G., 160
Fowler, Floyd, 256b
frame sampling, 184–85, 185f, 199, 261
framing surveys, 264b
Fraser, N. M., 366
free writing, 56–57, 66
frequency, 327, 410–11, 410f, 439
FTF interviews. *See* face-to-face interviews
Fujiyama, T., 141

Gaddis, S. Michael, 224
GAGV. *See* Growing Against Gangs and Violence
gang members, 14, 84, 192–93, 281, 288, 359, 465
Gardner, W. M., 139–40, 146–47
Gariglio, Luigi, 293–94
gatekeepers, 293–94, 310
gender, 215–16, 216t, 385
General Causal Model of Penal Transformation, 338f
generalizability, 308
generalization, 174, 175f, 183, 196b, 230, 265. *See also specific topics*
General Social Survey (GSS), 46b
  Cumulative Data file, 406b, 407f
  data, 128, 172, 402, 441–42
  data archives with, 321
  efficiency, 265
  FTF interviews and, 245–47, 245f, 246, 246f
  on gun control, 418–20, 418t, 419t
  harshness in, 214
  questions for, 268–69
general strain, 423–26, 424f, 426f
Gibbs, Graham, 448, 449t
Glaser, Barney, 452, 462–64
Goffman, Erving, 465–66
good research questions, 106b
Google, 46b, 48f
Gottfredson, D., 10–11
Gottfredson, Michael, 21, 32, 52
grade point average. *See* students
Graif, Corina
  erroneous convictions to, 204–7, 205, 209t
  research process of, 218, 219b, 220f, 222, 224, 229–30, 401
Gramling, L. K., 139–40, 146–47
grand tour questions, 302, 310
Green, Cherrell, 445–46, 450–55, 460
Greenleaf, R. G., 319b
Grimshaw, R., 281–82, 285
grounded theory, 369, 375, 452, 462–64
group interviews, 286–88
group research, 279, 291, 291f
Growing Against Gangs and Violence (GAGV), 359
GSS. *See* General Social Survey
Guerra, Nancy C., 383–84, 392
guiding questions, 290, 310
gun control, 418–20, 418t, 419t
gun violence restraining orders (GVROs), 369
Guttman, Louis, 157b
GVROs. *See* gun violence restraining orders

Hamilton, E. E., 35
Hanks, Tom, 464–65
harshness, 214
Havekes, Esther, 140
Hawthorne effect, 38, *38*, 41–42
higher education, 230–31
  cannabis and, 42
  CAS, 248–49, 262
  dorms in, 320–21
  IRB in, 86b, 87–88
  privacy in, 76b, 77t
  rankings in, 315
  research in, 2, 72, 72–73, 256b, 270
  university presses, 51
Hirschi, Travis, 21–22, 22, 30–32, 52
Hispanics, 142–43, 167–68. *See also* racism
histograms, 414, 414f, 439
history, 227b, 234, 340–41
Hodgkinson, W., 372–73
homelessness, 308
Hong, M., 15
Hu, Xiaochen, 123
Huberman, A. Michael, 460
human action, 121–22
human communication, 287
human elements, of science, 39
human perception, 122, *122*
human subjects training, 86b
Humphrey, Laud, 74, 91, 283, 393b
hypotheses
  concepts and, 153b
  in criminal justice research, 20, 30f, 134b
  data and, 50
  experiments and, 236–37
  hypothetical data, 77t, 432, 432t
  hypothetical research, 98–99
  null hypothesis, 420, 439
  observations and, 290
  preliminary hypothesis testing, 403f, 417–26, 418t, 419t, 421t, 424f, 426f, 428
  in research proposals, 67
  scholarship on, 41
  serendipity pattern and, 37–38
  testing, 323–24
  theory and, 30–31, 137

ICAT de-escalation training. *See* Integrating Communications, Assessment, and Tactics de-escalation training
ICPSR. *See* Consortium for Political and Social Research
identification, of concepts, patterns, and relationships, 447, 447f, 452–59, 454b, 456f, 457t, 458t

identity, 273, 279b, 283b, 284–85
ideology, 79, 93–96
illegal medical practices, 445, 454b
impact evaluations, 361, 375
improving reliability, 161
Improving Survey Questions (Fowler), 256b
imputation, 415, 439
incarceration rates. *See* prison
independent probability, 177
independent variables, 111, 127, 206, 212–13, 419–20, 419t, 442–43
in-depth interviews
  characteristics of, 276–77
  conducting, 200f, 300
  data analysis for, 304–5
  field research and, 13–14, 271–74, 310–13
  gathering data for, 303–4
  interview guides, 301–2
  with minorities, 167–68
  preparing for, 302b
  qualitative data analysis and, 445
  recruitment for, 300–301
  scholarship on, 17, 305b, 454b
indexes, 135, 157b, 170, 316
individual interviews, 286–88
individuals, 244
inductive inquiry, 167
inductive logic
  deductive logic and, 25–26, 33–34, 40b, 42
  inductive reasoning and, 26b, 29, 29b
  scholarship on, 41
  in social research, 30–35, 30f, 33f, 34f, 41
inference, 173–76, 176f, 197–98. *See also* sampling
inferential statistics, 401–2, 439
influence, 116–17
informed consent
  in experiments, 219, 219b, 220f
  research and, 73–74, 73f, 81–82, 97
  in surveys, 85b
inherent subjectivity, 133
inmates, 31–32
innocence, 205–6
inputs, 349, 350f, 375
inquiry
  deductive logic of, 30–35, 30f, 33f, 34f, 41
  inductive, 167
  LIWC, 330
  logic of, 38, 40b
  models of, 169b
inspection, data, 403f, 409–16, 410t, 411t, 413t, 414f

Institute for Social Research, 244
Institutional Review Board (IRB), 54, 97, 319b
  applications, 90–91
  approval from, 76, 88f, 124, 393b
  in higher education, 86b, 87–88
  research questions for, 105
  submissions to, 88f, 89–90
integrated designs, 396–97
Integrated Public Use Microdata Sample (IPUMS), 317–18
Integrating Communications, Assessment, and Tactics (ICAT) de-escalation training, 347–49, 361–63, 362b
intensity, in code variables, 327
interactive voice response (IVR) surveys, 249–50
inter-coder reliability, 160, 160, 452
internal consistency, 159–60, 160t, 170
internal validity, 380t, 381
  in experiments, 226–27, 234
  external validity and, 231
  research designs and, 227b
  threats to, 227, 227b, 234
Internet, 46b. *See also specific topics*
inter-rate reliability, 160, 160, 170
Inter-University Consortium for Political and Social Research, 321
interval estimates, 181
interval measurement, 147–48, 170
interval variables, 412–16, 413t, 414f, 423–26, 424f, 426f
intervening variables, 112, 112f, 118–19, 127
interviews. *See also* face-to-face interviews; in-depth interviews
  CAPI, 245f, 246, 246, 249–51, 267
  CASI, 245f, 249–52, 267
  CATI, 245f, 249–51, 263, 267
  consent for, 303
  group, 286–88
  individual, 286–88
  interview guides, 300f, 301–2, 304, 310
  interview protocol, 301
  interview schedule, 262, 267
  key informants in, 295
  life history, 465
  observation and, 287–88, 291f, 295, 357, 357f
  observations and, 122f, 124
  prison and, 273–82, 285, 289b, 290–95, 299b, 454b
  qualitative, 307
  for qualitative research, 275–77, 312–13

recruiting interviewees, 300–301, 300f
scheduling, 302b, 304
semi-structured, 285–86, 310, 446
settings for, 292–93
structured, 240–42, 267, 285–86
telephone, 247–49, 251t, 267
trust in, 273–74
unstructured, 285–86, 310
intimate partner violence (IPV), 456–57
invasion of privacy, 75–76, 76b
investigator bias, 380t
in vivo coding, 463, 468
involvement, 22
IPUMS. *See* Integrated Public Use Microdata Sample
IPV. *See* intimate partner violence
IQ tests, 39
IRB. *See* Institutional Review Board
Ireland, 72–73
Irvine, Jan, 70
Italy, 293
IVR surveys. *See* interactive voice response surveys

Jackson, N. A., 300–302, 304–5
Jackson, S. E., 147, 153
Jefferson, Gale, 466
Jeffersonian transcribing conventions, 466
Johnson, Ida, 102, 105, 123, 125, 445, 454b
judgmental sampling, 195, 197, 199
justice, 79, 94, 97
juvenile delinquency, 102, 105, 108–9, 111–12, 117b, 118

Kane, Robert J., 318
Karpinski, Aryn, 2
Katzer, Jeffrey, 64
Kelling, G. L., 140, 151–52
Kelly, C. L., 461
Kelly, Jane, 461, 465
Kennedy, A. C., 456–57, 457t
Kensey, A., 141
Kentucky, 348–50, 361–63, 362b
Keuschnigg, M., 140–41, 151–52, 157b, 320–21
key informants, 295, 310
King, R., 94, 96
Kleck, G., 15
knowledge
  production, 16
  scientific, 23, 36–41, 38
  students and, 6
  tentative, 36–37
  understanding and, 24

known probability, 177, 185
Kogel, C. J., 363
Krysan, Maria, 140
Kudkla, D., 327–28, 329t

laboratory experiments, 213–16, 214f, 216t, 225, 234, 236–37, 380t
LaFree, G., 415
Lahm, K., 318
Lane, David, 420–21
Lange, Matthew, 338–39
LaPrade, Jennifer, 52
large-scale probability sampling, 240
Latinos. *See* Hispanics
Law and Order (TV show), 324
law enforcement assisted diversion (LEAD) programs, 372
Law School Admissions Test (LSAT), 26b
Lawson, A., 160
leading questions, 256b, 267
LEAD programs. *See* law enforcement assisted diversion programs
length, of research reports, 64
Lerner Self-Esteem Scale, 162
"Let's Talk About Sex" (song), 70
libraries, 46b
life history interviews, 465
limits, 36–40, 38
Linguistic Inquiry Word Count (LIWC), 330
listwise deletion, 415, 439
literature
  research, 46, 46b, 48f, 49f, 50, 50f
  research reports and, 67
  review, 56, 58–59, 101f, 103–4, 128, 290
LIWC. *See* Linguistic Inquiry Word Count
Lofland, John, 292, 297–98, 450, 455
Lofland, Lyn, 292, 297–98, 450, 455
logic, of experiments, 204, 206–7, 208b, 208f, 209–10, 209t, 210b
logical reasoning, 25–26, 26b, 30
logic of inquiry, 38, 40b
longitudinal designs, 244–45, 245t, 265–66, 267
Lovaglia, Michael
  erroneous convictions to, 204–7, 205, 209t
  research process of, 218, 219b, 220f, 222, 224, 229–30, 401
low-wage labor markets, 388–90, 388f, 389f
LSAT. *See* Law School Admissions Test

Lucas, Jeffrey
  erroneous convictions to, 204–7, 205, 209t
  research process of, 218, 219b, 220f, 222, 224, 229–30, 401
Lulei, M., 141
Lumsden, K., 279b
Luo, L., 186, 401

mail surveys, 246–53, 251t
Malamuth, Neil, 345
mandatory arrest laws, 39
Manhattan Review, 26b
manipulated independent variables, 206, 210, 212–13
manipulation, experimental, 221
manipulation checks, 221–22, 234
manipulation operations, 138–39, 143, 143b
marginal frequencies, 419, 439
margin of error, 181
Marquart, James, 167
Martin, Liam, 273–82, 285, 289b, 290–95, 299b, 445, 454b
Marx, Karl, 332
Maslach, C., 147, 153
Maslach Burnout Inventory, 147, 153
Massachusetts, 240, 373
mass imprisonment, 332–35, 333t
mass media, 318
matrix of studies, 52t, 54
maturation, 228, 234
McClintock, Jenna, 70, 119, 190b
McKnight, P. E., 415
McPherson, G., 460–61
Meade, B., 62b
mean, 439
measurement
  conceptualization and, 131–34, 132f
  of dependent variables, 223
  direct, 162
  ease of, 380t
  error, 163b, 170
  feedback loops and, 167–69
  in field research, 172
  interval, 147–48, 170
  issues, 266
  measured dependent variables, 210
  measures of association, 422–23, 439
  of methodologies, 60
  models of inquiry for, 169b
  nominal, 145–46, 170
  nonreactive, 341, 380t, 381
  observations and, 140–41, 140f
  operationalization and, 132f, 134–37, 137b, 149b, 154b
  operations, 138–43, 140f, 143b

ordinal, 146–47, 170, 423
in politics, 147
process, 131–32, 132f, 137b
quality and, 131f, 154–57, 155f, 156, 157b
ratio, 148–49, 149t, 170
reactive measurement effects, 231–33, 234, 341
reliability assessment and, 158–61, 159t, 160, 160t
scaling techniques, 157b
scholarship on, 130–31, 166b, 170–72
in Self-Esteem Scale, 156, 156–62, 159t, 160t, 164–65, 165t, 168–69
in social research, 151–53, 153b
survey, 254–55
timing and, 211–12
validity, 155–56, 155f
validity assessment and, 161–65, 163b, 165t, 170
of variables, 108f, 110–13, 112f, 113b
mechanism, 365–66, 375
media, 18, 318, 326b. *See also* social media
median, 413, 439
Meier, E., 456–57, 457t
Meisenhelder, Thomas, 31–32, 102
Melander, Lisa, 326b
Meldrum, R. C., 152
Melvin, K. B., 139–40, 146–47
member checking, 461, 468
memory, 296
memo writing, 455, 462–64, 470
Mendeley, 46b, 51
mental illness, 323–27, 329–30, 341
Merton, Robert, 21, 38–39
meta-analyses, 5t, 37
methodologies. *See also* multiple methods
  applied research methods, 349, 374
  of debriefing, 83
  designs of, 59
  for evaluation research, 369–70
  for field research, 16
  measurement of, 60
  methodological approaches, 17b
  for qualitative research, 17b
  quantitative data and, 53b
microdata, 317–18
Miles, Matthew, 460
Milgram, Stanley, 74–75, 75, 83
mind-mapping, 465
Minneapolis Domestic Violence Experiment, 34–35, 37
minorities, 142–43, 167–68, 194, 326b
misconduct, in criminal prosecution, 204–6, 205, 213
missing data, 405–6, 406f, 439

Mitchell, M. M., 4
mixed methods research
   designs, 393, 393b, 395–96, 397b
   evaluation research and, 369–70
   multiple methods and, 379, 383–90, 385f, 387f, 388f, 389f, 397
   purposes of, 390–92, 392b
mixed-mode surveys, 251–52, 251t, 267
mode, 413, 439
models of inquiry, 169b
modes
   for data collection, 245–53, 245f, 246, 246f, 251t
   for survey designs, 243–53, 245f, 245t, 246, 246f, 251t, 253b
Monitoring the Future Study (MTF), 108–10, 117b, 183–87
MTurk. See Amazon Mechanical Turk
Mullainathan, Sendhil, 222–23
multicollinearity, 437b
multiple interpretations, 445
multiple methods
   with bullying, 383–85
   complementarity, 391
   for component designs, 395–96, 397
   in criminal justice research, 379–82, 380t, 382b, 393b
   development, 391
   with employers, 385–87, 387f
   expansion, 392
   for integrated designs, 396–97
   labor and, 388–90, 388f, 389f
   scholarship on, 377–79, 378f, 392b, 397–99, 397b
   for sequential designs, 395, 397
   triangulation, 378, 378f, 382, 390–91, 397
multiple regression, 433–37, 434t, 436t, 439
multistage cluster sampling, 187–89, 188f, 199
multivariate testing
   conducting, 429–38, 429f, 430t, 431t, 432t, 434t, 436t, 438b
   process, 403f
Murphy, Mike, 296–97
Murray, Cathy, 458, 458t
music, 329–30
mutual exclusivity, 145–46, 170
Myers, B., 330

N, 411, 439
narrative analysis, 464–65, 468
narrative comparison, 338–39, 343
National Center for Education Statistics, 316t

National Crime Justice Reference Service (NCJRS) Abstracts Database, 46b, 67
National Crime Victimization Survey (NCVS), 239–44, 253b, 259, 262
National Institute of Justice (NIJ), 94, 363, 376
National Institute on Drug Abuse, 316t
National Longitudinal Study of Adolescent to Adult Health (ADD Health)
   data from, 402–5, 410–14, 410t, 411t, 413t, 420, 422–23
   research for, 183, 187–89
National Research Act, 78
National Science Foundation (NSF), 94
National Survey on Drug Use and Health (NSDUH), 244
National Television Violence Study, 329
naturalistic approach, to qualitative research, 306
natural social settings, 230
Nazis, 72, 78
NCIS (TV show), 324
NCJRS Abstracts Database. See National Crime Justice Reference Service Abstracts Database
NCVS. See National Crime Victimization Survey
needs assessment, 352, 353t, 354–55, 354f, 375
negotiation, 294
Nelson, L. K., 464
nesting, 396–97
netnography, 287, 310
New Jersey, 357–58
The New Jim Crow (Alexander), 51
Newton, Isaac, 108
New York (state), 388–91, 388f, 389f
New York City Police Department, 318
New York Times Index, 316
New Zealand, 273–74
NIJ. See National Institute of Justice
Nixon, Richard, 334
NMPDU. See nonmedical prescription drug use
Nobles, M. R., 68
NodeXL, 318
Noel Monde, Melissa, 445–46, 450–55, 460
nominal measurement, 145–46, 170
nominal variables, 410–12, 410t, 411t, 418–23, 418t, 419t, 421t
nonequivalent control group designs, 372, 372f, 375
nonexperimental designs, 371, 373, 403–4

nonmedical prescription drug use (NMPDU)
   nuances of, 426f, 427b, 429f, 430t, 431t, 432t, 436t
   overview of, 426–32
nonparticipant observation, 281–82, 285f, 310
nonprobability sampling
   inference and, 197–98
   observations for, 195, 197
   qualitative research and, 277–78
   research sites for, 193–95
   scholarship on, 175–76, 175f, 176f, 192–93, 197–202, 199b, 201–2
nonreactive measurement, 341, 380t, 381
nonresponse error (bias), 189–90, 190b, 199
nonspuriousness (no common cause), 117–18, 429
nonspurious relationships, 371, 375
nonverbal evidence, 320–21
non-zero probability, 185
Northern Ireland, 72–73
notes
   code, 455
   EndNote, 46b, 51
   field, 310, 390, 453
   taking, 45–46, 46b, 48f, 49f, 50–52, 50f, 52t, 53b, 55b
NSDUH. See National Survey on Drug Use and Health
NSF. See National Science Foundation
null hypothesis, 420, 439
Nuremberg Trials, 72

observation
   covert, 282–85, 285f, 310
   of deviant behavior, 281
   interviews and, 287–88, 291f, 295, 357, 357f
   nonparticipant, 281–82, 285f, 310
   overt, 282–85, 285f, 310
   participant, 280–81, 310
   participation and, 282
   of public space, 312
   for qualitative research, 274–75
   scientific, 294–95
   systemic observation and analysis in, 23–25, 30
   of violence, 281–82, 285
observations
   coding, 124–25
   data and, 15
   empirical, 22
   hypotheses and, 290
   interviews and, 122f, 124

observations (cont.)
   measurement and, 140–41, 140f
   for nonprobability sampling, 195, 197
   sampling and, 175f
Office of Community Oriented Policing Services, 363
official data sources, 315, 316t
official records, 316–18
official statistics, 315, 316t
Oh, G., 319b
Ohio, 367b
online communities, 287–88
online panel, 196b, 199
online resources, 46b, 88b
online surveys, 85b, 195, 249–52, 251t
open-ended questions, 241–42, 267
operationalization
   assessment of, 154–57, 155f, 156, 157b
   conceptualization and, 167–69
   data from, 151–53, 153b
   interval measurement and, 147–48
   manipulation operations, 138–39, 143, 143b
   measurement and, 132f, 134–37, 137b, 149b, 154b
   measurement operations, 138–43, 140f, 143b
   nominal measurement and, 145–46
   operational definition, 136–37, 151, 154b, 170
   ordinal measurement and, 146–47
   ratio measurement and, 148–49, 149t
   reliability assessment for, 158–61, 159t, 160, 160t
   scholarship on, 166b, 170
   validity assessment for, 161–65, 163b, 165t
oral consent, 303
ordinal measurement, 146–47, 170, 423
ordinal-scale variables, 410–12, 410t, 411t, 418–23, 418t, 419t, 421t
organizing questions, 259–61
organ-trafficking, 283b
orientation, of evaluation research, 366–68, 367b
Oser, C. B., 156, 156–57
outcome evaluations, 360–63, 361f, 362b, 375
outcomes, 350, 350f, 361f, 375
outliers, 414–15, 439
outlines, 56
outputs, 350, 350f, 375
outsider status, 292, 294–95
overt observation, 282–85, 285f, 310
Owens, Timothy, 168–69

Pager, Devah, 213–14, 214f, 223, 230, 236, 385, 385–91, 395–96
panel studies, 244, 245t, 250, 267
Panel Study of Income Dynamics (PSID), 244–45
paper-and-pencil questionnaire surveys, 245f, 248–49, 267
Park, S., 50–51
Parnaby, P., 327–28, 329t
parole, 102, 105
Parrott, C. T., 323–27, 329–30, 341
Parrott, S., 323–27, 329–30, 341
partial regression coefficient/partial slope, 433–34, 434t, 439
partial tables, 431–32, 431t, 432t, 439
participants. See research participants
Pate, Margaret, 35, 70, 102, 119, 190b. See also depression
patterns, 447, 447f, 452–59, 454b, 456f, 457t, 458t
Pawson, R., 365–66
Pay It Forward (film), 399
Pear, V. A., 369
peer review, 51, 66, 68
Pell pilot program, 186
penal order, 333–35, 333t
penicillin, 73
Pennsylvania, 186
percentage distribution, 411–12, 411t, 419, 419t, 439
permission, in field research, 293–94
Perry, Gina, 83
personal characteristics, in research, 292
Pew Research Center, 2, 248
phases, of comparison, 462–63
Phillips, J., 141
physical, nonverbal evidence, 320–21
Piasentin, K., 160
Pickett, Justin, 196b
pilot-test reliability, 325f, 330
plagiarism, 64
Poledna, S., 141
police. See also use of force
   in Australia, 281–82, 368
   in Canada, 327
   in COVID-19, 50–51, 50f, 347
   drug offenders to, 370b
   on Facebook, 123
   in Kentucky, 348–50, 361–63, 362b
   LEAD programs, 372
   in Minneapolis Domestic Violence Experiment, 34–35, 37
   New York City, 318
   Office of Community Oriented Policing Services, 363

Police Executive Research Forum, 347–48
   racism by, 215–16
   reports, 205
   research with, 367b
   in US, 141–43
politics
   of APSA, 94–95
   crime and, 39, 333–39, 333t
   of elections, 115
   of ethical decision-making, 87–91, 88b, 88f
   ethics and, 69–70, 78–84, 85b, 86, 92–93, 93, 96–99
   ICPSR, 46b
   measurement in, 147
   political ideology, 93, 93–96
   public policy and, 96
   religion and, 145–46, 196b
   social research and, 92–97, 93
   in US, 111, 115–16, 115f, 116f
polling, 246, 246
population
   demography, 167–68, 239, 315, 316t, 317–18, 343, 344
   research and, 175–76, 175f, 176f, 199, 319b, 344
   target, 183–85, 185f, 200, 354f
   well-defined populations, 183
possibilities, 36–40, 38
possible solutions, 354f
posttest-only control group designs, 211–12, 234
posttests, 211–12, 227b, 234
potential harm, 72, 72–73, 75, 79–81
prejudice, 396
preliminary hypothesis testing, 403f, 417–26, 418t, 419t, 421t, 424f, 426f, 428
Presser, Stanley, 256
pretesting, 218–19, 227b, 234, 255–56, 255f, 261, 267
pretest-posttest control group designs, 211–12, 227b, 234
priming, 387
print media, 326b
prior research, 50–52, 52t
prison
   Attitudes toward Prisoners survey, 139–40, 146–47
   in Boston Reentry Study, 240
   BWCs in, 399
   Family History of Incarceration survey, 243–44
   Federal Bureau of Prisons, 316t

General Causal Model of Penal
  Transformation, 338f
guard experiments, 72, 72
interviews and, 273–82, 285, 289b,
  290–95, 299b, 454b
in Italy, 293
mass imprisonment, 332–35, 333t
penal order, 333–35, 333t
in Pennsylvania, 186
prisoners, 139–40, 146–47
racism and, 230
reading programs, 399
social research on, 167, 193–95, 445
Survey of Prison Inmates, 321
women in, 445–46, 450–55, 454b, 460
The Prison Community (Clemmer), 273
privacy, 75–76, 76b, 77t, 84
private documents, 318
private settings, 293
probability, 26b, 176–77, 199, 240
probability distribution, 176, 179–80,
  180t, 199
probability proportionate to size sampling, 186, 199
probability sampling
  nonprobability sampling and, 201–2
  nonresponse error and, 189,
    190b, 199
  random selection and, 176–77, 177b,
    178f
  sampling designs and, 185–89, 188f
  sampling error in, 179–80, 180t
  sampling frame for, 184–85, 185f
  scholarship on, 175, 175f, 182, 182b,
    191, 191b, 199
  statistical interference in, 180–81, 180t
  target population for, 183–84
probation, 140
probes, 301, 310
probing questions, 233
procedures, 60, 136–37
process analysis, 337–38, 343
process coding, 463
process evaluations, 358–59, 359b,
  360t, 375
Prock, K. A., 456–57, 457t
professional ethical guidelines, 78–84,
  85b, 86, 88, 92b
Profiles of Individual Radicalization, 415
program monitoring, 360t, 375
program outcomes, 361f
program process, 350, 350f, 375
program review, 356, 357f
program theory, 365–66, 375
Project S.T.O.R.M., 4, 5b, 5t

proportionate stratified sampling,
  186–87, 199
PSID. *See* Panel Study of Income
  Dynamics
psychology, 62b, 82–83, 89
*Publication Manual of the American
  Psychological Association*, 62b
public documents, 316–18
Public Health Service, US, 73, 73f
public policy, 96
public settings, 292–93
Public Use Microdata Sample (PUMS),
  317–18
punishment, 8–9, 9b, 11–12. *See also
  specific punishments*
purposive sampling, 195, 197, 199

qualitative data analysis
  coding in, 452–54, 454b
  coding terms in, 459b
  conclusions in, 447f, 460–61
  data displays and, 455–59, 456f, 457t,
    458t, 470
  data preparation for, 447–51, 448f, 449t
  memo writing and, 455, 470
  process of, 446–47, 447f
  scholarship on, 278–79, 279b, 396,
    444–46, 451b, 467b, 468–70
  variations in, 462–67, 467f, 470
qualitative interviews, 307
qualitative methods, 369–70
qualitative research
  benefits of, 385
  data gathering for, 124–25
  degrees of participation in, 280–82
  efficiency in, 309
  flexible research designs for, 307–8
  interviews for, 275–77, 312–13
  methodology for, 17b
  methods, 280–89, 283b, 285f, 289b
  naturalistic approach to, 306
  nonprobability sampling and, 277–78
  observation for, 274–75
  quantitative research and, 124, 312
  questions, 53b, 123, 126–27
  in research designs, 107b
  scholarship on, 8f, 9, 13–14, 17–18,
    280, 309, 310b
qualitative research methods, 280–89,
  283b, 285f, 289b
qualitative research questions, 106–7
Quality Education Data, Inc., 188
Qualtrics national online panel, 250
quantitative data analysis
  cleaning in, 408

codebook documentation and, 406b,
  407f
coding in, 404
concepts in, 416b
data entry in, 405–6, 406f
data modification and, 409–16, 411t,
  413t, 414f
editing, 404–5
of GSS Cumulative data file, 406b, 407f
multivariate testing and, 429–38, 429f,
  430t, 431t, 432t, 434t, 436t, 438b
preliminary hypothesis testing
  in, 417–26, 418t, 419t, 421t, 424f,
  426f, 428
process of, 403–4, 403f
scholarship on, 14, 53b, 60, 242, 354,
  400–403, 409b, 439–43
statistical assumptions in, 437b
statistical significance and, 427b
quantitative questions
  research and, 106, 113b, 127
  research designs and, 110b
  research strategies for, 108–9, 108f
  units of analysis in, 109–10
  variables and, 110–19, 112f, 113b, 115t,
    116t, 117b, 119b
quantitative research
  methods for, 369–70
  qualitative research and, 124, 312
  quantitative analysis, 168–69
  in research designs, 107b, 110
  surveys and, 442
quasi-experimental designs, 371–73,
  372f, 375
quasi-resisters, 458, 458t
questions. *See also specific topics*
  closed-ended, 241, 267
  data collection and, 245–53, 245f, 246,
    246f, 251t
  double-barreled, 256b, 267
  drafting, 301–2
  framing, 264b
  grand tour, 302, 310
  for GSS, 268–69
  guiding, 290, 310
  leading, 256b, 267
  open-ended, 241–42, 267
  organizing, 259–61
  questionnaires and, 240–42, 248–50,
    255–56, 255f, 267
  Question Understanding Aid, 256b
  in research proposals, 52, 53b, 54
  responses and, 275–76
  sampling and, 238–39, 254–56, 255f,
    256b, 259–66, 260b, 264b, 267b

questions (cont.)
    scholarship on, 267–70
    survey, 245t, 256b, 269–70
    survey research and, 239–42, 242b
    tour, 302, 310
    wording, 260b
    writing, 255–56, 256b
Quillian, Lincoln, 385–87, 395

R^2, 433–34, 434t, 439
racism
    criminal justice research and, 39, 142–43, 222–23
    by employers, 385–87, 387f, 396
    experiments on, 213–14, 214f
    against minorities, 194
    by police, 215–16
    prejudice and, 396
    prison and, 230
    studies on, 388–90, 388f, 389f
    surveys on, 386
    in US, 347
Ragin, Charles, 95–96, 336–37
random assignments, 206–7, 208b, 208f, 210, 234
Random Integer Generator, 177b, 178f
randomization, 118
randomized controlled trial designs, 348, 361, 362b
RANDOM.ORG, 177b, 178f
random selection, 176–77, 177b, 178f, 199
range, 413–14, 439
Rapley, Tim, 466
Rate My Professors, 2–3, 7, 131
ratio measurement, 148–49, 149t, 170
ratio-scale variables, 412–16, 413t, 414f, 423–26, 424f, 426f
reactive measurement effects, 231–33, 234, 341
reactivity effects, 283
readable text, 447–48, 448f
Reader's Guide to Periodical Literature, 316
readiness, 357, 357f
reading. *See also* communication
    abstracts, 18, 46b
    academic publications, 58
    criminal justice research, 53b, 76b, 157b, 163b
    note taking and, 45–46, 46b, 48f, 49f, 50–52, 50f, 52t, 53b, 55b
    prison reading programs, 399
    for research, 124
    writing and, 45–46, 45f, 67
Reagan, Ronald, 334, 338
recidivism, 372–73
reconstruction, 333–35, 333t

recorded communication, 325, 325f
recording units, 325, 343
recruiting interviewees, 300–301, 300f
recruit samples, 255f, 261–62
reference management software, 46b
references, 46b, 50–52, 61, 62b
refining searches, 46b
reflexivity, 278–79, 279b, 310
Reflexivity in Criminological Research (Lumsden and Winter), 279b
RefWorks, 46b, 51
regression analysis, 423, 425–26, 426f, 439
regression line, 439
Reisig, M. D., 46b, 49f
relationship building, 122f, 124
relationships, 447, 447f, 452–59, 454b, 456f, 457t, 458t
relevant negative cases, 337
reliability
    assessment, 158–61, 159t, 160, 160t, 170
    definitions of, 154–55
    domestic violence and, 172
    inter-coder, 160, 160, 452
    inter-rate, 160, 160, 170
    pilot-test, 325f, 330
    test-retest, 158–59, 159t, 170
    validity and, 308–9
religion, 145–46, 196b
renegotiation, 294
replication, 39–40, 41, 380t
reported surveys, 264–65
reports, 291f, 298
request for proposal, 369, 375
research. *See specific topics*
research designs, 227b
    evaluation research and, 374b
    flexible, 307–8
    preparation for, 106
    research questions in, 104–5, 106b, 107b
    research strategies, 108–9, 108f
    sampling and, 230–31
    scholarship on, 16, 100–102, 101f, 107, 127
    topic selection, 103
    units of analysis in, 109–10
    variables and, 110–19, 112f, 113b, 115t, 116t, 117b, 119b
research ethics, 88b
research evidence, 226
research findings, 96
research funding, 93–95
research interpretations, 38–39
research literature, 46, 46b, 48f, 49f, 50, 50f

research methods
    applied, 349, 374
    for criminal justice studies, 10–15
    qualitative, 280–89, 283b, 285f, 289b
    scholarship on, 1–4, 2, 5b, 5t, 6–7, 16, 17b, 18
    for social research, 7–9, 7f, 8f, 9b
research objectives, 399
research participants
    data collection and, 90–91
    deception with, 74–75, 75
    degrees of participation, 280–82
    ethics practice with, 78b
    experiments and, 204–6, 217–19, 218f, 227
    hypothetical data from, 77t
    informed consent from, 73–74, 73f
    participant observation, 280–81, 310
    participants' rights, 88f, 90–91
    participation, 282, 285f
    potential harm with, 72, 72–73
    privacy invasion with, 75–76, 76b
    in process evaluations, 360t
    roles of, 294–95
    scholarship on, 71, 77
    treatment of, 71–77, 72, 73f, 75, 76b, 78b
research process, 7–9, 7f, 8f
research proposals
    designs of, 54
    developing, 45
    ethical decision-making and, 88b
    hypotheses in, 67
    prior research for, 50–52, 52t
    questions in, 52, 53b, 54
    relevant literature for, 46, 46b, 48f, 49f, 50, 50f
    understanding, 55b
    writing, 45–46, 46b, 48f, 49f, 50–52, 50f, 52t, 53b, 55b
research questions. *See also specific topics*
    descriptive, 104–5
    expanding on, 119b
    good, 106b
    qualitative, 106–7
    quantitative, 113b
    in research designs, 104–5, 106b, 107b
    studies and, 7, 7f, 8f, 9b, 16, 52, 53b, 54
research reports
    citations for, 62b
    first drafts of, 56–61
    literature and, 67
    outlines for, 56
    parts of, 66b
    revisions in, 63–65
    scholarship and, 55

understanding, 66b
writing, 55–61, 62b, 63–65
research reviews, 126b
research sites, 193–95
research strategies, 108–9, 108f, 122f
research terminology, 370b
residuals, 425–26, 426f, 439
resisters, 458, 458t
resolving errors, 448, 449t
respect for persons, 79, 97
response rates, 246–48, 251, 253, 267
results, 60–61
review articles, 46b
revisions, 63–65
risk, 79–81. See also *specific topics*
Roberts, Donald, 329–30
Roethlisberger, F. J., 38
Rogers, P. J., 366
Rokkan, T., 141
Rosen, Leonard, 65
Rosenberg, Morris, 156, *156*, 158, 164
Roth, Wendy, 168
Rubin, H. J., 276, 304
Rubin, I. S., 276, 304

Saldaña, Johnny, 275, 302b, 452–53, 460
Salerno, Jessica, 215–16, 222
Salt-N-Pepa, 70
sample units, 325f, 328–30
sampling
 cluster, 187–89, 199
 convenience, 195, 199
 in criminal justice research, 190b
 data collection and, 245–53, 245f, 246, 246f, 251t
 designs, 185–89, 188f, 254–55, 255f
 disproportionate stratified, 186–87, 199
 error, 179–80, 180t, 199, 265
 in experiments, 208b, 208f
 frame, 184–85, 185f, 199, 261
 inference and, 173–76, 176f
 judgmental, 195, 197, 199
 large-scale probability, 240
 multistage cluster, 187–89, 188f, 199
 nonprobability, 175–76, 175f, 176f, 192–95, 196b, 197–202, 199b, 201–2, 277–78
 population and, 175–76, 176f, 199
 probability, 176–77, 177b, 178f, 179–89, 180t, 182b, 185f, 188f, 191, 191b, 201–2
 probability proportionate to size, 186, 199
 process, 174–76, 175f, 176f
 proportionate stratified, 186–87, 199
 purposive, 195, 197, 199

questions and, 238–39, 254–56, 255f, 256b, 259–66, 260b, 264b, 267b
recruit samples, 261–62
with replacement, 177b, 179, 199
without replacement, 177b, 179, 200
research designs and, 230–31
sample accuracy, 240
sample and, 59, 175f, 177, 185–86, 189–90, 199–200
sample quality, 190b
scholarship on, 199–202, 199f, 267–70
select sample, 261
snowball, 197, 200, 273–74, 300–301
survey research and, 239–42, 242b
Sanborn, J. B., 214
Sanchez, Justin, 215–16, 222
Sapci, O., 402–4, 410–12, 410t, 411t, 414, 420, 422–23
satisfaction surveys, 360t
saturation, 198, 200, 462–63
Savelsberg, J. J., 94, 96
scale
 large-scale probability sampling, 240
 Lerner Self-Esteem Scale, 162
 ordinal-scale variables, 410–12, 410t, 411t, 418–23, 418t, 419t, 421t
 ratio-scale variables, 412–16, 413t, 414f, 423–26, 424f, 426f
 scholarship on, 157b, 170
 Self-Esteem Scale, *156*, 156–62, 159t, 160t, 164–65, 165t, 168–69, 415
Scarce, Rik, 91
scatterplots, 424–26, 424f, 426f, 439
Schaefer, L., 139–40, 146–47, 152
scheduling interviews, 302b, 304
Scheper-Hughes, Nancy, 283b, 284–85, 445, 454b
Schoenfeld, Heather, 333–39, 333t
Scholastic Aptitude Test, 164–65
science
 communication in, 45
 goal of, 30
 human elements of, 39
 inquiry in, 30–35, 30f, 33f, 34f
 logical reasoning in, 25–26, 26b
 of memory, 296
 research findings in, 96
 scientific knowledge, 23, 36–41, 38
 scientific observation, 294–95
 scientific process, 37–38, 38
 scientists, 20, 39
 social research and, 19–20, 20f, 41–43
 sociohistorical aspect of, 38–39
 systemic observation and analysis in, 23–25, 30

theory in, 21–22, 22, 30
verifiable data in, 22–23, 23b
scientific research, 7
secondary analysis, 265, 267
selection, 227, 234, 261
selective deposit, 342, 343
selective survival, 342, 343
self-esteem, 384
Self-Esteem Scale (Rosenberg), *156*, 156–62, 159t, 160t, 164–65, 165t, 168–69, 415
self-reports, 139–40
semi-public settings, 292–93
semi-structured interviews, 285–86, 310, 446
sequential designs, 395, 397
serendipity patterns, 37–38, 41
sex offender registration and notification (SORN), 4
sex offenders, 456–57, 456f, 457t
sexual behavior, 283
sexuality, 385
Sherman, L. W., 34–35, 37, 39, 58, 62b
Shirk, J. L., 367–68
shock experiment, 74–75, 75, 83
"Silver Blaze" (Doyle), 25
simple random sample, 185, 200
Simpson, A., 366
Singleton, Royce, 20, 211, 227b, 256b
Sloan, J. J., 163b
slope/regression coefficients, 424–26, 424f, 426f, 439
Small, Mario, 395
Smith, Andrew, 212
Smith, Robert, 307
Smith, Tom, 404
Snapchat, 2
SNAP-ORP. *See* Stop Now and Plan-Under 12 Outreach Project
snow, 122, *122*
Snow, David, 450, 308–9
Snow, Marcia, 296–97
snowball sampling, 197, 200, 273–74, 300–301
sober delinquency, 118
social artifacts, 109
social bond theory, 21–22, 22, 30–33
social change, 340–41, 345
social desirability effect, 163b, 170, 387
social facilitation, 42
social groups, 123, 129
social media
 education and, 2, 2
 Facebook, 14, 123, 319b
 gang members on, 14
 students on, 2–3

social media (cont.)
  studies on, 123
  Twitter, 319b, 327–28, 329t
  viral videos, 347
"Social media addiction takes toll on academic performance," 2
"Social media usage negatively impacts the schoolwork of students from adolescence to college research suggests," 2
social research
  communication in, 67
  ICPSR, 46b
  identity in, 283b, 284–85
  inductive logic in, 30–35, 30f, 33f, 34f, 41
  Institute for Social Research, 244
  Inter-University Consortium for Political and Social Research, 321
  interval measurement in, 148
  measurement in, 151–53, 153b
  operational definition in, 151
  politics and, 92–97, 93
  on prison, 167, 193–95, 445
  quantitative analysis in, 168–69
  research methods for, 7–9, 7f, 8f, 9b
  on resisters, 458, 458t
  science and, 19–20, 20f, 41–43
  scientific knowledge and, 36–40, 38
  themes in, 465
  women and, 102, 105, 123, 125, 177b
social scientists, 16
social service referral telephone program (SSRTP), 355
social standing, 327
social structure, 340–41
socioeconomics, 335–36
sociohistorical aspect, of science, 38–39
sociology
  crime in, 21–22
  free writing in, 56–57
  ideology of, 93, 93
  research in, 52, 54
  social scientists, 71, 114–15
  sociological disclaimers, 95–96
Solymosi, R., 141
Soor, Sadhika, 52
Soriano, F. I., 352, 354
SORN. See sex offender registration and notification
South Africa, 283b, 465
South Carolina, 4, 5b, 5t
specification errors, 437b
Spinner, Barry, 345
spurious relationships, 118, 127
SSRTP. See social service referral telephone program

staff perception data, 360t
stakeholders. See also specific topics
  assessment and, 354, 354f, 357, 357f
  evaluation research and, 350f, 351, 361f, 366–68, 367b, 375
standard deviation, 414, 439
standard error, 181, 200
standardized regression coefficients, 435–36, 436t, 439
Stanford University, 72, 72
Stanley, Julian, 227b
Starr, S., 236
statistics
  Bureau of Justice Statistics, 316t
  data and, 401
  descriptive, 401–2, 439
  inferential, 401–2, 439
  National Center for Education Statistics, 316t
  official, 315, 316t
  statistical analysis, 169, 429
  statistical association, 129
  statistical assumptions, 437b
  statistical control, 112–13
  statistical inferences, 197–98
  statistical interference, 180–81, 180t
  Statistical Package for the Social Sciences, 405, 410–12, 410t, 411t
  statistical significance, 116, 117b, 127, 420–22, 421t, 427b, 439
  test of statistical significance, 116, 117b, 127, 439
  vital, 316–17, 343
Stephens, D. W., 367b
stereotypes, 215, 323
The Steve Harvey Show (TV show), 4
Stokes, N., 368
Stop Now and Plan-Under 12 Outreach Project (SNAP-ORP), 363
Straits, B. C., 211, 227b, 256b
Stratford, Michael, 95
stratified random sample, 186–87, 200
Strauss, Anselm, 452, 462–64
Street Corner Society study, 193
strength of association, 427b
strength variance, 445
stress, 423–26, 424f, 426f
structured interviews, 240–42, 267, 285–86
Stuart, Forrest, 14–15, 287–89, 312
students
  academic performance of, 119
  alcohol and, 179–81, 180t, 190b
  to Baumer, 183–86, 401
  bullying, 383–85, 392
  in campus surveys, 406f

  in CAS, 248–49
  cluster sampling with, 187–89
  cumulative scaling with, 157b
  employers and, 7
  evaluations from, 76b, 77t
  in experiments, 72, 72, 74–75, 75, 83
  general strain of, 423–26, 424f, 426f
  grading, 24
  knowledge and, 6
  NMPDU and, 426–32, 426f, 427b, 429–30, 429f, 430t, 431t, 432t, 436t
  plagiarism by, 64
  Rate My Professor for, 2–3, 7
  research on, 110–13, 112f, 176–77, 179–87, 180t, 227b, 383–85
  Scholastic Aptitude Test, 164–65
  on social media, 2–3
  student task forces, 399
  in surveys, 164
studies. See also specific topics
  ADD Health, 183, 187–89
  on alcohol, 281–82, 285
  audit, 213–14, 214f, 234, 385–90, 387f, 388f, 389f, 396
  on black market, 283b
  Boston Reentry Study, 240
  case, 193–94, 200
  Chicago gang study, 281, 288
  Comparative Neighborhood Study, 194
  on education, 110–13, 112f
  evaluation of, 55
  on female parolees, 102, 105, 123, 125
  on film ratings, 344–45
  on gang members, 84, 465
  matrix of, 52t, 54
  on mental illness, 323–27, 329–30, 341
  MTF, 108–10, 117b, 183–87
  National Television Violence Study, 329
  panel, 244, 245t, 250, 267
  PSID, 244–45
  on racism, 388–90, 388f, 389f
  references and, 46b, 50–52
  research questions and, 7, 7f, 8f, 9b, 16, 52, 53b, 54
  on sex offenders, 456–57, 456f, 457t
  on social change, 340–41
  on social media, 123
  Street Corner Society study, 193
  trend, 244, 245t, 267
  Tuskegee Syphilis study, 73–74, 78
  on violence, 329
subjective understanding, 307
substance abuse, 135–36, 162–63, 163b, 192–93

summative evaluation, 352, 353*t*, 375
supplementary archival data, 277
surveys. See also *specific surveys*
   African Americans in, 168
   assessment of, 380–81, 380*t*
   Attitudes toward Prisoners survey, 139–40, 146–47
   campus, 406*f*
   causal relationships in, 265–66
   concepts in, 172
   for criminal justice research, 9, 11–13, 17*b*
   data collection modes for, 245–53, 245*f*, 246, 246*f*, 251*t*
   descriptive, 242, 267
   explanatory, 242, 267
   Family History of Incarceration survey, 243–44
   focus groups and, 383
   framing, 264*b*
   FTF interviews and, 262
   generalization in, 265
   in-depth interviews compared to, 302*b*
   IVR, 249–50
   mail, 246–53, 251*t*
   margin of error in, 181
   mixed-mode, 251–52, 251*t*, 267
   NCVS, 239–44, 253*b*, 259, 262
   NSDUH, 244
   online, 85*b*, 195, 249–52, 251*t*
   paper-and-pencil questionnaire, 245*f*, 248–49, 267
   processes for, 254–56, 255*f*, 256*b*, 259–63, 260*b*, 264*b*
   quantitative research and, 442
   on racism, 386
   reported, 264–65
   satisfaction, 360*t*
   scholarship on, 17, 238–39, 267–70, 267*b*
   students in, 164
   survey-based experiments, 214–15, 234
   survey data, 392
   survey designs and modes, 243–53, 245*f*, 245*t*, 246, 246*f*, 251*t*, 253*b*
   Survey of Prison Inmates, 321
   survey questions, 245*t*, 256*b*, 269–70
   survey research, 239–42, 242*b*
   US, 250–51
   versatility in, 265
Sussman, S., 355
Sutherland, A., 133–36, 138–39, 144*b*, 145, 401
Sutherland, Edwin, 21
Sydes, Michelle, 399

syphilis, 73
systemic observation and analysis, 23–25, 30

Tahamont, Sarah, 185–86
target population, 183–85, 185*f*, 200, 354*f*
Taub, Richard, 194
taxonomies, 455–56, 456*f*, 468
"Teachers Say B.C. school teens showed improved grades and social skills after a ban on phones," 2
technological developments, 287–88
teenage resisters, 458, 458*t*
telephone interviews, 247–49, 251*t*, 267
temporal order, 116
temporary restraining orders, 296–97
tentative knowledge, 36–37
Terrill, W., 46*b*, 49*f*, 62*b*
test-retest reliability, 158–59, 159*t*, 170
tests of statistical significance, 116, 117*b*, 127, 439
Texas, 167, 309–10
themes, 465
theory. See also concepts; *specific theories*
   abstract, 29
   broken windows, 140–41, 151–52, 320–21
   causation and, 118–20
   concepts and, 111
   data and, 30*f*, 35, 41
   grounded, 369, 375, 452, 462–64
   hypotheses and, 30–31, 137
   literature review and, 103–4
   program, 365–66, 375
   revising, 34, 34*f*
   scholarship on, 41
   in science, 21–22, 22, 30
   social bond, 21–22, 22, 30–33
   theoretical definitions, 132
   theoretical explanations, 26*b*
   theoretical inferences, 198
   theorists, 20
   theory-data relationship, 20, 20*f*
   top-down approach in, 33, 33*f*
Thomas, Robert, 296–97
Thompson, Andrew, 196*b*
Thorne, S., 460–61
threats, to internal validity, 227, 227*b*, 234
Tik Tok, 2, 8, 123, 131
Tilly, N., 365–66
time-space measures, in code variables, 327
timing, 211–12

top-down approach, 33, 33*f*
topic selection, 93–95, 103
tour questions, 302, 310
Townsley, M., 281–82, 285
train coders, 325*f*, 330
trauma-informed care, 350
treatment, of research participants, 71–77, 72, 73*f*, 75, 76*b*, 78*b*
trend studies, 244, 245*t*, 267
triangulation, 378, 378*f*, 382, 390–91, 397
Trump, Donald, 115–16, 115*f*, 116*f*
truth tables, 343
Tucker, T. A., 163*b*
Turning Point software, 286
Tuskegee Syphilis study, 73–74, 78
Twitter, 319*b*, 327–28, 329*t*
typologies, 458–59, 458*t*, 468, 470

UCR. See Uniform Crime Report
Underwood, Alex, 4, 5*t*
unidimensionality, 157*b*, 170
Uniform Crime Report (UCR), 23*b*, 43, 141–42, 319*b*
United Kingdom, 72–73
United States (US). See also *specific topics*
   Attorney General, 72–73
   CDC in, 247
   Census, 167–68, 239, 315, 316*t*, 317, 344
   crime dramas in, 323–27, 329–30, 341
   criminal justice system, 93–94
   death penalty in, 29*b*, 42, 104–5
   discrimination in, 222–23, 389–90
   experiments in, 34–35, 37
   General Causal Model of Penal Transformation in, 338*f*
   mandatory arrest laws in, 39
   mass imprisonment in, 332–35, 333*t*
   MTurk in, 196*b*
   National Research Act in, 78
   NSDUH in, 244
   Pew Research Center in, 2, 248
   plagiarism in, 64
   police in, 141–43
   politics in, 111, 115–16, 115*f*, 116*f*
   Profiles of Individual Radicalization in, 415
   Public Health Service, 73, 73*f*
   Quality Education Data, Inc., 188
   racism in, 347
   Supreme Court, 36
   surveys in, 250–51
   Violent Crime Control and Law Enforcement Act in, 334–35
   war on drugs in, 215

units of analysis
    in content analysis, 325, 326b
    in quantitative questions, 109–10
    research and, 108f, 112f, 113b, 115t, 116t, 117b, 119b, 127, 325f
    in research designs, 109–10
univariate analysis, 409–12, 410t, 411t, 439
University of Hawaii, 29b
university presses, 51
unstructured interviews, 285–86, 310
US. See United States
use of force
    gender and, 215–16, 216t
    research on, 48f, 49f, 133–36, 138–39, 144b, 145
    scholarship on, 144, 401

validity. See also internal validity
    assessment, 161–65, 163b, 165t, 170
    experiments and, 380–81
    external, 229–31, 234, 380t
    measurement, 155–56, 155f
    reliability and, 308–9
variables
    antecedent, 112, 112f, 127, 129
    associated, 371
    association between, 207, 226–27
    code, 325f, 327, 330
    control, 112, 127
    dependent, 111, 127, 210, 211–12, 223, 335, 442–43
    description of, 407f
    dummy, 433–34, 434t, 439
    extraneous, 111–12, 127
    identifying, 120b
    independent, 111, 127, 206, 212–13, 419–20, 419t, 442–43
    individuals and, 244
    interval, 412–16, 413t, 414f, 423–26, 424f, 426f
    intervening, 112, 112f, 118–19, 127
    manipulated independent, 206, 210, 212–13
    measured dependent, 210
    measurement of, 108f, 110–13, 112f, 113b
    nominal, 410–12, 410t, 411t, 418–23, 418t, 419t, 421t
    ordinal-scale, 410–12, 410t, 411t, 418–23, 418t, 419t, 421t

ratio-scale, 412–16, 413t, 414f, 423–26, 424f, 426f
relationships among, 110–19, 112f, 113b, 115t, 116t, 117b, 119b
variations
    of experimental method, 211–16, 214f, 216t, 217b
    in qualitative data analysis, 462–67, 467f, 470
    in qualitative research methods, 280–89, 283b, 285f, 289b
    in survey designs and modes, 243–53, 245f, 245t, 246, 246f, 251t, 253b
Vasquez, J., 285–86, 301, 304
Venkatesh, Sudhir, 281
verbal measures, 223
verbal reports, 139–40, 170
verifiable data, 22–23, 23b
versatility, in surveys, 265
victimization, 307
Vietnam War, 177b
violence
    criminal justice research and, 281–82, 285, 323–24, 329
    domestic, 34–35, 37, 50–51, 50f, 172, 372–73
    GAGV, 359
    GVROs, 369
    IPV, 456–57
    Minneapolis Domestic Violence Experiment, 34–35, 37
    National Television Violence Study, 329
    Violent Crime Control and Law Enforcement Act, 334–35
vital statistics, 316–17, 343

Wallace, George, 334
Ward, Catherine, 461, 465
war on drugs, 215
Warren, P. Y., 141–42, 144b
Weber, Max, 93, 93, 332
weighting, 186–87, 200
Weiss, Robert, 303
well-defined populations, 183
Wertz, F. J., 470
Western, Bruce, 388–91, 388f, 389f
Western Electric Hawthorne plant, 38, 38
"What Facebook Users Share," 2
White, Michael D., 318
WHO. See World Health Organization

"Why social media diminishes student performance and wellbeing," 2
Whyte, William Foote, 193
Wichita Jury Study, 75–76
wild-code checking, 408, 439
Wildeman, C., 194–95
Williams, G. C., 139–40, 146–47, 152
Willie T. Donald Exoneration Advisory Coalition, 300
Wilson, J. Q., 140, 151–52
Wilson, William Julius, 194
Winter, A., 279b
Wisconsin, 35, 230, 385–86, 389, 396
within-case analyses, 337–38
Wolbring, T., 140–41, 151–52, 157b, 320–21
women
    in prison, 445–46, 450–55, 454b, 460
    social research and, 102, 105, 123, 125, 177b
wording questions, 260b
worker productivity, 38, 38, 42
World Health Organization (WHO), 316t
World War II, 71
Wozniak, K., 250
writing. See also communication
    field jottings, 296–97
    first drafts, 56–61
    free, 56–57, 66
    memo, 455, 462–64, 470
    questions, 255–56, 256b
    reading and, 45–46, 45f, 67
    reports, 291f, 298
    research proposals, 45–46, 46b, 48f, 49f, 50–52, 50f, 52t, 53b, 55b
    research reports, 55–61, 62b, 63–65
written consent, 303

Yale University, 83
Yamagishi, Toshio, 75
Yemen, 246, 246
Y-intercept, 424–26, 424f, 426f, 436, 436t, 439
YouGov, 11–12
YouTube, 2

Zgoba, K. M., 4
Zhang, Y., 319b
Zimbardo, Philip, 72, 72, 91
Zimmerman, Don, 466–67, 467f
Zotero, 46b, 51